Dickens at Work

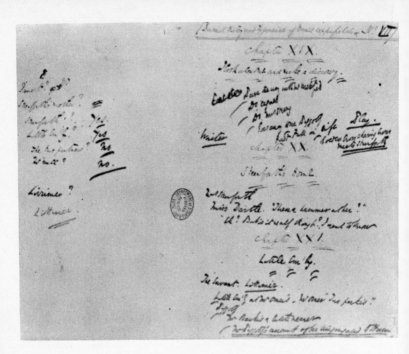

Dickens' 'Number Plan' for *David Copperfield*, No. VII
(Victoria and Albert Museum)

Dickens at Work

JOHN BUTT

AND

KATHLEEN TILLOTSON

METHUEN & CO. LTD
II NEW FETTER LANE · LONDON E.C.4

First published July 18, 1957
Reprinted 1963 and 1968
1.3
SBN 416 58880 3

First published as a University Paperback 1968
1.1
SBN 416 29710 2

Type set by The Broadwater Press,
Reprinted lithographically in
Great Britain by
John Dickens & Co Ltd
Northampton

Contents

Illustrations

Abbreviated Titles
of works frequently referred to

COUTTS LETTERS = *Letters from Charles Dickens to Angela Burdett-Coutts, 1841–1865*. Selected and edited . . . by Edgar Johnson (London, 1953).

FORSTER = John Forster, *The Life of Charles Dickens* (Library edition, 2 vols., revised, 1876; originally published in 3 vols., 1872–4). [Reference is by book and section].

HATTON AND CLEAVER = Thomas Hatton and Arthur H. Cleaver, *A Bibliography of the Periodical Works of Charles Dickens* (1933).

JOHNSON = Edgar Johnson, *Charles Dickens, his Tragedy and Triumph* (2 vols., London, 1953).

LETTERS = *The Letters of Charles Dickens*, edited by Walter Dexter (3 vols., 1938, the Nonesuch Dickens).

Preface

IN this book we have examined several of Dickens's novels in the light of the conditions under which he wrote them. The surviving evidence of these conditions is extensive and has been generally neglected hitherto, but if we are right in our estimate of the importance of this material, it suggests more than one new direction in the criticism of his work.

Many writers, taking their point of departure from Dickens's childhood reading, have seen him as continuing the tradition of Fielding and Smollett; but he also continues another eighteenth-century tradition. In the original Preface to *Nicholas Nickleby* (1839) he chose to call himself a 'periodical essayist', and took leave of his readers in the words of Henry Mackenzie in the last paper of the *Lounger*:

> Other writers submit their sentiments to their readers, with the reserve and circumspection of him who has had time to prepare for a public appearance. . . But the periodical essayist commits to his readers the feelings of the day, in the language which those feelings have prompted.

It is to the recovery of Dickens as a writer of 'periodical' novels that this book is especially devoted: how he responded to and conveyed 'the feelings of the day', what methods of work he evolved as best suited to his own genius and to the demands of monthly or weekly publication, and above all, how he eventually defeated Mackenzie's antithesis by learning to combine the 'circumspection' of preparation with the immediate and intimate relation to his readers which he valued so highly.

Our emphasis accordingly falls upon the process rather than the result, upon Dickens's craft rather than his art; but the inspiration and justification of our work is none the less a conviction of Dickens's greatness as a creative artist. This is widely shared. Yet, despite some excellent interpretative criticism and much zealous biographical enquiry, Dickens studies have hardly passed beyond the early nineteenth-century phase of Shakespeare studies; while the study of his text seems arrested in the early eighteenth century. With the lifting of this spell, which can only come with a full critical edition, much that Dickens originally wrote and had to discard, but would have retained had he been writing three-volume novels, will be restored to readers, as well as passages in the early works which for a variety of reasons he removed or revised in later editions. In some of our chapters we give a few examples of such passages; more will be found in recent issues of *The Dickensian*, and in *Dickens Romancier* (1953) by Professor Sylvère Monod, whose approach resembles ours in his use of the rich material of the Forster collection in the Victoria and Albert Library.

All of Dickens's writings have claims to be included in a study of 'Dickens at work', but our present choice fairly represents different stages of his career and different kinds of work. The variations and development of his method of work in early and late novels, in weekly and monthly instalments, are thus indicated; and also the persistence of his journalistic response to events of the day, from the 'no popery' cry of the late eighteen-thirties to the war in the Crimea—a response which is more varied and more extensive than is usually recognized or than we have had full opportunity of showing.

We arrived at our common concern in these matters by rather different routes: one of us starting from a specific interest in the effect of serial writing upon Dickens's novels, and the other from a more general interest in the conditions of publication of Victorian fiction. Some results of our earlier and largely independent investigations are to be seen in John Butt's article 'Dickens at Work' in 1948, and Kathleen Tillotson's *Novels of the Eighteen-Forties* in 1954. The beginnings of collaboration appeared in John Butt's centenary articles on *David Copperfield* in 1949-50, and in the same year we converged upon *Dombey and Son*—the earliest of the fully-documented novels—on which we published a jointly-written essay.

The other studies were written in close association. Chapters i, vi, vii, and viii are mainly the work of John Butt, chapters ii, iii, iv, and ix mainly the work of Kathleen Tillotson; but we are jointly responsible for the whole book, and for chapter v in particular. That chapter is the only one which has been published hitherto in substantially its present form: it appeared in *Essays and Studies 1951*, published for the English Association by John Murray. Parts of chapters i, vi, and vii have appeared in *The Durham University Journal*, *The Listener*, *The Dickensian*, *The Review of English Studies*, and *Nineteenth Century Fiction*. Chapter iv incorporates most of the introductory essay to *Barnaby Rudge* in the New Oxford Illustrated Dickens. To the editors of the journals mentioned, to the English Association, John Murray Ltd, and the Oxford University Press, we are indebted for permission to reprint.

For quotations from manuscripts, proof sheets, and memoranda in the Forster collection we acknowledge the permission of the Director of the Victoria and Albert Museum. Letters owned by the Henry E. Huntington Library, the Pierpont Morgan Library, the Albert A. Berg Collection of the New York Public Library, and the Rare Book Department of the Free Library of Philadelphia are quoted by permission of the owners. Permission to quote from hitherto unpublished material has been given by Mr Henry C. Dickens, O.B.E.

We are also grateful to Professor Geoffrey Tillotson for his constant advice and assistance; to Mr K. J. Fielding and Mrs Madeline House for several details which their unrivalled knowledge of unpublished letters could alone supply; to Miss Margaret Cardwell for valuable help in checking quotations and references; and generally, to members of discussion classes on Dickens at King's College, University of Durham, and Bedford College, University of London.

J. B.
K. T.

Preface to the 1968 edition

SINCE the writing of the foregoing Preface in 1957, the publication of additional material has fortunately outdated a few of its statements, though not, except in a few minor instances, the substance of the book itself. The 'full critical edition' of which we could then speak only with cautious hope was launched, under the general editorship of the authors, with the publication in 1966 of the first volume (*Oliver Twist*) of the Clarendon edition; among the several other novels of which the editing is in progress is *David Copperfield*, on the basis of extensive work done by John Butt before his lamented death. Further, many of the 'unpublished letters' to which we made a general reference are now available in the first volume of the Pilgrim edition; these naturally throw much further light on 'Dickens at work', in our sense of the phrase, and will sometimes enable the reader of our chapters to substantiate or modify our occasional conjectures or to supply additional dates. As far as I am aware, none of our conclusions is seriously affected, and no revision has been attempted. But I welcome the opportunity of this new edition to repair one oversight affecting the number plans and to add information on two small points.

P. 39, n. 1. 'Sentiment' first appeared in *Bell's Weekly Messenger*, 7 June 1834.

P. 59, n. 2. The song, 'I'll not believe love's wreath will pain', is from Thomas Haynes Bayly's farce *Perfection*, acted in 1830.

Pp. 115-6. The MSS. of the number-plans of No. 1 of *David Copperfield* and *Little Dorrit* were preserved, and are in the Forster collection (Forster MS. 168) but separated from the other numbers and uncatalogued. To the transcript on p. 116 the following, cut off in Forster's facsimile, should now be added: 'Chapter III./ I have a change./ The stranded boat./ The life there./ comes home "father"/ Black whiskers and black dog.'

The complete number-plans of *Little Dorrit* were reproduced by P. D. Herring in *Modern Philology*, LXIV (1967) and those of *Bleak House* by H. P. Sucksmith in *Renaissance and Modern Studies*, IX (Nottingham, 1965).

K. T.

CHAPTER I

Dickens as a Serial Novelist

I

IT is a commonplace in the criticism of early drama that the conditions in which a dramatist worked must be taken into account. He wrote for a theatre of a certain shape, with certain structural features, which permitted him to use certain dramatic effects. The analogy can be applied to the novelist who, though he has greater freedom than the dramatist, must also suit what he has to say to the current conventions of presentation. Just as Shakespeare thought in terms of a theatre without drop curtain, artificial lighting, or scenery, and of a theatrical company of male actors only, so Dickens was accustomed to think in terms of publication peculiar to his time. Today novels are customarily published in single volumes. A hundred and fifty years ago this form of publication was unusual. In the eighteenth century, novels had appeared in five volumes, or even in as many as seven; but by the time of Scott and Jane Austen the usual number was three or four. The prices varied: it was not uncommon to charge as much as half a guinea a volume, which made novel-reading exceedingly expensive to those who did not belong to a circulating library. These were still the conditions ruling when Dickens began to write. His first novel, *Pickwick Papers*, shows him attempting to reach a larger number of readers by cutting the price to suit their pockets. The method chosen was to publish in 'what was then a very unusual form, at less than one-third of the price of the whole of an ordinary novel, and in shilling Monthly Parts'.[1]

1. Dickens's address announcing the 'cheap edition' of his works (1847). It is preserved in a scrap-book of cuttings in the British Museum (shelf mark K.T.C. 1.b. 5 (21)), and is reprinted in the 'National' edition, XXXIV (1908), p. 433.

After the first few numbers of *Pickwick*, each monthly 'part' or number consisted of three or four chapters, covering thirty-two pages of print, with two plates, and several pages of advertisements. It was issued in green paper covers and was published at a shilling, nominally on the first day, actually on the last day, of each month. This form of publication was chosen for *Pickwick* by Chapman and Hall, but Dickens found it so suitable that he adopted it for *Nicholas Nickleby*, *Martin Chuzzlewit*, *Dombey and Son*, *David Copperfield*, *Bleak House*, *Little Dorrit*, *Our Mutual Friend*, and *Edwin Drood*. Each of these novels, except *Edwin Drood*, was planned for completion in nineteen monthly numbers, the last being a double number priced at two shillings, and containing, besides forty-eight pages of text and four plates, the title-page, frontispiece, preface, and other preliminaries. *Edwin Drood*, of which only six numbers were written, was planned for completion in eleven, the last to be a double number. Five of the other six novels were published in serial in weekly magazines and produced distinct problems of composition and form, which are touched upon in later chapters.

Although it might be supposed that Dickens would wish to complete a novel before permitting serial publication to begin, in fact he never wrote more than four or five numbers before the first was published, and by the middle of the novel he was rarely more than one number ahead of his readers. As might be expected, his practice differed at different stages of his career. Whereas *Little Dorrit* III was finished before the first number appeared and an even larger portion of *Our Mutual Friend* was ready before publication day, he had lightly embarked upon *Pickwick Papers* with nothing in hand;[1] and it seems that no more, or very little more, than the first numbers of *Nicholas Nickleby* and *Martin Chuzzlewit* were complete when publication began.[2] Furthermore, the writing of *Pickwick Papers* overlapped with *Oliver Twist*, and *Oliver Twist* with *Nicholas Nickleby*. In circumstances such as these, it is not surprising to learn that each number of *Nickleby* had been completed 'only . . . a day or two before its publication';[3] and

1. See Forster, VIII i, IX v, and below, p. 66.

2. 'The first chapter [of *Nicholas Nickleby*] is ready . . . so you can begin to print as soon as you like. The sooner you begin, the faster I shall get on' (*Letters*, I 161; 22 Feb. 1838). The first number of *Martin Chuzzlewit* was 'nearly done' on 8 Dec. 1842, with a little more than three weeks to go before publication day (*Letters*, I 493).

3. *Letters*, I 170.

this in turn meant that when something compelled him to stop working for a prolonged period, a gap in the series supervened. Thus the death of Mary Hogarth, his sister-in-law, on 7 May 1837 moved him profoundly, and the effect upon his serial publication was immediate: there were no June numbers of *Pickwick Papers* and *Oliver Twist*. On the other hand, when he himself died on 9 June 1870 there was enough of *Edwin Drood* written to permit the publication of three more numbers, the third being only two pages short of the normal complement.

The disadvantages of this method seem obvious. As Trollope remarked, 'an artist should keep in his hand the power of fitting the beginning of his work to the end'.[1] And the difficulties seem equally great. Writing in serial involved maintaining two focuses. The design and purpose of the novel had to be kept constantly in view; but the writer had also to think in terms of the identity of the serial number, which would have to make its own impact and be judged as a unit. Incident and interest had therefore to be evenly spread, since 'the writer . . . cannot afford to have many pages skipped out of the few which are to meet the reader's eye at the same time'.[2] Chapters must be balanced within a number in respect both of length and of effect. Each number must lead, if not to a climax, at least to a point of rest; and the rest between numbers is necessarily more extended than what the mere chapter divisions provide. The writer had also to bear in mind that his readers were constantly interrupted for prolonged periods, and that he must take this into account in his characterization and, to some extent, in his plotting. So early as the original preface to *Pickwick*, Dickens showed his recognition that not every story is suited to this type of publication.[3]

Great as these difficulties were, they were felt to be worth overcoming. To the reader the system meant not merely eager expectation of the day which brought a fresh batch of green covers to the bookstall, but also the impression that the story was in the making from month to month. Thus Lady Stanley is found addressing a friend in 1841 about the weekly progress of *The Old Curiosity Shop*:

How *can* you read Humphrey's last number and not *indulge* me with an ejaculation or two about it? Are you satisfied with the disposal of Quilp? My Lord is not, says it is too easy a death and that he

1. *Autobiography* (World's Classics revised text), p. 127.
2. Ibid., p. 132.   3. See below, p. 65.

should have more time to *feel* his punishment. Will Nelly die? I think she ought.[1]

To the author it meant a larger public, but also a public more delicately responsive, who made their views known during the progress of a novel both by writing to him and by reducing or increasing their purchases. Through serial publication an author could recover something of the intimate relationship between story-teller and audience which existed in the ages of the sagas and of Chaucer; and for an author like Dickens, who was peculiarly susceptible to the influence of his readers, this intimate relationship outweighed the inherent disadvantages of the system.[2]

II

Yet the disadvantages were none the less apparent, and they could be mastered only by more systematic planning than this impulsive man has been credited with. Publication day was the last day of each month, known in the trade as 'magazine day'.[3] By that date Dickens had to plan and write the equivalent of thirty-two printed pages and to give his illustrator instructions for two engravings. The manuscript had to be sent to the printer in London, perhaps from Broadstairs or the Isle of Wight, or even from as far off as Lausanne.[4] Proofs were to be corrected and sent to press, and copies were to be sewn and distributed to booksellers. The publishers' agreement for *Nicholas Nickleby* specified that the manuscript should be delivered on the fifteenth day of each month.[5] During the progress of this novel it seems to have been recognized that the twenty-fourth would serve as the last

1. *The Ladies of Alderley*, ed. N. Mitford (1938), p. 2.

2. On serial publication see Kathleen Tillotson, *Novels of the Eighteen-Forties* (Oxford, 1954), pp. 21–47.

3. For an account of the scene on 'magazine day' in Paternoster Row see Charles Manby Smith, *The Little World of London* (1857), pp. 45–6. The arrangements were different for weekly serials. When W. H. Wills, the assistant editor of *All the Year Round*, was arranging for contemporaneous publication of a German version of *Great Expectations*, he told the German publishers that the translated portion was not to anticipate the original: 'we publish on the Wednesdays before the date upon our numbers, which is that of each Saturday. Therefore you can bring out each weekly portion every Wednesday after Wednesday the 28th Instant; when (and not before) you may issue the first portion.' (copy, dated 15 Nov. 1860, in the *All the Year Round* letter-book, Henry E. Huntington Library.)

4. Part of *Copperfield* was written at Broadstairs, part in the Isle of Wight; part of *Dombey* was written at Lausanne, part in Paris.

5. Forster, II ii.

date for a number,[1] but Dickens's subsequent practice was to aim at the twentieth. Frequently he had to go straight from one number to the next; but often he could allow himself a few days' respite at the end of the month before beginning the next month's instalment. Occasionally he resumed work as late as the seventh day.[2] Thus he had about a fortnight for writing his three or four chapters.

He did not always complete his number before sending it to the printer. Sometimes it was delivered in batches with instructions for a proof to be forwarded to the illustrator.[3] Hablôt Browne was accustomed to work to orders. At best he had a proof to go upon; at worst his instructions were verbal.[4] Sometimes he had a letter such as this, which embodies directions for the first illustration in *Dombey* VII:

> ... The first subject which I am now going to give is very important to the book. *I should like to see your sketch of it, if possible.*
>
> I should premise that I want to make the Major, who is the incarnation of selfishness and small revenge, a kind of comic Mephistophilean power in the book; and the N° begins with the departure of Mr. Dombey and the Major on that trip for change of air and scene which is prepared for in the last Number. They go to Leamington, where you and I were once. In the Library the Major introduces Mr Dombey to a certain lady, whom, as I wish to foreshadow dimly, said Dombey may come to marry in due season. She

1. *Letters*, I 177.
2. Occasionally even later. On 9 Mar. 1847 he told Miss Hogarth that he had 'not yet written a single slip' of *Dombey* VII (*Letters*, II 17).
3. Thus Dickens wrote to Evans from Broadstairs about *Copperfield* No. IV (10 July 1849): 'I send you, by this Post, 9 slips of copy, containing Mr. Browne's second subject. Get it up *with all speed*, and send a proof to him. . .' (*Letters*, II 160).
4. 'It is due to the gentleman, whose designs accompany the letterpress, to state that the interval has been so short between the production of each number in manuscript and its appearance in print, that the greater portion of the Illustrations have been executed by the artist from the author's mere verbal description of what he intended.' Original preface to *Pickwick Papers*. David Croal Thomson, *Life and Labours of Hablôt Knight Browne 'Phiz'* (London, 1884), pp. 63f, 73f, prints instructions for *Dombey*, plate VII, and *Nickleby*, plate XXXIII; manuscript instructions for the plates XVIII, XXXVII, and XXXVIII, frontispiece, and title-page vignette of *Martin Chuzzlewit* are preserved in the Henry E. Huntington Library. On the instructions for plate XVIII, *The thriving city of Eden as it appeared in fact*, Browne has pencilled a mild protest: 'I can't get all this perspective in—unless you will allow of a long subject—something less than a mile'. Nevertheless he produced a sketch, on which Dickens commented 'The stump of the tree should be *in* the ground in fact a tree cut off two feet up. Too wide—cannot it be compressed by putting Martin's label on the other side of the door, and bringing Mark with his tree forwarder. Qy is that a *hat* on his head?'

is about thirty, not a day more—handsome, though *haughty* looking —good figure. Well dressed—showy—and desirable. Quite a lady in appearance, with something of a proud indifference about her, suggestive of a spark of the Devil within. Was married young. Husband dead. Goes about with an old mother, who rouges, and who lives upon the reputation of a diamond necklace and her family. Wants a husband. Flies at none but high game, and couldn't marry anybody not rich. Mother affects cordiality and *heart*, and is the essence of sordid calculation. Mother usually shoved about in a Bath chair by a Page who has rather *outgrown and outshoved his strength*, and who *butts at it* behind like a ram, while his mistress *steers herself languidly* by a handle in front. *Nothing the matter with her to prevent her walking*, only was once *sketched (when a Beauty) reclining in a Barouche*, and having *outlived the beauty and the barouche* too, still *holds on to the attitude* as becoming her uncommonly. Mother is in this machine in the sketch. Daughter has a *parasol*.

The Major presents them to Mr. Dombey, gloating within himself over what may come of it, and over the discomfiture of Miss Tox. Mr. Dombey (in deep mourning) *bows* solemnly. Daughter bends. The Native in attendance, *bearing a camp-stool and the Major's greatcoat*. Native evidently afraid of the Major and his thick cane.

If you like it better, the scene may be in the street or in a green lane. But a great deal will come of it: and I want the Major to express that, as much as possible in his apoplectic Mephistophilean observation of the scene, and in his share in it.

Lettering: *Major Bagstock is delighted to have that opportunity.*[1]

The letter is typical of the attention to detail which Dickens paid in all his undertakings. At a time when it might be expected that his energies would be fully expended upon writing his monthly instalment, he must turn aside to create a scene in Browne's imagination, letting him into secrets, appropriately enough, which less privileged readers were left to guess, and speaking out straight on matters which in the novel he is content to hint at, but embodying here and there with little verbal change significant details from the manuscript before him.[2] Browne responded rapidly. The directions were dated 10 March 1847; on the evening of 15 March Dickens was writing to express his delight at the sketch which Browne had furnished, and to ask him to re-dress the Native ('who is prodigiously good as he is') in European costume ('He may wear ear-rings and look outlandish,

1. D. C. Thomson, op. cit., pp. 68–71; *Letters*, II 17–18.
2. We have italicized these passages in the second and third paragraphs.

and be dark brown') and to make the Major older, and with a larger face.[1]

The last book which Browne illustrated was *A Tale of Two Cities*. For *Our Mutual Friend*—neither the weekly serial nor the first 'volume' edition of *Great Expectations* was illustrated—Dickens chose Marcus Stone, the son of an old friend. Though Stone was only twenty-five when he began work on *Our Mutual Friend*, Dickens seems to have given him a freer hand than he allowed Browne. Stone used to get proofs and select his own subjects, though Dickens reserved the right to criticize and to demand alterations, and was always 'ready to describe down to the minutest details the personal characteristics, and . . . life-history of the creations of his fancy'.[2] But though Stone was allowed to draw the cover of *Our Mutual Friend* without more than the first two monthly numbers to go upon, Dickens's son-in-law Charles Collins, who drew the cover of *Edwin Drood*, admitted that he did not in the least know the significance of the various groups in the design, which were drawn from instructions given him personally by Dickens.[3]

III

Much is known about Dickens's habits at the desk. In the middle of his career, it was his normal custom to work in the mornings only from nine o'clock till two; but he was no clock-work performer like Trollope. He described himself beginning *Little Dorrit*, in a letter to Mrs Watson (21 May 1855),

walking about the country by day—prowling about into the strangest places in London by night—sitting down to do an immensity—getting up after doing nothing—walking about my room on particular bits of all the flowers in the carpet—tearing my hair (which I can't afford to do)—and on the whole astonished at my own condition, though I am used to it. . .[4]

1. D. C. Thomson, op. cit., p. 65; *Letters*, II 19. Thomson (p. 234) also prints a table of work, without mentioning book or year, which shows that Browne received his instructions for the first plate on Friday, 11 Jan., posted his sketch to Dickens on Sunday, received it back on Monday evening with instructions for the second plate, forwarded his sketch for that on Tuesday, and received it on Wednesday. The first plate was finished on Tuesday, 22 Jan., and the second on Saturday, 26 Jan.

2. Notes of an interview with Stone, quoted in *The Dickensian*, Aug. 1912, pp. 216–17.

3. Luke Fildes in *The Times*, 3 Nov. 1905.

4. *The Dickensian*, June 1942, pp. 165–6.

As a young man he had been a fluent writer, able to drive himself to work all day; and the surviving sheets of manuscript of his earliest novels suggest a hand racing to keep pace with the mind's conceptions. As Heminge and Condell said of Shakespeare, 'We have scarce received from him a blot in his papers.' His letters to Forster written at this time suggest that eleven or twelve of these sheets, or 'slips' as he called them, could be written in a day, or, at a push, as many as twenty.[1] But at the height of his powers, he found more difficulty in satisfying himself, and from *Dombey and Son* onwards his manuscripts are characterized by frequent erasures and interlineations. Of these slips Georgina Hogarth is witness[2] that an average day's work was two or two-and-a-half, and 'a very, *very* hard days work was 4 of them'. The different shades of ink which he used from time to time show that his habit was to correct as he wrote, sentence by sentence, and that though he subsequently read through the whole of his chapter, he rarely needed to make any later alteration.

IV

The manuscripts he sent to press were these corrected first drafts. He never dictated to an amanuensis, nor used a secretary to make a fair copy, and only in a few instances can we be sure that he took the trouble of rewriting a much-corrected slip.[3] Indeed there was no time for what a modern printer regards as normal courtesy from his author; and as for dictation, it would only have hindered him, for he relied upon the knowledge that he had to fill about thirty slips in his normal handwriting to com-

1. Forster, II ii, iii, iv.

2. Letter to F. Harvey, 15 Dec. 1880, accompanying the MS. of *The Battle of Life* (Pierpont Morgan Library).

3. When sending Charles Edward Lester a sheet of the MS. of *Oliver Twist* on 19 July 1840, he remarked, 'I should tell you perhaps as a kind of certificate of the Oliver scrap, that it is a portion of the original and only draught.—I never copy' (letter in the New York Public Library, Berg Collection). But this does not represent his invariable practice later in life. The sheet on which Staggs's Gardens is described in *Dombey and Son*, ch. vi, is so clean and so conspicuously different from its neighbours in that respect as to suggest that he had decided to make a fair copy of a passage which had involved him in unusually heavy corrections. On the same reasoning it seems likely that he rewrote the first MS. slip of *Hunted Down* and of *A Holiday Romance* (both in the Pierpont Morgan Library), and certain passages in *Barnaby Rudge* (see p. 81 n.). In the MS. of *Little Dorrit* there are traces of rough draft on the versos of some sheets of the first and last numbers; three leaves of the last number have been pasted on to slips concealing an earlier version.

plete a monthly number. Thus Bradbury and Evans, his printers, had to make do with 'copy' obscure enough to daunt the most experienced compositor. Not only was it written in a small hand with all too little space left between lines for the numerous inter-lineations, but the text was sprinkled with peculiar proper names —not Cox but Tox, not Tomlinson but Towlinson—and with phonetic spellings of standard English. The difficulties presented even to a compositor accustomed to Dickens's hand may be gauged from the printer's setting up 'Mr. Dick was very partial to going abroad' for 'Mr. Dick was very partial to ginger bread'. But the compositors were picked men,[1] clean, quick, and accurate. To ensure rapid despatch they were accustomed to distribute copy amongst several hands by dividing each slip across the centre and endorsing the lower half with a starred numeral corresponding to the number of the original slip.[2] Their accuracy cannot be properly attested until the manuscripts have been carefully collated with the proofs by some future editor of a standard text of the novels; but it may be said that neither Dickens nor Forster, who also read the proofs, found much to need correction.

Surviving copies of proof sheets suggest that the printer was instructed to provide galley-proof when time permitted. Thus corrected proofs of *Copperfield*[3] consist of two sets of galley-proof of Number I, one set of page-proof of Numbers II to XVIII, and two sets of page-proof of Number XIX–XX. It seems unlikely that Numbers II to XIX–XX were first set up in galley, for time was short; and, as will be seen, the bulk of correction was necessarily done in page. We can be almost certain that Number II (chapters iv–vi, published on 31 May 1849) was not set up in galley, for Dickens sent the end of the number to Evans on 5 May 1849 with the note, 'If it should make a little too much (as I think it may) let them begin Chapter 5 on page 46, where there is now a great blank.'[4] A reasonable inference is that he had already seen page-proofs of at least chapter iv and possibly of chapter v as well.

There was not infrequently 'a little too much', for though he used the numbering of his slips as a guide to quantity—30 slips would yield about 32 pages of print—the reckoning was only

1. Mamie Dickens, *My Father as I recall him* [1897], p. 63.
2. See letter to Mrs Procter, 29 Oct. 1865 (*Letters*, III 442).
3. Victoria and Albert Museum Library, 48 B 16.   4. *Letters*, II 152.

approximate. In every number of *Copperfield* except V, X, XI,
XIV, XVI, XVIII, and XIX–XX, the proofs show what was
called 'over-matter' extending, in Number VI, to as much as 96
lines of print. Dickens was so well accustomed to this happening
that he could write to a correspondent on 28 January 1848, when
Dombey and Son was drawing to a close:

> I never accept an engagement for about this day in the month:
> being always liable, if my *proofs are late, to have to revise them at the
> printers*, and if there is too much matter (as is the case this month)
> to take it out, and put them all to rights and leave them on the
> press.[1]

But the amount taken out rarely corresponded at all exactly with
the amount of 'over-matter'. Thus in *Copperfield* VI Dickens
saved little more than 50 of the 96 lines excess; and in Number
IX, where there were 58 lines excess, he saved 40 but inserted the
equivalent of six more, adding as a note to the printer, 'the over-
matter must be got in somehow—by lengthening the page'. This
expedient was needed only in extreme cases, a 51-line page then
taking the place of a page of 50 lines of type. Where the over-
matter was small, less drastic methods were employed. In *Copperfield* XIII, for example, where there were a mere 11 lines too
many, the printer preferred to save the space by resetting a letter,
quoted at the end of chapter xi, in smaller type; and on numerous
occasions a small saving was readily made where the final words
of a paragraph overlapped into a new line.

When forced to lop and crop, Dickens was accustomed to make
his cuts at the expense of the comedy. In *Dombey and Son*, where
passages of greater significance were also removed, Mrs Chick,
Miss Tox, and Major Bagstock originally had longer parts;[2] so
had Skimpole in *Bleak House* II and Honeythunder in *Edwin
Drood* V; and in *David Copperfield*, chapter xxi, he had to remove
a capital scene in which Steerforth successfully exerted his charms
upon the lugubrious Mrs Gummidge and entered into a league
with her to be lone and lorn together.[3] The future editor of
Dickens will have to consider restoring these passages to the text,
since they were removed only because of the fortuitous demands
of serial publication.

---

1. *Letters*, ii 70.   2. See below, pp. 97, 98.

3. First published in *Review of English Studies*, new series i (1950), p. 251. It is
obvious, too, that space is most easily saved in dialogue, where short lines of print are
frequent.

But too little copy was even more troublesome than too much. 'Fancy!' Dickens wrote to Forster[1] early in July 1865, while *Our Mutual Friend* was on the stocks, 'fancy my having under-written number sixteen by two and a half pages—a thing I have not done since *Pickwick*!' He had forgotten *Dombey and Son* VI and *Bleak House* XVI where in each instance he was two pages light, and numerous other numbers deficient by half a page or more, notably *Little Dorrit* X, which concludes the first book with the release of Old Dorrit from the Marshalsea Prison. On that occasion he was the best part of a page too short even after he had added in proof a long paragraph describing the friends who assembled at the prison gate to welcome Mr Dorrit on his discharge. He disliked giving his readers short measure. The text of a number must usually end well down on the thirty-second page. 'Couldn't the end of the *next* chapter, which is crowded, be brought over to the following page?' he asked on the proofs of *Copperfield* XV, 'then, the blanks at the end of the No would be avoided'.

Proofs also provided opportunity for other types of alteration. Sir Leicester Dedlock's hair is turned from white to grey in *Bleak House* I, Richard Carstone's age is increased from seventeen to nineteen, and it is only at this stage that Skimpole's first name is changed from Leonard to Harold—one of a number of changes designed to weaken the resemblance to Leigh Hunt—that Jobling's assumed name is altered from 'Owen' to 'Weevle', that Matthew Bagnet's nickname is changed from 'Number Seventy Four' to 'Lignum Vitæ' and Minnie Meagles's from 'Baby' to 'Pet'. It is more surprising to discover that until proof Miss Flite had been 'Maggie'—a name to be used in *Little Dorrit* for another crazy woman[2]—and that even then Dickens had toyed with 'Flighty'.

Forster had also been accustomed to lend a hand ever since 1837.[3] He provided another pair of eyes for detecting errors of the press, and he was trusted as a judge of what the average reader would stand. Proofs show that he softened such expletives as Dickens himself had overlooked, and removed the description of Miss Tox ejecting the bugs from the wainscoting of her house by means of a brush dipped in paraffin. Furthermore, Forster was

1. Forster, IX v.
2. Her surname also is changed in proof—from Flinx to Bangham.
3. Forster, II i.

usually in London and could deal with last-minute adjustments sent from Broadstairs or further afield. Thus in July 1841 Dickens wrote from the Highlands—a 'place which no man ever spelt but which sounds like Ballyhoolish'—inquiring 'whether the blind man, in speaking to Barnaby about riches, tells him they are to be found in *crowds*. If I have not actually used that word, will you introduce it? A perusal of the proof of the following number (70) will show you how, and why.'[1] The addition was needed in chapter xlvii in the next number. A few years later on, as the last number of *Dombey* was going to press, he recollected that in the final parade of his pantomime one character had been overlooked—the dog Diogenes; he therefore sent Forster alternative versions, leaving to his judgement which was to be inserted in proof. There is no evidence of his consulting anyone else at proof-stage, except for a mystifying reference in a letter of 15 May 1861, where he tells Lytton that 'a woman' had frequently shown, when proofs were read to her, 'an intuitive sense and discretion that I have set great store by'.[2]

V

Such were the conditions in which he worked from writing the first words of the novel till the moment of publication. But the system only began to work when planning was completed. The nature of his planning is very largely revealed in the notes bound with his manuscripts. Those of *Pickwick Papers*, *Nicholas Nickleby*, and *Oliver Twist* are imperfect;[3] but judging by the sparseness of notes in the first complete manuscript, that of *The Old Curiosity Shop*,[4] the notes for these early novels are likely to have been very slight indeed. The beginnings of a change in practice are first noticeable in the manuscript of *Martin Chuzzlewit*, and it is not

1. Forster, II ix.

2. *Letters*, III 220. Could the unknown woman have been anyone but Georgina Hogarth?

3. Fragments of *Pickwick* are in the British Museum and in the Berg Collection of the New York Public Library; about two-thirds of *Oliver Twist* is in the Victoria and Albert Museum, and a page in the Berg Collection; and the Dickens House in Doughty Street has some fragments of *Nickleby*.

4. This MS. and those of all subsequent novels, with two exceptions, were bequeathed by Forster to the Victoria and Albert Museum. The MS. of *Great Expectations* was given by Dickens to Chauncy Hare Townshend and by him to the Wisbech Museum where it still lies. The MS. of *Our Mutual Friend* was given by Dickens to E. S. Dallas, and is now in the Pierpont Morgan Library.

without significance that Dickens claimed in the original preface to this novel:

> I have endeavoured in the progress of this Tale, to resist the temptation of the current Monthly Number, and to keep a steadier eye upon the general purpose and design. With this object in view, I have put a strong constraint upon myself from time to time, in many places; and I hope the story is the better for it, now.

Some evidence of this growing restraint is to be found in the manuscript notes for contents of two numbers of *Martin Chuzzlewit*, IV (chapters ix and x) and VI (chapters xiii–xv). Thereafter each novel from *Dombey and Son* to *Edwin Drood*, except for *Great Expectations* and *A Tale of Two Cities*,[1] has its full quota of notes, one page to each number.

The precise function which these notes fulfilled is difficult to determine. Dickens himself never mentions them; and Forster, who reproduced in his *Life of Dickens* part of the notes prepared for the first monthly numbers of *Little Dorrit* and *David Copperfield* to show 'in the former the labour and pains, and in the latter the lightness and confidence of handling',[2] was either ignorant of their function or insufficiently curious about them.

From *Dombey and Son* onwards the notes are uniform in appearance. A sheet of paper has been folded across the centre, thus forming two conjugate half-sheets. The left-hand half-sheet is invariably filled with general memoranda: the right-hand sheet is invariably headed by the title of the novel and the number of the monthly part, and is then sub-divided into chapters. A glance at the photograph of the notes relating to *David Copperfield* VII will show that the chapter numbers and chapter titles have been written down before the succeeding notes, since Dickens has left himself insufficient space between chapter xix and chapter xx for all the jottings he wanted to make. The *Edwin Drood* notes confirm that this was his practice, for the notes for Numbers V and VI contain no more than the chapter numbers and chapter titles.

What Dickens did after mapping out his memoranda sheet into chapters may be inferred from the appearance of the ink. He seems to have had three sorts in general use, one a blue-black, another a vivid blue, and a third which has now faded to a

---

1. It is not easy to account for Dickens's abandoning his practice in his last two weekly serial novels. The MS. of *Great Expectations* contains notes of other kinds; see below, pp. 30–1.

2. Forster, VIII i.

watery yellow. The supplies appear to have been uncertain, since changes from one to another occur with baffling irregularity. But though the irregularity is puzzling in itself, the frequency of change in ink in some of the manuscripts throws some light upon the process of composition. Thus the supply of watery ink with which *David Copperfield* was begun gave out on the eleventh leaf of Number IV, three-quarters way through chapter x, and Dickens then changed over to vivid blue which lasted him until the end of Number VII; but in Number VIII (chapter xxii) he reverted to the watery ink. We should expect the ink with which the notes were written to alter with these changes, if we assume that Dickens wrote the notes at the same desk at which he was writing the novel. But this does not happen. In the notes for Number IV[1] the chapter titles of chapters xi and xii, the line 'on my own account, and don't like it' on the left-hand side, and the passage 'neglect Quinion.–arrangement/"Behold me" &c' on the right-hand side are written in vivid blue ink unlike the surrounding notes, which are written in watery ink. This suggests that the passages written in vivid blue were jotted down after the supply of watery ink had temporarily failed and therefore *after* Dickens had begun to compose the number. But it also suggests that the notes under the headings of chapters xi and xii were written *before* the chapters were composed. More surprising is to find the resumption of watery ink in Number VIII anticipated in the summary for Number VII, where the only jottings in vivid blue are the memoranda on the left-hand side, the three chapter numbers, and the first two chapter titles. The inference is that all the notes on the right-hand side and the last chapter title ('Little Em'ly') were written after finishing the monthly number itself.

There is further evidence to support this. On the left-hand side Dickens can be seen trying out two names for Steerforth's servant: 'Lirrimer? Littimer'. 'Lirrimer' was his first choice; and so the name stands, though corrected to 'Littimer' on its first two occurrences in the second paragraph of chapter xxi—'Nothing could be objected against his surname, ⟨Lirrimer⟩ Littimer, by which he was known. Peter might have been hanged, or Tom transported; but ⟨Lirrimer⟩ Littimer was perfectly respectable.' But by the time he came to write the fourth paragraph of the same chapter, he was quite decided upon the name. 'Littimer was in my room in the morning' needed no correction, and 'Lit-

1. See below, pp. 126–7.

timer' he was from that point onwards. But 'Littimer' was also the form used in the notes to chapter xxi, showing that the notes for this chapter—or at least a part of them—were written after the chapter was completed.

It will be recalled that Mr Vholes in *Bleak House* supported an aged father in the Vale of Taunton. The manuscript reveals that he was originally intended to support an aged mother: 'father' is a correction in the manuscript, but it is the word 'father' we find in the summary for that chapter. Similarly, a comparison of chapter titles in the notes and in the text of *Bleak House* and of passages from the text quoted in the notes shows that the version in the notes often, but not invariably, records the corrected and not the original version.

It is clear, therefore, that Dickens was not entirely consistent in his practice. Sometimes he wrote his chapter notes before the corresponding chapter was written, sometimes after. And this inconsistency in his practice seems to imply an inconsistency of purpose. For while those chapter notes which were written after the chapter was finished cannot have been intended to help him in the composition of the chapter, those which were written before the composition of the chapter they relate to may well have been intended as a rough plan of the direction the chapter was to take. The closing notes for chapters vii and ix in *Copperfield* III are almost certainly notes of this kind.[1] But that he should have taken the trouble to jot down chapter notes after the chapter was written suggests that though he did not always need a rough plan to work by in composing his chapter, he did feel the need of a summary of the chapter afterwards. The function of this summary may have been to refresh his memory of the details of the preceding number before embarking upon the next.

The chapter notes on the right-hand side, then, seem to fill a double purpose. Sometimes they serve to rough out the direction the chapter will take and to emphasize its salient points; but except for the last numbers, they always serve to summarize the contents and to put Dickens into the mood of the last monthly number when beginning upon another.

The function of the notes on the left-hand side seems to have been different. They are jotted down haphazardly and bear no relation to the chapter divisions on the right-hand side. Dickens is seen in the process of meditating what ingredients shall go into

1. See below, p. 123.

the number to be written. Both the form of the entries and the quality of the ink show that there were frequently two stages in this process. The questions represent the stage of indecision; and the conviction of the replies, often underlined more than once, suggests that the shape of the number was rapidly forming in his mind.

This indecision must not be read as evidence of mere opportunism, as though Dickens relied upon the inspiration of the moment for filling his number. That indeed must have been his temptation in the days of *Pickwick* and *Nickleby*, and we learn from Forster that the theme of *The Old Curiosity Shop* took gradual form as he wrote it, 'with less direct consciousness of design on his own part than I can remember in any other instance throughout his career'.[1] But from *Martin Chuzzlewit* onwards readers could feel assured that though a Sairey Gamp or a Wilkins Micawber might wrest temporary control of the story, yet the novel was proceeding in however leisurely a fashion to some predestined end. 'The whole pattern . . . is always before the eyes of the story-weaver at his loom', he said in the Postscript to *Our Mutual Friend*; and it is hoped that later studies in this volume will confirm the remark. The master plans of *Dombey and Son*[2] and of subsequent novels almost certainly existed, but they have not survived on paper and in all probability they were never written down. 'I never commit thoughts to paper', he told a correspondent, about the time of *Copperfield*, 'until I am obliged to write, being better able to keep them in regular order, on different shelves of my brain, ready ticketed and labelled to be brought out when I want them.'[3]

The number plans were not primarily concerned with these master plans. At most they drew occasional attention to some prominent thread in the pattern, as when Dickens notes in the plan for *David Copperfield* XII: 'Carry the thread of Agnes through it all', or 'Carry through, the unravelling of Uriah Heep. always by Mr Micawber' in the plan for Number XVI, or 'The man who, being utterly sensual and careless, comes to very much the same thing in the end as the Gradgrind school', a sentence in which he characterizes James Harthouse in the first number plan of *Hard Times*. In short, the number plans show us Dickens not in the moments of creation, but in the moments of translating ideas

1. Forster, II vii.   2. See below, pp. 90, 94.
3. *Harper's New Monthly Magazine*, June–Nov., 1862, p. 379.

into practice,[1] deliberating how best to achieve a certain effect ('Louisa to be acted on by Harthouse, through Tom? Yes', *Hard Times* IV), when to introduce a predetermined theme ('Dora in declining health. First intimation? Yes', *David Copperfield* XVI), how to finish off a number ('Little Em'ly and Mr Peggotty. qy. To close the N° with her discovery? Yes', ibid.), or defining the dominant theme of a number ('David's Marriage to Dora', Number XIV; 'The Emigration N°', Number XVIII). Sometimes he will review possible characters and defer their re-entry to a subsequent number; thus Miss Mowcher's claim is rejected in Number X (chapters xxviii–xxxi) with the note 'Impossible. Try next time', and Mr and Miss Murdstone are kept waiting in the wings for a call which is deferred from month to month from Number XIII till the final number. Sometimes, when at work on one number, he can be discovered turning to consider an episode in a future number. Thus in the memoranda for *Little Dorrit* XVIII there is an entry 'The Merdle Image smashed?'. But it had been smashed in the previous month, and a later entry, '(Done last N°.)', takes account of the fact. This can only mean that the original entry, and presumably the two preceding entries, on the plan for Number XVIII were written before Number XVII was finished. Such evidence, however, is exceptional; and equally exceptional is the use of these memoranda to plan a scene at some length, as the storm scene in Yarmouth Roads is planned in *Copperfield* Number XVIII.[2] Often the briefest of notes suffices: 'Miss Murdstone comes on a donkey' is enough to suggest that generously comic incident in chapter xiii. Though indeed the majority of these jottings are related to incidents in the story, almost as many record the names of characters only. Their names, it would seem, were enough to suggest the parts the characters were to play.

1. For several years Dickens kept a notebook in which he jotted down notions as they darted into his mind; for example, 'The unwieldy ship taken in tow by the snorting little steam Tug', subsequently endorsed 'Done in Casby and Panks'. This notebook, which was used by Forster for his *Life of Dickens*, is now in the Berg Collection of the New York Public Library. He is also reported to have kept 'a series of small paper bags, filled with scraps of paper containing various memoranda' upon his writing-table (F. G. Kitton, *Charles Dickens by Pen and Pencil*, 1889, pp. 173–4, on the authority of Arthur Locker, a contributor to *All the Year Round*); but no memoranda other than those mentioned in this chapter have survived.

2. See below, pp. 168–9.

VI

Such would seem to have been the purposes Dickens had in mind when making these memoranda. Other notes associated with the memoranda can be more confidently accounted for. There are several sheets on which possible titles have been drafted. Occasionally—but this is rare—he makes a calculation about the age of a character so as to assure himself that all the evidence tallies. Thus there is a note on Florence's age in *Dombey and Son* XV based on the statement in Number VI that she was then not yet fourteen. An even more detailed calculation is made of the ages of the ten principal characters 'in the last stage of Pip's Expectations'.[1]

For *Great Expectations* he had been able to manage without number plans, but he found that he could not entirely dispense with all memoranda. In addition to the note on the ages of the characters, there is a calculation on the state of the tides for use in the great scene of Magwitch's recapture (chapter liv),[1] and there is a sketch of the conclusion of the novel[1] headed 'General Mems' which reads as follows:

> Miss Havisham and Pip, and the Money for Herbert. So Herbert made a partner in Clarriker's.
> Compeyson. How brought in?
> Estella. Magwitch's daughter.
> Orlick and Pip's entrapment—and escape
>   —To the flight
>   Start
>   Pursuit
>   Struggle—Both on board
>   together—Compeyson drownd [sic]—
>   Magwitch rescued by Pip. And
>   taken—
> Then:
>   Magwitch tried, found guilty, & left for
>   Death
>   Dies presently in Newgate
>   Property confiscated to the Crown.
> Herbert goes abroad:
>   Pip perhaps to follow.
> Pip arrested when too ill to be moved—lies in the Chambers in Fever. Ministering Angel Joe.

1. Printed in *The Dickensian*, Mar. 1949, pp. 78–80.

recovered again, Pip goes humbly down to the
   old marsh Village, to propose to Biddy.
     Finds Biddy married to Joe
So goes abroad to Herbert (happily married to Clara
Barley), and becomes his clerk.
   The one good thing he did in his prosperity,
the only thing that endures and bears good fruit.

Although there is no comparable sketch for the conclusion of any other novel, it is not altogether surprising that one was needed for a novel written without the help of number plans. The last double number had often proved to be troublesome. In *Dombey and Son* the final number plan is dense with notes; two or three scenes are sketched in some detail; and as each memorandum is used, a tick is placed against it in the plan. The last of these reads 'Q^y Order of chapters—'. An answer was found in the customary manner on the right-hand side of the number plan. But when the same problem arose in *David Copperfield*, the solution was reached only after canvassing three different orders in the memoranda.[1] In *Little Dorrit* also the order of chapters had to be settled ahead; but there the difficulty was, in the words of the chapter summary, to 'tell the whole story, working it out as much as possible through Mrs Clennam herself, so as to present her character very strongly'. Even the author himself seems to have been hard pressed to recall the precise connexion between Arthur Clennam, his father, his uncle, and Frederick Dorrit, Mrs Clennam, Flintwinch, and Flintwinch's brother. Accordingly an additional memorandum in two columns was compiled for the double number, one column being entitled 'Mems: for working the story round.—Retrospective' and the other 'Mems: for working the story round.—Prospective'. The 'retrospective mems.' summarize what was already known to the reader, and append page references; the 'prospective mems.' succeed, after what was clearly a struggle, in finding an answer to the initial question, 'How [were the Clennams] connected with the Dorrits?'

The conclusion of *Great Expectations* was straightforward by comparison, though 'the general turn and tone of the working out and winding up, will be away from all such things as they conventionally go', and 'the planning out from week to week' was declared to be unimaginably difficult.[2] The interest of the

1. See below, p. 174.   2. *Letters*, III 216–17.

sketch printed above lies in the stage of the story at which Dickens took his bearings, and the details which he altered in the course of writing. The last stage of Pip's expectations begins in chapter xl with Magwitch's return. Of the succeeding twelve chapters—dealing with Magwitch's story, Estella's marriage to Drummle and her parentage, the arrangements for Magwitch's escape by river, and Miss Havisham's death—the summary has little or nothing to say. It is only after Pip's entrapment by Orlick in chapter liii and his rescue that the events are forecast in detail. It would therefore appear that the sketch was written either immediately before or immediately after the completion of chapter liii, and that the first three entries are notes about matters still to be kept prominently in view. It was in chapter xxxvii that Pip had begun to buy Herbert a place in Clarriker's business, and the transaction was completed by Miss Havisham in chapter xlix. But it remains a live issue; for this was, in the words of the sketch,

> the one good thing he did in his prosperity, the only thing that endures and bears good fruit.

That this was not a mere afterthought, but one of the 'morals' of the book, is shown by the anticipation of these words at the end of chapter xxxvii:

> At length, the thing being done, and he having that day entered Clarriker's House, and he having talked to me for a whole evening in a flush of pleasure and success, I did really cry in good earnest when I went to bed, to think that my expectations had done some good to somebody.

'Compeyson. How brought in?' This query seems to refer to a problem of tying up loose ends at the conclusion of the novel, for Compeyson had been 'in' from the beginning. He had been actively shadowing Pip and Magwitch since the first chapter of the final stage, and his relations with Miss Havisham had been explained at a time when Dickens was still calling him 'Compey'. It was in chapter xlii that he was first given a name, and the last three letters are first added to it in the manuscript of chapter xlv. Not until chapter xlvii, where he next enters, is the name 'Compeyson' written without hesitation, as it is written in the 'General Mems'. On any explanation of them, therefore, the memoranda cannot have been drawn up until after chapter xlii was written, in which Magwitch tells the story of his life. 'How brought in?' must refer to something other than Compeyson's connexion with

Miss Havisham, and to what else can it refer but to the scene of Magwitch's capture?

'Estella. Magwitch's daughter' was almost certainly a part of the original design: it bears at least as closely upon the 'moral' of the book as the purchase of Herbert's partnership. Though the parentage is revealed before chapter liv, it was still to be kept in mind for use in the scene of Magwitch's death and later.

The sketch seems therefore to have been designed to cover the course of the last six chapters, or what is called in the manuscript the 'Ninth Monthly Portion'. The course as planned was not strictly followed. Magwitch and Compeyson were not on board together, nor was Magwitch rescued from drowning by Pip. Herbert's departure occurs before the trial, and there is no hint given of Wemmick's wedding or of the last meeting with Uncle Pumblechook. The variations are small, the additions mentioned are scarcely significant; so narrowly does Dickens diverge from the path he had plotted.

But there was to be one other addition to the scheme, the final scene with Estella. In the novel as we read it, all but the opening paragraphs of chapter lix, describing Pip's visit to the old forge, are a revised version urged upon Dickens by Bulwer Lytton.[1] The original was preserved and published by Forster,[2] who regarded it as 'more consistent with the drift, as well as natural working out, of the tale'. From this we see that the book was to end with a casual meeting between Pip and Estella. 'I was very glad afterwards to have had the interview', Pip commented,

> for, in her face and in her voice, and in her touch, she gave me the assurance, that suffering had been stronger than Miss Havisham's teaching, and had given her a heart to understand what my heart used to be.

Perhaps this seemed obvious before Lytton made his sentimental plea—something which could be left, like Wemmick's marriage, for the improvisation of the moment. It was at least more appropriate that Pip, who had lost Magwitch's money, should also lose his daughter, than that he should marry her in the end.

These were the kind of notes which experience showed that his system of publication and his manner of work required of him. They do not determine the pattern of the novel, they do not define the path of the story, but they ensure that, the pattern

1. *Letters*, III 225.   2. Forster, IX iii.

once determined, the threads do not go awry, and, the path once set, there is no serious deviation in a course of as much as nineteen months. Furthermore, they have an abiding interest in that they shed light on the design in the pattern and serve to show the measure of control which Dickens exercised. They reveal a calculated emphasis at one point, a calculated suspense at another, a problem of arrangement solved or a conclusion settled; they will accordingly be examined more closely in subsequent chapters in relation to the novels whose composition they served. The first ten years of Dickens's career present problems of a different kind. Though the documentation is sparser, enough evidence survives to answer some of the more interesting questions raised, and to these the next three chapters are devoted.

CHAPTER II

Sketches by Boz:
Collection and Revision

———

I

EVERY biographer has described how Dickens began by contributing tales and sketches to magazines and newspapers,
later collected and enlarged in the two series of *Sketches by
Boz*; and many since Forster have followed Dickens's own cue in
high-lighting that dramatic moment in December 1833 when the
twenty-one-year-old gallery reporter bought a copy of the *Monthly Magazine* and his eyes were 'dimmed with joy and pride' on
seeing his first story 'in all the glory of print'.[1] But there are many
aspects of this crucial first phase of his writing that have been
under-emphasized or even neglected: not only the sheer merit of
the *Sketches*, but their signal importance as an event in literary
history, and the effect of their contemporary fame on Dickens's
literary career; and, most neglected of all, the care which he
took in revising them. That revision—its extent, direction, and
probable motives—is the primary concern of this essay; it deserves a fairly full treatment, both for its obvious relevance to the
theme of this book and for the light thrown on the inter-relations
of journalistic and creative writing, a question of central interest
to Dickens's early career, and perhaps to the whole.

The *Sketches by Boz* are too apt to be seen as a mere prelude to
Pickwick Papers, instead of as, in Forster's words, 'a book that
might have stood its ground, even if it had stood alone'.[2] They
have been seen from a distance as 'early Dickens', and seldom as
writings which suddenly appeared to dazzle the 1830s with their
brilliance. And this has affected the whole interpretation of those

1. Preface to 1847 edition of *Pickwick Papers*.   2. Forster, I v.

first three years; too exclusive an emphasis has been laid on the 'ascent of the rocket'[1] with the fame of *Pickwick* and its immediate consequences, whereas it was the success of the *Sketches*, first in periodicals and then more decisively in book form, that really inaugurated Dickens's career as a writer. Indeed, as subsequent chapters suggest,[2] it appeared as the beginning of a different kind of success. When we try to recover Dickens's own point of view in the winter of 1835–6 and that of the contemporary readers who gave the First Series of the *Sketches* its glowing reception in February and March, we see that the *Pickwick* project cut across the planned career at an unexpected and slightly disturbing angle; and it was not of *Pickwick* that Dickens was thinking when he promised 'connected works of fiction of a higher grade' as a result of the 'unlooked-for success' of the *Sketches*.[3] The deflection of his ambition was, as we know, permanent; against all probability and expectation he discovered in that 'monthly something' his full creative powers and the beginnings of his large-scale constructive powers; he also, almost accidentally, initiated his characteristic mode of publication; and that is certainly one reason[4] why in maturity he tended himself to belittle the *Sketches*, and left too many later readers content to take them at the author's retrospective valuation. 'They were written', said Dickens, looking back from the peak of 1850, the year of *David Copperfield*, 'when I was a very young man . . . sent into the world with all their imperfections (a good many) on their heads . . . I am conscious of their often being extremely crude and ill-considered, and bearing obvious marks of haste and inexperience'.[5] This is very different from the tone of the original Preface of February 1836, which, despite its tactful modesty—the *Sketches* are a 'pilot balloon' in which the author ventures with the 'assistance and companionship' of an already famous illustrator, 'GEORGE CRUIKSHANK'—

1. The phrase, adapted from the review in the *Quarterly* (Oct. 1837), is used by Johnson as a chapter heading for III 3, in the year following the completion of *Pickwick* (1838). This criticism applies less to him than to other post-Forster biographers.

2. See pp. 63, 76 below.

3. Preface to second edition of First Series, 1 Aug. 1836; that is, just before *Pickwick* began to succeed.

4. Another reason may be that the later history of the *Sketches* involved him in his first disillusioning clash with a publisher.

5. Preface to 1850 edition (reprinted without change in all subsequent editions); this was the seventh volume in the 'Cheap edition'. It was Dickens's wish to put it late, since otherwise 'the Sketches would make a dangerous break in the continuity of the Sale, and perhaps damage what followed' (*Letters*, II 148).

asserts a high claim in the classic phrase of all literary revolutions
—'his object has been to present little pictures of life and manners
as they really are', which is echoed in the challenge of the sub-
title: 'Illustrative of Every-Day Life, and Every-Day People'.
As such they were applauded on all sides: next to the 'variety',
the mingling of the exquisitely ridiculous and the grim, what was
most praised was the 'startling fidelity';[1] ' "Boz" is a kind of Bos-
well to society.'[2] The *Sketches* were acclaimed for their novelty and
accuracy both in the kind of life observed, and the penetration
of the observer accepting and transforming the commonplace,
'bringing out the meaning and interest of objects which would
altogether escape the observation of ordinary minds',[3] 'the romance, as it were, of real life'.[4] Throughout the reviews there is
gratitude for the discovery of 'every-day life' in neglected but
immediately recognized pockets of urban and suburban society.
This sense of revelation cannot be fully recovered by readers unaware of the deficiency of such a quality in the popular prose-
literature of the time, of the sharpness of the difference between
the world of Boz and the worlds of 'silver-fork' novels, of the
Annuals, of romantic-historical thrillers and 'political-economy'
tales, or of the less sharp but still distinctive difference from the
comic worlds of Hood and Hook[5] and the lower-grade imitators
of Egan's *Life in London*. Unlike *Pickwick*, which for all its incidental topicality is upheld in timeless splendour by the illusion of
a self-sustaining world, the *Sketches* have more to give to a modern
reader who knows something of their literary and social context.
But this approach, though helpful, is by no means indispensable.
The tales and sketches themselves, without annotation, give us the
world which the young Dickens saw; and what is more import-

1. *Metropolitan Magazine*, Mar. 1836, p. 77.
2. *Court Journal*, 20 Feb. 1836, p. 123.   3. *Examiner*, 28 Feb. 1836, p. 133.
4. *Spectator*, 20 Feb. 1836, p. 183.
5. Some reviewers compared Boz's 'caricature of Cockney life' with Hook's;
others found it noticeably superior, and the *Sunday Times* (21 Feb. 1836) predicted
that Boz 'would one day make Tom Hood look to his laurels'. None mentions what
seems much more akin to Dickens's work, the tales in John Poole's *Sketches and
Recollections* (1835; mainly from the *New Monthly Magazine* of 1826–34). Sketches on
the recreations of Londoners (such as Greenwich Fair, Astley's, Vauxhall Gardens)
were very common, but the likeness here is merely of substance.

The closest contact, recognized by several reviewers, was between the tales and
contemporary theatrical comedy; they do not suggest derivation, but note Boz's
promise as a comic dramatist. Two tales were soon to be dramatized, 'The Bloomsbury Christening' and 'The Great Winglebury Duel', the latter by Dickens himself
as *The Strange Gentleman*.

ant, they give us Dickens seeing it, with that curious, all-absorbing
eye—the child's eye of David Copperfield, which he never lost.

Contemporary reviews are cited here, because the comments
of critics saluting an almost unknown writer have a special value
as testimony; but Forster's summary,[1] which includes and recalls
their sense of discovery, has also the distinctive authority of its
date and writer, and much of it deserves to be quoted for its
general critical direction as well as its information:

> The *Sketches* were much more talked about than the first two or
> three numbers of *Pickwick*, and I remember still with what hearty
> praise the book was first named to me by my dear friend Albany
> Fonblanque, as keen and clear a judge as ever lived either of books
> or men. Richly did it merit all the praise it had, and more, I will
> add, than he was ever disposed to give to it himself. He decidedly
> underrated it. He gave, in subsequent writings, so much more per-
> fect form and fullness to everything it contained, that he did not
> care to credit himself with the marvel of having yet so early anti-
> cipated so much. But the first sprightly runnings of his genius are
> undoubtedly here... The observation shown throughout is nothing
> short of wonderful. Things are painted literally as they are; and,
> whatever the picture, whether of every-day vulgar, shabby genteel,
> or downright low, with neither the condescending air which is
> affectation, nor the too familiar one which is slang... Of course
> there are inequalities in it, and some things that would have been
> better away: but it is a book that might have stood its ground, even
> if it had stood alone, as containing unusually truthful observation
> of a sort of life between the middle class and the low, which,
> having few attractions for bookish observers, was quite unhacknied
> ground. It had otherwise also the very special merit of being in no
> respect bookish or commonplace in its descriptions of the old city
> with which its writer was so familiar. It was a picture of every-day
> London at its best and worst, in its humours and enjoyments as well
> as its sufferings and sins, pervaded everywhere not only with the
> absolute reality of the things depicted, but also with that subtle
> sense and mastery of feeling which gives to the reader's sympathies
> invariably right direction, and awakens consideration, tenderness,
> and kindness precisely for those who most need such help.

II

'He decidedly underrated it'. This underrating has already
been illustrated from Dickens's 1850 Preface; and his view, how-

1. Forster, I v.

ever disputable, is a valid personal judgement, a fact about Dickens in 1850. But two other statements in that Preface, both coloured by this critical view, are open to objection from their manipulation of facts.

> The whole of these sketches were written and published, one by one, when I was a very young man.

But since six[1] out of the total of over fifty had made no previous periodical appearance,[2] and since his letters of 1835–6 show that some at least were written especially for the collection, this is only an approximate statement; and his exaggeration is probably motivated, consciously or not, by a wish to extenuate their 'obvious marks of haste'. What follows is misleading, if not disingenuous:

> They were collected and republished while I was still a very young man; and sent into the world with all their imperfections (a good many) on their heads . . .
>
> But as this collection is not originated now, and was very leniently and favourably received when it was first made, I have not felt it right either to remodel or expunge, beyond a few words and phrases here and there.

This description would not lead one to suppose that when Dickens first collected his sketches he made extensive cuts, rewrote whole paragraphs, and made innumerable minute changes both of substance and style; nor that he continued to revise in successive editions including the very one for which this Preface was written. Only an edition with heavy textual apparatus could exhibit the full extent of these changes; but a general account of them is for the first time[3] attempted here. The docu-

1. Three tales ('The Black Veil', 'The Great Winglebury Duel', and 'Sentiment', first appearing in First Series); and three sketches ('A Visit to Newgate', First Series, 'Our Next-door Neighbours' and 'The Drunkard's Death', Second Series).

2. Fifty-three items were previously published; all but one are recorded by Hatton and Cleaver, pp. 91–103, and 'Brokers' and Marine Store Shops' was further noted by W. J. Carlton (*The Dickensian*, Mar. 1951, p. 67) as published in the *Morning Chronicle*, 15 Dec. 1834. The fifty-three are reduced to fifty when collected, as two tales originally appeared in two instalments each, and two sketches were later combined into one.

3. Some of the cut passages are given, and the fact of revision noted by Hatton and Cleaver; and F. J. H. Darton (*Dickens, Positively the First Appearance*, 1933) reprinted the original version of 'A Dinner at Poplar Walk' ('Mr. Minns and his Cousin'). W. J. Carlton (*The Dickensian*, June 1954, pp. 100–9; see below, p. 52, n. 2) makes some use of the original versions of 'A Parliamentary Sketch'. The intermediate revisions of 1837–9 ('monthly parts') and 1850 have, so far as we know, never been mentioned; Darton even says (p. 131) that 'the earliest volume texts

ments are straightforward; no manuscripts or proof sheets survive, but all the periodicals are accessible in national libraries,[1] and also most of the important editions:—First Series, [February] 1836;[2] Second Series, 1837 [December 1836]; Monthly Parts of combined series, November 1837 to June 1839, complete in one volume, May 1839;[3] 'Cheap edition', October 1850.

The story necessarily begins with the process of collection and selection. The plan of a collection was evidently formed, at the suggestion of the publisher John Macrone, early in the October of 1835. By 27 October[4] the scheme was well under way: Cruikshank had been secured as illustrator, and the title was being discussed. Something like 'Bubbles from a Brain' had apparently been considered;[5] but Dickens now put forward, as 'more modest', 'Sketches by Boz and Cuts by Cruikshank', a title which shows his appreciation of his good fortune[6] as well as his awareness of the strikingly visual quality of his own writing.[7] He offered to write additional sketches 'if the whole collection falls short of the two volumes', mentioning several possible topics from his 'memoranda'; his enthusiasm makes it plain that he meant to

(1836) remained virtually the same in all later editions'. Yet the 'monthly parts' were actually advertised as 'revised by the author'. The Macmillan edition of 1892, which purports to reprint the 'first' edition, gives the 1839 text.

1. The British Museum lacks the 1833-4 volumes of the *Monthly Magazine*.

2. The second edition appeared in Aug. 1836, the third in Mar. 1837 (see below, p. 50, n. 3).

3. We have not seen the actual monthly parts in wrappers, but there was no possibility of revision between these and the volume edition.

4. *Letters*, I 46-7 (letter to Macrone); this is the first known reference to the collection. Dickens was introduced to Cruikshank by Macrone in Nov. (I 49, 52), not, as Johnson (p. 104) implies, by Ainsworth.

5. 'Are you particularly attached to the retention of the word "Brain"—when we can't preserve the parody on Head's title?' (*Letters*, I 46). This must refer to *Bubbles from the Brunnens of Nassau*, By an Old Man [Sir Francis Bond Head], published by John Murray in 1834. The reason against such 'parody' was that both Dickens and Macrone now saw that the notion of 'bubbles coming direct from a steel instrument' was unacceptable; which suggests that some pun on 'springs' may have been thought of.

6. Cruikshank had been before the public as caricaturist and illustrator for some twenty-five years. He had illustrated, for example, John Wight's *Mornings in Bow-street* (1824-7), *Sunday in London* (1833), and *The Comic Almanack* (1835-47), all works showing some general likenesses of material to Dickens's tales and sketches. By this time he had probably also agreed to illustrate the fourth edition of Ainsworth's *Rookwood*, which Macrone published in 1836.

7. Apart from the quasi-pun, 'Sketches' was a natural choice, as Dickens had used it for two of the newspaper series; it was also fashionable (especially for accounts of travel) and appropriately recalled Washington Irving's *Sketch-Book* (1820), which Dickens greatly admired (*Letters*, I 315), as well as a popular success of the year, John Poole's *Sketches and Recollections* (1835).

write 'A Visit to Newgate' whether more material was needed or not. There was no thought at this stage of publishing anything less than 'the whole collection'; but the letters show that Dickens had not yet looked over the available material as a whole, and it was more extensive than he evidently remembered.

The sketches proper, as distinct from the tales, fell into two distinct and complete series; the five 'Street Sketches' which had appeared in the *Morning Chronicle* in the autumn of 1834;[1] and the twenty 'Sketches of London' in the *Evening Chronicle* from January to August 1835.[2] Soon after the conclusion of the latter, Dickens had begun a new series of twelve 'Scenes and Characters', in *Bell's Life in London*,[3] over a new signature, 'Tibbs'; these too were no doubt also regarded as possible material, though in fact only four of the twelve got into the first collected series, as against twenty-two of the earlier twenty-five. Besides the sketches, there were the seven tales which had appeared in the *Monthly Magazine*.[4] The last of these was published in February 1835, Dickens having notified the editor of the *Monthly* that he could no longer contribute without payment; he seems however to have expected to publish 'The Great Winglebury Duel' there in December[5]

1. 'Omnibuses', 26 Sept.; 'Shops and their Tenants', 10 Oct.; 'The Old Bailey', 23 Oct.; 'Shabby and Genteel People', 5 Nov.; 'Brokers' and Marine Store Shops', 15 Dec.

2. 'Hackney-coach stands', 31 Jan.; 'Gin Shops', 7 Feb.; 'Early Coaches', 19 Feb.; 'The Parish', 28 Feb.; 'The House', 7 Mar.; 'London Recreations', 17 Mar.; 'Public Dinners', 7 Apr.; 'Bellamy's', 11 Apr.; 'Greenwich Fair', 16 Apr.; 'Thoughts about People', 23 Apr.; 'Astley's', 9 May; 'Our Parish' (ctd), 19 May; 'The River', 6 June; 'Our Parish' (ctd), 18 June; 'The Pawnbroker's Shop', 30 June; 'Our Parish' (ctd), 14 July; 'The Streets by Morning', 21 July; 'Our Parish' (ctd), 28 July; 'Private Theatres', 11 Aug.; 'Our Parish' (concluded), 20 Aug.

The 'Parish' sketches, though irregularly spaced, form a kind of serial, and were probably intended as a novel variation of that popular success, Miss Mitford's *Our Village* (1824–32).

3. 'Seven Dials', 27 Sept.; 'Miss Evans and "the Eagle"', 4 Oct.; 'The Dancing Academy', 11 Oct.; 'Making a Night of It', 18 Oct.; 'Love and Oysters', 25 Oct.; 'Some Account of an Omnibus Cad', 1 Nov.; 'The Vocal Dress-Maker', 22 Nov.; 'The Prisoners' Van', 29 Nov; 'The Parlour', 14 Dec.; 'Christmas Festivities', 27 Dec.; 'The New Year', 3 Jan. 1836; 'The Streets at Night', 17 Jan. 1836.

As biographers are uninformative about *Bell's Life*, it may be worth noting that it was a four-page sevenpenny weekly, liberal in politics but non-party, giving sporting and comic features as well as news; according to James Grant (*The Great Metropolis*, first series, 2 vols., 1836, II 134) it had a larger circulation than any daily or weekly except the *Dispatch*.

4. 'A Dinner at Poplar Walk', Dec. 1833; 'Mrs. Joseph Porter over the way', Jan. 1834; 'Horatio Sparkins', Feb. 1834; 'The Bloomsbury Christening', Apr. 1834; 'The Boarding House', May and Aug. 1834; 'The Steam Excursion', Oct. 1834; 'Passage in the Life of Mr. Watkins Tottle', Jan.–Feb. 1835.

5. *Letters*, I 47.

(perhaps changing his mind when he decided to dramatize it as 'The Strange Gentleman'); and he may have kept 'Sentiment' by him with the same purpose.[1] The other newly published tale, 'The Black Veil', is known to have been written in November,[2] expressly for the collection. The addition of these three, and of the long new sketch, 'A Visit to Newgate', suggests that where Dickens rejected earlier sketches it was not merely for lack of space; though it may of course have been thought advisable to attract readers by the inclusion of some unpublished material.

On the whole, it seems fair to regard work published by the beginning of November and omitted from the First Series of *Sketches by Boz* as deliberately rejected; though sketches published later might be left out simply for lack of space, since the new ones were by then already written. (One published as late as 27 December 1835 was in fact included, but probably as an after-thought—'Christmas Festivities', now called 'A Christmas Dinner', which concludes the first volume.) The 'rejected' material therefore consists of seven sketches: 'The Streets—Morning', 'Seven Dials', 'Some Account of an Omnibus Cad', 'The House', 'Bellamy's', 'The Old Bailey', and 'Love and Oysters'; and one tale, 'A Dinner at Poplar Walk'. Of these the first represented half a pair, and appears in the 'memoranda'[3] quoted in Dickens's letter of 27 October as 'The Streets—Noon and Night'; he did not publish its companion piece until 17 January 1836, too late for inclusion. 'Some Account of an Omnibus Cad' was eventually expanded into twice its length, as 'The Last Cab-driver and the First Omnibus Cad'; it may be that Dickens already had this expansion in mind, but had not time to effect it. 'The House' and 'Bellamy's', two *Evening Chronicle* sketches, were later combined into 'A Parliamentary Sketch', with some drastic rewriting to make them less allusive and topical; while 'A Dinner at Poplar Walk' was, when it finally appeared in the Second Series as 'Mr.

---

1. Its position, last in Vol. II, rather favours the supposition that it was written late; but in substance and manner it resembles the 1834 tales. The title in the first edition is 'Sentiment!', perhaps in error.

2. *Letters*, I 54; and compare the reference to 'an extraordinary idea for a story of a very singular kind' in a letter to Catherine Hogarth, undated but soon after 20 Nov. (*Mr. and Mrs. Charles Dickens*, ed. W. Dexter, 1935, p. 36).

3. These memoranda include one other heading for which Dickens subsequently wrote a sketch—'The Prisoners' Van'. The others (The Cook's Shop and Bedlam, Banking-Houses, Fancy Lounges, Covent Garden, Hospitals, and Lodging-Houses) were never used. (This is probably the earliest reference to literary memoranda of any kind.)

Minns and his Cousin', the most thoroughly revised of all the tales, in a way that shows Dickens's dissatisfaction with his earliest publication. The rejection of all these might then be attributed to lack of time; for the dropping of 'Love and Oysters',[1] 'Seven Dials', and 'The Old Bailey'[2] it is difficult to see a reason, unless the last-named was felt to be superseded by 'A Visit to Newgate'.

No tale or sketch which does appear in the first collection was revised so thoroughly as those mentioned above; but not one was reprinted exactly as originally published. To begin with, they were rearranged and the original series broken up. The grouping as 'Scenes', 'Characters', 'Tales' was not yet made,[3] but the six *Evening Chronicle* sketches which had dealt with 'Our Parish' were brought together, and opened the first volume. Except for sketches which close this volume, and probably owe their position to their late date of composition, the order seems unplanned; there are two early tales, two *Morning Chronicle* 'Street Sketches', seven *Evening Chronicle* 'Sketches of London', three *Bell's Life* 'Scenes and Characters', and the newly written 'A Visit to Newgate'. There is no juxtaposition of sketches alike in subject matter; if there is any principle at work it is rather the emphasizing of variety. The second volume is slightly less miscellaneous in character, since 'tales' predominate (five old and two new), the other contents being two 'Street Sketches', four 'Sketches of London', and one 'Scenes and Characters'.

One form of revision, then, was simply mechanical: the removal of the original 'series' heading, and where necessary, as in the 'Parish' sketches, the provision of a new title. Almost equally formal was the re-paragraphing; the newspaper column was usually broken into only a few paragraphs. It is possible that this affected the original calculation of material to be included, and dictated some of the cuts.

The material omitted from the sketches and tales would almost make a small volume on its own, and it is extraordinary that no attempt has been made to recover it for modern readers. It is not

1. Later entitled 'Misplaced Attachment of Mr. John Dounce'. It is a slightly *risqué* story, but that may not have been the reason for its omission, since Dickens did not tone it down (except for the title) until the monthly parts edition of 1837–39.

2. Later entitled 'Criminal Courts'.

3. These headings apparently first appeared in 1839, the first volume edition which combined the two series; the order was that of the 'monthly parts' edition of Nov. 1837–June 1839. (Hatton and Cleaver's account of the parts does not mention the sub-headings there.)

of course all of equal interest; but no one who has read it would willingly lose the first half of the sketch of 'The Prisoners' Van', a passage not only exceptionally racy and vivid, but providing the best early example of Dickens's trick (to be elaborated in *Oliver Twist*) of dealing with low life in a detached and whimsical style. This is the beginning of the omitted section:

> We have a most extraordinary partiality for lounging about the streets. Whenever we have an hour or two to spare, there is nothing we enjoy more than a little amateur vagrancy—walking up one street and down another, and staring into shop windows, and gazing about as if, instead of being on intimate terms with every shop and house in Holborn, the Strand, Fleet-street and Cheapside, the whole were an unknown region to our wandering mind. We revel in a crowd of any kind—a street "row" is our delight—even a woman in a fit is by no means to be despised, especially in a fourth-rate street, where all the female inhabitants run out of their houses, and discharge large jugs of cold water over the patient, as if she were dying of spontaneous combustion, and wanted putting out. Then a drunken man—what can be more charming than a regular drunken man, who sits in a door-way for half an hour, holding a dialogue with the crowd, of which his portion is generally limited to repeated inquiries of "I say—I'm all right, an't I?" and then suddenly gets up, without any ostensible cause or inducement, and runs down the street with tremendous swiftness for a hundred yards or so, when he falls into another doorway, where the first feeble words he imperfectly articulates to the policeman who lifts him up are "Let's av—drop—somethin' to drink?"—we say again, can anything be more charming than this sort of thing? And what, we ask, can be expected but popular discontent, when Temperance Societies interfere with the amusements of the people?

This may be suspected as an omission dictated by space;[1] 'The Prisoners' Van' did not appear until 29 November 1835, and by that date the manuscript had already left Cruikshank's hands and printing had begun.[2] The only critical reasons one could suggest are that the passage is a long introduction to the real subject of the sketch, and perhaps impairs its unity; and that the self-portrait with which it opens might be thought too revealing.

Few omissions were as drastic as this, and some were of more or less 'formal' introductions and conclusions; recalling a pre-

1. The whole passage is three times as long as what is quoted here.
2. *Letters*, I 53-4.

vious promise to his readers, wishing them a merry Christmas, suggesting the subject of the next sketch, and such-like journalistic patter.[1] But even these sometimes involve the omission of characteristic sentiments; as in the omission of the last paragraph of 'Astley's', obviously removed because of its relation to a later sketch, 'Private Theatres', and perhaps felt to be superseded by that sketch.

It is to us matter of positive wonder and astonishment that the infectious disease commonly known by the name of "stage-struck," has never been eradicated, unless people really believe that the privilege of wearing velvet and feathers for an hour or two at night, is sufficient compensation for a life of wretchedness and misery. It is stranger still, that the denizens of attorneys' offices, merchants' counting-houses, haberdashers' shops, and coal sheds, should squander their own resources to enrich some wily vagabond by paying—actually paying, and dearly too—to make unmitigated and unqualified asses of themselves at a Private Theatre. Private theatres, so far as we know, are peculiar to London; they flourish just now, for we have half a dozen at our fingers' ends. We will take an early opportunity of introducing our readers to the Managers of one or two, and of sketching the interior of a Private Theatre, both before the curtain and behind it.

The original closing paragraph often 'opens out' in this way; the end of 'London Recreations' touches on less harmless recreations than the gardening and frequentation of tea-gardens dealt with in the body of the sketch—such as standing in vaults drinking bad spirits, knocking at doors and running away, leaning against posts at street corners; it concludes with a militant statement of tolerance:

Whatever be the class, or whatever the recreation, so long as it does not render a man absurd himself, or offensive to others, we hope it will never be interfered with, either by a misdirected feeling of propriety on the one hand, or detestable cant on the other.

Setting this beside other changes, one is tempted to wonder whether discretion sometimes dictated the omission of a closing paragraph; Boz as a journalist liked a strong curtain-line, some-

1. E.g. the omitted closing paragraphs of 'Our Parish', I, II, and III; 'Thoughts about People'; 'Greenwich Fair'; 'Brokers' and Marine Store Shops'; 'The Pawnbroker's Shop'; 'A Christmas Dinner'; 'The Boarding-House' (ch. i). But the apology at the end of 'The River' survives into the first collected edition, to be removed only in 1839.

times with a political flavour. The original form of the conclusion of 'Thoughts about People' is much more clearly partisan than the revised version of 1836. Here is part of the omitted passage:

> . . . we see no reason why the same gentleman of enlarged and comprehensive views who proposes to Parliament a measure for preserving the amusements of the upper classes of society, and abolishing those of the lower, may not with equal wisdom preserve the former more completely, and mark the distinction between the two more effectually, by bringing in a Bill "to limit to certain members of the hereditary peerage of this country and their families, the privilege of making fools of themselves as often and as egregiously as to them shall seem meet". Precedent is a great thing in these cases, and Heaven knows he will have precedent enough to plead.

When Dickens recast the conclusion of this sketch[1] he suggested a similar social criticism, but in a much more urbane manner:

> We may smile at such people as these [the London apprentices in their Sunday best], but they can never excite our anger. . . And if they do display a little occasional foolery in their own proper persons, it is surely more tolerable than the precocious puppyism of the Quadrant, the whiskered dandyism of Regent-street and Pall-mall, or gallantry in its dotage any where.[2]

Here we have a typical instance of the modification of the journalistic manner of the original sketches—not only in the substitution of the bland smile of the periodical essayist for the glare of the propagandist, but in the removal of a too ephemeral allusion; for the original reference was to the notorious 'Sunday' bill[3] persistently introduced in several successive sessions by Sir Andrew Agnew, the 'Lord's-Day-Bill Baronet' referred to in another sketch.[4]

The sketches containing specifically 'political' allusions—'The House', 'Bellamy's', and 'The Parlour'—were passed over, no doubt deliberately, when Dickens made his selection for the

1. He also omitted the promise of subsequent sketches on the same subject.

2. 1836, p. 95. In the 1850 edition the criticism was perhaps a little further softened by the addition (before 'And if') of 'Besides, they are always the faint reflections of higher lights' and the change of 'of' to 'in' before 'the Quadrant' and 'Regent-street'.

3. Attacked by Dickens in his pamphlet *Sunday under three Heads*, written some time after Apr. 1836 when the bill was re-introduced, and published in June under the name of 'Timothy Sparks'.

4. 'Bellamy's', *Evening Chronicle*, 11 Apr. 1835 (see 'A Parliamentary Sketch' in Second Series), published two weeks before 'Thoughts about People'.

First Series, and revised with particular care for the Second Series, as we shall see. But Dickens was alert to remove incidental topicalities in other sketches. The Irish orator from Exeter Hall, mentioned at the end of 'The Ladies' Societies' ('Our Parish' VI), was presented to the *Evening Chronicle* readers of 1835 as 'Mr. Somebody O'Something, a celebrated Catholic renegade and Protestant bigot'; in the first edition of 1836 he became 'Mr. Mortimer O'Silly-one', later 'a celebrated oratorical pedlar', and in the monthly parts edition 'a celebrated orator . . . an Irishman'.[1] In the tales, he removed, for example, the references to 'the Duke of Wellington waiting for a *peal*', 'Mr. Barnett's "Salamanders"', and the 'individual to whose eager appetite [at 'the Edinburgh dinner'] we find allusion made in *The Morning Chronicle* of a few days since'.[2] Apart from the topicality of this, Dickens (or Hogarth) may have decided that it was improper to refer in his sketches to the journal which employed him; he also removed a reference to the 'clock at *The Chronicle* office' in 'Thoughts about People'.

The change in the name of one of the characters in the revised tale 'Mrs. Joseph Porter' shows Dickens avoiding a different kind of particularity; 'Mr. Harfield' in the *Monthly Magazine* version was the name of an actual friend and *Morning Chronicle* colleague.[3] In changing it to 'Harleigh', Dickens perhaps substituted another allusion, this time a friendly private joke; at the time when he was revising the *Sketches* for publication, he was in constant touch with John Pritt Harley, the actor and stage-manager for whom he was writing his farce *The Strange Gentleman*. He also removed two names, 'the Stubbs', the Halfpennys' from the list of the 'rank and fashion' of Clapham who attended the amateur theatricals; perhaps these were recognizable as real people in

1. The reference was to the Reverend Mortimer O'Sullivan, an Irish controversialist, who had come to England on a deputation from the Irish Protestant clergy; he had described their condition at meetings in Exeter Hall on 20 June and 11 July, and had also been 'going about this country like a showman . . . addressing [meetings] in the most bombastic, frothy, nonsensical style' (*Morning Chronicle*, 2 July).

2. 'The Steam Excursion'. Dickens was reporting the banquet given to Earl Grey at Edinburgh for the *Morning Chronicle* in Sept. 1834 (see *The Dickensian*, Dec. 1934, pp. 5–10), and the tale appeared in Oct. Johnson, 1 96, quotes from his report what is clearly the passage referred to, but is unaware of the reference in the original version of the tale.

3. *Letters*, 1 34 [1834]; see also 1 63. The tale (published in Jan. 1834) is supposed to reflect Dickens's amateur production of *Clari* at Bentinck Street on 27 Apr. 1833; it may also bear some relation to his burlesque *O'Thello*, written about this time.

Clapton?[1] The only other change of name in a tale—from 'Bagshaw' to 'Budden' in 'Mr. Minns and his Cousin' (the revised 'Dinner at Poplar Walk' collected in the Second Series)—was evidently made to avoid the appearance of plagiarism, since 'Claudius Bagshaw' was the name of the hero in John Poole's story, 'Preparations for Pleasure'.[2]

Another type of revision of substance partly dictated by the transition from newspaper to book was the removal of the (very occasional) touches of indelicacy and profanity; Boz's column in the newspaper would probably be read only by men, but a book which wished to pass through the 'needle's eye' into 'families' must be more circumspect. Dickens modified a reference to pregnancy in 'The Four Sisters' ('Our Parish', chapter iii) by the omission of the bracketed words in the following sentence:

> . . . a circumstance of the most gratifying description [Coming events cast their shadows before, and events like that at] which [we hint with becoming delicacy and diffidence] *will* happen occasionally in the best regulated families [—indeed the best regulated are usually supposed to be the most subject to such occurrences]

And he removed the phrase 'or half undressed' from the picture of the dancing revellers at the end of 'Greenwich Fair'. But he seems hardly to have begun altering 'God' to 'G—' or 'gum' or 'Heaven', or 'damned' to 'd—d', until the collection of the Second Series a year later;[3] one wonders whether this was in response to criticism of the First Series,[4] or the result of his growing consciousness of himself as a widely popular author, after the success of *Pickwick*. The revision in the Second Series, and the further revision of both series for the monthly parts edition, is thorough, and hardly an oath escaped in the end.

Of course Dickens's revision was also sometimes stylistic—even

1. Marianne Leigh, the girl who made mischief between Dickens and Maria Beadnell, and annoyed him on the evening of the theatricals, lived at Clapton; her mother is supposed to be represented in the malicious Mrs Joseph Porter.

2. *New Monthly Magazine*, Oct. 1829; republished in *Sketches and Recollections* (1835). The general situation and several details of Poole's story are also recalled in 'The Steam Excursion'; and one of Poole's minor characters is named 'Frederick Snodgrass' (see K. Tillotson, *The Dickensian*, Mar. 1956, pp. 69–70).

3. One of the very few examples in the First Series is in the last paragraph but one of 'Miss Evans and the Eagle'. The *Bell's Life* version reads 'You and your friend be damned!', which becomes 'd—d' in 1836, and 'hanged' in the monthly parts.

4. No objection to the oaths has been found in any reviews, but the most influential criticism is not necessarily printed.

at this early stage, when he was often revising sketches written only a month or so before. He had written often in great haste ('a day's time is a handsome allowance for me—much less than I frequently had when I was writing for The Chronicle')[1] and in looking over the sketches he saw several places in which punctuation and expression could be improved. This revision was not at all systematic; but here and there the style is formalized by the removal of colloquialisms such as '–n't' from the narration or description; a few grammatical solecisms are detected, and awkward repetitions smoothed away. Very occasionally there is a change that suggests a more critical view of his own humour: in 'The Bloomsbury Christening', for instance, he noticed that he had spoilt an epigrammatic phrase 'He was never happy but when he was miserable' by adding the facetious 'pardon the contradiction', and removed it. But there is very little of this kind of revision compared with what is found a year later; it is worth mentioning only because it indicates the lines of later revision.

Not surprisingly—in view of the amount of work required from Cruikshank, Dickens's reporting engagements out of town,[2] and the habitual dilatoriness of Macrone—the collected *Sketches* were not ready in time for Christmas, as had been hoped;[3] but by 7 January 1836 Dickens was able to say 'the greater part, if not the whole of the book, is worked off';[4] and two days later it was advertised in the *Morning Chronicle* as 'nearly ready'.

It was published on 6 February; there was some unexplained delay in sending out review copies, but it had a good send-off with 'Hogarth's beautiful notice' in the *Morning Chronicle* on 11 February;[5] the subscription was 'an excellent one',[6] the reviews numerous and favourable; by 24 March the agreed payment of £150 had been made, and by the end of the month Dickens was able to refer to 'the great success of my book, and the

1. *Letters*, I 47.

2. During one such absence the proofs were read by George Hogarth (*Letters*, I 57).

3. *Letters*, I 54.

4. *Letters*, I 61. At this eleventh hour Macrone appears to have suggested some change in the title. But the *Morning Chronicle* advertisement gives the title in its full final form.

Some difficulty with Cruikshank at this stage seems to be implied by the advertisement of the *Sketches* (*Athenæum*, 6 Feb.) which specifies '20 illustrations' instead of the correct number of 16.

5. *Letters*, I 65. There was also a 'puff' in the issue of 2 Feb.

6. *Letters*, I 66.

name it has established for me among the publishers'.[1] Meanwhile *Pickwick* was begun[2]—though its success was not to supersede that of the *Sketches* for some months to come—and a real three-volume novel was in contemplation; and though the series of 'Scenes and Characters' in *Bell's Life* had been concluded, Dickens seemed to have found a new vehicle for his tales in Charles Whitehead's *Library of Fiction*. The success of the *Sketches* had many consequences, but the only one which concerns us here is the collecting of a Second Series.

III

The letters suggest that this began early in the summer; perhaps as soon as the success of the First Series was assured.[3] Cruikshank was at work at least by July, and in August Dickens told Macrone of a projected new series in the *Carlton Chronicle* which he proposed to call 'Leaves from an unpublished Volume by Boz'.[4] Two volumes were planned, and an advertisement to this effect appeared early in October,[5] but it must already have been clear that Dickens's other commitments (*Pickwick*, his farce and his opera, reporting for the *Morning Chronicle*, and the two novels promised to Bentley) would prevent him from writing enough new sketches to fill them;[6] and in November came the quarrel

1. *Letters*, 1 68 (letter to his uncle Thomas Barrow announcing his forthcoming marriage).

2. See below, p. 62.

3. Johnson (1 149) quotes from an unpublished letter of 30 July, in which Dickens says he is revising the proof sheets of the second edition and 'preparing another series which must be published before Christmas'.

The second edition of the First Series is advertised in the *Athenæum* on 30 July; this is the first appearance in print of the author's name ('Mr. Charles Dickens' Sketches by Boz'), much earlier than has been generally supposed. A similar advertisement appeared on 13 Aug.; subsequent advertisements in Aug. and Sept. omit Dickens's name, perhaps at his insistence. The first published volume with Dickens's own name was *Pickwick Papers*, in Nov. 1837, where the dedication is signed; *Oliver Twist* (Johnson, 1 223) was therefore merely the first to have his name on the title-page.

4. *Letters*, 1 77. The first sketch, 'The Hospital Patient', appeared three days later, with the heading as given in the letter, plus the words 'which will be torn out once a fortnight'; but no other followed, perhaps because the 'Carlton Club' was not as 'liberal' as Dickens had expected. Its unauthorized printing of three sketches formerly published elsewhere, in the issues of 17 Sept., 8 Oct., and 15 Oct., indicates that there had been some trouble; Dickens protested against the piracy in a letter to Easthope, owner of the *Morning Chronicle*, on 1 Nov. (*Letters*, 1 87).

5. *Athenæum*, 8 Oct., as 'Mr Charles Dickens' New Work'.

6. Some of the tales intended for the collection may instead have been included in *Pickwick*; see below, p. 73.

with Macrone over the Bentley agreements. So the Second Series consisted of a single volume, advertised as such on 3 December[1] and published on 17 December, just in time for the Christmas season in 1836.

This time there was no problem of selection. Emboldened by the success of the First Series, Dickens simply swept up all the items published in 1833–5 but omitted from the collection of February 1836. These are (in chronological order) one tale, 'A Dinner at Poplar Walk'; one 'Street Sketch', 'The Old Bailey'; two 'Sketches in London': 'The House' and 'Bellamy's'; six 'Scenes and Characters': 'Seven Dials', 'Making a Night of It', 'Love and Oysters', 'Some Account of an Omnibus Cad', 'The Vocal Dressmaker', and 'The Parlour'. To these he added the two last 'Scenes and Characters', published early in 1836: 'The New Year' and 'The Streets at Night'; and two isolated sketches: 'A Little Talk about Spring, and the Sweeps'[2] and 'The Hospital Patient'. The general heading of the latter in the *Carlton Chronicle* shows that it was written with the new collection in mind; and it is probable that the newly-published sketches, 'Our Next-door Neighbours' and 'The Drunkard's Death', which are similarly grim in tone, were also intended for this projected series in the *Carlton Chronicle*. Also designed for the new volume were the four which appeared as 'Sketches by "Boz". New Series' in the *Morning Chronicle* in the autumn: 'Meditations in Monmouth-Street', 'Scotland Yard', 'Doctors' Commons', and 'Vauxhall-Gardens by Day'.[3] (This series also should have continued, but was checked by Dickens's quarrel with the proprietors.) The only periodical item which Dickens omitted was 'The Tuggs's at Ramsgate',[4] presumably because of its length. In the Preface to the new volume (dated from 'Furnival's Inn, December 17, 1836'), Dickens was sufficiently explicit about the chronological range of its contents:

> Some of these Sketches were written before the appearance of the former series, and the remainder have been added at different periods since that time.

1. The *Athenæum* advertisements give 'In a few days', 3 Dec.; 'nearly ready', 10 Dec., the latter with Dickens's name.

2. *Library of Fiction*, June 1836; the title was changed to 'The First of May'.

3. 24 Sept., 4, 11, 26 Oct. All were reprinted in the *Evening Chronicle* and the last three also printed elsewhere (see Hatton and Cleaver, 102–3, and *Letters*, 1 87); an interesting testimony to the enhanced value of the author's signature.

4. *Library of Fiction*, Apr. 1836.

But this is perhaps deliberately vague about the proportion of new work in the collection, and contains no hint of the amount of revision.

All of the previously published sketches underwent some alteration, but especially the earlier work. The earliest of all, 'A Dinner at Poplar Walk', had not only a new title, 'Mr. Minns and his Cousin', and a new surname for its hero, but three or four paragraphs entirely rewritten[1] with minor changes in substance, such as the omission of some of the cousin's garrulity and the tiresome behaviour of the boy Alick at the end, and the addition of the will. On the whole the motive seems to have been simply literary improvement, and there is nothing to regret except for one simile ('Minns . . . looked as merry as a farthing rushlight in a fog') and a detail of the pageboy's outfit ('with a parsley-and-butter border').

The omission of personal allusions and political or other topical references, already noted above, is most fully illustrated in the revision of 'The House' and 'Bellamy's'.[2] These are unusual in their direct use of material gathered by Dickens as a gallery reporter; he had already apologized for their allusiveness in the *Chronicle*, and the appearance of 'Bellamy's' was twice postponed, which perhaps suggests editorial doubts. They were run into one long sketch, under the title of 'A Parliamentary Sketch—with a few portraits'.[3] It is the individual portraits that are modified; one, the 'elderly man with the bald head and thin face . . . who has lived for two-thirds of his whole existence exactly one minute and a quarter's walk from Blackfriars'-bridge', is removed altogether. The portrait of the 'ferocious-looking gentleman' (Colonel Sibthorp) is toned down by the omission of such phrases as 'a brain slightly damaged', and perhaps made less easily identifiable by the omission of 'You must often have seen him in the box-lobbies of the theatres during the vacation.' The description of the 'awkward and ungainly-looking man' is considerably shortened, and the reference to his 'awkward scrape with his consti-

---

1. The whole text of the original version is accessible to modern readers in F. J. H. Darton's *Dickens, Positively the First Appearance* (1933), pp. 51–68, with some comments on pp. 73–7.

2. W. J. Carlton in 'Portraits in "A Parliamentary Sketch" ', *The Dickensian*, June 1954, quotes some of the omitted matter and discusses the whole sketch; he identifies several 'portraits', but not the 'awkward and ungainly-looking man' or the 'young Member'.

3. This became 'A Parliamentary Sketch' in the monthly parts.

tuents . . . at the commencement of the present session' is left out; the identifying traits of the 'young Member' talking to '"Jane", the Hebe of Bellamy's'—his 'large quantity of hair', his near relation 'to the noble leader of a "section" of the House' are similarly omitted, along with his flirtatiousness and his consumption of brandy-and-water. Throughout, the motive is probably as much caution as the wish to eliminate ephemeral matter; much of the original matter, as Mr Carlton says,

> would almost certainly be deemed libellous to-day, and it would be surprising if [it] did not provoke a protest from some readers of the *Evening Chronicle*.

But enough salt remains to make the sketch one of the liveliest in the whole collection, whether we recognize the originals or not.[1]

Similar instances of 'political and topical' revision are found in other sketches. The legal dignitaries in 'Doctors' Commons' were evidently also portraits, and the suppressed details about the 'doctor of civil law'—'an ecclesiastical dignitary in the cinque ports, and a not very distant relation to a commissioner of lunacy' —must have made the identification immediately obvious to contemporaries.[2] The 'radiating sentence' with which the red-faced man in 'The Parlour Orator' banged out of the room 'in which such adjectives as "dastardly", "oppressive", "violent", and "sanguinary", formed the most conspicuous words', was originally much longer; he spoke of ' "dastardly Whigs", "sanguinary Tories", "Mr. Roebuck", "depreciation of the currency", and "voluntary principle".' In the same sketch the greengrocer's reply 'I got no good out of the twenty million' to the accusation 'you *are* a slave', was evidently thought too allusive, and so was provided with a gloss 'that was paid for 'mancipation'.

The conclusion of this sketch was originally a good deal more

---

1. The *Spectator*, reviewing the Second Series (24 Dec. 1836, pp. 1234–5), said that no one who had ever seen the originals could fail to recognize them.

2. He was identified by Henry Jenner (*T.L.S.*, 22 Oct. 1931, p. 820; cf. *The Dickensian*, Dec. 1931, p. 5) with Dr Joseph Phillimore, Regius Professor of Civil Law at Oxford and at that time also Judge of the Court of Admiralty of the Cinque Ports. His brother, William Phillimore, was Chief Commissioner in Lunacy (*The Family of Phillimore*, Devizes, 1922). Mr Jenner regarded the descriptions as 'so recognizable as to be really actionably libellous'. He also identified 'the very fat and red-faced gentleman' with Sir Herbert Jenner-Fust, Dean of the Arches.

The case of 'Bumple against Sludberry' was drawn from an actual case reported by Dickens (W. J. Carlton, *Charles Dickens, Shorthand Writer*, 1926, ch. iv).

indignant in tone than the two paragraphs which were substituted and it is partly the indignation of one who is sated with
official oratory:

> "Great ass," thought we,—"a very common character and in no
> degree exaggerated. Empty headed bullies, who by their ignorance
> and presumption bring into contempt whatever cause they are con-
> nected with: equally mischievous in any assembly from the highest
> to the lowest, and disgusting in all. There is a red-faced man in
> every 'parlour'."

In that context, 'parlour' almost achieves the status of a pun on
'parliament'.

There is also a more challenging tone in the superseded last
paragraph of the 'Omnibus Cad', with its emphasis on the
futility of imprisonment:

> You may confine his body between four stone walls, or between
> four brick walls and a stone coping, which is much the same in
> effect—he cares not—you may cramp his body by confinement, or
> to prevent his body's getting the cramp, you may exercise his legs
> upon the mill—he defies your tyranny; he appeals from your
> oppressive enactments to the Paddington committee; and flies
> back to his profession with an ardour which persecution and in-
> voluntary abstinence have in no wise diminished. Like many other
> great men, Mr. Barker is a rigid predestinarian, or to advert once
> again to his own pointed and eloquent form of speech, he reasons
> thus:— "If I am to get into trouble for this 'ere consarn, I may as
> vell get into trouble for somethink as for nothink,"—and acting
> upon this logical mode of reasoning, he sacrifices at the altar of
> philosophy any little scruples he might otherwise entertain, and
> gets into trouble with great ease and coolness, getting out of it as
> well as he can; and losing no opportunity of getting into it again.

Two minor changes elsewhere illustrate the rebellious or imper-
tinent attitude to those in high places of the earlier Boz:

> We never saw a green so drunk, a lord so quarrelsome (except in
> the house of peers after dinner)[1]

where 'except' is slightly softened, to 'no: not even'. In 'The Old
Bailey' ('Criminal Courts') the following sentence was cut out:

> We never can help thinking that a full-dressed Lord Mayor looks
> like a South Sea idol, on which grateful devotees have hung a

1. 'A Little Talk about Spring, and the Sweeps', *Library of Fiction*, June 1836
('The First of May'). In the Second Series 'green' becomes ' "Green" '.

variety of gorgeous ornaments without the slightest regard to the general effect of the whole.

Two sketches were shorn of their long introductory paragraphs: 'The Parlour' began with a general account of different types of parlour, and its unity is improved by the concentration on the 'Orator'; and 'Scotland Yard' began with a general lament over the changes in the London scene, of which this is the first half:

> If our recollection serves us, we have more than once hinted, confidentially, to our readers that we entertain a strong partiality for the queer little old streets which yet remain in some parts of London, and that we infinitely prefer them to the modern innovations, the wide streets with broad pavements, which are every day springing up around us. The old Exeter 'Change, for instance, and the narrow and dirty part of the Strand immediately adjoining, we were warmly attached to. The death of the elephant was a great shock to us; we knew him well; and having enjoyed the honour of his intimate acquaintance for some years, felt grieved—deeply grieved—that in a paroxysm of insanity he should have so far forgotten all his estimable and companionable qualities as to exhibit a sanguinary desire to scrunch his faithful valet, and pulverize even Mrs. Cross herself, who for a long period had evinced towards him that pure and touching attachment which woman alone can feel.

The detail about the elephant was perhaps thought too topical to perpetuate.

Oaths were occasionally but still not consistently removed. For example, for the curse 'Flare up!' used by the boy at the end of 'Criminal Courts' a circumlocution in the Bill Sikes manner is substituted, though the same imprecation survives (with inverted commas added) in 'Making a Night of It'. There are many minor changes of expression, but the only one of interest is the substitution of 'we' for 'I' throughout 'The Hospital Patient', to bring it into line with the other sketches.

At about the same time as the planning of the Second Series, Dickens was preparing the second edition of the First Series; he added a new Preface, and either then or in the third edition[1] he made further small changes on the lines of those already noted in the first edition. Again he was on the watch for unsuitable collo-

---

1. No copy of the second edition is at present available; there is none in the British Museum, the Bodleian, Cambridge University Library, National Library of Scotland, nor in the Forster collection.

quialisms, and certain kinds of facetiousness. The old gardener in 'London Recreations' was described as 'digging, and sweeping and cutting, and messing about'; for the last two words, Dickens substituted 'planting'. For the apprentices' 'oh-no-we-never-mention-'ems' in 'Thoughts about People' he substituted 'summer trousers'. Some exuberance of simile in 'The Boarding-House' was reduced; in 'He was as empty headed as the great bell of St. Paul's, and had about as long a tongue', Dickens cut out the last seven words; Mrs Bloss's watch was compared to 'a small tea-cup' instead of a breakfast-cup.[1] A few topicalities were removed from 'Horatio Sparkins': 'to see St. George and the Dragon' becomes 'to the theatre', and 'he talks like a second Pelham' is cut out, perhaps in deference to Bulwer.[2]

IV

The most minute and careful revision was applied to the first combined edition of the two series for the monthly parts published (after much controversy)[3] by Chapman and Hall from November 1837 to June 1839, and as a single volume, uniform with *Pickwick*, in May 1839.

One item, 'The Tuggs's at Ramsgate', was collected for the first time, and the sketches were put in the order which survives in modern editions. They are grouped as follows: 'Seven Sketches from our Parish' (the six of the First Series, with 'Our Next-door Neighbour' rather incongruously tacked on); twenty-five

1. The latter comparison disappeared altogether in the monthly parts, along with others in the sentence; see below, p. 58.

2. 1839 has 'he talks like an oracle'. (This is one of many instances which suggest that the revision for 1839 was based on the first edition, not the second or third.)

3. See Forster, II 1; *Letters*, I 110–11; Johnson, 183–5, 208–9. Chapman and Hall's edition had probably been under consideration since their purchase of the copyright from Macrone in mid-June, and this would allow time for revision, even with Dickens's commitments to *Pickwick*, *Oliver Twist*, and *Bentley's*. It was first advertised in the Sept. number of *Pickwick*, as 'revised by the author', and again in Oct.; the *Athenæum* advertisement (21 Oct.) and the title-page lack this phrase, calling it simply 'New Edition'. Thirteen additional illustrations were provided by Cruikshank, to make up the two plates to each number, as in *Pickwick*; the text, however, is usually shorter (24 pp. each in Nos. I–XVIII, 56 pp. in No. XIX, and 38 pp. in No. XX), and the end of a number never coincides with the end of a sketch.

The pink cover was used possibly at Dickens's wish to distinguish it from *Pickwick*, as it was not a new work; he had especially objected to Macrone's project of monthly parts in 'just the same form' (*Letters*, I 110). The cover was originally drawn by Cruikshank for Macrone's projected edition; see *The Dickensian*, June 1937, p. 175.

'Scenes'; twelve 'Characters'; and twelve 'Tales'. Within the groups there is some system in the order: six pieces on recreations and entertainments, for example, now fall into a natural sequence.

The whole series was further revised, not excepting the tales and sketches that had been specially written for the previous collections; these therefore are changes that cannot be attributed simply to the shift from periodical to book. By the autumn of 1837 Dickens was established as a popular 'family' author, and also as the editor of a periodical himself; he had a keener sense of his audience and of his responsibilities towards it; he was rising socially, and possibly especially sensitive to imputations of vulgarity.[1] And by this time he had the benefit of Forster's advice.[2]

Sometimes the impression of the writer's personality is modified; in 'The New Year' he takes out 'quaffing our grog' and omits the original conclusion, in which he had dismissed 'all gloomy reflections' with the words

> We were happy and merry in the last [year], and will be, please God, in this. So as we are alone, and can neither dance it in, nor sing it in, here goes our glass to our lips, and a hearty welcome to the year one thousand eight hundred and thirty-seven, say we.

He is now more particular about anything verging on indelicacy. The speculation, at the appearance of the prisoners' van, 'upon the possibility of the Duke of Cumberland being brought up on a warrant for assaulting the Princess Victoria', is omitted; the aphrodisiac effect of the oysters upon Mr John Dounce is toned down by two cautious alterations.[3] Not only is most of the strong language modified or removed,[4] but also slang expressions (in the

1. The reviews of the First Series can hardly have influenced Dickens in this direction; in about twenty notices, many of them long ones, there are hardly any unfavourable comments of any kind, and only one objection to 'sheer vulgarity' (in the *Atlas*, 21 Feb., p. 123). The *Examiner*'s notice (28 Feb., pp. 132–3) found 'too much' of the 'caricature of Cockneyism'; the *Court Journal* (20 Feb., p. 123) found some sketches 'coarse, it is true, but very real. The subjects of "Boz" generally preclude refinement.' The *Observer* (8 May, p. 3) noted that 'The vernacular idiom is given in all its truth and richness, yet free from grossness'. But the *Quarterly*'s comment, in its generally favourable article on *Pickwick* (Oct. 1837, pp. 484–518), that 'Mr. Dickens may well afford to disregard the imputation of vulgarity' suggests that there was more criticism of this kind than survives in print.

2. Forster does not mention the *Sketches* in this connexion, but states clearly (II i) that his help with proofs began in June 1837.

3. Perhaps in deference to the *Athenæum*'s review of the Second Series (31 Dec. 1836, p. 916): 'Mr. John Dounce is one of the best papers, but is a little too broad to suit our pages.'

4. E.g. 'God' to 'Heaven', 'by G—d' to 'by gum', 'God bless you' to 'Bless you';

narrative) such as 'goes of gin', 'regular good ones, and never a bit the worse for it', 'come-up-to-the-scratch kind of manner' and even simple colloquialisms like ''em' and 'wasn't'.[1] There is some cutting of humorous similes;[2] the stout Mrs Bloss no longer 'looked like a pin-cushion on castors', nor does the man in 'Early Coaches' start up in bed 'as if . . . rehearsing the tent-scene in *Richard*'. Two of these cuts fall into a special category:

which certainly was 'rayther warm', as the child said when it fell in the fire.[3]

ev'ry one to his liking, as the man said when he pisoned hisself.[4]

Dickens evidently came to feel that this locution should be the monopoly of Sam Weller; and with a similar protectiveness towards a later-born character, he altered the name 'Fitz Winkle' in 'Public Dinners' to 'Fitz Binkle'. One or two of his more elaborate puns are also removed; Mr Calton in 'The Boarding-House' is habitually compared to a 'knocker', and on his last appearance he has to pay damages for breach of promise 'because he had declined to *ring* the *belle*'. In the same tale, the simile for Mrs Bloss's watch, already modified,[5] disappears, with two others in the same paragraph, 'a chain like a gilt street-door chain' and 'stones about the size of half-crowns'.

Dickens no longer assumes his readers' easy familiarity with London inns. In 'Mr. John Dounce' a reference to 'the Rainbow' in 1835 becomes 'the Rainbow in Fleet-street' in 1836, and 'the Rainbow Tavern in Fleet-street' in 1837; and 'the Albion' in 'Making a Night of It' is similarly glossed with 'in Little Russell-street'. A few references to passing events that had survived the first revision, and had become more out-of-date with the further passage of time, were altered; Mr Potter is no longer looking for

---

'damn' to 'hate', 'confound', 'damning' to 'execrating', 'a d—d sight' to 'a deal', 'damned odd' to 'odd'. At the end of 'Private Theatres' the Shakespearean 'bloody officer' becomes 'bleeding officer'; an early appearance of a well-known schoolboy joke.

1. This kind of revision is fairly consistent, and also that of ''Tis 'or 'It's' to 'It is'.
2. Cf. p. 56 above.
3. 'London Recreations' (*Evening Chronicle*, 17 Mar. 1835); this therefore is Dickens's earliest Wellerism.
4. 'The Great Winglebury Duel'. The *Quarterly* (p. 515) had quoted this passage and remarked on the family likeness.
5. See above, p. 56.

the comet but for the moon, and the comparisons 'like Ward in Gustavus' and 'with all the dignity of a minor Manners Sutton'[1] are omitted. One of the drawing-room ballads sung at the Bloomsbury christening-party—'Can I believe Love's Wreath will pain?'[2]—goes out, and several names of newspapers; it is a loss that John Evenson's reading of the *Examiner* no longer survives to define his radicalism.[3] An added footnote in 'A Visit to Newgate' explains that conditions have changed since the sketch was first published; on the other hand, another footnote complimenting Ainsworth on his portrayal of Dick Turpin in *Rookwood*, introduced since the first edition, is removed.[4] The hinted prospect of further stories about Mrs Tibbs's boarding-house goes out, since the tally of Dickens's early stories was now complete,[5] and the collection would not be further enlarged.

V

The final clean-up was made for the cheap edition of 1850, which carries the apologetic Preface quoted at the beginning of this essay. Here the language was further softened, even 'cursedly' and 'the deuce' and the mere reference to imprecations and kicks in 'The Pawnbroker's Shop', being expurgated; 'taken to prigging' in 'Criminal Courts' becomes 'got into trouble'; the 'legs' of the young lady in 'The Dancing Academy' become 'ankles'; an added phrase in 'A Parliamentary Sketch' makes it clear that Jane's 'friskings and rompings . . . in the passage' 'are very innocent'; one more reference to the effect of oysters on gallantry was detached; in 'The Boarding-House', Mrs Bloss's 'two grain calomel pill' becomes 'a pill', and Mrs Tibbs no longer distributes 'all the *et ceteras*' as well as 'towels and soap'. The tales received particular attention; the harshness of their humour, especially towards women, is sometimes softened, and once again some lively comparisons are cut out. Horatio Sparkins formerly 'looked as handsomely miserable as a Hamlet sliding upon a bit

1. 'The Boarding-House'; 'The Steam Excursion'.
2. We have not yet succeeded in tracing this song.
3. 'The Boarding-House'; 1839 substitutes 'a Sunday paper'.
4. *Rookwood* was as popular as ever, but Dickens's view of it had changed.
5. An American reprint of 1839 (Philadelphia 1842) adds 'The Public Life of Mr. Tulrumble' and 'The Pantomime of Life' from *Bentley's*, which Dickens never collected.

of orange-peel'; Teresa blushed 'like a full-blown peony'; the Miss Tauntons in 'The Steam Excursion'

> advanced to the table, with that ballet sort of step which some young ladies seem to think so fascinating—something between a skip and a canter.

Perhaps that particular affectation had gone out of fashion; and it is probably a loss of topicality that deprives us of the comparison of the draper's price-figures:

> a seven with a little three-farthings in the corner, something like the aquatic animalculae disclosed by the gas microscope,[1] "perfectly invisible to the naked eye".

It is these small cuts that are typical of the 1850 revision; but a few are more extensive, and suggest some change of sentiment or social attitude. Dickens's work for Miss Coutts's Ragged School is surely reflected in the change of 'irreclaimable wretches' to 'creatures of neglect' in the description of the juvenile delinquents of 'A Visit to Newgate'. In 'The First of May' the closing phrase, 'How has May-day decayed!' was formerly expanded into a condemnation of the 'profligate and vicious customs', the 'degradation and discontent', that had replaced the 'merry sports' of the past. The revision of the close of 'Gin-shops' shows the substitution of practical social reform for ironic defiance:

> Gin-drinking is a great vice in England, but poverty is [1850, 'wretchedness and dirt are'] a greater; and until you can cure it [1850, 'improve the homes of the poor'] . . . gin-shops will increase in number and splendour. If Temperance Societies could suggest an antidote against hunger and distress [1850, 'would suggest', 'hunger, filth, and foul air'] . . . gin-palaces would be numbered among the things that were. Until then, their decrease may be despaired of. [1850 omit 'Until . . . of'.]

And one minute but significant change also comes in a 'curtain-line'; a family Christmas dinner, Dickens says, does more

> to awaken the sympathies of every member of the party in behalf of his neighbour, and to perpetuate their good feeling during the ensuing year, than all the homilies that have ever been written, by all the Divines that have ever lived.

---

1. 'Horatio Sparkins'; the words 'something . . . microscope' are omitted in 1850. The gas microscope had been a popular public exhibit of the 1830s, and contributed a point to one of Sam Weller's famous ripostes to Sergeant Buzfuz.

In 1850, whether from conviction, or from caution prompted by Forster, Dickens altered this to read:

> than half the homilies that have ever been written, by half the Divines that have ever lived.

This account of Dickens's revisions is by no means exhaustive, and has been almost confined to points of substance; but it is enough to show that the suppression of the original versions in modern editions brings some loss of understanding, both of Dickens's methods and of the very nature of the original sketches, which critics have followed Dickens rather than Forster in under-rating. The establishment of a critical text of the *Sketches by Boz* is surely a prerequisite for a true estimate of these 'first sprightly runnings of his genius'.

CHAPTER III

From Sketches to Novel: *Pickwick Papers* (1836-7)

I

IN a letter of 31 March 1836, Dickens speaks of 'the great success of my book, and the name it has established for me among the publishers . . .' One immediate consequence of the *Sketches by Boz*, published on 6 February 1836, was the well-known offer from Chapman and Hall[1] on 10 February:

> I was a young man of three-and-twenty, when the present publishers, attracted by some pieces I was at that time writing in the Morning Chronicle newspaper (of which one series had lately been collected . . .), waited upon me to propose a something that should be published in shilling numbers. . . The idea propounded to me was that the monthly something should be a vehicle for certain plates to be executed by MR SEYMOUR; and there was a notion . . . that a "NIMROD club", the members of which were to go out shooting, fishing, and so forth, and getting themselves into difficulties through their want of dexterity, would be the best means of introducing these.[2]

The terms offered for providing the letterpress for Seymour's plates were £14 a month for an instalment of about twelve thousand words. 'The emolument', wrote Dickens, 'is too tempting to resist'.[3] At the same time, it must have seemed to cut across

---

1. Chapman (Forster, I v) gave a slightly different account, explaining that he and his partner William Hall were attracted by the *Monthly Magazine* stories, and wished to enlist the writer as a contributor to their new periodical the *Library of Fiction*, edited by Charles Whitehead (his first story there, 'The Tuggs's at Ramsgate', appeared at the end of March), and that having opened this connexion, they naturally applied to him for *Pickwick*. For a summary of most of the evidence, see W. Dexter and J. W. T. Ley, *The Origin of Pickwick*, 1936.

2. Preface to 1847 edition of *Pickwick Papers*.   3. *Letters*, I 65.

his plans, which were apparently to use such leisure as he had from his full-time reporting for further sketch-writing, and, above all, for the three-volume novel already in his mind. The Preface to *Sketches by Boz* refers to that publication as a 'pilot balloon'; there was already a real balloon designed for launching if it succeeded—the 'proposed novel' referred to as early as 1834,[1] but now presumably re-forming in his mind as *Gabriel Vardon, the Locksmith of London*.[2] Such a design at least helps to explain the implied wish to 'resist' the 'tempting' emolument; and also the remark (ironic by then) in the 1847 Preface to *Pickwick*:

> My friends told me it was a low, cheap form of publication, by which I should ruin all my rising hopes . . .[3]

The 'friends', one supposes, were the only two established novelists whom Dickens already knew—Harrison Ainsworth and Edward Bulwer, both with respectable three-volume novels to their credit; perhaps the editors among his acquaintance, Laman Blanchard, Douglas Jerrold, and William Jerdan, may have added their arguments. Dickens's 'rising hopes' early in 1836 were literary rather than journalistic; he was working his way out of journalism, with the collection and revision of his *Sketches*, his comedy and his burletta, and his plans for a novel; Chapman and Hall's proposal must have seemed to pull him back into hack work again. For his position was only that of a salaried partner in the proposed monthly enterprise: the artist was already commissioned, and the subject more or less prescribed; four of Seymour's plates were to be illustrated by twenty-six pages of text, and the anticipated circulation of the 'serial' was about four hundred copies. The shilling number, so soon to be transformed in public estimation, had then no status: even two years later, in 1838, the *Edinburgh Review* noted the paradox of the form of Dickens's novels—that of 'literary *ephemerae* . . . the lightest kind of light reading'.[4] When the proposal was made to Dickens, he associated the form only with

> a dim recollection of certain interminable novels in that form, which used, some five-and-twenty years ago, to be carried about

---

1. *Letters*, 1 29: 'I shall cut my proposed novel up into little magazine sketches'.
2. See below, p. 76.
3. The corrected proof (in the Forster collection) shows that Dickens originally wrote 'Everybody' for 'My friends'.
4. Oct. 1838; p. 76.

the country by pedlars, and over some of which I remember to have
shed innumerable tears, before I served my apprenticeship to Life;[1]

an association which perhaps affected his choice of a picaresque
fiction, with reminiscences of his favourite Smollett. The artist's
plan of plates illustrating the comic misadventures of a Nimrod
Club of Cockney sportsmen[2] was of course derived rather from
the popular series in annuals (such as Cruikshank's *Comic Almanack*) and monthly magazines (such as the *New Sporting Magazine*,
in which Surtees's *Jorrocks* series had recently appeared, and the
New Monthly, where John Poole had a series called 'A Cockney's
Rural Sports'); and from the publication in numbers, in the previous decade, of Pierce Egan's *Life in London* ('Tom and Jerry'),
with illustrations by Cruikshank and others.

It is clear that Seymour was the initiator of the plan, and was
seen from the start as the dominant partner; and although
Dickens at once demanded and was conceded certain modifica-
tions so as to give him a 'freer range of English scenes and people',
Seymour might conceivably have maintained his position had he
lived. But his sudden death decisively shifted the emphasis; first,
it 'brought about a quick decision' to reduce the plates from four
to two and increase the text to thirty-two pages;[3] and then, by
the substitution of a very young artist, Hablôt K. Browne, who
was virtually Dickens's own choice, ensured the dominance of
the author. By the third number the external pattern of *Pickwick*
was established; all that was wanting was success. His 'rising
hopes' had not, as his friends prophesied, been ruined by *Pick-*

1. Preface to Cheap edition, 1847. In his autobiographical fragment Dickens,
according to Forster, had named the 'cheap series of novelists then in course of publication' which his father bought and in which he, like David Copperfield, first met
the eighteenth-century classics. The series has not been identified, but probably
resembled Cooke's *British Novelists*, referred to by Hazlitt, and published in six-
penny numbers in 1792.
    There had been a recent revival of the method for the reprinting of popular suc-
cesses; see M. Sadleir, *XIX Century Fiction* (1951), II 94ff.
2. The plan survives in Seymour's cover-design, which is not very appropriate to
Pickwick as we have it, but evidently represents Seymour's own intentions before
Dickens's views were 'deferred to'. Seymour had illustrated Richard Penn's *Maxims and Hints for an Angler, and Miseries of Fishing* (1833); the frontispiece shows a fat
spectacled man fishing, and the 'maxims' are presented as 'extracts from the Common Place Book of the Houghton Fishing Club'.
3. The 'Address from the Publishers' in No. III (dated 30 May) claimed that the
change was made 'on a suggestion which has been made to them from various influential quarters' and pointed out that it entailed 'considerable expense, which
nothing but a large circulation would justify them in incurring'—a cunningly
ambiguous phrase.

wick; but they had certainly not been stimulated, with the circulation of the 'monthly something' still in the region of five hundred copies, and very few press notices. He must still have felt doubtful about this 'low, cheap form of publication' which he had consented to adopt simply because 'the emolument'[1] was 'too tempting to resist'; which he had adopted, moreover, without regarding it as other than one of several journalistic sidelines, for after two numbers of *Pickwick* had appeared, he signed a contract with Macrone, the publisher of *Boz*, to supply for £200 a three-volume novel to be completed by the following November.[2] The coincidence of events is suggestive; he was still seeing *Pickwick* as journalism, as distinct from a real novel, which he saw as a considered work 'compact in three separate and indiwidual wollumes'—the one form that he was never to use for the first publication of a novel.[3]

As we know, Dickens was to learn how to reconcile the foresight and planning which a novel required with writing in numbers; but he began *Pickwick* before he had learnt it, and before he even knew that the lesson was relevant. Looking back from ten years' experience, he wrote that:

> no ingenuity of plot was attempted, or even at that time considered very feasible by the author in connexion with the desultory mode of publication adopted.

—here recalling what he had written in the 1837 Preface:

> it was necessary—or it appeared so to the author—that every number should be, to a certain extent, complete in itself, and yet that the whole twenty numbers, when collected, should form one tolerably harmonious whole, each leading to the other by a gentle and not unnatural progress of adventure.
>
> It is obvious that in a work published with a view to such considerations, no artfully interwoven or ingeniously complicated plot can with reason be expected.

The qualifying clauses in the first sentence suggest that he was already changing his mind. And by 1847 he had come to realize that 'experience and study' had now taught him something in that respect, and to wish that the separate papers had been

1. This was raised to £16 when the amount of text was increased, after being reduced to 10 guineas in May.
2. See below, p. 76.
3. *Oliver Twist* and *Great Expectations* were published in this form after serial publication.

strung together on a stronger thread of general interest; still, what they are, they were designed to be.

Plotting and planning, even had Dickens thought it 'feasible', was in any case virtually ruled out by the exigencies of the calendar. *Pickwick* is unique among Dickens's novels, not in being written from month to month 'almost as the periodical occasion arose'—all his novels were so written—but in being *begun* in response to an external demand, instead of gradually taking shape in his mind. There was no preliminary period of imaginative incubation, such as is found even for the other early novels. Between contract and first instalment for *Oliver Twist*, six months elapsed; for *Nicholas Nickleby*, four months (partly spent in visiting Yorkshire); and for *Barnaby Rudge* the quite extraordinary period of at least five years. For later novels the period of preparation is well documented by reference in letters ('vague thoughts', 'agonies of plotting and contriving'), and sometimes by such evidence as the preliminary design of *Dombey and Son* and *The Chimes*; and from 1846 on, he usually began publication with a few numbers in hand. Improvisation thereafter was within the limits of a foreseen plan, which might be modified in detail, but not radically. But for *Pickwick* the time-table is: Chapman and Hall's offer, 10 February; its final acceptance, 16 February; writing begins, 18 February; first number promised to the publishers early in March; second number by the end of March; Number I on sale 31 March.

How it was done is a matter largely of inference. No complete manuscript, no number plans, no proof sheets, very few letters to Forster (whom Dickens did not meet until December 1836) are available here.[1] It may be assumed that as publication proceeded, Dickens watched the sales, that he noticed that they began to rise in July with the introduction of Sam Weller; certainly he took notice of William Jerdan's advice to 'develop' this character 'to the utmost';[2] and the soaring success, from the fifth number on, buoyed him up on a rising wave of confidence, doubled, after

1. The series of notes to Catherine Hogarth in Feb. and Mar. is undated, and the dating supplied by the late Walter Dexter (in *Mr. and Mrs. Charles Dickens: his Letters to her*, 1935, and again, with some changes in dating, in the few extracts also given in *Letters*) is difficult to accept. For example, the remark that 'the sheets are a weary length—I had no idea there was so much in them' seems likely, in its suggestion of inexperience, to refer to the writing of No. I in late Feb. or early Mar., and there is nothing in this or other letters to contradict such dating; but Dexter dated it '[18 March]', without query or explanation, and subsequent writers on Dickens have so accepted it.

2. *Autobiography* (1852), IV 364.

the eleventh number, by the simultaneous success of *Oliver Twist* as a serial in *Bentley's Miscellany*. The peculiar advantage of hand-to-mouth writing—its immediate sensitiveness to public response—must have been disclosed to him in the course of *Pickwick*. But how he began, as an unknown author in an unprecedented form, with merely the experience of his sketch and story writing behind him, can be seen only by looking closely at the early numbers themselves. (As the object is to show the improvised nature of the early instalments, in contrast to the emerging unity of the novel, detailed commentary is not carried further than Number V, chapters xii–xiv.)

II

The first number (chapters i–ii, and the first two pages of chapter iii) is essentially a single 'sketch' combined with the first part of a farcical episode such as we find in the *Monthly Magazine* tales. The 'sketch' is the Pickwickians' meeting in chapter i, supposed to be taken from the Transactions of the Club. Besides its obvious expository function, it has an evident satirical purpose, for the oration and debate 'bear a strong affinity to the discussions of other celebrated bodies'. It is the reporter who is speaking, with recollections of Parliament and political meetings and innumerable other public meetings in mind; and with more than a side-glance, in the Theory of Tittlebats, at the proceedings of the recently established British Association[1] (already a target in Cruikshank's *Comic Almanack* of 1835); the chapter is virtually a further variant on the committee meeting in 'The Steam Excursion' of 1834.[2] From his earliest to his latest writings Dickens loved to set his characters speechifying; 'The Election for Beadle' already foreshadows the humours of the United Metropolitan Improved Hot Muffin and Crumpet Baking and Punctual Delivery Company in *Nicholas Nickleby* and the Mudfog Association for the Advancement of Everything, and John Willet at the Maypole may be seen taking shape in 'The Parlour

1. The notice in the *Bath Herald* called this number 'a squib directed against the British Association' (*The Dickensian*, June 1936, p. 216).

2. 'He had the highest esteem for Mr. Percy Noakes as an individual, but he did consider that he ought not to be intrusted with these immense powers (oh, oh!) He believed that in the proposed capacity [as organizer of a picnic] Mr. Percy Noakes would not act fairly, impartially, or honourably; but he begged it to be distinctly understood that he said this, without the slightest personal disrespect'—that is, in a Pickwickian sense. (*Sketches by Boz*, First Series.)

Orator'. When Dickens is writing under pressure, the guying of public debate is the humorous device that he most readily turns to; deflating the pomposities of the self-intoxicated orator, amateur and professional, was his revenge for the years of enforced listening to speech-making recorded in *David Copperfield*:

> Night after night, I record predictions that never come to pass, professions that are never fulfilled, explanations that are only meant to mystify. I wallow in words.[1]

The first chapter also prepares for the travels of the four Pickwickians, which begin accordingly in the second, with the journey to Rochester, the meeting with Jingle,[2] and the first stage of the embroilment with Dr Slammer. Tracy Tupman's ambition to cut a dash in company and his amorous bent, the empty pretensions of Mr Winkle's claims to sportsmanship, are illustrated in the manner of 'humours'; the whole episode is from stock, clearly recalling the duel in *The Rivals*. Dickens expected Jingle to make 'a decided hit'; but there is nothing as yet to suggest that he is more than a transient character; and the desultory form of the papers is confirmed by the appearance, at the end of the number, of 'dismal Jemmy', who prepares to tell a tale. Thus the conclusion of the farcical episode is left in suspense, and the third chapter is interrupted for a month at the foot of its second page.

In the second number (chapters iii–v) the interrelation is still loose; the grim 'Stroller's Tale' is first narrated, with no other apparent purpose than to exhibit Boz's versatility[3] and his independence of Seymour's designs; its impact is nullified by the immediate return of the farce. Chapter iv introduces an entirely new episode with the field-day at Fort Pitt and a new group of characters with the Wardle party; which results in the invitation to Manor Farm, and the humours of the journey with the horse and trap.[4]

---

1. Ch. xliii.

2. Dickens had written thus far, the equivalent of eight printed pages, by 21 Feb. (*Letters*, I 67; the date is confirmed by the letters to Chapman and Hall in the same week.)

3. Compare such a sketch as 'The Black Veil' (*Sketches by Boz*, First Series). It is possible that this, like other intercalated tales, was originally designed for separate publication. Dickens was working under considerable pressure, for the MS. of No. II was in the publishers' hands by 29 Mar. (Dexter and Ley, op. cit., p. 43), presumably to allow time for his honeymoon (2–?14 Apr.) and for the four illustrations, of which Seymour had done three before his death on 19 Apr.

4. The review in the *Sun* (2 May) describes it as 'the second number of an entertaining, miscellaneous collection of tales, anecdotes, etc., collected and arranged by Boz'.

The third number (chapters vi–viii), more obviously a miscellany than any, inaugurates a new amorous adventure for Mr Tupman, provides sporting humour with Mr Winkle's shooting and the cricket match, and some more comic oratory; it also includes a set of verses, 'The Ivy Green', known to have been written independently,[1] and the second intercalated 'grim' story, 'The Convict's Return'. The characters remain in the flat, the situations stock; though the farce is diversified and enlivened by means of minor characters like the Fat Boy. But this number also suggests some planning ahead, through the recurrence of Jingle, now cast as a rival to Tupman; and the number ends on a note of suspense:

> The host was in high spirits, for he had satisfied himself that there was no ground for the charge against Mr. Tupman. So was Mr. Tupman, for Mr. Jingle had told him that his affair would soon be brought to a crisis. So was Mr. Pickwick, for he was seldom otherwise. . . So were Mr. Jingle and Miss Wardle, for reasons of sufficient importance in this eventful history, to be narrated in another chapter.

This simple type of number-ending is Dickens's favourite in *Pickwick*.

The fourth number (chapters ix–xi) makes no marked departure from the pattern. The elopement of Jingle and Miss Wardle, his pursuit, exposure, and buying-off apparently complete the second farcical episode, and the retreat of the disconsolate Tupman sets the Pickwickians on their travels again; the self-contained incident of 'Bill Stumps his Mark' reminds us of the antiquarian researches of the Club, and there is the usual dose of the macabre in 'The Madman's Manuscript'. The only anticipation of the next number is the prospect of the election at Eatanswill, 'a scene so interesting to every Englishman'. Thus far there is no reason why the sales of *Pickwick* should at this point have shown a spectacular rise; this must be partly attributed[2] to the appearance of a particularly racy though apparently transient minor character in the exposure scene—the Boots at the White Hart, Sam Weller. It is unlikely that his full possibilities were as yet foreseen. Writing to a friend, Dickens draws attention to him

---

1. F. G. Kitton, *The Poems and Verses of Charles Dickens* (1903), p. 35.
2. This is the explanation usually given, but in any case three or four months seems about the right time for a new publication, unusual in form, to make its impact.

simply as a 'specimen of London life'[1]—a true-to-life Cockney 'character', that is, of the order of 'the Omnibus Cad' in the *Sketches*. Nothing of his future relation to Mr Pickwick is as yet suggested; but the characteristic anecdote of his father, and still more, the skilful use of his observations so as to show the whole Jingle incident from a fresh and unexpected point of view, seem to promise a more than merely episodic function. Perhaps Dickens had vague designs for him as the stock comic servant in the eighteenth-century tradition, sharpened up with Cockney humour and with verbal reminiscences of Simm Spatterdash in Beazley's popular comedy.[2] Whatever he foresaw, he at once responded to Jerdan's suggestion to 'develop' this character 'to the utmost', not only by ever-resourceful comic invention of detail, but by integrating the character with the plot and themes of the novel.

The 'development' of Sam in subsequent numbers gives a new depth and a new motive force to *Pickwick*; henceforward it is built, not simply upon events, but upon the deepening relation between him and his master. Much weight, in criticism of *Pickwick*, is commonly given to Dickens's well-known account of its beginnings—'My views being deferred to, I thought of Mr. Pickwick'; but Pickwick is not 'thought of' as a character distinct in kind from the other Pickwickians until he is connected with Sam Weller. Until then, he is simply the benevolent butt, the fat man who loses his hat and is upset in a postchaise, differentiated from the amorous Tupman and the would-be sporting Winkle only by being less clearly ticketed with a single 'humour'; with Sam, he becomes that most fruitful of all comic archetypes, the innocent at large, with a touch of the chivalrous crusader. Not only Smollett, but Cervantes, was Dickens's model here, as several contemporary reviewers recognized.[3]

Chapter xii, which opens the fifth number and includes Mr Pickwick's engagement of Sam as his servant, is crucial in another way too: and this, no doubt, is what Dickens had in mind

1. *Letters*, I 73.

2. *The Boarding House*, 1811. Simm is a cheeky servant who acts as a go-between in the 'love'-plot; the only specific resemblance is in his use of 'Wellerisms' ('as the — said'), which Dickens had already adopted in his *Sketches* (see above, p. 58). The review in the *Westminster Review*, July 1837, referring to 'those imaginary speeches . . . after the fashion of Cockney wags', suggests that they were taken from life.

3. E.g. *Edinburgh Review*, Oct. 1838: 'the modern Quixote and Sancho of Cockaigne'.

in its descriptive title, 'A very important Proceeding on the part of Mr. Pickwick; no less an epoch in his Life than in this History'. The importance of Mrs Bardell's misunderstanding of Mr Pickwick's intentions, which dawns upon the reader in the sixth number with the letter from Dodson and Fogg, is here proclaimed; and this supplies a plot-interest which continues to the end of the novel. Thus, a quarter of the way through its course, *Pickwick* discovers its shape, with the emergence of Sam and the beginning of the action of Bardell v. Pickwick.

The new plot-material sprang directly from a recent journalistic experience. Dickens wrote the fifth number in July; on 22 June, as a reporter on the *Morning Chronicle*, he had attended the Norton-Melbourne case, his report occupying twenty-six columns of the paper next day. He saw the possibilities of the trial, not only the prosecuting counsel's comments on the formal notes of Lord Melbourne[1] and the browbeating of witnesses,[2] but more soberly, as material for satiric exposure of social corruption, for it was a flagrantly deliberate attempt to damage the character of innocent persons. Dickens's treatment is serious as well as comic, producing what the *Edinburgh Review* was to call

> one of the most acute and pointed satires upon the state and administration of English law that ever appeared in the light and lively dress of fiction.[3]

It is the earliest and one of the most successful instances of Dickens's use of topical appeal in his novels and an excellent

1. ' "I will call about half past 4. Yours, Melbourne" ... The style and form of these notes, Gentlemen, seems to import much more than they contain. Cautiously, I admit, they are worded; there are no professions of love ... but still they are not the letters of an ordinary acquaintance'. The final speech for the defence ridiculed the argument, quoting the notes again; 'Are Lord Melbourne's declarations very violent? Are his protestations exceedingly warm? (*Laughter*).' The *Quarterly Review* (Oct. 1837) quotes Buzfuz on 'Chops and tomata-sauce' as 'a fair specimen of Mr. Dickens's tact in stimulating the reader's attention by little sly allusions to contemporary events'.

2. Compare also the exchange between Mr Thesiger and Sir William Follett in the examination of a lady's maid, obviously the source of the little judge's flat contradiction of Mr Winkle:

Witness: I have often known Lord Melbourne there but I could never get a look at him. *Sir William Follett:* What? *Mr Thesiger:* She said she had often known Lord Melbourne there but could never get a look at him. *Sir William Follett:* No, she did not.

3. Oct. 1838, p. 80; and compare Charles Buller's review in *Westminster Review*, July 1837. F. G. Kitton, in his notes to the Autograph edition (1903), says that Dickens was helped in his account of the trial by Talfourd, who revised the proof.

example of how he selected and reassembled facts[1] (for Justice Gaselee and Serjeant Bompas, notoriously the models for Stareleigh and Buzfuz, did not appear in the case) and transformed them by exaggeration and invention into a timeless comic fantasy. Nor is the immortal Trial merely a star episode; it is one of the key scenes of the novel, in displaying the main characters, especially Pickwick, Winkle, and the Wellers, at their most characteristic. It appeared in the twelfth number, in March 1837; but Dickens had surely had it in mind for several months before.

III

This is the clearest instance of foresight and planning. But alongside the Bardell–Pickwick plot and the deepening relation of master and servant, the looser, more miscellaneous pattern proceeds as before; adventures at Eatanswill, Ipswich, Bath; the shooting party, the skating scene, the medical students' party, with inset tales and verses, diversify the numbers. As it grew into a novel, *Pickwick* did not lose its character as a miscellany, with a 'free range of English scenes and people', nor its loosely picaresque form. The *Athenæum*, reviewing the first nine numbers, summed up their ingredients as—

> two pounds of Smollett, three ounces of Sterne, a handful of Hook, a dash of a grammatical Pierce Egan—[2]

rightly recognizing the basis of the mixture as Smollett, though with a significant difference—'Smollett without his coarseness'.[3] Dickens had also in mind such periodical series as the De Coverley papers—on the whole the nearest precedent offered by the eighteenth century for the serial novel. *Pickwick* remains to the

1. Other *crim. con.* trials may be recalled; in *Birch v. Neale* (Court of Common Pleas, 25 June 1835) a good deal is made to depend on what the servants can see through the cracks of a bedroom door. Charles Philips, the Irish barrister, was notorious for his pleadings in such cases, and was 'a great practical patron of the brow-beating system' (James Grant, *Portraits of Public Characters*, 2 vols., 1841, I 212; and see *Edinburgh Review*, Oct. 1815 and Nov. 1817).

2. 3 Dec. 1836; compare *New Monthly Magazine* (Sept. 1836): 'his spirit is akin to that of our Fieldings and Smolletts'.

3. But not all readers agreed. Lockhart told Ainsworth that he thought *Pickwick* ' "all very well—but" with one of his usual laughs—"damned low!" ' (S. M. Ellis, *William Harrison Ainsworth and his Friends*, 1911, I 336) and two members of a circulating Book Society opposed the notion to take in the numbers because 'they considered the work vulgar' (MS. notes in a British Museum copy of first edition).

:nd more strictly 'periodical' than any of his later novels. The
high proportion of inset tales seems to show that he pursued, perhaps in a crude form, the principle of variety within a single number; the episodes are farcical, the inset story macabre. (In the
Fleet numbers, where the main content is more serious, no such
tales occur.) A more practical and economical motive may have
contributed. Dickens had written many short tales when he began *Pickwick*; very likely he had some in his desk and used them
to eke out his numbers.[1] Seven of the nine stories occur in the first
half of the novel; they are almost completely disconnected from
their contexts, related casually by unimportant people, and seldom making any impact on their hearers. In one case the immediate source in recent experience is evident; Dickens visited
Bedlam in June 1836 (he had planned a 'sketch' on the subject
and was also probably already thinking of *Barnaby Rudge*) and in
the July number inserted 'The Madman's Manuscript'.

The 'journalistic' nature of *Pickwick* is also evident in one
curious and unique feature: the consistent relevance of the numbers to the time of year in which they appeared, so that, for example, the cricket match falls in the June number, the shooting
scene in October, and the skating scene in February. Some numbers are slightly retrospective in dating; Christmas at Dingley
Dell is in the January number, the September number opens
with a description of August, Sam Weller writes his Valentine in
the March number, and the final (November) number opens
with Mr Pickwick going to Gray's Inn 'in the healthy light of an
October morning'. Dickens appears to have imagined his readers
asking themselves on the first of the month, What have the Pickwickians been doing since we saw them last? and to have reported accordingly. The duration of the action matches the nineteen
months of publication, running from May (1827) to October
(1828), parallel with the serial appearances from April 1836 to
November 1837. The law terms are observed, and when, after
the trial, Mr Pickwick is told that 'they can issue execution just

1. Bibliography seems to confirm this in one instance; the story of Prince Bladud
in the thirteenth (Apr.) number was set up separately with a blank space before
and after. Dickens might well be pressed for time just then, having recently begun
the editing of *Bentley's* and the writing of *Oliver Twist*; and February, as he often
ruefully notes, is a short month.

He reverted to the practice only once in a later novel; the second number of
Nicholas Nickleby contains two tales, whose presence is explained by a letter to
Forster: 'I . . . have yet five slips to finish, and don't know what to put in them for
I have reached the point I meant to leave off with' (*Letters*, 1 162).

two months hence', the necessary interval is occupied with the visit to Bath in the next two numbers. This exact correspondence is not observed in any later novel, though isolated instances of 'seasonal relevance' can be found, such as Little Nell's death in January; and the pointed reference to the date in chapter xiii of *Barnaby Rudge*, published on 4 April:

> It was, in fact, the twenty-fifth of March, which, as most people know to their cost, is, and has been time out of mind, one of those unpleasant epochs termed quarter-days.[1]

But the novels after *Pickwick* were each worlds of their own, not tied to the reader's calendar.

The other external circumstance which may have affected the direction of *Pickwick* was the writing of *Oliver Twist*, which overlapped with it after the first nine numbers. Its success may have emboldened Dickens to introduce a more serious kind of social satire into *Pickwick*. Just after the new serial had begun to appear comes the Trial; it had been running for three months when Mr Pickwick enters the Fleet prison. 'The next Pickwick', he wrote to Forster, 'will bang all the others';[2] he was right; the sales rose to forty thousand.

The interlocking of the first three novels is indeed made clear by a remark in the Preface to *Nicholas Nickleby*. He says he had had the evils of the Yorkshire schools in his mind for many years; and 'at last, having an audience, resolved to write about them'.[3] 'Having an audience': this was assured to Dickens, and for his lifetime, after the fifth number of *Pickwick*; and 'having an audience', he resolved to expose the corruptions of the law, the plight of the pauper child, the evils of prison, school, and workhouse. But, having captured that audience by his power as an entertainer, he never abused his position:

> the rascalities of those Yorkshire schoolmasters *cannot* easily be exaggerated, and I have kept down the strong truth and thrown as much comicality over it as I could, rather than disgust the reader with its fouler aspects.[4]

So Stiggins, Bumble, and Squeers remain comic characters, and

---

1. See also the description of Chancery Lane in the hot days of a long vacation, in *Bleak House*, No. VI (ch. xix), published in August 1852, and of late autumn weather in No. IX (ch. xxix), published in November.
2. *Letters*, I 124.   3. Preface to *Nicholas Nickleby*, Cheap edition, 1848.
4. *Letters*, I 185.

the trial of Bardell v. Pickwick shows no trace of the revolting coarseness of the testimony of the suborned witnesses in the Norton-Melbourne trial. He was first a creator and entertainer:

> The author's object in this work, was to place before the reader a constant succession of characters and incidents; to paint them in as vivid colours as he could command; and to render them, at the same time, life-like and amusing.

Thus the opening of the 1837 Preface to *Pickwick*. But looking back ten years later he saw something more:

> I have found it curious and interesting, looking over the sheets of this reprint, to mark what important social improvements have taken place about us, almost imperceptibly, ever since they were originally written. The license of Counsel, and the degree to which Juries are ingeniously bewildered, are yet susceptible of moderation; while an improvement in the mode of conducting Parliamentary Elections (especially for counties) is still within the bounds of possibility. But legal reforms have pared the claws of Messrs. Dodson and Fogg; . . . the laws relating to imprisonment for debt are altered; and the Fleet Prison is pulled down!

Forster's words were true in more senses than one:

> The book itself, in teaching him what his power was, made him more conscious of what would be expected from its use; and this never afterwards quitted him.[1]

*

Dickens had discovered his power; he had also discovered his medium in the monthly number.

> My friends told me it was a low, cheap form of publication, by which I should ruin all my rising hopes; and how right my friends turned out to be, everybody now knows.

Other experiments in form were still to be made; but with *Pickwick*, Dickens embarked upon his lifelong love-affair with his reading public; which, when all is said, is by far the most interesting love-affair of his life.

1. Forster, II i.

CHAPTER IV

Barnaby Rudge:
The First Projected Novel

I

BARNABY RUDGE, though it is now one of the least read of Dickens's novels, deserves special attention on account of two unusual features: the length of time which Dickens had it in mind, and the particular kind of 'work' it involved, in research upon original sources. Also notable, though not unusual, is the way he makes his historical romance a tract for the times, relating it to some of the social and political preoccupations of the years of writing.

He had it in mind for at least five years. For it should have been his first published novel, instead of his fifth. Instead of coming out in the threepenny numbers of *Master Humphrey's Clock* in 1841, it should have appeared in all the traditional dignity of 'three compact indiwidual wollumes' at the end of 1836, when Mr Pickwick had progressed no farther than Ipswich. That, at least, was the agreement made in May with Macrone, publisher of *Sketches by Boz*.[1] What interfered was the soaring circulation of *Pickwick*; by August a contract for an outright payment of £200 and an edition of a thousand copies, welcome enough for the young beginner, could only seem derisory. The agreement was eventually cancelled and the projected novel (its title now changed from *Gabriel Vardon, the Locksmith of London* to *Barnaby Rudge, a tale of the Riots of '80*) transferred to Bentley.[2] In Septem-

1. *Letters*, I 71–2. The 'entire manuscript' was to be delivered 'on or before' 30 Nov. or 'as soon afterwards as I can possibly complete it'.

2. Dickens believed himself released from the Macrone agreement and on 22 Aug. agreed to provide two novels (unnamed) for Bentley. Macrone however wished to hold him to his contract and in Dec. was advertising *Gabriel Vardon*; the release was only obtained, on consideration of a reduction in the sum paid for the copy-

ber 1837 its delivery was promised by October 1838; but this was soon found incompatible with the claims of serial writing, and the next project, to run it as a monthly serial in *Bentley's Miscellany* in 1839,[1] also broke down. It was postponed again to January 1840 ('as a novel, and not in portions') ;[2] in the following July transferred to Chapman and Hall as a novel 'of matter sufficient for ten monthly numbers',[3] and finally appeared weekly in the *Clock*[4] from 13 February to 27 November, 1841. This complicated and harassing history has a more than biographical interest; the novel was affected by the change of form, and still more by its exceptionally long period of incubation. Dickens's persistence in his plan for 'a tale of the Riots of '80' is evidence of his tenacity of purpose and the grip of the original idea on his imagination; not, as has been suggested, of the grudging performance of a task. There were difficulties; being committed to the weekly appearances of the *Clock*, he had to begin with all his 'thoughts and interest hanging about'[5] the just-concluded *Old Curiosity Shop*; and to the last he was, as he told his readers, 'often cramped and confined in a very irksome degree' by the short weekly instalments.[6] But after 'warming up' in the middle chapters, he could write to Forster: 'I was always sure I could make a good thing of *Barnaby*, and I think you'll find that it comes out strong to the last word . . . I am in great heart and spirits with the story'.[7]

What then was the original idea which he had held in mind for so long? We know from the Preface that Dickens began with the object of writing about the Gordon Riots, which he believed to be new material for fiction,[8] 'presenting many very extraordinary

rights of the *Sketches*, in Jan. 1837. These and later agreements were published in *The Dickensian*, Sept. 1935, pp. 241–54 and June 1937, pp. 199–204, and the whole story of Dickens's publishing troubles for the four years 1836–40 was first clearly set out, with extracts from unpublished correspondence, by Johnson in *The Dickensian*, Dec. 1949, pp. 10–17, and Mar. 1950, pp. 76–83.

1. It is advertised in the first edition of *Oliver Twist* (published 9 Nov. 1838) as to be 'published forthwith, in *Bentley's Miscellany*', and again in the *Miscellany* itself, 1 Dec. 1838.

2. *Letters*, 1 198; letter of 31 Jan. 1839. The payment on delivery of the manuscript was now to be £2,000.

3. *Letters*, 1 263; the publishers had the option of publishing 'in fifteen smaller numbers'. The terms for six months' copyright were now £3,000.

4. Nos. 46–87.   5. *Letters*, 1 297.

6. 'To the Readers . . .'; see below, p. 88.   7. *Letters*, 1 345.

8. Thomas Gaspey's *The Mystery or, Forty Years Ago* (3 vols., 1820), in which three chapters are concerned with the riots, was possibly not known to him; yet he must have known the author as a member of the staff of the *Evening Chronicle*. James Grant, *The Great Metropolis* (first series, 2 vols., 1836), II 47–8, describes Gaspey

and remarkable features'. This means that in 1836 he set out to write a serious historical novel, and by his choice of subject challenged comparison with Scott. The storming of the Tolbooth in the opening chapters of *The Heart of Midlothian* is the literary inspiration of his central scene, as Madge Wildfire is of his central figure—who also recalls (especially in appearance) Davie Gellatley, the daft servant in *Waverley*.[1]

All this, however, is secondary to the direct inspiration of Newgate itself, both as place and symbol. Its exterior had been a familiar and awesome sight to Dickens as a schoolboy.[2] In 1835 he visited it, in order to write the sketch for the collected First Series of *Sketches by Boz*,[3] and was struck by the aspect and the imagined suffering of three condemned men, of whom two, he learnt, were afterwards executed, and one respited during His Majesty's pleasure. There is the germ of chapters lxxvi–lxxvii of *Barnaby*. His essay also emphasized the massiveness of the walls and gates, the hopelessness of escape; a perception closely connected with his triumphant letter of September 1841: 'I have just burnt into Newgate, and am going in the next number to tear the prisoners out by the hair of their heads.'[4] One may suspect that it was this incident in the riots that first fired his interest in the subject. In contemporary accounts, the burning of Newgate appears more terrifying than all the attacks upon Catholic chapels and property in its expression of the lawlessness of the mob; and to the next generation it carried the shadow of a far greater historical event, the fall of the Bastille. Dickens's imagination was also stirred by a rumoured scheme of violence still more terrifying—the release of the lunatics from Bedlam. This,

---

as also 'favourably known as the author of several novels, which he wrote some years ago'. Dickens's only known reference to him is in his Diary for 31 Jan. 1839: 'Gaspey. Chapter on Executioners' (*Letters*, 1 191). The entry looks like a memorandum to read such a chapter, and it is natural to connect it with *Barnaby Rudge*, which is mentioned in a letter of the same date (*Letters*, 1 198). The 'chapter' may be ch. vii of *The Mystery*, vol. 1, in which 'Ned Dennis' appears, accompanied by the same kind of macabre jesting as in *Barnaby Rudge*, though this hardly seems to account for the plural, 'executioners'. Another general parallel in a novel of Gaspey's is found in *George Godfrey* (3 vols., 1828) where there is an execution scene (III i) in which one of the three condemned criminals is reprieved at the last moment.

1. This parallel was noticed as early as June 1841, in Patrick Robertson's speech at the Edinburgh banquet.

2. See the opening paragraph of 'The Old Bailey' (*Morning Chronicle*, 23 Oct. 1834), included in the Second Series of *Sketches by Boz* under the title 'Criminal Courts'.

3. 'A Visit to Newgate'; see above, pp. 40–1.   4. *Letters*, 1 349.

along with the mad streak in Gordon's own character, contributed to his conception of Barnaby; at one time he had even
thought of making good the rumour, and showing three Bedlam-
ites as the unsuspected leaders of the rioters.[1] Forster's sober
counsels deterred him, and indeed the ironic social point is better
made by his actual choice of leaders—Hugh, the bastard of a fine
gentleman and a gipsy hanged at Tyburn; Barnaby, the imbecile
son of a murderer; and Dennis, the public hangman.

The two titles of the projected novel suggest that the outline of
his main design respecting the riots was already formed in 1836.
He may also have had it in mind on his visit to Bedlam 'for the
new series' (of *Sketches by Boz*) and certainly on his second visit to
Newgate in 1837.[2] The writing, however, is not known to have
begun until the autumn of 1839; early in October, hard upon the
conclusion of *Nickleby*, he was 'going . . . tooth and nail at
Barnaby',[3] and by February 1840 two chapters[4] were written,
substantially chapters i–iii of the published novel, which introduce the main characters and provide clear evidence of an elaborated plan for the whole. *Master Humphrey's Clock* and *The Old
Curiosity Shop* then intervened and occupied him for the rest of the
year. In January 1841 he revised and redivided the two opening
chapters,[5] and began to write the fourth chapter;[6] but he soon
lost the advantage of starting with material for two numbers in
hand, and by April was 'getting on very slowly'.[7] But with the
riots he wrote more rapidly, and by mid-September was again a
few weeks in advance.[8] Although he still complained of lack of
room ('Oh! If I only had him . . . in monthly numbers.')[9] the

1. Forster, II ix. Dickens refers to the rumour in ch. lxvii.

2. On 27 June 1837, with Macready, Forster, Cattermole, and 'Phiz' (*Diaries of
W. C. Macready 1833–1851*, ed. William Toynbee, 2 vols., 1912, I 401–2). Chigwell
was also perhaps in his mind as one of the settings; a picnic there 'last year' is
described in his *Sketches of Young Gentlemen* (1838).

3. *Letters*, I 231, to Cruikshank, who was then expected to illustrate it.

4. *Letters*, I 249.

5. *Letters*, I 296. Ch. i originally ended with 'and galloped away', and ch. ii included the whole of what is now ch. iii. In revision, several passages were added,
and some references to Barnaby as 'the idiot' were omitted. John Willet was called
'Peter Badge' for the first few pages.

6. He sent Cattermole '4 slips' on 30 Jan. (*Letters*, I 298); this was the beginning
of No. III (48), published on 28 Feb.

7. *Letters*, I 317.

8. *Letters*, I 353 (18 Sept.): 'I have let all the prisoners out of Newgate, burnt
down Lord Mansfield's, and played the very devil' (chs. lxv–lxvi, published
1 Oct.); see also the letters to Cattermole of 6 and 19 Aug. and 12 Sept.

9. *Letters*, I 343.

problem was less acute than in the earlier numbers, where he h:
committed himself to the careful laying-down of clues for t!
Haredale–Rudge murder-mystery part of the plot. This, mu:
more appropriate to a three-volume novel than to short week
instalments, set him a problem in exposition, and no dou
accounts for the anxiety shown in the letters of the early month

The manuscript survives, but without the proof sheets; t!
considerable differences between manuscript and printed te
show that much revision must have taken place in proc
Dickens's space was indeed small. With two exceptions,[1] ea:
number consisted of two chapters, and twelve pages of print,
which the illustrations were inset.[2] Sixteen and a half of Dicken:
quarto pages or 'slips' went to a number. Cutting in proof w
frequently necessary, both for length and other reasons, an
Forster's assistance was often sought:

> if there be anything here you object to, knock it out ruthlessly[3]

> Don't fail to erase anything that seems to you too strong[4]

> It was too bad of me to give you the trouble of cutting the numbe
> but I knew so well you would do it in the right places.[5]

Nothing of particular interest has, however, been lost. Th
description of eighteenth-century London at the beginning
chapter iv originally included the following:

> receiving Houses for the sick, which are now blocked up to swarm
> ing labyrinths—hotbeds for the constant growth of all the wor
> diseases they receive—were then upon the very borders of the tow
> The Middlesex Hospital, and those at Westminster and Hyde Pa:
> Corner, were of this kind. Their several sites selected with a view
> the healthiest and purest air, they were at that time in the outskirt
> beyond them were florists' gardens, widespread fields, green lan
> and country roads. Half a century appears but a little time for s
> much growth, but it is with cities as with human beings—on:
> dropsical they rapidly increase in size, and in a short space becom
> more overgrown and more unwieldy than in all their lives befor

---

1. No. I (*Master Humphrey's Clock*, No. 46), and No. VII (No. 52). The latter w
a short number, as it closed vol. II of the *Clock* and included the frontispiece, tit!
page, and preface.

2. Dickens sometimes indicates in the manuscript where he wishes the illustr
tion to come, and his instructions were usually followed.

3. *Letters*, I 309.

4. *Letters*, I 312; letter of 5 Apr., apparently referring to chs. xvii–xviii (publishe
18 Apr.) as just written.

5. *Letters*, I 317.

A passage which was possibly one of those 'knocked out' by Forster occurs in chapter xvii; it is a continuation of the stranger's threat, which ends in the text at 'if you betray me':

> 'By this right hand whose history you know and by this Devil's seal stamped upon me you remember when, I will!'
> He pulled his slouched hat from his brow, and pointing, as he spoke, to the gash upon his cheek, replaced it, and sat awaiting her decision.

Solomon Daisy's revelations in chapter xxxiii were delayed in the original, and Mr Willet's impatience was thus emphasized:

> They waited so long, and questioned him so often, without receiving any more satisfactory answer than a wild start, that Mr. Willet had entertained serious thoughts of [throttling him *deleted*] inserting a fork in his arm or leg by way of opening a vein, and had indeed begun to polish one of those instruments with his apron, and to look intently at the little man as if considering where to have him, when Solomon Daisy, with tears in his eyes, implored them to have patience for a minute longer and to fill his glass once more, to the end that he might rally his scattered spirits and be coherent in his speech.
> 'If he don't tell us now,' said John as he stirred the liquor and held it to his lips to take, 'if he don't tell us now in a quarter of a minute what's the matter, I shall do him a mischief. Mind that.'

But after the riots are reached there is much less revision,[1] and everything points to this part of the novel being written easily, by an author thoroughly familiar with his material: 'Many thanks for your kind offer', he writes to Charles Ollier, 'but I don't need the Trials'. He had made up his mind about his reading of Lord George Gordon's character and does not appear to have made any concessions to Forster's objections here.[2]

His favourable view was emphasized in the closing chapter, where he related the circumstances of Gordon's death in Newgate, five years after the riots.

> The prisoners bemoaned his loss, and missed him; for though his means were not large his charity was great, and in bestowing alms among them he considered the necessities of all alike, and knew no distinction of sect or creed. There are wise men in the highways of

1. In one or two places, however, it is clear that the manuscript itself is a fair copy.

2. *Letters*, 1 324; Forster had just read chs. xxxv–xxxvi, and thought 'some points . . . stated much too favourably'; the letter (3 June 1841) gives Dickens's defence.

the world who may learn something, even from this poor crazy Lord who died in Newgate.

The general moral of the story is made explicit in the Preface, written in November 1841:

> those shameful tumults, while they reflect indelible disgrace upon the time in which they occurred, and all who had act or part in them, teach a good lesson. That what we falsely call a religious cry is easily raised by men who have no religion, and who in their daily practice set at nought the commonest principles of right and wrong; that it is begotten of intolerance and persecution; that it is senseless, besotted, inveterate, and unmerciful; all History teaches us. But perhaps we do not know it in our hearts too well, to profit by even so humble and familiar an example as the "No Popery" riots of Seventeen Hundred and Eighty.

But this was only one of the many lessons for the times to be drawn from Dickens's tale.

II

The five years' delay between design and publication had increased the novel's topicality. At any time in the 'thirties and 'forties, it would have suggested (as most historical novels did) 'new foes with an old face', for the revolution that never happened seemed always imminent. But the events of 1836–41 made the novel almost journalistically apt. The Poor Law riots, the Chartist risings at Devizes, Birmingham, and Sheffield, the mass meetings on Kersal Moor and Kennington Common, and most pointed of all, the Newport rising of 1839 with its attempt to release Chartist prisoners—all these, with their aftermath of trials, convictions, and petitions against the punishment of death, gave special point in 1841 to 'a tale of the Riots of '80'. The imperfections of the historical parallel, the vital difference between agitation directed to limited and specific ends and the madness of the underworld let loose, were less obvious then than now. What most often repeats itself in history is the fear that history will do so. Dickens was responding not to enlightened historical analysis, but to the average man's horror of looted chapels and distilleries, armed robbery in the streets, prisons and mansions ablaze— sights imprinted ineffaceably upon the memories of many living individuals, and the family memories of thousands more.

There were other topical parallels. 'It is a common but dangerous error', wrote Thomas Hood,[1] rebuking Dickens for a too charitable view of Gordon, 'to attribute all moral to mental obliquities'. The question of criminal responsibility and degrees of insanity had been newly raised by the 1840 trial of Edward Oxford, who shot at the Queen and was found guilty but insane.[2] (Three years later the M'Naghten rules were framed.) Dickens recognized that in the popular mind madness, crime, and revolutionary agitation ran into and coloured each other; but he saw the need for discrimination, and suggests it by his emphasis on Gordon's abnormality and the reprieve of Barnaby. These questions are also related to the growing pressure of capital punishment, and especially of public executions, upon the conscience of the thoughtful; Courvoisier's execution (which Dickens witnessed)[3] and Thackeray's harrowing account of it in 'Going to See a Man Hanged'[4] are also part of the contemporary context of Barnaby.

In his Preface Dickens gives most emphasis to the dangers of the unscrupulous exploiting of Protestant bigotry, and the timely relevance of this warning is less likely to be grasped by modern readers. But his contemporaries were well aware of the Protestant Association, newly founded in 1839, with local branches for 'operatives', great meetings in Exeter Hall, and petitions to the government against favours supposedly shown to Catholics, especially in education. Though violent only in language, and dissociating itself emphatically from social agitation, it gave grounds, not least by its defence of the Association of 1779–80,[5] for fears of another 'false religious cry'. The unexpected religious animus in the novel also expresses Dickens's general dislike of puritanism, whether in Little Bethel or the 'Protestant Manual'; as a defender of the humble, he strikes a blow for the domestic happiness of Mrs Nubbles and of Gabriel Varden. In Mrs Varden (and Mr Chester) he must have had his eye especially on the Evangelicals; Crabb Robinson noted in his diary that 'Dickens will lose popularity with the saints, for he too faithfully exposes

1. Athenæum, 22 Jan. 1842.

2. Dickens regarded him not as mad, but 'brimful of conceit, and a desire to become, even at the cost of the gallows (the only cost within his reach) the talk of the town', and saw in such cases a further argument against capital punishment (letter to the Daily News, 9 Mar. 1846; Miscellaneous Papers, ed. B. W. Matz, 1914, p. 27).

3. With Maclise and Henry Burnett, his brother-in-law; see F. G. Kitton, Charles Dickens by Pen and Pencil (1889–90), pp. 142–3.

4. Fraser's Magazine, Aug. 1840.

5. Protestant Magazine, Jan. 1840.

cant'.[1] Thomas Hood, in his review, comparing 1841 with 178
saw 'the same—nay, a worse fanatical demon abroad . . . a Zea
of-the-Land Busy' attacking 'Art, Science, Literature, the Dram
and all other public amusements'; which itself would expla
Dickens's bias in making all his 'Protestants' objectionable. To
years later he would have had other axes to grind, and the writ
of the *Child's History of England* would hardly have drawn tl
Catholics Langdale and Haredale sympathetically: indeed, 18.
was only just in time. During that year the waves from Oxfor
(Tract 90 was published in March) were to reach London; ear
in 1842 Dickens's friends in *Punch* were attacking the 'Pussyites

III

Barnaby, then, is related to the events and mood of the exa
years of its writing and publication. Further, as a novel of rece
history, history at the ideal distance of 'sixty years since',[3] it dre
support from the memories, oral[4] and written, of men living
recently dead. One passage (at the end of chapter lxv) sugges
that Dickens had talked to eyewitnesses, and he is likely to hav
read many recently published reminiscences—those, for i
stance, of Frederick Reynolds the actor (1827) and Hen
Angelo (1828).[5] He would read too the published letters of I
Johnson, Horace Walpole, and Crabbe; and if he wante
general inspiration for description of mob violence, there wa
Carlyle's *French Revolution* (1837), 'that wonderful book'. But h
main sources were undoubtedly the brilliantly written *Narrati*
of 'William Vincent' (Thomas Holcroft),[6] Robert Watson's *Li*
of Lord George Gordon (1795), and the reports in the newspapers

1. *Books and their Writers*, ed. Edith Morley (3 vols., 1938), p. 599.
2. 'Punch's Pencillings', no. xxxii (vol. II, p. 109). Dickens himself satirized rit
alism in his article on Oxford in the *Examiner* (3 June 1843); see *Miscellaneo
Papers*, p. 97, and below, p. 180.
3. See the defence in *Waverley*, ch. i.
4. 'It is a matter of pride with some of our old citizens, to remember the Grea
Riots of '80 . . . they seem to recall every particular of the tumult' (*Athenæum*, 2
Jan. 1842).
5. Reynolds lived till 1839 and Angelo till 1841.
6. See the Bibliography in J. P. de Castro, *The Gordon Riots* (1926), for this an
other contemporary pamphlets. Dickens owned copies of Holcroft's *Narrative* and
Watson's *Life*; the latter was annotated by him (see F. G. Kitton, notes to Auto
graph edition, III 336).
7. Several are named in ch. xxxix: 'the *St. James's Chronicle*, the *Herald*, *Chronicl*
or *Public Advertiser*'. Dickens presumably had access to the files of the *Mornir*

Dickens's use of his historical sources, which has never received the detailed consideration it deserves, can only be summarized here. What is most remarkable in his powerful narrative of the riots (chapters xxxvi–lxxiii) is the way he combines fidelity to fact with the doings of his fictitious characters. He adds, but never falsifies. The main events of eight days (2 June to 9 June) are all brought in, with accurate particulars of time and place; almost every action ascribed to the mob in London or to unnamed individuals is factual, down to such telling anecdotes as the burning of the canary-birds and the young man hanged in Bishopsgate. *The Thunderer* and *England in Blood* really existed, some released convicts did return voluntarily to the jail, and the attack on the Bank was led by a man on 'a brewer's horse . . . caparisoned with fetters'. The break into Newgate and the burning of Langdale's distillery are described often in the very words of contemporary accounts. No rioters are known to have gone as far as Chigwell, but several country mansions were threatened, and the mob's attempt 'to burn the Warren' (i.e. the Woolwich Arsenal) probably gave Mr Haredale's house its name. 'The Boot' was an actual inn, in Lamb's Conduit Fields. General Conway, Sir John Fielding, Lord Mansfield, Akerman the keeper of Newgate, and the Lord Mayor acted or suffered just as Dickens describes. The appearance, manner, and after-history of Gordon, and some of his words (as in the warrant of protection conveyed to Gabriel Varden) are faithfully given, and Dickens's interpretation of his character and actions, if coloured by Robert Watson's *Life*, represents at least a legitimate reading of the evidence.

For the actions and motives of other characters, fact and fiction are mingled in varying proportions. At one end of the scale is Mr Langdale, historic except for his dealings with the invented characters; at the other, Gabriel Varden, whose valiant refusal to break the lock of Newgate is based on a mere hint—the resistance

---

Chronicle; he also had a reader's ticket for the British Museum, and F. G. Kitton recorded in 1891 that 'Dr. Bullen, of the Museum, remembers having seen Dickens in the Reading-room, where he used to go for the purpose of consulting the newspapers about the London Riots in 1780, when he was writing "Barnaby Rudge" ' (*Charles Dickens by Pen and Pencil: Supplement*, p. 15).

A good short account of the riots was published in 1837 by Charles Knight, as chs. ii–iii of *Sketches of Popular Tumults*, in the series 'Contributions to Political Knowledge'. It is interesting evidence of current interest in the events of 1780, but can hardly be regarded as a source, though it may possibly have led Dickens to such pamphlet-sources as Holcroft's *Narrative* and the anonymous *Fanaticism and Treason*, which it quotes freely.

of a Moravian blacksmith, urged under threats to strike off the prisoners' irons. Dickens may have noticed that idiots, gipsies, apprentices, and a 'one-armed man' were among the rioters; and he surely caught hints for Miggs and Sim from a description of 'debating societies' with 'female orators' and the 'apprentice who spent the night 'in rehearsing harangues' and 'wasted the day (the property of his master)' in dreams of political power.[1] In two characters, Gashford and Dennis, the interweaving of fact and fiction is especially curious, and in the former case still a matter of conjecture. Something is borrowed from the career of the secretary Robert Watson[2] (whose suicide was fully reported in 1838) and the treachery of James Fisher; but Gashford exists mainly as an ingenious means of connecting Dickens's sympathetic interpretation of Gordon with his view of the riots. His plot and his picture alike require a cold-blooded villain manoeuvring in the dark, and the presence of such an agent is a plausible reading of events. With Dennis he worked more imaginatively. The presence of 'Edward Dennis, the public hangman' among the rioters convicted of helping to burn a private house, was sufficient basis:[3] Dickens's sense of ironic fitness extended Dennis' activities to the burning of Newgate, had him hanged instead of respited, and elaborated his craftsman's pride in his calling in a way both diverting and horrible. In him Dickens continues the studies of evil begun in Sikes and Quilp. But Dennis, though a grotesque, is less of a bogey-man than Quilp, and more closely related to the themes of the novel. He embodies Dickens's open concern with the social horror of hanging and his less conscious obsession with the man about to be hanged; and he also derives something from literary tradition—from the first chapter of Charles Whitehead's *Autobiography of Jack Ketch*, and, more generally, from the irony of *Jonathan Wild*.

Dickens's complex intentions are fulfilled in the almost allegorical juxtaposition of Dennis, Hugh, and Barnaby, and their discriminated attitudes to violence and death. Through Hugh

1. *Fanaticism and Treason* (anon.; 1780), p. 22. This is also obviously topical. Sim may be compared with 'a journeyman carpenter' who took the chair at meetings of a Radical Association in Marylebone (James Grant, *The Great Metropolis*, second series, 1837, I 91ff).

2. Watson has been claimed as the original of Gashford (*The Dickensian*, June 1933, pp. 175ff).

3. Thomas Gaspey's novel, if he knew it, provided a precedent for fictional treatment.

nd Barnaby the fictitious and historical parts of the novel are
irmly related; and they, perhaps alone of the invented charac-
ers, gain in interest under the pressure of public events. Dickens's
low approach to his historical subject, though it has many
dvantages, brings certain difficulties. The first third of the novel
s all fiction: the Haredale–Rudge murder-mystery and Mr
Chester's intrigues, diversified with the domestic comedy of the
Willet and the Varden households, are set out in a leisurely way
vithout much 'period' colouring and with hardly a hint of his-
ory to come. Then, after a silent lapse of five years, the tide of
uistory advances, slowly at first, then with increasing force, involving all the characters; as it recedes, the mystery is resolved,
ind the nemesis, tragic and comic, fulfilled. Although the
nystery-plot could be detached (as was done in two dramatic
versions, presented before publication was complete),[1] it loses
hereby much of its interest, for Dickens's integration of the two
nain lines of narrative, which, as we realize later, he is quietly
preparing throughout the early chapters, is excellently managed.
By reserving the history till later he conveys the irony of the com-
non assumption that private lives are immune from public
events, an irony pointed by his presentation of the same scene
under two different lights; the snugness of the Maypole makes us
hare John Willet's sense of its devastation as an almost personal
nsult, while we also enjoy the nicely contrived nemesis by which
history' converts the innkeeper from invincible stupidity to imbecile stupor, and from petty tyranny to submissiveness. But the
change in tempo in the middle chapters is exacting, and the rush
of events in what Dickens called 'the thick of the story' made him
chafe, as we have seen, at his 'want' of 'elbow-room'.[2]

IV

Dickens's experience in the writing of *Barnaby* fixed his preference for the 'monthly number' as a form of publication. The
period of experiment was over. He had introduced the new plan

hoping that to shorten the intervals of communication between

1. One, by Charles Selby and Charles Melville, was acted at the Lyceum on 28
June 1841, another at the New Strand in August. The former, which Dickens saw
(*Letters*, I 339), was published in August. (A third version, including the riots, was
put on at the Adelphi in December.)
2. *Letters*, I 353 (when writing chs. lxv–lxvi).

himself and his readers would be to bind more closely [their
pleasant relations.[1]

The disadvantages had proved too great. In October 1841 he
published his manifesto, which because of its clear statement of
the drawbacks of the weekly part (and its inaccessibility to
modern readers)[2] deserves reproducing in full:

TO THE
READERS OF "MASTER HUMPHREY'S CLOCK".

DEAR FRIENDS,

NEXT November, we shall have finished the Tale, on which we
are at present engaged; and shall have travelled together through
Twenty Monthly Parts, and Eighty-seven Weekly Numbers. It is
my design, when we have gone so far, to close this work. Let me tell
you why.

I should not regard the anxiety, the close confinement, or the
constant attention, inseparable from the weekly form of publication
(for to commune with you, in any form, is to me a labour of love)
if I had found it advantageous to the conduct of my stories, the
elucidation of my meaning, or the gradual development of my
characters. But I have not done so. I have often felt cramped and
confined in a very irksome and harassing degree, by the space in
which I have been constrained to move. I have wanted you to know
more at once than I could tell you; and it has frequently been of the
greatest importance to my cherished intention, that you should do
so. I have been sometimes strongly tempted (and have been at some
pains to resist the temptation) to hurry incidents on, lest they should
appear to you who waited from week to week, and had not, like me,
the result and purpose in your minds, too long delayed. In a word,
I have found this form of publication most anxious, perplexing, and
difficult. I cannot bear these jerking confidences which are no
sooner begun than ended, and no sooner ended than begun again.

Many passages in a tale of any length, depend materially for their
interest on the intimate relation they bear to what has gone before,
or to what is to follow. I sometimes found it difficult when I issued
thirty-two closely-printed pages once a month, to sustain in your
mind this needful connexion; in the present form of publication it is
often, especially in the first half of a story, quite impossible to preserve it sufficiently through the current numbers. And although in
my progress I am gradually able to set you right, and to show you
what my meaning has been, and to work it out, I see no reason why

1. Preface to *Master Humphrey's Clock*, vol. 1 (Sept. 1840).
2. It is reprinted only in the National edition (vol. XXXIII, pp. 342–4).

you should ever be wrong when I have it in my power, by resorting to a better means of communication between us, to prevent it.

Considerations of immediate profit and advantage, ought, in such a case, to be of secondary importance. *They* would lead me, at all hazards, to hold my present course. But, for the reasons I have just now mentioned, I have, after long consideration, and with especial reference to the next new Tale I bear in my mind, arrived at the conclusion that it will be better to abandon this scheme of publication, in favour of our old and well-tried plan, which has only twelve gaps in a year, instead of fifty-two.

Therefore, my intention is to close this story (with the limits of which I am, of course, by this time acquainted), and this work, within, or at about, the period I have mentioned. I should add, that for the general convenience of subscribers, another volume of collected numbers will not be published, until the whole is brought to a conclusion.

Taking advantage of the respite which the close of this work will afford me, I have decided, in January next, to pay a visit to America. The pleasure I anticipate from this realization of a wish I have long entertained, and long hoped to gratify, is subdued by the reflection that it must separate us for a longer time than other circumstances would have rendered necessary.

On the First of November, eighteen hundred and forty-two, I purpose, if it please God, to commence my new book in monthly parts, under the old green cover, in the old size and form, and at the old price.[1]

I look forward to addressing a few more words to you, in reference to this latter theme, before I close the task on which I am now engaged. If there be any among the numerous readers of Master Humphrey's Clock who are, at first, dissatisfied with the prospect of this change—and it is not unnatural almost to hope there may be some—I trust they will, at no very distant day, find reason to agree with

ITS AUTHOR.

SEPTEMBER 1841.

1. *Martin Chuzzlewit* in fact began publication in Jan. 1843.

CHAPTER V

Dombey and Son:
Design and Execution

═══

I

WHEN the first instalment of *Dombey and Son* appeared on 30 September 1846 in the familiar green covers, Dickens was embarking once more upon his favourite form of publication. Since the early numbers of *Pickwick* he had been paying increasing attention to problems of structure, as previous essays have shown. In the Preface to his latest novel, *Martin Chuzzlewit* (1844), he had claimed that he had from time to time 'put a strong constraint' upon himself and had kept 'a steadier eye upon the general purpose and design'. This and other statements indicate his belief that there was no insuperable obstacle to writing, barely ahead of its publication in monthly instalments complete in themselves, a novel with a well-defined purpose worked out by such an 'artfully interwoven or ingeniously complicated'[1] plot as he had once felt that he must eschew. In *Dombey and Son*, when for the first time he planned each instalment on paper before he began writing, he went a great way toward realizing the intention he had so clearly formulated. It may, in fact, be said that with *Dombey and Son* he began a new chapter in his work.

Apart from the text itself, the available sources of evidence for 'the strength of his mastery over his first design' and the degree of consistency with which he maintained his purpose, fall under five heads:[2] (1) the title, (2) the cover-design, (3) the letter (especially the letter to Forster on 25 July 1846,[3] accompanying

---

1. See above, p. 65.
2. No 'master plan' survives, and there is no reason to suppose that such a plan was set on paper.   3. Forster, VI ii.

the first four chapters), (4) the manuscript, including the number plans, (5) the proof sheets. An examination of (1) and (2) and the letters of the three months preceding publication will throw light on the nature of that 'first design' at a stage when the writing of the novel had barely begun.

It is impossible to say just when the design took shape, but it was evidently growing in the author's mind for six months before he put pen to paper. 'A new book in shilling numbers' was in his thoughts at the end of January 1846; between then and his departure for Switzerland at the end of May he was clearing the decks for action. In March the publishers were approached; in mid-April the first announcement appeared in the press—'A New English Story, By Mr. Dickens, to be published in Twenty Monthly Parts, price 1s. each, is now in preparation'; and on 18 May the author committed himself also to a date—'No. 1 will be published on the First of October'.[1] Such open self-commitment would nowadays imply some pre-existent writing of the novel; for Dickens it was enough that 'the characters . . . were growing in his mind'. Not until he was well settled at Lausanne, at the end of June, did he 'plunge straight over head and ears into the story . . . BEGAN DOMBEY'.[2]

Forster had been, as usual, his sole confidant over the unwritten book, though he has unfortunately not extended much of his confidence to us. To him the word 'Dombey' must have already carried a whole train of associations; the title had undoubtedly been decided on some time before. No hesitance over it, and no alternative forms (as for *Copperfield*, *Bleak House*, and *Little Dorrit*) are recorded; but Dickens showed what store he set by it in emphasizing the need for secrecy, 'the very name getting out would be ruinous' (18 July),[3] and to another correspondent 'the name shall not pass these lips, until the bills proclaim it' (9 July).[4] The bills proclaimed it at the end of August:

> Dealings with the Firm of Dombey and Son, Wholesale, Retail, and for Exportation.

Immediately after the announcement of the title, Dickens wrote to Mitton, 'I think it is an odd one, and therefore a good one'.[5] It was the most provocative he had yet devised. The need for

---

1. This information, not given by any of Dickens's editors or bibliographers, is all available in Forster's *Life*, the *Letters*, and the contemporary press.
2. Forster, v ii.   3. Forster, v iii.   4. *Letters*, 1 766.   5. *Letters*, 1 783.

secrecy is clear; in contrast to titles of Dickens's earlier novels, this is to some extent declarative of purpose and defines a new field of operations. (A 'business' novel, from Boz?) Titles were a special problem for the serial-writer, since no title could be modified to suit a subsequent change of intention: yet readers must be attracted. Hitherto Dickens had played for safety, usually with the 'life and adventures' type of title; but in this, the first of his novels to be thoroughly designed in advance, he could risk committing himself more deeply. The title promised the fortunes of a firm; while the author's name (although the famous words were as yet unwritten) guaranteed 'the firm of Human Interest Brothers, with a rather large connexion in the fancy goods line'. The title also indicated an increased concern with contemporary life. And possibly the particular collocation 'Dombey *and Son*' suggested the history of a relation between two characters as distinct from the 'life and adventures' of one, and that a relation in two fields, business and domestic. Deliberately, too, the title exploits the serial-writer's special privilege of misleading as well as capturing attention. The evidence of correspondence shows that the whole design of Mr Dombey's history as a parent had been worked out before the title was announced; and the first number was already written, emphatically concluding with Walter Gay's toast, 'So here's to Dombey—and Son—and Daughter!' The title kept a bigger secret than it disclosed.

Meanwhile, during August, Dickens must have been instructing his illustrator Hablôt K. Browne about the cover-design, which was to appear on the first number and be repeated for each monthly instalment; for early in September he approved it as 'very good; perhaps with a little too much in it'.[1] This also was a new departure in the extent to which it foreshadowed the story, though its general method bears an evident relation to the cover of *Chuzzlewit*. Dickens spoke of the *Dombey* cover later as 'shadowing out [the] drift and bearing' of the story,[2] and his choice of phrase is a useful pointer. Previous commentators[3] have interpreted the cover over-literally and have therefore found consistency or inconsistency according to what they thought they saw. The story in its development shows a *general* consistency with the

1. Forster, vi ii.

2. In a letter of 29 Oct. 1846 on *The Battle of Life*, his current Christmas book (Forster, v vi).

3. E.g., Kentley Bromhill, *The Dickensian*, Sept. 1942, pp. 219f; F. G. Kitton, *The Novels of Charles Dickens* (London, 1897), p. 103.

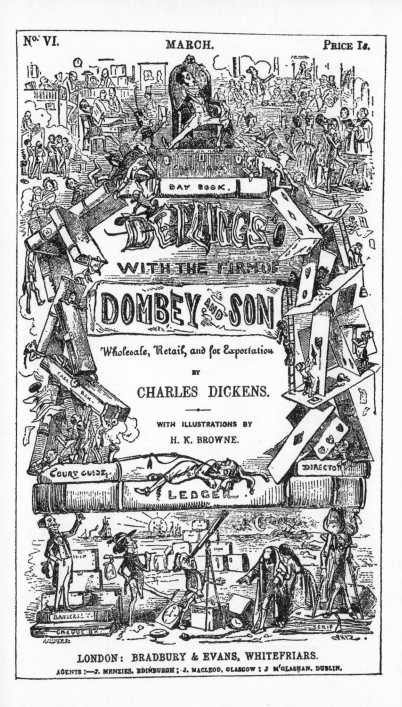

DAY BOOK.

DEALINGS

WITH THE FIRM OF

DOMBEY AND SON

Wholesale, Retail, and for Exportation

BY

CHARLES DICKENS.

WITH ILLUSTRATIONS BY

H. K. BROWNE.

COURT GUIDE.   LEDGER   DIRECTORY

LONDON: BRADBURY & EVANS, WHITEFRIARS.

AGENTS :— J. MENZIES, EDINBURGH ; J. MACLEOD, GLASGOW ; J MᶜGLASHAN, DUBLIN.

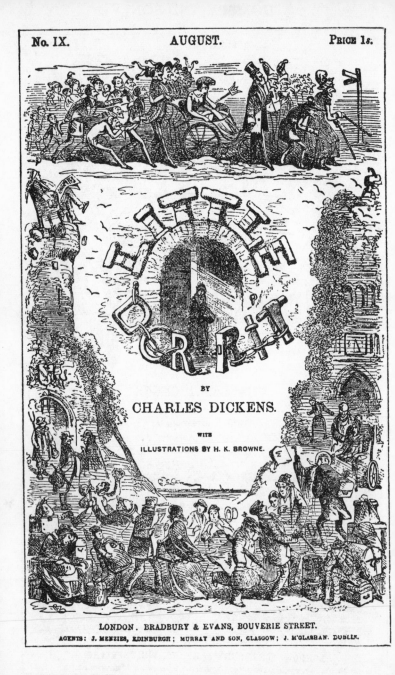

cover, within the elastic limits of a semi-allegorical or 'shadowing' method. The cover-design of *Chuzzlewit* is built up on a system of simple contrasts; roses on the left balance thorns on the right, dream balances nightmare and riches poverty. But there is no narrative line running through these disconnected symbols. In the *Dombey* cover there is such a line, which also suggests part of the moral curve of the narrative. The line of prosperity and promise runs upwards from the left of the centre, through the precariously balanced ledgers, to where the hero sits enthroned in an office chair on the platform of a cash box, and down through the tumbling house of cards on the right. The allegorical scenes at the foot emphasize the turn of Fortune's wheel. Hopeful youth sets out to seek its fortune, with a background of rising sun, smooth-sailing ships, and calm sea; at the other side is the evening of life—a broken-down figure set against a night sky, shipwreck, and storm. At one side, 'rising' Mr Dombey lightly balances his wealth on brow and thumb; on the other, 'fallen' Mr Dombey, old and crippled, is nearly crushed by the descending money bags. At the top are more realistic scenes, in general illustration of his seemingly secure prosperity: his hopeful heir (baby with nurse, and boys' classroom); his power in the office; his distinction in public life (a House of Commons scene);[1] and the new turn in his social and domestic fortunes (bridegroom at a society wedding, with a military witness). The figure of Mr Dombey dominates the whole. Other characters are there only to substantiate his background, and the little goblin-like creatures among the ledgers and cards are as impersonal as the decorations on Doyle's *Punch* cover. The figure at the bottom centre certainly bears some relation to the Wooden Midshipman (not, as has been thought, to Sol Gills),[2] but its significance in the 'drift and bearing' surely rests rather on the surrounding symbols of Time, and the blind confidence in the future implied by the closed eye at the telescope. The whole method is allegorical; if readers of the first number tried to 'look at the end' by scanning the cover they would find little to help them.[3] It would need

1. See below, p. 103, n. 1.

2. There is no likeness to Sol as he is shown in the plate to ch. ix. But it is conceivable that Browne, when doing the cover, had confused the descriptions of shop-emblem and shop-owner in ch. iv.

3. The *Athenæum* reviewer of Nos. I–II (31 Oct. 1846) disclaimed prediction, but commented with some acuteness:

The title-page reveals something of the prominent idea, in whatever forms em-

exceptional discernment even to detect the despised little daughter of chapter i in the young female figure who gently attends the fallen hero. This may have been where Dickens found 'a little too much in' the cover, if by this remark he meant that it was too revealing and not merely too crowded. Secrets are kept—notably the death of Paul. The only specific event predicted is the second marriage; and this is hardly a close secret, since it is already prepared for (though with a false lead as to candidate) in Mrs Dombey's death and its aftermath. The cover does what Dickens wanted; it 'shadows out the drift and bearing' of the whole, not disclosing secrets, not committing the author, but still picturesquely confirming and enlarging the promise of the title, and clearly showing the existence of a ruling general design for the unwritten story. The novel's centre is the head of a great firm, its main concern is the intertwining of his domestic and his business life (the falling cards are hearts and diamonds), and to this is added the overshadowing, menacing moral—that Pride of Wealth must have a Fall.

Dickens's early letters to Forster confirm this intention, but, since they are private, add more detail of its projected execution. Before the letters begin, conversation with Forster had established one part of the intention; the novel 'was to do with Pride what its predecessor [*Martin Chuzzlewit*] had done with Selfishness',[1] and this presumably is the 'leading idea' of the letter of 12 July.[2] The letters themselves survive only in the extracts Forster selected. But the main document in the case, the letter of 25 July, is probably given with little omission, for Forster printed it in 1873 partly to rehabilitate Dickens as a serious designer, to counter criticisms (such as Taine's) that Paul's death and Mr Dombey's final relenting were improvised as adventitious aids to interest. This important letter, somewhat similar to the letter of 18 October 1844 sent with the first part of *The Chimes*, is our substitute for a 'master plan'. In it the design is seen from another angle; the emphasis is almost wholly on the family situation, the dynamic relation between Dombey and Son and Daughter.

bodied, which is intended to be wrought out by the plastic hand of Mr. Dickens in this new work;—and the first chapter confirms the revelation. His hero . . . is to personate one of those representatives of a long commercial line in whose contracted and exclusive minds selfishness takes the quality of reflecting the single figure of its own commercial importance on all the objects which surround it.

1. Forster, vi ii.   2. Forster, v iii.

Florence here takes the prominent place deliberately and ironically withheld from her in title and picture.[1]

> I will now go on to give you an outline of my immediate intentions in reference to *Dombey*. I design to show Mr. D. with that one idea of the Son taking firmer and firmer possession of him, and swelling and bloating his pride to a prodigious extent. As the boy begins to grow up, I shall show him quite impatient for his getting on, and urging his masters to set him great tasks, and the like. But the natural affection of the boy will turn towards the despised sister; and I purpose showing her learning all sorts of things, of her own application and determination, to assist him in his lessons: and helping him always. When the boy is about ten years old (in the fourth number), he will be taken ill, and will die; and when he is ill, and when he is dying, I mean to make him turn always for refuge to the sister still, and keep the stern affection of the father at a distance. So Mr. Dombey—for all his greatness, and for all his devotion to the child—will find himself at arms' length from him even then; and will see that his love and confidence are all bestowed upon his sister, whom Mr. Dombey has used—and so has the boy himself too, for that matter—as a mere convenience and handle to him. The death of the boy is a death-blow, of course, to all the father's schemes and cherished hopes; and 'Dombey and Son,' as Miss Tox will say at the end of the number, 'is a Daughter after all.' . . . From that time, I purpose changing his feeling of indifference and uneasiness towards his daughter into a positive hatred. For he will always remember how the boy had his arm round her neck when he was dying, and whispered to her, and would take things only from her hand, and never thought of him. . . At the same time I shall change *her* feeling towards *him* for one of a greater desire to love him, and to be loved by him; engendered in her compassion for his loss, and her love for the dead boy whom, in his way, he loved so well too. So I mean to carry the story on, through all the branches and off-shoots and meanderings that come up; and through the decay and downfall of the house, and the bankruptcy of Dombey, and all the rest of it; when his only staff and treasure, and his unknown Good Genius always, will be this rejected daughter, who will come out better

1. It is accorded to her in the frontispiece to the first edition, which first appeared as one of the plates in the concluding double number. This is another semi-allegorical composition, summarizing the novel in retrospect, when the need for keeping secrets is past. Florence occupies the centre, seated on a sea-beach beside Paul's wheel-chair. Above, an angel points upwards to a heavenly choir; and below, a rough sea beats against the shore. Besides taking precedence over Paul in the central scene, Florence also appears in most of the surrounding scenes—at the two deathbeds, with Polly, with Edith, struck down by Mr Dombey, welcoming the literally shipwrecked Walter, and rescuing her symbolically shipwrecked father.

than any son at last, and whose love for him, when discovered and understood, will be his bitterest reproach. For the struggle with himself, which goes on in all such obstinate natures, will have ended then; and the sense of his injustice, which you may be sure has never quitted him, will have at last a gentler office than that of only making him more harshly unjust.

This forecasts the main development up to about the seventh number ('positive hatred' is clearest in chapter xx), and the references to the downfall of the firm and the redemptive power of Florence's persistent love reach forward to the close. (The prediction is fulfilled, save for the hinted active rôle for Florence.) The heart of the design is now exposed: the theme is the opposition of pride and love, with Mr Dombey as the meeting-point. The novel is thus to be a new departure for Dickens—a novel founded upon a relation, and upon a character's inner conflict.

The letter goes on to mention only two minor characters, Susan Nipper and Polly Toodle (who are to 'go over' to Florence, 'like everybody else'). Dickens sums up his outline as 'the stock of the soup', to which 'all kinds of things will be added'. It was 'stock' in the sense that it would not change;[1] doubts and deliberations affected other persons—notably Walter Gay—but not Mr Dombey, Paul, and Florence.

The 'stock', the main design, already posed a problem to which Dickens perhaps did not yet penetrate: the interweaving of Dombey's domestic and business fortunes. This interweaving is achieved, partly by chapter headings, in the first few numbers, but it wears thin after Paul's death, and Carker, who had probably been designed as the canker of both office and family, becomes much more prominent in the latter capacity.

II

So far as Paul's death the way lay clear ahead and the number plans record little that can be interpreted as hesitation. Proofs and letters to Forster show that the chief difficulty was to find space for all that needed saying. Paul, the 'Boy born, to die' (in the words of the first number plan) was originally to die at the

---

1. This is interestingly confirmed by an entry in the diary of the Hon. Mrs Watson, who records on 12 Sept. 'a Soiree at Mr. Dickens to hear him read the first number. . . The career of Dombey, Son, and Daughter are settled, but I think none of the others'. (*The Dickensian*, Dec. 1950, p. 18.)

end of Number IV, but the pace in the first two numbers was so leisurely that Forster was asked,[1] while III was being planned, whether Paul should not be killed in V. Even this respite was not sufficient, for each of the first four numbers proved to be over-written by amounts varying from one page to six. When faced with the need of extensive cuts at proof stage, Dickens was accustomed to economize at the expense of the comedy. The luxuriant growth of fancy displayed in Mrs Chick and Major Bagstock was accordingly pruned;[2] but passages of greater significance were removed as well. One of them, describing Mr Dombey's destruction of a letter written by his dead wife, was retrieved by Forster[3] who regarded it as evidence 'thus early . . . of the struggle with itself that such pride must always go through'. Less ambiguous are Mr Dombey's comments (chapter i) when Florence disregards his invitation to 'go and look at [her] pretty brother':

> 'Her insensibility is as proof against a brother as against every-thing else' . . . and he seemed so confirmed in a previous opinion by the discovery, as to be quite glad of it,

and the 'expression of positive pain—pain that was suffering to him; that he could not conceal, and was ashamed to show' which appeared in Mr Dombey's face (chapter xi) as he confided to Mrs Pipchin that Paul had concentrated too much of his childish affection on his sister. Perhaps nothing essential to our under-standing of the novel's purpose was lost by cuts such as these, but the book as we now have it is weaker by some distinct loss of emphasis.

Restrictions of space were also felt in other ways. The third number plan (chapters viii–x) shows that Miss Tox was to have

1. Forster, vi ii.
2. Readers who enjoy the partnership of Mrs Chick and Miss Tox will regret that Dickens could find no room for the following passage (deleted in proof from ch. viii), in which Mrs Chick once more insinuates Miss Tox's claims on Mr Dombey's serious consideration:

'My dear Paul,' returned Mrs. Chick, 'with your usual discrimination, which I am weak enough to envy you, every time I am in your company; and so I think is Miss Tox—'

'Oh my dear!' said Miss Tox, softly, 'how could it be otherwise. Presumptuous as it is to aspire to such a level; still, if the bird of night may—but I'll not trouble Mr. Dombey with the sentiment. It merely relates to the Bulbul.'

Mr. Dombey bent his head in stately recognition of the Bulbul as an old-established body.

3. Forster, vi ii.

given a party at which 'Her uncle the Magistrate' (a character
who never appeared, though already named in chapter v to
impress Towlinson and the cabman) and 'The Major' were to
have been present and would have been introduced, we may
safely assume, to Mr Dombey. Carker was also to appear in this
number, and the 'Offices in the City' were to have been described, for it was time for the firm to take a larger share of the
reader's attention. But there was no room in Number III and the
two scenes were marked in the plan 'To stand over'. The party
was never to take place; Major Bagstock, however, characteristically introduced himself to Mr Dombey at Brighton later in
this number (chapter x). Thus the irony of Miss Tox presenting
the man who was to undermine her position in the Dombey
household was necessarily dropped; but the change seems to
square with the general intention of reducing Miss Tox from her
prominence in the opening numbers. A description of the counting-house was deferred till the next number, and meanwhile the
glimpse of Dombey and Son in a business transaction is supplied
by the loan of money to 'pay out' the broker at the Little Midshipman's. 'You will consider that it is done by Master Paul',
says Mr Dombey, as he hands the note to Walter. This is his
effective answer at the end of the number to the question, so
simple yet so powerful in irony, which Paul had asked at the
beginning, 'Papa! What's money . . . what can it do?'

Restricted though he was for space, Dickens might have had
room for the scenes marked 'to stand over' if he had fully determined what to do with Walter Gay. The notion of showing
Walter 'gradually and naturally trailing away . . . into negli-
gence, idleness, dissipation, dishonesty, and ruin'[1] required an
appropriate setting of characters. We know that Florence was to
have been 'always at the bottom of it', and we may suspect that
Carker the Junior would also have played an important part.
'The strangest man, Mr. Carker the junior is', Walter is made
to remark to Florence, as he conducts her (chapter vi) to his
uncle's shop;

> 'If you could understand what an extraordinary interest he takes
> in me, and yet how he shuns and avoids me; and what a low place he

1. From the close of the letter of 25 July. Forster, so often a check to Dickens's
gloomier notions, represents himself as responsible for discouraging Dickens from
this plan, 'for reasons that need not be dwelt on here' (vi ii); one may guess that
they were connected with sales, perhaps also with the danger of too close portrayal
of some actual person.

holds in our office, and how he is never advanced, and never complains, though year after year he sees young men passed over his head . . . you would be as much puzzled about him as I am.'

The passage was removed in proof after Dickens had decided to reserve Walter for a happier future, but it remains to motivate a character who is unnecessary to the story as it developed. We may be sure that Carker the Junior's 'extraordinary interest' in Walter Gay was an interest in a young man who was to fall as he had fallen.

Dickens told Forster that he could also 'bring out Solomon Gills and Captain Cuttle well, through such a history' of deterioration as Walter's might have been. Cuttle remains an important figure in Walter's happier fate. But Gills, whose heart seems made to be broken, had no place in Dickens's revised intentions. He could only duplicate Cuttle's rôle, so he is cleared off at an early opportunity. 'Uncle Sol to die?' Dickens inquires in the eighth number plan (chapters xxiii–xxv); but though he immediately relents ('No, run away, to look after Walter'), he can find no use for him until the eighteenth number (chapter lvi) when he returns to crown the happiness of Walter and Florence.

But these are blemishes in an otherwise faultless exposition. Our attention is mainly directed to 'that one idea of the Son taking firmer and firmer possession of [Mr Dombey], and swelling and bloating his pride to a prodigious extent'. The theme of Pride is not merely developed in the father's regard for his son, in the 'family humbug' of Mrs Chick, and in the use of honest and dishonest toadies, Tox and Bagstock, but is expounded with remarkable thoroughness in Mr Dombey's treatment of his social inferiors, Polly Toodle and her son. He would make the relations between Paul and his wet nurse 'a mere matter of bargain and sale. . . It is not at all in this bargain that you need become attached to my child, or that my child need become attached to you. I don't expect or desire anything of the kind. Quite the reverse'. Dickens, we may be sure, has already determined upon an affectionate relationship between Paul and Polly even though he may not have foreseen the incident where Paul summons his old nurse to comfort him on his death bed, or the still later scene when all Mr Dombey's dependants have left his house and Polly returns to look after him. So closely are we bound together, Dickens implies, despite what a sense of class can do to separate us. Polly's immediate recompense for her services was to have her

eldest son nominated to a vacancy in the Charitable Grinders'
School, where Mr Dombey was assured that he would be taught
to know his position and conduct himself properly. Again we may
safely infer that Dickens relished the retribution in store for Mr
Dombey, though he might not then have decided precisely how
Rob the Grinder would assist Mr Dombey's enemy. But he
shows that he was keeping Rob's development in sight by placing
in Mrs Chick's mouth the solemn and ironic rebuke:

> 'If it was *my* ungrateful case . . . and I had *your* reflections,
> Richards, I should feel as if the Charitable Grinders' dress would
> blight my child, and the education choke him.'

A reader need not be particularly shrewd to suspect that Pride
of such a kind will have a fall. He might forecast Mr Dombey's
bankruptcy and expect that in some way Paul would disappoint
his father. But Paul's death was intended as 'a great surprise', and
Dickens thought his friend Mrs Marcet was clever to have guessed
it when he read the first number to her.[1] In Number II it is clearly
enough forecast in the chill of the christening and the ominous
conclusion of chapter v: but already in Number I, the distinction
drawn by Susan Nipper—'Miss Floy being a permanency,
Master Paul a temporary'—carries ironic overtones.[2]

In the same sentence in which Dickens told Forster of the
'great surprise', he spoke of 'a new and peculiar sort of interest,
involving the necessity of a little bit of delicate treatment'.[3] It is
possible that he was looking ahead to Paul's final illness in Number V (chapter xiv) and the decision recorded in the number
plan that 'His illness [should be] only expressed in the child's
own feelings—Not otherwise described'. It is reasonable to suppose that it was the novelty of this treatment that brought tears
to the eyes of so many readers.[4]

Meanwhile the 'neglected daughter' motif of the plan has been
steadily developed throughout the first number, though its im-

1. Forster, v v.

2. But the secret is not betrayed, since the words could be read with Susan's own
meaning—the necessary impermanence of the suckling period and so of the wet-
nurse.

3. Forster, v iii.

4. It was also in keeping with Dickens's decision to take the child's point of view
so far as possible, notably in the Brighton scenes both at Mrs Pipchin's boarding-
house and at Dr Blimber's academy. This also was 'a new and peculiar sort of
interest', and its success no doubt prompted the extension of this treatment in his
next novel, *David Copperfield*.

portance is not realized until we reach the last chapter (chapter iv). That was the chapter which Dickens at one point thought of removing when he discovered that the number was too long. The alternative was to substitute a shorter version of what later became chapter vii (where Major Bagstock is introduced as Miss Tox's neighbour in Princess's Place). It is altogether fortunate that this was not done, for pleasing as chapter vii is it does not open up such possibilities in the development of character and theme as chapter iv. Here is our first glimpse of the firm of Dombey and Son, seen from the point of view of a promising young recruit; and (though Dickens was still undecided whether to disappoint Walter's prospects) here is the young 'Sir Richard Whittington [who] married his master's daughter'. Sol Gills and Captain Cuttle admit that 'the Son's a little in our way, at present', but the chapter and the number end with the toast 'So here's to Dombey—and Son—and Daughter!' Thus the importance of 'Dombey and Daughter' is emphasized from the very beginning; and lest we should overlook it, that toast is echoed at the end of Number V (chapter xvi), which concludes the first movement of the novel:

'Dear me, dear me! To think,' said Miss Tox, bursting out afresh that night, as if her heart were broken, 'that Dombey and Son should be a Daughter after all!'[1]

III

The plan of Number VI begins with an important memorandum for the second movement of the novel, 'Great point of the No. to throw the interest of Paul, at once on Florence'[2] and accordingly the whole of Number VI (chapters xvii–xix) is devoted to this. Chapter xviii, originally intended to open the number (but moved, presumably to avoid two successive Cuttle chapters), is given the half-misleading title 'Father and Daugh-

1. The sentence is dropped from all editions after 1858, except the two reprints of the first edition (Macmillan, 1892–5, and Glasgow, n.d.). See K. Tillotson, 'A Lost Sentence in *Dombey and Son*', *The Dickensian*, Mar. 1951, pp. 81f.

2. Jeffrey's complimentary letter of 31 Jan. 1847 must have been in one respect disquieting: 'After reaching this climax in the fifth number, what are you to do with the fifteen that are to follow?' (Lord Cockburn, *Life of Lord Jeffrey*, 1852, II 407). After receiving it, Dickens wrote to Forster: 'To transfer to Florence, instantly, all the previous interest, is what I am aiming at. For that, all sorts of other points must be thrown aside in this number.' (VI ii.)

ter'. The two should be drawn together by Paul's death; instead
there is first cold neglect, then open repudiation of the child's
timid advance. The latter is kept subdued, by a cautious memorandum

> not to make too much of the scene with the father, or it may be too
> painful.

Accordingly, some suspense remains; there is no open break.
This is important to the other aspect of Florence's status—she is
now the possible 'heir' to the firm, and the interest is also
'thrown' on her by hints of the webs being spun round her.
Though this is not shown as part of Mr Dombey's consciousness,
and indeed is never really explicit, it is henceforth a vital contribution to the course of the narrative, and a means of foreshadowing its close. Number VI, in which to all appearances Florence's
fortunes are steeply declining (Paul dead, Walter going abroad,
her father slighting her), contains also a clear hint of how the
firm is to be perpetuated—she asks Walter to be a brother to her,
and he sails in the *Son and Heir*. And—a brilliant stroke of economy—Captain Cuttle artlessly reveals his fairy-tale hopes to
Carker, who now dawns on the reader as Walter's rival:

> 'There's a son gone; pretty little creatur. Ain't there?'
> 'Yes, there's a son gone,' said the acquiescent Carker.
> 'Pass the word, and there's another ready for you.'
>
> (chapter xvii)

When Carker thinks (in the next chapter) of 'some obstacle
removed' he has Walter as well as Paul in mind. All this is un-
emphasized, but carefully planted; it is followed up in the next
two numbers by Carker's setting his spy on Florence's visits to
Sol Gills (chapter xxii) and his seeking her out at the Skettleses
(chapter xxiv).

But the situation has the triplicity of fairy-tale; the 'king's fair
daughter under a spell' has three suitors—Fairy Prince, Demon
King, and Fool. Number VI also re-introduces Mr Toots, whose
visit with the gift of Diogenes does most to 'throw the interest on
Florence', while also maintaining the link with Paul and Blimber's Academy. And by closing the number with the symbolic
incident of Toots's meeting with Carker on Mr Dombey's doorstep, and Diogenes' instinctive bite, Dickens emphasizes the re-
assuring effect of the protective squire. Mr Toots makes no
appearance in the original plan, and never figures prominently

in the number plans; but he is perhaps the most tasty of the 'all kinds of things' that were 'added to' the stock of the soup.

Florence is again the centre of Number VIII (chapters xxiii–xxv). On one of her few excursions into the world, her visit to the Skettleses (of whom surely more was meant to be made),[1] she observes and overhears things that sharpen her sense of deprivation; and her desirability as a match is reiterated. The three suitors are not forgotten; Toots rows past Fulham, Carker pays his sinister call, and brings bad news of the *Son and Heir*. With her prominence fairly established, Dickens can devote himself to the more dynamic relationship of Mr Dombey, Edith Granger, and Carker (Numbers VII and IX). Since the early stages of the plan say nothing of the second marriage, we may guess that it grew under Dickens's hand, partly from its intrinsic interest (and especially the possibilities he finds in Edith), partly from the unforeseen limitations of Florence as a plot-producing character. Her silent presence modifies all events, and much revolves round her; but her rôle is to feel and inspire (in all save her father) admiration and affection and to suffer from his neglect. Her very virtues, as well as her age and social status, preclude her from taking any initiative.

The second marriage is the real storm-centre of the novel. Mr Dombey's courtship is presented as we should expect—in the shape of a business deal. He is ready to buy a wife with 'blood' and accomplishments, to grace his house and provide him with another son (and, as one symbolic piece of description suggests, to stand between him and his daughter).[2] He meets a woman who is prepared to be bought: this is how the notes for Number VII prepare for Mrs Skewton and Edith Granger:

> The mother and daughter. The mother, and her cant about 'heart', and nature— Daughter who has been put through her paces, before countless marrying men, like a horse for sale— Proud and weary of her degradation, but going on, for it's too late now, to try to turn back.

The social implications do not escape Dickens;[3] and he develops

1. The snobbish and ambitious Sir Barnet was an M.P., and the cover shows Mr Dombey speaking in the House. Parliament does have its share in the novel, but only through the faded reminiscences of Cousin Feenix.

2. Near the end of ch. xx ('He saw her image . . . what was there he could interpose between himself and it?').

3. It was at just this time (1846–7) that he was corresponding with Miss Burdett-Coutts about her scheme for establishing a home for fallen women.

them ironically by providing a counterpart to Edith in Alice
Marwood, introduced in Number XI (chapter xxxiii) but prepared for as early as Number II, when Good Mrs Brown, the
kidnapper of Florence, speaks of 'a gal of my own—beyond seas
now—that was proud of her hair'. The difference in social status
is as nothing to the identity of the situation; Dickens evidently
asked, like his contemporary Florence Nightingale,

> The woman who has sold herself for an establishment, in what is
> she superior to those one may not name?[1]

Carker is connected with both; he has been the agent of Alice's
degradation (another social point is made when she nevertheless
refuses to take his money) and schemes to be that of Edith's; her
recognition that he can read her thoroughly is the climax of
Number IX[2] (chapters xxvi–xxviii), whose business was, in the
words of the plan:

> To bring on the marriage gradually—connect Carker with
> Edith, before the wedding, and get in Florence.

Florence is 'got in' (chapter xxviii) by the scene in which Edith
treats her with affection, and the complex of relationships is thus
completed. We shall see how Edith's sole escape from 'degradation' is through her affection for Florence, which proves no
escape since it turns Mr Dombey more against them both; how
it leads him in his sultan-like pride to use Carker as his emissary,
thus allowing Carker to strengthen his hold upon Edith. The
situation is wonderfully planned for its ultimate purpose—the
'fall' and late enlightenment of Mr Dombey. But though the
main design is still kept in view, the 'thickening' of the situation
here raised some problems for Dickens, and he was driven to
unforeseen economies among characters who could not directly
contribute to it. Florence's protectors and 'reflectors' (Nipper,
Toots, Cuttle) must of course remain; but Mrs Chick will have
to give way, though in a superbly comic scene (chapter xxix).
Major Bagstock and Mrs Skewton, having served their purpose
by contriving the marriage, will not reap their expected reward,[3]

1. In 'Cassandra', written about 1852, and first published as Appendix to Ray
Strachey's *The Cause* (1928), p. 412.
2. Singled out for emphasis in the plan, 'First interview between Carker and
Edith. Very important'.
3. The shift in emphasis comes in the plan for ch. xxxi, where the Major is
deleted as proposed speechmaker at the wedding in favour of Cousin Feenix. This is

which the Major's words promise in chapter xxvi: 'Cleopatra the peerless, and her Antony Bagstock . . . sharing the elegance and wealth of Edith Dombey's establishment'.

More important still, there will be no room for the firm, until Mr Morfin appears in Number XVII (chapter liii; after waiting in the wings since Number XIII, when he first appears in the number plans, 'to stand over') and 'shadows forth Mr Dombey's ruin'. This shrinking of the firm is perhaps the one considerable modification of the main design; the letter to Forster had hinted at an almost symmetrical rise-and-fall line for the firm's fortunes; in the event, the 'decay and downfall of the house', and the 'bankruptcy of Dombey' are not only deferred until very late (to the closing double number) but occur in an unchronicled year, just before chapter lviii ('After a Lapse'). The moral shape of the novel, however, is not really affected; the pervasive suggestion remains that a family cannot be run on business lines; Mr Dombey's fall still begins from the story's mid-point, his second marriage; the hastener of the catastrophe is still the 'trusty agent', 'Mr. Carker the Manager'.

IV

The converging lines that lead towards both catastrophe and resolution first stand out clearly in Number XIII (chapters xxxix–xli). The number caused trouble in the writing—it 'requires to be so carefully done';[1] for it must mark clearly (though not coarsely) the breakdown of the marriage. The climax of the big central chapter, 'Domestic Relations', is a show-down between the two whom we now see as 'mighty opposites' in pride, Mr Dombey and Edith; its setting is 'her own apartment', which he will not see again until 'a very different occasion'—one of many indications that her flight with Carker was already designed. The catastrophe is also prepared for by further isolation of the four main characters; Mrs Skewton is to die, Mrs Pipchin to be installed as housekeeper (which will mean the routing of her old enemy Nipper, and thus leave Florence unprotected). All this is calculated in the notes: as is also the confronting of the two base mothers and their proud degraded daughters, which, contrived

---

more plausible, and also prepares for Cousin Feenix's final vindication of the family honour.

1. Forster, VI i (19 Sept. 1847).

and theatrical though it is, again foreshadows Edith's fate.

This is the half-way point; it is time not only to provide for the future, but to round back upon the past. Themes of the first movement reappear: Mrs Skewton is taken in her fatal illness to Brighton, Blimber's Academy is revisited, and voices in the waves are heard once more.

Chapter xli was a calm before storm; events now hurry to the catastrophe, the flight of Edith and Carker, which first appears in the plans in the note on chapter xlv (Number XIV). The rôle devised for Edith is that of an unwilling adulteress, still claiming the reader's sympathy in her resistance to a doubly intolerable situation, and meeting her final defeat only when her one refuge —her love for Florence—is turned into a weapon against them both. 'She . . . relenting by force' is the note for chapter xlv;[1] a little later he wrote to Forster, 'Of course she hates Carker . . . I have relied on it very much for the effect of her death'.[2] He was then writing the chapters just before the elopement; his change of plan for Edith was late, but he was unconsciously prepared for it. For in engaging the reader's sympathies he had entrapped his own, and so was ready to welcome one influential reader's incredulity at Edith's guilt, as an excuse to swerve from his course. But this was later; when he was leading up to and describing the elopement he still designed Edith for guilt, and consequently a repentant deathbed—we may guess, with Florence at her bedside, matching Harriet, whose main function is to attend at Alice's and to forgive.[3] The reader would not suspect the change of plan; Dickens's hold on his main design conceals the swerve of his intention. This is an 'offshoot', if not a 'meandering'; the fall of pride and its redemption are unaffected by it.

From the opening of Number XIV the pace quickens in both plot and counterplot. The 'headline' note in the plan is 'Carker employed as go-between to reduce proud Edith'; and this manœuvre is accelerated by the riding accident, which immobilizes Mr Dombey in the downstairs apartments and gains Carker unhampered admission to Edith. It also gives an opportunity for Nipper to speak her mind, Paulina-like, so that a good reason is

1. Before proofs showed that a cut was necessary, the chapter ended by emphasizing her despair: 'If he has spoken truth, she is lost to me, and I have no hope left'.

2. Forster, vi ii.

3. Foreshadowed in Alice's 'I'll thank you when I die' at the end of ch. xxxiv.

supplied for her banishment; and with Mr Toots as appointed escort, a consolation prize is prepared for the faithful squire; not the rose, but something that grows near it. The finer threads in the pattern are never forgotten. Susan Nipper's explosion is a double preparation for Florence's flight; it isolates her, and also, through its substance, seems a casting-up of accounts, preparing for the final reckoning. And it follows Florence's first doubts of her father (chapter xliii).

All was ready for Number XV (chapters xlvi–xlviii). But in the original plan 'The Thunderbolt' would have fallen last, making the number conclude with Florence's stricken flight, but not its destination and consolation. The serial reader would then have remained in horrified suspense through December 1847. But as the chapter was written first, Dickens had time to change his mind; 'to leave a pleasanter impression on the reader' (had he perhaps the Christmas season in mind?) he pushed this chapter back into the middle place, and added the chapter (xlviii) which shows Florence safely under Captain Cuttle's protection, with mystified but not mystifying hints from Toots of 'a person' awaiting him round the corner. (The note is 'Preparation for Walter'.) The first chapter (xlvi)[1] was ostensibly a 'counterplot' chapter, opening with Carker's diligence at business and closing with his vengeful vision of Edith; it nevertheless prepares ingeniously for his defeat, for he is recognized by Good Mrs Brown, and is warned that his brother is watching Mr Dombey's interests. We may observe that Dickens had not yet decided to use Edith herself as a means of Carker's defeat, for diligence at business suggested to the Stock Exchange 'that Jem was going to marry a rich widow'; and, for contrast with Edith in her degradation, Alice once more appears refusing to touch any money which Carker has to bestow. The views of the Stock Exchange can be interpreted ironically in the light of what is to come; but there are no ironic overtones in the last long paragraph of this chapter, which summarizes the 'slow and sure degrees' by which Edith was to become Carker's mistress and was thus to obtain

the dark retaliation [i.e., upon Mr. Dombey], whose faintest

1. The letter of 19 Nov. 1847 seems to suggest that as originally planned the first chapters (when 'The Thunderbolt' came last) were to be 'light'. But Forster is here perplexing, for he refers to the writing of the 'fourteenth' number, which was already published. It is late even for the writing of No. XV; perhaps date and not reference is mistaken.

shadow seen once and shuddered at, and never seen again, would have been sufficient stain upon her soul.

Number XVII is now prepared for, and the intervening Number XVI (chapters xlix–li) can be mainly devoted to the idyll of Florence and Walter; the solitary general note is 'Return of Walter', and this dominates the number. Dickens had privately prepared for the betrothal in a way which reveals his care over detail, and the peculiar problems of the serial-writer. Before writing chapter xlvii, he went over earlier numbers from VI onwards working out Florence's age, and satisfied himself that she could be 'almost seventeen'. Her age is then specified in that chapter, with a reference to her diminished hopes of her father's love and to 'the change from childhood to womanhood'.[1] It was necessary to 'bring on' Florence's marriage, partly to remove her from the scene of action and partly so that the third generation might arrive in time for the reconciliation. But while it is suitable for the balance of interest[2] that the actual wedding should be deferred till Number XVIII (chapter lvii) this involves Dickens in another time-problem: what to do with the year which nature dictates, when he has only five chapters left. The closing chapter of Number XVI is another 'pause', a quiet preparation for the final rush of events around Mr Dombey, Carker, and Edith. In 'Mr. Dombey and the World' the full irony of the proud man's exposure is brought out, by presenting him in his humiliation through a series of choruses; as the memoranda summarize it:

The Major & Cousin Feenix / The clerks—the city—Perch / Miss Tox / The servants.

The dominant theme of Number XVII (chapters lii–liv) is pursuit; the notes reiterate it—'pervading the number'—and each of the three chapters is built up to a 'pursuit-ending, quick and fierce'. Mr Morfin, at last justifying his dim existence, tells the good Carkers about their brother, 'shadowing forth Mr. Dombey's ruin', and incidentally revealing Dickens's modification of his first design:

1. Dickens also in these notes works out the duration of the second marriage, which he puts at exactly two years; which is longer, perhaps, than accords with the reader's impression (for by this calendar eighteen months must elapse from ch. xl to ch. xlvii) but is not contradicted by any of the time-indications.

2. No. XVII is the only number in the whole novel in which Florence neither appears nor is mentioned.

The distractions of death, courtship, marriage, and domestic un-happiness, have left us no head but your brother for this long, long time.

That is, for nearly three years, and three-quarters of the novel, Mr Dombey has neglected Dombey and Son, and Dickens has let private life overrun his 'business' novel. The situation has its own irony, but the cover and the letter to Forster are evidence that it was not what was originally intended.

Number XVII concludes with the great chapter of Edith's repudiation of Carker at Dijon; here the change of plan already noted[1] was devised only three weeks before the number went to press. On 21 December 1847 Dickens wrote to Forster:

> Note from Jeffrey this morning who won't believe (positively re-fuses) that Edith is Carker's mistress. [Jeffrey had read chapter xlvii, published at the beginning of the month.] What do you think of a kind of inverted Maid's Tragedy, and a tremendous scene of her undeceiving Carker, and giving him to know that she never meant that?[2]

Forster agreed, and it went down in the notes—'Edith not his mistress'. Jeffrey's protest provided occasion rather than cause; the change chimed with Dickens's own view of Edith, who 'hates Carker in the most deadly degree', and whose revenge is only thus completed. The change also lightened his task in the closing numbers; the business of the self-explanation, repentance, and death of an Edith guilty in fact as well as appearance could hardly have been enclosed in the shambling amiabilities of Cousin Feenix, and must have left a lingering shadow on Florence's hap-piness. The diagrammatic equivalence between Alice and Edith, already overemphasized by the revelation of their cousinship in chapter lviii, would have been too starkly obtruded. And, not least in importance, by this change of plan Carker's isolation in evil is sustained to his end.

The first chapter of Number XVIII, with its brilliantly half-revealing title 'Rob the Grinder loses his place', not only wipes out Carker; by concentrating upon the progress of his flight, swift yet protracted, it emphasizes one of the big transitions in the nar-rative, even as Mr Dombey's railway journey to Leamington had done. The same devices are even repeated—the whirling thoughts

---

1. See p. 106 above.   2. Forster, vi ii. Jeffrey's note has not survived.

that accompany the wheels, the symbolically intended railway
junction. But this journey makes a full stop; with it the only
irredeemable evil in the novel's world is abolished—not merely
destroyed, but torn to fragments.

V

There could be no doubt in either author's or reader's mind
about the general content of the closing chapters (lviii–lxii, in the
final 'double number', XIX–XX). The main action must fulfi
itself in the undermining of Mr Dombey's pride from within and
his reconciliation with Florence, and there must be news of all
the other characters, as satisfactory as their conditions and
deserts allow, leading to a final fireside or sunset glow. There was,
however, the problem of time: for that reconciliation to carry
conviction, time must not only pass but be felt to pass, and it
must be the time of heart-throbs as well as clocks and calendars.
Mr Dombey has been unseen, save for oblique glimpses, for
several chapters; we are behindhand even with events, still more
with his response to them. He is now to be seen at close quarters
after a year has passed; but not at once. The first chapter (lviii)
seems leisurely and quiet, but is packed with useful information.
Its purpose is to expound the changed situation, both by narrative and dialogue, to give Mr Dombey his final prominence, first
through choric commentary from Mr Perch, Major Bagstock,
and Mrs Chick, then more fully through the conversation of Harriet and Mr Morfin, which also ties in many other loose ends.
(Dickens's instinct for economy leads him, while he has Harriet
in hand, to dispose of her consoling visit to Alice's repentant
deathbed, though she is not an obvious confidante for Good Mrs
Brown's revelation of family history.) Turning from the world
and the firm to the 'great house in the long dull street' (chapter
lix), the approach to Mr Dombey is still gradual, through the
chorus of the 'kitchen council',[1] the sale, the refrain 'the house is
a ruin and the rats fly from it', and the glimpse of Toodle and
Tox, ghosts of past loyalty lurking in the shadows. A bare five
pages are devoted to Mr Dombey himself, but so thorough has
been the preparation, and so concentrated and searching is the

1. From Dickens's running title added in the edition of 1867. The intention was
calculated; in the number plan for X he notes 'carry on the servants as a sort of
odd chorus to the story', and he had indeed already initiated this in earlier chapters.

ight shed upon him as he roams the memory-haunted house,
hat the picture of his fallen pride seems to dominate the entire
lumber. The main design is at last fulfilled,

> for the struggle within himself, which goes on in all such obstinate
> natures, will have ended then,

and so intense is our sense of his retributive suffering that the
almost theatrically opportune return of Florence can be accepted
as morally earned. Miss Tox's last comment, with its echo ('So
Dombey and Son, as I observed upon a certain sad occasion, is
really a daughter after all!') draws a concluding line under the
climax. The notes in the plan include 'q^y order of chapters'; but
there is no doubt that chapter lix is rightly placed.[1] The stage is
now left clear for the final grouping of the other characters, whom
Dickens's plan conscientiously lists for a final round-up, with
ticks added when they had been disposed of. Not one was forgotten,[2] not even Master Bitherstone and Miss Pankey, though
the Skettleses and the last glimpse of Miss Tox were inserted only
at proof stage. The return to Brighton (chapter lx) helps to link
the final chapters to the close of the first movement, and again
enforces the sense of passing time, and of changelessness in
change. The detail of Mr Bunsby's wedding is at first sight surprising in its amplitude; but apart from the attraction of one
broadly comic scene at the close, it makes an adequate last
appearance for that somewhat petted character Captain Cuttle.
There is no one for him to marry, so we must be shown by means
of this awful warning how glad he is to have escaped marriage.

But throughout the 'matrimonial' winding-up the epilogue of
Florence and her father is kept before us; the movement of chapter lx is traced in the notes, with a final lead back to the central
figures:

> Open with Blimber's—lead to Bunsby, through the Captain, &
> end with Susan and Florence.

Mr Dombey's illness (predicted on the cover) is persuasively
used to emphasize his change of heart, and is also an excuse to

1. Possibly the original intention was to include a Florence-chapter; the first note
is 'The birth of Florence's child and her relenting towards her father', then 'The
scene in his own room'.

2. At least of the humans; and the dog Diogenes was remembered a week before
publication. Dickens wrote to Forster (vi ii; 25 Mar. 1848) asking for him to be
inserted in proof, and a brief addition stands on the last page of the proof sheet:
'and an old dog is generally in their company'.

'distance' him, so that even our glimpse of him in recovery improbably clinking glasses with Captain Cuttle (like Scrooge and the Cratchits'), does not seem incongruous.

One item on the agenda of the plan was doubtful; the note shows an unexpected hesitation over the meeting between Edith and Florence:

> Edith—q[y] Edith and Florence—certainly, Edith and Cousin Feenix. Yes, all three.

Edith has her just place; shadowed herself,[1] but removing the one remaining shadow on Florence. The substance and style of their speeches could be predicted; but the scene draws a surprising extra vitality from the rôle of Cousin Feenix. His gentility is at last revealed as the genuine article (Edith is to reveal the truth 'not for the honour of the family . . . but because it *is* wrong, and not right'), and his oratory is for the first time effectual; but he retains all his native absurdity, and while ministering to the mood of the epilogue he is not subdued (as is Nipper) into a mere contributor to the chorus.

Echoes reverberate in the closing number; incidents and scenes are recalled, themes reappear, dominant images and even words are repeated.[2] But one echo planned for the conclusion of the final chapter was removed in proof:

> End with the sea—carrying through, what the waves were always saying, and the invisible country far away.[3]

That popular sentiment which added an apocryphal wildness to the waves in a drawing-room song might have preferred it so.

1. The gradations of poetic justice are delicate; her destination is the south of Italy, whereas little Em'ly must go to Australia.

2. E.g., Miss Tox's comment, quoted above, and 'Let him remember it in that room, years to come'; the latter also the caption of an illustration.

3. In correcting proof Dickens had to reduce his number by seven lines, yet wished to find room for Skettles and Miss Tox. It was the last two paragraphs he chose to sacrifice. They read as follows:

The voices in the waves speak low to him of Florence, day and night—plainest when he, his blooming daughter, and her husband, walk beside them in the evening, or sit at an open window, listening to their roar. They speak to him of Florence and his altered heart; of Florence and their ceaseless murmuring to her of the love, eternal and illimitable, extending still, beyond the sea, beyond the sky, to the invisible country far away.

Never from the mighty sea may voices rise too late, to come between us and the unseen region on the other shore! Better, far better, that they whispered of that region in our childish ears, and the swift river hurried us away!

But the conclusion is comparatively restrained, and comes no nearer that echo than a last 'long shot' of the sea-beach in autumn, and a natural grandfatherly recollection of the other Paul. It is with the two Florences that Dickens ends; mindful in valediction of his main design.

CHAPTER VI

David Copperfield
Month by Month

T HE last number of *Dombey and Son* was published in April 1848, and before the year was out Dickens was brooding upon his next novel *David Copperfield*. As for *Dombey*, no master plan survives, and there is no reason to suppose that such a plan was set on paper. Other evidence bearing upon the nature of his first design is slight, and when compared with what survives about the design of *Dombey*[1] is disappointing. It is true that on one page of the manuscript are written as many as seventeen draft titles, but all are variants upon a single pattern. What began as 'Mag's Diversions: Being the personal history, experiences, and observations of Mr. Thomas Mag the Younger, of Blunderstone House' ended as 'The Personal History and Experience of David Copperfield the Younger'. After promising so much in the title of *Dombey*, he would seem to be returning to the noncommittal type of *The Life and Adventures of Nicholas Nickleby*: even 'Mag's Diversions', an old saying like 'the deuce and all', was no more compromising than *As You Like It*. The cover-design of the monthly numbers, which had foreshadowed the drift of *Dombey*, tells no secrets here. It shows indeed that the story will begin in earliest childhood, but that is no more than the first number itself reveals. Forster, it is true, found the 'unity of drift or purpose ... apparent always', and added, in explanation:

> By the course of the events we learn the value of self-denial and patience, quiet endurance of unavoidable ills, strenuous effort against ills remediable; and everything in the fortunes of the actors warns us, to strengthen our generous emotions and to guard the purities of home.[2]

1. See above, pp. 90–6.   2. Forster, vi vii.

This is well said; but it is said after the event. Of the seminal period Forster could afterwards recall only his suggestion in 1848 that Dickens should write his next book in the first person—a suggestion 'which he took at once very gravely ... though as yet not dreaming of any public use of his early personal trials',[1] and that when his sixth son was born in January 1849 he decided to call him Henry Fielding 'in a kind of homage to the style of work he was now so bent on beginning'.[2] All this amounts to little. Substantial evidence of a commanding purpose at the outset must be found, if at all, inside the book and in the number plans, which are now published *in extenso* for the first time.[3]

Number I: May 1849
Chapters i–iii: written in April 1849

The plans of the first numbers of *David Copperfield* and *Little Dorrit* were removed from their manuscripts by Forster. He had facsimiles of them made and used these in his *Life of Dickens* to show in *Dorrit* 'the labour and pains' and in *Copperfield* 'the lightness and confidence of handling'. The plans were never restored, and have disappeared with the rest of Forster's manuscript. This would not have mattered so much if Forster had reproduced the plans in their entirety; but his purpose of contrast was served by a two-thirds facsimile of each, and this truncated specimen (printed on pp. 116–17) is all that now survives.

---

1. Ibid., VI vi. But the successful adoption of the child's point of view in *Dombey and Son* (see p. 100, n. 4) had awoken an interest in his own childhood which had led him to write some chapters of an autobiography probably in 1847. 1847 was also the year of publication of an impressive novel written in the first person, *Jane Eyre*. See Tillotson, *Novels of the Eighteen-Forties* (Oxford, 1954), pp. 114, 192, 260.

2. Forster, VI vi.

3. Though it is impossible to convey in print all that the number plans reveal, in their manuscript form, of hesitation and decision, of haste and excitement, and of afterthought squeezed into what might seem the least inconvenient space unfilled, our transcription is as exact as it is practicable to make it. A line in the manuscript is invariably represented by a line of type, and in position it matches as closely as possible an entry on the half-sheet of paper facing it. Capitalization and underlining have been preserved. Erasures, where legible, are printed within angle-brackets. Compare frontispiece, and see pp. 25–9.

Lobsters & Crawfish
The people living on the Barge.

Mr Hasden
    Murdle Murdstone
    Murden

The progress of his mother's second courts

Brooks of Sheffield
    Goes to Peggotty's

The first number is a charming and lavish piece of exposition. Apart from the rich possibilities latent in the Peggottys and Betsey Trotwood, Dickens had provided himself in this number with three possible themes for future development. The first, though the least important, is the mystery of Betsey Trotwood's husband. That this mystery was no casual embellishment of his preliminary sketch of her character, but was intended for future use, the number plan seems to confirm, for the note 'Her old wrongs' may have served to keep in mind something for later use.

The second theme is David's relations with Mr Murdstone, whose well-chosen name is determined after three attempts. It is likely that Mr Murdstone's harsh treatment of David was already foreseen, if not the form which that treatment was to take, for the reader receives more than one covert warning. The autobiographical mode of writing is employed with notable irony when David and Peggotty discuss the subject of marriage and when David relates the tiff between Peggotty and Mrs Copperfield after Mr Murdstone's visit. The unwitting David is made to convey, without expressly stating, that Mrs Copperfield has been too easily won by flattery, and that Peggotty has good reason to disapprove the coming marriage. After this it is not altogether surprising that the first number should end with a flutter of ominous excitement. David and Peggotty return from their visit to Yarmouth, but Mrs Copperfield is not at the door to greet them.

nal History and Adventures of David Copperfield—N⁰ I)

chapter I.
I am born

Father dead—Gravestone outside the house
Young mother—Tendency to weakness and vanity
    Miss Betsey—Her old wrongs   Peggotty
    Why rookery?   Ham Peggotty
        Morgan the Dr

chapter II.
I observe

The things that come out of the blank of his infancy on
looking back.—child at church—
—The future father in law "at this minute I see him
turn round in the garden with his damned black eyes"—&c

Peggotty with difficulty explains to David that he has 'got a Pa
.. A new one', and her agitation affects David too. The scene in
the parlour when David is at last brought to his mother is described with an economy of words for which Dickens is not often
credited:

> My mother dropped her work, and arose hurriedly, but timidly
> I thought.
> 'Now, Clara my dear,' said Mr. Murdstone. 'Recollect! controul
> yourself, always controul yourself! Davy boy, how do you do?'
> I gave him my hand. After a moment of suspense, I went and
> kissed my mother: she kissed me, patted me gently on the shoulder,
> and sat down again to her work. I could not look at her, I could not
> look at him, I knew quite well that he was looking at us both; and
> I turned to the window and looked out there, at some shrubs that
> were drooping their heads in the cold.

The agony to come is implied briefly but sufficiently. The droop-
ing shrubs are an emblem of the cold which has invaded the
home; and with another emblem, of the man who has come to
ruin their domestic happiness, the number is concluded:

> My old dear bedroom was changed,[1] and I was to lie a long way off.
> I rambled downstairs to find anything that was like itself, so
> altered it all seemed; and roamed into the yard. I very soon started

---

1. He had formerly slept 'in a closet within my mother's room'.

back from there, for the empty dog-kennel was filled up with a
great dog—deep-mouthed and black-haired like Him—and he wa
very angry at the sight of me, and sprung out to get at me.

The third theme is as ominous as the second: it is Little Em'ly'
future. The manuscript shows that the scene at Yarmouth wa
elaborated in two respects after the draft of the first number wa
completed.

(1) As Dickens first conceived her, Mrs Gummidge had no
character at all. It was only after completing chapter iii that he
turned back and interpolated the long episode beginning 'I soon
found out that Mrs. Gummidge did not always make herself so
agreeable as she might have been expected to do, under the circumstances of her residence with Mr. Peggotty.' It is then that
she becomes 'a lone lorn creetur', and thus helps to exemplify the
forbearing character of Mr Peggotty.

(2) The second interpolation is more important. In the first
draft Em'ly is no more than the little girl whom young David
adored, though the sequel shows that even this first affair of
David's undisciplined heart is of some importance. But on completing the chapter Dickens added the long passage, beginning
'"You're quite a sailor, I suppose?" I said to Em'ly' and ending
'This may be premature. I have set it down too soon, perhaps.
But let it stand.' In this passage is revealed Em'ly's wish 'to be a
lady' so as to prevent Mr Peggotty and Ham from risking their
lives at sea in stormy weather. She is afraid of the cruel sea for
their sake, but not a whit for her own; and she demonstrates her
fearlessness by running 'along a jagged timber which protruded
from the place we stood upon, and overhung the deep water at
some height, without the least defence'. She seemed to spring forward to her destruction; and David, recalling the scene, reflected
'there has been a time since . . . when I have asked myself the
question, would it have been better for little Em'ly to have had
the waters close above her head that morning in my sight; and
when I have answered Yes, it would have been'.

This interpolated passage forecasts the part which Em'ly is to
play. With his mind occupied by Miss Coutts's project for establishing a home for fallen women,[1] Dickens reverts to one of the
themes of *Dombey and Son*, the repentant prostitute: someone, it is
clear, will offer to make Em'ly a lady on speciously honourable

1. See below, p. 148.

terms, and she will fall in attempting to improve the lot of Mr Peggotty and Ham.[1]

Thus in the first number many incidents are already forecast. In one direction Dickens could see as far perhaps as Number V, where David comes to live with Betsey Trotwood; in another he might see as far as Number XVI (in which Mr Peggotty at last finds Em'ly in hiding), or even as far as the great storm in Number XVIII, though it is not at all likely that he yet knew all that he would meet on either road. The contemporary reader who recognized these two themes might have speculated upon their ultimate connexion. Since David himself could not have been cast for Em'ly's seducer, was he then to effect her rescue, perhaps even to marry her? Or was he, whose caul forecast immunity from drowning, to rescue her in a final storm which the interpolation so clearly promises? Much would depend upon the identity of the seducer. He was to be revealed in the next number, the plan of which is presented overleaf.

1. The interpolation of this important passage in the first draft of the number invites speculation. Did the theme first occur to Dickens after finishing the number, or had he already meditated it and set it aside for fuller treatment on a future occasion? The first number was evidently written in haste. Though publication was set for 1 May, it was not finished on 19 April (*Letters*, II 150). The opportunities of the story may therefore have been imperfectly recognized and have opened before him as he wrote. On the other hand, it should be noted that there are thirty sheets of manuscript in the first draft, which is rather more than his normal monthly stint. Proofs, however, would show him that he had more space at his disposal than the number of manuscript sheets had led him to believe, and he may have decided thereupon to broach this important theme at the earliest possible moment.

      Miss Murdstone
      Their religion
      Picture of all that, and its effect on Davy's life.
      Cast off and getting sullen.
      qy His books and reading?
      His offence, and confinement upstairs. Child's rem
      brance of the latter.
      Sent away

      ⟨I attend church.⟩

         ⟨hospitably received⟩
      ⟨I am received∧by Mr Peggotty⟩

The first number had ended with the reader's curiosity roused
about David's relations with Mr Murdstone. Dickens decided to
satisfy it immediately in the first chapter of Number II. The
memoranda relate entirely to chapter iv and, with the summary,
cover all the incidents in their order of narration, except Peggotty's visit to David in his confinement. It might be deduced
that chapter iv required particular care and that the details of
the journey to school and the boys' return could be improvised in
the act of writing. The only memorandum bearing upon the
journey is scored out, perhaps because a second visit to Mr

experience
'ersonal History and ⟨adventures⟩ of David Copperfield—N° II.)

chapter IV.
I fall into disgrace

Progress of his mother's weakness under the Murdstones.
Miss Murdstone

> Beat's him
> Bites
> Shut up and dismissed

chapter V.
—And am sent away from home.

The carrier & Peggotty.
Waiter—Glass of ale—chops—pudding—himself
journey
to be left till called for
School with the boys all at home
"Take care of him. He bites"

chapter VI.
I enlarge my circle of acquaintance.

Mr Creakle.
return of the boys
spending his money
Steerford
Steerforth.

Peggotty's barge would have conflicted with the impression of friendlessness in which David makes his way to Salem House. Though the bareness of the summary of chapter v contrasts with the lavishly fanciful expansion of the incidents in the text, it is enough to recall what is essential and, in the instance of 'the carrier and Peggotty', to keep in mind the one point for future development. But the summary of chapter vi is even more bare and brief; yet this is the chapter in which Steerforth is introduced, the foundations of whose character are laid with obvious care. How deftly Dickens suggests by the confiscation and disposal of David's pocket-money that Steerforth's actions are not in keeping with his heroic demeanour; and any reader who doubts that Steerforth is already reserved for a dark future need only turn to the description of him lying asleep and observe there the first anticipation of the final scene on Yarmouth sands in chapter lv:

I . . . raised myself, I recollect, to look at him where he lay in the moonlight, with his handsome face turned up, and his head reclining easily on his arm. He was a person of great power in my eyes; that was of course the reason of my mind running on him. No veiled future dimly glanced upon him in the moonbeams.

Number III : July 18

School. Master

                    The Afternoon

Steerforth

                    Peggotty's enquiries about schoo
                    Tells her of Barkis

Goes home   Mother says she is not to leave h
                    It may not be for long.

Mother with a baby.
comes back, & receives news of her death.

            again,
Goes home ∧ to the funeral.

⟨I enjoy one afternoon's holiday⟩

⟨The holidays are concentrated into one afternoon.⟩

⟨My holidays.⟩

He is, so far, the only possible seducer for Little Em'ly, and that he was already destined for this rôle may be guessed from a hint of the young libertine, undeveloped as yet, but casual and untrustworthy in his approaches to women:

'You haven't got a sister, have you?' said Steerforth, yawning. 'No,' I answered.

'That's a pity,' said Steerforth. 'If you had had one, I should think she would have been a pretty, timid, little, bright-eyed sort of girl. I should have liked to know her. Good night, young Copperfield.'

pters vii–ix: completed by 21 June 1849

sonal History and Experience of David Copperfield—Nº III.)

chapter VII.
My First half at Salem House.

School—His progress
 Steerforth's character.
 Traddles. Dº
 Mr Mell's poverty and mother, and dismissal.

Visit from ⟨Peggotty⟩ Mr Peggotty? Yes. And Steerforth
     Summing up, & going home.

chapter VIII.
My holidays. Especially one happy Afternoon

The Afternoon. The baby
Peggotty & his mother.
The Murdstones—progress of their influence &c
Holding up the baby

chapter IX.
I have a memorable Birthday.

Mrs Creakle breaks it to him
 His state of mind—childish incidental whimsicalities
 The undertaker's, Mr Omer's
 State of home, and recollection of funeral
 Peggotty's narrative
    close with the idea of his
    mother as she was, with him
    as he was, in her arms.

The confidence which Dickens felt in his story at this juncture is reflected in a letter to Forster dated 6 June 1849.[1] '*Copperfield* half done', he wrote; 'I feel, thank God, quite confident in the story. I have a move in it ready for this month; another for next; and another for the next.' It seems not unlikely that the first 'move' was the meeting of Mr Peggotty and Ham with Steerforth at Salem House in chapter vii. The number plan shows that Dickens had first chosen Peggotty as David's visitor. It was a natural choice to make; but it seems to have flashed across his mind—the form of the summary supports this—that if Mr Peggotty, a less likely visitor, came instead of his sister, the way lay open for a meeting between him and Steerforth, which might in turn give rise to a meeting between Steerforth and Em'ly. Steerforth himself is presented throughout with notable irony. Every adult reader recognizes how meanly he behaves; but David 'could not help thinking . . . what a noble fellow he was', and every unworthy action of his patron is given a suitably heroic and generous interpretation.

With Steerforth's character sufficiently shaped in chapter vii, Dickens could turn back to pursue the Murdstones' influence in the two remaining chapters. Once decided that David's mother shall die, it is obvious that her death must occur in the last chapter of the number. 'Get a clean pocket-handkerchief ready for the close of Copperfield N° 3;' he wrote to Lemon on 25 June; ' "simple and quiet, but very natural and touching."—*Evening Bore*.'[2] Manuscript and proof disclose some adjustment of emphasis in the pathos. The 'RAT-tat-tat' of Mr Joram's hammer on the coffin was an afterthought, and so was the first passage of repartee between Minnie Omer and her father.[3] A paragraph describing the morning of the funeral was deleted in proof. It read as follows:

> When the day came, I remember being awakened in the morning by the sharp strokes of a spade, and that I looked out of the window, and saw men working in the churchyard, underneath the tree, and went to bed and wept. I remember that I lay there, sobbing, until

1. The letter is misdated 6 June 1850 in the Nonesuch edition (II 218), and Forster (VI vi) is wrong in referring it to the second number which was already published.

2. *Letters*, II 157.

3. The passage beginning ' "Father!" said Minnie, playfully. "What a porpoise you do grow!" ' and ending 'Mr. Omer took me back into the parlor, breathing with some difficulty on the way.'

Peggotty came up to help me dress myself, and that being in her black dress for the first time, she wrung her hands—a thing it turned my very blood to see her do—and gave way to her sorrow before me, for the only time in all my knowledge.

When proofs of Number III reached him, Dickens found that he had overstepped his monthly allowance of thirty-two pages by thirty-five lines of type. Something had to go, and this was one of the passages cut. Its omission involves a small but appreciable relaxing of tension.

(Continued overleaf.)

what I know so well

I become neglected and am provided for

I begin life on my ⟨account⟩ own account.

I go on with life, rather uncomfortably
                    on my own account and don't like

I make a resolution

Though he had already made use of his unpublished autobiography in Number II, it is in this number that he relies most
heavily on his past experiences. The memoranda are accordingly
brief, amounting to little more than drafts of chapter titles, and
the manuscript itself shows unusually few corrections. It was not
a mere question of transcribing, however; 'I really think I have
done it ingeniously,' he wrote to Forster on 10 July, 'and with a
very complicated interweaving of truth and fiction.'[1]

A change which Dickens made in the colour of his ink while
writing this number shows that the summaries of chapters xi and
xii were made before chapter x was written, and that the items in
the summary of chapter x were jotted down concurrently with
the episodes to which they refer. They reveal little. He was not

1. *Letters*, II 160.

Chapters x–xii: written during the first fortnight of July 1849

(Personal History and Experience of David Copperfield—N° IV.)

chapter X.
I become neglected, and am provided for.

Go away with Peggotty—Barkis
Mr Peggotty's
Her marriage ride with the two children
neglect
Quinion.—arrangement
"Behold me" &c

chapter XI.
I begin life on my own account, and don't like it.

all the ⟨Murdstone and⟩ life at the warehouse
Murdstone and Grinby
M^r and Mrs Micawber—Prison—Insolvent Court

chapter XII.
Taking life on my own account no better, I form a great resolution.

The young man with the donkey cart

run away to Aunt Betsey

accustomed to sketch his characters in these plans, and accordingly 'M^r and Mrs Micawber' and 'the young man with the donkey cart' stand starkly with no indication of how they will develop under his hand. More surprising is to find no record of Em'ly's interest in the account which David and Mr Peggotty give of Steerforth.

(*Continued overleaf.*)

Chatham—Canterbury sunshine
Tramps—pint of beer?

Your sister, Betsey Trotwood

Mr Dick's history? qy Yes, very briefly. by Miss Bet

Donkies
Miss Murdstone comes on a donkey

Mr Dick and his memorial

His delusion

Introduction of the real heroine

Dickens was not fully persuaded of the advantages of dividing a long novel into books until later in his career. These divisions guide the reader; but the author may be presumed to be aware of them even though he does not mark them. Such a division comes at the end of Number IV: one movement of the novel ends with David running away to Aunt Betsey, and another begins in Number V with the introduction of fresh characters representing fresh contributions to the principal theme. His first duty to his readers was to resume the flight to Dover which the demands of the serial form had interrupted at so important yet so convenient a juncture. The prospect opening upon David—the new home and its inmates, the dismissal of the Murdstones, and the preparation for a new start in life at Canterbury—might seem to require a number in itself: this new prospect was doubtless the 'move'

Chapters xiii–xv: finished and proofs read by 22 August 1849

Personal History and Experience of David Copperfield—Nº V.)

chapter XIII.
The sequel of my resolution.

His journey
Goes to his aunts
Miss Betsey—"Janet! Donkies!"
Mr Dick

chapter XIV.
My Aunt makes up her mind about me.

Mr Dick again
Mr and Miss Murdstone come
conversation—ends with his Aunt adopting him.
Trotwood Copperfield

chapter XV.
I make another beginning

old House at Canterbury
Mr Wickfield
His one motive. Agnes Wickfield
Uriah Heep.

ready for September, as Forster had been told in June, just as David's experiences at the blacking factory were the 'move' prepared for August. But though the briefness of the memoranda might be thought to indicate that Dickens saw clearly every turn in the path before him, a phrase in a letter to Forster written on 10 August, when nearly half the number was done, shows that all was not straightforward: 'I have not worked quickly here yet', he wrote from the Isle of Wight; '. . . Divers cogitations have occupied my mind at intervals, respecting the dim design'.[1]

The nature of some of these cogitations is revealed in the memoranda. The query about Mr Dick's history seems to imply a doubt whether this was the right moment to relate it. He may well have been faced with the temptation to make a mystery of

1. *Letters*, II 167.

Mr Dick's past. This would have involved the provision of a group of subordinate characters related to Mr Dick and the cumbersome apparatus of a sub-plot. Dickens was never averse to such additional complication, but in his mature work a mystery was of interest only in so far as it clarified another purpose, as Lady Dedlock's mystery clarifies the inescapable responsibility of her social class for the condition of such a slum as Tom-all-alone's. The purpose of Mr Dick is to illustrate and commend such humane treatment of the partly imbecile as Betsey Trotwood administers. It was not beyond Dickens's powers to demonstrate this purpose by means of a mystery; but he may have reflected that it could be made equally clear without, and that by revealing Aunt Betsey's treatment of Mr Dick at this point he contributed effectively to the exposition of her character on which he was then engaged.

Forster was the first to mention that Mr Dick's topical[1] obsession with King Charles's head replaced the Bull in the China Shop at proof stage. But an even more significant alteration in proof has escaped notice. David's original vision of Mr Dick was of 'a florid, pleasant-looking gentleman, with a grey head, putting his tongue out against the glass, and carrying it across the pane and back again; who, when his eye caught mine, squinted at me in a most terrible manner, laughed, and went away'. The tongue is removed in proof, and the terrible squint is softened to an eye shut up 'in a grotesque manner'. If Dickens had not softened this description, he might well have been charged, as Coleridge charged Wordsworth in 'The Idiot Boy', with not taking sufficient care 'to preclude from the reader's fancy the disgusting images of *ordinary morbid idiocy*, which yet it was by no means his intention to represent'.[2]

Another point of interest in the memoranda is the note, 'Introduction of the real heroine'. It might be deduced from this note that Agnes Wickfield is to serve not merely as David's 'good angel', a rôle in which David commends her performance all too frequently, but that she is eventually to become his wife. A 'real' heroine also implies an illusory heroine, and though he may have been thinking of Em'ly in that part, it is more probable that he had already had Dora Spenlow in mind. If Agnes, then, as the real heroine, is destined to marry David eventually, Dora is also

---

1. 1849 was the bicentenary year of Charles I's execution.
2. *Biographia Literaria*, ed. J. Shawcross (Oxford, 1907), II 35.

destined to make way for her, assuming that she is indeed to marry David in the first place. Yet Forster records[1] that in the latter part of the story 'his principal hesitation occurred in connection with the child-wife Dora, who had become a great favourite as he went on', and this is confirmed by a letter of 7 May 1850, written during the course of Number XIV, 'Still undecided about Dora, but MUST decide to-day.' This hesitation may be explained as an attempt to avoid a harsh but necessary decision made at an earlier stage. But there is a truly Dickensian alternative. Had Dora been allowed to live, Agnes might have maintained her part as 'the real heroine' by educating Dora, by superintending the household, and by caring for the children, the very part which Georgina Hogarth—'my little housekeeper', as he calls her in a letter of 29 August 1850[2]—was playing in Dickens's own family. Such a development in this 'autobiographical' novel would have been embarrassingly close to life; but it would have had the advantage of saving Dora, and Dickens may well have reviewed this possibility before deciding upon her fate.

(*Continued overleaf.*)

1. Forster, VI vi.   2. *Letters*, II 229.

Dictio

The good old Doctor & the young wife
Uriah Heep? qy <u>Yes.</u>
Mr Micawber? qy <u>Yes. and M^{rs}</u>
"Turn his attention to coals." <u>The Medway Coal T</u>

Mr Micawber's letter

<u>The Progress from childhood to youth.</u>

My aunt? qy <u>No. only generally</u>

Mr Dick? qy Yes. <u>With the D^r.</u>

Peggotty's half guinea to be repaid.

<u>Mems for the Progress.</u>
The cathedral

Miss Wilkins—<u>No. Shepherd</u>

Head boy.
Tail-coat
Loving a grown woman, much too old.

This number plan is appreciably more elaborate than the last, and shows that the story demanded more detailed planning at this stage. It is not difficult to see why this should have been. Two new themes are introduced—the themes of Dr and Mrs Strong's relations with Jack Maldon and of Uriah Heep's ambitions—whose connexion with David's story is of far-reaching complexity.

The Strong–Maldon theme engages his first attention. At first sight its relationship either to David's story or to the story of Steerforth and Em'ly may seem remote, but when in Number

sonal History and Experience of David Copperfield—N⁰ VI.)

chapter XVI.

I am a new boy, in more senses than one.

Doctor Strong's
The Doctor and his young wife
Mr Jack Maldon   Wife's mother. The old soldier
Mr Wickfield & Agnes.
Uriah Heep.
Mr Jack Maldon's going away. The cherry colored ribbon.
Close with her face.

chapter XVII.

Somebody turns up.

Mr Dick—The man who frightens my aunt.

Mr Dick & the Doctor walking up & down
Uriah Heep and his mother
Their lemon-squeezing process
Mr & Mrs Micawber. Mr Micawber makes Uriah's acquaintance.

chapter XVIII.

A Retrospect.

Two loves.
    Miss Shepherd. In the responses—put her in
among the Royal family.
    Fight with a butcher
    Growing up—Agnes grows up.
    In love with the eldest Miss Larkins
        ring—Bear's grease—&c &c

XV Dickens explains what has been happening, it is clear that
Annie Strong's experiences bear upon David's affection for Dora
Spenlow. His eyes are opened by her words to see that he too has
suffered from the 'mistaken impulse of an undisciplined heart'.
There is little doubt that this was part of the original intention,
although in Number VI the reader has not yet heard of Dora.
The theme of The Undisciplined Heart had been touched long
before Dora appears. David had told Em'ly in chapter iii that he
'adored her, and that unless she confessed she adored me I should

be reduced to the necessity of killing myself with a sword'. His love for the eldest Miss Larkins was as extravagantly expressed:

> If the eldest Miss Larkins would drive a triumphal car down the High Street, and allow me to throw myself under the wheels as an offering to her beauty, I should be proud to be trampled under her horses' feet.[1]

Before Miss Larkins there had been Miss Shepherd, 'the one pervading theme and vision of my life'; and before Miss Shepherd, Agnes:

> I love little Em'ly, and I don't love Agnes—no, not at all in that way—but I feel that there are goodness, peace, and truth, wherever Agnes is.[2]

The distinction is already clear between the 'rock' on which his later love was founded and the mistaken impulses of his undisciplined heart.

Annie Strong's experiences serve to enforce this. She too had been deceived by childish love. When Dr Strong's proposal was made, she was as little able as David to recognize the future source of her happiness. '"Mama," she said, crying,'—the report is Mrs Markleham's—'"I am extremely young ... and I hardly know if I have a heart at all."' But in this same chapter (chapter xvi), the very chapter in which David fails to recognize the substance of his love for Agnes, Annie Strong is brought by Jack Maldon's behaviour to recognize the difference between her old feelings for him and what she has since learned to feel for the Doctor. Jack Maldon's behaviour on leaving for India aroused that look of 'penitence, humiliation, shame, pride, love, and trustfulness' with which she regarded the Doctor, and which David was to remember 'a long time afterwards'. When at last he falls in love with Dora in Number IX, the reader feels no surprise because the quality had been foreseen and prepared for in Numbers I, V, and VI.

Did Dickens also foresee the use of Mr Dick to effect the reconciliation between Dr and Mrs Strong in Number XV? It is not impossible, since Dr Strong and Mr Dick are already placed in close association. The picture of these two men, each with his

---

1. This and other passages describing David's infatuation were removed from ch. xviii in proof when it was discovered that the 'over-matter' in No. VI extended to 96 lines of print.
2. Ch. xvi.

harmless obsession, walking together 'by the hour, on that side of the courtyard which was known among us as The Doctor's Walk', is a pleasing contribution to the pattern of the novel. It seems to suggest, as gently as possible, that the Doctor's notion of compiling a dictionary is as futile as Mr Dick's notion of writing a memorial, and as little likely to be completed. Dickens's purpose in creating Mr Dick should also be recalled. If he was aware of the best contemporary treatment of lunacy,[1] it seems not unlikely that he was already preparing to show Mr Dick engaged in the humane office of reconciling husband and wife.

Another strand in the pattern of the novel can be observed in the Strong episode and in other episodes of this number. In each of the prominent themes a shadow is cast upon a scene of domestic happiness: the Murdstones' shadow darkens the happiness of Blunderstone Rookery, and Steerforth is to darken the Peggottys' happiness. In the same way Jack Maldon casts his shadow over the Strongs, and Mr Dick reveals to David—at greater length before proofs showed the need for pruning—that an unknown man has been frightening Aunt Betsey. Uriah Heep's ambitions are announced lightly but surely, and they will cast their shadow over the happiness of Agnes and her father.

The memoranda disclose some uncertainty in the use of both Uriah and Mr Micawber at this stage, yet the pointedness of the coincidence by which Micawber discovers David at tea with the Heeps suggests that Dickens, in the moment of plotting Uriah's schemes, provides an instrument for unveiling them.

(*Continued overleaf.*)

---

1. A reviewer of *Maud* in *Fraser's Magazine*, Sept. 1855, remarks: 'The wonders which have been worked of late years, even in idiots and cretins, simply by drawing out their humanity, by interesting them and employing them, by giving them something to love, something to do, seem to open a boundless door of hope'.

Janet?   qy?
Steerforth's mother?   ⟨Ye

Steerforth?   Ye

Little Em'ly?   Ye

The two partners?   N
Mr Mell?   N

Lirrimer?
Littimer.

This brilliant and confident number shows Dickens in full sail with no apparent hesitation about the course before him. But the number plan reveals once more that he took his direction immediately before writing the number, and took it not without deliberation. A close examination of the number itself might have suggested as much, for complete as it is, it foreshadows doom.

David has now left school and is sent away for a change of scene to help in choosing a profession. Dickens must therefore take a last look at two Canterbury themes which he was not likely to resume in the near future. When David goes to take leave of Agnes, she mentions her anxiety about the 'gradual alteration in Papa' and Uriah's growing ascendency. Short as the episode is, it serves its purpose; but the passage had been longer before proofs showed the need for cuts, and two paragraphs describing a dinner

ᵒnal History and Experience of David Copperfield—Nᵒ VII.)

chapter XIX.
I look about me, and make a discovery.

Pave the way with Mʳ Wickfield
Dᵒ Agnes
Dᵒ Mʳˢ Strong
Goes away to see Peggotty
First Fall in life   Play.

Waiter   Golden Cross Charing Cross
                         meets Steerforth

chapter XX.
Steerforth's Home.

Mʳˢ Steerforth
Miss Dartle. "Threw a hammer at her?"
"Eh? But is it really though? I want to know

chapter XXI.
Little Em'ly.

The servant. Littimer.
Little Em'ly at Mʳ Omer's—Mʳ Omer "Two parties."
Peggotty
Mʳ Barkis a little nearer
Mʳ Peggotty's account of her being engaged to Ham.

---

at Mr Wickfield's had to go. These added some slight emphasis to the points made in David's conversation with Agnes. The other Canterbury theme concerns the Strongs and Jack Maldon, and after glancing at that, Dickens was ready to convey David to London for the principal subject of the number, his reunion with Steerforth.

The memoranda show Dickens in doubt whether to use Steerforth and his mother, Em'ly, Littimer, Mr Mell, and 'the two partners'. He decided against Mr Mell, who would presumably have served once more to illustrate Steerforth's churlishness, and who might have encouraged backward glances when so much lies ahead; and 'the two partners', Spenlow and Jorkins—though they had not yet received those names—were deferred until the following month. The remaining characters are employed and form the staple of chapters xx and xxi. Other characters enter too. Em'ly's appearance involves the reappearance of the Peg gotty, Barkis, and Omer households, who therefore did no require specific mention. But it is perhaps surprising that though Littimer is mentioned in the memoranda, Rosa Dartle is not Littimer is to become an important agent:

> He was very often by [David observes, in a passage subsequently removed in proof] for his attention to Steerforth, at all times, wa most remarkable. Without obtruding it, or watching him, he seem ed to have the power of divining his wants, and supplying them at the very moment when it was agreeable to him that they should be supplied. He never showed the least sense of there being anything meritorious in this; neither did his master.

Miss Dartle, on the other hand, seems to have been regarded at this stage as a passive figure. She serves in this number as a chorus of sarcastic comment on Steerforth's brutalities. But her relative prominence in the summary, probably written after completing the number, suggests that she may have grown in importance while chapter xx was being written.

The future is foreshadowed in the Yarmouth gossip, retailed to David by the Omers, that Em'ly had not been keeping 'to her own station in life', that she 'wanted to be a lady . . . to do so and so for her uncle—don't you see?—and buy him such and such fine things'. It is foreshadowed even more ominously in Steerforth's remark that 'the sea roars as if it were hungry for us'.

Steerforth is delineated with great pains, and indeed with great success. The measure of his importance can be gauged by the number of mirror-characters who surround him to reflect facets of his personality—Mrs Steerforth, Rosa Dartle, Littimer, and, in the following number, Miss Mowcher. Even Mrs Gummidge is pressed into this service, for in a scene which, alas, was removed in proof[1] she succumbs to his undoubted charm and ceases to think of 'the old 'un'. But for all this superficial fascination, there is no difficulty in recognizing, thanks to a score of deft touches, that his feelings are false and his moral responses undependable. The most startling revelation is his reply to David's rhapsody as they leave the barge after interrupting the celebration of Ham's betrothal to Em'ly:

1. Reprinted by John Butt in 'David Copperfield: From Manuscript to Print', *Review of English Studies*, n.s. i (1950), 251.

'A most engaging little Beauty!' said Steerforth, taking my arm. 'Well! It's a quaint place, and they are quaint company, and it's quite a new sensation to mix with them.'

'How fortunate we are, too,' I returned, 'to have arrived to witness their happiness in that intended marriage! I never saw people so happy. How delightful to see it, and to be made the sharers in their honest joy, as we have been!'

'That's rather a chuckle-headed fellow for the girl; isn't he?' said Steerforth.

His final comment—'Daisy, I believe you are in earnest, and are good. I wish we all were!'—is scarcely needed to show what is brewing.

(*Continued overleaf.*)

Aiguille and Tanguille	⎤	For the Proctors
Tranguille and Jorker	⎦	No. Spenlow & Jo
Miss Croodledey Miss Croodledy Miss Croodlejeux	⎱⎰	No. Miss Mowcher.

His first time of getting tipsy.
Description of it exactly.

'A smashing number' was Dickens's comment to Forster on this instalment: 'His first dissipation I hope will be found worthy of attention, as a piece of grotesque truth.' That was written after completing the number on 20 November. Five days earlier he was still in chapter xxiii, turning over in his mind a suitable profession for David. 'I think it is necessary to decide against the special pleader', he wrote: '... I am not sure but that the banking house might do. I will consider it in a walk.' By 17 November he had rejected the banking house 'on account of the confinement: which would stop the story, I foresee. I have taken, for the present at all events, the proctor.'[1] None of this uncertainty is reflected in the summary, which was probably written, therefore, after completing the number. Yet the notes for chapter xxii at least are interesting since they show how consciously Dickens massed his

1. Forster, VI vi.

Chapters xxii–xxiv: completed 20 November 1849

Personal History and Experience of David Copperfield—N° VIII.)

chapter XXII.
Some old scenes and some new faces.

Steerforth's misgivings ⎤ still tending onwards, <u>Miss Mowcher</u>
Em'ly's misgivings   ⎦

<u>Ham</u>   Martha. The girl already lost.
                        Omer. haberdasher &c

chapter XXIII.
I corroborate Mr Dick and choose a profession

Aunt Betsey—Afraid of fire
Proctor's   —Doctors Commons
Chambers in Buckingham Street
Mrs Crupp

Chapter XXIV.
My First Dissipation

Dinner Party
Guests
"A man" &c
Agnes at the Theatre
Amigoarawayso?

---

contrasts. The chapter which opens with Steerforth's misgivings
closes with the misgivings of Em'ly as she sees herself mirrored in
Martha Endell, 'the girl already lost'.

These two complementary scenes are divided by his most irresistibly and powerfully vulgar sketch, Miss Mowcher. She was
undoubtedly to serve with Littimer as an agent of Steerforth's
purpose; but before this could be brought about, Mrs Hill, a
professional chiropodist and manicurist, recognized herself in
this portrait, and instructed her solicitor to protest. Dickens promised that the character should be amended; but he pointed out,
in a letter of 21 December,[1] that this could 'only be made in the
natural progress and current of the story. Even if the next number
were not already in the Press, it would be impossible to be made
there, because the character is not introduced, and the course of

1. *Letters*, II 193.

the tale is not at all in that direction'. He kept his promise: the plan for Number X shows him attempting to make amends there —'qy Miss Mowcher? <u>Impossible.</u> Try next time'—and suc- ceeding ('Miss Mowcher. <u>Yes</u>') in Number XI.

In so far as the summaries provided a record of contents of

Number IX: January 18

<u>No Steerforth this time. Keep him o</u>

Doctors Commons?	Yes
Traddles?	Yes
Dora Spenlow?	Yes
Uriah Heep?	Yes
The Micawbers?	Yes

'No Steerforth this time. <u>Keep him out.</u>' With eleven numbers still ahead of him, Dickens presumably reflected that he must not bring the Steerforth–Em'ly theme to a too sudden issue, and also that the reader might well be kept in suspense. Instead of Steer- forth, he reviews other possibilities, and accepts them all: old themes and old friends are to be kept in mind, and a new episode, foreseen at least as early as Number V, is now begun, David's subjection to the charms of Dora Spenlow.

For this episode Dickens was drawing once more upon per-

chapters, the detail in this number is surprisingly chosen. A guest at David's party, Markham, is recalled in his manner of speech (' "A man" &c'), as Rosa Dartle is recalled by a mannerism in the previous number plan; but the appearance of Betsey Trotwood's husband and his effect upon her are not recorded.

pters xxv–xxvii: completed before 21 December 1849

onal History and Experience of David Copperfield—Nº IX.)

chapter XXV.
Good and bad Angels.

Start from last point, with Agnes—His good angel. Steerforth,
she tells him, his bad

at Papa's agent's—Mr Waterbrook.
Dinner—Aristocracy—Blood
Tommy Traddles.
Uriah Heep and Agnes—told to David at his chambers
sleeps there.

chapter XXVI.
I fall into captivity.

In love with Dora Spenlow
Miss Murdstone, her duenna
all his love
close with Mrs Crupp

chapter XXVII.
Tommy Traddles.

Traddles engaged
His furnishing
His story
Mr and Mrs Micawber.
all engaged to dine with David

sonal recollections. The evidence is contained in a letter written on 15 February 1855 to Mrs Winter, whose maiden name was Maria Beadnell:

> You may have seen in one of my books a faithful reflection of the passion I had for you . . . and may have seen in little bits of 'Dora' touches of your old self sometimes and a grace here and there that may be revived in your little girls, years hence, for the bewilderment of some other young lover—though he will never be as terribly in earnest as I and David Copperfield were. People used to say

to me how pretty all that was, and how fanciful it was, and how
elevated it was above the little foolish loves of very young men and
women. But they little thought what reason I had to know it was
true and nothing more nor less.[1]

But though the account is true, it is not related uncritically, for
it is witnessed by the affectionate yet steady eyes of an older
observer. 'Some beautiful comic love' is a description of a later
scene in the love-making.[2] It is beautiful; but it is also faintly
absurd, and the presence of Mrs Crupp at the end of the chapter.

Number X: February

qy Em'ly to go? <u>No.</u> —<u>Yes.</u>

qy Aunt ruined?—Next time

qy Miss Mowcher? <u>Impossible.</u> Try next

Littimer? <u>Yes</u>
Steerforth? <u>Yes</u>

First chapter funny

Then on to Em'ly.

Gauntlet to society
"Going out with the tide"

Divide last chapter in two

Mrs Gummidge

The number plan shows Dickens divided between the pursuit
of two themes. Should he deal with Em'ly's elopement or with
Aunt Betsey's ruin and its effect upon David's prospects? After

1. *Letters*, II 629.   2. Forster, VI vi.

nsures that the absurdity is recognized. ' "It was but the gentleman which died here before yourself", said Mrs. Crupp, "that
fell in love—with a barmaid—and had his waistcoats took in
directly, though much swelled by drinking".' David protests,
with justification; yet a reader might pause to reflect that love for
the real heroine' would not be related in such a context. Agnes,
moreover, had already been playing her part of 'the Good Angel'
in the first chapter of this number, and was thus placed at the
very beginning in some measure of competition with Dora.

oters xxviii–xxxi: begun 29 December 1849, proofs corrected
fore 23 January 1850

---

onal History and Experience of David Copperfield—N⁰ X.)

---

chapter XXVIII.
Mr Micawber's Gauntlet

M^r & Mrs Micawber
  & Traddles   Glimpse of Littimer
         Mr Micawbers relieving himself by legal
         phraseology
Mrs Micawber's projects
Mr Micawber's letter.   Steerforth

chapter XXIX.
I visit Steerforth at his home, again.

Rosa Dartle.
    "Never more to touch that passive hand"

chapter XXX.

    A loss.   Omer and Joram—lead up.
              Barkis is willin

chapter XXXI.

    A greater loss.   The candle in the window
              Ham comes alone & takes Davy
              outside
        Her letter.
Close with Mrs Gummidge

---

some hesitation he decided that Em'ly should elope now, and
that Aunt Betsey's ruin should be reconsidered next month. If
Mrs Hill and her solicitor had not intervened, Miss Mowcher
might have had a task to perform in assisting Em'ly's elopement;

but though there could be no place for a reformed Mowcher there was obviously little hesitation about using both Littimer and Steerforth.

Before proceeding with Em'ly, the first chapter was to be 'funny'; and what more convenient than to take advantage of the opportunity provided in the last chapter of Number IX and stage a dinner, with Traddles and the Micawbers as guests, at which Mr Micawber should throw down his gauntlet to society. But the number is Em'ly's, and the comedy is interrupted by the Em'ly theme in the form of Littimer entering to inquire for his master. Before the chapter is over, Steerforth himself has arrived with the news that Barkis cannot last much longer, thus providing a motive for David to be in Yarmouth at the time of Em'ly's disappearance. Em'ly will disappear in the last chapter; thus room is left in the second to show Rosa Dartle's jealous love and, more important, to present once more the prophetic picture of Steerforth 'fast asleep; lying, easily, with his head upon his arm, as I had often seen him lie at school'.

When the last chapter came to be written, Dickens decided to divide it into two. A chapter must be given to Barkis, 'willin'' to the end, but 'going out with the tide'; yet even here Em'ly is kept

Number XI: March

Mr Peggotty to begin his search. ✓
Mrs Steerforth. qy Yes. And Rosa Dartle

Miss Mowcher. ✓   Yes
The Doctor and his wife. qy. No
Agnes? qy. Only an allusion
Aunt & Mr Dick   Yes
Is engaged to Dora. Yes (Miss Mills)
Tommy Traddles   qy

What an idle time! What an unsubstantial, happy, fool time! of all the times of mine, that ⟨he⟩ Time has in his there is none that in retrospection I can smile at half so much, and think of half so tenderly!

---

in view. She is seen through Mr Omer's eyes, as pretty as ever, working as well as 'any six', and clinging to her uncle 'tighter and tighter, and closer and closer, every day', but unsettled; and a later scene allows the reader to confirm Mr Omer's judgement from his own observation. This is the preparation for the final chapter in which Peggotty and her brother, Mrs Gummidge and David, are gathered together in the old barge waiting for Em'ly to come home with Ham. The talk turns upon Em'ly and shows Mr Peggotty's unchanged affection for her. The candle will always stand in the window to greet her return, burning as an emblem of unchanging love. Then Ham comes in alone, with a letter which explains what has happened. The light in the last moments of the scene is cast not upon what Em'ly has done, nor upon Steerforth's crime, nor even upon Ham, but upon Mr Peggotty, showing that Em'ly's elopement is to serve as a test of the heart's affections. Anger is expressed; but not shame: what Mr Peggotty is mainly impelled to do is 'to find my poor niece in her shame,'—the shame is hers, not his—'and bring her back'. The heart's affections stand up to the test; the emblematic candle will not cease to burn.

pters xxxii–xxxiv: completed 21 February 1850

sonal History and Experience of David Copperfield—N⁰ XI.)

chapter XXXII.
The beginning of a ⟨pilgrimage⟩ long journey.

chapter XXXIII.
Blissful.

The used-up young friend. Miss Mills—blighted affection. Sings about the echoes in the Caverns of Memory.

chapter XXXIV.
My Aunt astonishes me.

'Mr Peggotty to begin his search': that was the obvious opening for the number following upon Em'ly's loss. The second
memorandum determines where the search shall begin, and the
third finds the first favourable opportunity of making amends to
Mrs Hill. These are the basic materials of the first chapter, but
they do little to indicate what its tone and structure were to be.
A letter written to Cerjat on 29 December 1849, and a passage in
a letter to Miss Coutts written (4 February 1850) during the
composition of this number, show the drift of Dickens's thought
at this time: to Cerjat he wrote:

> I had previously observed much of what you say about the poor
> girls. In all you suggest with so much feeling about their return to
> virtue being cruelly cut off, I concur with a sore heart. I have been
> turning it over in my mind for some time, and hope, in the history
> of Little Em'ly (who *must* fall—there is no hope for her), to put it
> before the thoughts of people in a new and pathetic way, and per-
> haps to do some good.[1]

A full treatment of the moral and social problem of prostitution
would have been beyond the scope of the novel, perhaps even
beyond the scope of the novelist, though Dickens, as Miss
Coutts's principal adviser on the home for fallen women at
Shepherd's Bush, was in an exceptionally favourable position to
study the problem. Besides, as he wrote to Miss Coutts,

> the sad subject . . . is difficult to approach, in pages that are intended
> for readers of all classes and all ages of life; but I have not the least
> misgiving about being able to bring people gently to its considera-
> tion. You will observe that I am endeavouring to turn their
> thoughts a little that way, in Copperfield.[2]

He was not interested in tracing, as George Eliot was to trace
nine years later in *Adam Bede*, how one heedless act of vicious
folly could bring disaster upon the community; but he could
show how the community regarded the act. Em'ly had become
an outcast. There was no question about that. But Dickens, with
his mind on the girls of Miss Coutts's Home, was anxious to soften
the Victorian reader's heart towards such an outcast. Mr Peggotty's heart had already withstood the test, and the reader is
told once more that the emblematic candle 'must be stood in its
old pane of glass, that if ever she should see it, it may seem to say
"Come back, my child, come back!" ' But what of the other

1. *Letters*, II 194.   2. *Coutts Letters*, p. 165.

haracters? Minnie Joram thought Em'ly 'a deceitful, bad-\
earted girl. There was no good in her, ever!' Yet when David\
emonstrated, she 'tossed her head, endeavouring to be very\
tern and cross; but she could not command her softer self, and\
)egan to cry.' 'I was young, to be sure;' is David's comment, 'but\
thought much the better of her for this sympathy, and fancied it\
)ecame her, as a virtuous wife and mother, very well indeed.' As\
o Mr Omer, he 'had taken it so much to heart . . . that he had\
)een very low and poorly all day, and had gone to bed without\
iis pipe'. By contrast, Mrs Steerforth receives Mr Peggotty in a\
nood of stern selfishness and uncompromising condemnation.\
3ut Mr Peggotty is not downcast, and the words he is given show\
hat Dickens shared that unusual power which Jeffrey had\
letected in Scott, namely, the power of displaying the noble\
qualities of humble characters.

Two passages foreshadow future scenes. When David asks\
Ham on what his thoughts are bent, he replies: 'On what's afore\
ne, Mas'r Davy; and over yon.' 'On the life before you, do\
you mean?' David asks. 'He had pointed confusedly out to sea.\
"Ay, Mas'r Davy. I doen't rightly know how 'tis, but from over\
yon there seemed to me to come—the end of it like." ' Evidently\
the main incidents in the storm in chapter lv were already clear\
in Dickens's mind.

The second is a foreshadowing of the melodramatic scene in\
Number XVI (chapter l) where Rosa Dartle pours her re-\
proaches upon Em'ly's head. The scene seems also to have been\
planned long in advance, for when Rosa and David part in chap-\
ter xxxii, Rosa declares that if ever she could reproach Em'ly\
with her infamous condition, she would go anywhere to do so.

Amongst the remaining memoranda it is noticeable that\
though the engagement to Dora is so enthusiastically chosen,\
Agnes is uppermost in Dickens's thoughts. 'The real heroine'\
cannot be overlooked, and the reader must keep her in mind, too,\
if only by 'an allusion'. The 'allusion' comes in the final chapter\
(which announces Betsey Trotwood's ruin), and is ambiguous.\
David had written to her announcing his engagement, and\
remembered

> that I sat resting my head upon my hand, when the letter was half\
> done, cherishing a general fancy as if Agnes were one of the ele-\
> ments of my natural home. As if, in the retirement of the house\
> made almost sacred to me by her presence, Dora and I must be

happier than anywhere. As if, in love, joy, sorrow, hope, or disappointment; in all emotions; my heart turned naturally there, and found its refuge and best friend.

For what part was Agnes destined when those words were writ-

Number XII: April

Agnes. ⟨Her   ⟩   Yes
D^r & Mrs Strong? Yes
Jack Maldon?   Yes.
Mr Micawber engaged by Uriah.

Progress of David to a working state, still tinged, romantically, by his youth and character, and overdone. No similar progr on the part of Dora. Poor little Dora, not bred for ⟨the world⟩ a working life
      My aunt
   ⟨Miss Betsey⟩ "And not silly?"

Express that, very delicately

Carry the thread of Agnes through

After confirming the use of certain characters,[1] Dickens sets out the theme for the number in an unusually long memorandum. Aunt Betsey's ruin in the last chapter of Number XI pro-

1. The form of the memorandum relating to Jack Maldon seems to imply that the decision to bring him back from India was taken in the moment of planning. Compare the form of memorandum in No. XIV where he is not dissociated from the Strongs.

ten? They seem to look forward to David's later discovery that his love for Dora was the 'mistaken impulse of an undisciplined heart'; yet they are not incompatible with Agnes's rôle as the Georgina Hogarth of David's household.

pters xxxv–xxxvii

sonal History and Experience of David Copperfield—N° XII.)

chapter XXXV.
Depression.

My Aunt.
"and not silly?
"Blind, Blind, Trot!"
Agnes
My Aunt's Property
Mr Wickfield and Uriah. Agnes—Blind, blind, blind

chapter XXXVI.
Enthusiasm.

David's New State. Forest of Difficulty
  Glimpse of Rosa Dartle
Bring up Dr Strong and Annie, & Mr Jack Maldon. Mr Dick
                                                    useful
  Mr Micawber "a member of one of the learned professions
I.O.U. Foot on his native heath—Judge or Chancellor. Kettle Drums.
"Walks erect before his
ellow men"

chapter XXXVII
A little cold water.

⟨   ⟩ Poor little Dora
"Oh Take me to Julia Mills and go away, please!"
Taking a Guitar case through the Forest of difficulty.
"I used to sit thinking of it of a night, sometimes,
until I felt quite grey

vides the motive for David to become self-supporting; but even though his resolve leads to little more than a part-time secretary-ship to Dr Strong, what is tonic to David proves dispiriting to Dora, as the conclusion of the number amply shows. The contrast between the two heroines is completed by the part which Agnes is made to play. 'Carry the thread of Agnes through it all' is the direction; and accordingly it is Agnes who makes in the first

chapter the only practical suggestion of the secretaryship, and
who, in a general way, 'was like Hope embodied, to me':

> she filled my heart with such good resolutions, strengthened my
> weakness so, by her example, so directed . . . the wandering ardor
> and unsettled purpose within me, that all the little good I have
> done, and all the harm I have forborne, I solemnly believe I may
> refer to her.

The contrast between Agnes's practical support in the first
chapter and Dora's impractical weakness in the last is strong
enough. But Dickens was not content to leave it so. Agnes and
Dora must be placed in even more marked apposition.

> 'Agnes!' I joyfully exclaimed. 'Oh, my dear Agnes, of all people
> in the world, what a pleasure to see you!'
> 'Is it, indeed?' she said, in her cordial voice.
> 'I want to talk to you so much!' said I. 'It's such a lightening of
> my heart, only to look at you! If I had had a conjuror's cap, there is
> no one I should have wished for but you!'
> 'What?' returned Agnes.
> 'Well! perhaps Dora, first,' I admitted, with a blush.
> 'Certainly, Dora first, I hope,' said Agnes, laughing.
> 'But you next!' said I.

The reader does not need exceptionally clear eyes to see that
Agnes is 'the real heroine'. And Betsey Trotwood sees it too. She
tenderly questions David about his love, makes him reflect
whether Dora is not silly or light-headed; and when David protests that he could never love anyone else or cease to love her,
Betsey Trotwood can only shake her head and smile gravely,
murmuring, 'Ah, Trot! Blind, blind, blind!' At this point
Dickens was forced to cut out in proof a sentence which glosses
this remark:

> whether her tone of pity [he had written] was for me, or for herself,
> or for anybody else, I could not decide—did not ask myself, per-
> haps; but I know that it made me feel uneasy afterwards, and that
> it sounded in my fancy like a sorrowful strain of music I had some-
> times heard at a distance, before that night.

Dickens relies heavily for his pointing upon these musical *motifs*.
Betsey Trotwood's observation, which may be read as a comment both upon David's infatuation and upon his inability to recognize where his heart lay, is echoed at the end of the chapter in

a passage describing Agnes sitting at the window and speaking to
him of Dora:

> Oh, Agnes, sister of my boyhood, if I had known then, what I knew
> long afterwards!—
>
> There was a beggar in the street, when I went down; and as I
> turned my head towards the window, thinking of her calm,
> seraphic eyes, he made me start by muttering, as if he were an echo
> of the morning:
>
> 'Blind! Blind! Blind!'

This is the most prominent theme, and the minor detail stands in
close relationship to it. If indeed Annie Strong represents one
who has withstood the first mistaken impulses of an undisciplined
heart, she is introduced here because her self-knowledge (supported by a visit to Agnes) contrasts with David's blindness.

The introduction of Uriah Heep and Mr Micawber is not inappropriate in a number dealing with Betsey Trotwood's ruin,
even though no direct association is made. Uriah Heep is reported to be increasing his hold upon Mr Wickfield's affairs; and in
preparation for Uriah's eventual exposure, Mr Micawber is
shown on the eve of departure for Canterbury to take up his post
as Uriah's confidential clerk.

(*continued overleaf*)

The Doctor, Annie, and Mr Jack Maldon?

Agnes and her father?　<u>Yes</u>

Mrs Heep?　Yes. Touched

<u>To carry on the thread of Uriah, carefully, a</u>
<u>not obtrusively, also of David and Agnes</u>

Mr Spenlow.　Dead
Mr Peggotty's story of his search.
Miss Murdstone ⎫
Mr Murdstone　⎬　qy　<u>Not yet</u>

Traddles　<u>Next N^o</u>

The two principal chapters, xxxviii and xxxix,[1] maintain the
balance of Agnes and Dora established in Number XII. Ostensibly they deal with two partnerships, the dissolution of the firm
of Spenlow and Jorkins by Mr Spenlow's death in chapter
xxxviii, and the effectual subordination in chapter xxxix of Mr
Wickfield to Uriah in the partnership of Wickfield and Heep.
But the state of these partnerships is, in fact, used to show the

1. It was Dickens's frequent, but not invariable practice, to design his first two
chapters of equal length and importance, leaving the final chapter as a short
appendix to them. The following distribution of manuscript sheets between chapters may be noted: No. II, 13, 12, 5; IV, 13, 10, 6; V, 12, 10, 5; VI, 13, 10, 5; XI,
12, 11, 6; XII, 13, 10, 5; XIII, 10, 12, 5; XIV, 10, 12, 5; XVII, 12, 14, 4.

Personal History and Experience of David Copperfield—N⁰ XIII.)

chapter XXXVIII.
A Dissolution of Partnership.

David found out
Mr Spenlow & Miss Murdstone
Will-making   Two Maiden Aunts
                                    Putney
Miss Mills's Journal. "Self and Young Gazelle. J.M."

chapter XXXIX.
Wickfield and Heep.

Touting in Doctors Commons.
Canterbury. Agnes.
Uriah and his mother. Why "Umble"
Mr Wickfield. Agnes.

chapter XL.
The Wanderer

Snowy night.
Martha.—a shadow of it.
Mr Peggotty.
His travels.
Letter from Little Em'ly. Close with him
going away again—through the snow—hushed.

---

effect upon Dora (and therefore upon David) of the dissolution of Spenlow and Jorkins, and the effect upon Agnes (and therefore upon David) of the subordination of Wickfield to Heep.

The memoranda indicate that this pattern, obvious as it now appears, did not immediately occur to Dickens as he set to work. His first impulse was to resume the Strong theme, but this he set aside. He then passed the Wickfields under review, and having accepted this theme for present treatment, he decided upon the nature of the episode and some of its threads. Mr Micawber was also to be used, but so far as planning was concerned, he could evidently be left to look after himself.

The longest and most detailed chapter is placed at the centre of the number. The memoranda for chapter xxxviii are even briefer, consisting of the single entry 'Mr. Spenlow. <u>Dead</u>'. The careful and ingenious balance of Dora and Agnes in these two chapters would therefore seem to have arisen after planning was complete. It was in the act of writing, evidently, that the detail of his diptych was determined: of Agnes, on one side, in whom David felt 'rest and peace', though he 'had perversely wandered

Number XIV: June 18

David's Marriage to Dora
<u>===================</u>

Back to the Strong incidents, and clear the w

Mr Dick

Clear Julia Mills off

Bring Agnes and Dora together.

'Have begun *Copperfield* this morning', wrote Dickens on 7 May 1850; 'Still undecided about Dora, but MUST decide to-

away from the voice' of his own heart; of Dora, on the other, incapable of mastering her grief or of affording any support or encouragement.

The short concluding chapter gives an opportunity of keeping Mr Peggotty and Em'ly in mind. By introducing Martha Endell once more, Dickens was providing himself with the means of discovering Em'ly in a future number.

hapters xli–xliii: begun 7 May 1850

---

ersonal History and Experience of David Copperfield—N⁰ XIV.)

chapter XLI.
Dora's Aunts.

Traddles & David go to them
Their house at Putney
The old ladies like birds
arranged—Little Dora behind the door
"If I should like a nice Irish Stew for instance.

chapter XLII.
Mischief.

Uriah Heep, jealous of interlopers, works it out, about the Strongs
Old Doctor, generous & good.   Agnes & Dora
Slap Uriah's face   Dora—suppose—to David
Close chapter with Mrs Micawber's letter describing change in Micawber

chapter XLIII.
Another Retrospect.

Let me stand aside, and see the phantoms of those
days go by me.
Licence—dressmaker—Agnes, Sophy, church
Peggotty in the gallery   Dora   Jip
                              House. Aunt don't live with them
          "Are you happy now, you foolish boy?"

---

day.'[1] Neither the number begun nor the decision to be taken is

1. Forster, vi vi.

known for certainty; but unless he had got well ahead of the printer in previous months and had subsequently lost ground, the number must have been the XIVth; and the difficult decision is more likely to have been Dora's death than her marriage to David, which is announced with confidence in the memoranda, a confidence bred by the trend of the narrative in recent numbers. This is the most prominent incident of the number, and it necessarily finds its place in the final chapter. For there was much to be done before the ceremony. There were Dora's aunts to be reconciled to the match, and there was the contrast with Agnes to be maintained. The contrast is carried through by the decision to bring Agnes and Dora together. Not only is the reader intended to see Dora to her disadvantage, but Dora herself is made to recognize it, a recognition which prepares the way for her later recommendation of a second marriage.

Here perhaps is the first effect of the decision to get rid of Dora. But her fate affected not merely the fate of Agnes, but the future development of the novel. Dickens had contrived a number of entanglements: Em'ly has eloped with Steerforth, thus bringing sorrow to her family, and (since Steerforth's intentions are dishonourable) bringing shame and hardship to herself; Annie Strong is entangled in an old love affair, which the stupidity of her mother keeps alive, and which Uriah Heep reveals to Dr Strong in this number; Mr Wickfield and Agnes are entangled in Uriah's web; David is entangled in marriage with Dora, of whose incapacity he is becoming aware. The unravelling of one entanglement will affect the unravelling of the others. Em'ly could become another Martha Endell: Annie could break Dr Strong's heart: Uriah could marry Agnes: Dora could continue to live and make David more and more aware of his mistake. But if one of the solutions were rejected, all would be rejected, since the mood of the novel must be sustained: all shadows must be withdrawn from domestic happiness. Of these solutions one certainly and one probably must be rejected: Uriah, as much as Jonas Chuzzlewit or Carker, is a villain made for unmasking; and an ultimately happy future seems assured for Em'ly at a time when fallen women were being reclaimed at Shepherd's Bush by Miss Coutts or shipped off to a new life in Australia by Mrs Chisholm. If some such reflections as these occurred to Dickens, they would ease his decision to get rid of Dora and determine his interpretation of the story of Dr and Mrs Strong and Jack Maldon. A veil has been drawn in this number between husband and wife, which Mr Dick will remove; and thus the way is cleared for the interpretation, which can scarcely be deferred much longer than Number XV in the interest of David's recognition of his undisciplined heart.

Lastly, Mr Micawber's reserve, evident in Number XIII, has now become so pronounced as to make Mrs Micawber write to David about it. The exposure of Uriah seems imminent.

(Continued overleaf.)

M^r and Mrs Strong. <u>To be adjusted</u>—Mrs Markleham—Mr Jack Maldo

<u>David's Married Life.</u>

qy. M^r and Miss Murdstone? <u>No. consider for next N^o</u>

qy Little Em'ly? And through Martha??

qy My Aunt's persecutor? And any indication of M^r
Micawber in communication with her?—<u>No consider for next N^o</u>

Mrs Steerforth and Miss Dartle. <u>Carry Steerforth through
by means of them.</u>

The contents of this number were largely dictated by the contents of the last. The reader, impatient to learn something of David's married life with Dora, is provided with ample detail of their housekeeping. '<u>Carry through incapacity of Dora—but affectionate</u>' is Dickens's direction; he does not add, '<u>Carry through the contrast with Agnes</u>', though there it is, discreetly maintained:

'I wish,' resumed my wife, after a long silence, 'that I could have gone down into the country for a whole year, and lived with Agnes!'

Her hands were clasped upon my shoulder, and her chin rested on them, and her blue eyes looked quietly into mine.

Personal History and Experience of David Copperfield. Nº XV.)

chapter XLIV.
Our Housekeeping

<   > Mary Anne—Paragon
Ordeal of Servants
First quarrel Carry through incapacity of Dora—but affectionate
Salmon. One pound six.

chapter XLV.
Mr Dick fulfils my aunt's prediction.

The Explanation brought round by Mr Dick
Shew the faults of mothers, and their consequences
"No disparity in marriage like unsuitability of mind and
purpose"—"Saved from the first mistaken impulse of an undisciplined
heart"—"My love was founded on a rock."
all brought to bear on David, and applied by him to himself
old unhappy feeling going
by, upon the wind

chapter XLVI.
Intelligence.

Miss Dartle—<   > Garden seat—Prospect
respectable Mr Littimer, and his account of
Em'ly's having left Steerforth, and why
"Don't address yourself to me"—"Nor to me"—
"You have no mother? It is a pity she would have
been proud of you
closing prospect, and mist like a rising sea. Next
time seen, sea risen.—Then with Mr Peggotty following
Martha

'Why so?' I asked.

'I think she might have improved me, and I think I might have learned from *her*,' said Dora.

But the memoranda show that Dickens's first consideration was to finish off the Strong sub-plot, which he had left so favourably placed in Number XIV. The entry 'Mr and Mrs Strong. To be adjusted—Mrs Markleham—Mr Jack Maldon' precedes 'David's Married Life', though it seemed proper to describe the housekeeping first. The scene is set in the following chapter for a passionate explanation by Annie Strong, not indeed so passionate as Edith Dombey's, though almost equally obscure. But the bearing of the scene upon the main plot is clear and is epitomized in the summary of chapter xlv, written in all probability after the chapter was completed.

The theme of the remaining chapter was determined after some deliberation. The number plan shows several topics being passed under review and deferred, until finally the Steerforth theme is chosen, the pursuit of Martha being picked up as a conclusion which will conveniently serve to open the next number. The summary may have been written after the chapter was com-

Number XVI: August 1

Carry through, the unravelling of Uriah Heep. always by Mr Micaw

Carry through, also, the married life ✓

Dora in declining health. First intimation? Yes.

Little Em'ly and Mr Peggotty. qy. To close the N^o with her discovery? Yes

qy Omer and Joram? No

qy. M^r and Miss Murdstone? From last Number

No.

qy. My Aunt's Persecutor? From last Number

Yes.

pleted, and one piece of external evidence seems to confirm this. No title had been found for chapter xlvi before the manuscript was sent to press, and the word 'Intelligence' is supplied in proof. But the title stands at the head of the summary in the number plan. If the summary, with the title, had been written before the chapter was composed, it seems unlikely that the title would have been omitted from the manuscript.

~pters xlvii–l: written during July 1850

~sonal History and Experience of David Copperfield. No XVI.)

chapter XLVII.
Martha

Vauxhall Bridge
Oh the river oh the river!
Emily will be the means of her redemption.

My Aunt's husband
"This is my grumpy
frumpy, story Trot."

chapter XLVIII
Domestic.

Dora & David again—Page—transported page
    Progress of his mind about his marriage—Tries to "form
        Dora's mind."
David's mind—old feeling—suppose not married—
Dora's illness begun—Jip growing old   Carrying her upstairs

Little Blossom. O what a
fatal name it was, and
how the blossom withered
in its bloom!

chapter XLIX
Mysterious.

Mr Micawber's letter to David—fallen tower
Mrs Micawber's letter to Traddles. Oyster knife at the twins
Mr Micawber contemplating King's Bench
rascal-Heep––Gray's Elegy. Pastoral note.

chapter L.
Mr Peggotty's dream comes true.

Martha takes them to her
    old street—about Golden Square
    Scene between Emily and Rosa Dartle
    "Uncle!"
        covers her face with a handkerchief.

While at work on the number Dickens wrote to the Rev. James White (13 July 1850) '. . . I have carefully planned out the story, for some time past, to the end, and am making out my purposes with great care.'[1] It is difficult to accept the statement without qualification. He had indeed foreseen the implications of Dora's death and much of what is to occur at Yarmouth, but the number plans show that plenty of detail was left to be arranged from month to month. In Number XVI there is ample opportunity for such decisions. Two themes had been specifically deferred from the last number: one, 'Mr. and Miss Murdstone', is deferred yet again; but the other, 'My Aunt's Persecutor', is accepted and dealt with briefly at the end of the first chapter, whose main theme, the pursuit of Martha and through her of Em'ly, had already been determined by the manner in which Number XV was concluded. With this disposed of in the first chapter, the way is open for Em'ly's reappearance, and this also is decided in the memoranda, though without resolving how and where she is to be discovered. A hint had been offered in Number XI of a scene in which Rosa Dartle would load Em'ly with reproaches; yet the entry, 'qy Omer and Joram? No', following directly upon 'Little Em'ly and Mr Peggotty', suggests that Dickens was contemplating her discovery in Yarmouth, or at least bringing her straight back from London; for it must be remembered that Mr Omer was physically incapable of leaving his shop. In the end he decided to stage the discovery in London and to leave the return to Yarmouth for a future number.

Yet though these points required consideration, the number plans indicate that his attention was primarily occupied with other matters. The 'unravelling of Uriah Heep' is to be 'carried through'—carried, in fact, to a point at which it can be completed in a later number; and in resuming 'the married life', a first intimation is to be given of Dora in declining health.

The unusually large number of corrections in the manuscript provides evidence of the trouble Dickens took in adjusting the melodramatic scene of Em'ly's discovery. Nor was he finally satisfied when he sent the manuscript to the printer, for he found several details to correct in proof. Besides some short additions to Rosa Dartle's part, he altered the timing of Mr Peggotty's arrival. In the manuscript Mr Peggotty arrives in time to hear the last of Rosa Dartle's tirade, and waits till it is over:

1. *Letters*, II 223.

Mr. Peggotty waited until she was gone, as if his duty were too sacred to be discharged in such a presence, and then passed into the room.

This was cancelled in proof and the following short paragraph substituted:

The foot upon the stairs came nearer—nearer—passed her as she went down—rushed into the room!

(*continued overleaf*)

Dora to die in this N⁰? Yes. at the end. "I
want to speak to Agnes." alone with her, before dying.

Smash Uriah Heep, by means of Mʳ Micawber.

Mʳ Micawber triumphant. restored to Mʳˢ Micawber's a▮

Brought from last N⁰.   Omer & Joram?   Yes.

Mʳ and Miss Murdstone?   Not yet.

The planning of this number cannot have caused much difficulty. Em'ly's discovery at the end of the last number demanded
that the first chapter be reserved for her story, with a visit to Yarmouth to collect characters for the emigration[1] and to take leave

1. The contemporary reader was not likely to have been surprised by Aunt
Betsey's proposal that Em'ly should go to Australia. The British Ladies' Female
Emigration Society had held their first annual meeting in April 1850. 'It recognizes that a large emigration is going on', wrote a reporter in *Household Words*, 'and
it seeks to provide an agency of moral improvement to the emigrants by establishing
homes for the reception of female emigrants before they leave this country'. Under
their auspices, as many as six parties of young women left Gravesend for Australia

pters li–liii: completed 22 or 23 August 1850

onal History and Experience of David Copperfield—N⁰ XVII.)

chapter LI.
The beginning of a longer journey.

Mr Peggotty's narrative
    Fever—forgot recently acquired language—"Fisherman's daughter
'here's a shell!" / saved by Martha
        David & Peggotty go down to Yarmouth
Clear the way for Emigration   Farewell of old boat
                    Mrs Gummidge

Chapter LII.
I assist at an Explosion.

Uriah Heep's office
    Mr Micawber's letter—revelation—Traddles. my Aunt's
property.
Mrs Heep "Be umble Ury, and tell all!
    Emigration proposed by my Aunt
                restoration of mutual confidence
                            between Mr & Mrs
                                Micawber.
        Chapter LIII.   Australia.
        Another Retrospect.

Three times—White line before each [?]
        Speaks of herself as past.
                            Jip grown old. The
chinese House before the fire. David looking at him
Present little Dora's death, through Jip's Death. David sees him lie
down on the rug, and die—Agnes comes down—all over—

___

of Omer and Joram. The form of the first memorandum suggests

during the summer. It appears that many of them were redeemed prostitutes. One party, whose departure was reported in *Household Words* on 26 June, was described as consisting 'almost entirely of needlewomen, and most of them have been inmates of the "Home", and have received certificates of good conduct while domiciled there'. A 'Family Colonization Loan Society' was inaugurated during the summer by Mrs Caroline Chisholm for the purpose of lending money without interest to these emigrants, and it was in support of this Society that Dickens wrote an article, 'A Bundle of Emigrants' Letters' for the first number of *Household Words* (30 Mar. 1850): money is well spent, he declared, 'in sending a steady succession of people of all laborious classes . . . from the places where they are not wanted, and are miserable, to places where they are wanted, and can be happy and independent'.

a doubt whether Dora's death should be deferred, but the doubt
must soon have been settled by the reflection that a decent interval must elapse between her death and David's marriage to
Agnes in the last number. Her death determined, the most suitable position for it was the last chapter (liii), thus leaving the
central chapter to be filled. But Dickens was already pledged by
Mr Micawber's last letter in chapter xlix to unveil Uriah Heep at

Number XVIII: October 18

To finish from last Nᵒ—Uriah
To bring up—Mʳ and Miss Murdstone?   No.   last No.
The Emigration Nᵒ = Mʳ Peggotty ⎫
                     Mʳˢ Gummidge⎪
                     Em'ly   ⎬
                     Martha   ⎭

                     Mʳ Micawber ⎫
                     Mʳˢ Micawber ⎬
                     The children ⎭

Agnes. Carry through.
Ham and Steerforth. Steerforth in a sinking ship
in a great storm in Yarmouth Roads. Ham goes
off in a life boat,—or with a rope round his waist?—
through the surf. Both bodies washed ashore together?
                                        No.
a mighty wind.

To remember—the last parting—"he was lying easily with his
head upon his arm".

Mʳˢ Micawber—Her "family" and "never will desert Mr Micawbe

Close with David going on a tour abroad.

(Lapse between this Nᵒ and the next)

the earliest possible moment. The appointment for David to meet Mr Micawber was for 'this day week' and therefore could scarcely be deferred until Number XVIII. But there was no need to consider deferment, since the exposure of cunning by Micawber and Traddles, those two innocents in the ways of the world, makes a contrast of mood with the chapters before and after it such as Dickens loves to provide.

pters liv–lvii: finished between 17 and 22 September 1850

sonal History and Experience of David Copperfield—N° XVIII.)

chapter LIV.
Mr Micawber's Transactions

& Mrs Micawber

family.

h Heep's business finished

Micawber arrested—over and over again

Aunt's money recovered. She composed.

husband. "He is gone, Trot. God forgive us all!

chapter LV.
Tempest.

id goes down to Yarmouth with letter from Emily to Ham

storm

wind—The spray—the coming to the sea

town—Flying sand, seaweed—and flakes of foam seen

ck.   Bell   at Broadstairs here, last night. Flying

t, blown down   in blotches.

w him lying with his head upon his arm, as I had often seen him lie at school.

chapter LVI.
chapters here. The New wound and the old

Home to Mrs Steerforth & Rosa Dartle.

"I loved him better than you ever did! I loved him better

than you ever did!" Mother, a mere statue

chapter LVII.
The Emigrants.

Micawbers. Preparation and Nauticality   arrested again   Hungerford

her family   Sunset

Tween Decks

close with Emily & her uncle

The number plan shows two small items to be disposed of before attention could be given to the principal episode, signalized by the entry 'The Emigration Nᵒ'. Finishing off Uriah, recovering Aunt Betsey's money, settling the Micawbers' affairs, and disposing of Aunt Betsey's husband provided enough business for a chapter, which as a chapter of mere business is suitably placed first. The emigration itself must conclude the number. Thus the central chapter is left for the disposal of Steerforth in the great storm for which preparations were made in the first number of all. But an additional chapter was then required, to provide for David's breaking the news to Mrs Steerforth and Rosa Dartle.

No scene in the book was given such careful preparation as the storm scene. The number plan shows the outline of events being sketched on the left-hand side, with a separate memorandum for the detail so frequently anticipated: 'To remember—the last parting—"he was lying easily with his head upon his arm".' Dickens then seems to have turned to the right-hand side to make a note of subordinate details, drawing for them upon a storm which conveniently rose 'at Broadstairs here, last night'.[1] The labour involved in writing this scene is conveyed in a letter to Forster of 15 September: 'I have been tremendously at work these two days', he writes; 'eight hours at a stretch yesterday, and six hours and a half to-day, with the Ham and Steerforth chapter, which has completely knocked me over'.[2] Two days later he told Wills that the 'most powerful effect in all the Story [is still] on the Anvil'.[3] Thus the writing of this chapter occupied at least four days.

Proofs showed that the number would end high on the thirty-second page. Honest dealing with the reader demanded that he should get full measure for his shilling, and the page must therefore be completed. Additions could be made most conveniently in the last chapter where they would cause least disturbance of type. Accordingly no more than one adjustment is made in the earlier chapters (the omission of a macabre detail at the end of the third paragraph of chapter lvi),[4] and the space is devoted to embellishing the last moments of the Micawbers.

1. *The Times* weather reports for 10–20 Sept. record no storms during this period.
2. Forster, VI vii.   3. *Letters*, II 234.
4. Steerforth's body has been covered with a flag—'While I tried to consider what it would be best to do, the wind plucked at the flag, as if it were eager to get underneath and see its work.'

The number ends, as is indicated in the summary, with a last sight of Em'ly and her uncle;

> surrounded by the rosy light, and standing high upon the deck, apart together, she clinging to him, and he holding her, they solemnly passed away. The night had fallen on the Kentish hills when we were rowed ashore—and fallen darkly upon me.

This marks an unusual change of intention, for the memorandum reads, 'Close with David going on a tour abroad'. But the calm, symbolic lights of the concluding picture could scarcely be improved, Em'ly suffused by the rosy expectations of a new life overseas, David returning to the darkness of his widowhood. Second thoughts were best.

(*Continued overleaf.*)

after Lapse—dreamily described—in Italy &c
David to come back from abroad
All his love for Agnes and all her love for him to be worked out

Traddles married, & living in chambers. Himself and his
wife putting themselves to all kinds of inconvenience for her
sisters

Uriah Heep "a Pet Prisoner"—continually singing hymns
and exhorting everybody who visits him—regarded as a model
Penitent—but quite true to himself & exactly the same infernal
scoundrel as ever.

His Mother, ditto. Never were people so "umble".
No. Change that. Let him profess to be
‗‗
        converting her.

Order
Absence
Return
Agnes
Interesting Penitents
Agnes
Visitor
Retrospect

Peggotty. Little Em'ly. The Micawbers

David and Agnes married.
    Close with ⟨   ⟩ a Retrospect
What Dora said to Agnes, to come out <u>at last</u>.

            To bring up.
            ‗‗‗‗‗‗‗‗
        a
Creakle, as ∧ Middlesex Magistrate. remember his son
Mr Mell?
Mr and Miss Murdstone
Janet—Donkeys—Dr & Mrs Strong—<u>Julia Mills</u>
            ⟨order⟩

Transition state	Visitor?
return home? Murdstones? Agnes?	Mrs Steerforth and Ros
Agnes 1	Last Retrospect
Traddles and his wife	
Interesting Penitents & Miss Mowcher?	
Agnes 2. and marriage	

Personal History and Experience of David Copperfield—N°s XIX and XX.)

chapter LVIII.

Absence

His state of mind
  Despondency changed by Agnes—Switzerland
  Loves her and finds dreamily that he has long loved her.

Too late. For he made
chapter LIX.   her his sister! Her, & her
Return.   own noble heart

Gray's Inn Coffee House
unpromising appearance of England

Happiness of Traddles married. Hope for him, after all.

Mr Chillip

chapter LX.

Agnes.   Tells of the Murdstones.

Finishes them

My Aunt (1st time)
The old house
Looking out of a window how he had looked out as a boy
Brother and sister   Agnes mother

chapter LXI.

I am shewn two interesting Penitents

Middlesex Magistrates Separate System
Uriah Heep & Mr Littimer

The Beef & the Cocoa. "Hoping you and your families will
amend & see
your wickedness"!
"Everybody ought to come here"

Mowcher

chapter LXII.

A light shines on my way Agnes—

My Aunt (2nd time) David declares "I have loved you all my life"
  "That only I should occupy this
vacant place"

chapter LXIII.

A Visit

Mr Peggotty. Tells of them all. "That's Em'ly"—Mrs Gummidge
Port Middlebay newspaper. Micawber.   Dr Mell of
Colonial Salem House

chapter LXIV.

A last Retrospect.

Wind up. Julia Mills &c.
Traddles a Judge
Close with Agnes.

Though the last number plan is densely covered with memoranda, it does not reveal all that had to be considered at the last stage. David, of course, was 'to come back from abroad' and 'All his love for Agnes and all her love for him' were still 'to be worked out'; the remaining characters, or the most important of them, were also to be paraded, as in the last scene of a pantomime, to make their final bow; but the stages of deliberation by which the final decisions were reached can only be inferred. The prominence given to Traddles in the memoranda is borne out by his prominence in the text; but though he seems at first to have been given the second chapter, at a subsequent stage (shown at the foot of the memoranda) he was evidently demoted to fourth place before being restored to his original position, where the description of his domestic happiness lends a more hopeful colour to David's prospects on his return.

It appears to have been only at the second stage of deliberation that more than one scene with Agnes was planned. The first stage seems to have envisaged a single episode, perhaps in the penultimate chapter, leading up to the marriage, followed by a final chapter of retrospect in which 'What Dora said to Agnes [was] to come out at last'. But if this inference is correct, the single episode was abandoned in favour of a more gradual process. Two visits to Agnes were then planned, and these two visits were to be separated by two other episodes. Perhaps it was felt that too much intervened between the visits, and in a revised order, enclosed within a box on the plan, this was remedied. It is the second of these visits which leads to the marriage and, eventually, to the revelation of Dora's last words.

Thus the memoranda appear to reveal three stages of deliberation, the essential difference between the second and third being a reduction in what intervenes between the two visits to Agnes and between the second visit and the last retrospect. But it was already decided at the second stage that these three main scenes should be interrupted by principal characters taking their final bow. Uriah Heep and his mother, Peggotty (but surely *Mr* Peggotty is intended), Em'ly, and the Micawbers stand out prominently in the number plan and are awarded two chapters; but several others are canvassed, and only the Dover donkeys fail to appear.

Uriah Heep owes his appearance in a Model Gaol to Dickens's

recollection of an article called 'Pet Prisoners',[1] which he had written for *Household Words*, 27 April 1850, censuring the system of separate confinement at Pentonville and the lavish feeding of the prisoners. The memoranda show that, by the time he had reached the second stage of deliberation, he had resolved to send Littimer there to join Uriah—after being captured by Miss Mowcher—and to put Mr Creakle in charge of them. This irrelevant excursus into sociology recalls an earlier manner, that of the disciple of Smollett.[2] But in spite of this, it affords a racy and economical disposal of four characters.

Although 'Visitor' is qualified with a query on its second entry in the memoranda, the form in which Mr Peggotty, Little Em'ly, and the Micawbers could be recalled admitted little scope for choice. A visit from so important a character as Mr Peggotty was more suitable than a letter, and by this stage he was committed to bearing news of Mr Micawber making good. However improbable this may seem, the tide of the novel was flowing too strongly in favour of retrieving past errors. The venial errors of David and Annie Strong can be retrieved in England; Australia is the place where more serious offenders and social misfits make good. Once the Micawbers are safe on the emigrant ship in Number XVIII, their fate is sealed.

There remain amongst the major characters Mrs Steerforth, Rosa, and the Murdstones. It appears that Mrs Steerforth and Rosa were at one time considered for a prominent position; but in the process of condensation which occurred after the second stage of deliberation, they were allotted a more modest place in the last retrospect. The Murdstones had been kept waiting in the wings since Number XIII, and even at the end their fate is to remain off stage. But just as Mr Creakle is economically recalled to present Uriah Heep and Littimer, so Mr Chillip, an even more remote acquaintance, is recalled to report that a second Mrs Murdstone is suffering like the first at the hands of her husband and his sister. The characters are thus presented at different distances in the final parade.

On 21 October 1850 Dickens reported to Forster that he was

1. Suggested, perhaps, by one of Carlyle's *Latter-Day Pamphlets*, 'Model Prisons', published in Mar. 1850.
2. See below, p. 178.

'within three pages of the shore'.[1] Two days later the novel was completed, and the last chapter, the preface, and a page of errata were sent off to Evans for printing.

1. Forster, VI vii.

CHAPTER VII

The Topicality of
Bleak House

═══

I

NONE of Dickens's novels is innocent of topical appeal. His naturally keen eyes were sharpened by a journalist's training to render his account of contemporary men and manners, and his sympathies were trained in the same school to detect social abuses. In the early novels he followed the practice of his master Smollett and kept shifting his scene to permit the light to play on a wide diversity of experiences. Thus in the first number of *Nicholas Nickleby* we are prepared, by meeting Squeers, for a visit to Dotheboys Hall; but we have already attended a public meeting held 'to take into consideration the propriety of petitioning Parliament in favour of the United Metropolitan Improved Hot Muffin and Crumpet Baking and Punctual Delivery Company'; and later in the novel we are to learn what life is like in a strolling players' troupe. There is no connexion between Squeers's slum and Crummles's more genial slum except that Nicholas Nickleby lives for a time in each—the Company Meeting he did not even attend—and there might have been even greater diversity of scene, if Dickens had acted upon an impulse, after a visit to Manchester, of striking a blow for the cotton-mill operatives.[1]

---

1. Dickens wrote to Edward Fitzgerald on 29 Dec. 1838: 'I went, some weeks ago, to Manchester, and saw the *worst* cotton mill. And then I saw the *best. Ex uno disce omnes.* . . So far as seeing goes, I have seen enough for my purpose, and what I have seen has disgusted and astonished me beyond all measure. I mean to strike the heaviest blow in my power for these unfortunate creatures, but whether I shall do so in the *Nickleby* or wait some other opportunity I have not yet determined' (E. Hodder, *Life and Work of the Seventh Earl of Shaftesbury*, ed. of 1888, p. 120). At the time of writing this letter, he had just completed No. X (chs. xxx–xxxiii), in which

This discursiveness of incident is gradually controlled in later novels, but it is not until the eighteen-fifties that a unifying principle can be detected in these heterogeneous topicalities. As late as *David Copperfield* such unrelated topics of contemporary discussion as model prisons, the redemption of prostitutes, and the treatment of lunatics, can be discovered cheek by jowl. But in the next novel, *Bleak House*, a great and largely successful effort was made to integrate the diversity of detail into a single view of society. The 'Condition-of-England question' was perfectly familiar. It was Carlyle who had raised it as long ago as 1839 in his *Chartism*, and he had recently presented another formulation of it in *Latter-Day Pamphlets*:

> The deranged condition of our affairs is a universal topic among men at present; and the heavy miseries pressing, in their rudest shape, on the great dumb inarticulate class, and from this, by a sure law, spreading upwards, in a less palpable but not less certain and perhaps still more fatal shape on all classes to the very highest, are admitted everywhere to be great, increasing and now almost unendurable.[1]

Carlyle goes on to define two attitudes currently adopted, one being to admit the miseries and pronounce them to be incurable except by Heaven, the other being to alleviate the evil by charities, 'to cure a world's woes by rose-water':

> A blind loquacious pruriency of indiscriminate Philanthropism substituting itself, with much self-laudation, for the silent divinely awful sense of Right and Wrong;—testifying too clearly that here is no longer a divine sense of Right and Wrong; that, in the smoke of this universal, and alas inevitable and indispensable revolutionary fire, and burning up of worn-out rags of which the world is full, our life-atmosphere has (for the time) become one vile London fog, and the eternal loadstars are gone out for us!

There is no need to ask whether Dickens recalled these particular passages. This in general terms was the diagnosis he accept-

---

Nicholas returns to London, after leaving Crummles's troupe of players, removes his sister from Mrs Wititterly's, and establishes her once more with his mother in Miss La Creevy's apartments. In the following number (chs. xxxiv–xxxvi) he begins life afresh as a clerk in the Cheeryble Brothers' counting-house. The originals of the two Cheerybles are well known to have been Daniel and William Grant of Ramsbottom and Manchester (F. G. Kitton, *Charles Dickens: His Life, Writings, and Personality*, 1902, p. 65). By placing the Cheerybles' business in Lancashire and sending Nicholas to work there, Dickens would have taken a satisfactory stance for striking his 'blow' in *Nickleby*.

1. 'Model Prisons', Mar. 1850.

ed of the troubles of mid-Victorian England; and in *Bleak House*
he set himself to translate this diagnosis into the terms of his own
art, choosing individual characters and groups of characters to
represent 'the great dumb inarticulate class', those who regarded
social iniquities as inevitable, and the rose-water philanthrop-
ists; finding symbols in the images of fog and fire; and representing by a plot the way the evil spreads upwards till it impinges 'on
all classes to the very highest'.

'The great dumb inarticulate class' is represented by Jo the
crossing-sweeper, and to a lesser extent by the brickmaker's
family. These are the typical inhabitants of Tom-all-Alone's, a
typical slum. They are the victims of our social iniquities, and in
a different way they are victims of such ineffectual philanthrop-
ists as Mr Chadband and Mrs Pardiggle. The class who admit
that the country is in a parlous state are represented by Sir
Leicester Dedlock and those attending his house parties at Chesney Wold. These Regency survivals are content with their old-
established ways—just as the lawyers are content with their antiquated routine—and are scornful of such men as Mr Rouncewell
who tackle the problem by providing productive work. Fire will
sweep away the confusion of the Law, as Spontaneous Combus-
tion disposed of Lord Chancellor Krook; and Chesney Wold will
slowly decay in the persistent rain. But before that happens, its
secrets will have been found buried in Tom-all-Alone's, for that
is where Lady Dedlock's lover lay and that is where she herself
comes to die. Tom-all-Alone's must have its inescapable effect
upon society; this is as unavoidable, in the present state of affairs,
as the smallpox which Esther catches from Jo. It is not surprising
to find that 'Tom-all-Alone's: The Ruined House' was the first
title drafted for the novel in the manuscript.

The fable has indeed been frequently interpreted, but what
has hitherto been overlooked is the topicality of Dickens's par-
ticularization. This was a fable for 1852, related to a large extent
in terms of the events, the types, and the social groups which the
previous year had thrown into prominence.

II

1851 was the year of the Great Exhibition in Hyde Park. It was
also a time of public anxiety caused by the establishment of
the Roman Catholic hierarchy in England during the previous

twelve months. Dickens was aware of both. As to what Lord John
Russell called 'papal aggression', he seems to have followed the
Prime Minister's lead in blaming it upon the Puseyites: 'if the
Universities', he wrote to Miss Coutts on 22 August 1851, 'had
been forced to adjust themselves to the character of the times,
we never should have had to bless Oxford for the intolerable
enormity it has dug out of the mire'.[1]

The principal representative of the Puseyites in *Bleak House* is
Mrs Pardiggle. Her allegiance is not asserted, but it is clearly
enough implied, in the names she has given to her sons—Egbert,
Oswald, Francis, Felix, and Alfred, the names of saints or heroes
of the primitive Church—and in her custom of pressing her
young family to attend Matins with her '(very prettily done), at
half past six o'clock in the morning all the year round, including
of course the depth of winter'. But she is not the only Puseyite in
the novel. Other suspects are the ladies who pestered Mr Jarndyce for a subscription 'to establish in a picturesque building
(engraving of proposed West Elevation attached) the Sisterhood
of Mediæval Marys',[2] and the ladies and gentlemen of the newest
fashion assembled at one of Sir Leicester Dedlock's country house
parties. Theirs was a 'dandyism' in religion:

> in mere lackadaisical want of an emotion, [they] have agreed upon
> a little dandy talk about the Vulgar wanting faith in things in
> general; meaning, in the things that have been tried and found
> wanting, as though a low fellow should unaccountably lose faith in
> a bad shilling, after finding it out! Who would make the Vulgar
> very picturesque and faithful, by putting back the hands upon the
> Clock of Time, and cancelling a few hundred years of history.[3]

Bearing in mind the terms of his letter to Miss Coutts, we must
attribute this attack upon the Oxford Movement in 1852 to
Dickens's disgust at the establishment of the Roman Catholic
hierarchy in England in 1850. The Puseyites were to blame for
this 'intolerable enormity'.

No one in 1851 could escape being aware of the Great Exhibition, least of all the editor of a weekly journal. But readers of
Household Words could not complain of being satiated with

1. *Coutts Letters*, p. 186.
2. *Bleak House*, ch. viii. The first Anglican Sisterhoods had been founded in the
eighteen-forties. Miss Sellon's Sisterhood of Mercy at Devonport had been in the
news in 1849 owing to an inquiry conducted by the Bishop of Exeter. See H. P.
Liddon, *Life of Pusey*, III (1894), ch. viii.
3. *Bleak House*, ch. xii.

description and comment. The third in a series of articles by Charles Knight on 'Three May Days in London' was devoted to the Great Exhibition, and William Howitt was allowed to describe a 'pilgrimage' to Hyde Park; but when his wife offered an article on the May Festival at Starnberg, Dickens wrote impatiently to Wills (10 August 1851):

> In the May Festival of Miss [sic] Howitt (very good) for the Lord's love don't let us have any allusion to the Great Exhibition.[1]

This is what earlier letters might have led us to expect. He is 'used up' by the Exhibition, he tells Mrs Watson on 11 July:

> I don't say "there is nothing in it"—there's too much. I have only been twice; so many things bewildered me. I have a natural horror of sights, and the fusion of so many sights in one has not decreased it;[2]

and he left Miss Coutts to take the children. In fact, he had always had 'an instinctive feeling against the Exhibition', so Wills was told on 27 July, 'of a faint, inexplicable sort'.[3] Some explanation of this feeling, however, may be found in an article, which he wrote for *Household Words* (published 4 January 1851), entitled 'The Last Words of the Old Year'. The Old Year lies dying; on his death bed he surveys his life, and makes his bequests to his successor. It is a melancholy retrospect. ' "I have been," said the good old gentleman, penitently, "a Year of Ruin".' Farmers have been blighted, and the land destroyed; many valuable and dear lives have been sacrificed, in steamboats, 'because of the want of commonest and easiest precautions for the prevention of those legal murders'; forty-five persons in every hundred are found to be incapable of reading or writing; starving children who stole a loaf out of a baker's shop have been sentenced to be whipped in the House of Correction. ' "I have seen," he presently said:

> "a project carried into execution for a great assemblage of the peaceful glories of the world. I have seen a wonderful structure, reared in glass, by the energy and skill of a great natural genius, self-improved: worthy descendant of my Saxon ancestors: worthy type of ingenuity triumphant! Which of my children shall behold

1. *Letters*, II 336. To complete the tally, mention must be made of two articles by Henry Morley, one on the future of the Crystal Palace (19 July) and one on the Catalogue of the Exhibition (23 Aug.) which was reviewed by Dickens, and one by Horne contrasting the Great Exhibition with the Little (Chinese) Exhibition beside it.
2. Ibid., II 327.   3. Ibid., II 333.

the Princes, Prelates, Nobles, Merchants, of England, equally united, for another Exhibition—for a great display of England's sins and negligences, to be, by steady contemplation of all eyes, and steady union of all hearts and hands, set right?"'

The Great Exhibition, he seems to infer, may encourage, rather than temper, the mood of self-satisfaction, which the mechanical achievements of the age have aroused. In a novel where the life of England in 1851 is otherwise fully represented, the Great Exhibition is deliberately, even conspicuously, excluded.

III

At the end of his survey the Old Year makes some bequests. Not all of them are relevant to this discussion, but a note of prophecy may be easily detected in the following:

> "I bequeath to my successor . . . a vast inheritance of degradation and neglect in England; and I charge him, if he be wise, to get speedily through it . . . I do give and bequeath to him, likewise, . . . the Court of Chancery. The less he leaves of it to his successor, the better for mankind."

The centre of *Bleak House* is the great chancery case of Jarndyce and Jarndyce. Dickens himself had suffered from chancery proceedings in 1844, when he had attempted to stop publication of a plagiarism of *A Christmas Carol*, and had ultimately dropped a chancery suit against the bankrupt pirates. More recently he had published two papers, entitled 'The Martyrs in Chancery', in *Household Words*.[1] Those papers show that he was aware of the injustices of chancery as early as 7 December 1850, when the first of them was published; but they do not foreshadow the treatment of chancery in *Bleak House*. There he complains of intolerable delays and legal obfuscation: the articles revert to a theme which he himself had already touched in *Pickwick Papers*, chapters xli and xliii, and deal with the cases of men who have languished in prison over long periods of years, because as executors they had failed to defend a suit in which another party was interested, or to hand over property of which they were never in possession. His theme in the *Pickwick* chapters, and his contributor's theme in the *Household Words* articles, is long-term imprison-

1. The *Household Words* contributors' book shows that the author, A. Cole, was assisted in the second article by Dickens's assistant editor, W. H. Wills.

ment.[1] It is possible to see how that might have turned his mind
to the theme of *Little Dorrit* or of *A Tale of Two Cities*, but scarcely
to the theme of *Bleak House*.

What had directed Dickens's attention to the Court of Chancery in 1851 was the interest which everyone was taking in chancery that year. The reader of *The Times* who opened his newspaper on 1 January would have noticed a leading article on the
subject, in the course of which the writer remarked:

> We believe that the time is rapidly approaching when the public
> necessities and the public will must triumph over the *inertia* of an
> antiquated jurisprudence and the obstacles raised by personal or
> professional interest . . . the community suffers . . . from a confused
> mass of laws, from costly and dilatory procedure, and from an in-
> adequate number of Judges . . . This opinion has now become so
> strong and universal in the country that active measures for the
> reform of the law . . . are becoming the test by which a large pro-
> portion of the Liberal party are disposed to try the sincerity and the
> capacity of their present leaders. We could crowd our columns day
> after day with the remonstrances which are addressed to ourselves,
> especially with reference to the present state of the Court of
> Chancery.

The words are not such as Dickens would have used, but the indictment is Dickens's indictment. The writer points, as Dickens
was a few months later to point, to the inertia, the confusion, the
costly and dilatory procedure, and (most significantly) to the
vested interests impeding reform, 'the obstacles raised by personal or professional interest'.

In *The Times* of 24 December 1850, there had been an even
stronger protest, and once again the complaint has a familiar
ring:

> If a house be seen in a peculiarly dilapidated condition, the be-
> holder at once exclaims, "Surely that property must be in Chan-
> cery;" and the exclamation very correctly expresses the popular

1. In Sept. 1852, Lord Denman, a former Lord Chief Justice, attacked Dickens
in a series of articles in the *Standard*, which were reprinted as a pamphlet with the
title, *Uncle Tom's Cabin, Bleak House, Slavery and Slave Trade* (1853). Commenting on
it in a letter to Lord Denman's daughter, Mrs Cropper, 20 Dec. 1852, Dickens
wrote: 'The pamphlet . . . objects that I come in at the Death of Chancery and
might have attacked it before.—The most serious and pathetic point I tried with
all indignation and intensity to make, *in my first book*, (Pickwick) was the slow tor-
ture and death of a Chancery prisoner. From that hour to this, if I have been set on
anything, it has been on exhibiting the abuses of the Law.' For the reasons for Lord
Denman's attack see *Letters*, II 445 and note.

> opinion as to the effect of legal proceedings generally upon all property which unluckily becomes the subject of litigation in any shape. . . Success and defeat are alike fatal to litigants.

and again, later in the same article,

> the lingering and expectant suitors waste their lives as well as their substance in vain hopes, and death robs them of their wished-for triumph, if ruin have not already rendered it impossible.

Richard Carstone, Miss Flite, and Gridley, as well as Tom-all-Alone's can there be seen casting their shadows before. Gridley's case is known to have been based upon an actual case in Staffordshire. Forster mentions that a certain Mr Challinor of Leek had sent Dickens a pamphlet setting out its details after the publication of the first monthly number of *Bleak House*, and that Dickens had embodied the facts in a later chapter.[1] Challinor had already drawn attention to the case at a meeting of the Chancery Reform Association on 30 January and *The Times* carried a long report of it the following day. At that meeting a barrister told an anecdote which might have appealed to Conversation Kenge:

> A man young in his profession . . . came to tell his father-in-law that he had at last succeeded in bringing a suit long in dependence to a termination. "You simpleton," said the grave senior; "it was by means of that Chancery suit that I accumulated the money by which I was able to give a portion to my daughter, your wife. If you had known which side your bread was buttered on, you might have made that lawsuit a patrimony for your children's children";

and another barrister reported that in a case where the parties desired to get out at any sacrifice, 20,000 sheets of brief paper would have to be looked over before the estate could be sold.

Thus in December and January alone the columns of *The Times* contain most of the charges in Dickens's indictment of chancery. There was more to come. A new session of Parliament was opened early in February, and in the course of the Queen's speech it was predicted that the administration of justice in the several departments of law and equity would 'doubtless receive serious attention'. The announcement was welcomed; but a week

1. Forster, VII i. The pamphlet was *The Court of Chancery; Its Inherent Defects as Exhibited in Its System of Written Proceedings* . . . By a Solicitor. London. Stevens and Norton, 26, Bell Yard. 1849. Dickens wrote to Challinor on 11 Mar. 1852 sending him a formal 'receipt of his pamphlet and obliging note'. In a letter to Wills of 7 Aug. 1853 Dickens asked for details of the Day case, which had been instituted in Chancery in 1834 and was still incomplete (*Letters*, II 481).

later *The Times* had already heard rumours that legislation might be delayed till the end of the session, although 'the state of the Court of Chancery is an evil . . . of extreme magnitude'. The rumour proved to be correct. Several weeks were consumed in the search for a Prime Minister who would form a government, and when at last Russell was persuaded to resume office he had first to complete the discussion of the Ecclesiastical Titles Bill which the establishment of the Roman Catholic hierarchy had prompted. It was not until the Act had been placed on the statutes at the end of March that Russell was able to propose a measure of chancery reform. At first *The Times* was inclined to welcome any bill which promised to improve existing conditions:

> To the common apprehension of Englishmen the Court of Chancery is a name of terror, a devouring gulf, a den whence no footsteps return. Ask why such a family was ruined, why the representatives of a wealthy man are wanderers over the face of the earth, why the butlers, and housekeepers, and gardeners of the kindest master in the world, in spite of ample legacies in his will, are rotting on parish pay, why the best house in the street is falling to decay, its windows all broken, and its very doors disappearing, why such a one drowned himself, and another is disgraced,—you are just as likely as not to hear that a Chancery suit is at the bottom of it. There is no word so terrible to an Englishman as this. An honest, industrious man . . . will turn pale and sick at heart at the bare mention of Chancery. A suit in that court is endless, bottomless, and insatiable. (28 March.)

But second thoughts were not so favourable. Russell's proposals were discovered to be quite insufficient, and less than a week after its first article *The Times* was remarking that the bill was nothing and would come to nothing. *The Times* was right again, for within a month of introducing his bill, Russell withdrew it in deference to legal criticism in the House of Lords.

A revised bill was not ready until the middle of June at almost the last possible moment before the end of the Parliamentary session. Though the bill was welcomed by Lord Brougham as 'a step—not a great or a long step, but still a step—in the right direction',[1] and though it passed all its readings before Parliament was prorogued in August, criticism was by no means silenced. *The Times*, which was describing the feeling of the public as 'one of angry and restless impatience',[2] permitted itself to adopt a

1. *The Times*, 15 July.   2. Ibid., 4 July.

more sardonic approach to the question. A clever young leader-writer, Robert Lowe,[1] later to become Chancellor of the Exchequer, discovered a chancery suit which had been introduced as long ago as 1815:

> Thirty-six years [he commented] are something in the life of a man, of a nation, of a dynasty, or even of a planet, but in the history of a Chancery suit they are a brief interval . . . a mere decent pause in the slow and stately march by which parties proceed to what, by a fine irony, we are in the habit of calling "equitable relief." When this old suit was new, the counsel who have succeeded to its management were probably babes in arms, and the judge before whom it is heard a truant schoolboy. Since the parties first applied to this dilatory tribunal for the determination of their rights three Monarchs have succeeded to the aged Prince in whose reign it was commenced. . . The occupant of every throne in Europe, and every prominent office in the English church and State, has been changed, but still the inexorable Chancery suit holds on its way, permanent in the midst of never-ending change, the only immutable thing in an era of restless transition. . .

And he continues, in words which bring Richard Carstone to mind:

> It is usual to speak of lawsuits as embittering the lives of those who embark in them; but such an expression does but little justice to the hereditary curse which a suit in equity on the present system hands down to the children who are to inherit it. We leave our suits to our children just as we bequeath to them too often our mental peculiarities and bodily infirmities. The little plaintiffs and defendants grow up for the benefit of Chancery; and she adopts them as naturally as they succeed to us. (14 June.)

Bleak House was not begun until the end of November, though Dickens's letters show that as early as 7 September his 'new book [was] waiting to be born'.[2] By that date, Russell's Chancery Reform Act was a month old; but the public was still critical. Throughout those weeks when the new story was 'whirling through' Dickens's mind,[3] *The Times* kept hammering at the inadequacies of legal education, and at the eminent members of the legal profession who were thwarting legal reform. The opening of

1. *The History of The Times 1841–1884* (London, 1939), II 130.
2. *Letters*, II 341. The first reference to the new novel is even earlier: on 17 Aug. he had written to Miss Coutts, 'I begin to be pondering afar off, a new book' (*Coutts Letters*, p. 184).
3. *Letters*, II 349.

the law courts on 3 November had provided one more occasion for insisting that 'not one whiff of wholesome fresh air has been let into the Court of Chancery and its purlieus'.

Thus Dickens's indictment of chancery was more than merely topical. It followed in almost every respect the charges already levelled in the columns of *The Times*. In both we read of houses in chancery and wards in chancery, of dilatory and costly procedure, of wasted lives, and of legal obstructionists. *The Times*, as befitted a national newspaper, was concerned to report the efforts made in Parliament to procure reform, even while it deplored the delays in Parliament itself. Dickens had no faith in the powers of Parliament to bring any good thing about. He makes no reference to Russell's bills. But the behaviour of Parliament during these months had not escaped him. Some of the most brilliant scenes in the novel display, with evident mockery of Disraeli's manner, a country house party of the governing classes at Chesney Wold. Like their fellow guests the Puseyites, these are Dandies too—'of another fashion, not so new, but very elegant, who have agreed to put a smooth glaze on the world, and to keep down all its realities'. Among them is my Lord Boodle, who 'really does not see to what the present age is tending', who finds that 'the House is not what the House used to be; even a Cabinet is not what it formerly was', and who 'perceives with astonishment, that supposing the present Government to be overthrown, the limited choice of the Crown, in the formation of a new Ministry, would lie between Lord Coodle and Sir Thomas Doodle—supposing it to be impossible for the Duke of Foodle to act with Goodle'.[1]

IV

Lord Boodle was not the only politician to be voicing his discontent with Parliament and Government in 1851. Scarcely had the session opened in February before Russell was defeated and the country was without a government for a fortnight, while first one statesman and then another tried to form an administration. And when a government was formed, it was clearly too weak to last. It is not surprising that Greville should record in his diary that 'there is no respect for, or confidence in, any public men or man' and that 'there is a lack of statesmen who have either

1. *Bleak House*, ch. xii.

capacity to deal with political exigencies, or who possess the confidence and regard of the country'.[1] Throughout this period *The Times* was unsparing in its attacks upon Parliament and Government alike for failing to perform their duties. One leading article in particular has a familiar ring. Lansdowne, Stanley, and Russell, however much they differed in policy, were all 'wonderfully agreed about the very small number of men at all fit, or likely, for power'. Lansdowne in particular 'is so honestly persuaded that orthodox statecraft is vested in a very small clique, that he is convinced it would be a national calamity to let in new hands. His is a wholesome jealousy and depreciation of outsiders. It is the old quarrel between 'the trade' and interlopers, between fully qualified artisans and independent workmen'.

The moral may be taken in the words of Dickens or in the words of *The Times*, for it amounts to the same thing.

> It is an insult [said *The Times*] to a free people and a constitutional State to allege that the faculty of government is confined among us just to a score or two hands. What becomes of all our numerous institutions for self-government . . . if, with all this apparatus of political training, the sacred gift of government, is after all, an heirloom in two or three families? (5 March.)

and Dickens:

> as to some minor topics, there are differences of opinion; but it is perfectly clear to the brilliant and distinguished circle, all round, that nobody is in question but Boodle and his retinue, and Buffy and *his* retinue. These are the great actors for whom the stage is reserved. A People there are, no doubt—a certain large number of supernumeraries, who are to be occasionally addressed, and relied upon for shouts and choruses, as on the theatrical stage; but Boodle and Buffy, their followers and families, their heirs, executors, administrators, and assigns, are the born first-actors, managers, and leaders, and no others can ever appear upon the scene for ever and ever.[2]

Contemporary readers could be trusted with so obvious a reference; and when they reached chapter xl, published in March 1853, where Sir Leicester and his circle comment on the election campaign then in progress, they would readily recall the general election of July 1852, of which Greville considered that the most

1. *Journal of the Reign of Queen Victoria from 1837 to 1852* (London, 1885), III 391, 406.
2. Ch. xii.

leplorable feature was 'the exclusion of so many able and re-
pectable men'.[1]

V

Dickens's indictment of Boodle and Buffy is that they are con-
ent to fiddle while Rome is burning: and *The Times* would have
igreed. On 5 March it declared that the most serious evil of the
political *deadlock* was 'the indefinite postponement or defeat of
various measures of great public utility, but yet unconnected
with the passions, the prejudices, or the interest of political
parties'. A modern reader, recalling the conditions in which the
brickmaker and his family lived and the filth of Tom-all-Alone's,
might ask whether there could have been any more important
measure of great public utility' than a bill for cleansing the
slums. Thinking people in 1851 were fully aware of these horrors.
Dr Simon's report on the Sanitary Condition of the City, presented to the Commissioners of Sewers, was reviewed in *The
Times* at great length on 31 December 1850, and 2 January 1851.
In that review the reader would have learned

> that the main conditions which constitute the unhealthiness of
> towns are definite, palpable, removable evils; that dense over-
> crowding of a population; that intricate ramification of courts and
> alleys, excluding light and air; that defective drainage; that the
> products of organic decomposition; that contaminated water and a
> stinking atmosphere—are distinct causes of disease and death . . .
> that each is susceptible of abatement or removal, which will at once
> be followed by diminution of its alleged effects upon the health of
> the population.

Sanitary reform was not so actively canvassed in the columns of
The Times as chancery reform; but no careful reader could have
overlooked it. He would have been impressed by the resolution
with which Lord Shaftesbury was campaigning for better housing
conditions; he would have noticed Shaftesbury's description, in
The Times of 9 April 1851, of the squalor in the cheap lodging
houses of London, and very probably he would have approved of
the Lodging Houses Bill sponsored on 8 July by Shaftesbury, who
pointed out the consequences of overcrowding in the spread of
disease and the undermining of morality. He would probably
have approved of Shaftesbury's bill, for *The Times* on 6 August

1. Op. cit., III 459.

declared that on sanitary questions there is happily a general
measure of agreement. Perhaps it was because of this general
agreement that *The Times* was less active in pressing sanitary
reform than in pressing chancery reform where there were vested
interests to be overcome; but even so, there was no attempt to
minimize the ghastly truth. In a leading article written on
4 September, when Dickens was meditating his new book, *The
Times* reported as established fact that

> In English towns generally half the attainable period of life is lost to
> all who are born... This loss of life is in no degree attributable either
> to the situation, soil, or climate of a locality, or to the density of a
> population, or to the employments generally prevailing. ... The
> destroying agent is typhus fever, generated by localized filth and
> excessive moisture... Bad drainage and immoderate dampness,—
> that is to say, too little water where it is needed, and too much where
> it is out of place, are the generating elements.

In illustration of those generating elements of typhus, 'localized
filth and excessive moisture', no more is needed than two details
in the description of Tom-all-Alone's and the brickmaker's
house and garden: 'the stagnant channel of mud which is the
main street of Tom-all-Alone's'; and in the earlier chapter of Mrs
Pardiggle's visit: 'miserable little gardens ... growing nothing
but stagnant pools. Here and there, an old tub was put to catch
the droppings of rain-water from a roof, or they were banked up
with mud into a little pond like a large dirt-pie'.

Dickens did not need *The Times* to draw his attention to sanitary reform. The author of *Oliver Twist* knew something of 'the
foul and frowsy dens, where vice is closely packed and lacks the
room to turn'. This was an old campaign of his to which he
proudly alludes in the Preface to a new edition of *Martin Chuzzlewit* in November 1849: 'In all my writings, I hope I have taken
every available opportunity of showing the want of sanitary
improvements in the neglected dwellings of the poor'. The recognition of his claim may have led to his choice as speaker at the
dinners of the Metropolitan Sanitary Association in February
1850 and again in May 1851. At the first of these dinners the
Bishop of London, who presided, referred to plans for the clearance of Jacob's Island, the very slum described in *Oliver Twist*,
and paid a tribute to Dickens who had first drawn attention to
this scandal. But in spite of the general measure of agreement on

sanitary matters discerned by *The Times*, it was not everyone who recognized the need. A few days later Alderman Sir Peter Laurie, the Mr Filer of *The Chimes*, told a vestry meeting of the parish of St Marylebone that Jacob's Island existed only in Dickens's imagination. The opportunity was too good to miss; and having occasion to reissue *Oliver Twist* in a cheap edition the following month, Dickens made a sarcastic retort:

> Remembering that when Fielding described Newgate, the prison immediately ceased to exist; that when Smollett took Roderick Random to Bath, that city instantly sank into the earth . . . I was inclined to make this preface the vehicle of my humble tribute of admiration to Sir Peter Laurie. But, I am restrained by a very painful consideration—by no less a consideration than the impossibility of *his* existence. For Sir Peter Laurie having been himself described in a book (as I understand he was, one Christmas time, for his conduct on the seat of Justice), it is but too clear that there CAN be no such man!

The same Preface also bears witness to Dickens's abiding concern for slum clearance:

> I have always been convinced that this Reform must precede all other Social Reforms; that it must prepare the way for Education, even for Religion; and that, without it, those classes of the people which increase the fastest, must become so desperate and be made so miserable, as to bear within themselves the certain seeds of ruin to the whole community.

This shows that his mind was already alive to the wider issues involved. In his speech at the second Metropolitan Sanitary Association dinner he explored the subject further, and in his remarks can be detected some of the interrelated themes of *Bleak House*. The smallpox infection which Charley and Esther catch from Jo is the novelist's way of expressing a truth already perceived by the orator:

> That no man can estimate the amount of mischief grown in dirt, —that no man can say the evil stops here or stops there, either in its moral or physical effects, or can deny that it begins in the cradle and is not at rest in the miserable grave, is as certain as it is that the air from Gin Lane will be carried by an easterly wind into Mayfair, or that the furious pestilence raging in St. Giles's no mortal list of lady patronesses can keep out of Almack's.[1]

1. *The Speeches of Charles Dickens*, ed. R. H. Shepherd (London, 1884), p. 127:

Mrs Pardiggle visiting the brickmaker and Allan Woodcourt succouring the dying Jo are foreshadowed in the following questions:

> Of what avail is it to send missionaries to the miserable man condemned to work in a foetid court, with every sense bestowed upon him for his health and happiness turned into a torment, with every month of his life adding to the heap of evils under which he is condemned to exist? What human sympathy within him is that instructor to address? what natural old chord within him is he to touch? Is it the remembrance of his children?—a memory of destitution, of sickness, of fever, and of scrofula? Is it his hopes, his latent hopes of immortality? He is so surrounded by and embedded in material filth, that his soul cannot rise to the contemplation of the great truths of religion. Or if the case is that of a miserable child bred and nurtured in some noisome, loathsome place, and tempted, in these better days, into the ragged school, what can a few hours' teaching effect against the ever-renewed lesson of a whole existence? But give them a glimpse of heaven through a little of its light and air; give them water; help them to be clean; lighten that heavy atmosphere in which their spirits flag and in which they become the callous things they are; take the body of the dead relative from the close room in which the living live with it, and where death, being familiar, loses its awe; and then they will be brought willingly to hear of Him whose thoughts were so much with the poor, and who had compassion for all human suffering.[1]

It is interesting to note that during the next two years, while *Bleak House* was in the course of publication, Dickens was himself engaged in the preliminaries of slum clearance by advising Miss Coutts on acquiring ground in a suitable locality for building blocks of flats.[2] On 7 January 1853, he paid a visit to Bermondsey to inspect a possible site adjoining Jacob's Island, and sent Miss Coutts a description.[3] It is not unlikely that this visit served to

---

the point had been forcibly made by Carlyle (*Past and Present*, 1843, III 2) when telling the story of a widow refused charity by the Charitable Establishments of Edinburgh:

> The forlorn Irish Widow applies to her fellow-creatures, as if saying, 'Behold I am sinking, bare of help: ye must help me! I am your sister, bone of your bone; one God made us: ye must help me!' They answer, 'No; impossible; thou art no sister of ours.' But she proves her sisterhood; her typhus-fever kills *them*: they actually were her brothers, though denying it! Had human creature ever to go lower for a proof?

1. Ibid., pp. 128-9.
2. Letters of 13 Jan., 16 Mar., 18 Apr. 1852; *Coutts Letters*, pp. 191-200.
3. Ibid., pp. 219-20.

supply his mind with some details in the description of Tom-all-Alone's in *Bleak House*, chapter xlvi, published in Number XIV the following April.

Even without any external evidence showing that Dickens habitually read *The Times*, the internal evidence would be strong enough. Of the five subjects to which *The Times* kept recurring during the months immediately preceding the inception of *Bleak House*, three take a prominent place in the novel, and one of the remaining two is memorably represented. What is of greater significance is that both the policy of the newspaper and its interpretation of facts are represented without much distortion in the novel. Dickens followed *The Times* in deploring the ineffectuality of Parliament, its incapacity for dealing with the important issues of the day; he shared *The Times*'s view that the unhealthiness of the towns was a removable evil, and an evil which must be removed unless the whole community was to suffer; and he agreed with *The Times* in thinking that chancery reform was a crying need, and was being obstructed by certain lawyers who profited from the existing system.

VI

The characters are no less of their time than the action which they support. Mention has already been made of Mrs Pardiggle, the representative of Puseyism. She and her fellow-worker, Mrs Jellyby, are not the only managing females in the novel. There were also Mr Jarndyce's numerous correspondents amongst 'the Women of England, the Daughters of Britain, the Sisters of all the Cardinal Virtues separately, the Females of America, the Ladies of a hundred denominations', all of them consumed with 'rapacious benevolence': 'excellent people, you know', confessed Mr Jarndyce, in a passage removed in proof from chapter viii,

> excellent people, you know, . . . Mrs. Pardiggle and all the rest of 'em. Excellent people! Do a deal of good, and mean to do a good deal more. But they want one pattern out of all varieties of Looms, they *must* be in extremes, they *will* knock in tin tacks with a sledge hammer, they make such a bustle and noise, and they are so confoundedly indefatigable!

One or two of these women make a more extended appearance at Caddy Jellyby's wedding in chapter xxx, notably Miss Wisk, whose mission 'was to show the world that woman's mission was man's mission; and that the only genuine mission, of both man and woman, was to be always moving declaratory resolutions about things in general at public meetings'.

In no other novel does Dickens make so much play with female emancipation and female management, and perhaps in no other novel could he have used these themes so satisfactorily. Every reader of *Bleak House* can see in what directions the energy of these women might more properly have been turned; but the contemporary reader would have recognized their living prototypes. A few might have seen in Mrs Jellyby a representation of Mrs Caroline Chisholm, whose Family Colonization Loan Society, established in May 1850, won Dickens's support, but whose housekeeping and dirty-faced children haunted his dreams;[1] but more readers would have recalled the failure of an expedition in 1841 to abolish the slave trade on the River Niger and to introduce there an improved system of agriculture. Dickens reviewed the published narrative of the expedition in the *Examiner* on 19 August 1848. The expedition appeared to him an exemplary instance of the type of misguided philanthropy associated at that time with Exeter Hall in the Strand:

> It might be laid down as a very good general rule of social and political guidance, that whatever Exeter Hall champions, is the thing by no means to be done. If it were harmless on a cursory view, if it even appeared to have some latent grain of common sense at the bottom of it—which is a very rare ingredient in any of the varieties of gruel that are made thick and slab by the weird old women who go about, and exceedingly roundabout, on the Exeter Hall platform—such advocacy might be held to be a final and fatal objection to it, and to any project capable of origination in the wisdom or folly of man.
>
> The African Expedition . . . is in no respect an exception to the rule. Exeter Hall was hot in its behalf, and it failed. Exeter Hall was hottest on its weakest and most hopeless objects, and in those it failed (of course) most signally.

The Niger expedition succumbed to fever, the few surviving colonists of the model farm were murdered by 'King Boy', and 'King Obi' returned to his profitable trade in slave selling: Borrioboola Gha failed 'in consequence of the King of Borrioboola

---

1. See 'A Bundle of Emigrants' Letters' in the first issue of *Household Words*, and a letter of 4 Mar. 1850 (*Coutts Letters*, p. 166). See above, p. 166 n.

wanting to sell everybody—who survived the climate—for Rum'. The connexion between the actual and the imagined episodes would have been clear enough, even if Hablôt Browne had not inserted on his cover-design the figure of a woman embracing two black children, and by her side a man who wears a foolscap and carries a sandwich board bearing the legend 'Exeter Hall'.

The moral, as Dickens expressed it in his review, was that 'the work at home must be completed thoroughly, or there is no hope abroad. To your tents, O Israel! but see they are your own tents! Set *them* in order; leave nothing to be done *there*; and outpost will convey your lesson on to outpost, until the naked armies of King Obi and King Boy are reached, and taught'.[1] But Mrs Jellyby did not see her disappointment in that light; we learn that 'she has taken up with the rights of women to sit in Parliament . . . a mission involving more correspondence than the old one'.

The only occasion for surprise is that Mrs Jellyby did not reject the petticoat in favour of the trousers. In the early summer of 1851 *Punch* received the intelligence that an American lady, 'a Mrs Bloomer', had adopted male attire: 'so far so good', was the comment; 'when does the lady begin to shave?' Whether Mrs Bloomer's initiative was followed to any great extent in England is uncertain; but interest was excited, and the pages of *Punch* in the late summer and autumn were stuffed with fantastic prophecy of the 'tremendous accession of physical energy to the ladies if they once get into trousers'. *Punch* foresaw the new garb

1. Lord Denman, in a pamphlet already quoted (p. 183 n.), fell foul of Mrs Jellyby, through whom 'the attempt at commerce and cultivation is to be ridiculed as a wilder absurdity than even the preaching of religion'. In defending himself Dickens restates his moral, but surprisingly and untenably claims that he was 'inventing' the notion of an African expedition: 'Mrs. Jellyby gives offence merely because the word "Africa", is unfortunately associated with her wild Hobby. No kind of reference to Slavery is made or intended, in that connexion. It must be obvious to anyone who reads about her. I have such strong reason to consider, as the best exercise of my faculties of observation can give me, that it is one of the main vices of this time to ride objects to Death through mud and mire, and to have a great deal of talking about them and *not* a great deal of doing—to neglect private duties associated with no particular excitement, for lifeless and soulless public hullabaloo with a great deal of excitement, and thus seriously to damage the objects taken up (often very good in themselves) and not least by associating them with Cant and Humbug in the minds of those reflecting people whose sympathies it is most essential to enlist, before any good thing can be advanced. I *know* this to be doing great harm. But, lest I should unintentionally damage any existing cause, I invent the cause of emigration to Africa. Which no one in reality is advocating. Which no one ever did, that ever I heard of. Which has as much to do, in any conceivable way, with the unhappy Negro Slave as with the Stars.' (Letter to Mrs Cropper, 20 Dec. 1852, in the Free Library, Philadelphia.)

becoming generally adopted; but in the van of the movement was the 'most superior and very strong-minded woman, settling into the forties, and owning to thirty-six . . . full of enthusiasm for "isms", and of scorn for conventionalities', the type of managing female who asserts her equality with the male.[1]

It was not long before Dickens offered his comments. In an article entitled 'Sucking Pigs', published in *Household Words* on 8 November 1851, he showed his strong distaste, not so much for the change of fashion, as for the state of mind implied in the change and for the proselytizing fervour accompanying it. Even if a woman

> chooses to become, of her own free will and liking, a Bloomer, that won't do. She must agitate, agitate. She must take to the little table and water-bottle. She must go in to be a public character. She must work away at a Mission. It is not enough to do right for right's sake. There can be no satisfaction . . . in satisfying her mind after due reflection that the thing she contemplates is right, and therefore ought to be done, and so in calmly and quietly doing it, conscious that therein she sets a righteous example which never can in the nature of things be lost and thrown away.

This article was published a few weeks before the first pages of *Bleak House* were written, and assuredly it expresses the mood in which Mrs Pardiggle, Mrs Jellyby, and their associates were conceived. They did not adopt the bloomer costume, but in all other respects they were enlisted under the banners of Bloomerism. When it came to defining the missions at which they should work, Puseyism lay ready to hand in the year of 'papal aggression' (as the pages of *Punch* bear witness), and though it was three years since he had touched upon the Niger expedition, 'the Nigger question', as Carlyle called it, was still a lively issue, and Exeter Hall with all it stood for was still a powerful force.

VII

Another dateable character is Inspector Bucket, whose identity was soon guessed. The detectives were a recently-formed[2] branch of the Metropolitan Police Force, and Dickens himself

1. *Punch*, XX 220, XXI 168, 192. Mrs Chisholm herself was described by Lord Shaftesbury as having attained 'the highest order of Bloomerism' in that she had 'the heart of a woman, and the understanding of a man.' (XXI 156.)

2. In 1842; see G. Dilnot, *The Story of Scotland Yard* (London, n.d.), p. 207.

had given them ample publicity in *Household Words*. An article of
13 July 1850, on 'The Modern Science of Thief-taking', explained the organization of the branch and described instances of the
detective at work; his duty, it may be noted, was 'not only to
counteract the machinations of every sort of rascal . . . but to
clear up family mysteries, the investigation of which demands the
utmost delicacy and tact'. A fortnight later (27 July), an article
entitled 'A Detective Police Party' recounted an interview in
Dickens's Wellington Street office with Inspectors Wield and
Stalker, and was designed to convey 'some faint idea of the extraordinary dexterity, patience, and ingenuity, exercised by the
Detective Police'.

Inspector 'Wield' was to become familiar to readers of *Household Words*. In Number 18 (27 July) he is described as 'a middle-
aged man of portly presence, with a large, moist, knowing eye, a
husky voice, and a habit of emphasizing his conversation by the
aid of a corpulent forefinger, which is constantly in juxtaposition with his eyes or nose'. (Mr Bucket also was 'a stoutly-
built, steady-looking, sharp-eyed man . . . of about the middle
age';[1] and as to his forefinger, 'when Mr Bucket has a matter of
this pressing interest under his consideration, the fat forefinger
seems to rise to the dignity of a familiar demon. He puts it to his
ears, and it whispers information; he puts it to his lips, and it en-
joins him to secresy; he rubs it over his nose, and it sharpens his
scent; he shakes it before a guilty man, and it charms him to destruction'.)[2] In Number 25 (14 September 1850) his experience
was called upon to supply three 'detective' anecdotes, and in
Numbers 63 and 64 (7 and 14 June 1851) he appears again, the
last time under his proper name of Field, and shows his familiarity with the criminal underworld and his easy jocular intercourse
with its inhabitants. It was therefore not an unwarrantable
assumption that Bucket, so similar in build and manner and so
well acquainted with the warrens of Tom-all-Alone's, was a
representation of Field. But when *The Times* on 17 September
1853, reprinted an article from the *Bath Chronicle* ('A Detective in
his Vocation'), which credited Dickens with making 'much use
of Mr Field's experiences in Inspector Bucket, of the *Bleak House*',
and with being 'engaged in writing his life', Dickens issued a
denial (20 September): 'Allow me to assure you that, amid all the
news in *The Times*, I found nothing more entirely and completely

1. Ch. xxii.   2. Ch. liii.

new to me than these two pieces of intelligence'. Had Pope written this letter, he might have boasted of having equivocated
pretty genteelly. Dickens may have had no intention of writing
Field's life, and may not have 'availed' himself of Field's 'experiences', even though they extended to clearing up 'family mysteries'; but it seems clear that he saw Bucket as Field, and en-
dowed him with Field's peculiar yet limited sagacity, his energy,
his good nature, his mannerisms, and above all with his intimate
knowledge of the haunts of vice. Tom-all-Alone's, which Bucket
knows so well, is a slum overripe for clearance. A similar association of mind led Dickens to think of Field when Miss Coutts was
looking for an appropriate slum to clear; but just as Allan Woodcourt, a doctor, sees the human problem of Tom-all-Alone's
more clearly than Bucket, so Southwood Smith's advice was
considered more dependable than Field's:

> I am disposed to doubt the efficacy of [Field's] peculiar sort of
> knowledge and sagacity in this stage of the matter. A locality
> chosen, I have no doubt that, at a small expence, his assistance in
> the beginning would be of immense service; or, a locality suggested,
> that his observations upon it would also be very important—for, if
> there were a serious objection, he would be certain to know it. But
> the habits of his mind hardly lead him . . . to the present point
> before us.
> . . . Dr Southwood Smith is the man, of all others, to consult first.
> His fever-practice has made him, for many years, well acquainted
> with all the poor parts of London . . . and he knows what work there
> is in this or that place; and how the people live; and how their tene-
> ments are held; and all about them.[1]

VIII

At least two more characters, Mrs Bagnet and Mr Rouncewell,
can be shown to have been in the public mind as well as in
Dickens's mind in the early eighteen-fifties. A brief note in
Household Words on 6 September 1851 had drawn attention to the
difficult conditions in which soldiers' wives were living. Only five
per cent of private soldiers could marry; and if they did, they
received no more than 7s. 7d. a week with no married quarters,
though a sergeant would be permitted to curtain off a narrow

1. *Coutts Letters*, pp. 191–2. Letter of 13 Jan. 1852, written during the composition
of *Bleak House*, No. I.

space from the public dormitory for himself and his wife. The
contributor of this note was herself the wife of an officer. In
twenty years' experience of her husband's regiment, she could
not single out three respectable women, for in such conditions
only 'a will strong in virtue can set temptation at naught'. These
then were the conditions in which Mrs Bagnet had learned to
practise her virtues, conditions which had recently been brought
to light in Dickens's own journal.

Mrs Rouncewell's eldest son was a manufacturer whose sturdy
independence we are asked to admire. Some trade he needs must
practise, but Dickens seems not to have chosen haphazardly in
making him an ironmaster. It is possible that he had been reading
The Times reports of the ironmasters' quarterly meetings at Dud-
ley. Those were difficult days in the iron trade, for the demand
for iron was much reduced; but the action of the ironmasters was
exemplary, as *The Times* showed in its report on 29 March 1851:

> A reduction of make, or a reduction of wages, [was] suggested, but
> [either way] the work people must be the sufferers. The ironmasters
> of South Staffordshire are, and ever have been, particularly
> anxious not to curtail the employment or reduce the remuneration
> of their men; to such an extent has this considerate feeling been
> exhibited that many works have been carried on which, if profit
> only had entered into the masters' minds would have been closed,
> for the purpose of giving employment and support to the neigh-
> bouring population.

Whether or not this report had caught his eye, Dickens knew the
ironmasters and respected them. Having occasion, a year later,
to advise Miss Coutts where to send her 'suggestion-paper' on
slum clearance and the principles of building a model community, he recommended the 'large ironmasters—of whom there are
some notable cases—who have proceeded on the self-supporting
principle, and have done wonders with their workpeople'.[1] It
seems probable, therefore, that when Dickens was deciding what
trade Mr Rouncewell should practise, he recollected the behaviour of a large group of manufacturers which he could whole-
heartedly admire.

1. 18 Apr. 1852; *Coutts Letters*, p. 199.

IX

As in *Martin Chuzzlewit*, *Little Dorrit*, and other novels, so in *Bleak House* there are certain indications that Dickens intended to place the action at a greater distance in time. Thus it has been observed that for the details of chancery procedure he was drawing upon his memories of his career as a reporter in the Lord Chancellor's court in the late 'twenties, that the Spanish refugees who were neighbours of Harold Skimpole in Somers Town (chapter xliii) were known to be living there at much the same period;[1] and that Esther wrote the last section of her narrative 'full seven years' after the story was ended.[2] Contemporary readers who were well acquainted with chancery procedure might be trusted to note the discrepancies between chancery as it had been and chancery as it then was; but it is safe to say that the majority would fail to notice them and that Dickens himself can never have intended them to be used in evidence of the date of the action. He was content to draw upon his memory of chancery procedure without reflecting, or perhaps even caring, whether in every respect his knowledge was up to date. Nor are those 'full seven years' to be taken at their face value, for he is repeating once more the device, already used at the end of *Dombey and Son* and *David Copperfield*, of distancing the action of the story in time so as to emphasize the calm of mind which rewards the surviving actors.

More difficult to reconcile is the appearance of the Spanish refugees,[3] and the description (chapter lv) of preparations for the coming of the railways to Lincolnshire, where at the time of the action no railways evidently existed. But neither of these isolated references is enough to counteract the strong flavour of contemporaneity in the action and in the characters. *Bleak House* began as a tract for the times, and the more fully this is recognized, the more fully we shall appreciate the 'esemplastic power' which imposed upon a mass of seemingly heterogeneous material a significant and acceptable form.

1. The Dickens family also was living in Somers Town (No. 13 Johnson Street) from July 1824 till January 1829 (Kitton, op. cit., p. 19 n.)

2. The case is argued by Humphry House in *The Dickens World* (London, 1941), pp. 30–3.

3. Though Dickens could have recalled them from his boyhood recollections of that district of London, it seems possible that his memory was stimulated by reading Carlyle's *Life of Sterling* (1851), where they are described in Part 1, ch. ix.

CHAPTER VIII

Hard Times: The Problems
of a Weekly Serial

I

HOUSEHOLD WORDS had been running for some eighteen months when *Bleak House* was completed at the end of August 1853. While Dickens was engaged with his book he had no time to write anything for his magazine more substantial than articles; but once the book was out of the way, he could listen to the persuasions of Forster, Bradbury and Evans, and Wills. 'There is such a fixed idea on the part of my printers and copartners in *Household Words*, that a story of me, continued from week to week, would make some unheard of effect with it that I am going to write one'; so he told Miss Coutts on 23 January 1854.[1] The decision had been taken some time earlier, however. On 20 January he sent Forster a list of fourteen titles for 'the *Household Words* story', begging him to look at them 'between this and two o'clock or so, when I will call. It is my usual day, you observe, on which I have jotted them down—Friday! It seems to me that there are three very good ones among them. I should like to know whether you hit upon the same.'[2] Though he had not yet set himself to write, it would seem that he had already discussed the theme of the novel with Forster; for if he had not, he could scarcely have expected Forster to choose between titles for a single story so strictly committing as these: *According to Cocker, Prove it, Stubborn Things, Mr Gradgrind's Facts, The Grindstone, Hard Times, Two and Two are Four, Something Tangible, Our Hardheaded Friend, Rust and Dust, Simple Arithmetic, A Matter of Calculation, A Mere Question of Figures, The Gradgrind Philosophy.*

1. *Letters,* II 537.   2. Ibid.

These rejected titles and those in the manuscript—*Fact,
Hard-headed Gradgrind, Hard Heads and Soft Hearts, Heads and Tales,
Black and White*—remain of interest, since they seem to indicate
the limits within which the book would move. The irony implicit
in *Something Tangible, A Matter of Calculation,* and *A Mere Question
of Figures* suggests that the novel will open up areas of experience
beyond the reach of Mr Gradgrind's philosophy, and the importance of feelings, disregarded by the political economists, is represented in *Hard Heads and Soft Hearts,* while *Heads and Tales*
seems to forecast the opposition of fact and fancy so prominent in
the scenes at Sleary's Circus troupe. These titles show that the
story would appropriately appear in the columns of *Household
Words,* whose policy Dickens had defined in an initial address
(30 March 1850):

> . . . No mere utilitarian spirit, no iron binding of the mind to grim
> realities, will give a harsh tone to our *Household Words.* In the
> bosoms of the young and old, of the well-to-do and of the poor, we
> would tenderly cherish that light of Fancy which is inherent in the
> human breast; which, according to its nurture, burns with an
> inspiring flame, or sinks into a sullen glare, but which (or woe betide
> that day!) can never be extinguished.

The same day on which he consulted Forster about the title,
Dickens sat down to plan the book. On a sheet of paper preserved
in the manuscript he wrote first the date and then a memorandum on quantity, which reads as follows:

> One sheet (16 pages of Bleak House) will make 10 pages and a
> quarter of Household Words. Fifteen pages of my writing, will
> make a sheet of Bleak House.
> A page and a half of my writing, will make a page of Household
> Words.
> The Quantity of the story to be published weekly, being about
> five pages of Household Words, will require about seven pages and
> a half of my writing.

and at the head of the first number plan he has, subsequently,
written:

> Write and calculate the story in the old monthly N^os.

These calculations conceal the real difficulty. They amount to
saying that one monthly number is the equivalent of four week-
lies; but they do not emphasize that the weekly number is now

the unit, and that within its brief limits characters must be presented, background sketched, and atmosphere created. A monthly number of thirty-two pages had been a convenient unit for two or three episodes; one or two episodes had now to be related in the equivalent of eight pages. It is no wonder that Dickens found himself hampered. In February he wrote to Forster:

> The difficulty of the space is CRUSHING. Nobody can have an idea of it who has not had an experience of patient fiction-writing with some elbow-room always, and open places in perspective. In this form, with any kind of regard to the current number, there is absolutely no such thing.[1]

The sense of this restriction never left him: 'I am in a dreary state,' he told Wills on 18 April, 'planning and planning the story of *Hard Times* (out of materials for I don't know how long a story)'[2] and in the end he was forced to enlarge his weekly stints to ten pages of his manuscript.[3]

But though the difficulties of the weekly number exasperated him, and though there is reason to suppose that some material was forcibly excluded, there is no doubt that Dickens was able to adapt his manner to the new conditions, and it might be argued that the discipline was good for him. The necessary shortness of the chapters is matched by an economy in detail, noticeable throughout the novel and especially obvious if the opening chapters of *Hard Times* are compared with the opening chapters of *Bleak House*. It is appropriate, no doubt, that the symbolical fog of *Bleak House* should be more leisurely presented than the symbolical fact of *Hard Times*; but it is difficult to believe that in any monthly novel Dickens would have been content with those mere eight but sufficient words which set the scene, 'a plain, bare, monotonous vault of a schoolroom'. The initial description of Mr Gradgrind's square appearance is conveyed in a traditional manner, but it is considerably shorter than the initial descriptions of Sir Leicester Dedlock and Mr Tulkinghorn in *Bleak House*, chapter ii; and more remarkable still, both in economy and in power, is the symbolically contrasting appearance of Sissy Jupe and Bitzer as the sunlight plays upon them:

> whereas the girl was so dark-eyed and dark-haired, that she seemed to receive a deeper and more lustrous color from the sun, when it shone upon her, the boy was so light-eyed and light-haired that the

1. *Letters*, II 543.   2. Ibid., 551.   3. See below, p. 216, n. 2.

self-same rays appeared to draw out of him what little color he ever possessed. His cold eyes would hardly have been eyes, but for the short ends of lashes which, by bringing them into immediate contrast with something paler than themselves, expressed their form. His short-cropped hair might have been a mere continuation of the sandy freckles on his forehead and face. His skin was so unwholesomely deficient in the natural tinge, that he looked as though, if he were cut, he would bleed white.

It is not merely that Bitzer's body has been deprived by Coketown smoke of the life-giving sun, or that his mind has been repressed by a lifeless education, but that he is emptier and shallower than Sissy; there is no depth to him. The monthly novels are not without comparable moments. The juxtaposition of Miss Flite and the young wards at the end of *Bleak House*, chapter iii, is equally well contrived, she suitably enough at the *bottom* of the steep, broad flight of stairs, they looking down upon her, and her words are equally powerful to suggest more than they say,

> 'Youth. And hope. And beauty. And Chancery. And Conversation Kenge! Ha! Pray accept my blessing!'

This, however, is only a small part of a much larger episode. It lacks the rounded completeness of the scene in *Hard Times*.

But though Dickens recognized how his manner required adapting to weekly presentation, he was also determined to 'write and calculate the story in the old monthly N^{os}'. This is shown not only by the memorandum but by the whole appearance of the manuscript. In it the novel is divided into five monthly parts, each separately foliated as his custom was when writing a monthly serial, and each represented by a separate number plan. The first of these makes clear that after deciding what shall happen during the month he arranged this material in chapters before distributing the chapters into weekly issues. He evidently felt the need to see these chapters grouped into units larger than a weekly number, even though the monthly unit could not force itself upon the reader's attention and might not even be apparent to him. These larger monthly units would serve as stages by which to measure the progress made and the distance still to be covered. Thus the opening words of chapter viii, the last of the first monthly 'part'—'Let us strike the key-note again, before pursuing the tune'—seem to indicate that the exposition is completed; and the ending of the second 'part' with Louisa Grad-

grind's marriage to Bounderby, the third with Stephen Blackpool leaving Coketown, and the fourth with the breakdown of
Louisa's marriage, all mark important stages completed in the
development of the story.

Though the reader may appreciate the completion of the stage
without observing that a monthly 'part' is completed also, his
attention is called to still larger movements in the story by the
division of the novel into 'books'. The device had frequently been
used since its adoption from the epic by Fielding in *Joseph
Andrews*. But Dickens had not hitherto employed it.[1] Perhaps he
had taken notice of Thackeray's refinement in *Esmond* (1852) of
not merely numbering his books, as the custom was, but of nam-
ing them. The second number plan of *Hard Times* shows him con-
sidering this device ('republish in 3 books? / 1. Sowing / 2. Reaping / 3. Garnering'). By then it was perhaps too late to adopt it in
serial publication: we do not know whether the first weekly issue,
without an indication of book number, was already in print when
the second monthly 'part' was under consideration. But the
notion was kept in mind, and when the novel was reissued in
volume form it was divided into books with the titles already
determined, the divisions coinciding with what had been the
end of the second and fourth monthly 'parts'.

Of earlier novels, only *Dombey and Son* lends itself to a similar
division, with well-marked stages reached at the end of Number
V (the death of Paul), Number X (Mr Dombey's second marriage), and Number XV (the flight of Florence). But from *Hard
Times* onwards each novel, except for *Edwin Drood*, is divided into
books even in the serial issues. This is further evidence of the
attention which Dickens was now paying to construction. He was
quite justified in telling Carlyle that *Hard Times* was 'constructed
. . . patiently, with a view to its publication altogether in a compact cheap form'.[2]

II

Dickens's first purpose was to establish the dominion of Fact
and of its high priest, Mr Gradgrind. The draft titles show that
Mr Gradgrind was to be the representative of a theory. It is therefore appropriate that he should first appear in his own school

1. Except in the serial version of *Oliver Twist*, of which ch. xxii in Part XI is num-
bered the first of the Second Book. The book-division of this novel was abandoned
in the first 'volume' edition.   2. *Letters*, II 567.

impressing his theories upon the rising generation, who will show the effect of his teaching as the story develops.

Although Dickens had settled upon the name, opinions, and perhaps the nature of his principal character before beginning to write, he was still undetermined about his supporters. Mr Gradgrind was to have two children—the first number plan specifies 'Louisa Gradgrind' and 'Young Thomas'—who would doubtless exist to disappoint him in different ways; but whether his wife was still alive was not yet decided. Dickens was evidently tempted to produce another repellent widower with a sister in attendance, as Miss Murdstone had attended upon Mr Murdstone, and Mrs Chick upon Mr Dombey. The number plan shows his purpose settling: 'Mrs. Gradgrind—or Miss? Wife or Sister? Wife.' Having fixed upon that, he turned to consider the remainder of the household: 'Any little Gradgrinds?

Say 3.   Adam Smith ⎫
          Malthus   ⎬   no parts to play'
          Jane   ⎭

Jane Gradgrind is later to play a small, yet not unimportant, part; and Mrs Gradgrind is to become one more of Dickens's ineffectual mothers, closer in type to Mrs Matthew Pocket in the future than to Mrs Nickleby in the past. Her entry is carefully timed—postponed from chapter iii ('Mrs. Gradgrind—badly done transparency, with not enough light behind it. No not yet') to chapter iv ('Now, Mrs. Gradgrind'). No member of his household could have had less effect upon Mr Gradgrind or upon his children, and that was perhaps the reason that she displaced the sister in Dickens's choice: she serves to emphasize more powerfully than any sister that Mr Gradgrind alone influenced the course of his children's career.

Gradgrind is to be recognized not only in his house and family, but also by the company he keeps. He is seen in school with a representative of the Department of Practical Art, who in his determination to remove flowers from the design of carpets and foreign birds and butterflies from the design of crockery, is as anxious as Gradgrind to submit the imagination to the chains of fact and real circumstance. But the representative of the Department of Practical Art has served a limited purpose by the end of chapter ii, and no more is seen of him.[1]

1. See further K. J. Fielding, 'Charles Dickens and the Department of Practical Art', *Modern Language Review*, xlviii (1953), 270–7.

Much more prominent among Gradgrind's friends is Josiah
Bounderby, for whose appearance the reader's expectations are
raised at the end of the first weekly number (chapter iii). 'What
would Mr. Bounderby say?' cried Mr Gradgrind on finding
his elder children peeping through a hole in the circus tent. But
Dickens himself had not pronounced the name with equal confidence when meditating his number: "What will Mr. Bound
say?" is the version on the number plan (and in the manuscript
of chapter iii), subsequently altered to 'Bounder' and finally to
'Bounderby'. Dickens may already have known his man; certainly the very next entry on the number plan shows that he
knew what parts he was to play ('Mr. Bounderby, the Bully of
humility. Dawn of Bounderby and Louisa'), and in their partnership Gradgrind supplies the ethos of heartless calculation in
which Bounderby can oppress the Coketown operatives; but the
momentary hesitation over his name shows that Bounderby was
not so prominent in Dickens's scheme as Gradgrind.

A final entry on the first number plan points to Gradgrind's
third associate: 'The man who, being utterly sensual and careless, comes to very much the same thing in the end as the Gradgrind school? Not yet.' This was James Harthouse, who is not
introduced until the third month. He is a young man of good
family who had found army and diplomatic life a bore, and had
now been persuaded by an elder brother in Parliament to 'go in'
for statistics, make a place for himself amongst the 'hard Fact
fellows', and canvass one of the industrial seats. Finding Coketown as much of a bore as the army and the diplomatic service, he
whiles away his time there by attempting to seduce Louisa
Bounderby. If Dickens had already foreseen this rôle, it is surprising that he should have contemplated introducing Harthouse in the first month, since he could not perform his function
in the plot until Bounderby and Louisa were married. A possible
explanation is that Dickens, with his mind on the fable, needed
Harthouse as a supporter to Gradgrind; but recognizing that
Harthouse could best be employed as a seducer of Louisa, he permitted the requirements of the fable to give place temporarily to
the requirements of the plot.

Bounderby also has his supporter. Just as Captain Cuttle is
incomplete without Mrs MacStinger and Captain Bunsby, and
Mr Toots without the Game Chicken, so Bounderby is incomplete without Mrs Sparsit. The distance he has reached from the

humblest origins, born in a ditch and abandoned by his mother, is most readily measured by his now employing as a housekeeper this lady of seemingly the highest family connexions. But Mrs Sparsit's aristocratic connexions are of doubtful authenticity, and so are Bounderby's origins. The reader is left to guess this and merely to suspect that the eminently respectable countrywoman, Mrs Pegler, is betraying a suspiciously maternal interest in a most unlovable mill-owner. Dickens is already preparing the ground for the scene of Bounderby's exposure, or rather of his deflation, for at his first appearance he is seen to have

> a great puffed head and forehead, swelling veins in his temples, and such a strained skin to his face that it seemed to hold his eyes open, and lift his eyebrows up. A man with a pervading appearance on him of being inflated like a balloon, and ready to start.[1]

But though all but the most unsophisticated reader can see that a rich retribution is in store for Bounderby, this assumption of humility on his part and of gentility on Mrs Sparsit's serves a more immediate purpose. Here at the very centre of the dominion of Fact are people indulging in Fancy, a peculiarly repulsive Fancy maybe, but Fancy still. Here, in the punning of one of the rejected titles, is a man proud of his head but flourishing his tale. This apposition of Fact and Fancy is forcibly presented throughout the first three weekly parts. The young Gradgrinds have been brought up on Fact, but when we first meet them they are contriving to satisfy their starved Fancy by peeping through a hole in a circus tent. Coketown too is 'Fact, fact, fact, everywhere in the material aspect of the town; fact, fact, fact, everywhere in the immaterial'; but in an obscure corner of Coketown, Fancy is ensconced in the shape of a circus. The district is so obscure that Mr Gradgrind and Mr Bounderby, like two evil characters in *The Pilgrim's Progress*, do not know where to find it and are forced to enlist the help of the clown's daughter. The circus people are lodged at an inn named, in a suitable frolic of Fancy, the Pegasus's Arms, and are expert in all sorts of fanciful behaviour, in dancing upon rolling casks, standing upon bottles, catching knives and balls, twirling hand-basins, and dancing upon the slack wire and the tight-rope. But for all that they are the salt of the earth:

> there was a remarkable gentleness and childishness about these

1. Ch. iv.

people, a special inaptitude for any kind of sharp practice, and an untiring readiness to help and pity one another, deserving often of as much respect, and always of as much generous construction, as the every-day virtues of any class of people in the world.

And their leader, Mr Sleary, has a philosophy adapted to the world of Fancy just as Mr Gradgrind's is adapted to the world of Fact:

> 'People must be amuthed, Thquire, thomehow,' continued Sleary, rendered more pursy than ever, by so much talking; 'they can't be alwayth a working, nor yet they can't be alwayth a learning. Make the betht of uth; not the wurtht. I've got my living out of the horthe-riding all my life, I know; but I conthider that I lay down the philothophy of the thubject when I thay to you, Thquire, make the betht of uth: not the wurtht!'[1]

This is the milieu from which Sissy comes to be an inmate of the Gradgrind household, there to be educated in Mr Gradgrind's system. It is some measure of the man's inherent goodness that he receives her as an inmate. He is redeemable, and the course of the novel shows that he will be redeemed by Sissy. He fails to educate her head, but she succeeds in educating his heart.

III

Within a week of setting to work, Dickens had paid a visit to Preston. The Lancashire towns had been suffering from a succession of strikes, and *The Times* had kept its readers fully informed about them by frequent reports, leading articles, and correspondence. The Preston strike, which had begun in the summer, had been especially stubborn. Forster relates that the choice of subject for *Hard Times* made Dickens anxious to observe it at first hand; but he was disappointed, and reported to Forster 'I am afraid I shall not be able to get much here'.[2] If his intention had ever been to introduce a strike into the novel, he changed his mind and recorded his resolution in a letter (21 April) to Mrs Gaskell, who was also at work on an industrial novel and interested in avoiding an overlap:

> I have no intention of striking. The monstrous claims at domination made by a certain class of manufacturers, and the extent to which

1. Ch. vi. 2. *Letters*, II 538.

the way is made easy for working men to slide down into discontent under such hands, are within my scheme; but I am not going to strike.[1]

If a strike was ever entertained, the decision not to strike must have been taken early. The only position for a strike in the novel as we have it would have been in the second or the third month; a strike could have made no difference to the course of the plot or to the relations of the principal characters; but the number plans never canvass the possibility. They are not even concerned with industrial unrest. 'Mill Pictures' are indeed mentioned, and Bounderby's slander upon the operatives is rehearsed ('Turtle and Venison & a gold spoon. "That's what the Hands want Sir!"' —'); but the subject of principal importance here is 'Law of Divorce' and the name of the sufferer, first 'John Prodge?' then in succession 'Stephen? George? old Stephen?' and eventually, the notion of martyrdom winning approval, 'Stephen Blackpool'. Another memorandum keeps Harthouse in mind but still defers his entry ('Man of N° 1?—Not yet'). These are the principal memoranda; the others remind him to 'carry on' Tom, Louisa, and Sissy, the last designated as 'Power of affection'.

The weekly numbers in the second month confirm this impression. Four of the eight chapters, ix, xiv, and the whole of the eighth weekly number, are devoted to the children: Sissy, a mere child in matters of political economy and statistics but uttering such wisdom as is given only to babes and sucklings, and ingratiating herself so effectively with the family that Mr Gradgrind, though disappointed in her development, freely admits that she is 'an affectionate, earnest, good young woman—and—and we must make that do'; Tom selfishly pressing Louisa upon Bounderby; Louisa coldly accepting Bounderby's proposal made through her father, and eliciting from Sissy a look of wonder, pity, sorrow, and doubt.

The remaining four chapters 'open the Law of Divorce', in the words of the number plan.[2] The Matrimonial Causes Act came

1. *Letters*, II 554.

2. The subject was topical. In 1853 a Royal Commission had reported on the Ecclesiastical Courts, one of whose functions was to try divorce petitions before their submission to Parliament, and had recommended transferring their functions to other bodies. A second reading was given in the House of Lords to a Divorce and Matrimonial Causes Bill on 13 June 1854, seven weeks after Dickens's fifth weekly number where the Law of Divorce was 'opened'. In the Debate the Lord Chancellor admitted that Divorce on other grounds than adultery had been suggested in

into force three years after the novel was written, and permitted a husband to obtain a decree in a divorce court on the ground of his wife's adultery. Hitherto a divorce could only be obtained by Act of Parliament, and was therefore so expensive as to lie beyond a poor man's reach: Bounderby in fact reckoned it to cost 'from a thousand to fifteen hundred pound. Perhaps twice the money'. The plight of the poor man is depicted in Stephen's interview with Bounderby and in the two subsequent chapters which illustrate Stephen's married life. It is a plea for greater latitude than the Act of 1857 was to permit. Stephen's wife may have been an adulteress, but more emphasis is laid upon her habitual drunkenness, a condition chosen perhaps because it permits a more harrowing scene of martyrdom to be displayed. As for Bounderby and Mrs Sparsit, they are not merely scandalized by Stephen's wish to be free to marry again, but they point out that the law cannot help such as Stephen is. There is one law for the rich and one for the poor. If Dickens had in mind at this stage to point the contrast between Stephen and Bounderby, he takes no pains to press it upon the reader. Bounderby is not yet married to Louisa, and the time is still far ahead—twenty chapters, in fact— when Bounderby, like Stephen, will feel that he 'mun be ridded o' her', and will take the law into his own hands by returning Louisa to her father. The ironic foreshadowing of an event is characteristic of Dickens's art at this period, but there is no premonition in chapter xi of the power which Bounderby will possess over his wife but which Stephen does not possess, and in chapter iii of Book 3 he offers no reminder of chapter xi of Book 1. A novelist so adept at linking his episodes is unlikely to have overlooked such a favourable opportunity of pointing at least one of the morals in his story. It is more probable that the crushing demands of the weekly serial compelled him to leave it out.

The Law of Divorce is 'opened' in Weekly Number VI (chapters xi and xii). It is not until Weekly Number XI that Dickens approaches the question of industrial unrest. In the first chapter of that number (Book 2, chapter iv) we find the 'hands' assembled to listen to the popular leader, Slackbridge. 'Stephen won't join', adds the number plan, 'and is sent to Coventry'. Here without

---

various quarters, but that he considered that the Bill should be confined to adultery. Lord Redesdale, opposing the Bill, allowed that a divorce could at present be obtained only by the rich, but denied that there was 'the least expression of a desire for a cheap tribunal for granting divorces'. See *Parliamentary Debates*, 3rd ser. cxxxiv (1854), coll. 1–20. The Bill never reached the House of Commons.

doubt Dickens was drawing upon his Preston experiences, for he had attended just such a meeting and had noted the attitude of the strikers as they listened to a delegate from another district. He was inevitably contributing to the knowledge of his south-country readers in describing the scene, and he was also exercising their sympathies for the Lancashire operatives both here and in other scenes where the Coketown landscape is described; but he made little attempt to discuss the problems of industrial unrest. In fact he scarcely went beyond the comments of *The Times* reporter who, in an article of 8 November 1853, found in the Preston operatives 'a certain rough vigour and independence of thought and feeling which one cannot help respecting', and blamed the masters 'for a generally stern and unbending demeanour towards their operatives, which freezes their sympathy, and lays the groundwork for constant suspicion and occasional violent ruptures, like the present'. These characteristics are exhibited in Book 2, chapter v, the second chapter of Weekly Number XI, where Stephen expounds 'the Slackbridge question' (in the words of the number plan) to an unsympathetic Bounderby, who proceeds to discharge him. Stephen's exposition is certainly rough, vigorous, and independent, but it contributes little to the problem and perhaps was not intended to contribute much. Why Stephen was sent to Coventry by his fellows we are not informed—perhaps there was insufficient space to offer a reason; it is enough that he suffers a further degree of martyrdom by first adopting an independent line and then defending it before Bounderby. That is the limited service of this theme; Coketown with its troubles is merely the purgatory in which individuals suffer. After a scene in which Tom Gradgrind projects his robbery of Bounderby's bank and arranges for suspicion to fall upon Stephen, Dickens provides (in the words of the number plan) a 'Morning picture of Stephen going away from Coketown out of the cruel ashes on to the country dust'. So ends the twelfth weekly and the third monthly number, and at that point Stephen and the industrial theme walk out of the novel until Weekly Number XIX.

IV

Meanwhile Dickens was occupied in developing that much-favoured theme, the education of the heart. At the beginning of the third month (Book 2, chapter i), Bounderby has set up house in the country[1] with Louisa, and the stage is set in the number plans for the destruction of this nominal marriage:

Mrs Sparsit's life at the Bank?   Yes

Bitzer, Light Porter   Yes

Tom's Progress   Yes

Louisa's married life—Dawn of knowledge of her

    immaterial self—Too late   Scarcely yet.

Man dropped in N° 1?   Yes.   Percy Harthouse
                                   Jem
                                   James

Here are the means by which Louisa will return to her father's home at the end of the fourth month (Book 2, chapter xii), and say to him

'I do not know that I am sorry, I do not know that I am ashamed, I do not know that I am degraded in my own esteem. All that I know is, your philosophy and your teaching will not save me. Now, father, you have brought me to this. Save me by some other means.'

The movement in the third month is somewhat slow. One weekly number and much of another had to be devoted to Stephen's isolation; but two entries on the number plan suggest some infirmity of purpose ('Lover for Sissy? No. Decide on no love at all / Sissy and Rachael to become acquainted? No.'), and the time to show the 'dawn of knowledge' of Louisa's 'immaterial self' was deemed to be not yet ripe. In the event Dickens did little more during this month than establish Harthouse in a convenient relationship with Tom Gradgrind, and place Mrs Sparsit and Bitzer in a strategic position to watch what is to come.

The stream of action moves rapidly once more in the fourth month and reaches the climax at the end of the sixteenth weekly number without apparent hesitation. We should have suspected

1. In moving Bounderby out into the country, Dickens was doubtless describing what many a millowner was doing at that time. Though he does not specifically condemn the action, it may be assumed that he would disapprove since it would tend to separate the master still farther from his men. But the move to the country is convenient in several other ways: the bank is more readily robbed; Harthouse and Louisa are more clearly isolated; and Tom, the betrayer of the sister who loved him, is more suitably shown (in 2, vii) biting and tearing rosebuds, the emblems of love.

none had it not been for the number plan. The first three entries
for the fourth month are confirmatory:

> Tom to rob Bounderby?   Yes
> Louisa to be acted on by Harthouse, through Tom?   Yes
> Louisa's danger slowly drawn about her.   Yes.

Since these plans had already been sketched in the previous
month, the entries here can only mean that now was the time to
put them into force. But the following entries betray some doubt
where else the course of the story might stray during this important month:

> Sissy?   No?
> Rachael?
> Bring her with Louisa again?   No.
> Stephen?
>   No

It is not surprising that Sissy, whose healing powers will prove so
valuable, should be passed in review at this point, though reflection must soon have shown that her time was not yet;[1] and to
consider at least a passing reference to a now distant Stephen is
equally understandable. But that there should ever have been a
question of bringing Rachael to Louisa in her distress seems to
imply some doubt of the final issue of Louisa's actions which the
firm control of the narrative denies. A visit from Rachael before
Louisa's flight could only have been distracting, for it is essential
that Tom and Harthouse alone have power to direct the course
she takes. A visit to Rachael after the flight, or even a chance encounter, could only have delayed the inevitable return to Mr
Gradgrind with its decisive effect upon his belief in his system.
Though we cannot tell how long these entries were deliberated,
their rejection would seem to have been inevitable, and the remaining entries return to the heart of the action:

---

1. She makes a brief appearance at the end of 2, ix, the scene of Mrs Gradgrind's death. But though we see little of her in that scene, we are made to feel her
presence both in the difference which Louisa notices in her sister and in the
thought with which the dying Mrs Gradgrind struggles, a thought more effectively
presented in the number plan than in the text itself: ' "Mr. Gradgrind must have
forgotten some ology. Can't have had them all taught".' Though nothing in Mrs
Gradgrind's life became her like the leaving of it, we recognize that the scene
really belongs to Sissy.

To shew Louisa, how alike in their creeds, her father
and Harthouse are?—How the two heartless things come
to the same in the end?

Yes,   But almost imperceptibly.

Louisa
     "You have brought me to this, father.   Now, save me!"

Louisa is therefore to be denied such guidance as Sissy or as
Rachael (another fount of affectionate guidance) might have
offered in a matter where the heart must decide. Tom had been
the subject of all the little tenderness of her life;[1] Harthouse had
used Tom to gain her confidence and having gained it had shown
that he recognized the emptiness of her marriage. Louisa is to be
reduced by degrees to a situation in which she can bear her marriage no longer; she seeks refuge in flight, and returns a broken
creature to her father's house. Weekly instalments were desper-
ately short for representing these degrees; and to help us in recognizing them, Dickens offers his readers almost apologetically the
image of Mrs Sparsit's staircase:

> Now, Mrs. Sparsit was not a poetical woman; but she took an idea
> in the nature of an allegorical fancy, into her head. Much watching
> of Louisa, and much consequent observation of her impenetrable
> demeanour, which keenly whetted and sharpened Mrs. Sparsit's
> edge, must have given her as it were a lift, in the way of inspiration.
> She erected in her mind a mighty Staircase, with a dark pit of shame
> and ruin at the bottom; and down those stairs, from day to day and
> hour to hour, she saw Louisa coming.
>
> It became the business of Mrs. Sparsit's life, to look up at her
> staircase, and to watch Louisa coming down. Sometimes slowly,
> sometimes quickly, sometimes several steps at one bout, sometimes
> stopping, never turning back. If she had once turned back, it might
> have been the death of Mrs. Sparsit in spleen and grief.[2]

Mrs Sparsit, so often likened to a bird of prey, is an appropriate
observer of this gradual descent, and the arrangement by which
the reader views the relationship of Louisa and Harthouse
through her eyes is admirably managed, for while he relishes her
misapprehension of it, he is prevented from regarding it as a
romance.

     Yet there is something ambiguous in the relationship. Louisa
is attracted to Harthouse, and in her final confession to her father

1. The words are Louisa's (2, xii).   2. Book 2, ch. x.

she finds herself unable to say whether or not she loves him. Those 'almost imperceptible' steps by which Dickens hoped to show her recognition of the identity of Harthouse's and Gradgrind's creeds are difficult to discover. Were they too jettisoned because the difficulties of space were crushing? The equation of Harthouse with Gradgrind suggested in the number plan is neither clear nor satisfactory.[1] He is closer to Bounderby. Gradgrind is honestly persuaded of the truth of his system, and for him there is hope as the next monthly part will show; but Bounderby and Harthouse merely use the system for their own ends, and for them there is no hope.

V

The fifth month is co-extensive with the third and last book named 'Garnering'. Gradgrind, of whom little has been seen, except in the last chapter, during the two previous months, is now to return to the centre of the action. He was first observed at the beginning of the novel impressing the system upon the rising generation; it is time to see how the system has worked. The reader has been made fully aware of its failure both in Louisa and in Tom, and in that premonitory scene of Mrs Gradgrind's death he has received some hint of another force at work in Stone Lodge during Mr Gradgrind's absence; but it is only in the last chapter of the fourth month (Book 2, chapter xii), when he sees Louisa 'the pride of his heart and the triumph of his system, lying, an insensible heap, at his feet' that Gradgrind himself begins to recognize the failure and its cause. The requirements of the weekly serial[2] ensure that the recognition is both swift and clear. Grad-

1. The best that Dickens offers to convince his readers of the likeness of the two men is a passage at the beginning of the first chapter of this month (2, vii):

The not being troubled with earnestness was a grand point in his favour, enabling him to take to the hard Fact fellows with as good a grace as if he had been born one of the tribe, and to throw all other tribes overboard, as conscious hypocrites.

'Whom none of us believe, my dear Mrs. Bounderby, and who do not believe themselves. The only difference between us and the professors of virtue or benevolence, or philanthropy—never mind the name—is, that we know it is all meaningless, and say so; while they know it equally and will never say so.'

Why should she be shocked or warned by this reiteration? It was not so unlike her father's principles, and her early training, that it need startle her. Where was the great difference between the two schools, when each chained her down to material realities, and inspired her with no faith in anything else? What was there in her soul for James Harthouse to destroy, which Thomas Gradgrind had nurtured there in its state of innocence!

2. The demands of the story required additional space for this last monthly num-

grind meets his daughter the morning after her return, and confides to her:

> 'It would be hopeless for me, Louisa, to endeavour to tell you how overwhelmed I have been, and still am, by what broke upon me last night. The ground on which I stand has ceased to be solid under my feet. The only support on which I leaned, and the strength of which it seemed, and still does seem, impossible to question, has given way in an instant. I am stunned by these discoveries. I have no selfish meaning in what I say; but I find the shock of what broke upon me last night, to be very heavy indeed.'

and later in the same chapter:

> 'Louisa, I have a misgiving that some change may have been slowly working about me in this house, by mere love and gratitude: that what the Head has left undone and could not do, the Heart may have been doing silently...'

Of course it had. The reader, who has previously seen what 'the Heart' had done even for Mrs Gradgrind, has already noticed its effect upon Jane Gradgrind, or rather has seen its effect through Louisa's eyes:

> 'What a beaming face you have, Jane!' said Louisa, as her young sister—timidly still—bent down to kiss her.
> 'Have I? I am very glad you think so. I am sure it must be Sissy's doing.'

Of course it is; and before the chapter is over, Sissy, the representative of 'the Heart', has begun to exert her influence over Louisa too:

> 'Forgive me, pity me, help me! Have compassion on my great need, and let me lay this head of mine upon a loving heart!'
> 'O lay it here!' cried Sissy. 'Lay it here, my dear.'[1]

The remaining chapter of Weekly Number XVII (Book 3, chapter ii) completes the victory of Heart over Head, or at least is so intended. Sissy, like Jack the Giant-killer, goes resolutely forth to dispose of James Harthouse and succeeds in touching him 'in the cavity where his heart should have been'. Both Harthouse and the reader agree that it is 'very ridiculous' that a stroller's

---

ber. Dickens's note at the head of the number plan reads: 'Weekly N^{os} to be enlarged to 10 of my sides each—about', i.e., an extension of about two and a half sheets of manuscript for each weekly number.

1. Book 3, ch. i.

child should succeed in evicting a parliamentary candidate from his prospective constituency; but that is how things happen in fairy tales, and Dickens could never entirely resist the satisfaction of giving the victory over the forces of evil to the children of light. Another consideration might also have influenced him. If, as he supposed he had made clear, Gradgrind and Harthouse were alike in their creeds, it was appropriate that Sissy, who had penetrated Gradgrind's complacency, should succeed in wounding Harthouse also.

After the scene to which reference has already been made, where Bounderby repudiates his marriage with Louisa, the story returns to the robbery of the bank, and therefore to the suspected Stephen and his reappearance, and to Tom the real culprit.[1] The suspense—'Still no Stephen' is thrice repeated in the number plans—is admirably contrived.[2] It is not merely a question of what can have happened to Stephen. That is perplexing enough when the bills have been posted offering Twenty Pounds reward for the apprehension of a man whom the reader knows to be innocent, and of whose innocence many characters in the story are convinced. But his disappearance has also an important bearing upon Tom. The reader knows him to be guilty, Louisa and Sissy darkly suspect his guilt, but as yet their suspicions are not shared by Mr Gradgrind, who does not therefore recognize what further humiliations may be in store for him.

Stephen's discovery is presented in one of Dickens's most allegorically lurid scenes. His hat is found by Rachael and Sissy at the mouth of an abandoned mineshaft. The faith and hope of

1. The anxiety which Dickens experienced in the composition of these episodes is reflected in a letter to Forster of which, alas, Forster (VII i) transcribed only an extract:

Tavistock House. Look at that! Boulogne, of course. Friday, 14th of July, 1854. I am three parts mad, and the fourth delirious, with perpetual rushing at *Hard Times*. I have done what I hope is a good thing with Stephen, taking his story as a whole; and hope to be over in town with the end of the book on Wednesday night... I have been looking forward through so many weeks and sides of paper to this Stephen business, that now—as usual—it being over, I feel as if nothing in the world, in the way of intense and violent rushing hither and thither, could quite restore my balance.

Weekly No. XIX, in which Stephen is at last found, is endorsed in the number plan 'The great effect'.

2. It may be remarked that the suspense is scarcely interrupted by the capital scene of Mr Bounderby's deflation, for when Mrs Sparsit brings Mrs Pegler into Bounderby's presence she supposes that she has captured a material witness to the robbery and to Stephen's disappearance.

Rachael are insufficient and she gives him up as lost, but Sissy's charity is equal to the situation; she controls Rachael, and fetches help. After several hours, Stephen is brought to the surface, still alive, and makes a dying statement before the large throng which has collected in the torchlight. It seems that he had set out immediately to vindicate his innocence, had taken the nearest cross-country route to Bounderby's villa, and had fallen down Old Hell Shaft, a mine whose foul air had formerly killed many who worked in it:

> 'When it were in work,' [Stephen comments,] 'it killed wi'out need; when 'tis let alone it kills wi'out need. See how we die an' no need, one way an' another—in a muddle—every day!'

He had begun his journey in anger with Louisa and Tom for plotting against him as he thought; but while in Hell a star shone down upon him ('I thowt it were the star as guided to our Saviour's home'), and by its light he saw more clearly and therefore more charitably, making it his dying prayer

> 'that aw th'world may on'y coom toogether more, an' get a better unnerstan'in o' one another, than when I were in 't my own weak seln;'

and commending Mr Gradgrind to clear his name—'Yor son will tell yo how', the martyr dies with the appropriate reflection (picked out in the number plan)

> 'in our judgments, like as in our doins, we mun bear and forbear'.

The utter failure of his system has its physical effect upon Mr Gradgrind, as a similar failure had had upon Mr Dombey: 'aged and bent he looked, and quite bowed down; and yet he looked a wiser man, and a better man, than in the days when in this life he wanted nothing but Facts' (Book 3, chapter vii). But the system does not invariably fail, and almost as appalling as its failure is its success. Tom is to be smuggled abroad through the agency of Sleary and his circus troupe, and all is going well with their plans when Bitzer appears and arrests the culprit. We have now come full circle. In the first weekly number, the reader had seen Bitzer a model pupil returning model answers to Mr Gradgrind's questions; now in the last number Bitzer is 'true to his bringing up', as the number plan remarks, and once more returns model answers to the questions put to him:

'Bitzer,' said Mr. Gradgrind, broken down, and miserably sub-
missive to him, 'have you a heart?'

'The circulation, Sir,' returned Bitzer, smiling at the oddity of
the question, 'couldn't be carried on without one. No man, Sir,
acquainted with the facts established by Harvey relating to the circulation of the blood, can doubt that I have a heart.'

'Is it accessible,' cried Mr. Gradgrind, 'to any compassionate
influence?'

'It is accessible to Reason, Sir,' returned the excellent young
man. 'And to nothing else.'

In response to a final appeal to the sense of gratitude for schooling
received, Bitzer dismisses this 'untenable position' with the comment that his schooling was paid for and the bargain ended when
he left. Dickens's point is made; but he cannot leave a dying
story like that, and he cannot consent to the further punishment
of a reforming character. Besides, Gradgrind in his unreformed
days had taken pity upon Sissy and now he is to garner the
reward which, by her presence in his house, he had already begun
to reap. 'The Thquire thtood by you, Thethilia,' says Sleary,
'and I'll thtand by the Thquire'; Sleary knows a trick worth
two of Bitzer's, and Tom escapes.

It is the end, except for that dip into the characters' future with
which Dickens always assuages the curiosity of his readers. But
before the epilogue is reached, he gives the last word to Mr
Sleary, who had had to apologize on a previous occasion for being
'too muth of a Cackler'. The payment which he accepts for
services rendered is altogether appropriate. It was a fundamental
principle of the Gradgrind philosophy that everything was to be
paid for; and Mr Gradgrind pays. Five pounds, it is true, went to
Mr Childers, who had assisted Tom's escape; but Childers was a
family man, and the money 'mightn't be unactheptable'. Apart
from that, the philosopher of Fact 'very willingly undertook' to
stand a collar for the dog, 'a thet of bellth for the horthe', brandy
and water for Mr Sleary, and 'a little thpread for the company'.
After so willingly paying in kind, and agreeing, it would seem, to
'give a Hortheriding, a bethpeak' whenever he could, the expo-
nent of calculable Fact has to listen to a tale about the instinct of
the faithful dog Merrylegs, and we can readily accept his giving
tacit assent to the moral which Mr Sleary sees in the depths of his
brandy and water:

'one, that there ith a love in the world, not all Thelf-interetht after all, but thomething very different; t'other, that it hath a way of ith own of calculating or not calculating, whith thomehow or another ith at leatht ath hard to give a name to, ath the wayth of the dogth ith!'

What remains for this brandy-sodden Fairy Queen to do but to pronounce a benediction and repeat the philosophy of fancy:

'People mutht be amuthed. They can't be alwayth a learning, nor yet they can't be alwayth a working, they an't made for it. You *mutht* have uth, Thquire. Do the withe thing and the kind thing too, and make the betht of uth; not the wurtht!'

CHAPTER IX

From 'Nobody's Fault'
to *Little Dorrit*

I

Dickens completed *Hard Times* in July 1854. By October the familiar symptoms of restlessness which presaged the beginning of a new book were appearing once more:

> visions of living for half a year or so, in all sorts of inaccessible places, and opening a new book therein. A floating idea of going up above the snow-line in Switzerland, and living in some astonishing convent, hovers about me.[1]

Early in February 1855 he was still 'in a dishevelled state of mind,' seeing 'motes of new books in the dirty air';[2] both public and personal life bore hardly upon him—this was the worst phase of the Crimean War, the beginning of his friend Layard's agitation for administrative reform, and also of the reappearance of his old love Maria Beadnell. To her he wrote on 3 April (partly perhaps in the wish to escape from his embarrassing disillusionment with his 'Flora') to say that he was 'going off, I don't know where or how far, to ponder about I don't know what'.[3] A month later, the 'wandering-unsettled-restless uncontrollable state of being about to begin a new book' still persisted; but in a few days his plans were taking shape—Folkestone for the autumn, Paris for the winter—and the form and date of the new book were fixed—'a new, long, twenty-number Green book (publication to

---

1. *Letters*, II 596. Dickens had visited the St Bernard in 1846 and recalled it when writing Bk 2, chs. i–ii of *Little Dorrit* ten years later (*Letters*, II 803, 828).

2. *Letters*, II 620; 'January' is the editor's conjecture, but comparison with letters of 9 Feb. makes the later date more probable.

3. *Letters*, II 650.

begin in November)'. Its 'first page' was before him, with 'all kinds of notes' and 'a capital name'.[1]

The 'capital name' stands at the head of the early number plans, as *Nobody's Fault*;[2] and this persisted in his mind through at least five months, throughout the writing of the first eleven chapters. He announced it to Mrs Watson on 16 September, but said it would not be made public until the end of October. On 13 October, however, it was advertised as *Little Dorrit*.[3] Why did Dickens choose *Nobody's Fault* as a title, why did he change it, and how is the original title related to the completed novel? Though this work has drawn much critical attention in recent years, no one since Forster has attempted to answer any of these questions.

Forster's explanation is simple, but unsatisfying:

> The book took its origin from the notion he had of a leading man for a story who should bring about all the mischief in it, lay it all on Providence, and say at every fresh calamity, "well, it's a mercy, however, nobody was to blame, you know!"

(a notion evidently related, though the connexion is not made by Forster, to the notebook entry:

> The people who lay all their sins negligences and ignorances, on Providence).[4]

This man, unnamed, makes two brief appearances in the number plans; first in Number II (chapters v–viii):

> The man who comfortably charges everything on Providence?
> Not yet

and then in Number IV (chapters xii–xiv):

> Charging everything on Providence? No

Even there, he hardly looks like a 'leading man', for by that time most of the main characters have appeared, and he cannot be identified with any of them. The trait might be compatible with

1. *Letters*, II 658–9, 660. The 'name' is referred to in a letter of 8 May, and the 'Green book' in a letter to Mrs Watson (*The Dickensian*, June 1942, p. 165) of 21 May; but 'a new tree with the old green leaves' had been mentioned in a letter of 5 Mar. (*Letters*, II 639).

2. Later deleted and *Little Dorrit* substituted.

3. A good deal earlier, therefore, than Forster's 'on the eve of publication' (VIII i) which was 30 Nov. Forster (followed by Johnson, II 846) is also wrong in supposing that four numbers were then written; the fourth number plan is headed simply *Little Dorrit*, and No. IV, though begun in Oct., was completed only on 31 Dec.

4. Forster, IX vii; for the notebook, see p. 29 n. above.

the passivity of Mr Dorrit, or the hypocrisy of Casby, or the non-chalance of Henry Gowan; but Mr Dorrit appears by name in the notes for Number II, and Casby in the notes for Number IV; and none of these fulfils the other function mentioned by Forster, of bringing about all the 'mischief' in the book.[1] Indeed, such personal responsibility for evil seems foreign to the whole book as we have it. In so far as any individual is responsible, rather than 'society', it is Mrs Clennam; but she is fully aware of what she has done and sure of her righteous motives. More probably the notion of this man was only accidentally the 'origin' of the book, and had he survived into the written story he would have been a mere exemplum of the wider theme of 'Nobody's Fault'; the title could hardly have persisted through the writing of so many chapters if it was to be fulfilled only by this vanished character.

The general notion of 'Nobody's Fault' may also have been connected with an abandoned suggestion for Number I: that of people meeting and parting as travellers do, 'and the future con-nexion between them in the story, not to be now shown to the reader';[2] 'being in the same place, ignorant of one another, as happens in life; and to connect them afterwards, and to make the waiting for that connection a part of the interest'[3]—meeting, that is, through Providence, not their own contrivance. But only a trace of this remains, in the juxtaposition in Marseilles of the two prisoners with the travellers; for although the Meagles family, Clennam, and Miss Wade, 'meet and part as travellers do', the connexion between them *is* already shown, at least as much as one normally expects in any introductory chapter.

But the early number plans and Forster's information are not our only evidence of Dickens's preliminary view of the dominant themes of the novel. Some weeks before publication began, the design for the cover must have been discussed with Browne, and prepared by him. Unfortunately no correspondence survives,[4] and we do not know whether the original design carried the old title. Certainly the words *Nobody's Fault* in the centre would em-phasize the irony of the design. Its two sides seem to typify society in decay, and images of doom are combined with com-

1. The one possibility is another character who disappears early from the notes—Miss Wade's father, suggested for No. III (chs. ix–xi), with a 'Not yet', and again by implication in No. IV: 'Miss Wade. Her surroundings and antecedents? No'.

2. No. I, memoranda.   3. Forster, VIII i.

4. A letter of 19 Oct. complains of hearing nothing from Browne, 'although I have communicated at full explanatory length'. (*Letters*, II 698.)

placence and self-absorption. On the left is part of a crumbling castle, on whose tottering top is seated a sleeping man in an arm-chair with a handkerchief over his eyes and a newspaper on his knee. Against the castle lies a falling tree; the 'supporters' of the coat of arms are rats. This is 'the world' in its material aspect. Opposite stands part of a church, crowned by a raven, while a child plays leap-frog among the graves, and in a wheel-chair sits the life-in-death figure of Mrs Clennam attended by Flintwinch. So much for 'religion'. Overlapping these two scenes, and extending across the bottom of the design, is a motley crowd of travel-lers, each clinging to his belongings, all moving different ways, colliding, harassed, unhappy. Across the top of the design is what is virtually a political cartoon. Two aged figures, crippled and half blind, lead the procession, followed by a line of dotards and a dandy; Britannia in a bath-chair, asleep, is propelled by a line of men in fools' caps, followed by a crowd of toadies, behind whom are women and children; all, save the last, are smiling inanely. The centre-piece is Little Dorrit herself, at the gate of the prison, in a shaft of sunlight.

Here then, strongly emphasized, are the political, social, and ethical themes of the novel; there is no narrative line, as in the *Dombey* cover, but the inner meaning of the story is clearly 'shadowed forth'. For our purpose, the most interesting feature is the prominence of the political idea; it is clear from the cover-design that chapter x, 'Containing the Whole Science of Govern-ment' was foreseen from the start, and that its satire was a funda-mental part of Dickens's conception of the novel—more so, per-haps, than the working-out of the story suggests, since the Bar-nacles remain rather episodic in the plot. To the readers of Num-ber I, the prominence of the political satire must have been baffling; there is nothing so far in Marseilles or London to suggest a political theme. But the month was December 1855; the state of things pictured at the top of the cover had become dismally fami-liar to every reader. Its promise was fulfilled for them two months later in the brilliant sketch of chapter x, 'How Not to Do It':

> Sometimes, angry spirits attacked the Circumlocution Office.
> Sometimes, parliamentary questions were asked about it, and even parliamentary motions made or threatened about it, by dema-gogues so low and ignorant as to hold that the real recipe of govern-ment was, How to do it. Then would the noble lord, or right honor-able gentleman, in whose department it was to defend the Circum-

locution Office, put an orange in his pocket, and make a regular
field-day of the occasion. Then would he come down to that House
with a slap upon the table, and meet the honorable gentleman foot
to foot. Then would he be there to tell that honorable gentleman
that the Circumlocution Office not only was blameless in this
matter, but was commendable in this matter, was extollable to the
skies in this matter.

The chapter is the second in Number III, which Dickens was
writing in the latter half of September. He was evidently pleased
with it. He writes to Collins on 30 September:

I have relieved my indignant soul with a scarifier[1]

and to Macready a few days later:

In No. 3 of my new book I have been blowing off a little of indignant
steam which would otherwise blow me up, and with God's leave
I shall walk in the same all the days of my life; but I have no present
political faith or hope—not a grain.[2]

The context of this sentence makes his despair more specific:

As to the suffrage, I have lost hope even in the ballot. We appear
to me to have proved the failure of representative institutions without an educated and advanced people to support them. What with
teaching people to "keep in their stations," what with bringing up
the soul and body of the land to be a good child, or to go to the beer-
shop, to go a-poaching and go to the devil; what with having no
such thing as a middle class (for though we are perpetually bragging
of it as our safety, it is nothing but a poor fringe on the mantle of the
upper); what with flunkyism, toadyism, letting the most contempt-
ible lords come in for all manner of places, reading The Court Circular for the New Testament, I do reluctantly believe that the English people are habitually consenting parties to the miserable imbecility into which we have fallen, *and never will help themselves out of it.*
Who is to do it, if anybody is, God knows. But at present we are on
the down-hill road to being conquered, and the people WILL be content to bear it, sing "Rule Britannia," and WILL NOT be saved.

The last sentence is strongly suggestive of the 'cartoon' on the
cover.

Dickens had been led to this position by the events of the past
twelve months. The Crimean War began in March 1854; in
October, William Howard Russell's revelations of mismanagement and disaster were appearing in *The Times*; in January 1855

1. *Letters*, II 694.   2. *Letters*, II 695.

the Roebuck Committee was appointed, and Lord Aberdeen's government fell—to Dickens, and to many others, merely substituting Coodle for Doodle.

The general evidence of inefficiency and corruption, 'a confused heap of mismanagement, imbecility, and disorder, under which the nation's bravery lies crushed and withered'[1], gave Dickens the material he wanted for the Circumlocution Office, in which he also made use of the abuses exposed by the Northcote–Trevelyan report of 1853. As usual, the sharp truth is softened by his artist's delight in the creation of a satiric fantasy; there is more relish than indignation in his picture of the Barnacles. But the full animus of his attack is seen elsewhere, and in the very months in which the novel was first forming in his mind—seen in his letters, in *Household Words*, and in his speech for the Administrative Reform Association.

The first reflection of his political disgust is in the scheme, communicated to Forster in August 1854, of 'occasional papers in Household Words called the Member for Nowhere',[2] which would have shown his 'contempt for the House of Commons'; this was reluctantly given up in the following month. Dickens instead made an indirect attack. Seeing that 'the war will be made an administrative excuse for all sorts of shortcomings'[3] and that 'the old cannon-smoke and blood-mists obscure the wrongs and sufferings of the people at home',[4] he proceeded to ventilate these wrongs in an article 'To Working Men', published on 7 October and followed by a series, by himself and Henry Morley, on public health and sanitary reform.

A letter of February 1855 shows him moving nearer the Barnacle idea:

> I am hourly strengthened in my old belief that our political aristocracy and our tuft-hunting are the death of England.[5]

and the same letter mentions his 'bright idea' for a political skit on the *Arabian Nights*, 'The Thousand and One Humbugs'. This series appeared a few weeks later;[6] the undesirable characters bear such names as Scarlitapa, Jobbiana, and Palmerstoon, or Twirling Weathercock. The last of these sketches brings us to the

---

1. 'That Other Public', in *Household Words*, 3 Feb. 1855; Dickens reverted to the subject in a satirical fairy tale, 'Prince Bull', in the issue of 17 Feb., where the wicked fairy godmother is called 'Tape'.

2. *Letters*, II 584–5.   3. *Letters*, II 600.   4. *Letters*, II 603.

5. *Letters*, II 622.   6. 21, 28 Apr., 5 May.

month in which the actual writing of the novel began; and its
relation to his political preoccupations is clear from a letter
which was written some weeks earlier:

> You see what we have been doing to our valiant soldiers. You see
> what miserable humbugs we are. And because we have got involved
> in meshes of aristocratic red tape to our unspeakable confusion,
> loss, and sorrow, the gentlemen who have been so kind as to ruin us
> are going to give us a day of humiliation and fasting the day after
> to-morrow. I am sick and sour to think of such things at this age of
> the world. . . I am in the first stage of a new book, which consists in
> going round and round the idea, as you see a bird in his cage go
> about and about his sugar before he touches it.[1]

In May the Administrative Reform Association was formed;
Dickens immediately became a member, and on 27 June made a
speech at the meeting at Drury Lane Theatre.[2] The Prime Minister had taken advantage of an earlier meeting in the same place
to jeer at the Association's 'private theatricals'; Dickens made a
telling comparison with the 'public theatricals' of politics:

> so full of "walking gentlemen", the managers have such large
> families and are so bent upon putting those families into what is
> theatrically called "first business"—not because of their aptitude
> for it, but because they *are* their families. . . We have seen "The
> Comedy of Errors" played so dismally like a tragedy . . .

At the same time he disclaimed any intention of changing his
sphere of action from literature to politics:

> By literature I have lived, and through literature I have been con-
> tent to serve my country; and I am perfectly well aware that I can-
> not serve two masters. In my sphere of action I have tried to under-
> stand the heavier social grievances, and to put them right.[3]

His mind was turning back to his novel, *Nobody's Fault*; by September the failure of Layard's movement was clear, and Dickens

---

1. *Letters*, II 712; undated; the editor conjectures 'November', but the 'day of
humiliation and fasting' was 21 Mar., which makes this one of the earliest references to the new book. Compare also the letters to Layard on 10 Apr. (I 651–2) and
to Forster on 27 Apr. (I 655–6).

2. A reporter who was present recalled the speech as 'a masterpiece of raillery
and rebuke to a "how-not-to-do-it" Government' (F. G. Kitton, *Charles Dickens by
Pen and Pencil, Supplement*, 1890, p. 45).

3. *Speeches*, ed. R. H. Shepherd. Forster, who probably did not approve, makes
only a passing reference to the Association, making Dickens's share in its work
merely an instance of the 'unsettled discontent' of this summer (VII ii).

was 'blowing off . . . indignant steam' in his description of the Circumlocution Office.

Enough has been said to demonstrate his concern with the evils of 1854–5, and his intention of exposing them in his writings;[1] it is necessary only to add that in the ironic formula 'Nobody's Fault', he was catching up a current notion. Revelations of mismanagement of the war at once led to the attempt to pin down the responsibility; which failed, as usual, owing to the skill of officials and ministers in 'passing the buck'. 'Who's to Blame?' was the question everyone was asking (it was the title of an article in the *Catholic Standard* by Newman in January 1855); and the answer was 'Nobody'.[2] If the man who was to assert that nobody was to blame survives in the novel at all, he is surely a Barnacle.

When he was half-way through *Little Dorrit* (a few weeks after writing the chapter 'A Shoal of Barnacles') Dickens summed up the situation in *Household Words* in an article called 'Nobody, Somebody, and Everybody':[3]

> The power of Nobody is becoming so enormous in England, and he alone is responsible for so many proceedings, both in the way of commission and omission; he has so much to answer for, and is so constantly called to account; that a few remarks upon him may not be ill-timed.

1. Much more of course would need to be said in a full study of the topicality of the novel, which would involve a fuller treatment of the Civil Service report of 1853 and would have also to include the 'Sunday question' (the Hyde Park riots on Lord Robert Grosvenor's bill receive their comment in the picture of a London Sunday as it strikes the returned traveller in ch. iii, and this relevance was generally recognized) and the contemporary rage for speculation in England and France, including the suicide of John Sadleir in Feb. 1856, reflected in the history of Mr Merdle. Several reviews of the completed novel were on partly political lines; see especially 'The License of Modern Novelists' (*Edinburgh Review*, July 1857); *The Train*, Aug. 1857; and two articles in the *Saturday Review*, 3 Jan. and 4 July 1857. The writer of the last of these concluded with the hope that Dickens would not again offer his readers 'the cold cabbage of Crimean inquiries and Royal British Banks, Administrative Reformers, Tottenham Court Road accidents, Messrs. Redpath, Cameron, and John Sadleir'.

2. Compare the cartoon in *Punch* (Mar. 1855, xxxvii 85) 'Mr Bull wants to know "the Reason Why"' and the title of a pamphlet of the autumn of 1854, 'Whom Shall We Hang?' That it really was 'nobody's fault' but the fault of the whole structure of administration became steadily clearer with successive hearings before the Committee. Roebuck wrote 'I felt corruption round about me, but I could not lay my hand upon it' (Asa Briggs, *Victorian People*, 1954, p. 84). A typical contemporary comment is 'there has been any amount of short-comings and blunderings, causing . . . a fearful and needless quantity of misery . . . yet it seems quite hopeless to attempt to find out who is to blame' (*Illustrated London News*, 24 Mar. 1855).

3. 30 Aug. 1856.

The hand which this surprising person had in the late war is amazing to consider. It was he who left the tents behind, who left the baggage behind, who chose the worst possible ground for encampments, who provided no means of transport, who killed the horses, who paralysed the commissariat, who knew nothing of the business he professed to know and monopolised, who decimated the English army. It was Nobody who gave out the famous unroasted coffee, it was Nobody who made the hospitals more horrible than language can describe, it was Nobody who occasioned all the dire confusion of Balaklava harbor, it was even Nobody who ordered the fatal Balaklava cavalry charge. The non-relief of Kars was the work of Nobody, and Nobody has justly and severely suffered for that infamous transaction.

In civil matters we have Nobody equally active. When a civil office breaks down, the break-down is sure to be in Nobody's department. I entreat on my reader, dubious of this proposition, to wait until the next break-down (the reader is certain not to have to wait long), and to observe, whether or no, it is in Nobody's department. A dispatch of the greatest moment is sent to a minister abroad, at a most important crisis; Nobody reads it. British subjects are affronted in a foreign territory; Nobody interferes. Our own loyal fellow-subjects a few thousand miles away, want to exchange political, commercial, and domestic intelligence with us; Nobody stops the mail. The government, with all its mighty means and appliances, is invariably beaten and outstripped by private enterprise; which we all know to be Nobody's fault. Something will be the national death of us, some day; and who can doubt that Nobody will be brought in Guilty?

II

Meanwhile the novel had become *Little Dorrit*: a title which, Dickens said, 'has a pleasanter sound in my ears, and which is equally applicable to the same story'.[1] Its application is however very different. 'Nobody's Fault' represents the 'one idea and design' of social criticism of which 'Society, the Circumlocution office and Mr. Gowan' are 'three parts';[2] *Little Dorrit*, the optimism about humanity which sets the rest in perspective. In her Dickens repeats, more subtly, a leading idea of *Oliver Twist* and *The Old Curiosity Shop*: that of the strength and indestructibility of natural, innocent virtue. As with Oliver and Nell, her goodness,

---

1. To Mrs Watson, 10 Nov. 1855. (*The Dickensian*, June 1942, p. 166.) Mrs Watson was one of the few to whom he had confided the original title.
2. *Letters*, II 766.

with such an upbringing, may be thought implausible; but it must be seen as expressing what still survived of Dickens's own indestructible faith—expressing it almost allegorically, with the validity of fairy tale. It seems likely that Little Dorrit was not at first intended to be so important a character; indeed, in manuscript, proofs, and letters we can trace the way she grew in importance, and even see her acquiring her name.

She was introduced in the third chapter, merely as an unknown girl seen in Mrs Clennam's room and inquired about by Arthur Clennam. In the manuscript her name does not appear; Affery only says 'Oh! *She*'s nothing; she's a whim of hers.' Her name is added in proof as 'Dorrit', which is then altered in a different coloured ink to 'Little Dorrit'. This change must have been made a good deal later, for her name is 'Dorrit' whenever she appears, in manuscript and proof, right up to chapter xii, and even in the memoranda for Number IV (chapters xii–xiv); the first appearance of 'Little Dorrit' in the manuscript is an addition made on the back of a leaf in that chapter. The text of chapter xii is indecisive as evidence, since she does not appear, and is referred to naturally by Plornish as 'Miss Dorrit' and only by Clennam (in the later addition) as 'Little Dorrit'; but the decision as to the title must already have been taken when that chapter was written, for the heading of the number plan, which stands on the right-hand side, is plain from the start as *Little Dorrit*. The dawning of the change may go back to chapter ix, where Maggie calls her 'Little mother', and which ends with Clennam's farewell in the prison yard:

> Little as she had always looked, she looked less than ever when he saw her going into the Marshalsea lodge passage, the little mother attended by her big child.

And it is noticeable that in chapter xiv, where Arthur asks if he may call her by this name, Maggie corrects him to 'Little mother'. The emphasis also falls on the name at the close of chapter xiii, which ends with her softly opening the door; and this was prepared for in the summary in the number plans:

> Lead up, through the state of Arthur Clennam's mind to "Little Dorrit"

in contrast to the general note in the memoranda, 'How he stands towards Dorrit?'

Having made his decision, Dickens went back and changed the name in all previous chapters,[1] which by now were in proof; and also added the title,[2] and presumably drafted the advertisement for 13 October. (It would be tempting to take the earlier advertisement of 6 October, where the novel was simply 'New Work by Mr. Charles Dickens', as defining the date of the change within a week; but such a preliminary advertisement in general terms was not unusual.) No change in her description in the early chapters was necessary; she was already a 'diminutive figure' with 'all the manner and much of the appearance of a subdued child'. But it is conceivable that if Dickens had had time to rewrite, he would have led up more clearly to the first appearance of the name in chapter v.

'I can make Dorrit very strong in the story, I hope', he had written to Forster on 16 September (during the writing of Number III);[3] and from this expectation dates the growing concentration upon her. That number in fact shows the double emphasis very clearly; the 'Little Mother' chapter (ix) being juxtaposed to 'Containing the Whole Science of Government' (x), in which Arthur, actuated by his interest in the Marshalsea family, applies to the Circumlocution office; and the further tangling of the threads is foreshadowed by his meeting there with Mr Meagles, the father of Pet,[4] who is to be the first object of his affections. Arthur Clennam's misunderstanding of his own feelings towards Little Dorrit is the result of his thinking of her as a child; so the diminutive is an essential part of the plot. It is also picturesque and symbolical—the small frail figure who is nevertheless the fount of moral strength; the protectress, the neglected, loved by all and, until the end, understood by none.

Dickens's decision was surely a wise one. He was writing a novel of individuals, not preaching a sermon or making a political speech; the pathetic, human appeal was more appropriate than the didactic 'Nobody's Fault', which in any case was almost

1. But he did not catch all the instances, so that there is a whole patch of ch. ix where she is still called 'Dorrit', surviving into modern texts.

2. No title appears on the proofs of I–III.

3. *Letters*, II 689. Mr William Dorrit is never called simply 'Dorrit', so there is no doubt that Little Dorrit is meant here.

4. 'Pet' was called 'Baby' in No. I, and this was altered only in proof; this also was a late revision (she is still 'Baby' in the memoranda of No. III) and it is very likely that it was consequent upon the addition of 'Little' to 'Dorrit', for two child-women in one novel would be awkward.

too narrowly topical.[1] On the most practical level of attracting sales, the new title had the advantage of recalling the most popular of all his characters, Little Nell; and its oddity was useful in arousing curiosity.

> For, let us say at once, that "Little Dorrit" is not a broom, not a village, not a ship,—as has been variously surmised at various tea-tables,—where the book in the green cover is as eagerly expected as the news of the last battle,—but a live flesh and blood little girl.[2]

Yet 'Nobody's Fault' survives, and not only in the Barnacles. Its meanings are multiple. Beginning as irony, a comment on the tendency to shift responsibility, it becomes a gloomy truth pervading all parts of the novel, as a ground-tone of despair about society. As in *Bleak House*, the calamities of the novel spring not so much from a single evil will but from the corruption of the whole condition of things: Mr Merdle and Mrs Clennam are themselves victims. The Marshalsea is more than a prison; it is a microcosm of the world. Gaining wealth, Mr Dorrit escapes only from one prison into another: the prison of society—with Mr Merdle's butler and Mrs General as half-comic jailers. We are shown the prison of poverty in Bleeding Heart Yard, the prison of administration in the Circumlocution Office, the prison of heredity and temperament in Mrs Clennam and Miss Wade. We are all each other's prisoners; there is no way out, for it is 'nobody's fault'. Individual happiness is possible for few; for the selfless servant of the community, like Daniel Doyce; for the Plornishes, against all odds, in 'Happy Cottage'; and for Arthur and Little Dorrit, when the curse of prison, wealth, and heredity is lifted from them. The novel ends with their marriage at the Marshalsea gates; but the very last words are not of them. They are of the crowds in the streets, the prisoners of society:

> They went quietly down into the roaring streets, inseparable and blessed; and as they passed along in sunshine and in shade, the noisy and the eager, and the arrogant and the froward and the vain, fretted, and chafed, and made their usual uproar.

1. As a 'formula' it was much more appropriate to the period when the first numbers were being written than to the time of publication.

2. *Athenæum*, 1 Dec. 1855. Can this be echoed by the inimitable Flora in ch. xxiii? '... and of all the strangest names I ever heard the strangest, like a place down in the country with a turnpike, or a favourite pony or a puppy or a bird or something from a seed-shop to be put in a garden or a flower-pot and come up speckled.'

INDEX

Thomas Hardy: *The Poetic Structure*

Novelists and Their World

General Editor: Graham Hough
Professor of English at the University of Cambridge

Thomas Hardy

The Poetic Structure

Jean R. Brooks

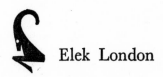

Elek London

© 1971 Jean R. Brooks

ISBN 0 236 15416 8

Published in Great Britain by
ELEK BOOKS LIMITED
2 All Saints Street London N I

Printed in Great Britain by
W & J Mackay & Co Ltd
Chatham

Contents

Acknowledgements

Quotations from Hardy's published works are made by kind permissions of The Trustees of the Hardy Estate and Macmillan London Ltd., and the Macmillan Company of New York.

My thanks are due to the staff of the Dorset County Museum, the British Museum, the Fitzwilliam Museum, Cambridge, the Bodleian Library, Oxford, and the Birmingham City Museum and Art Gallery, for permission to examine manuscripts.

My inexpressible thanks go to the help and encouragement of my family and friends; especially to the constructive criticism of my husband, Professor Harold F. Brooks, to fellow Hardeians Dr C. J. P. Beatty of the University of Oslo and Mr R. F. Dalton, former Curator of the Dorset County Museum; and to the students of Rose Bruford College, whose lively discussions and appreciation of Hardy from the viewpoint of drama students contributed to my chapter on *The Dynasts* and the final assessment of Hardy's place in the modern world.

Jean R. Brooks
Welwyn Garden City
April 1971

I
Introduction: The Heart and Inner Meaning

Hardy scholarship is a flourishing industry. The reader may question the need for yet another book of criticism. But for an author whose place in literature has always been controversial, constant reassessment is essential to keep the balance between modern and historical perspective. The strong disagreements about what is 'good' or 'bad' in Hardy's work prove only the relativity of judgement and the vitality of the author. Time has revealed Hardy's anti-realistic devices to be imaginative truths about cosmic Absurdity rather than the author's incompetence. Modern depth psychology has vindicated his profound intuition of character in terms of irrational drives. A. J. Guérard rightly draws attention to features which modern preoccupations have taught the reader to appreciate:

'We are in fact attracted by much that made the post-Victorian realist uneasy: the inventiveness and improbability, the symbolic use of reappearance and coincidence, the wanderings of a macabre imagination, the suggestions of supernatural agency; the frank acknowledgement that love is basically sexual and marriage usually unhappy; the demons of plot, irony and myth.'

(Thomas Hardy: The Novels and Stories)

But Guérard, like many other modern critics, assumes a too inclusive scepticism of values which the modern failure of nerve can ignore, but cannot displace.

'And we are repelled or left indifferent by what charmed that earlier generation: the regionalist's ear for dialect, the botanist's eye for the minutiae of field and tree, the architect's eye for ancient mansions, and the farmer's eye for sheepshearings; the pretentious meditation on Egdon Heath; the discernible architecture of the novels and the paraphrasable metaphysic; the Franciscan tenderness and sympathy—and, I'm afraid, the finally unqualified faith in the goodness of a humanity more sinned against than sinning.'

One must respect the values of Hardy both as an individual and as a product of his age to avoid the temptation to assess his work according to twentieth-century obsessions. In the Overworld perspective of *The Dynasts*, these will stand as local cults. An age which suspects Henchard's strong affection for Farfrae, which can define Giles Winterborne's sacrifice for Grace's reputation as 'close to absurd' and the selfless self-control of Oak, Winterborne and Venn as an 'immature refusal to accept life and enjoy it', reveals its own limitations rather than Hardy's. The things which Guérard finds repellent, in fact, constitute Hardy's intense celebration of life in all its physical manifestations and metaphysical mystery in face of the full look at the worst advocated in 'In Tenebris II'—less repellent than the modern trend to reduce plain goodness to perverted ulterior motive. Recent biographical conjecture stemming from Lois Deacon's unproved contention in *Providence and Mr Hardy* that Hardy's relationship with his cousin Tryphena was incestuous and produced a son, distorts both the man and his work by attributing to this cloudy episode both his lifelong—and constitutional— tragic vision and much of the material in his works.* To substitute biography, conjectural or otherwise, for imaginative truth is to replace the profound mystery of the suffering artist's creative indictment of the cosmos with a cause small and personal enough for unawakened minds to grasp.

The critic's first concern at this point of time (1971) is to stress once more Hardy's power—the poetic power—to make real those great commonplaces of heroic, though doomed, human nature which the modern Iago thinks he has seen through because, if they exist, their beauty makes him ugly. The reader will find them given weight by critics of an earlier generation: Lascelles Abercrombie, Edmund Blunden, David Cecil, H. C. Duffin, Lionel Johnson, Arthur McDowall. Other critics, in the light of modern social and psychological theory, have profitably explored certain aspects of Hardy's complex richness. W. R. Rutland and H. C. Webster set him in the context of nineteenth-century thought. Evolution through natural selection, the origin of man, the long stretch of geological time behind him, the displacement of a transcendent personal Deity by immanent process without mind or purpose, the

*Research done on the photographers responsible for the two portraits alleged to be of Hardy's son (*Providence and Mr. Hardy*; Lois Deacon, *Tryphena's Portrait Album*, Toucan Press, 1967) seems to prove that both had gone out of business at the address on the reverse of the portraits long before the alleged son could have reached the age of the subjects portrayed. See R. F. Dalton, 'Thomas Hardy's Alleged Son', *Notes and Queries*, ccxiii, July 1968, and C. J. P. Beatty, *Notes and Queries*, Vol. 17, No. ix, Sept. 1970.

'Higher Criticism' of sacred texts, Herbert Spencer's philosophy of the Unknowable, John Stuart Mill's essays on the religious and social liberty of the individual—all left their mark on Hardy's vision of man's place in nature. Douglas Brown stresses the destructive effect on a stable peasant culture of the revolution in industry that joined with the revolution in thought to define man as product and victim of a soulless mechanism. The insecurity of a displaced peasantry contributes to several of the tragedies, notably *The Woodlanders, Tess of the d'Urbervilles* and *Jude the Obscure*. A. J. Guérard and Richard Carpenter have rescued the grotesque, antirealistic elements from derision and shown them to be powerful expressionistic images of existential absurdity and the irrationality of subconscious drives. R. C. R. Morrell has corrected the view that Hardy weights the scales unfairly against his characters, by drawing attention to the recurrent rhythm of reprieves and second chances, and the responsibility of the human will to direct fate at those neutral moments 'when the mighty necessitating forces . . . happen to be in equilibrium'.

The poetry has received less critical attention than the novels, though the balance has recently been redressed by Samuel Hynes's *The Pattern of Hardy's Poetry* and Kenneth Marsden's *The Poems of Thomas Hardy: A Critical Introduction*. Both have useful chapters on Hardy's revisions, and the kind of 'development' to be expected in a poet whose eight volumes of verse, most of them containing work widely separated in date of composition, were published in the last thirty years of a very long creative life. Hynes devotes his study to a demonstration of a common (but not invariable) principle of order in Hardy's poetry—'the eternal conflict between irreconcilables'. Like J. G. Southworth's earlier study, and many recent articles and chapters on the poetry, Hynes's book leaves a general impression of Hardy's weaknesses rather than his strengths. Marsden's introduction, however, is a model of balanced judgement in this respect as in others, clarifying clichés and misconceptions about Hardy's poetic method, philosophy, and reputation.

Hardy's flaws as poet, novelist, and dramatist have attracted enough attention. The present study concentrates on a body of successful work which is large enough to give him the status of major artist: a fair proportion of the poems, a few short stories, six major novels, and *The Dynasts*, in the definitive published form in which Hardy left them to the public.

The critic who follows a host of capable predecessors wonders at times whether anything new can be said. One can only reiterate that in a new encounter with Hardy the light falls differently from of old. When the obvious has been repeated, a need has been felt to stress the basic qualities that may have been pushed aside in the excitement of following a specialized trail. When the obvious has been passed over, other critics have explored it thoroughly and space is limited.

What are the basic qualities of Hardy's creative power to give new beauty to old commonplaces? They are an amalgam of traditional moulds and personal vision, harmonized by poetic associative structures and a deeply-felt poetic emotion that affirms and links subjective experience to the universal commonplaces of the race—birth, death, love, suffering, work.

'Nobody can deny Hardy's power—the true novelist's power—to make us believe that his characters are fellow-beings driven by their own passions and idiosyncrasies, while they have—and this is the poet's gift—something symbolical about them which is common to us all.
(Virginia Woolf, 'The Novels of Thomas Hardy',
The Common Reader, Second Series)

The poet's gift has not gone unremarked, but what it means to Hardy's art has not been explored in great detail in the light of modern poetic structure. One could, without much profit, compare some of Hardy's poems with their prosed counterparts to discover the link between poet and poetic novelist. Different kinds of poetry—philosophical, lyrical, elegiac, narrative/dramatic—isolate microscopically various ingredients which unite in the novels to produce the true Hardeian flavour. They crystallize a certain mood or moment of vision which are emotional arias in the novels. 'Beyond the Last Lamp', 'Tess's Lament', 'Proud Songsters', and 'A Light Snow-fall after Frost' (*Tess of the d'Urbervilles*); 'The Pine Planters' and 'In a Wood' (*The Woodlanders*); 'Childhood among the Ferns' and 'Midnight on the Great Western' (*Jude the Obscure*) are fine poems in their own right, because Hardy has added or subtracted features which re-create them in terms of lyric. Usually, however, the prosed poems are more successful in the novels, where they are an organic part of narrative structure and emotional accumulation of detail. To compare 'The Puzzled Game-Birds' with the end of Chapter XLI of *Tess* proves the futility of computer exercises.

The poetic strain is more complex. It is a way of looking at and ordering experience. It includes the ballad qualities of Hardy's narrative, poetic presentation of event and character, his poetic sense of place and history in the re-creation of Wessex, his imaginative blending of new Victorian science and old folk superstition, and the Gothic strangeness of his vision and style. It includes a sensuous apprehension of daily life that embraces the contemplative and metaphysical. Virginia Woolf reminds us ('Impassioned Prose', *Granite and Rainbow*) that the novelist has his hands full of the facts of daily living, so 'how can we ask [him] . . . to modulate beautifully off into rhapsodies about Time and Death . . .?' Hardy's achievement of this difficult transition vindicates him as a poetic novelist.

The poetic impulse, expressing the basic but multiple faces of experience, defines the Hardeian quality. He thought of himself as 'an English poet who had written some stories in prose', and in prose tried to preserve the poetry.

'He had mostly aimed at keeping his narratives close to natural life and as near to poetry in their subject as the conditions would allow, and had often regretted that those conditions would not let him keep them nearer still.'

(*Life*)

It reconciles all the seeming contradictions of Hardy's subject, style, and philosophy by giving them equal weight but no synthesis. Hardy anticipates the modern anguish of unresolved tensions in the stylized forms which contain the undirected chaos of life; the traditional character types who reveal Freudian subtleties of psychology; grand gestures punctured by absurd and vulgar intrusions; the dichotomies of common and uncommon, simple and complex, protest and acquiescence. Yeats's definition of the double face of poetry is appropriate to the powerful tensions that constitute the Hardy vision:

'The passion . . . comes from the fact that the speakers are holding down violence or madness—'down Hysterica passio'. All depends on the completeness of the holding down, on the stirring of the beast underneath . . . Without this conflict we have no passion only sentiment and thought.'

(Letter to Dorothy Wellesley, Aug. 5, 1936)

The multiple perspective of poetry is more often a strength than a weakness. It gives simultaneously the personal and formal vision; the subjective feel of experience falling on 'all that side of the mind

11

which is exposed in solitude' (Virginia Woolf, op. cit., *Granite and Rainbow*) and the bold epic relief of those characters who 'stand up like lightning conductors to attract the force of the elements' (op. cit., *The Common Reader*) in their mythopoeic relation to time, death, and fate, both enhanced and diminished by the time-marked Wessex scene that rings their actions. It is the source of Hardy's distinctive ironic tone and structure, his tragi-comedy, his blend of fatalism and belief in the power of chance, and his profound sense of tragedy.

Hardy's ironic mode is the reverse face of his compassion. The pattern of what is runs in tension with the pattern of what ought to be according to human values. Mismatings, mistimings and undesired substitutions for an intended effect point to the 'if only' structure of Hardeian irony. If only Newson had entered the tent a few minutes earlier or later; if only Angel had danced with Tess on the green; if only Tess had not been 'doomed to be seen and coveted that day by the wrong man' instead of by the 'missing counterpart' who 'wandered independently about the earth waiting in crass obtuseness till the late time came'. Hardy's notorious use of coincidence to demonstrate cosmic absurdity is shadowed by its traditional function as an agent of cosmic design. As Barbara Hardy points out in *The Appropriate Form*, the use of coincidence in *Jane Eyre* is directed by Charlotte Brontë's belief in Providence; in *Jude the Obscure* by Hardy's belief in the absence of Providence. In Victorian melodrama the 'heroine' of *Tess of the d'Urbervilles* would have been rescued providentially by the 'hero' from the 'villain'. Hardy has neither hero, villain, nor Providence, and the alternative reasons he suggests for Tess's seduction point to the impenetrable mystery of the cosmic scheme.

When passionate personal emotion counterpoints the control of a traditional form, the ironic double vision thus obtained questions the unthinking acceptance of cosmic and social arrangements implied by the patterns Hardy took over from popular narrative and drama. Received morality is shaken and measured by the morality of compassion; poetic and Divine justice by the honesty that allows Arabella and Fitzpiers to flourish while Jude and Winterborne suffer unjustly and die, in a world where personal worth does not decide the issue. The internal tensions between the betrayed-maid archetype of balladry and the fallen woman of Victorian moral literature, set against the intense subjective world of Tess, provoke a complex reaction to her story. The psychological study of a frustrated woman strains against the breathless action of the sensation novel in *Desperate Remedies*. The Golden-Age pastoral exposes the cosmic dissonances of *Far from the Madding Crowd* and *The Woodlanders*. The expected end of the story in marriage or death takes on a bitter irony in *Jude the Obscure*, where the marriage of Sue is more tragic than the death of Jude. The hymn metres behind some of Hardy's poetic questionings of the First Cause; the ballad of revenge behind his ballads of generous action; the popular conception of romantic love behind the cruel, blind, sexual force that sweeps his characters to ecstasy, madness, suffering, and death, make the ironic mode of double vision inseparable from style. The puzzled game-birds in the poem of that name sing their bewilderment at man's inconsistent cruelty in a graceful triolet. 'The Voice' sets Hardy's grief for his wife's death to the gay tune of a remembered dance. The harsh physical facts of death deflate the pattern of the consolation poem in which 'Transformations' is written. Marsden points out that the beautiful patterns made on the page by 'The Pedigree' bring out the subtle variations and irregularities of structure which enact personal defiance of the realization of heredity to which the poem moves—'I am merest mimicker and counterfeit!—'

Hardy's multiple vision of experience brings him close to the modern Absurdist form of tragi-comedy or comi-tragedy.

'If you look beneath the surface of any farce you see a tragedy; and, on the contrary, if you blind yourself to the deeper issues of a tragedy you see a farce.'

(*Life*)

The comic court-room scene of *The Mayor of Casterbridge* in which the furmity hag works Henchard's downfall, the comic constables who take the foreground while Lucetta lies dying from the shock of the skimmity ride their incompetence has been unable to prevent; the rustics who discuss, at length, folklore remedies as Mrs Yeobright lies mortally wounded from snakebite; the two lovers who quarrel about their precedence in Elfride's affections when they have travelled unknowingly with her dead body; the farcical conjunctions of Ethelberta's three lovers; the love-sick de Stancy's undignified eavesdropping on Paula's gymnastic exercises in pink flannel; the Kafka-like distortions of figure or scene, stress the ironic deflation of romance, heroism, and tragedy by the objective incursion of absurdity; without, however, denigrating the value of romance, heroism, and suffering. 'All tragedy is grotesque—if you allow yourself to see it as such' (*Life*).

In all his work Hardy's personal voice, with its humane values, its Gothic irregularities, its human contradictions and rough edges, its commonness and uncommonness, strains against the rigidities of traditional patterns and expectations. The first two paragraphs of *The Mayor of Casterbridge*, for example, can provide the mixture to be found in all the other novels, *The Dynasts*, and most of the poems—the amalgam of homely simplicity, awkward periphrasis, triteness, and sharp sensuous vision that invests an ordinary scene with the significance of myth and Sophoclean grandeur. The dissonance of the multiple vision dramatically enacts Hardy's metaphysic of man's predicament as a striving, sensitive, imperfect individual in a rigid, non-sentient, absurd cosmos, which rewards him only with eternal death.

The predicament is tragic. A poetic ambiguity of perspective is inherent in the nature of tragedy. It is part of the texture of human hope.

'The end of tragedy . . . is to show the dignity of man for all his helpless littleness in face of the universe, for all his nullity under the blotting hand of time.'

(Bonamy Dobrée, *The Lamp and the Lute*)

In Hardy's tragedy one finds the tragic protagonist, defined for his role by a tragic greatness (not in high estate, as in Sophocles and Shakespeare, but in character alone) that intensifies the sense of life, and flawed by a tragic vulnerability that unfits him for the particular tragic situation he has to face. Jude's sexual and self-degrading impulses are disastrous in view of the obstacles to higher education for working men. Henchard's rash and inflexible temper cannot ride the agricultural changes that overtake Casterbridge. In the tragic universe human errors become tragic errors which co-operate with Fate (those circumstances within and without, which man did not make and cannot unmake, incarnated as natural forces, the clockwork laws of cause and effect, the workings of chance, coincidence, and time, irrational impulses, man-made conventions, and the search for happiness) to bring evil out of his goodness and good intentions, and to bring down on him, and innocent people connected with him, tragic suffering and catastrophe out of all proportion to its cause. The irresponsible sending of a valentine, the concealment of a seduction until the day of the wedding to another man, the careless sealing of love letters and choice of an untrustworthy messenger, release forces of death and destruction which inspire tragic terror at the contemplation of the painful mystery of the workings of inexorable law. Tragic pity is aroused, as Dobrée points out, 'not because someone suffers, but because something fine is bruised and broken'—something too sensitively organized for an insentient world of defect.

But the sense of tragic waste is tempered by tragic joy, because in the tragic confrontation with futility and absurdity Hardy affirms some of the highest values men and women can achieve.

'The great writer of tragedy manages to convey that though this be the truth, it is well that men should behave thus and thus; that in spite of all the seeming cruelty and futility of existence, one way of life is better than another; that Orestes is right and Clytemnestra wrong, that Othello is fairer than Iago. Not that fault is to be imputed to the wrongdoer; he also is a pebble of fate, destined to play his part in the eternal drama of good and evil.'

(Dobrée: op. cit.)

These values remain unchanged when the people who embodied them are destroyed, and whether the gods are alive or dead. Giles Winterborne's death may contain a criticism of his former backwardness and of Victorian sexual hypocrisy, but in its essence it celebrates the selfless love that can see further than temporary satisfaction of physical desire to the preservation of Grace's image untarnished to posterity. Modern permissiveness cannot change his nobility or the value of his suffering. Giles, Clym, Henchard, Tess, Jude, and Sue are not fulfilled in the eyes of the world. But their tragedy asserts the values for which they suffered (even Eustacia, whose selfishness limits our sympathy, asserts the value of self-assertion), stripped of all recommendations of success.

Hardy's tragic figures, rooted in an unconscious life-process more deterministic than their own, try to mould their lives according to human values, personal will, feeling, and aspiration. Though their self-assertion is overcome by the impersonality of the cosmos, including those instinctive drives they share with the natural world, their endeavour to stamp a humane personal design on cosmic indifference makes them nobler than what destroys them. Hardy had no time for Nietzsche. 'To model our conduct on Nature's apparent conduct, as Nietzsche would have taught, can only bring disaster to humanity' (*Life*). His characters' close and conscious relationship to unconscious nature defines the hope that is contained in the tragic suffering. Hardy's greatest novels are tragic actions which demonstrate the incomplete evolutionary state of man, a throb of the universal pulse, suffering as the pioneer of a more compassionate cosmic awareness—the hope towards which the whole of *The Dynasts* moves. His poems are the cries of tragic love, tragic error, tragic injustice, tragic waste, and tragic awareness with which tragic poets and dramatists from Aeschylus to Beckett have defined the sense of life.

> HAMM: What's he doing? . . .
> CLOV: He's crying . . .
> HAMM: Then he's living.
>
> (Samuel Beckett: Endgame)

That Hardy's voice still has the authentic tragic note defines his importance to the modern world. Recent assertions (as in George Steiner's *The Death of Tragedy*) that tragedy died with the gods and an ordered system of Hellenic or Christian values shared by artist and audience, which gave reasons for the suffering and struggle, can hardly stand against the tragic experience of Hardy's work. Hardeian man, sustained only by his own qualities as a human being, defies the chaotic void as Hellenic and Shakespearean man, placed in reference to cosmic myth, defied powers which were, if cruel and unknowable, at least *there* to be defied.

> Then would I bear it, clench myself, and die,
> Steeled by the sense of ire unmerited;
> Half-eased in that a Powerfuller than I
> Had willed and meted me the tears I shed.
>
> ('Hap')

A strong plot, 'exceptional enough to justify its telling', explicit in the novels and implicit in many poems, was Hardy's formal correlative for the tragic vision of man confronting his destiny. As Bonamy Dobrée points out, plot ('this is how things happen') is a more important symbol for tragedy than character ('this is what people are like'), 'since the tragic writer is concerned with the littleness of man (even though his greatness in his littleness) in the face of unescapable odds'. The hammer strokes of a clockwork universe on human sensitivity are enacted in a pattern as rigid as scientific law, likened by Lascelles Abercrombie to a process of chemistry, in which the elements

16

'are irresistibly moved to work towards one another by strong affinity; and the human molecules in which they are ingredients are dragged along with them, until the elemental affinity is satisfied, in a sudden flashing moment of disintegration and re-compounding.'

(*Thomas Hardy*)

There is no inconsistency between Hardy's determinism and the important role in his works of chance and coincidence. Chance is direction which we cannot see; but it is the direction of a blind, groping force, unrelated to anything we can conceive as conscious purpose. Once more the double perspective of chaos and determinism conjures up a richly complex poetic response to the fate of living creatures subject to inhuman cause and effect.

The symmetry and intensity of Hardy's plots, with every link in the chain of cause and effect made clear, join with his poetic vision of natural rhythms, and traditional devices of dramatic development, in a disproportioning of reality to bring out the pattern of the larger forces driving the cosmos and its creatures. Sensational events, disastrous coincidences, untimely reappearances, overheard or revealed secrets, present a universe where every action is a hostage to a predetermined and hidden fate. The supernatural detail, the rural superstitition and folk belief, stand in for the missing Providential direction. Without Providence, everything contributes to the longing for significance. Besides giving the poetic *frisson* at inexplicable mysteries, Hardy's use of superstition is integral to the characters' relation to fate. The tragedy of *The Woodlanders* is touched off by old John South's anthropological involvement with a tree. The primitive emotion conjured up by the events at the Midsummer Eve 'larries' lays the foundation of Grace's marriage, her separation, and Mrs Charmond's death. As J. O. Bailey demonstrates in 'Hardy's Visions of the Self' (*Studies in Philology*, LVI, 1959) the Hardeian 'ghost' (a waking vision, a dream, a real sight suggesting guilt, or a mental image presented to the reader) plays the part of a directing Nemesis in revealing to the character his own inner nature, causing him to accept responsibility for disasters he had blamed on circumstances, and to take the action that brings the novel to a conclusion.

The characters too have a simple epic and tragic strength. They are types, though not without individuality. All the subtleties of psychology and sociology that might obscure the pattern of their ritual interaction with Fate are stripped away. Life is reduced to its basic elements: birth, mating, death, the weather, man's pain

and helplessness in an indifferent universe; the passions and conflicts that spring from an enclosed rural community with its roots
in an ancient past and an ancient countryside, its pagan fatalism
and ballad values and personal loyalties, being gradually invaded
by modern urban restlessness and alienation. The catastrophic
passions of the main characters are set off by a peasant chorus
quietly enduring the realistic slow trivialities of daily living, which
shape human fate by steady accumulation. They are as slow to
change as the natural rhythms they are part of. Hardy creates a
fundamental persistence from the tension between the two kinds of
stability; the eternal recurrence of the natural cycle and the re-
current finiteness of men.

'They compose a pool of common wisdom, of common humour, a
fund of perpetual life. They comment upon the actions of the hero and
heroine, but while Troy or Oak or Fanny or Bathsheba come in and out
and pass away, Jan Coggan and Henry [sic] Fray and Joseph Poorgrass
remain. They drink by night and they plough the fields by day. They
are eternal. We meet them over and over again in the novels, and they
always have something typical about them, more of the character that
marks a race than of the features which belong to an individual. The
peasants are the great sanctuary of sanity, the country the last strong-
hold of happiness. When they disappear, there is no hope for the race.'
(Virginia Woolf, op. cit., *The Common Reader*)

They are equivalent to Camus's nostalgia for a lost paradisal homeland of harmony with things as they are.

The human emotional force of the characters counterpoints the
regularity of plot and scientific process; a process which they both
obey and defy. Hardy's double vision of man's greatness in values
and littleness in the cosmic scheme keeps the tragic balance between fate—the impersonal nature of things—and personal responsibility. When Henchard disregards his wife's last wishes and
reads the letter in which she discloses that Elizabeth-Jane is not his
child,

'he could not help thinking that the concatenation of events this evening
had produced was the scheme of some sinister intelligence bent on
punishing him. Yet they had developed naturally. If he had not
revealed his past history to Elizabeth he would not have searched the
drawer for papers, and so on.'

The doubt reflects the painful ambiguity and inscrutability of
things; a poetic asset. While it is true that Hardy's poetic pattern

stresses the action of fate, it does so to stress too the human responsibility to deflect fate from its path before it is too late. Misery, which teaches Henchard 'nothing more than a defiant endurance of it', teaches Clym to limit his ambitions and Oak to keep one step ahead of an infuriated universe. The adaptive resourcefulness of Farfrae, the loving-kindness of Viviette which triumphs over her sexual passion for Swithin, the determination of Paula to follow her lover through Europe regardless of etiquette, modify a fate that seemed predetermined. Their conscious purpose redefines the concept of fate as what must be *only if no resistance is made*.

In the complexity of things resistance itself has a double edge. The greatest value ephemeral man can find to stand against the threat of meaninglessness is love. It promises to satisfy the thirst for happiness and harmony with cosmic purposes. Hardy's definition of love is unfashionably wide. It includes, as well as the physiological fact and frank relationship between the sexes which he wanted to show his Victorian readers, Viviette's sublimated maternal love for her young lover Swithin, Mr Melbury's for his daughter and Mrs Yeobright's for her son, Henchard's for Farfrae and the girl who is not his daughter, Charley's idealized love for his mistress Eustacia, Clym's for suffering mankind, and the life-loyalties of the interrelated Hintock community. But because its roots are in the impersonal sexual impulses that drive the natural world, love contributes to the tragedy of human consciousness. Respect for the real being of the beloved is lost in illusory wish-projections which cause suffering when they clash with reality. Angel's image of Tess as an inhumanly pure woman, Clym's vision of Eustacia as a school matron and Eustacia's of Clym as a gay Parisian escort, Bathsheba's defence of Troy as a regular church-goer, Jude's intermittent treatment of Sue as the 'average' woman, are nature's devices, working on the human tendency to idealization, to accomplish the mating process. The projection causes pain when it moves from lover to lover; love rarely ceases for both at the same moment. But though agony is the inevitable corollary of ecstasy, the pain affirms the life-enhancing quality of love. The caprice it inspires in women—a type of the cosmic caprice of fate—is also a measure of their vitality and truth to life. The will to enjoy, inseparably bound up with the opposing will to suffer (part of 'the circumstantial will against enjoyment'); the instinctive zest for existence modified by the modern view of life as a thing to be put up with, can bring maturity and even happiness. Bathsheba

19

attains maturity and a realistic appraisal of Oak's controlled fidelity. Even Tess is only robbed of the purely human Paradise promised in Talbothays by the inhumanity of man.

Virginia Woolf accepts the great emotional crises as part of Hardy's poetic pattern.

> 'In all the books love is one of the great facts that mould human life. But it is a catastrophe; it happens suddenly and overwhelmingly, and there is little to be said about it.'
>
> (op. cit., *The Common Reader*)

T. S. Eliot, on the other hand, attacks the 'emotional paroxysms' which seem to him a 'symptom of decadence' expressing

> 'a powerful personality uncurbed by any institutional attachment or by submission to any objective beliefs . . . He seems to me to have written as nearly for the sake of "self-expression" as a man well can; and the self which he had to express does not strike me as a particularly wholesome or edifying matter of communication . . .'
>
> (*After Strange Gods*)

His criticism suggests the distrust of someone who feels the meaning of orthodox allegiances threatened by the affirmation of a life without God or ultimate purpose. But in a world where Eliot's own poetry has revealed the dehumanization of hollow men living in an emotionless waste land, the intense emotion of Hardy's characters and Hardy's personal voice affirm the response of living passion to the human predicament. 'The function of the artist is to justify life by feeling it intensely' (J. E. Barton, 'The Poetry of Thomas Hardy'). Far from robbing the characters of their human individuality, as Eliot claims, heightened emotion stresses both their basic humanness and the resistance of the unique personality to the habit of despair which Camus found worse than despair itself ('None of us was capable any longer of an exalted emotion; all had trite, monotonous feelings'—*The Plague*), and which Matthew Arnold had defined in a letter to Clough (14 December 1852) as 'the modern situation in its true *blankness* and *barrenness*, and *unpoetrylessness*'.

Hardy's poetic persona is untouched by the modern taboo on tenderness and top notes, though the understatement of deep feeling also forms part of his vision. His emotional scenes are operatic rather than melodramatic; arias which reveal the inner quality of life, with all its dissonant primary passions reconciled in the musico-poetic form, while the outer action is suspended. The effect of Boldwood's final gesture, with its poignant return of his old courtesy, 'Then he broke from Samway, crossed the room to Bathsheba, and kissed her hand', in the context of his murder of Troy, can only be compared with the return of the love leitmotif at the end of Verdi's *Otello*. (The *Life* proves that Verdi was a composer with whom Hardy felt some affinity.) As the emotional persuasiveness of music suspends disbelief in what would be absurd in spoken drama, Hardy's poetic heightening carries him through operatic implausibilities of action and clumsinesses of style. The unrealistic 'libretto' of the quarrel between Clym and Eustacia, reminiscent of the quarrel of Brachiano and Vittoria in *The White Devil*, directs attention away from the technicalities of expression to the white-hot emotion underneath that compels the jerky speech rhythms, the trembling of Eustacia's hands, and the agony of a man still in love with the wife he is rejecting on principle, who while he ties her bonnet strings for her, 'turned his eyes aside, that he might not be tempted to softness'.

It is the emotion of Hardy's work which one remembers. It expresses the whole of his many-sided personality, spilling over the barriers of artistic form to make his work an experience which is musical and artistic as well as literary. Virginia Woolf's definition of the special quality of Hardy's characters—

'We recall their passions. We remember how deeply they have loved each other and often with what tragic results . . . But we do not remember how they have loved. We do not remember how they talked and changed and got to know each other, finely, gradually, from step to step and from stage to stage . . .'

(op. cit., *The Common Reader*)

—places his work with those sister arts (in which Hardy was a competent practitioner) which create a universal image of the essence of things to transcend the personal and local details that gave it birth. As W. H. Auden remarked about his experience of writing opera libretti (the T. S. Eliot Memorial lectures given at the University of Kent at Canterbury, 1967): 'Music can, I believe, express the equivalent of *I love*, but it is incapable of saying whom or what I love, you, God, or the decimal system.' In the extraordinary states of violent emotion that distinguish the operatic mode, all differences in social standing, sex, and age are

21

abolished, so that even in a foreign language one can tell the emotion that is being expressed.

Hardy's equivalent for the operatic state often takes a form that is both musical and pictorial. Dance and song are linked with ritual survivals of fertility rites that are an 'irresistible attack upon . . . social order', as in the village gipsying on Egdon and the dance that inspires the change of marriage partners in 'The History of the Hardcomes'. The folk or church music that was part of Hardy's heritage often moves a sexual or compassionate emotion that precipitates a definite step in the story. The step is not always disastrous. The sound of children's voices singing 'Lead kindly Light' re-establishes Bathsheba's relationship with Oak after her tragedy; Farfrae's song stops Henchard from killing him in the loft. Boldwood feels encouraged to consider himself as good as engaged to Bathsheba after their exhibition of harmony at the shearing supper. Wildeve feels that there is nothing else to do but marry Tamsin after they have been celebrated by Grandfer's crew as a married couple. Farfrae's modest dance with Elizabeth-Jane at his entertainment precipitates a half-declaration of love. Tess's interest in Angel's music rivets his attention on this unusual milkmaid, whose 'fluty' tones had interrupted his meditations on a music score. The hymn tune of the Wessex composer, which made Sue and Jude clasp hands by an 'unpremeditated instinct', gives rise to her confession of an 'incomplete' marriage with Phillotson, and points to her search for spiritual harmony with Jude. Even Melbury's irritation at Cawtree's low ballad, which contributes to his rejection of Giles as a suitable mate for his daughter, is a refusal to recognize the primitive side of Grace's nature which is in harmony with the sentiments of the song and the simple woodland company who sang it. The effect of ritual music becomes a correlative for the operations of the Immanent Will, moving people through their emotions to obey its own inscrutable purposes.

Ritual itself is, in modern terms, total theatre. The ritual character of Hardy's operatic scenes—the village gipsying, the skimmity ride, the Egdon bonfires, the arrest at Stonehenge—is stressed by his balletic groupings and his description of scene and characters in terms of the strong contrast of light and shade. This pictorial treatment abstracts personality from the actors and leaves their faces mask-like, with no 'permanent moral expression'. The silhouette, employed most frequently in descriptions of the rustic chorus, expresses a communal emotion rather than individual idiosyncrasy. The figure defined in sharp relief against a dun background, like Clym against the settle or Mrs Yeobright against the heath, or suddenly illuminated, Rembrandt-fashion, in a long shaft of light (Marty at the window, Eustacia in the light from Susan Nunsuch's cottage), suddenly fixes the moving characters through the distancing of pictorial art as eternal tableaux of the littleness of conscious human experience in the surrounding darkness. (Alastair Smart, 'Pictorial Imagery in the Novels of Thomas Hardy', *Review of English Studies*, xII, 1961.) As Cytherea's father falls to his death from the tower, shafts of light falling across the room become for her an objective correlative of tragedy. The essential nature of Arabella and of her opposite Sue Bridehead is caught in the framed picture of Delilah and the comparison of Sue to a Parthenon frieze. When the heart and inner meaning has thus been established in a frozen image, it dissolves once more into the drama of people in motion acting out that reality, leaving the reader with a new perspective of their place in the cosmic scheme. This technique provides a major principle of dramatic development in *The Dynasts*.

Hardy's emotionally charged poetic pattern integrates all his personal interests into a new artistic unity. Different forms of art—architecture, sculpture, painting—and different schools add to the complex richness of his multiple perspective. The Impressionist view of Marty's hair, as it strikes the barber; of Grace through the Romantic vision of Fitzpiers, 'a sylph-like greenish-white creature, as toned by the sunlight and leafage'; of landscape, weather and people toned to the mood of the observer, opposes subjective reality to the homely detail of a Dutch painting, seen to perfection in *Under the Greenwood Tree* and 'The Homecoming'—the unheroic objective reality to which the human spirit must adjust. Even the unartistic facets contribute to the artistic whole. Hardy's much-criticized philosophical incursions and 'heavy lumps of social reform' are essential to the emotional texture of the work. The long passage on rural migration to the towns that begins Chapter LI of *Tess* falls into place as a re-creation in social terms of the central poetic image of purposeless mechanical process driving units of life in an unnatural direction. If one places the modern cult of the disappearance of the author into proper perspective as only one form of literature among many equally valid, the expansive scope of the novel can afford the author's compassionate voice pointing to the scheme of things that motivates his action. In the smaller compass of a poem, the charge that Hardy's philosophy was intrusive may carry more weight. But in his successful work the 'sentiment and thought' (in Yeats's phrase) is carried by the passion of Hardy's total portrayal of the cosmic predicament. The totality is the achievement of the poetic vision.

'Life offers—to Deny':
The Philosophical Poems

> It says that Life would signify
> A thwarted purposing:
> That we come to live, and are called to die.
>   Yes, that's the thing
>   In fall, in spring,
>   That Yell'ham says:—
>   "Life offers—to deny!"

The tragic paradox expressed in 'Yell'ham-Wood's Story' is the recurring theme of several poems that put forward a philosophic view of the universe. Hardy disclaimed the title of systematic philosopher: repeatedly his Prefaces insist that 'no harmonious philosophy is attempted in these pages' (*Winter Words*); that his poems are 'unadjusted impressions' . . . 'written down in widely differing moods and circumstances' (*Poems of the Past and the Present*); mere '"questionings" in the exploration of reality' (*Late Lyrics and Earlier*). As an explorer of reality he is, like every other serious artist who has a controlling vision of man's relation to the cosmos, a man with a personal slant on reality that can be called a philosophy. Hardy's tragic vision of the 'thwarted purposing' evident in the conflict between the fine potentialities of conscious man and the indifference of the unconscious universe which had produced him, informs the bulk of the *Collected Poems*. There are many poems which seem designed to give prominent expression to Hardy's philosophical concepts: 'The Bedridden Peasant', 'The Lacking Sense', 'The Mother Mourns', 'The Convergence of the Twain', 'God-Forgotten', 'The Subalterns', 'Hap', 'Agnosto Theo', 'Nature's Questioning', 'A Dream Question', 'Before Life and After', spring immediately to mind. And among these are some overtly philosophical poems in which the poet uses some of the tools of the professional philosopher—direct statement, logical argument, analysis, abstract concepts placed in the foreground as subject instead of providing an undercurrent of implication in a concrete illustration of the human predicament—to explain or suggest why things are as they are.

While the poems which state philosophical beliefs are obviously the product of careful thought on man's predicament, their speculations are diverse enough to justify Hardy's denial of the charge that he tried to build up a system of organized philosophy. His personification of the ultimate Cause of things moves from God ('God-Forgotten', 'A Dream Question', 'By the Earth's Corpse') to Nature ('The Mother Mourns', 'The Sleep-Worker', 'The Lacking Sense') to the 'Willer masked and dumb' of 'Agnosto Theo' and the neuter 'It' of 'A Philosophical Fantasy' and 'The Absolute Explains'. In some poems two or more manifestations of the ultimate Cause share responsibility; Doom and Nature in 'Doom and She'; in 'Hap', Time and Chance; the elements and all the ills of the flesh, driven by Necessity, in 'The Subalterns'. His tentative conclusions on the origin of human suffering range from the traditional theological view of 'severance, self-entailed' from God in 'God-Forgotten' and 'The Bedridden Peasant', the indifference of an unknowing and unknowable God in 'A Dream Question' and 'A Philosophical Fantasy', to the more charitable impressions of the purposeless workings 'by vacant rote' of a blind necessitating force, liable to make mistakes ('The Sleep-Worker', 'The Mother Mourns', 'The Lacking Sense', 'Nature's Questioning'). Nevertheless, it is a force which may one day grow sensitive to the sufferings of its creatures ('Agnosto Theo') and either restore a state of universal unconsciousness ('Before Life and After') or 'patiently adjust, amend, and heal' ('The Sleep-Worker').

The variety of Hardy's 'mood-dictated' impressions does not conceal his belief that presentation of a world-view or views is as proper a function for the poet as for the novelist, and may make for easier reception by the public. A note written in 1896 after the shocked public reaction to his arraignment of the universe in *Tess of the d'Urbervilles* and *Jude the Obscure* leaves no doubt that he intended to continue the 'application of ideas to life' in poetry:

'Perhaps I can express more fully in verse ideas and emotions which run counter to the inert crystallized opinion—hard as a rock—which the vast body of men have vested interests in supporting. To cry out in a passionate poem that (for instance) the Supreme Mover or Movers, the Prime Force or Forces, must be either limited in power, unknowing, or cruel—which is obvious enough, and has been for centuries—will cause them merely a shake of the head; but to put it in argumentative prose will make them sneer, or foam, and set all the literary contortionists jumping upon me, a harmless agnostic, as if I were a clamorous atheist, which in their crass illiteracy they seem to think is the same thing. . . .

The proposition that 'the Prime Force or Forces must be either limited in power, unknowing, or cruel' does not always produce a passionate poem.

I asked the Lord: "Sire, is this true
Which hosts of theologians hold,
That when we creatures censure you
For shaping griefs and ails untold
(Deeming them punishments undue)
You rage, as Moses wrote of old?

When we exclaim: 'Beneficent
He is not, for he orders pain,
Or, if so, not omnipotent:
To a mere child the thing is plain!'
Those who profess to represent
You, cry out: 'Impious and profane!'"

He: "Save me from my friends, who deem
That I care what my creatures say!
Mouth as you list: sneer, rail, blaspheme,
O manikin, the livelong day,
Not one grief-groan or pleasure-gleam
Will you increase or take away.

"Why things are thus, whoso derides,
May well remain my secret still. . . . . .
A fourth dimension, say the guides,
To matter is conceivable.
Think some such mystery resides
Within the ethic of my will."
                                        ('A Dream Question')

The answer to the dreamer's question—that there is no answer to the riddle of pain—has elsewhere produced the true poetic thrill of awe at the mystery of things. But here there is no resonance beyond the unemotive question and statement. Both speakers are too dispassionate for the poem to take fire in a reader's mind. Shadowy

27

Causes 'vacant of feeling', 'labouring all-unknowingly', which can ask:

> "World-weaver! what *is* Grief?
> And what are Right, and Wrong,
> And Feeling, that belong
> To creatures all who owe thee fief?
> Why is Weak worse than Strong?"
> ('Doom and She')

are not the most fitting mouthpieces to express or respond to the passionate human indictment of creation, since 'nor joy nor pain/ It lies in [them] to recognize'. The 'incensed Deity' of Milton has no parallel in the indifferent First Cause of Hardy. Where such a metaphysical mouthpiece does spring to passionate life it is, significantly, as the fantasy of a primitive 'vengeful god' conceived and communicated in personal terms by the human mind of the 'suffering thing'—one of the 'infallible estimators' of pain:

> If but some vengeful god would call to me
> From up the sky, and laugh: "Thou suffering thing,
> Know that thy sorrow is my ecstasy,
> That thy love's loss is my hate's profiting!"
>
> Then would I bear it, clench myself, and die,
> Steeled by the sense of ire unmerited;
> Half-eased in that a Powerfuller than I
> Had willed and meted me the tears I shed.
>
> But not so. How arrives it joy lies slain
> And why unblooms the best hope ever sown?
> —Crass Casualty obstructs the sun and rain,
> And dicing Time for gladness casts a moan. . . .
> These purblind Doomsters had as readily strown
> Blisses about my pilgrimage as pain.
> ('Hap')

Here, crass Casualty and dicing Time do not exceed their function as abstract concepts of the blind and dumb arbiters of man's fate, conceived as such by the same ordering human mind which created the illusion of cosmic design in the first eight lines of the sonnet. The philosophical idea develops, not in bare statement or debate, but in a human context of moral and dramatic confrontation which compels an immediate shock of recognition. To rejoice in the downfall of one's enemy acknowledges his importance. To bear pain with resignation, 'half-eased in that a Powerfuller than I/Had willed and meted me the tears I shed', suggests acknowledgement of the importance of the divine antagonist's design. The clash of two meaningful opposites—Captain Ahab and the white whale, Hemingway's Old Man and the big fish, Job and his God—is easier to realize in a concrete poetic image than an encounter between a puzzled representative 'manikin' and an unmoral, loveless and hateless force which cannot realize passion.

'But not so'. The honest colloquial shrug at the turn of the sonnet rejects the comforting illusion of a personal God to whom human suffering is meaningful for the less flattering truth of an impersonal absurdity. A cosmos operated by impersonal abstractions is delicate ground for a poet whose interests in philosophical concepts lies predominantly in their bearing on human life. But the precise dramatic image of one man's confrontation of fate, enriched by the poet's emotional response to this aspect of human experience, has generated enough poetic feeling to impregnate the abstractions of the sestet. The world of abstract concepts is held in constant and fruitful tension, fundamental to Hardy's best poetry, with specific images from the world of sense experience, felt on the pulses of an individual human being.

'Hap' is shaped by the basic conflict implied in much of Hardy's poetry; usually a variation of Yell'ham-wood's theme song "Life offers—to deny". It grows out of the tensions between human and inhuman, personal and impersonal, concrete and abstract, feeling and thought. The knotted strength of the poem comes from the simultaneous presence of the opposing worlds, maintaining the powerful unresolved balance of two wrestlers sculptured in granite. The human mind of the protagonist, within which both terms of the opposition are conceived, creates the poetic emotion from his simultaneous acceptance of the truth of the nineteenth-century scientific view of man's unimportance to the cosmic scheme, and his desire to go on believing in the traditional significance of individual man. The divided allegiance to harsh absurd truth and meaningful fantasy is acknowledged by the reader as authentic, because it is communicated as a deeply-felt cry—the whole poem—from a sensitive and tormented individual experiencing as a human being 'the inherent will to enjoy, and the circumstantial will against enjoyment'.

Life and its denial, the tensions inherent in personal experience of the impersonal cosmos, are presented in a pattern of thought and emotion, structure, diction and word-music, balance and disturbance of rhythm, that is peculiarly Hardy's own, where his quirks of style are major assets inseparable from the thought. When 'Crass Casualty obstructs' the sun and rain, the obstruction to the smoothly-singing monosyllables from the world of simple sense experience is caused by the overwhelming polysyllabic sonority of the Latin abstraction with its hard alliterative consonants. The concept of a fundamental disharmony inheres in the wrestle of words taken from every level of language, which combine and strain against each other. The archaic 'Doomsters' (judges) exists in ironic tension with the unusual but still extant 'purblind'. Judges are not expected to be blind, obtuse, or dull; Fate is, and because the root of 'Doomsters' evokes Fate a musical discord is set up between the worlds of human and inhuman values. The outmoded, but Biblical, second person singular invests the dramatic scene with the emotional resonance that belongs to every mythical confrontation of a heroic human being with a primitive god made in man's tribal image. The coinage 'unblooms', in its characteristic Hardeian use of the negative particle, which has been happily defined by Viola Meynell as 'the *un* that summons in order that it may banish, and keeps the living word present to hear sentence and denial', is concrete and precise in its evocation of the reversal of an expected natural process. The question in which the word occurs realizes imaginatively the denial of the meaning of life, growth, and sense experience which is mirrored in the answer. The negating 'unblooms' is linked to the abstract causes of denial, not only by the sound echo in 'Doomsters', but also by their parallel positions of stress in the line.

Hardy's concern with stress and rhythm, which has caused so much bafflement to readers and critics with other than Hardeian expectations, constitutes a major contribution to the poetry of tension and paradox. His fascination with the technical problems of scansion, and impatience with critics who could not see that 'those oft are Stratagems which Errors seem', is demonstrated by the many notes on rhythm and metre found among his papers:

'Years earlier he had decided that too regular a beat was bad art . . . He knew that in architecture cunning irregularity is of enormous worth, and it is obvious that he carried on into his verse, perhaps in part unconsciously, the Gothic art-principle in which he had been trained—the principle of spontaneity, found in mouldings, tracery, and

30

such-like—resulting in the 'unforeseen' (as it has been called) character of his metres and stanzas, that of stress rather than syllable, poetic texture rather than poetic veneer . . . He shaped his poetry accordingly, introducing metrical pauses, and reversed beats; and found for his trouble that some particular line of a poem exemplifying this principle was greeted with a would-be jocular remark that such a line "did not make for immortality."'

(*The Life of Thomas Hardy*)

In 'Hap', the reader who respects the metrical stress of the normal iambic pentameter of the sonnet form will get into difficulties, for example, with the fourth line, where natural emphasis in the speaking voice demands three consecutive heavy stresses on the opposing phrases 'thy love's loss' and 'my hate's profiting'. But a reader sensitive to the authentic speech rhythms of an idiosyncratic human voice in the grip of a deeply-felt emotion, responding painfully, precisely, to the affirmations and denials of life, will re-create the heroic confrontation that is forced on his senses by the balancing stresses on 'My . . . thy' and 'Crass Casualty . . . sun and rain.'

The speaking voice realizing in its own personal music the double face of the universe is a varied instrument. Hardy reproduces it faithfully, warts and all, in all its human contrariness—its smoothness and roughness, simplicities and complexities of expression, colloquialisms and bookish clichés, clipped phrases and prosinesses, sublime harmonies and harsh dissonances, pauses, passions, and meditations, broken rhythms, quickenings and retardings of pace. But the human voice alone, however faithfully reproduced, is not enough to make poetry. Hardy, like Camus, was too honest and too aware of human dignity to leave out of his formal structure the mechanical insentient universe against which conscious man shatters himself.

'Negating one of the terms of the opposition on which he lives amounts to escaping it . . . To impoverish that reality whose inhumanity constitutes man's majesty is tantamount to impoverishing him himself.'

(Camus: *The Myth of Sisyphus*)

The individual speaking voice responding fully to experience runs in counterpoint against the rigidity of an expected metrical structure; often, as in 'Hap', of a conventional poetic form such as the sonnet, sometimes obeying the underlying structure, sometimes straining against it. The resulting tension creates a striking re-enactment of a conscious human being painfully striving to impose order and significance on the mechanical insentience of the universe, 'that reality whose inhumanity constitutes man's majesty', by the very qualities of unmechanical imperfection that constitute his humanness.

The characteristic tension of Hardy's verse is most noticeable in short poems. Concentration of form often seems to produce concentration of thought, emotion, mood, and image. The borrowed philosophy of constant change as the ultimate stable reality can hardly have been summed up in a more succinct paradox than '"According to the Mighty Working"':

> When moiling seems at cease
>   In the vague void of night-time,
>   And heaven's wide roomage stormless
>   Between the dusk and light-time,
>   And fear at last is formless,
> We call the allurement Peace.
>
> Peace, this hid riot, Change,
>   This revel of quick-cued mumming,
>   This never truly being,
>   This evermore becoming,
>   This spinner's wheel onfleeing
> Outside perception's range.

Here, though Hardy denies himself the aid of a specific human context to give dramatic realization to his philosophic concepts, the poetry is not unbalanced by the philosophy. The poetic emotion, often created by some personal pressure of suffering, is here implied in the title, taken from the Burial Service, which had both a personal and universal relevance for many of Hardy's readers in 1917. Though the speaking voice in this poem is less personal than representative of all those for whom the war was a symbol of the ceaseless elemental hostilities of the cosmos, the Hardeian tensions are still present in the very structure of the poem, framed as it is between the key-words of the paradox inherent in existence—cease-Peace, Change-range. Peace is reduced to its opposite Change in the space of one economical six-syllable line by the pivotal 'hid riot' implied in the 'moiling' of the first stanza. Hardy's idiosyncratic word-music of dissonance is captured in the tensions between abstract idea and vivid specific image ('mumming' is a favourite Hardeian metaphor for the automatic processes of the cosmos); between a resonant mixture of unusual diction ('moiling', 'roomage', 'onfleeing') and plain words, often juxtaposed in evocative combinations ('light-time', 'quick-cued'). The long open vowels of the first stanza, which bring to the ear vast formless reaches of space and time in a state of seeming suspension, are set in opposition to the short rapid vowels of the second, which presents the eternal 'onfleeing' in a whirl of accelerating activity that returns over and over again to the fixed point of assonance in 'revel . . . never . . . evermore'. The diction of each stanza is carefully chosen and combined to give to each its appropriate rhythm and movement, as a comparison, for example, of the second line of each stanza makes clear. The slow monosyllables of 'In the vague void of night-time', which retard the swift Swinburnian metre, also retard the speaking voice, while the sound as well as the sense of 'This revel of quick-cued mumming' calls for accelerated reading. One can hardly read the poem aloud without becoming conscious of the paradox at the heart of existence being enacted in every detail of the structure.

'"According to the Mighty Working"' succeeds as poetry because Hardy has resisted the temptation to explain the workings of the contradictory mysteries of life. He leaves them as a presented image of unresolved tension. The speculative definitions of the Peace-Change paradox in the second stanza, reminiscent of Vaughan's metaphysical 'Son-Days', draw no conclusions that are beyond the limits of human knowledge. The same reticence operates, in spite of reference to the Immanent Will and the Spinner of the Years, in 'The Convergence of the Twain' to make this longer poem a successful poetic image of 'thwarted purposing' in its unexplained juxtaposition of human purpose—the 'smart ship' —and its denial, the 'sinister mate' of ice that was to be the agent of its destruction. The sexual terms in which the disaster is seen makes the final 'consummation', in which the separately-developing 'twin halves of one august event' come together for the first time, when Time and Chance coincide, a symbol of cosmic mismarriage that is central to Hardy's universe. In such a mismarriage, as Hynes points out in *The Pattern of Hardy's Poetry*, there can be no resolution of discord, only honest recognition of its unreconciled ironies. The question of the sea's natural inhabitants,

"What does this vaingloriousness down here?"

receives no answer from the accident that jarred two hemispheres, for there is no answer known to humankind to the mystery of suffering. The possible absurdity of the universe is presented by letting the inexplicable contraries of the event speak for themselves in the various 'mismarriages' of idea and structure. The bare, direct language of dignified abstraction that clothes the philosophy of predestination in the second half of the poem ('A Shape of Ice, for the time far and dissociate', 'In shadowy silent distance') is ironically mismated to the rich, grotesque, sensuous diction and evocative imagery of the first half, the specific context of 'vaingloriousness' which the experience of the second half is predestined to contradict. The two short lines of each stanza are contrasted with the long final lines, which in the first half coil in and out of the poem with the inevitability of the fatal sea. In stanzas VI to XI, however, the rhythm of these final lines is changed by simpler, smoother diction into a movement that is colder, more inhuman. That the contrasts and juxtapositions have no meaning to 'mortal eye' is the meaning of this poem, and many others. Human lack of knowledge, man's inability to impose rational order on the incongruities of life, is powerfully suggested by what Hardy does *not* say. As G. K. Chesterton points out in his book on Browning, 'there is a certain poetic value . . . in this sense of having missed the full meaning of things. There is beauty, not only in wisdom, but in this dazed and dramatic ignorance.'

When Hardy rejects the poetic value of the human individual's 'dazed and dramatic ignorance' for discursive argument with and through vague non-human mouthpieces, the poetic impact is often blunted by an overweight of philosophic content that disperses the instigating passion. The cry of passion, by its very nature, cannot be long sustained. The presentation of the same idea—for example, the idea of Nature's unreflecting blindness—is more effective in the concentrated sonnet 'The Sleep-Worker'* than in the long argument of 'The Lacking Sense'. The sonnet begins with a direct cry of passionate protest from the human sufferer to the Cause of his suffering:

When wilt thou wake, O Mother, wake and see . . .?

Her nature and mode of operation are implied only through simile and metaphor—the usual bridge between the known of the physi-

*The diversity of critical viewpoint can be illustrated by referring to Hynes's judgement of 'The Sleep-Worker' as a failure.

cal world and the metaphysical unknown. No explanation is demanded; relief from pain is of more immediate concern to the sufferer than explanation of its cause. The mystery of life's dissonances is simply presented, and left unsolved. The poem ends, as it begins, with a question—a natural human speculation on the wished-for development of cosmic awareness which has grown inevitably out of the original cry of protest. The personal cry from an individual who has felt in his 'palpitating tissues' the effects of Nature's faulty workmanship is more powerful than the questioning and explanation of 'the Mother's moody look' in 'The Lacking Sense'. The direct expression of pain is curiously distanced both by the concern of the human questioner for the Mother's moody look rather than for his own suffering, and by the third-party intervention of Time. Hardy's Time, except possibly in the *Dynasts*, which is a deliberate attempt to create a new mythology in the temper of the modern age, is too shadowy to have the traditional reverberations of the scythe-and-hour-glass figure familiar to readers of George Herbert's dialogue-poem 'Time'. And even with his reliance on the seventeenth-century conditioned response to the partly humanized figure, Herbert gives most of the argument to his controlling human character, whereas four out of the six stanzas of 'The Lacking Sense' are spoken by Hardy's specification of a Time whose nature, to the nineteenth and twentieth centuries, is unknown. Distancing of emotion has its effect on the language too. Abstractions and literary clichés replace the vivid visual and aural dissonances of 'The Sleep-Worker'. The general language of statement and explanation—

> Into her would-be perfect motions, modes, effects, and features
> Admitting cramps, black humours, wan decay, and baleful blights,
> Distress into delights

—has no reverberation beyond itself. But the emotional response to 'Strange orchestras of victim-shriek and song' takes on a rich complexity when one reflects on the directly-experienced discords combined in the same line with an evocation of the harmony of individual instruments working together in an orchestra. The language of poetry, as opposed to the language of prosaic statement, requires an emotional and imaginative contribution from the reader to blossom into full meaning.

Hardy's humanizing compassion for all things groaning together in creation gives distinction to some poems whose ingredients would seem to invite complete failure. 'The Subalterns' has a higher measure of success than some other poems in which non-human mouthpieces speak because man's antagonists Sickness, Death, and the elements are imbued with his own compassion. Human and non-human manifestations alike are driven by the force of necessity, which is allowed to remain outside the poem, potent in its unknowable mystery. Its 'subalterns' make no attempt to explain or justify the mystery of necessity; the poem is a simple concrete presentation of the effects of their orders from 'laws in force on high' on the body of an individual human being, with a disclaimer of responsibility which turns these former antagonists into fellow-victims. 'Nature's Questioning', though less successful than 'The Subalterns' in its use of inanimate poetic mouthpieces, owes its memorable quality to Hardy's feeling that human and non-human nature alike are fellow-sufferers from the First Cause. Both human and non-human manifestations appear in the first stanza in a sympathetic relationship; the First Cause does not appear except as speculations of 'pool, field, flock, and lonely tree', though its effects are felt, as in 'The Subalterns', throughout the poem. The alternative guesses at an explanation of the faulty cosmic scheme are among Hardy's most striking realizations of the metaphysical in terms that bring it within the range of human comprehension but do not rob it of all mystery by too concrete an image. His characteristic mixture of the physical with the metaphysical, the high poetic style with the colloquial, as in

> Or are we live remains
> Of Godhead dying downwards, brain and eye now gone?

the abstract Miltonic majesty of 'some Vast Imbecility', the hymn-like dignity of the metre with its unexpected long final line (an Alexandrine) breaking the pattern to focus attention on the effects of the First Cause on its manifestations, all work together to give these three verses a high rank in philosophical poetry. But when they are placed in the context of the whole poem, one wonders whether language worthy of a Miltonic angel could be the 'lippings mere' of cowed inanimate things, still less of the 'chastened children sitting silent in a school' to which they are compared almost before their identity as inanimate things has been established. The metaphors in this poem are perhaps too strong for the realities they represent, and the poet's philosophy too strong for the metaphors. The dramatization of the First Cause as a schoolmaster

36

humanizes it into something very close to the personal God of primitive myth, which injures its presentation as a nonhuman force. The poem is pulled in two directions by the poet's fellow-feeling for 'things around': the tension is not tight enough to be fully creative. Nevertheless, a kind of unity operates through the consciousness of the poet as passive observer, registering through his imaginative fantasy the universal questioning of the mystery written on the face of all nature:

> . . . . No answerer I . . .
> Meanwhile the winds, and rains,
> And Earth's old glooms and pains
> Are still the same, and Life and Death are neighbours nigh.

The sense of impenetrable mystery informing the human being's relationship to the laws of the cosmos produces the most authentic poetic emotion when it is left as a question mark:

> Why joys they've found I cannot find,
> Abides a mystery.
> ('The Impercipient')

> Wilt thou destroy, in one wild shock of shame,
> Thy whole high heaving firmamental frame,
> Or patiently adjust, amend, and heal?
> ('The Sleep-Worker')

> Ere nescience shall be reaffirmed
> How long, how long?
> ('Before Life and After')

> Perhaps Thy ancient rote-restricted ways
> Thy ripening rule transcends;
> ('Agnosto Theo')

Human knowledge of the unknowable cannot go beyond a speculative 'perhaps' or 'how much' or 'as if':

> How much of consciousness informs Thy will,
> Thy biddings, as if blind,
> Of death-inducing kind,
> Nought shows to us ephemeral ones who fill
> But moments in thy mind.
> ('Agnosto Theo')

But human ignorance can allow the human heart to hope; and the hope of growing awareness in the unconscious cosmos at the end of 'Agnosto Theo' is all the more powerful for the honest admission at the beginning of ignorance of the unknown and unknowable:

> Long have I framed weak phantasies of Thee,
> O Willer masked and dumb!

While the Willer remains masked and dumb, a mere fantasy of human speculation, its lack of definition can arouse the proper poetic awe and terror at the unknowable. A God made in man's image, like the vengeful god of 'Hap' and even Milton's rather unorthodox deity, has enough traditional authority to give him credibility when he opens his mouth to argue, justify, or explain. But in a transitional age when, as Leslie Stephen said in a note quoted by Hardy in the *Life*, 'the old ideals have become obsolete, and the new are not yet constructed', it is difficult to respond to a Prime Force which is neither one thing nor the other. The question which Hardy so often asks of the universe:

"And how explains thy Ancient Mind her crimes upon her creatures?"

postulates a being which has enough mind to reason—a humanized conception which neighbours uneasily with the mindless mechanical Causes of nineteenth-century science that Hardy's integrity compelled him to present. Insensitive mindless mouthpieces which have no recognizable reverberations from tradition are not qualified to justify the cosmic scheme, to explain or withhold explanation, to mourn 'man's mountings of mindsight' ('The Mother Mourns', 'New Year's Eve', 'God's Education'), to be schoolmaster to natural phenomena ('Nature's Questioning') when, as God remarks in 'God's Education':

> "Forsooth, though I men's master be,
> Theirs is the teaching mind!"

or to give moral advice on man's function in the cosmos ('The Lacking Sense', 'A Plaint to Man'). Moral speculation on man's possible relationship to cosmic laws as conscious 'pioneer' of Nature's growth of awareness comes more naturally as a personal response of the maker of 'weak phantasies' to the unknowable:

Part is mine of the general Will,
Cannot my share in the sum of sources
Bend a digit the poise of forces,
And a fair desire fulfil?

('He Wonders About Himself')

Only suffering man is qualified to mourn, hope, make moral resolutions, admit shortcomings, or entertain contradictory speculations on the nature and power of the First Cause, since, as the 'phasm' of God admits in 'A Plaint to Man',

My virtue, power, utility,
Within my maker must all abide,
Since none in myself can ever be.

Only he can choose to absolve God from his crimes and keep up the fantasy of a merciful deity while facing the harsh truth of his neglect, as in the fine lyric 'The Bedridden Peasant'.

'Human beings, in their generous endeavour to construct a hypothesis that shall not degrade a First Cause, have always hesitated to conceive a dominant power of lower moral quality than their own; and even while they sit down and weep by the waters of Babylon, invent excuses for the oppression which prompts their tears.'

(*The Return of the Native*)

The vivid dramatization of this idea in the archetypal figure of the bedridden peasant makes this poem superior in poetic quality to 'God-Forgotten', which appears on the previous page in *Poems of the Past and the Present*: poems which are close neighbours often show different attempts to work out the same thought. The idea common to both 'God-Forgotten' and 'The Bedridden Peasant' is God's neglect of the human race. 'God-Forgotten' is written in the form of a dialogue between a God who does most of the talking and a respectful but dogged representative of humankind, 'Sent thither by the sons of Earth, to win/Some answer to their cry.' The poem develops logically and straightforwardly from the first encounter, when the supercilious and absent-minded deity is prodded into vague remembrance of creating 'Some tiny sphere I built long back (Mid millions of such shapes of mine)'; into admission of lost interest at the time of Earth's 'severance, self-entailed'; into self-justification of his continuing neglect—

"Thou shouldst have learnt that *Not to Mend*
For Me could mean but *Not to Know*:"

and finally into a plan to 'straightway put an end/To what men undergo'. In spite of the admirable persistence of the human representative, the dialogue is too distanced from the specific human context to rouse much emotion. It pales before the direct prayer of the suffering peasant to an unknowing God, who does not have to state his ignorance like the God of 'God-Forgotten', for he is conspicuous by his absence throughout the poem. The absence of what ought to be there, ironically pointed up by the simple prayer form and hymn metre of 'O God Our Help in Ages Past', creates a fruitful tension with what *is* there—the nobility of a human individual who hesitates to conceive a dominant power of lower moral quality than his own, and so is prepared to give his absent God the benefit of the doubt. The self-revelation of the God of 'God-Forgotten' does not reveal so much of the contrast between man and God as the endeavour of the forgotten victim to protect the good name of his Maker. Shut in by the 'dead wall' of the physical world, that is the physical wall of his bedridden confinement as well as the metaphysical wall of his alienation from God and meaning, he can only reason from his limited human experience; and when the actions of God are judged by the moral standards of men, God is seen by the reader to be the inferior being:

> For, say one puts a child to nurse,
> He eyes it now and then
> To know if better it is, or worse,
> And if it mourn, and when.

But his conception of the God made in man's image remains stubbornly charitable. It is hard to conceive of a deity who would allow meaningless pain when no human being would, 'For Thou art mild of heart'. The very limitations of the peasant's philosophical point of view, which we all recognize when faced with the mystery of pain, creates the poetic emotion. If it was difficult to sympathize with an all-powerful deity which is so inhuman that it has to be prodded into remembrance of earthly pain, it is not difficult to thrill to the human nobility and compassion of the powerless peasant who makes a deliberate choice to stand by his fantasy of what God ought to be, in face of the truth of what God is—unknowing and unknowable.

> Then, since thou mak'st not these things be,
> But these things dost not know,

> I'll praise Thee as were shown to me
> The mercies Thou wouldst show!

The great strength of a poem like 'The Bedridden Peasant' with its sublime human response to the unknowable couched in the simple, direct, often Biblical language of the sufferer, is a strength of tension between the poet's intellectual allegiance to scientific truth and his emotional nostalgia for the Christian God and the Christian myth. The emotion of poignant regret for the loss of traditional belief while accepting the harsh truth of a meaningless world motivates and permeates such fine short lyrics as 'The Impercipient', 'The Oxen', and 'A Drizzling Easter Morning'. In these poems, the tension is first of all objectified in the poet's physical situation—among the gravestones on a wet Easter morning, 'By the embers in hearthside ease' on Christmas Eve, hovering on the outskirts of a Cathedral service—the archetypal alien from the harmony of a God-directed universe. He both observes and suffers the assaults of a physical world that has lost hope of Christian salvation, while his mind reaches back to the lost belief that would give meaning to suffering. The physical presence of the poet throughout, experiencing the divided allegiances of his time, gives emotional resonance to the simple but traditional details without which a poem like 'A Drizzling Easter Morning' would hardly rise above the factual observation of a wet day. His observation of the eternally heavy-laden as he stands amid the eternally at rest makes an ironic comment on the meaning of the Resurrection referred to in the first line: 'And is he risen? Well, be it so', which modifies the tone of the repetition in the last:

> And toilers with their aches are fain
> For endless rest—though risen is he.

The poet's figure within the poem, at once both a private individual and universal representative, throwing his mood of regret for lost faith over the whole poem, can make a success of a longer work such as 'God's Funeral', whereas 'A Plaint to Man', which presents the same idea—the growth and decay of man's conception of the deity—is less happy in its point of view. The dead God of 'A Plaint to Man'—one 'thin as a phasm on a lantern-slide'—can hardly transmit the powerful personal pressure of human nostalgia for a lost value that resides in the traditional associations of a funeral procession seen through the eyes of a stricken mourner.

> I saw a slowly-stepping train—
> Lined on the brows, scoop-eyed and bent and hoar—
> Following in files across a twilit plain
> A strange and mystic form the foremost bore.

The visual scene, with its vivid details of death and sorrow in the second line and its evocation of crowds engaged in some strange symbolic action, is reminiscent of Dante. So is the sad observing figure of the poet, whose sympathy with the figures of his vision sustains and unifies a poem of seventeen stanzas. The sympathy with this image of human sorrow, as yet unexplained, is established in the second stanza by 'contagious throbs of thought', and followed in stanzas III and IV by a changing image of what the dead shape had meant in all its 'phantasmal variousness' to the poet. Only when his personal response and mood has been clarified does he draw 'towards the moving columns without a word'. From stanzas VI to XII his personal response becomes involved with the general lament, which he overhears, of the human race for its 'man-projected Figure, of late/Imaged as we'. The explanation in these stanzas is not the emotionless explanation of cosmic operations given by a deity or Cause, but of the vision of human sorrow we have just seen, suffused with the grief of the observer. The growth of man's conception of God, and his grief at the loss of his comforting fantasy, is more comprehensible to the human mind than explanations of the cause of pain, which is inexplicable. The question 'And who or what shall fill his place?' returns the poem in stanza XIII to the personal response of the poet.

> I could not buoy their faith: and yet
> Many I had known: with all I sympathized;
> And though struck speechless, I did not forget
> That what was mourned for, I, too, long had prized.
>
> XV
> Still, how to bear such loss I deemed
> The insistent question for each animate mind . . .

Standing in the cold light of a godless day, without belief in a man-made God, or in a God that has survived the 'requiem' of his false man-made mockery, the insistent question of how to live in a meaningless absurdity is faced by the human individual with courage and integrity. Characteristically, Hardy does not place too much reliance on the small gleam of hope on the horizon, perhaps a new God still to make himself manifest, but ends in the dazed and dramatic ignorance of the human being, isolated from his ordering fantasy, accepting the inexplicable mystery of a dissonant godless world:

> Thus dazed and puzzled 'twixt the gleam and gloom
> Mechanically I followed with the rest.

God is dead: all we can know of him is the value of his image to the human mind that created him. That value is developed in the poem through Hardy's dramatic use of the human consciousness, with its capacity for emotion, vision, fantasy, and truth, shaping the structure of the poem itself.

The importance of a tenable philosophy in a poem like 'God's Funeral' pales before the strength of the poet's feeling of regret for the passing of one which had imposed order on chaos. The strain of living without a comforting fantasy gives rise in countless shorter poems to the bewildered cry of personal pain that lifts poems like 'Hap' and 'Before Life and After' into the rank of major poetry. But the directionless bewilderment can also succeed at lower tension when it takes an ironic or humorous turn, as in 'The Respectable Burgher on "The Higher Criticism"' and 'Drinking Song'. A characteristic tone of humorous and resigned regret can be found in the chorus of 'Drinking Song'—

> Fill full your cups: feel no distress;
> 'Tis only one great thought the less!

—which punctuates the roll-call of man's diminishing importance as reflected in the history of Western philosophy, from Thales' conjecture that 'everything was made for man' to Darwin's 'We are all one with creeping things'. The encompassing image of bewildered man, facing the dark with cheering cup in hand and an unshakeable faith in the one value he is left with, the value of human action ('We'll do a good deed nevertheless!'), to set against the loss of all sustaining philosophies, has more power to move than all the explanations of the Absolute. The colloquial language, such as the homely dialect word 'rathe' in the middle of Einstein relativity, and the awkward syntax that clothes the Copernican theory—

> We trod, he told,
> A globe that rolled
> Around a sun it warmed it at. . . .

present a vivid impression of the muddled human mind stutteringly trying to formulate incomprehensible abstractions in down-to-earth concrete terms. Einstein's 'notion' of relativity ('just a sort of bending-ocean') is more effective, by reason of the honest admission with which it begins, that it is

> Not yet quite clear
> To many here—

than its long scientific analysis in 'The Absolute Explains'.

To laugh at the absurdity of his tragic predicament in the universe is man's prerogative. God's attempts at grim humour in 'A Philosophical Fantasy' are not successful, any more than his attempts at thinking and feeling in other poems where he is the mouthpiece for Hardy's ideas. In spite of the wry rejection of man-centred philosophies in 'Drinking Song', the human being, with his capacity to feel, was always the centre of Hardy's universe. When the human cry is submerged in argumentative verse of direct statement or analysis, the poem is liable to fall flat. But when the cry of protest at 'the intolerable antilogy/Of making figments feel' is passionate enough to shape substance and style from the philosophy, a major poem is born.

> A time there was—as one may guess
> And as, indeed, earth's testimonies tell—
> Before the birth of consciousness,
> When all went well.
>
> None suffered sickness, love, or loss,
> None knew regret, starved hope, or heart-burnings;
> None cared whatever crash or cross
> Brought wrack to things.
>
> If something ceased, no tongue bewailed,
> If something winced and waned, no heart was wrung;
> If brightness dimmed, and dark prevailed,
> No sense was stung.
>
> But the disease of feeling germed,
> And primal rightness took the tinct of wrong;
> Ere nescience shall be reaffirmed
> How long, how long?
>> ('Before Life and After')

44

Here, the whole poem moves towards the passionate cry of human suffering in the last line. The germinal idea is one expressed by Hardy many times—'that the human race is too extremely developed for its corporeal conditions, the nerves being evolved to an activity abnormal in such an environment . . . This planet does not supply the materials for happiness to higher existences.' (*Life*)

Much of Hardy's overt philosophical poetry, in which the idea takes precedence over unadjusted impression of life, differs little in its presentation from such a prose statement, and at times descends to doggerel:

> But seeing indications
> That thou read'st my limitations,
> And since my lack of forethought
> Aggrieves thy more and more thought . . .
>
> ('A Philosophical Fantasy')

But in 'Before Life and After', the concept is a consequence of the immediate experience—the instigating cry of agony at the insensitivity of the cosmos. The idea of dissonance is modified by the poet's personal emotion, which imposes a complex pattern of structure, rhythm, and diction on the prose facts of the world he is reacting to. Poetry is, for Hardy, 'emotion put into measure', and 'the Poet takes note of nothing that he cannot feel emotively'. The poet's job is to order his materials in such a way that the reader is infected with his own feeling about the experience that inspired the poem. In this poem, the simple objective statement of primal harmony in the world, with its economical but evocative glance at the long sweep of evolutionary history ('earth's testimonies') is framed between two mood-inducing echoes of earlier poetry. 'A time there was' smuggles in a memory of Wordsworth's 'Ode on the Intimations of Immortality', which begins likewise in a mood of regret for a lost sense of harmony. But the resonance is ironic. Wordsworth's nostalgia is for the loss of a child's heightened awareness, Hardy's for a time 'before the birth of consciousness', since heightened awareness is so often awareness of suffering. The slow, dignified movement of the four monosyllables 'When all went well', which one can hardly speak without placing a major stress on each word, catches the deathly calm of Keats' 'And no birds sing', and so enriches by association the sense of a landscape without life. The complex ironies contained in these reverberations, added to the prose sense of the words, have already established the tension between conscious man and the unconscious universe which produces both poem and poetic emotion.

The tensions, strains, stresses and hesitations which characterize human life make themselves felt in the very different movement and music of the second stanza. The 'nescience' of things before life, implied in the negation of the pronoun 'one', is combined significantly with active verbs that affirm the moral values which developed with human consciousness. These three phrases, placed in parallel positions of emphasis at the beginning of the line, hold balance in the stanza with general definitions of the ills that flesh is heir to, which *then* were unfelt. The 'now' which in a Hardy poem is set in inevitable opposition to the 'then', is expressed in the various pains of a conscious world fighting strenuously against the expected beat of the line, which has been set in a fairly smooth-running pattern by the first stanza. The reader's uncertainties on the placing of speech stress may be art rather than incompetence— a required imaginative contribution to the sense of the difficulties of emergent human consciousness struggling with the intractable denseness of matter. Does one, for example, place heavy stresses on both components of 'starved hope' and both root-syllables of 'heart-burnings'? Or even on all three syllables (as Benjamin Britten has done in his musical setting of the poem), which is suggested by the rhyme-word 'things', and would be a practice in keeping with the medieval ballad level of diction which Hardy drew on for this particular compound? Does one stress both subject and verb of 'None suffered . . . none knew . . . none cared'? To do so is to retard the movement of the second line at least with heavy stresses, but the very weight of the line, added to the increased alliteration of the whole stanza, points up the straining tensions between life and no-life which make the reader's perplexities part of the poem's creative process.

The third stanza reverses the placings of negative and positive elements. The negative of the person, 'none', is replaced at the beginning of the line by the positive abstractions 'something' and 'brightness', while the negative connotations move over to the verbs—'ceased', 'winced and waned', 'dimmed'. The human pain evoked by these verbs is brought nearer home by the diction of this stanza—'tongue' and 'heart' are parts of the human body traditionally associated with the expression of feeling.

Hardy's emotional manipulation of negation is masterly. The

response of consciousness *after* the appearance of life is continually implied in his vision of the world *before* life by denial of the responses we have come to recognize as human. 'None suffered . . . None knew . . . none cared . . . no tongue bewailed . . . no heart was wrung . . . no sense was stung.' The last stanza brings to birth the cry of human pain that has been implicit through its denial in the first three stanzas. The passion behind it inspires that imaginative, evocative use of words and word-music that turns what could have been an emotionless scientific analysis of the relationship between man and his environment into a poetic experience of the highest quality. In the context of a longing for 'nescience' the word 'dis-ease' evokes its original meaning of discomfort and disharmony, as well as the more usual sense of illness, which in turn requires a double response to 'germed' in its suggestions of springing and decaying life, and to the rare poetic 'tinct' with its connotations of moral taint as well as impregnated colour. The preciseness with which Hardy invests the words taken from every level of language can be felt in the unpretentious 'if something winced'. Wincing is defined as an *involuntary* shrinking, therefore a movement that is appropriate to the state of unconsciousness that existed before human knowledge of pain.

Simplicity and something which is almost the opposite of simplicity—terms in which Leonard Woolf described the man Hardy —can be seen in rich tension in 'Before Life and After', as in all Hardy's best poetry. The simple phrases, the sonorous dignity of the abstractions 'consciousness', 'nescience', 'rightness', 'wrong', set against the concrete vision of human suffering; the echoes of Biblical and traditional literature with its ready-made emotional associations—'If brightness dimmed, and dark prevailed'; the subtle vowel progressions and assonances in the key-words 'burnings— things—wrung—stung—wrong—long': all work together to produce a poem which has the idiosyncratic simplicity and complexity of the man, and yet achieves universality and objectivity through the very depth of his personal reaction to the universe.

In his philosophical poetry, Hardy sometimes succumbs to the temptation to attempt an explanation of the inexplicable dissonances of life. They cannot be explained by unrepresentable Forces; they can only be felt in the power of their mystery on the pulses of a human being. The vividly communicated personal pain of 'How long, how long?' would make Hardy rather less than the perfect artist of T. S. Eliot's ideal in 'Tradition and the Individual

Talent': 'the more perfect the artist, the more completely separate in him will be the man who suffers and the mind which creates'. But perfection is not a human quality. As Hardy remarks in a note (*Life*) 'It is the incompleteness that is loved, when love is sterling and true'.

'Hardy . . . put everything he felt, everything he noticed, everything he was, into his poetry. As a result he wrote a great many bad poems—far more than Mr Eliot will ever have written: but also, because what he gave so unreservedly was the impressions of a magnanimous heart, the thoughts of a mind closely engaged in the problems of its own time and possessed of a strong historical sense, the experience of a man thoroughly versed in human suffering, his poetry has that breadth of matter and manner which only a major poet can compass.'

(C. Day Lewis, 'The Lyrical Poetry of Thomas Hardy', *Proceedings of the British Academy XXXVII*, 1951)

It is the note of personal suffering which makes Hardy speak truly to those human beings who think humbly, deeply, and in jagged personal rhythms about their relationship to the mysteries of the cosmos.

'The Homeliest of Heart-Stirrings': Shorter Lyrics

'I believe few persons have read *Faust* without disappointment . . . A masterpiece excites no sudden enthusiasm; it must be studied much and long, before it is fully comprehended; we must grow up to it, for it will not descend to us. Its influence is less sudden, more lasting. Its emphasis grows with familiarity. We never become disenchanted; we grow more and more awestruck at its infinite wealth. We discover no trick, for there is none to discover. Homer, Shakespeare, Raphael, Beethoven, Mozart, never storm the judgment; but, once fairly in possession, they retain it with increasing influence . . . With *Faust* my first feeling was disappointment. Not understanding the real nature of the work, I thought Goethe had missed his aim, because he did not fulfil my conceptions. It is the arrogance of criticism to demand that the artist, who never thought of us, should work in the direction of our thoughts.'
(G. H. Lewes: *The Life and Works of Goethe*)

Lewes' experience with *Faust* mirrors the road which many readers of Hardy's non-dramatic lyrics must travel, Whereas the best of his philosophical poetry is shaped by passionate personal feeling, the cry of unadulterated joy or sorrow which certain theories of poetry regard as indispensible to lyric form seems to be missing, or to exist at low tension, in many of Hardy's successful lyrics. Nor can one find the subtleties and ambiguities on which the modern reader of Eliot or Empson has been trained to exercise his talent for the elucidation of mysteries. It is perhaps difficult not to feel a sense of disappointment on first reading, for example, 'Life and Death at Sunrise':

> The hills uncap their tops
> Of woodland, pasture, copse,
> And look on the layers of mist
> At their foot that still persist:
> They are like awakened sleepers on one elbow lifted,
> Who gaze around to learn if things during night have shifted.

A waggon creaks up from the fog
With a laboured leisurely jog;
Then a horseman from off the hill-tip
Comes clapping down into the dip;
While woodlarks, finches, sparrows, try to entune at one time,
And cocks and hens and cows and bulls take up the chime.

With a shouldered basket and flagon
A man meets the one with the waggon,
And both the men halt of long use.
"Well," the waggoner says, "What's the news?"
"—'Tis a boy this time. You've just met the doctor trotting back.
She's doing very well. And we think we shall call him 'Jack.'

"And what have you got covered there?"
He nods to the waggon and mare.
"Oh, a coffin for old John Thinn:
We are just going to put him in."
"—So he's gone at last. He always had a good constitution."
"—He was ninety-odd. He could call up the French Revolution."

There are no tricks to discover here. It is difficult for the most
ardent student of ambiguity to make the poem carry a meaning
other than the one intended by the poet. Hardy has ventured so
near the prosaic in matter and manner that one is tempted to think
that he set out to prove to himself how much 'poetry' he could do
without. Yet, like Wordsworth's deceptively simple 'A Slumber
Did My Spirit Seal', the poem grows in depth and richness until
one realizes that its centrality of theme has subtly changed one's
awareness of life.

The observation of a chance encounter between two country-
men, and their fragment of completely natural conversation, seems
at first sight too trivial to carry much significance. Yet the prosaic
conjunction of two men is made poetic by the conjunction of life
and death embodied in their meeting. Quiet acceptance of the
eternal rhythms of human life is reflected in their brief unemotional
exchange of news. The baby, taking the name of the dead man
whose memory reaches so far back into the past, promises for the
future the only kind of continuity the human race can hope to
attain. Hardy's hawk-like vision, which so often in his poetry and
novels sets tiny individual figures in a landscape, gradually extends
to link his two speakers, through the old man and baby and the
distant figure of the doctor, mediator of life and death, not only to

their local social context but also to the whole of human history. Finally these ephemeral human lives are set firmly in the larger rhythms of nature. Their conjunction takes place to the dawn chorus of wild birds and farm livestock. Hardy's affectionate and slow-moving enumeration by species suggests the eternal recurrence of natural things, and with them, of leisurely funeral waggons eternally meeting and passing the hurry of new life. These things go onward the same though Dynasties pass. And the whole of sentient life—birds, farm animals, human beings—is set in the vast timeless context of the insentient universe in which they live and die—the landscape of hill, wood, pasture, copse, and morning mist.

Like so many of Hardy's lyrics, 'Life and Death at Sunrise' (subtitled 'Near Dogbury Gate, 1867') begins with a precise evocation of time and place. The details of the moment when 'the hills uncap their tops' to reveal their reality while human figures emerge from and disappear into the fogs that 'still persist' at the foot, show a naturalist's exact observation of phenomena, yet they are emotionally charged with the imponderable mystery of life and death. Natural features of the landscape, night, and mist arouse deep traditional responses which turn the hills into watchers from an Overworld of unobscured reality, and the foggy lowland into the darkling plain of blinkered human action. Apart from the one simile of the hills as 'awakened sleepers', which brings overtones of resurrection into this poem of life and death, and the personalizing metaphors of 'uncap' and 'look', the details of the poem are not of the kind to satisfy the image-hunter. Hardy seems to depend more on factual statement than suggestion; yet the steady piling up of observed detail of this moment of sunrise manages to suggest more than the content of the statements. When the scene has been set, human action appears in the second stanza. The movement of sentient life counterpoints the stability of the insentient landscape with another kind of stability—the perpetual recurrence of the life cycle. Things have not shifted during night; only the individual actors in the drama are likely to be different. The last two stanzas focus on the two individual figures—the most important features of Hardy's landscape—to bring the dramatic immediacy of homely colloquial speech into the descriptive but as yet non-dramatic scene. At this pivotal point of time and space evoked by the details of the first two stanzas, no extraneous comment from the poet is needed to realize the conjunction of light and dark inherent in the exchange of words.

The effect of the poem springs from the reality of a normal everyday experience honestly recorded and felt; the moment of insight into our relationship to the rhythms of the universe from the unflinching response of Hardy's senses to all facets of the objective world. Lyric ecstasy gives way to loving fidelity to what he sees and hears; yet this very devotion to fact produces lyric emotion.

'The only way of expressing emotion in the form of art is by finding an "objective correlative"; in other words, a set of objects, a situation, a chain of events which shall be the formula of that *particular* emotion; such that when the external facts, which must terminate in sensory experience, are given, the emotion is immediately evoked.'

(T. S. Eliot: *Selected Essays*)

In this homely Wessex scene Hardy has found an objective correlative for his intuitions about life and death. In the simple but precise diction, the natural speech rhythms straining against metrical rigidity, in the verse form itself, he has found the means to infect his readers with those intuitions. While all four stanzas keep roughly to the metrical pattern of three stresses in the first four lines and six in the last two, the wide variations in speech stress and number of syllables to the stress make the movement of each stanza very different. Syllabic and speech stress do not pull too far apart in the first stanza. As the stability of the landscape gives way, however, to the eccentricites of human and animal life, the tension between regular metre and irregular speech stress becomes more elastic: a crisp six-syllable line of alternating stress and unstress, such as 'The hills uncap their tops', has grown to nine syllables of completely natural speech rhythm in

"Well," the waggoner says, "What's the news?"

as human speech and movement gradually dominate the insentient natural scene. The 'closeness of phrase to his vision' which Hardy admired in his fellow Dorset poet William Barnes has been achieved here.

The unpretentious nature of both phrase and vision may call for a redefinition of lyrical quality. Hardy himself, in his Preface to *Select Poems of William Barnes*, objected to too severe a classification that would exclude much of the finest English poetry as well as his own characteristic mixture of lyrical, dramatic, narrative, and contemplative elements in the same poem.

'. . . many fine poems that have lyric moments are not entirely lyrical; many largely narrative poems are not entirely narrative; many personal reflections or meditations in verse hover across the frontiers of lyricism . . . the same lines may be lyrical to one temperament and meditative to another; nay, lyrical and not lyrical to the same reader at different times, according to his mood and circumstance . . .

'One might, to be sure, as a smart impromptu, narrow down the definition of lyric to the safe boundary of poetry that has all its nouns in the vocative case, and so settle the question by the simple touchstone of the grammar-book, adducing the *Benedicite* as a shining example. But this qualification would be disconcerting in its stringency, and cause a fluttering of the leaves of many an accepted anthology.'

Other 'impromptu' definitions are just as wide of the mark. The gnarled and knotted nature of much of Hardy's thought and diction does not accord with the singing quality once thought to be essential to a lyric, though the technical challenge they present to musicians has produced several successful settings, notably Benjamin Britten's 'Winter Words'. There are some exceptions: few people would disagree with Hardy's estimate that 'When I Set Out for Lyonnesse' has 'the song-ecstasy that a lyric should have', but in general he found 'So little cause for carolings/Of such ecstatic sound' that his poetic impulse took other directions. And though much of that impulse is personal, it is difficult to make 'Life and Death at Sunrise', 'An Unkindly May', or 'The Sheep-Boy' fit exactly the definition of Ruskin: 'Lyrical poetry is the expression by the poet of his own feelings'. There is too much fact within the feeling for most of his poetry to exist as simple cries of joy or sorrow; too much contemplation for the complete merging of poet and subject that takes place in 'pure' lyric, though 'Weathers' approaches this rare purity. But the isolated details of experience that he selects to relate in the significant pattern of a poem imply his subjective response where it is not explicit, and the complex of objective reality and subjective response add up to a poetic unity (not invalidated by the contrasts of mood and experience which may be contained within a single poem) that can be called lyrical, however mixed the genres within the poem may be.

Hardy's best lyrics are moments of vision that have found their objective correlative in something close to common experience which yet evokes the underlying deeper reality that he admired in Turner's late paintings. All the unremarkable and usually unremarked aspects of routine life are brought into consciousness by

Hardy's penetrating vision in a search for the attainable significance that does not aspire beyond the world of here and now. He finds it in the burning of an old photograph, a car 'whanging' down a country road, a thrush singing in the gloom of a death-marked landscape at the turn of the century, an old woman raking up leaves, a girl who 'passed foot-faint with averted head' the scene of her former love, a boy at midnight on the Great Western,

> Bewrapt past knowing to what he was going,
> Or whence he came,

a mysterious couple promenading beyond the last lamp on Tooting Common, whose human quality of sadness immortalizes the scene in the poet's memory, 'the mould of a musical bird long passed from light' in a museum, the loss of a drinking glass, a broken appointment, a moment of indecision whether to meet or not, the memory of imperfections in a face or in social graces, the scene of youthful pleasures, old furniture, a dream of the loved one in old age, a map on the wall, a family pedigree which mocks illusions of individual free will and significance, a glance in the mirror, a visit to his first school, the death of a cat, a superstition that 'this candle-wax is shaping to a shroud', a flash of sunlight reflected from the coffin of a fellow-poet and friend. Poems like 'After the Last Breath' and 'The Announcement' catch the imperceptible moment when the death of a person makes an undefinable difference to routine rhythms:

> They came, the brothers, and took two chairs
>   In their usual quiet way;
> And for a time we did not think
>   They had much to say.
>
> And they began and talked awhile
>   Of ordinary things,
> Till spread that silence in the room
>   A pent thought brings.
>
> And then they said: "The end has come.
>   Yes: it has come at last."
> And we looked down, and knew that day
>   A spirit had passed.
>   ('The Announcement')

Our awareness of the moment when things have changed their look and quality is enlarged by the quiet prosaic observation of habitual actions that sustain life, the suggestion of regular recurrence in the repetition of 'And', the sudden tightening of natural speech rhythms to end the second stanza on three stressed monosyllables which bring expectation of change; the dramatization of that change, as in 'Life and Death at Sunrise', in colloquial speech; the respectful embarrassed gesture 'And we looked down' in the presence of the reluctantly-voiced mystery which has brought the larger rhythms of the cosmos into intersection with the ordinariness of the daily round.

Often in Hardy's world, as in Samuel Beckett's, 'nothing happens, nobody comes, nobody goes', as a glance at some of his titles may indicate—'A Commonplace Day', 'A Broken Appointment', 'Nobody Comes', 'She did not Turn', 'You were the Sort that Men Forget'. Yet, like Beckett, Hardy extracts significance from the insignificant. The moment of awareness can be projected as strongly from what does not happen as from a dramatic conjunction of persons, time, and place, as in 'A Commonplace Day':

> Wanly upon the panes
> The rain slides, as have slid since morn my colourless thoughts; and yet
> Here, while Day's presence wanes,
> And over him the sepulchre-lid is slowly lowered and set,
> He wakens my regret.

The poet's attempt to define the quality of an uneventful day begins, characteristically, at the twilight hour, which in many poems ('Nobody Comes', 'At Day-Close in November', 'Birds at Winter Nightfall', 'The Darkling Thrush', and others) carries a traditional emotional charge of loneliness, sadness, loss and regret. The striking metaphor 'turning ghost' gives the lead to 'the pale corpse-like birth . . . bearing blanks in all its rays', and the images of colourlessness which define the insubstantiality of the day. The colloquial 'scuttles' suggests the undignified character of its insignificance in a precise concrete verb which, in true Hardy fashion, is immediately swallowed up like the day itself in the abstract Latinate grandeur of 'the anonymous host/Of those that throng oblivion' and the formal 'ceding his place, maybe,/To one of like degree'. But the cautious colloquial 'maybe' which punctuates the formal phrase and the personification of the day cast doubt on the poet's complete assent to its insignificance.

When the time of day has been precisely set, stanza II brings place and person into conjunction with it. The fireside seems to be a favourite spot for contemplation, as poems like 'The Photograph', 'Logs on the Hearth', and 'Surview' bear additional witness. The poet's physical presence in the poem by a physical fireside gives authenticity to an experience that can only be made significant by the human capacity to feel and think. His precise, orderly actions reinforce the 'end-of-the-day' atmosphere, which closes in again with the dragging extent of the fourth line, unpunctuated by the pauses that characterize the human action of the previous lines, and the overwhelming alliterative weight of 'beamless black'. In stanza III his meditating mind brings human values into fruitful tension with the uneventfulness of the day through pondering on what he has *not* done to make it significant—a characteristic Hardeian affirmation through negation. His relationship as a human being to 'this diurnal unit' is suggested by the compound of cancelling opposites in 'corpse-like birth' and the 'blanks' in its 'rays', for only conscious human action can realize the dormant potentialities that each day is born with. The preponderance of cloddish 'u's and heavy alliterating 'b's and 'd's end the stanza with the brutish thump of the cosmic insignificance which the conscious human mind has to face and transform.

Stanza IV develops the link between the poet's human consciousness and the dull world he inhabits by the simile of colourless thoughts; outer and inner environments slide, with the long vowels and repetitions of 'n', to one dead level of insignificance, until the positive turn 'and yet'. The humanized image of Day as a dead person returns, in a context which stresses the actualities of place—'Here'—and time—'while Day's presence wanes'—and these antidotes to insubstantiality are joined by the most powerful positive of all—human emotion. Stanza V moves in closer to the poet's meditating mind to turn over the irrational feeling of regret.

The idiosyncratic rhythm of the overheard voice is now in full swing, with all the stops and starts, slow hesitations, and eccentricities of thought in process, so the stanza can carry such Hardeian medievalisms as 'that I wot of' and 'toward'—which gives a better sense of forward motion than a commoner word. Hardy's unflinching look at the worst in this stanza—the commonplaceness of the day, unmarked by any significant human action that he knows of—is immediately and characteristically balanced in stanza VI by his tendency to hope for the best and believe that there was some extra-sensory reason for his emotion. The scrupulous hesitancy of 'Yet, maybe'—for he will not pretend to absolute conviction—serves to emphasize the outward swing from the personal to 'the wide world' which began in stanza v and is carried on in 'some soul,/In some spot undiscerned on sea or land', and the unpunctuated rush of the 'enkindling ardency' which brings the imagined positive impulse to a soaring conclusion in the last three lines. The fire of matter and manner in this penultimate stanza balances the dying embers of the second; the prefix of the unusual compound 'upstole' gives a lift to the 'waning' imagery that predominated in the first half of the poem. The final stanza does not lose the impetus of the upward lift, though Hardy's respect for truth qualifies the hope of the noble intent by making it potential rather than actual; 'benumbed at birth/By momentary chance or wile'—a misfire. Yet the human emotion of regret for the 'thwarted purposing' of the day which created his moment of vision remains valid, as the most important thing in the poem, and ends it with an affirmation of waking awareness that balances all its corpses. The feeling cannot be explained by reason, but the irrational and supernatural which Hardy's respect for scientific truth rejected intellectually persists in powerful emotional tension with that scrupulously presented truth in the 'undervoicings' of the poem.

'A Commonplace Day', like many of Hardy's successful lyrics, has a quietness that comes of contemplating the values of life from the standpoint of their denial. The poetic significance to him of what does not happen can be gauged from the number of fine poems in which negative statements occupy a key position. They may begin a poem:

> Breathe not, hid Heart: cease silently . . .

> For Life I had never cared greatly . . .

>> You did not come . . .

> Not a line of her writing have I,
>> Not a thread of her hair . . .

> Her laugh was not in the middle of her face quite . . .

> You were the sort that men forget;
>> Though I—not yet!—

They may bring the poem to a close:

> "He hears it not now, but used to notice such things".

> . . . And nobody pulls up there.

> O never I turned, but let, alack,
>   These less things hold my gaze!

> As we seemed we were not
>   That day afar,
> And now we seem not what
>   We aching are . . .

> . . . But none replies:
> No warnings loom, nor whisperings
> To open out my limitings,
> And Nescience mutely muses: When a man falls he lies.

A negative statement in the body of the poem often points to the contrast between the potentialities of life and their denial:

> Alas, I knew not much of her,
> And lost all sight and touch of her!

> Now no Christmas brings in neighbours,
>   And the New Year comes unlit;
> Where we sang the mole now labours,
>   And spiders knit.

A pattern of denial running through all the stanzas of a poem can act as a refrain which is a powerful instrument of the irony contained in two contrasted states. The harsh denying present is brought into violent juxtaposition with pleasant memories of the past in 'During Wind and Rain' by the repeated refrain of the years; and in 'Molly Gone' by the first line pattern of each stanza, 'No more summer [planting, jauntings, singing] for Molly and me', and by the memory-denying actions that begin each stanza of 'Shut out that Moon'. The sinister denial of evidence of the senses in the first three stanzas of "Who's in the Next Room?" prepares the way inevitably for the affirmation of negation—death's world of no-sense—in the final stanza. What is not seen or heard or said or done or known can create a more potent mood of dread than the most explicit statements of positive knowledge. The repeated determination in each stanza of 'He Resolves to Say No More' to 'keep the rest unknown' says all that Hardy wished to say about the harsh conditions within which value and meaning must be achieved. But other, tenderer moods can be evoked too by his negative refrains and repetitions. The comments of the animal, human and stellar world which end each stanza of "I Am the One" paint an affirming picture of 'one for whom Nobody cares' enough to interrupt their normal rhythms; a gentle, unassuming character whose reticence is not due to any lack of interest or observation, but to a genuine humility about his place in nature and a feeling of kinship with all its parts, which provides the final affirmative: 'He is one with us/Beginning and end.' On the other hand, the refrain-like repetitions in 'The Fallow Deer at the Lonely House' of 'One without looks in tonight' and 'We do not discern those eyes' intensify the central opposition between the natural bleakness without and the unnatural bleakness within. Hardy often uses an animal to crystallize a human attitude to life: here, the cold landscape is given affirmative significance by the movements of body and mind that characterize a living creature—on tiptoe, wondering, watching, 'aglow' with the dynamic fire that is missing from the silent unobservant couple nursing the fireside, who shelter in their passive ('lit') comfort from the pain of a full response to life. 'The Reminder' shows that Hardy knew the penalty of a full response, as he sits in a similarly cheerful Christmas blaze:

> Why, O starving bird, when I
> One day's joy would justify,
> And put misery out of view,
> Do you make me notice you!

A poem like 'The Photograph' dramatizes a painful affirmation of living warmth in the very act of negating it. The woman's photograph is burned 'in a casual clearance of life's arrears', but as the flame moves over her pictured sexual attractions

> . . . I vented a cry of hurt, and averted my eyes;
> The spectacle was one that I could not bear,
> To my deep and sad surprise.

Hardy himself was no life-denier. Poems such as 'Let Me Enjoy' and 'Great Things' bear direct witness to his pleasure in the simple sensuous joys of the world as it is. Even "For Life I had never Cared Greatly" denies the initial denial by admitting the ebb and flow of life's appeal, 'till evasions gave in to its song'. Only a man who loved life in every fibre of his being could feel so keenly the betrayal of its potentialities in the sight of a starving thrush, a blinded bird, or an unwanted pauper child. His inability to put misery out of view is a direct corollary of the intense wish to justify life and joy, and the interaction of these two emotions a major source of his resonant power. Only a man who upheld the value of life and the individual human being is capable of the compassion that begins 'To an Unborn Pauper Child' with

> Breathe not, hid Heart: cease silently,

and consistently negates the negating injunction by the living personal rhythms of his own voice affirming painfully, honestly, against the rigid metrical pattern, the value of human emotion—'unreasoning, sanguine, visionary'—which

> can hope
> Health, love, friends, scope
> In full for thee; can dream thou'lt find
> Joys seldom yet attained by humankind!

The affirmation is all the more impressive for refusing to deny the life-denying realities of travails, teens, and Time-wraiths their power and place in human experience. The manuscript shows Hardy's indecision between 'seldom' and 'never' in the last line. His final choice of 'seldom' is more accurate; but the hope of joys remains a hope rather than a conviction. However, its truth is accepted without question because it has been hardly won through a struggle with life's denials. Where the tension between what is and what ought to be is missing in thought and structure, the result is a lesser poem. 'To C.F.H. on Her Christening Day' and 'The Unborn' make the same indictment of birth, but without the sense of painful personal involvement that springs from Hardy's conflicting allegiances to scientific truth and human aspiration. The beginning of 'To C.F.H.':

> Fair Caroline, I wonder what
> You think of earth as a dwelling-spot,
> And if you'd rather have come, or not?

pales before the immediate dramatic power of an injunction to stop breathing. The equivalent question to the pauper child, 'Wilt thou take Life so?' comes, not as a desultory speculation to start a poem, but as a fitting climax to the failure of life's illusions set out in the previous stanza, and it gains resonance from the poet's knowledge, which he never allows us to forget as he voices his desires for the child, that it is *not* free 'To cease, or be', but 'Must come and bide'. The prayer for 'good things with glad' in the last stanza of 'To C.F.H.' is less effective than the scrupulously cautious hope that ends 'To an Unborn Pauper Child' because it does not rise out of the travails and teens that invariably balance good things and glad. The sense of painful personal struggle towards affirmation of life is less effective in 'The Unborn', where it is left distanced and un-dramatic. The tension in 'the news that pity would not break/Nor truth leave unaverred' does not come to life in the verse form, the clichés, the abstractions, the generalized vagueness of 'crowding shapes'. But it can be felt in the anguished hesitations and broken personal rhythms of a man experienced in life's travails and teens addressing a potential human being who comes to stand for the human predicament.

In 'To An Unborn Pauper Child' the Hardeian idiosyncrasies of rhythm and diction enact what it means to be human, with illusions of freedom, against the predestination of the verse pattern. It means dignity and tenderness: Hardy has managed to suggest both by using the second person singular throughout, hallowed by Biblical and traditional associations and the intimacy of its con-tinuing usage in dialect. It means sublimity and simplicity: the rolling Latinate grandeur of 'unreasoning, sanguine, visionary' and 'Ere their terrestrial chart unrolls' is followed immediately by short monosyllabic statements. The Revelations image of cosmic power in Stanza IV leads to a stanza on man's weakness in which only one of the Anglo-Saxon words is not a monosyllable. It means losing the concrete joys of life—'songsingings'—to ghostly abstrac-tions in the march of Time, and human aspirations to the process of physical decay:

> Hark, how the peoples surge and sigh,
> And laughters fail, and greetings die:
>   Hopes dwindle; yea,
>   Faiths waste away,
> Affections and enthusiasms numb;
> Thou canst not mend these things if thou dost come.

It means being part of the cosmic rhythm of suffering as an individual, and as a member of the human race; and it means companionship in suffering, helplessness, and loss of illusion. It means accepting fully the human being's inability to change the nature of things: the dream of doing so as a 'vain vow'—but nevertheless a positive contribution to the value of life, as the hammer-blows on 'Health, love, friends, scope' indicate. It means, finally, feeling the complex emotion that inspired the poem: the love-hate relationship with life; the compassion and reverence for the human individual subjected to its ills; the irrepressible desire to hope for the best while believing that it cannot be, which affirms the significance of life denied to it by the cosmic scheme.

Only a rare reverence for the phenomena and potentialities of life could rebel so passionately at the injustice of finding them meaningless. Hardy loved them well enough not to see eternity in a grain of sand. In 'A Sign-Seeker', the poetic emotion is generated from the tension between his desire to believe that the beauty, sublimity and horror of the physical world, including man, are part of a cosmic design which will justify their existence, and his reluctant conviction that they are not. The poet's usual position as observer within the poem becomes a symbol of man's predicament in the physical universe, helpless to alter its course, able only to endure the effects of its phenomena on his senses while remaining in ignorance of their ultimate cause and meaning. 'I mark . . . I see . . . And hear . . . have felt . . . And trodden . . . I learn . . . I witness . . .' but he cannot say 'I understand'. Yet the full response to the physical world as the only world that exists, by the whole man—human being, lover and hater of life, scholar, philosopher, observer—in the idiosyncratic Hardy voice, paradoxically evokes 'undervoicings' from the details of natural phenomena which deny portents of meaning. The characteristic mixture of simplicity and complexity, prosaic and rare, archaic, dialect, and literary expression, unusual forms and coinages, awkward constructions, and jagged personal rhythms fights against the simple verse form with its enclosed rhyme scheme and long last line that hammers home with alliteration and assonance the denseness of matter and passage of time which mock at man's search for significance—

And hear the monotonous hours clang negligently by.

Hardy's choice of words sets up reverberations that extend far beyond a mere record of the physical world. The 'eyeless countenance of the mist' juxtaposes the blank face of nature with the groping 'view' of its human observer, conscious but hardly less blind in his search for meaning. The accuracy of the rare Latinate 'subtrude' evokes the traditional and appropriate associations of night, and night as the image of death, *thrusting* its presence *stealthily* on the human being, as Hardy's first thought in the manuscript, 'I know the Nod of Night subdued', did not. And no other word but the coined 'outbreathing' could express so succinctly the desire that dead matter should give out a sign of continued existence to the living world. 'Eccentric' attached to 'orbs' revives its original astronomical meaning which, in conjunction with its more usual modern sense of caprice in human behaviour, points to the lack of a fixed centre of reference which would justify all things as part of an intelligent design. 'Moils' invests the human activity of work with the additional connotation of turmoil and confusion, which also mean 'a world alive'. The unusual form of 'solve' for 'dissolve' carries undertones of the solution of life's mysteries that is only to be found in dissolution.

The meaning of a search for meaning in a physical world that denies it is gradually revealed through the shifts in the seeker's viewpoint. Close observation of the familiar rhythms of hours, days, seasons, and weathers changes to observation of the extraordinary rhythms of nature at extremes, which distance and diminish the observer. Then the angle of vision suddenly soars to an Overworld view of humanity as a rhythmic, conglomerate mass of impulses involuntarily obeying the same fundamental force that powers 'the earthquake's lifting arm' and 'the leaping star':

> I witness fellow earth-men surge and strive;
> Assemblies meet, and throb, and part;
> Death's sudden finger, sorrow's smart;
> —All the vast various moils that mean a world alive.

When mass movement has abstracted all significance from the human individual, the viewpoint sweeps back to earth again, to the personal search for meaning among the last physical traces of a close human relationship, 'in graveyard green, where his pale dust lies pent'. Only the physical world exists for Hardy; only a physical sign would appease his hunger for justification—a voice from the grave, a 'print to prove her spirit-kisses real' from a dead Love's lips, 'one plume as pledge that Heaven inscrolls the wrong' to witness that earthly injustice is part of heavenly design. The honest admission of the faith of others emphasizes the final return to Hardy's sole surety—the existence of the physical world, meaningless as it is. The denseness of unresponsive matter is present in the weight of monosyllables in

> I have lain in dead men's beds, have walked
> The tombs of those with whom I had talked . . .

and also in the simple finality of 'When a man falls he lies'—the inescapable physical fact that makes a mockery of man's search for metaphysical meaning. Yet the wide-ranging movements of the conscious human mind in its deep hunger for metaphysical truth and its refusal to deny the physical world its own truth, 'even if despair', relates all things within the poem to invest it with the design that is missing from the cosmic process.

In the absence of cosmic significance, affirmation of life is wrested out of those things which seem to deny it value. The large and small phenomena of the physical world have no small value to a man who can hardly bear to attribute them to the void, and they take their place with the less tangible values of life and love, friendship and justice, in a Hardeian pattern of poetry where denial infers the value of the things denied. The call in 'Shut out that Moon' to deny the joys of the senses leaves no doubt of what they had meant to Hardy

> When living seemed a laugh, and love
> All it was said to be.

The vivid factual details of the natural world in 'Afterwards', the fleeting actions of small creatures which the poet tries to fix against the flux of time and relate to the exact moment of his own fixity in death, suggest how much they mean in themselves, without metaphysical justification, to 'a man who used to notice such things'. And the attraction that natural phenomena held for him adds a rich complexity to the mood of regret that ends 'Overlooking the River Stour':

> And never I turned my head, alack,
>> While these things met my gaze
>> Through the pane's drop-drenched glaze,
> To see the more behind my back . . .
> O never I turned, but let, alack,
>> These less things hold my gaze!

The details of the riverside scene fix by repetition his immersion in a sense of the present moment; the obvious attraction for him of 'these less things' comments on and enhances the value of 'the more behind my back'—the human relationship with his wife that his position at the window denies.

Hardy's fidelity to factual presentation of the physical world needs no intimation of hidden signs and portents to stir delight in recognition of its truth. He brings the naturalist's ultra-sensitive eye and ear to the sights, sounds, and processes of nature in poems like "I Watched a Blackbird", 'Throwing a Tree', 'On Sturminster Footbridge', and 'Snow in the Suburbs'; an artist's eye for colour, shape, line, and contrast, and a musician's ear for evocative sounds. Yet the unflinching integrity of his response to the physical world, along with a poet's command of language and rhythm, provides him with one of the most powerful weapons of poetry to replace metaphysical significance—a sense of wonder at the mysteries of the cosmos. 'I feel that Nature is played out as a Beauty, but not as a Mystery' he wrote in a note of 1887. There are strange conjunctions in the natural world—as of poet, longlegs, moth, dumbledore, and 'sleepy fly, that rubs its hands' in 'An August Midnight'—

> Thus meet we five, in this still place,
> At this point of time, at this point in space

—which bring, not the expected elucidation of their significance, but a sense of humility and awe at the mystery of things:

> "God's humblest, they!" I muse. Yet why?
> They know Earth-secrets that know not I.

In 'The Darkling Thrush' the defiant bird-song speaks to him, cautiously, of 'some blessed Hope, whereof he knew/And I was unaware': but more often, not even a tentative conclusion is allowed to creep into his wonder at the mysterious rhythms contained in physical phenomena. In 'The Year's Awakening', the repeated question 'How do you know?' to the 'vespering bird' and the hidden crocus sufficiently points up the mystery of their instinctive knowledge of the vast movements of the Zodiac and transformation of light which are part of an intricate process that adds up to the miracle of Spring. Poems such as 'A Backward Spring', 'An Unkindly May', and 'The Sheep-Boy' do not even ask a question: the sense of wonder is generated from accurate report of the physical facts. The bees' foreknowledge of a change in the weather in 'The Sheep-Boy' is left without comment on their action except the contrasting ignorance of the human figure: 'Awhile he waits, and wonders what they mean'. Their sudden flight before the mist simply adds one more external detail to the process which describes the mystery, none the less a mystery for being so full of physical facts, of one of nature's sudden transformations. The vivid pictorial quality brings undertones of the greater mystery of the final blotting out of all human life and landscape, 'folded into those creeping scrolls of white'. The transformation is given ironical point by one of Hardy's rare similes, of the mist 'like the moving pillar of cloud raised by the Israelite', because the Biblical cloud was a meaningful sign from God. Even a poem so unemotively factual as 'Throwing a Tree' culminates in

> The tree crashes downward: it shakes all its neighbours throughout,
> And two hundred years' steady growth has been ended in less than two
>   hours

which hints at the mysteries contained in the transformations of Time. Such mysteries are treated variously: in a straightforward manner, as the continuance of human life in vegetable form, in 'Transformations'; humorously and ironically, in the appropriateness and inappropriateness of the transformations, in 'Voices from Things Growing in a Churchyard'. The best of these lyrics have in common an exact attention to the physical fact of the present moment, which, in poems like 'Proud Songsters' and 'At Day-Close in November', combines with a negation in the last stanza to invite us to wonder at the mystery of growth and transformation from one state to another. Twelve months ago the different species whose song is dwelt on so carefully 'no finches were, nor nightingales'; the tall trees which had been set 'in my June time' have become a permanent feature of the landscape to children who

> Conceive that there never has been
> A time when no tall trees grew here . . .

Time and transience are the great negations which deny meaning to the physical world. Hardy's constant concern, like Proust's, was to find credible values which could stand against the flux. Many of his nature poems are successful in catching and fixing the actual moment of transformation from one state to another by observation of the small physical detail that would have escaped the eye of anyone but a devoted naturalist, as, for example, in stanzas II and IV of 'A Light Snow-fall after Frost':

> The frost is on the wane,
> And cobwebs hanging close outside the pane
> Pose as festoons of thick white worsted there,
> Of their pale presence no eye being aware
> Till the rime made them plain.

> The snow-feathers so gently swoop that though
> But half an hour ago
> The road was brown, and now is starkly white,
> A watcher would have failed defining quite
> When it transformed it so.

But not Hardy; for 'he was a man who used to notice such things'. Only a poet who was also a countryman to his bones could have indicated the moment when an almost imperceptible change of temperature gives cobwebs the look of 'thick white worsted' because the snow and frost that covers them is wet. The mystery of the physical change remains unexplained; only the poignant significance of the transient moment can be felt through the careful accumulation of details that catch the moment and the scene— colour or lack of it, outline, movement, and most important of all for Hardy, the presence of central human figures.

'The method of Boldini . . . of Hobbema, in his view of a road with formal lopped trees and flat tame scenery—is that of infusing emotion into the baldest external objects either by the presence of a human figure among them, or by mark of some human connection with them.'

(*Life*)

Stanzas I and III are devoted to human figures whose connection with the elemental world of snow and frost provides the relevant emotion.

> On the flat road a man at last appears:
> How much his whitening hairs
> Owe to the settling snow's mute anchorage,
> And how much to a life's rough pilgrimage,
> One cannot certify.

A second man comes by;
His ruddy beard brings fire to the pallid scene:
His coat is faded green;
Hence seems it that his mien
Wears something of the dye
Of the berried holm-trees that he passes nigh.

Any emotional reverberation there may be in the first man's 'whitening hairs' is cautiously qualified and distanced by the observer's disclaimer of exact knowledge. The detail serves mainly to unite him to the landscape in a monotone of white. The details of the second man's colouring—the contrasting 'life' colours of red and green, which he shares with the evergreen holly—indicate that he has not travelled so far along 'life's rough pilgrimage' as the first man. But the physical transformation of snow and frost from one state to another in the intervening stanza, and the overwhelming of the brown road (related by colour to the ruddiness of the second man) by the lack of colour which characterizes the first man, gives intimations that the effects of time and transience are not confined to the landscape. At some undefinable moment the fire of the ruddy beard will be transformed by whitening hairs in one of the small undramatic defeats of life which Hardy knows so well how to suggest. The mood of regret for such transformations, and wonder at their mystery, is built up almost entirely by observation and selection of details from the world experienced by the senses—the only kind of truth available to the agnostic. Yet, as Hemingway said of the naturalistic details in his own *The Old Man and the Sea*:

'I tried to make a real old man, a real boy, a real sea and a real fish and real sharks. But if I made them good and true enough they would mean many things.'

The poems which are concerned to fix the transient moment bear a close relationship to the poems of regret at failing to catch its importance, and the solidity of the physical world takes a prominent place in both kinds. As in 'Overlooking the River Stour' it can prove to be a rival attraction that overwhelms the moment: or it can in itself present potentialities of significant moments which are overlooked in one's dreams of future happiness, as in 'The Temporary the All', "Known Had I", 'The Musical Box', and 'Before and After Summer':

When went by their pleasure, then?
I, alas, perceived not when.

The truth and stability of the physical environment turn nostalgia, which could be an enervating emotion, into something that is both more complex and more bracing. Hardy is above all a poet of memory, which dramatizes subjective isolation, and meditation. Memory of the relationship of a vividly-realized landscape with a human figure and human emotion can affirm the quality of a past moment in the teeth of a harsh denying present. 'Under the Waterfall' not only recaptures a moment of happiness in Hardy's courtship by a Proustian physical sensation—

"Whenever I plunge my arm, like this,
In a basin of water, I never miss
The sweet sharp sense of a fugitive day
Fetched back from its thickening shroud of gray"

—but also, through the details of the idyllic scene and loss of the glass which contains the memory of their love, 'intact' and purified by the waterfall, becomes an objective correlative of 'a real love-rhyme'. The value of the moment is also affirmed, more strikingly, through what may seem to deny it meaning—the death of love, or the death of the loved person—by the same fidelity to the Wordsworthian dictum that 'the passions of men are incorporated with the beautiful and permanent forms of nature'. Hardy's forms of nature are not always beautiful; but they have the beauty of truth which enables them to become part of the permanent emotional inner landscape of a painful love experience.

There are some lyrics scattered through the *Collected Poems* which re-create in memory the bitter end of a youthful passion. Most of them have the ring of personal experience, and some of the details are left obscure by the poet, but recent attempts to cast light on them by biographical speculation only respond 'to the desire of a good many readers that poetry should be explained to them in terms of something else' (T. S. Eliot, *On Poetry and Poets*). As Eliot asks apropos of conflicting views about Wordsworth's love affairs:

'. . . does it matter? does this account help me to understand the Lucy poems any better than I did before? For myself, I can only say that a knowledge of the springs which released a poem is not necessarily a help towards understanding the poem: too much information about the origins of the poem may even break my contact with it.'

All that matters in this group of poems is that Hardy or his poetic persona went through a common experience of 'misprized love' which seemed to deny the meaning of all that life offers, but out of the intensity of his pain re-created a sense of the abiding value of love itself that enabled him to fall in love again. The titles of many of these poems—'At Rushy-Pond', 'The Mound', 'The Place on the Map', 'On a Heath', 'In the Vaulted Way'—indicate a new and mature awareness of the human being's relationship to environment which had been burnt into him by the death of the passion that flourished in these places. The present sight of the mound, the pond, the place on the map, where 'she' told him something that would bring the affair to an end

> re-creates therewith our unforeboded troublous case
> All distinctly to my sight,
> And her tension, and the aspect of her face:

the reflected moon in Rushy-Pond becomes 'corkscrewed' with the human agony that is displaced from the end of the love affair and transferred to the natural scene. The most complete objective correlative of the emotion felt at the end of an affair comes, in this group of poems, in the desolate winter landscape of 'Neutral Tones'. The lovers' quarrel is integrated so fully with details of landscape in a potent image of the death of love that all future experience of love's pain comes to mean this particular landscape, person and mood:

> Since then, keen lessons that love deceives,
> And wrings with wrong, have shaped to me
> Your face, and the God-curst sun, and a tree,
> And a pond edged with grayish leaves.

Hardy is too honest to admit to any consolation for what has been taken from him: nevertheless, the stability of scene and objects associated with the lost person fixes the value of love, which includes pain at its loss, as a positive quality against the flux of time. 'Just here it was' he says of the painful experience at the Mound, and many of his poems start with such a definite statement of place. 'Here is the ancient floor', 'Here we broached the Christmas barrel', 'Where once we danced, where once we sang'. But it is not long before a memory of human activity appears to give the scene value:

Here was the former door
Where the dead feet walked in.
'(The Self-Unseeing')

Old furniture, a broken-down garden seat, a little creaking table, are valued for the time-defeating memories they bring of loved people associated with them. The stability of the scene enshrines the memory, but even when time and transience have taken the figure from the scene, the scene takes its significance from the figure:

Yet her rainy form is the Genius still of the spot,
    Immutable, yea,
Though the place now knows her no more, and has known her not
    Ever since that day.
('The Figure in the Scene')

'Curious quizzings' may see in his rain-blotted drawing of the figure, 'only her outline shown', the *lacrimae rerum* that takes away the solidity of the loved human being and leaves only the cragged slope and the rain. But the relationship of figure and environment has created something 'immutable, yea'—an affirmation out of life's denial.

Death, the greatest negation of all, affirms the life and love it denies through the strength of Hardy's feeling for the value of purposeful human activity in relation to the natural rhythms of death and seasonal renewal. In poems of elegiac memory, such as 'Molly Gone', 'During Wind and Rain', and 'The Five Students', work and play, energy and stillness, alternate. The diminishing number of students of life 'beating by' on their 'urgent way', now in harmony with the unexpected strenuous violence of spring that 'boils the dew to smoke by the paddock-path', now in discord with the summer heat and cold visual and aural deadness of the winter scene that mocks human aspiration with the icicles that 'tag the church-aisle leads' and the meaningless ghostly gibbering of the flag-rope, celebrate the human endeavour to make order in the absurdity of the physical world. Memory responds to the absence of human activity in its meaningful rhythm of work and play in 'During Wind and Rain' and 'Molly Gone': that there is no more 'making the pathways neat/And the garden gay,' planting, 'training the clambering rose', singing, 'jauntings' to well-loved places whose roll-call of names is a pledge of their stability, sets up the characteristic fruitful dissonance between their value and the refrains of

71

mortality and loss that restrain uninhibited indulgence in the past. The significance of the individuals exhumed in the vivid accuracy of the details of their relationship with scene is qualified in 'During Wind and Rain' by archetypal symbols of the anonymity of death —the 'sick leaves reel down in throngs', rain obliterates the names carved on their gravestones. The beginning of 'Molly Gone' and the end of 'During Wind and Rain' and 'The Five Students' present us with the harsh denying reality—'The Five Students' in a typical pattern of elimination that is repeated in many poems, for example, 'Looking Across' and "Ah, are you Digging on my Grave?" But in the best elegiac poems, we are also left with the stability of the landscape and the eternal rhythms of nature inseparable from the order-making activities of human beings linked by 'life-loyalties' and enshrined in the memory of the poet shuttling between past and present to make his own significant order in the pattern of the poem.

Hardy's achievement has been to make meaningful poetry out of experience that has no inherent meaning. For those sign-seekers 'who aspired beyond and above the human individual towards something they could not even imagine, there had been no answer' (Camus: *The Plague*). But, to quote Camus again, 'if there is one thing one can always yearn for, and sometimes attain, it is human love'. In Hardy's poetry the yearning may be more obvious than the attainment, but it is a yearning of memory that infers a high moral value in love and life-loyalties. Men are frail, and Fate indifferent to human values. An image of 'thwarted purposing' is implicit in the negations, silences, Pinteresque inadequacies and failures to connect, the missed opportunities while 'we were looking away', the unwanted substitutions, ironical mismeetings, mismatings, and mistimings when

> . . . the face,
> And the eyes,
> And the place,
> And the sighs,
> Were not, alas, the right ones—the ones meet for him—
> ('Mismet').

But though Hardy's vision gives full weight to the dissonances brought about by Time and Chance, it is important not to underestimate the emphasis he places on human responsibility to affirm human values against the negation of death and denial of meaning.

The darkling thrush in the death-marked landscape, made ironically resonant by echoes of poetic identification with the immortal ecstasy of Keats' nightingale and Shelley's skylark, points to a more acceptable identification with age, frailty, and endurance of mortality in the bird's irrational defiance. 'O never I turned my head, alack' suggests some culpability for missing 'the more behind my back'. In 'Thoughts at Midnight' Hardy calls Mankind to task for

> Acting like puppets
> Under Time's buffets.

'The Blinded Bird', with its strong three-beat pulse of throbbing indignation, its intimate and respectful use of the second person singular, as in 'To an Unborn Pauper Child', and its bold application of St Paul's words to one of the humbler species, is a passionate indictment of man's as well as God's consent to the bird's needless pain and indignity. In 'Nobody Comes', intoning telegraph wires and a car hint at the possibilities of human communication, yet the car 'has nothing to do with me/And whangs along in a world of its own,/ . . . And nobody pulls up there.' The great negation of death, which ends all human striving, makes the vacillating lover's indecision whether 'To Meet, or Otherwise' understandable. But the brilliant use of negative particles reverses the negation, and leaves no doubt about the value Hardy placed on human effort to make relationship:

> By briefest meeting something sure is won;
> > It will have been:
> Nor God nor Demon can undo the done,
> > Unsight the seen,
> Make muted music be as unbegun,
> > Though things terrene
> Groan in their bondage till oblivion supervene.

> So, to the one long-sweeping symphony
> > From times remote
> Till now, of human tenderness, shall we
> > Supply one note,
> Small and untraced, yet that will ever be
> > Somewhere afloat
> Amid the spheres, as part of sick Life's antidote.

In both 'To Meet, or Otherwise' and 'Nobody Comes' (the telegraph wires like a 'spectral lyre') communication is presented in terms of music as something that can impose harmony on life's discords. The pity of missing an opportunity to supply that one note of human tenderness runs through much of Hardy's poetry of small occasions. It strikes the keynote of the emotion in 'A Broken Appointment' and provides the positive value that is both inferred and framed by its denial in the repetitions of 'You did not come' and 'You love not me'.

> You did not come,
> And marching Time drew on, and wore me numb.—
> Yet less for loss of your dear presence there
> Than that I thus found lacking in your make
> That high compassion which can overbear
> Reluctance for pure lovingkindness' sake
> Grieved I, when, as the hope-hour stroked its sum,
> You did not come.

> You love not me,
> And love alone can lend you loyalty;
> —I know and knew it. But, unto the store
> Of human deeds divine in all but name,
> Was it not worth a little hour or more
> To add yet this: Once you, a woman, came
> To soothe a time-torn man; even though it be
> You love not me?

The importance Hardy gives to 'that high compassion' which missed fire is suggested by the characteristic inversion of the long-awaited main verb and subject. The rhythmic build-up of the long periodic sentence, logically, painfully and precisely forming the poet's feelings as he contemplates them, comes to rest, not on the individual sufferer 'I' but on the grief that is common to all. The personal pain of Thomas Hardy takes on the impersonal quality of great poetry: the failure of 'a woman' to respond to 'a time-torn man' becomes a universal loss to 'the store/Of human deeds divine in all but name'. But it is great personal poetry too: the impersonality flowers from a depth of personal feeling that will not deny even the negative aspects of human experience. Those negative aspects are presented physically as the destructive actuality of Time—the only visual image in a poem developed through pure statement, though the sound as well as the cancellations contained in 'the hope-hour stroked its sum' brings to the sense of hearing all the heaviness of human endurance of Time without hope. The failure implied in 'You love not me' (another significant inversion), stated simply and honestly in a personal rhythm of thought that is jerky and abrupt as each unit of the analysis is accepted and drops painfully into place, exists in tension with the understanding compassion for individual human frailty that tempers the dignified reproach and develops the main statement of the first line of the final stanza into the concessive clause of the last lines, which places the importance of this failure in 'lovingkindness' once and for all.

Hardy was no mean poet of great occasions as well as small, as 'The Convergence of the Twain' can demonstrate, and war stirred him as the most obvious expression of cosmic futility and missed opportunities for lovingkindness. Other poets have written better songs for the men who march away and the girls they leave behind them, and his heart was not in a call to National Service. But few have integrated more successfully an Overworld philosophy of war as an image of tragic cosmic absurdity with the microscopic details of its physical impact on human beings and lesser creatures; as in the impressive "And there was a Great Calm", written to celebrate the Armistice of 1918.

> Aye; all was hushed. The about-to-fire fired not,
> The aimed-at moved away in trance-lipped song.
> One checkless regiment slung a clinching shot
> And turned. The Spirit of Irony smirked out, "What?
> Spoil peradventures woven of Rage and Wrong?"
>
> Thenceforth no flying fires inflamed the gray,
> No hurtlings shook the dewdrop from the thorn,
> No moan perplexed the mute bird on the spray;
> Worn horses mused: "We are not whipped today";
> No weft-winged engines blurred the moon's thin horn.

He is nearer to Owen in 'The Man He Killed', where he emphasizes by the very limitations of the speaker's viewpoint the sinister distortion of communication that abstracts humanity from the ordinary kindly individual. But the internal rhyming and repetition, the hesitations of speech that recapture the perplexity of the common soldier as he tries to rationalize the absurdity of war which turns friend into 'foe' when they are 'ranged as infantry' on opposite sides, are pure Hardy. In this poem and "And there was a Great Calm", Hardy comments on the significance simple words may be made to carry. They can be destructive of communication, but he also finds in 'many an ancient word/Of local lineage like "Thu bist", "Er war" ', a more constructive significance in their similarity to the language that

> they speak who in this month's moon gird
> At England's very loins . . .
>> ('The Pity of It')

Hardy's view of patriotism was unfashionably catholic.

> Then said I, "What is there to bound
> My denizenship? It seems I have found
> Its scope to be world-wide."
>> ('His Country')

But it makes a poem like 'Drummer Hodge' more representative of the universal Unknown Soldier than Rupert Brooke's 'The Soldier'. Brooke's soldier is narrowly centripetal: his death means only 'that there's some corner of a foreign field/That is for ever England'. Drummer Hodge dies for a cause and in a country he does not understand, beneath foreign stars he cannot name,

> Yet portion of that unknown plain
> Will Hodge for ever be;
> His homely Northern breast and brain
> Grow to some Southern tree,
> And strange-eyed constellations reign
> His stars eternally.

Hardy's characteristic unsentimental response to a dead man's physical relationship to environment, creative and centrifugal, which is reported with a dignified simplicity and restraint that is indicative of deep feeling, gives the local lad from Wessex the importance of a citizen of the world and the cosmos that Brooke's 'richer dust' and 'pulse in the eternal mind' cannot compass.

The significance of death in war lies less in the 'glory and war-mightiness' than in 'the long-ago commonplace facts/Of our lives' ('The Souls of the Slain') enshrined in the memory of the living by death's very power to deny. This is the long-awaited revelation whose Pentecostal imagery and elemental setting at Portland Bill, where 'contrary tides meet', as Hardy's note tells us, provide 'undervoicings' of the intersection of the timeless with time that make 'The Souls of the Slain' a memorable war poem, in spite of the 'senior soul-flame' in incongruous military command of impalpable 'sprites without mould'. In time of the breaking of nations, significance resides in the individual human being asserting the eternal rhythms of life against the abstract negation of death—the transformed body of Drummer Hodge contributing to the true meaning of patriotism; the common soldier puzzling out in his own slow, country way why he killed another common soldier called 'the foe'; 'a maid and her wight' indulging in a passion older than the Anglo-Saxon words, and a man and an old horse engaged in the eternal occupation of taming the earth from which they grew.

Hardy's intensely personal yet universal affirmations of life against the negations of old age and death can perhaps be justly assessed by comparing them with the equally valid but very different affirmations of another poet who wrote some of his finest poetry in and about old age, W. B. Yeats. The insistent question of mortality is raised both in Yeats' 'Among School Children' and Hardy's 'He Revisits his First School' by the discrepancy between the youth of the children and their elderly visitor. In contrast to the detailed realism of the children in their schoolroom that begins Yeats' poem, Hardy's poem gives more prominence to the unwished-for physical presence of the poet, 'standing solidly there as when fresh', than to the children, who exist only as an undefined 'they' of the future in the third stanza. The whole poem develops from the half-humorous, half-apologetic deprecation of his intrusive physical body, unbecoming in its old age, to a fanciful superstition of his return as a ghost.

> Yes; wrong was the way;
> But yet, let me say,
> I may right it—some day.

The ghostly image, 'beglimpsed through the quaint quarried glass/ Of green moonlight, by me greener made', is more acceptable and more in harmony with place and children than the reality, but in spite of its whimsical treatment, Hardy can admit no transformation of the reality except through death.

To Yeats too the harsh reality of 'a sixty-year-old smiling public man' in the midst of children is one that cannot be denied. Yet 'Both nuns and mothers worship images'; the changeless conceptions of love-blinded eyes defeat the physical negation of 'Old clothes upon old sticks to scare a bird'. The poem, more complex than Hardy's single lyrical mood, develops from the realism of the encounter with children and nuns through a reverie on the poet's beloved Maud Gonne as a child and as an elderly woman, to an extended statement of his personal philosophy that ends in a symbolic image of tree and dancer which reconciles the mortality of the individual with the recurring cycle of life to whose changeless image the individual contributes her changing body.

> O chestnut-tree, great-rooted blossomer,
> Are you the leaf, the blossom or the bole?
> O body swayed to music, O brightening glance,
> How can we know the dancer from the dance?

Hardy makes the point more simply, and more physically, in 'Heredity':

> I am the family face;
> Flesh perishes, I live on,

and many of his lyrics (for example, 'At Waking', 'Thoughts of Phena', 'He Abjures Love'), realizing the bleakness of life without illusions, clearly recognize the value of images to worship.

There can be sad acceptance, but no reconciliation to perishing of the flesh in Hardy. Grief is the one note that suffuses 'I Look into My Glass', which presents the dissonance between passions still strong and the ageing physical body. There is none of the rage that batters the language and rhythm of Yeats' 'The Tower':

> What shall I do with this absurdity—
> O heart, O troubled heart—this caricature,
> Decrepit age that has been tied to me
> As to a dog's tail?
>   Never had I more
> Excited, passionate, fantastical
> Imagination, nor an ear and eye
> That more expected the impossible—

The passion of imagination that is so strong in Yeats is able to call up 'images and memories' of those who had peopled his environment, and of his own literary creations; and to leave to 'young upstanding men' those qualities which had affirmed him as a man —his full acceptance of both body and soul, his pride, and faith that 'Death and life were not/Till man made up the whole'

And further add to that
That, being dead, we rise,
Dream and so create
Translunar Paradise.

The strongest passion in Hardy is of human affection, as the second stanza of 'I Look into My Glass' bears witness. No triumph of imagination or compulsion on his soul to 'study/In a learned school' (Yeats) could make the distress of 'hearts grown cold to me' (Hardy) 'seem but the clouds of the sky' (Yeats). Yet the value of his passion is affirmed just as strongly through his sadness at its loss as Yeats' through his more complex assertion.

Hardy had no faith in a translunar Paradise to leave to anyone. Like Camus, he can leave no more than the experience of having known plague (by which Camus here means death) and remembering it,

'of having known friendship and remembering it, of knowing affection and being destined one day to remember it. So all a man could win in the conflict between plague and life was knowledge and memories . . . how hard it must be to live only with what one knows and what one remembers, cut off from what one hopes for!'

(Camus: *The Plague*)

Hardy has achieved this miracle of integrity by accepting Camus' definition of the double face of knowledge: 'Knowing meant that: a living warmth, and a picture of death'. His ability to touch the two chords simultaneously puts him in the front rank of elegiac poets. His first wife's death in 1912 released his full poetic power in the elegiac vein; but the death of a lesser creature suffices to bring out Hardy's idiosyncratic affirmation of living warmth through a vivid picture of its negation by death. 'Dead "Wessex" the Dog to the Household' misses fire, like some of his philosophical poems, because the mouthpiece—Wessex himself—is beyond the suffering his death causes, the verse form is rather too jaunty for its subject, and there are few concrete details about the dog or his relationship to Max Gate to give the quality of the loss. But in 'Last Words to a Dumb Friend', the tenderness of immediate memory recreates through tightly-controlled couplets and directly-felt observations the dead cat's relationship to his human family and environment. The natural first reaction of any pet-lover, never to have another, followed by factual details of the impossibility of blotting out his memory by blotting out 'each mark he made', rises to a deeply personal, creative meditation on the relationship of any living creature to the negation of death:

> Strange it is this speechless thing. . . .
> Should—by crossing at a breath
> Into safe and shielded death,
> By the merely taking hence
> Of his insignificance—
> Loom as largened to the sense,
> Shape as part, above man's will,
> Of the Imperturbable.

The negation inevitably calls up the affirmation of the value of life; the empty scene speaks of the importance of the missing figure.

> And this home, which scarcely took
> Impress from his little look,
> By his faring to the Dim,
> Grows all eloquent of him.

We are left with the harsh reality of knowledge, and the inextricably-linked pain and triumph of human memory and emotion that enshrine the significance of life in its relation to the physical fact of death:

> Housemate, I can think you still
> Bounding to the window-sill,
> Over which I vaguely see
> Your small mound beneath the tree,
> Showing in the autumn shade
> That you moulder where you played.

But Hardy, perhaps, like Camus' Tarrou, would have called that winning the match.

The Elegies: *Poems of 1912–13*

> Thy voice is on the rolling air;
>   I hear thee where the waters run;
>   Thou standest in the rising sun,
> And in the setting thou art fair.
>
> (Tennyson: 'In Memoriam', cxxix)

> Then through the great town's harsh, heart-wearying roar,
>   Let in thy voice a whisper often come,
>   To chase fatigue and fear:
> *Why faintest thou? I wander'd till I died.*
>   *Roam on! the light we sought is shining still.*
>   *Dost thou ask proof? Our Tree yet crowns the hill,*
> *Our Scholar travels yet the loved hillside.*
>
> (Matthew Arnold: 'Thyrsis')

> Woman much missed, how you call to me, call to me,
> Saying that now you are not as you were
> When you had changed from the one who was all to me,
> But as at first, when our day was fair.
>
> (Hardy: 'The Voice')

The difference in tone between these three voices of the dead is a measure of the difference Hardy has made to the elegy. Tennyson's friend Hallam, 'mixed with God and Nature', has attained a lofty metaphysical existence that consoles the poet for his physical death. Arnold's agnosticism makes Clough's voice less of a certainty, and less sublime as a Wordsworthian voice that rolls through all things; but it is nevertheless a stern Victorian voice of moral precept which gives metaphysical consolation by linking the temporal search for truth which he and Arnold pursued to the eternal symbol of the tree. Both voices—Clough's 'whisper' notwithstanding—are public voices, speaking through poets who have made the death of a close friend the occasion for a general meditation on Man's relationship to Death.

Emma Hardy's voice is just loud enough to be overheard. Hardy's elegy speaks in the intimate personal rhythms of twentieth century conversation of a private relationship between husband and wife, thrown into painful relief by Emma's death. The relationship was more troubled than Tennyson's and Arnold's to their dead friends; but there is no grasping at metaphysical consolation. The world of nature does not contain for Hardy the 'diffusive power' of the dead person that Tennyson felt: it is the harsh physical reality the poet is left with as Emma's phantom voice recedes:

> Can it be you that I hear? Let me view you, then,
> Standing as when I drew near to the town
> Where you would wait for me: yes, as I knew you then,
> Even to the original air-blue gown!
>
> Or is it only the breeze, in its listlessness
> Travelling across the wet mead to me here,
> You being ever dissolved to wan wistlessness,
> Heard no more again far or near?
>
> Thus I; faltering forward,
> Leaves around me falling,
> Wind oozing thin through the thorn from norward,
> And the woman calling.

'The Voice', which reaches a low water mark of desolation in the sequence of elegies published as 'Poems of 1912–13' in *Satires of Circumstance* after Emma's death, shows 'how hard it must be to live only with what one knows and what one remembers, cut off from what one hopes for'. Tennyson had to add faith to the inadequacies of knowledge ('for knowledge is of things we see'); without belief in a life after death, earth would, for him, be 'darkness at the core,/ And dust and ashes all that is'. Hardy, cut off from faith and the hope of ever being able to repair the errors of this life in another one, unable to believe in any far-off divine event that would justify pain and loss, accepts the darkness at the core but affirms through knowledge and memories alone the human value of the relationship with his wife, imperfect and incomplete as it was. The human quality of Clough and Hallam in their friendship with their elegists is not the primary concern of 'Thyrsis' and '*In Memoriam*'. The elegiac conventions distance the relationship too much to re-create the give and take between two people that we recognize as human. In 'The Voice', the complex nuances of such a relationship between two living people are projected into the tensions and uncertainties of thought and rhythm which mirror the grief-stricken response of the living survivor to the death of his partner. His mood of utter desolation, mingled with remorse and regret that the chance to perfect an imperfect relationship has been irrevocably lost, projects him wishfully into the past, 'when our day was fair', on the unexpected but brilliantly appropriate rhythm of a triple-time dance tune that carries the insubstantial voice of the 'woman much missed'. We know that music was a shared interest of the Hardys' courtship and marriage; it may be more than coincidence that the rhythmic pattern of 'The Voice' fits that of 'Haste to the Wedding', one of the traditional dance tunes notated in the Hardy family's music manuscript book. Our response to this metrical reminder of their early happiness counterpointing the poet's present desolation is rich and complex. Tune and voice rush inseparably on his musing memory: the personal loss is related to and ordered by the experience of the race in the lilting folk rhythm and curiously formal but deeply moving 'Woman much missed' and 'the woman calling' which frame the personal bereavement.

As the poem develops the rhythm of the dance begins to falter. The regular, distancing folk-beat gives way to the irregularity of the distressed human mind trying to grasp and clarify its vision of time past, with all the broken speech rhythms, hesitations and abrupt changes of emotional tempo that re-create the painful struggle towards affirmation as the aural appeal of the insubstantial voice turns to visual realization of the past in the second stanza. One cannot read

> Can it be you that I hear? Let me view you, then,

without placing heavy stress on the internal rhyme 'view' and the first 'you', which points up Hardy's uncertainty about the truth of the phantom voice: he is the same man who would only be satisfied by a physical manifestation of meaning in 'A Sign-Seeker'. The sense of the third line asks for a heavy stress on the final 'then'. Hardy's vision of Emma

> Standing as when I drew near to the town
> Where you would wait for me:

has been recaptured and held for a moment in perfect clarity; but in its very affirmation, as the rhythm gathers certainty—'yes, as I knew you *then*' (my italics) the vision has been doubted by the counterpointing speech stress that suggests the irrevocable pastness of time past. The clinching detail of the visual re-creation, 'Even to the original air-blue gown', draws attention to itself as an authentic groping after precise definition of the past by the poly-syllabic awkwardness of 'original' after two stanzas consisting almost entirely of monosyllables.

The moment of clear vision in the second stanza comes within and yet extends the scope of the usual elegiac convention. It corresponds to Arnold's sudden, almost involuntary, sight of the tree he had been vainly searching for, which leads to his final affirmation, and Tennyson's trance in which he holds mystic communion with Hallam and 'the deep pulsations of the world'. Hardy's memory of Emma does not move into the metaphysical dimension. There is no communication between living and dead: the phantom voice, a wish-fantasy born of the wind and mental confusion, makes no physical manifestation as a presence, though it intensifies an absence.

In Stanza III the idiosyncratic irregularity of the musing human voice becomes unsure of the truth of the vision. No longer in command of its pulsations, it responds to the drift of the listless breeze as the power of the vision recedes before the harsh encroach-ing reality of the physical world in which the poet is discovered 'faltering'. The dissolution that overtakes both vision and physical body is enacted in diction. The subjective 'you' who was so clearly defined in the previous stanza is swallowed up in the impersonal dragging indefiniteness of that strange but exact coinage from Anglo-Saxon, 'wistlessness'. 'Dissolved to wan wistlessness' (i.e. to a state of being without knowing) is a more precise evocation in sound and sense than the vague 'consigned to existlessness' of the manuscript: it negates the crisp firmness of 'as I *knew* you then' (my italics) of Stanza II. The active finite verbs 'hear', 'view', 'would wait', 'knew', which defined the human relationship between two people in the recaptured moment of time past, are replaced in Stanzas III and IV by past and present participles that cannot be modified by a subject. The unalterable presentness of present reality is felt in the present participles which contain the action of the fourth stanza. But they exist in tension with the human subject that lacks a verb to modify—'Thus I'—the lonely human figure now shown in dramatic close-up faltering through the desolation of an autumn landscape to a clipped faltering metre that has changed utterly from the dancing tune which had resurrected the past vision. Only the third line brings a suggestion of the old rhythm, and the difficulty of forcing vowels through the proliferating 'th' sounds halts the lilt sufficiently to place the phantom voice as an illusion projected on to the sound of the wind.

If, as Leslie Stephen remarked in a note that Hardy took down, 'the ultimate aim of the poet should be to touch our hearts by showing his own', then Hardy has achieved the ultimate aim in these sad tributes to his marriage. Never before had the elegy sounded such a note of purely personal grief. Yet they become representative of the universal experience of bereavement by the intensity of that grief, the integrity of Hardy's response and refusal to deny any part of the experience, and his truth to the feeling of remorse, justified or unjustified, which overtakes the survivor when the opportunities to improve a relationship are denied for ever by death. This most painful of common human emotions had not before complicated the simple sense of loss in the elegy, which usually meant eulogy. If tensions existed between Arnold and Clough, Tennyson and Hallam, they are kept hidden. Both the elegist and the elegized emerge as serene figures untroubled by the stresses and strains of an intimacy of thirty-eight years—the period of Hardy's marriage. A realistic literary treatment of marital incompatibility was made difficult by Victorian insistence on the sanctity of marriage, which ensured a horrified public reception of Ibsen's plays, Hardy's own *Jude the Obscure*, and Meredith's *Modern Love*. It is to *Modern Love*, not to an elegy, that one must turn for a courageous attempt to present in a series of poems the breakdown of a marriage. Meredith's wife was still living when he wrote them, so he was not forced, like Hardy, to a painful reappraisal of the relationship by his wife's death; but perhaps the form of Hardy's elegies would not have been quite the same if *Modern Love* had not broken new ground in the poetical treatment of marriage. Hardy's excellence and originality as an elegist lies in his individual blend of the elegy with the love lyric and the honest treatment of stress in marriage, for which *Modern Love* provided contemporary precedent, to produce one of the most intense artistic expressions of inseparably linked love and death since Wagner's *Tristan und Isolde*.

Modern Love, though considered very avant-garde for its period, lacks the unforced personal note that places Hardy's poems in the modern world. Meredith's work is a serious attempt to convey in a linked series of fifty poems the range of complex emotions that attend the breaking-point of a marriage; and the stresses, cruelties and deceits of keeping up appearances. The point of view switches from the subjective first person to an attempted detachment expressed in the third person, but it is always the poet who speaks, interprets, remembers and relates. There is no attempt to re-create the experience through the eyes of his wife, though there are moments of real sympathy for her predicament:

> Yet it was plain she struggled, and that salt
> Of righteous feeling made her pitiful.
> Poor twisting worm, so queenly beautiful!
> Where came the cleft between us? Whose the fault?

A woman who is only known through the interpretation of a prejudiced observer is inevitably more distanced in the role she played in the break-up than even the ghost of the dead Emma, who is given her say in three poems out of twenty-one, and a stanza of 'Your Last Drive'.

> When I could answer he did not say them [words]:
>   When I could let him know
> How I would like to join in his journeys
>   Seldom he wished to go.
>   ('The Haunter')

The pathos of the married couple's failure to communicate in life and death touches the quick more directly in the simplicity of speech that was apparently characteristic of Emma than the satirical tone of Meredith's dramatized account:

> Madam would speak with me. So, now it comes:
> The Deluge or else Fire! She's well; she thanks
> My husbandship. Our chain on silence clanks.
> Time leers between, above his twiddling thumbs.
> Am I quite well? Most excellent in health!
> The journals, too, I diligently peruse.
> Vesuvius is expected to give news:
> Niagara is no noisier. By stealth
> Our eyes dart scrutinizing snakes.

In spite of an attempt to reproduce the authentic rhythm of false give and take in defensive non-communication, Meredith's external view of his wife places emphasis on the persona of the poet himself. He is insufficiently distanced from his ironic exhibition of egotism, and so it is difficult not to take away from *Modern Love* an impression of the poet striking a melodramatic attitude appropriate to the role of Injured Husband, which inevitably places his co-star in the role of Erring Wife. The violent language and heavy sarcasm are further aids to the distancing of pain.

Self-dramatization is not necessarily a fault in poetry: in Yeats, for example, it is an essential virtue. In conventional elegiac poetry, when the poet is using the death of an individual as a springboard to generalizations about man's relation to death, a suitable persona is necessary. As Tennyson remarked of *In Memoriam*, ' "I" is not always the author speaking of himself, but the voice of the human race speaking through him.' Tennyson deliberately assumes the dignified mantle of Man and Poet. He suffers the expected grief and makes the expected recovery, in noble and serene diction and rhythm that are fitting to the voice of the human race. Hardy would never have dreamed of speaking for the human race, though in the event he did so by speaking as an individual. His elegies are quite innocent of self-dramatization: they are 'feeling confessing itself to itself' (John Stuart Mill). To him the individual was more important than the species: the loss of a particular woman to a particular man was an injustice that no grand vision of the future of the species could make up for. Though we are conscious all the time of the complexity of his relationship with Emma, 'Poems of 1912–13' stands as the finest tribute a wife could have, for she occupies the centre of a cosmos from which her husband has effaced all that makes up his persona except the quality of his naked grief.

The twenty-one poems which Hardy chose to make up the sequence, and others scattered through subsequent volumes of poetry, are devoted to a vivid imaginative re-creation of Emma in all her humanness—including her human imperfection—which gives her a second life, though one which must inevitably include the pain of remorse and of her physical absence. 'One looked back through the years, and saw some pictures; a loss like that just makes one's old brain vocal!' Hardy told A. C. Benson in 1913. We see her as 'a little girl of grace' in Plymouth; we see her in the early days of courtship in Cornwall, as a charming companion, ready like Desdemona to fall in love with the teller of a romantic tale ('of sunk Lyonnesse'); a practitioner of the arts that were 'great things' to Hardy too—painting and music—and sharer of his ideals: a woman of quick sympathy with animals, plants, and landscape. We see her independent and characteristic qualities; as a fearless rider and ardent walker; her child-like pleasure in simple things—flowers, parties, pretty clothes. We come to know her physical appearance—her fragility, 'her delicate head', her

> nut-coloured hair,
> And gray eyes, and rose-flush coming and going . . .

and the familiar habits that characterize her death as well as her life:

> It was your way, my dear,
> To vanish without a word
> When callers, friends, or kin
> Had left . . .

We see her simultaneously in three tenses, as in 'The Walk'. The remote past of 'earlier days', the recent past of her weakness when she could not take her usual walk, and her absence at the present moment combine in the poet's memory and emotion to give a sense, through the contrasting moods of his two walks, of the durable quality of their relationship, whatever its stresses. 'The look of a room on returning thence' after Emma's death has intimations of the significance of the lacking figure. Death was needed to 'couch' his eyes 'of the mis-vision that blurred me' ('The Spell of the Rose'). It puts a different perspective on the tensions that marred their marriage, which was denied to Meredith writing while still involved. Hardy is free of the temptation to blame Emma, and the even greater temptation to indulge in futile remorse and excessive self-accusation, though he accepts the burden of a certain amount of culpability:

> Well, well! All's past amend,
> Unchangeable. It must go.

Quietly he accepts that to give and receive pain is part of the human condition, and to remember is part of the pain that matures. 'The dark space wherein I have lacked you' affirms what was true and real in his relationship to Emma's life.

> Primaeval rocks form the road's steep border,
>   And much have they faced there, first and last,
> Of the transitory in Earth's long order;
>   But what they record in colour and cast
> Is—that we two passed.

And to me, though Time's unflinching rigour,
 In mindless rote, has ruled from sight
The substance now, one phantom figure
 Remains on the slope, as when that night
Saw us alight.

The figure in the scene, as always, gives significance to the scene
when it knows her no more.

The traditional elegy has always given scope for expression of
the profound link between human life and the natural world with
its recurring rhythms and promise of new life to come out of death.
Hardy's predecessors Arnold and Tennyson had managed to adapt
the old pastoral conventions of the elegy to a personal vision
nurtured by the spiritual unrest of the nineteenth century. Proser-
pine, who brought new life out of death, had trod the Sicilian fields
in classical myth,

But ah, of our poor Thames she never heard!
Her foot the Cumnor cowslips never stirr'd!
And we should tease her with our plaint in vain.

In the absence of gods of death and renewal we are left with the
Cumnor cowslips of the here and now, and the garden of Somersby
Rectory—real features of real English landscapes, where the
weather can be as uncomfortable as in the realistic-pastoral Forest
of Arden. But the bones of pastoral elegy show through, as in the
recurring seasonal poems of *In Memoriam* which define the poet's
progress in recovery from his bereavement, for their application
to Hallam is the traditional link of 'life re-orient out of dust.' The
value of such 'a friendship as had master'd Time' depends on the
feeling that death is not the end. If 'Man dies: nor is there hope in
dust', the effort to cherish love as a thing meaningful only in itself
would be lost in

The moanings of the homeless sea,
 The sound of streams that swift or slow
 Draw down Æonian hills, and sow
The dust of continents to be.

For Hardy, the passage of chronological time towards death
cannot alter the quality of love. In 'At Castle Boterel' he faces it
squarely in the primaeval rocks that form the background to
Emma's phantom figure, and in the loss that is remembered simultaneously with the joy of recaptured experience. But time's

89

'mindless rote' imaged in Hardy's hills is controlled by his projection against their insentient infinity of the moment of value contained in a human relationship: a moment measured not by time but by intensity.

> It filled but a minute. But was there ever
>   A time of such quality, since or before,
> In that hill's story? To one mind never . . .

Daily life is full of the time-sense, and something else, as E. M. Forster reminds us in *Aspects of the Novel*:

'We think one event occurs after or before another, the thought is often in our minds, and much of our talk and action proceeds on the assumption. Much of our talk and action, but not all; there seems something else in life besides time, something which may conveniently be called "value," something which is measured not by minutes or hours, but by intensity, so that when we look at our past it does not stretch back evenly but piles up into a few notable pinnacles, and when we look at the future it seems sometimes a wall, sometimes a cloud, sometimes a sun,but never a chronological chart. Neither memory nor anticipation is much interested in Father Time, and all dreamers, artists and lovers are partially delivered from his tyranny; he can kill them, but he cannot secure their attention, and at the very moment of doom, when the clock collected in the tower its strength and struck, they may be looking the other way. So daily life, whatever it may be really, is practically composed of two lives—the life in time and the life by values—and our conduct reveals a double allegiance. "I only saw her for five minutes but it was worth it." There you have both allegiances in a single sentence.'

'At Castle Boterel' indicates from the first that Hardy's moment of value is independent of time and local conditions. The place is the same, and the month is again March, but these constants only serve to highlight the difference between the present of the poet's reverie and the past scene that forms its subject. It was a March day of 1913, when he revisited the Cornish scenes of his courtship, which called into being his vision of a previous March of forty years ago, and the time of day was light enough for him to see the slope of the fading byway 'now glistening wet'. Yet what he sees in vision on the slope is

> Myself and a girlish form benighted
>   In dry March weather.

The contrast between past and present is further pointed by the solitude of the musing man as he *drives* in a waggonette, remembering the compassionate gesture that his younger self shared with Emma in *walking*

> Beside a chaise. We had just alighted
> To ease the sturdy pony's load
> When he sighed and slowed.

A direct vision is built up by each apparently trivial detail of setting and action, recalled in short, precisely-punctuated statements that move jerkily with the recollecting emotion across a metrical pattern of long and short lines which expand and contract in his memory with the two kinds of time. The minutely realized particulars of a chronological action—getting out of a chaise and climbing a hill—pile up into what Forster would call a notable pinnacle. It expands in his memory over forty years and the dark space wherein he has lacked his partner of the scene, to become an honest and joyous affirmation of the timeless quality contained in those apparently unimportant particulars of the daily life of time:

> What we did as we climbed, and what we talked of
> Matters not much, nor to what it led . . .

Their marriage, with its pain of misunderstanding, death and remorse marking the chronological chart, is accepted and enfolded into the life by values. But Hardy's integrity and fidelity to the world of here and now will not let him leave the last word entirely with the life by values. The timeless moment of value, in which a quality in life is discerned, gains strength from being placed in perspective at the peak of the poem against the hard primaeval rocks that image 'Time's unflinching rigour'. The double vision that can see the human relationship both as part of 'the transitory in Earth's long order' and as a triumph of human consciousness which can record on the rocks their importance to human emotional history—'that we two passed'—produces a poetic tension rich in complexity. The poem ends in absolute honesty, with Hardy's vision and the expansion of time it afforded now 'shrinking, shrinking', separated from him by time and distance as his waggonette drives forward into the future and away from the physical scene. As the harsh rain-washed reality of the time-ruled present breaks into, but does not destroy, the timeless quality of his recaptured vision, the natural movement of musing colloquial speech settles down into quiet acceptance of the daily life of time which must be lived through.

> I look and see it there, shrinking, shrinking,
>   I look back at it amid the rain
> For the very last time; for my sand is sinking,
>   And I shall traverse old love's domain
>   Never again.

The figure is inseparable from the landscape in Hardy's search for value after his loss. A comparison of the relationship between figure and landscape in Hardy's elegies and Arnold's 'Thyrsis' shows how personal to himself was each poet's use of the elegiac pastoral convention in this respect. Arnold's search, like Hardy's, is localized first of all in a world of nature familiar to the dead and the survivor. The natural scene calls up both pain at the loss of the missing figure and memory of a shared past there; and at Arnold's moment of deepest despair, it becomes the measure of his grief, for the cuckoo will return next year, while Clough-Thyrsis will not. But it also provides his moment of affirmation in the signal-elm—a symbol of the continuity of the search for truth which he had shared with Clough, only intermittently manifested to the disordered nineteenth century, but still there. The Cumnor world of cowslips, brambles, and garden flowers has been realized with a vivid detail that makes the world of here and now seem to be the most actual thing in the poem: it pushes Clough into the background. Yet it shows so many signs of time and change to the visitor that he wonders whether it is illusory, just as Hardy asks, in 'A Dream or No', 'Does there even a place like Saint-Juliot exist?' because the death of the woman who gave meaning to the place casts doubt on the permanence of things. Death, to the Victorian agnostic, invalidated the traditional pastoral convention of a death-less and timeless order of existence mirrored in the calm seclusion of a rural retreat where gods of life's renewal were part of the props. The shadow of the mythic world of elegiac tradition that is felt behind the real Oxfordshire countryside connected with Arnold's bereavement produces a complex vision. It points the distance between the modern world of uncertainty and the ideal mythic order which the agnostic can no longer accept unmodified, but it also lifts the personal temporal experience of Clough's death into the universal timeless order represented by the pastoral elegy.

The shadow of the timeless world of myth hovers also behind Hardy's personal tragedy, for the Cornish landscape of Emma's home was also the setting for the tragic death-marked love of Tristram and Iseult. Though Hardy makes no specific reference to their story in 'Poems of 1912–13', it was heavily marked in his copy of Malory, and a visit to Tintagel in 1916 with his second wife elicited the comment, in a letter to Sir Sydney Cockerell, 'I visited the place 44 years ago with an Iseult of my own, and of course she was mixed in the vision of the other.' His 'Iseult', described in terms that could have come straight out of a ballad-version of the legend—'Fair-eyed and white-shouldered, broad-browed and brown-tressed'—and placed in intimate connection with the scene that had witnessed the archetypal love-death relationship, acquires a significance that extends beyond the personal aspect of a marriage gone wrong and ended by death. Though Emma was a woman of thirty when he met her, Hardy stresses in many poems her child-like capacity to live with her whole undivided being—'Lament', 'Rain on a Grave', 'Places', 'Beeny Cliff', 'The Phantom Horse-woman'. One of his most recurring memories of Emma is of

> A ghost-girl-rider. And though, toil-tried,
>> He withers daily,
>> Time touches her not,
>> But still she rides gaily
>> In his rapt thought
>> On the shagged and shaly
>> Atlantic spot,
>> And as when first eyed
> Draws rein and sings to the swing of the tide.

There is an essential freedom in her harmonious relationship to this elemental scene of sea and primaeval rock which reminds one of the first Cathy's relationship to the moors in *Wuthering Heights*. There is also the same isolation from everyday concerns of someone in contact with absolutes.

>> There lonely I found her,
>> The sea-birds around her,
> And other than nigh things uncaring to know.

Emma's sea-birds and the shot lapwing of Cathy's delirium call up the limitless, timeless world of absolutes from which marriage has exiled them. Marriage brings maturity, compromise, complexity, and alienation from the child and folklore world of elemental harmony where past and present, near and far, natural and supernatural, love and death, are one. The world of absolute oneness which time cannot touch can only be regained, as in Wagner's version of the Tristram legend, through death.

> Yet her shade, maybe,
> Will creep underground
> Till it catch the sound
> Of that western sea
> As it swells and sobs
> Where she once domiciled,
> And joy in its throbs
> With the heart of a child.

In poems such as this one, "I Found Her out There", there is a feeling that it had been a betrayal of Emma's essential being to bring her 'here' and lay her to rest

> In a noiseless nest
> No sea beats near

when 'out there' she was vividly alive, in harmony with the violence of the Atlantic gales which she joyed in 'with the heart of a child'. The form of the poem, in its subtle interplay of speech stress and metre, dramatically enacts the woman's intimate association with the elements. The quiet, controlled two-beat line of the first two stanzas rises in the next two to an urgent pounding throb in which two or three syllables crushed to the beat are varied with lines in which almost every word demands a major stress:

> As a wind-tugged tress
> Flapped her cheek like a flail

as Emma's harmony with elemental violence reaches a peak of intensity. But the speech stress fighting strenuously against the inexorable throb of the sea suggests that it is a humanly-controlled harmony which does not allow the human identity to be submerged.

Emma's association with the stormy scene which imbues her with its own ambiguous vital energy dramatically revalues the initial threat of the 'hurricane [which] shakes/The solid land' in the first stanza, and by implication, the meaning of violence and death in the universe. Through the outrage of Emma's death

94

Hardy has regained an intensified sense of their lost love at a time and place when Emma was most alive, most herself. These scenes of time past

> Have a savour that scenes in being lack,
> And a presence more than the actual brings . . .
> ('Places')

As in *Wuthering Heights* country, there is a very thin line dividing natural and supernatural in what Hardy describes as the 'region of dream and mystery', where a ghostly voice calls out to him from forty years ago. Nevertheless, Emily Bronte's sense of the supernatural is not Hardy's: his feet are always firmly on the ground even in his moments of greatest confusion and distress, and he never doubts for a second that Emma has no life as a spirit beyond the grave. The Cornish scene, with its ambivalent destructive and creative energies, speaks strongly of the missing figure: Hardy's elegies are not original in this respect. It implies the contrast or contrasts on which his poems are so often constructed: between a happy companiable past and a harsh desolate present; between Emma's affection for the landscape when living and its indifference to her death; between the sensitivity of the living woman to the elements and her insensitivity when dead; between ignorance of the significance of a certain spot in the scene or a certain moment in human relationships and the importance they gain in retrospect from Emma's death and burial. Death is the moment that alters all: the event that gives retrospective meaning to the individual life in all its varied settings.

Hardy's search for the meaning of Emma's life in relation to his own returns constantly to the Cornish landscape around St Juliot, for 'much of my life claims the spot as its key'. But their married life at Max Gate forms part of the pattern too, and the first eleven poems of the sequence set Emma firmly, alive or dead, in Dorset. In these poems which centre on Max Gate or Stinsford (the place of her burial), written before Hardy's journey into Cornwall in March 1913, the fact of Emma's death is paramount. The general mood is one of unreconciled desolation: the key of Hardy's life, like the key that illustrates the manuscript of 'Nature's Questioning' in *Wessex Poems*, is broken and meaningless. The twelfth poem, 'A Dream or No', though written a month before his Cornish revisitation, begins in memory and recollected emotion the search for 'that time's renewal' in the places connected with Emma's youth and love. Slowly the shattered key starts to knit together and turn again as Emma's recaptured vitality brings a sense of time by values into the passage of chronological time that had robbed him of her presence.

The movement of the whole sequence develops according to the poetic and musical logic of a song cycle. Hardy's theme, of the mysterious relationship between love and death and the affirmative possibility of time's renewal through memory of past love, is a common theme of song cycles: Schubert's 'Winterreise' and Tippett's 'The Heart's Assurance' come to mind. 'Poems of 1912–13' has the unity of theme and mood that belongs to a song cycle, with its internal variations of feeling, tempo, and aspect, its peaks and troughs. As the 'cycle' stands now, it is constructed on the peaks of six major poems which form stages in the poet's acceptance of Emma's death: 'The Going', "I Found Her out There", 'The Voice', 'After a Journey', 'At Castle Boterel', and 'Where the Picnic Was'. The interspersed poems are generally of a lower tension and less complex in metre and form. Many of them use the strong two-beat line which by its descent from traditional folk rhythms serves to stylize and distance the poet's personal grief and so link it with the *lacrimae rerum* of the human race which lives and loves under the shadow of death.

'The Going' opens the sequence with Hardy's naked reaction to Emma's death. The abrupt mid-conversational opening which is so characteristic of Hardy (and which he shares with Browning, Pope, Donne, and Juvenal) takes the feel of the very moment of bereavement in its spontaneous cry of pain, surprise, remorse, and desolation. The poem is worthy of its position as the first poem in the cycle: it establishes straightaway the love/death theme. The suffering that must be faced in loneliness and remorse, the conscious-ness that death has given their alienation a finality which must be reckoned with in the survivor's reintegration into normal life, is present in this first poem. But so is the possibility of 'that time's renewal' to be sought in later poems through memory of the missing figure linked to the two landscapes of Dorset and Cornwall which are introduced in 'The Going' as symbols of the recent past of illusion and the remote past of reality; and the final sober recon-ciliation with what is 'past amend'. Above all, 'The Going' intro-duces the search for the source of Emma's true identity, which Hardy had lost not only through her death but through the change that overtook their relationship in their married life. Here, the rapid rush of recollection of the circumstances of her death, so typical in its non-communication of what their relationship had become, settles into two contrasting pictures of Emma's persona. The first, in stanza III, is of the married woman at Max Gate, exercising the power of the recently dead (in contrast to her quiet leavetaking of life) to create an illusion of her presence.

> Why do you make me leave the house
> And think for a breath it is you I see
> At the end of the alley of bending boughs
> Where so often you used to be . . .

But the vision is not a true recapture of time past; the hard consonants and varied 'a' sounds of 'darkening dankness' and 'yawning blankness', like the earlier 'Saw morning harden upon the wall', pull the stanza back to the unwelcome emptiness and heaviness of the physical world without Emma, unrelieved by any momentary flash of insight. A hint that the true hiding-place of her personality is to be found in the past is contained in the past tense—'You were she'—of stanza IV, which presents her in her Cornish setting, already linked with vital symbols of pulsing life—but a life related to death because it is transfixed in the primaeval rocks:

> You were she who abode
> By those red-veined rocks far West,
> You were the swan-necked one who rode
> Along the beetling Beeny Crest . . .

The next stanza holds to this vision as the true essence of Emma when it returns to painful questioning of their shattered marriage:

> Why, then, latterly did we not speak,
> Did we not think of those days long dead,
> And ere your vanishing strive to seek
> That time's renewal? We might have said,
> "In this bright spring weather
> We'll visit together
> Those places that once we visited."

The last stanza is typical of many poems in the sequence in that it swings back from illusion and regret for what might have been to the harsh denying reality the poet must live with.

> Well, well! All's past amend,
> Unchangeable. It must go.
> I seem but a dead man held on end
> To sink down soon . . .

The rhythm and sentence-structure that had the uninterrupted swing of folk-song suddenly collapses into the dry, jerky movement of an individual human voice controlling the emotion of a personal grief. Then, brilliantly, the counterswing from stoic soliloquy to passionate address affirms in broken, awkward phrases that could belong to no-one but Hardy, the intensity and quality of the sorrow from which the whole cycle springs:

> . . . O you could not know
> That such swift fleeing
> No soul foreseeing—
> Not even I—would undo me so!

This is not a man talking about his grief, but the essence of grief as a quality displaying itself through the unselfconscious motions of a passionate and deep-feeling human mind.

"I Found Her out There", flanked on either side by three poems concerning Emma's life and death in Dorset, sees what her marriage entailed, the breaking of her harmony with the violent Cornish scene, as a betrayal of her essential being, and a symbol of the human adult's alienation from meaning in the world. This poem holds a focal position in the cycle. It corresponds to those songs in which a change of key or an unexpected harmonic colouring presents the dual face of experience simultaneously. Though "I Found Her out There" is still concerned with Emma's death and burial, her vital relationship with the violence of the elements points to this equivocal natural energy as an essential part of the woman Hardy loved. Love and death are related in a harmony of dissonance. 'The Voice', coming between two dramatizations of Emma as a sad but solicitous ghost, swings to the depth of desolation without reconciliation in setting her illusory presence against her real absence in the physical world. Yet the unexpected ground base of a dance tune, steadying the confused uncertainty of the poet's speech-rhythms, again brings love into a vital harmonic tension with death, though at this stage the juxtaposition does not find any ultimate meaning in Emma's death. 'The Voice' is the last of the peak poems in the sequence to be controlled by the past.

'A Dream or No', a musical bridge to the poems that follow, develops the undervoiced change of harmonies in facing honestly the difficulty of distinguishing between fact and fiction, when 'nought of that maid from Saint-Juliot I see;/Can she ever have been here . . .?' The confusion of past and present is finally thrashed out, and both are valued and placed, in the next poem, the climactic 'After a Journey'.

Hardy did well to change the rather formal first line, 'Hereto I come to interview a ghost' to 'Hereto I come to view a voiceless ghost' in subsequent editions. 'View' introduces the major theme of clear vision that can at last accept and so penetrate the darkness to distinguish between illusion and reality: 'voiceless' characterizes the ghost as something different from the illusion of 'the woman calling' in 'The Voice'. The alliteration stresses the link between clear vision and departure of illusion. The only voice in the poem, of 'the cave just under', with

> a voice still so hollow
> That it seems to call out to me from forty years ago,
> When you were all aglow,
> And not the thin ghost that I now frailly follow!

is placed firmly, in its hollowness, in the perspective of the past, and with it, Emma in the illusion of her living presence. The heavy stresses on the 'then fair hour' and the 'then fair weather' point up the poet's clear recognition of the past for what it is, and his realization that he cannot return to 'then'. He comes through finally in this poem to a liberation from his lively and tantalizing ghost, but only because he does not refuse the experience of disorientation. The shifting perspectives of time and vision that cloud his memory—

> Where you will next be there's no knowing,
> Facing round about me everywhere . . .

affect sense, rhythm, structure, and sound. The flitting movement of his vividly-defined ghost, with her 'rose-flush coming and going', is mirrored in the jerky uncertainty of Hardy's own coming and going in pursuit—'Up the cliff, down, till I'm lonely, lost'; and the opening and closing vowels of 'the unseen waters' ejaculations awe me'. The clumsiness of this line has caused some protest; but it is a deliberate change from the first edition's 'unseen waters' soliloquies', and there is no doubt that its particular arrangement of reverberating vowels and clashing consonants helps to create the 'coming and going' of the ghost, of the throbbing sea which is a groundbase controlling all the other kinds of movement in the poem, of the different dimensions of time, of the waves of reality and illusion, of the poet's recollecting consciousness, and the urgent, intimate speech rhythm of a man gradually coming to terms with the onrush of his grief. Life offers—to deny: the rhythm of ebb and flow controls the lines, stretching out the voice from death to life to issue finally in the affirmative simplicity of

> I am just the same as when
> Our days were a joy, and our paths through flowers.

The nuances of uncertainty in the second stanza contribute towards a final honest reckoning with guilt for the past, for it is set clearly in its proper dimension of time. 'Through the years, through the dead scenes I have tracked you'. 'Your olden haunts' may be a common figure of poetic speech, but its semantic relationship to 'dead scenes' in the next line suggests that the ghost which has trespassed over its proper boundary of time is about to be laid. Time dominates the poem, and especially in the diction of this stanza.

> What have you now found to say of our past—
>   Scanned across the dark space wherein I have lacked you?
> Summer gave us sweets, but autumn wrought division?
>   Things were not lastly as firstly well
>   With us twain, you tell?
> But all's closed now, despite Time's derision.

The hollow mockery of time, which mingled past and present, no longer has power to confuse Hardy's definition of reality. His eyes are wide open and his vision unblurred: 'I see what you are doing: you are leading me on . . .' She leads him on from the 'dead scenes' into a fully-accepted present that balances two realities, equally valid: the reality of the present moment of dawn after physical and spiritual darkness, that is defined through the acute response of his senses to the eternal affirmations of waking animal life; and the reality of his vision, no longer the ghost tantalizing him with her physical absence, but a presence enshrined in his memory as the deepest truth he had known. He knows that the exchange of illusion for daylight reality brings pain, but his decision is firm:

> Soon you will have, Dear, to vanish from me,
> For the stars close their shutters and the dawn
> whitens hazily.

He does not need the deceptions of memory now; living through them has brought him to a quiet acceptance of what memory can give: a sense of 'that time's renewal' in perpetuating the most valued experience of his past, untouched by time's slow stain, into the present. Now he can say, with that simple tenderness which is one of Hardy's deepest notes,

> Trust me, I mind not, though Life lours,
> The bringing me here; nay, bring me here again!

for he can trust himself to keep a positive hold on life.

The note of quiet but positive contemplation is held in the next two poems, which ponder on the scene's indifference to Emma's death and its comparative immortality, with the steady vision of 'the woman whom I loved so, and who loyally loved me' placed in the past and holding its own against the physical bulk of Beeny Cliff. These two comparatively muted poems lead to the intense affirmation of that time's quality against the record of chronological time in 'At Castle Boterel'. The poet's steady look at physical reality in the last stanza, with his vision 'shrinking, shrinking', provides a diminuendo that leads to the less passionate tone of the next two poems, though the vision of Emma in all her youth and vitality, always balanced against the pain of her absence from the scenes that knew her, stays with him all the time. The second of these two poems, 'The Phantom Horsewoman', originally formed the last poem of the sequence. While in many ways it makes a fitting conclusion with its reiteration of the theme of the power of memory to perpetuate the poet's vision of the essential Emma, the three poems which follow in subsequent editions add something more to the cycle. The ballad form of 'The Spell of the Rose', which retells the story of their love-death romance with the appurtenances of romantic allegory, links their personal tragedy to the universal folk-experience of the human race. 'St. Launce's Revisited' moves tersely from allegory to the blunt reality he has to live with: the wish 'Slip back, Time!' is almost immediately denied by the strange faces of the servants, and the denial clinched by the final wry comment:

> Why waste thought,
> When I know them vanished
> Under earth; yea, banished
> Ever into nought!

Its tone prepares the way for the final peak of the sequence, 'Where the Picnic Was'. There is no ecstasy, and no affirmation; these are stages past. There is only retracing of the external act of human communion that a picnic represents, noting of the external signs of human occupation, by the 'last relic of the band/Who came that day'; and quiet acceptance of his isolation in the continuing scene. 'Yes, I am here': Hardy has survived an overwhelming grief, and has learned not to deflect its natural course, not to refuse those memories which give value and meaning to the broken relationship of love at the same time as they revive the pain of death that is the other deepest truth about life.

The life that is affirmed by 'Poems of 1912–13' and Hardy's other elegies is not one of inflated operatic grandeur. It moves us precisely because it is an ordinary unpretentious life of doing and suffering, often empty and commonplace, full of human imperfections. It is a life of prose quality such as most people live: W. H. Auden, who describes Hardy as his poetic father, has paid tribute to Hardy's peculiar power of investing the most prosaic of colloquial statements with the light that never was, to express the 'poetry in what is left [in life] after all the false romance has been abstracted' (*Life*).

> "There was a frost
> Last night," she said,
> "And the stove was forgot
> When we went to bed . . ."

> I see what you are doing: you are leading me on . . .

First lines in particular introduce and make memorable the prosaic quality of the little unremembered acts that constituted life at Max Gate or St Juliot: 'You did not walk with me', 'It was your way, my dear', 'How she would have loved/A party today!' 'It never looks like summer'—the last a poem made out of a chance remark of Emma's, which is pencilled on one of Hardy's sketches of the Cornish scene.

Sometimes the prosaic quality and stumbling awkwardness that expresses an inarticulate grief almost too great for expression, which make a poem like 'After a Journey' so powerful, do not produce poetry of the first rank. 'A Circular', with its predictable ending in a shroud, hardly goes beyond the form of the Fashion catalogue that inspired it. 'The Prospect', which starts promisingly with one of Hardy's vivid silhouettes of trees against a winter sky and develops through simile and metaphor an image of the season linked to old age, finishes its first stanza with a picture of Emma 'greeting a gathered band/Of the urban and the bland', in which the diction seems chosen more for the needs of rhyme than for precision of poetic statements. There is not here the intensity of feeling which inspires concise expression even in some of the 'variation' poems of the main cycle, such as 'Rain on a Grave', 'Your Last Drive', and 'Lament'. In the last, what might have been a routine description in the familiar before-and-after pattern of trivial social occasions at Max Gate, is exalted by the controlled passion of the ballad-like refrain, 'She is shut, she is shut', with its variations from stanza to stanza and its sudden tightening of rhythm and diction. In general, Hardy's fidelity to the truth of feeling, phrasing and syntax, diction and stress of common speech, and the rhythms of the ordinary human mind recollecting some great emotion, makes great poetry out of the elegiac experience mortal men must undergo. His achievement gives the lie to the view expressed in Joseph Wood Krutch's *The Modern Temper* and George Steiner's *The Death of Tragedy* that tragedy and other human values are not possible to modern man. Hardy brings the values of tragedy within the scope of the ordinary human individual. Tennyson's 'stars in their courses blindly run'; Hardy's 'stars close their shutters' in a homely image of human experience that is as undignified as the words 'flop' and 'flitting' in the same stanza. Yet 'After a Journey', which never leaves the world of common human experience, is one of the finest expressions of tragic values in any language.

The values by which an ordinary human being may live in a death-marked life can be traced in the hundred or so poems inspired directly by Hardy's relationship with Emma. Though sadness and regret for the waste recur in his deep self-questioning— ('An Upbraiding', 'We Sat at the Window', 'Best Times', 'Known Had I', 'Overlooking the River Stour', 'Near Lanivet')—there is a high proportion of poems devoted to happiness in this most tragic of poets. It is strongly implied by its negation in poems of the before-and-after type ('A Riddle', "It Never Looks like Summer", 'On the Doorstep', "The Curtains now are Drawn"); and such lyrics as "When I Set Out for Lyonnesse", 'The Wind's Prophecy', 'A Two Years' Idyll', 'At the Piano', 'She Opened the Door', and 'Once at Swanage' say Yea unequivocally to their love. In "The Curtains now are Drawn", he still hears the notes of her song, 'And death may come, but loving is divine'. The value of the dream as well as the reality is given its place too, when it can be clearly distinguished from illusion, as it can in 'The Shadow on the Stone', where Hardy determines not to 'unvision' the shape though he knows it cannot be 'her I long had learned to lack'.

Respect for what is due to any human being places high among Hardy's values love, tenderness, tolerance, a forgiveness that he extends to himself, and a fidelity that survives death while recognizing that death may render it futile:

> True: never you'll know. And you will not mind.
> But shall I then slight you because of such?
> Dear ghost, in the past did you ever find
> The thought, "What profit," move me much?

Posthumous existence in the memory of the living is the only kind of immortality Hardy can recognize. There, the essential truth of a person that has survived years of misunderstanding can be recaptured from death. The essential Emma lies not in the worn, dead body that 'looked quite other than theretofore,/As if it could not *be* you' ('Days to Recollect') but in the preceding memory of her, young and vital, collecting on her petticoat winged thistle seeds that 'sailed on the breeze in a nebulous stream/Like a comet's tail behind you'. Her immortality is here, in an intense moment of vision which burnt into the poet's mind vivid details of her relationship to the natural world that trembles with an inscrutable significance. This is how he remembers Emma; vital, human, imperfect. 'He Prefers Her Earthly' is the elegist's ultimate tribute to the ordinary individual that was Emma Hardy. He firmly rejects the kind of immortality that would rob her of her human qualities and change her 'mortal mould'

> to a firmament-riding earthless essence
> From what you were of old:

> All too unlike the fond and fragile creature
> Then known to me . . . Well, shall I say it plain?
> I would not have you thus and there,
> But still would grieve on, missing you, still feature
> You as the one you were.

V

Dramatic and Narrative Lyrics

Hardy is a poet who resists rigid classification. In the *Life* he quotes with approval a sentence from the *Edinburgh Review*

'which I might have written myself: "The division [of poems] into separate groups [ballad, lyrical, narrative &c.] is frequently a question of the preponderance, not of the exclusive possession, of certain aesthetic elements."'

So the poems to be considered as dramatic or narrative have merely a preponderance of story and dramatic expression. Dramatic conjunctions of people, time and circumstance do not preclude lyrical elements which would be equally at home in the 1912–13 poems. The lyrical emotion that sets the tone of 'The Peasant's Confession' —a first-person narrative of war-time action—

> I hid him deep in nodding rye and oat—
>   His shroud green stalks and loam;
> His requiem the corn-blade's husky note—
>   And then I hastened home . . .

is not vastly different from

> His crypt the cloudy canopy,
>   The wind his death-lament

of 'The Darkling Thrush', though the narrative modifies, and is modified by, the lyrical feeling. Nor have dramatic and narrative elements been excluded from reflective lyrics. Within the framework of his own poetic persona recollecting, Hardy re-creates in the 1912–13 poems the story of his marriage. A situation conceived in dramatic terms of action, figure, scene, and often dialogue provides an objective correlative to personal emotions. The strange couple eternally promenading in 'Beyond the Last Lamp' possibly dramatizes the unhappiness of his marriage: the travelling boy in

'Midnight on the Great Western' gives dramatic embodiment to Hardy's tragic vision of the unknown region into which man's birth thrusts him.

Hardy's Prefaces insist on the dramatic nature of his verse, 'even that which is in other than narrative form—much is dramatic or impersonative even where not explicitly so' (*Poems of the Past and the Present*). Even 'those lyrics penned in the first person . . . are to be regarded, in the main, as dramatic monologues by different characters' (*Time's Laughingstocks*). His insistence can be defended if one regards his poetic persona as a dramatic instrument in itself, recording the inner and outer conflicts of human experience. Intensity of lyrical feeling and personal reflection does not rob poems like 'The Going' and 'To an Unborn Pauper Child' of dramatic immediacy:

> Why did you give no hint that night
> That quickly after the morrow's dawn,
> And calmly, as if indifferent quite,
> You would close your term here, up and be gone
> Where I could not follow . . .

> Breathe not, hid Heart: cease silently,
> And though thy birth-hour beckons thee,
> Sleep the long sleep . . .

However, Hardy's dramatic monologues do not re-create the excitement of immediate experience as Browning's re-create Fra Lippo Lippi's escapade or the exposure of Mr Sludge the medium. More often, they are either past situations recollected by a speaker in present equilibrium, or they are heavy with nostalgia engendered by 'the long drip of human tears' behind the specific situation.

Even poems such as 'The Curate's Kindness', 'The Chapel-Organist', and 'At Shag's Heath', which appear to be related while the old man is actually being conveyed to the workhouse, the organist giving her last performance, and the guilt-haunted wife on her way to drown herself, are really completed actions. Past events condition the immediate situation. Though 'The Chapel-Organist' is in the form of a monologue being thought or spoken in a present action, a glance at Browning's 'Abt Vogler' or 'Master Hugues of Saxe-Gotha' will show how much Hardy's poem depends on a narration of past conflict. The organist's thoughts as she plays grow from the conflict of body and soul which her whole life-story expresses, and not from her present performance, which is rather the final consequence of that story. Abt Vogler's reflections on music as an expression of the Absolute are a direct result of 'the palace of music I reared' while extemporizing at the organ. The vision of the organist in 'Master Hugues of Saxe-Gotha' of life as 'God's gold . . . Palled beneath man's usurpature' develops spontaneously from his struggle to find meaning under the dusty fugue structures of an obscure composer as he plays them in the organ loft whose unusual perspective shows him both the cobweb-covered gold of the ceiling and the usurping human activities of the sacristan below sweeping the church. Neither a philosophy of life, the quality of the music, nor the character of the organist is re-created in Hardy's poem by the organist's present activity. She and her playing exist simply as a fundamental image of the cosmic disharmony between what is and what might be, shown in her story.

Browning's 'interest's on the dangerous edge of things' in character and motive: his situations merely contributory. Hardy, in spite of a fascination with the grotesque and melodramatic aspects of experience which he shares with Browning, has no revelation of complexity in his speakers to compare with the Bishop who orders his tomb, Fra Lippo Lippi, Andrea del Sarto, Porphyria's lover, or the protagonists of 'The Laboratory' and 'My Last Duchess'. In the form of monologue favoured by Browning and Tennyson, the objective events and other characters concerned in the situation are filtered through the subjective screen of a speaker whose self-knowledge is limited by the presentness of his perspective. Caliban's natural theology owes its physical concreteness and moral short-sightedness to the bottom of the swamp on which he is reclining; St Simeon Stylites' lofty distortion of the world below and clear vision of the angel, to his perch on top of a pillar. The organist's definition of meaning in Master Hugues' 'mountainous fugues' as gold hidden under a mass of cobwebs is inspired both by his unusual position in the organ loft and the physical attack of his fingers on the spidery texture of the old fugue. The speaker so committed to a present situation reveals more than he understands. Tennyson's old maid in 'The Spinster's Sweet'arts' avows her independence of men while fondling the cats she has named after her rejected lovers: the reader is left to complete her self-revelation by judging the extent of her substitution of manageable cats for unmanageable men. Similarly, it is the reader who comprehends and passes judgement on the Duke's insolent monomania as he talks about the failings of his last duchess to the official who is arranging the marriage to his next; and on the extent of Karshish's belief in the miracle he tries to explain by rational means. The dramatic effect of a double perspective, of reader and speaker, is lost when the subject of the monologue is a past action, unless its retelling is conditioned by the speaker's present situation, as it is in Andrea del Sarto's attempts to impress Lucrezia with his past achievements and Karshish's endeavour to pierce the scientific scepticism of his superior. Though a few poems like 'Rake-hell Muses' and 'The Pink Frock' gain some dramatic effect from the moral blinkers of their speakers, Hardy usually sacrifices the psychological subtlety that results from Browning's double perspective to a stress on the situation itself, which came nearer to expressing the quality of his personal vision. Whereas Browning's double viewpoint on the lover who steals his friend's mistress in 'A Light Woman' leads the reader to understand the lover's moral and emotional ambiguities better than he does himself, Hardy's emphasis in 'The Face at the Casement' falls on the lover's 'deed of hell' and the chance—'why I turned I know not'—that dictated it.

> It was done before I knew it;
> What devil made me do it
> I cannot tell!

> Yes, while he gazed above,
> I put my arm about her
> That he might see, nor doubt her
> My plighted Love.

There is no excuse or pretence of motive for the inexplicable. The deed is morally evaluated within the poem by a first-person narrator whose perspective is identical with the reader's. The complex emotions of 'Porphyria's Lover' are replaced by a simple archetype of the guilt-haunted man, and a final reflection which shows the speaker standing outside his own situation, understanding something at least about the quality of contradictory passions:

> Love is long-suffering, brave,
> Sweet, prompt, precious as a jewel;
> But jealousy is cruel,
> Cruel as the grave!

Complexity or development of persona would be out of place in Hardy's vision of man's predicament. It is the quirks of time and chance, best seen through a completed action which is necessary to the ironic perspective from which he reflects on the madness of circumstance, rather than quirks of character, which form Hardy's climaxes. 'The Slow Nature' is less a study of the motions of a shocked psyche than a study of the quixotic action of time, which a fortnight after her husband's death strikes the woman with grief, while the unwontedly grave messenger

> amazed that a wife struck to widowhood
> Thought first of her unkempt room

is restored to his usual humour. It is therefore no great matter whether the narrator is an actor in the story or a persona who views it objectively, since his perspective does not require a contribution from the reader to complete the total meaning of the poem.

In Browning's account of the medical experiences of 'Karshish, the Arab Physician' and Hardy's 'Panthera' and 'The Wood Fire', both poets employ the convention of the neutral narrator on the periphery of a great event—the story of Lazarus in Browning's poem, and the Crucifixion in Hardy's. 'Panthera', in addition, insets the narration of Christ's supposed father, who might be presumed to have a personal interest in the Crucifixion, inside the narration of an uncommitted character. But Panthera's calm account of the Crucifixion at which he recognized Mary as his former mistress and Christ as their son might have yielded Browning more psychological tension than

> "Though I betrayed some qualms, she marked me not;
> And I was scarce of mood to comrade her
> And close the silence of so wide a time
> To claim a malefactor as my son—"

The effect of the Crucifixion on the human mind is not Hardy's primary business. Browning's emphasis, however, is placed on the effect of Lazarus' experience, and 'how he takes up the after-life', on the uneasy paganism of Karshish, the physician who examined him. The full force of Karshish's revaluation of the scientific attitude, depending as it does on a non-rational feeling of 'peculiar interest/And awe indeed this man has touched me with', can only strike us because his character as a responsible citizen of the world and sober scientific witness, trusting in physical 'things of price'

like 'blue-flowering borage . . . very nitrous' that can be botani-
cally and chemically defined, has been established from the beginning. But his interest in Lazarus carries the meaning of the poem
beyond what he actually says; beyond his anxiety to define the
case to a sceptical superior in physical and rational terms as 'a
case of mania—subinduced/By epilepsy'. The end of the poem—
a contemplation on the 'madman's' idea of the 'All-Great' as 'the
All-Loving too'—implicitly denies Karshish's protestations that he
has been writing 'of trivial matters'.

Hardy's neutral narrators, like Browning's, distance the strangeness of events. We cannot give full assent to the story of Panthera
when the narrator warns

> That the said woman did not recognize
> Her lover's face, is matter for surprise.
> However, there's his tale, fantasy or otherwise.

Nevertheless, it is the strangeness of circumstance which is stressed
by the lack of psychological subtlety in the narrators. We see in
Panthera only one of Time's laughingstocks, like the soldier of
'San Sebastian' whose daughter supernaturally inherits the eyes of
'the maiden I wronged in Peninsular days'; the elderly returned
lover of 'The Revisitation' who learns from the sight of the lady in
full daylight that 'Love is lame at fifty years'; the mother of 'A
Sunday Morning Tragedy' whose procuring of an abortion for her
daughter kills the girl on the day her tardy lover had published
the banns. Neither the personal character of narrators, nor the
effect of the Crucifixion on them, is functional in Hardy's poems.
What is significant, in fact, is the *lack* of effect, which has its
dramatic function in eliciting the reader's response to the Crucifixion. What should have been a 'day of wont' to Panthera, when
'some three or four were stript, transfixed, and nailed,/And no
great stir occurred' has only an economical importance to the
Christopher Coney of Calvary in 'The Wood Fire'; he buys
the crosses 'bargain-cheap of the executioners' and commends the
piece that Christ was on for its cheery blaze in a bleak spring:
"And it's worthless for much else, what with cuts and stains
thereon." Poor people and Roman soldiers alike are more conscious
of the ever-present enmity of nature and the physical world, of
aches and wounds occasioned by active service and duties in damp
outposts, than the implications of the Crucifixion. The physical
struggle for survival leaves little room for speculation on the

miraculous. Browning, in contrast, gives little space to the *events* of Lazarus' 'death'. Hardy's concern with the fate of the human being —to be eternally active but ignorant of final causes—places stress inevitably on event rather than its effect on character.

Hardy's vision is expressed most succinctly through the bare statement of event that composes 'Satires of Circumstance in Fifteen Glimpses'. Here, the quintessence of a situation of human delusion is presented at a moment of crisis, the culmination of an implied drama, which reveals the situation for what it is. The means used are dramatic and narrative. The poet-narrator observes gesture, dialogue, tone, appearance, and allows them to speak for themselves. The danger that the effect of a shock revelation may stale on re-reading is largely avoided by variety of presentation. The series does not depend exclusively on the mechanical reversal of viewpoint from the apparent situation in the first stanza to the real situation in the second, by means of which the irony is shown, though this method can be seen at its best in 'At Tea', 'In the Nuptial Chamber', 'In Church', and 'In the Cemetery'. The ironic form is varied, for example, in 'In the Study', where it is present only in the narrator's compassionate piercing of the lady's nonchalant façade, by her hesitant speech rhythms as she offers her father's books for sale, by clauses of manner: 'as if necessity were unknown', 'as if to sell were a mere gay whim'; and details of appearance and gesture that show her poverty. 'In the Restaurant' is less an ironic reversal of attitude than a study of two different points of view—the man's and the woman's—towards marital deceit and the expected child of their illicit union. In 'At the Draper's' the incident which caused a double revelation to husband and wife—the wife's precipitate ordering of fashionable widow's weeds, observed by her still-living husband—is placed in the past, and the poem consists almost entirely of the husband's words as his knowledge of the incident strips her vanity bare. 'In the Moonlight' expresses its sense of life's grim irony in the question-and-answer form reminiscent of certain traditional ballads, which eliminates from the initial question—why the lonely workman stands staring at a grave—all its possible answers until the final stanza reveals the truth:

> "Ah—she was the one you loved, no doubt,
> Through good and evil, through rain and drought,
> And when she passed, all your sun went out?"

111

> "Nay: she was the woman I did not love,
> Whom all the others were ranked above,
> Whom during her life I thought nothing of."

'In the Room of the Bride-Elect' provides the shock at the beginning, in the bride's revelation that she would have married the man of her parents' choice with a little more parental pressure. The poem moves towards a bitter image of resignation to her self-imposed fate:

> "Ah! here he comes with his button-hole rose.
> Good God—I must marry him I suppose!"

Even in those poems which make use of the usual ironic antithesis there is normally enough variation to exempt them from the charge of overwhelming the human experience with a mechanical formula. They ring the changes on the ignorance or knowledge which a revelation of the reality under the appearance leaves with the actors. 'At Tea', 'At a Watering-Place' and 'In the Cemetery' leave the victims of duplicity or circumstance in blissful ignorance. 'In Church', 'Outside the Window', 'At the Altar-Rail' and 'In the Nuptial Chamber' depend for their irony on the presence of someone within the poem who has beheld a soul undraped. The victims in 'By her Aunt's Grave' and 'Over the Coffin' are dead: their dead presence is the touchstone which shows up the disloyalty of the girl who spends her aunt's headstone money on a dance (though the tone here is not unqualified by a suggestion of Christopher Coney's philosophy, "Why should death rob life o' fourpence?") and the narrow conventions of the eternal triangle that hinged on the man now in his coffin.

> "But now I am older, and tell you true,
> For life is little, and dead lies he;
> I would I had let alone you two!"

The effect of irony is also subtly varied according to the viewpoint and commitment of the narrator. The poet-narrator who observes the undercurrents which stir action, gesture, scene, dialogue, and tone in 'At Tea' distances the irony of ignorance as the actor-narrator of 'At a Watering-Place' does not. Whereas the apparent harmony of 'At Tea' is not destroyed by the observer-narrator pointing out the ironic cross-currents of wife, husband and mistress, the peaceful tone and scene of 'At a Watering-Place' is violently disrupted in the second stanza by the ex-lover's passionate details of his love-making to the girl who is to be married to another:

> "... How little he thinks
> That dozens of days and nights on end
> I have stroked her neck, unhooked the links
> Of her sleeve to get at her upper arm. ..."

A more compassionate, even humorous irony appears in the narration of 'the man of the cemetery' who, like the Overworld of *The Dynasts*, has knowledge denied to mothers squabbling over the empty graves of their children.

> "And then the main drain had to cross,
> And we moved the lot some nights ago,
> And packed them away in the general foss
> With hundreds more. But their folks don't know,
> And as well cry over a new-laid drain
> As anything else, to ease your pain!"

Occasionally, as in 'On the Death-bed', Hardy tries to pack too much incident into a form which makes its effect through stark statement of a dramatic situation stripped bare of all but the culminating crisis implying the steps that led up to it. But the best of these situations, told in the language of bare simplicity and natural cadences of the human voice in strong but controlled emotion, stand as memorable images of some essential quality of life. Even the titles have dramatic relevance as scene-setting and agents in the action. The restaurant carries an aura of snatched guilty meetings. The altar-rail, the room of the bride-elect, and the nuptial chamber are places which reveal the frailty of the eternal Eve: the grave and the coffin measure the importance of human actions: the draper's exposes their vanity, and the church their false professions. 'In Church', 'In the Cemetery', and 'Over the Coffin' crystallize that essential quality of life which is bounded by place and time. Every word contributes economically to the meaning. The connotations of falsehood as original sin are felt in the alliterating 'glide,' 'gloss or guile' of 'In Church', with its smooth flowing rhythm: the man of the cemetery's image of the dead children as 'sprats in a tin' implies their unimportance as human individuals to the First Cause. But the essence lies primarily in the vividly-sketched situations: the child's accidental sight of her adored minister's re-enactment in the vestry mirror 'in deft dumb-show' of the pulpit gestures that had so moved the congregation in the first stanza, before she had been initiated into the evil of false-seeming; the mothers' futile quarrelling over their children's graves; the confrontation, 'the coffin between', of 'his wife of old, and his wife of late' in a dramatic image that is reminiscent of the final scene of *John Gabriel Borkman*, when their struggles for the dead man have been valued by the timeless state into which he has disappeared:

> And the dead man whose they both had been
> Seems listening aloof, as to things past date.

All are really deft dumb-shows, manipulated by the narrator to illustrate the absurdity of active, passionate life. They look back to the Dumb Shows of *The Dynasts* and in some respects forward to Camus' image of the telephone booth in *The Myth of Sisyphus*:

'At certain moments of lucidity, the mechanical aspect of their gestures, their meaningless pantomime, make silly everything that surrounds them. A man is talking on the telephone behind a glass partition; you cannot hear him but you see his incomprehensible dumb-show: you wonder why he is alive.'

Hardy's vision needed anonymous voices speaking out of the human predicament, both as sufferers and reflective commentators on its absurdity and tragedy. The dramatic form alone does not suit his particular genius, as a glance at 'Aristodemus the Messenian' and the rather better 'At Wynyard's Gap' will show. His unsureness with dialogue crushed into stylized form, and (in 'Aristodemus') the overbalance of melodrama tell against him when the dramatic situation is not made poetic and reflective (a function supplied by the extended stage directions and the presence of the Overworld in *The Dynasts*). The ironies of 'cynic circumstance' need the perspective of a narrator. The strange behaviour of Mad Judy at weddings and christenings could not be seen in its true light as a criticism of life without the narrator's refrain, 'Judy was insane, we knew.' The delusion of the father scrubbing the Statue of Liberty until 'her shape looms pure as snow' would not be shown for what it is without the comment of the sculptor in the last stanza: 'His child, my model, held so saintly. . . ./In the dens of vice had died.' In 'At the Railway Station, Upway',

114

the 'pitying child', the 'grimful glee' of the convict who sings to the boy's violin

> "This life so free
> Is the thing for me!"

and the constable's tolerant smile, stand in for the Spirits of Pity and Irony who in *The Dynasts* comment on the dissonant forces of human life thus harmonized for a moment. The comment is of more significance than the narrator.

With stress falling so markedly on the ironies of action, it is not surprising that Hardy's personae do not create so strong an impression in their own right as Browning's. They take their life from the dramatic situation. The simple archetypal features of lover, wronged woman, returned soldier, tragic mother, guilt-haunted wrongdoer and victims of circumstance generally which Hardy's characters display, enable them to comment without unfitness in their creator's voice on the action which expresses his quarrel with the cosmic scheme. The chapel-organist, a kind of musical Tess, answers criticism of a 'bosom too full for her age; in her lips too voluptuous a dye' as Tess might have done when speaking in Hardy's voice: ('It may be. But who put it there? Assuredly it was not I.') The girl of 'Her Dilemma', forced into a false declaration of love out of pity for a dying man, reflects:

> But the sad need thereof, his nearing death,
> So mocked humanity that she shamed to prize
> A world conditioned thus, or care for breath
> Where Nature such dilemmas could devise.

If Hardeian reflections on life run the risk of destroying both dramatic illusion and the impersonal tone of ballad narration, one could answer that a modern poet cannot revive the original climate that produced traditional country ballads. Since then,

> Souls have grown seers, and thought outbrings
> The mournful many-sidedness of things.
> ('The Sick Battle-God')

If it is the business of a poet to express 'the emotion of all the ages and the thought of his own' (*Life*) an impersonal blow-for-blow account of a battle will not express the mournful many-sidedness of things so accurately for the war-sated nineteenth and twentieth centuries as the narrator's interpolation of the thoughts of the old folk at the battle of Leipzig:

> 'O,' the old folks said, 'ye Preachers stern!
> O so-called Christian time!
> When will men's swords to ploughshares turn?
> When comes the promised prime?'

Hardy's dual interest as a modern poet in action and emotion gives a resonance beyond bare statement of situation in concentrated dramatic lyrics like 'The Woman in the Rye' and 'The Whitewashed Wall'. They make their effect in simple diction and rhythms hardly different from those of prosaic speech, but their placing of stress, pause, and repetition invests ordinary speech with 'the emotion of all the ages':

> But she knows he's there. And when she yearns
> For him, deep in the labouring night,
> She sees him as close at hand, and turns
> To him under his sheet of white.
> ('The Whitewashed Wall')

> "I told him I wished him dead," said she.

> "Yea, cried it in my haste to one
> Whom I had loved, whom I well loved still;
> And die he did. And I hate the sun,
> And stand here lonely, aching, chill;

> "Stand waiting, waiting under skies
> That blow reproach, the while I see
> The rooks sheer off to where he lies
> Wrapt in a peace withheld from me!"
> ('The Woman in the Rye')

The situation is unfolded in spare, economical statement in answer to a leading question posed by an anonymous listener—usually the only function of Hardy's listeners—about an oddity of human behaviour, which elicits the tale of its cause. The mother's 'raptured rite' of kissing the blank wall of her cottage and the girl's stance in the dripping rye, 'cold-lipped, unconscious, wet to the knee', are explained by the answers received, but a great deal is left to the imagination. No reason is given for the girl's wish, though a passionate quarrel is implied: nor for the son's absence from home, though the date when the poem appeared—November 1918—suggests absence on military service, if not death. The tone of 'The Whitewashed Wall' does not seem correlative with an actual death; but the vivid details of the 'sheet of white' under which the shadow-drawn image lies, the whitener whose activity symbols the inevitable on-going of the world—

> The whitener came to cleanse the nook,
> And covered the face from view. . . .

> ". . . When you have to whiten old cots and brighten,
> What else can you do, I wonder?"

—and the drawing of the 'lifelike semblance' of the boy on the flame-lit cottage wall, evoke a complex response to the power of mothers to worship images in the Plato-cave of shadows when the substance shall be hidden under the final annihilating sheet of white.

In the swift telling of bare essentials in 'The Woman in the Rye' there is the same sense of inexplicable human action, and inexplicable fatal catastrophe, that one finds in 'Lord Randal' or 'The Three Ravens'. Ballad-like, the poem focuses on action and physical detail rather than meaning and motive. The solitary human figure standing against a dark backdrop of cosmic indifference expressed for Hardy, in many poems and novels, the plight of human consciousness and feeling waiting in an insentient universe for a lost harmony that can only be regained by death. The indifference of the elements to human significance conjures up the authentic ballad note, but the impersonality of

> Oer his white banes, when they are bare,
> The wind sall blaw for evermair

is very different from the emotive effect of Hardy's living, feeling woman making of the universe a vast reproach. The subjective emotion of the sufferer is essential here to answer the objective viewpoint of the observer; 'unconscious' is the one thing she is not. Her situation and her response to it crystallize sharply in a haunting visual image the high moral quality of a being who takes onto her own shoulders the guilt of a cosmic bad joke and, like the ballad protagonists of 'Edward', 'Mary Hamilton' and 'Bonnie

Annie', decrees her own punishment. The self-decreed death of the traditional ballad protagonists would have been easier: the death-wish is truer to modern psychology. It is objectified in the woman's hatred of the sun, her deliberate courting of nature's hostility, and her sight of the rooks which, in common with other black death-linked birds of folklore, know a harmony with cosmic purposes denied to alienated man.

Bare factual statement of situation and dialogue which is so effective in these two poems does not succeed without careful choice of evocative image and diction—'deep in the *labouring* night', 'waiting, waiting under skies/That blow reproach'; the woman in the wet rye watching the rooks fly to her dead lover, the haunting figure of the whitener and his annihilating sheet of white—to give cosmic significance to the specific situation. Some poems carry the elements of a good dramatic narrative without unifying their traditional features and modern sensibility. 'In Sherborne Abbey' begins with a fugitive couple flying the vengeance of kin, like so many ballad lovers, surrounded as they rest in a church by the forms of looming effigies, 'recumbent like their own,/Yet differing; for they are chiselled in frigid stone'. This striking visual image, full of dramatic and poetic potentiality to a century haunted by transience, leads in rather forced fashion to a revelation of the lovers' position, in uninspired dialogue:

> ". . . We two are not marble yet."
> "And, worse," said she; "not husband and wife!"

The final twist to the story—

> "Why did you make me ride in your front?" says she.
> "To outwit the law. That was my strategy.
> As I was borne off on the pillion behind you,
> Th' abductor was you, Dearest, let me remind you"

is a bit of irrelevant legal quibbling too trivial to carry the expectations aroused by the initial contrast between human passion and the stone passivity of the dead against which all departure from convention must be measured. Here, Hardy has allowed his love of a strange situation to run away with his artistic sense of unity. As Edmund Blunden remarks, in his book *Thomas Hardy*:

'so greatly did Hardy feel the incidents of life which had anything of the unexpected or peculiar in them, that he believed they would tell very well in some sort of ballad form, without much accompaniment of reflection or choice of phrase.'

'The Children and Sir Nameless', on the other hand, is successful in fusing the evocative possibilities of a stone effigy with the situation and story portrayed. In simple statement that hardly strays from common usage, yet is irradiated by the unifying concept behind the poem, it tells of the proud Sir Nameless' irritation with children, which leads him to seek 'green remembrance' not in offspring, but in a huge alabaster effigy.

> Three hundred years hied; Church-restorers came,
> And, no one of his lineage being traced,
> They thought an effigy so large in frame
> Best fitted for the floor. There it was placed,
> Under the seats for schoolchildren. And they
> Kicked out his name, and hobnailed off his nose;
> And, as they yawn through sermon-time, they say,
> "Who was this old stone man beneath our toes?"

The simply told story, and the vivid physical details, culminating in the attack by other people's posterity upon the effigy that was to be the proud man's 'green remembrance', becomes a striking objective correlative for the ironic operations of Hubris, Time, and Chance. The comment of 'green' on the lifeless whiteness of alabaster and the lively children who carry the seeds of human immortality shows a care for evocative language that characterizes Hardy at his best.

Hardy learned much about dramatic and narrative art from traditional ballad and folksong, which was the most common way of telling or hearing a story in nineteenth-century rural Dorset. One can point to his concern with a strong, often melodramatic, situation; with the staple food of village gossip which at its best expressed from the perspective of a shared and settled peasant culture the timeless truths of human life—the focal points of birth, love, death, and the primitive social code of human conduct centred on these points. In the ballad world the values in face of sudden death that was always round the corner are simple and self-supporting, based on the life-loyalties important to the survival of the rural community: courage, love, friendship, loyalty to friends and kin, swift vengeance on traitors and enemies, pride in human achievement wrested out of a mechanical universe that makes 'The

Old Workman' akin to 'John Henry'. Transgression of natural and social taboos brings guilt and self-punishment that is not resented:

> My punishment I cannot bear,
> But pray God *not* to pity me

cries the tragic mother of Pydel Vale in 'A Sunday Morning Tragedy', in the spirit of Michael Henchard. The action is primal and violent and ruled by an inexplicable fatality indifferent to man. It takes place in a metaphysical and social void which is filled instead with the tangible importance of physical things. The jilted lover of 'Rose-Ann', like Farmer Boldwood, objectifies his feeling in the goods he was putting by for the wedding:

> Down home I was raising a flock of stock ewes,
> Cocks and hens, and wee chickens by scores,
> And lavendered linen all ready to use,
> A-dreaming that they would be yours.

Circumstances and action are given barely: the tale tells itself in dramatic or semi-dramatic form. Dialogue and gesture objectify obliquely much of the action, situation, essential information, motivation, meaning, result, character, feeling, and mood; with much more left to the imagination. We are often introduced to the drama only in the fifth act, or even the epilogue, when a final conjunction of people, time and place illuminates the meaning of a past story inferred, Ibsen-like, through the present crisis.

Hardy's debt to balladry can be seen in tone and certain aspects of structure, adapted for modern consumption. 'Satires of Circumstance in Fifteen Glimpses' show what he could do with a strong situation and a drama that discloses itself only when it has reached the fifth act. In his concentrated lyrics generally he was able to draw on those ballad techniques of implication through economical speech and gesture which told a story as much through what was missed out as through what was put in. The mother-in-law situation which is so common in ballads, and which Hardy made good use of in *The Return of the Native*, is implied succinctly in 'The Nettles' through the mother's first words:

> This, then, is the grave of my son,
> Whose heart she won! And nettles grow
> Upon his mound; and she lives just below.

The 'strange phantasmal sight' of the lady dancing when she has heard of her husband's death ('Seen by the Waits'), seen as a mirror reflection by the waits who provocatively refuse to comment, speaks eloquently of her married life. 'The Dark-eyed Gentleman', like *Tess of the d'Urbervilles*, leaps over the act that produced 'a fine lissom lad' in the third stanza, though it is implied in the refrain lines by the gentleman's concern for the lady's garter and the lady's mixed emotions that she allowed him to tie it. 'A Practical Woman' —a poem in the common four-three ballad metre—likewise leaps over the means which the woman found to produce a healthy son after enumerating the defects of her seven (folklore magic number) sickly legitimate children. It has a ring of 'Sir Patrick Spens' in the abrupt beginning—"O who'll get me a healthy child"—the swift resolve, and the economical statement of action and result:

> She went away. She disappeared,
> Years, years. Then back she came:
> In her hand was a blooming boy
> Mentally and in frame.

In 'John and Jane', the incremental repetition of balladry, with a variation which advances the story in each repetition, implies the disillusionment that has taken place between the four stages of human life crystallized in the four stanzas. John sees the world as a boisterous place, 'Does John', comments the refrain line, implying his single state. 'They' find the world a pleasant place, 'Do John and Jane'. They see their cottage as a palace, containing a pearl, 'Do John and Jane with a baby-child.' They rate the world as a gruesome place, 'Do John and Jane with their worthless son.' The question-and-answer technique reveals the situation of 'The Ruined Maid' as very different from the Victorian conception of ruin, with the questioner pointing the contrast between the hardness of the village girl's lot and the refinements displayed by 'Melia, and the refrain-line answer varying the theme of 'ruined'.

Yet ballad technique alone would not account for the peculiar flavour of Hardy's narratives. His most original successes rely on our conditioned response to ballad and folksong, which contain the emotion of all the ages, counterpointing those touches of modern sensibility which mark the thought of our own. The intensity of lyrical feeling which comes from a modern and idiosyncratic outlook on human destiny is controlled by the impersonality which belongs to ballad technique. A complexity of response is added to

'The Dark-eyed Gentleman', 'A Practical Woman' and 'The Ruined Maid' when one recalls the tragedy, not infrequently the death of the lovers at the hands of husband or kin, that often attended a sexual slip in balladry. The positive attitude of the practical woman and the mother of the fine lissom lad, and the un-guilt-laden prosperity of the ruined maid, question traditional sexual codes. The husband's view, in the poem of that name—

> "And what with our serious need
> Of sons for soldiering,
> That accident, indeed,
> To maids, is a useful thing!"

criticizes not only the intolerance of sexual morality, but the morals of a modern society that needs sons for soldiering. There are several poems, including 'The Burghers', 'A Wife and Another', 'Her Death and After', which gain their effect from the ghost of the old ballad of vengeance walking behind the modern narrative in which the deceived husband or wife or lover acts nobly. The passionate treatment of love in balladry receives a sharp check from the progress of disillusionment briefly set out in 'John and Jane' in a form which more usually records the stages of passionate action.

The pattern of false assumption and elimination through question and answer—the pattern of 'Edward'—lies behind such poems as 'The Statue of Liberty', "Ah, are you Digging on my Grave?" 'Heiress and Architect', 'A Sound in the Night', and 'The Work-box', but Hardy does not use it merely as a mechanical formula. The initial situation which is stripped of the values implied in it in "Ah, are You Digging on my Grave?"—the idea of immortality through the memory of the living—gains added ironic point from fusion with the 'Unquiet Grave' convention of dialogue between the dead and the lover who will not let her sleep. For the dog, her last hope, has only disturbed the grave to bury a bone in it. In 'Heiress and Architect' the rigidity of this ballad form gives physi-cal check, like the 'arch-designer', to the soaring line of the heiress' romantic notions of a dwelling place, which are ruthlessly whittled down to the bare denying reality of the heavily-stressed

> ". . . Give space (since life ends unawares)
> To hale a coffined corpse adown the stairs;
> For you will die."

The question-and-denial form which inevitably advances the story of 'A Sound in the Night' towards solution of a mystery at the same time as it eliminates all possible answers except murder is a mani-festation (as in 'Edward') of the woman's dominant will, which dur-ing the course of the poem drives the farmer to kill his former mistress as it had driven him to marry her supplanter. In 'The Workbox' the discipline of this particular ballad form uncovers the deceit in the relationship of the married pair, through the wife's evasions of the true reason why she shrinks from her husband's gift of a workbox which had been made out of the coffin wood supplied for a lad from her home town. The eloquent gesture of the final stanza—

> Yet still her lips were limp and wan,
>   Her face still held aside,
> As if she had known not only John,
>   But known of what he died.

—implies the answer she does not give. 'In the Servants' Quarters' —Hardy's version of St. Peter's betrayal of Christ—gives a double twist to the form. It begins with the truth everyone knows— imaginatively presented, through recognition of Peter's dialect as akin to the 'criminal's'—and moves through Peter's denying answers to the counterdenial of the cock.

The importance of physical things in balladry is adapted vari-ously to Hardy's vision of the importance of the physical world. The traditional roll-call of familiar names and places, which implies a certain security in an unpredictable world, is extended to include dance tunes in 'The Dance at the Phoenix' and inns in 'A Trampwoman's Tragedy'. The role of the physical in determin-ing human fate is suggested by the part played by physical objects as agents of action, or as the measure of value and reality. The workbox which becomes a powerful image of the wife's relation-ship to the dead man and her unsuspecting husband—a relation-ship which is itself inextricably bound up with the proximity of life and love to death—

> "The shingled pattern that seems to cease
>   Against your box's rim
> Continues right on in the piece
>   That's underground with him"

—has dramatic importance as the cause of the wife's agony. In **'The Satin Shoes'**, the delicate shoes which unhinged the bride's mind when rain prevented her wearing them for her wedding, enact a sinister marriage with her when they persuade her to enter the un-fairytale coach which takes her to the madhouse. The gay trinkets in which ballad heroines usually deck themselves motivate the lover to rob a church in 'The Sacrilege', and ruthlessly show Jenny's age as she 'rose, arrayed, and decked her head/Where the bleached hairs grew thin' to go to the dance at the Phoenix. The 'raiment rare' which the wife in 'The Burghers' had heaped up to pay for her elopement, and the luxuries rejected by the wife who meets her lover 'On Martock Moor'—

> I'd feather-beds and couches,
>   And carpets for the floor,
> Yet brighter to me was, at eves,
>   The bareness of the moor

—value the superior wealth of love. In 'The Homecoming', which bears some resemblance to 'My Boy Billy', the vivid particulars of

> . . . great black beams for ceiling, and a floor o' wretched stone,
> And nasty pewter platters, horrid forks of steel and bone

and 'a skimmer-cake for supper, peckled onions, and some pears' provide a humorous objective correlative for the child-wife's disillusion and her elderly husband's crude but kindly comfort.

Hardy's use of refrains, too, shows a fusion of traditional and modern features which is both original and idiosyncratic. They range in kind from the repeated half-line of 'A Trampwoman's Tragedy' and 'A Sunday Morning Tragedy' to the detailed mood-and-landscape painting of 'The Homecoming' and 'The Sacrilege'. The balance between expectation and surprise is skilfully managed. Hardly ever does Hardy use a rigidly unvarying refrain. The keening 'alas for me' that ends the second line of most stanzas—not all—of 'A Sunday Morning Tragedy' adds a sense of obsessive grief and guilt to the effect of stifling enclosure caused by the thirty-two end rhymes in 'e'. And the guilt fixation caused by the recurrence of Monmouth's name in the last line of each stanza of 'At Shag's Heath' gives a literal truth to the end of the poem, which anticipates his betrayer's suicide:

> When comes the waterman, he'll say,
> "Who's done her thuswise?"—'Twill be, yea,
>   Sweet, slain King Monmouth—he!

One has only to compare this poem with Browning's 'The Confessional', on a similar theme, to see the difference made to mood by the obsessive refrain. The half-line repetition of 'A Tramp-woman's Tragedy' embodies the weariness of the travellers in the blazing sun, which played its part in encouraging the 'wanton idleness' that sets off the tragedy. Variations and word-stresses are important. One notes the added ironic affirmative, the emphasis on number that was soon to be decreased by a murder, a hanging, and a natural death, and a repetition of the emotive 'alone':

> For months we had padded side by side,
>   Ay, side by side . . .

> Inside the settle all a-row—
>   All four a-row . . .

> Thereaft I walked the world alone,
>   Alone, alone!

The alternative refrains of 'A Military Appointment'—'That soldier/lover of yours/mine'—advances the story to the inevitable point where the alternatives fuse for a moment, then neatly change partners in the sexual dance:

> "—Nell, him I have chanced so much to see,
> That—he has grown the lover of me!—
>   That lover of yours—
> And it's here our meeting is planned to be."

'The Sacrilege' and 'The Homecoming' make use of local landscape in the refrain in a way that recalls *The Return of the Native* though obviously in a much smaller compass. The wind that blows through 'The Homecoming' as a refrain is an active agent in the child-wife's adjustment to the reality of marriage. The basic refrain—

> *Gruffly growled the wind on Toller downland broad and bare,*
> *And lonesome was the house, and dark; and few came there*

embodies both the reality she must now face, very different from the farmer's 'pretty song of lovely flowers and bees,/And happy lovers taking walks within a grove o' trees', and her mood of desolation. Its variations are integrated into the story. The wind makes practical trial of the bride's discovery of 'a monstrous crock in chimney.' The sorely tried husband's threat to consign his wife to the mercy of the elements, "And leave 'ee to go barefoot to your d—d daddee!" is preceded by a hint of the wind's rough treatment of objects in its path:

> *Straight from Whit'sheet Hill to Benvill Lane the blusters pass,*
> *Hitting hedges, milestones, handposts, trees, and tufts of grass*

and followed by its diminuendo '*away down Crimmercrock's long lane*' as the wife capitulates. The last appearance of the refrain returns to its basic form: man has passed the trial of the elements, and they have no further power over him. In 'The Sacrilege', though the landscape of Exon and Dunkery Tor appears only in the second line of each stanza, it has something of the complex effect of Egdon Heath in evoking both the indifference of nature to human passions, and the close link between natural and human moods. The link gives birth to the style, for the landscape is integrated into the structure of the human sentence:

> "I said: 'I am one who has gathered gear
> From Marlbury Downs to Dunkery Tor . . .'"
>
> And all could see she clave to him
> As cleaves a cloud to Dunkery Tor . . .

Some narrative poems give the impression of being either too long or too short—a sign that Hardy was experiencing difficulties in adapting a traditional narrative form to modern sensibilities. They dissipate the concentrated drama that can be packed into a single moment of crisis, and miss the lyrical mood which needs room to expand, reflect, and connect the emotions and incidents to the natural world in which they happen. 'The Moth-Signal', for example, suffers from the lack of a lyrical mood which in 'The Sacrilege' was developed through landscape-refrain. The poetic conception of 'The Moth-Signal' needed for its fulfilment more than the situation itself, expressed in snatches of conversation and a statement of the lovers' meeting. Comparison with a similar incident in *The Return of the Native* shows how much it gains in the novel from the slow build-up of fire as a creative-destructive symbol to which Eustacia and Wildeve, like the moth Wildeve has released to Eustacia, are irresistibly attracted. And the grinning Ancient Briton of the poem who pops up from the tumulus in the last stanza to comment on the sameness of human destiny through time is no substitute for the presence of Egdon Heath that broods over the novel from beginning to end. When Hardy does manage to integrate the lyrical mood that comes out of his vision of nature with the ballad-swing of a good story, he produces a new and modern kind of ballad, such as 'A Sound in the Night' and 'Her Death and After'. The sounds of disturbed nature in 'A Sound in the Night', repeated though not formalized into a refrain, evoke not only mood and the farmer's guilty knowledge that the strange sound is human—

> "It may be a tree, bride, that rubs his arms acrosswise,
> If it is not the eaves-drip upon the lower slopes,
> Or the river at the bend, where it whirls about the hatches
>   Like a creature that sighs and mopes"

—but also the situation gradually revealed by their absence:

> "Nay, husband, you perplex me; for if the noise I heard here,
> Awaking me from sleep so, were but as you avow,
> The rain-fall, and the wind, and the tree-bough, and the river,
> Why is it silent now?"

'My Cicely' has received attention from many critics as a failure; it has been cited as an example of 'the most incredible and unnatural mish-mash of language.' The diction seems to reflect a fundamental disunity in imaginative concept. The poem falls uneasily between the two stools of ballad narrative and dramatic lyric, without fusion. Concentration on stark statement of the moment of revelation might have produced a poem like 'The Newcomer's Wife', in which an overheard conversation reveals to the newcomer that he has married 'the Hack of the Parade'. The splash in the fifth and final stanza, and the grim statement

> They searched, and at the deepest place
> Found him with crabs upon his face

say all that is necessary about his response to the news. But a similar technique in 'My Cicely' would have ignored the ironic relevance of the lover's spiritual and physical journey through ancient Wessex landmarks—the poem's lyrical element—to his wish to reverse Time. Its slow development as an image overbalances the dramatic moment of swift double revelation from a stranger that *his* Cicely is not the dead woman of the same name, and that he had failed to recognize his Cicely in the coarse barmaid at the Three Lions.

Comparison with another poem which has for its theme the same wish to reverse Time, 'The Revisitation', suggests why the latter is more successful in its fusion of traditional narrative and dramatic ballad tone with modern lyric personal intensity. In this long poem all the details of landscape—barrows, 'dateless' Sarsen stone, flint-tipt arrows trampled by living cattle, the wailing of peewits that

> Seemed the voicings of the self-same throats I had heard
> when life was green,
> Though since that day uncounted frail forgotten generations
> Of their kind had flecked the scene

—build up a vivid objective correlative to the emotion of a man 'living long and longer/In a past that lived no more.' The elusive and illusive flitting quality of life, which he forgets, is caught in the flashing of the 'spry white scuts of conies', the past peewits who had 'flecked' the scene and their present descendants who revealed 'their pale pinions like a fitful phosphorescence/Up against the cope of cloud', and 'the open drouthy downland thinly grassed' where 'an arid wind went past.' When the narrative of the lover's sentimental journey and his state of mind have been built up in this fashion, 'a figure broke the skyline—first in vague contour, then stronger', and as we move into his illusion that time has slipped back we move, rightly, into drama, the direct medium of illusion, with the immediacy of speech and gesture. The immediacy of drama has power to balance the poetic significance of landscape, as the stranger's report of Cicely's fortunes had not. Though there are some Hardeian clumsinesses in the dialogue—surely no-one ever started a sentence with the colloquial "Dear, I could not sleep for thinking" to end it with "of our trystings when twin-hearted"? —the hesitations and inflexions are true to the rhythms of emotion. Lyric narrative takes over again at the end of the scene, when the 'red upedging sun' that glorifies natural features, 'flinging tall thin tapering shadows from the meanest mound and molehill' cruelly lights up the daylight reality of 'Time's transforming chisel' on the lady's human features. An exit which is the dramatic reversal of her entrance—

And I saw her form descend the slopes, and smaller grow and smaller,
    Till I caught its course no more. . . .

leads to the narrator's quiet impersonal reflection, authentic
because it springs from the direct personal experience just dramatized, that 'Love is lame at fifty years.'

The strange conjunctions which appealed to Hardy's narrative
and dramatic sense are operatic in nature, and like opera libretti,
incomplete without a lyrical element to preserve the drama from
degenerating into either melodrama or prosaic short stories in
rhyme. Browning's objective viewpoint supplies the place of music
in his dramatic monologues. One could imagine what Browning
might have done in his own convention with the calm tale, in 'Her
Second Husband Hears her Story', of the lady who sewed up her
drunken first husband in a sheet, and the second husband's equally
phlegmatic response, "Well, it sounds strange—told here and now
to me". A more lyrical approach to such melodramatic material
would not, in Hardy's hands, produce the psychological subtleties
of 'The Confessional' or 'The Laboratory' or 'My Last Duchess',
but it did produce, when he allowed himself to expand beyond the
bare telling, 'A Trampwoman's Tragedy', 'The Revisitation', and
'Her Death and After'. The subjective exploration of emotion, or
complexity of mood, provided by the music of an operatic aria
finds its Hardeian equivalent so often in lyric touches, dramatic in
function as well as lyrical, which express his vision of man in relation to nature. In 'The Burghers', 'the Froom's mild hiss' which
can be heard 'from Pummery-Tout to where the Gibbet is' suggests the complexity of the husband's emotions which can hold
both charity and thoughts of murder: these are the sounds his
state of mind selects to listen to. In 'Her Death and After', the
change of mood after the dying woman's confession of love is shown
clearly by the change from a death-marked landscape presented in
slow-moving monosyllables—'And the trees shed on me their rime
and hoar'—to a new dynamic conception of life and landscape that
affects diction and rhythm:

      —When I had left, and the swinging trees
        Rang above me, as lauding her candid say,
        Another was I.

His decision to 'insert a deed back in Time' by claiming the unwanted child of his rival and the woman he loved subtly alters our
response to the Roman Amphitheatre, the 'Ring' of *The Mayor of*

Casterbridge, where it takes place. Henchard continues to feel the power of man's primitive past of which the Ring is a grim reminder: the lover of the poem neutralizes it through his disinterested kindness.

Lyric emotion inheres by nature in bare but well-chosen statement of a dramatic event; but when Hardy leaves the concentrated lyric of crisis for more leisurely narration of Wessex events his achievement is variable. Without the distancing effect that ballad form and cadence places on a strange story, and the evocative phrase that makes traditional form speak to the modern age, village gossip tends to remain the untransmuted trivia that it often is. The rural relish for scandal and a strange story can be seen too faithfully recorded in 'The Dame of Athelhall', 'The Flirt's Tragedy', 'In the Days of Crinoline', 'The Two Wives', 'The Whipper-in', 'One who Married above Him', 'Her Second Husband Hears her Story', 'The Moth-Signal', 'On the Death-bed', 'In Sherborne Abbey'. 'A Poor Man and a Lady', 'The Mock Wife', 'The Elopement', 'The Contretemps', 'The Duel', 'A Woman's Fancy', 'The Turnip-Hoer', 'The Noble Lady's Tale', and others, whose truth in local tradition was too often for Hardy the only excuse for writing them.

However, when the village gossip concerns either the supernatural or the great events of military history, he can make a firm success of local tradition in straight narrative of events. His skill can be judged first of all from the group of Napoleonic war poems which are perhaps relics of his first conception of *The Dynasts* as a ballad sequence. They are distanced by memory, and helped by the existing tradition of ballad-making on some memorable battle. Ironically, this war-hater succeeds in conveying the excitement of a military action, the ebb and flow of personal fortunes, the physical sight and sound and smell of carnage, often in traditional ballad metres, with traditional ballad features—the varying refrain line, the honourable roll-call of fighters and place-names, the narrator recounting events he knew by experience or hearsay. Heroic action there is in plenty, but the uncomplex glory of war in traditional balladry is qualified by the lyrical touches that relieve the stark telling of the action with personal emotion. Even the emotive adjective or simile—'And harmless townsfolk fell to die', 'when the Allies/Burst on her home like flame'—would be out of place in 'The Battle of Otterburn' or 'Andrew Barton'. The fine description of the blowing of Bridge Lindenau in 'Leipzig'—

130

When there surged on the sky an earthen wave,
    And stones, and men, as though
Some rebel churchyard crew updrave
    Their sepulchres from below

places the carnage of war as a cosmic death-wish of some nether tidal force which destroys men as indifferently as stones. The touches of natural description in these war ballads not only brings to mind the use of nature in traditional balladry, which sets human passions against the indifferent on-going of the world—

He's killed this may, and he's laid her by,
    Eh vow bonnie
For to bear the red rose company
    On the bonnie bank o' Fordie
            ('Babylon')

"We've fetched en back to quick from dead,
But never more on earth while rose is red
    Will drum rouse Corpel!" Doctor said
        O' me at Valencieën.
            ('Valenciennes')

but also sets against the destructive interruptions of war the eternal values of human relationships linked closely to the cycle of life. The precise evocation of time and place that begins 'The Alarm' presents the most tempting of the soldier's alternative choices—to return to his pregnant wife, or to march on and meet the invader. One can forgive Hardeian unevennesses in this poem, such as the unlikely peasant dialogue—"And if our July hope should ante-date", "Why courting misadventure shoreward roam?" for the genuine fusion of traditional ballad qualities (in an untraditional stanza form) with personal lyricism. No-one but Hardy could have saved the ballad 'prop' of the guiding bird-omen from the suspicion of synthetic tone by the acutely and compassionately observed incident of its release by the soldier from the river vegetation:

While he stood thinking,
A little bird, perched drinking
Among the crowfoot tufts the river bore,
Was tangled in their stringy arms and fluttered, almost sinking
Near him, upon the moor.

The reality of the bird, its stringy trap and the compassionate act of the soldier that releases its power as an agent of fate together with its trapped body, and the events that follow from its release, become a reverberating image of the longing of the human heart which guides it back through a roundabout route of military duty to the homestead in the ferny byway of Wessex. The lyric emotion that inheres for Hardy in the natural cycle is skilfully and movingly integrated with the military event in 'Valenciennes':

> I never hear the zummer hums
> O' bees; and don' know when the cuckoo comes;
> But night and day I hear the bombs
> We threw at Valencieën. . . .

The traditional 'props' of spring and summer—the sounds of nature which should be a human birthright—revalue the unnatural sounds of military 'humming' in the first stanza, when stanza IX reveals that the narrator is a soldier for whom time stopped revolving when he was deafened by the shells of Valenciennes. His personal reflections, unemotional as they are (for his deafness shuts him off from passion) add the many-sidedness of modern thought to the extravert war ballad.

> 'Twas said that we'd no business there
> A-topperèn the French for disagreeën;
> However, that's not my affair—
> We were at Valencieën.

'We were at Valencieën'. The common soldier's part is to experience and suffer, to take part in the eternal human predicament of acting without understanding. His dialect and touches of fumbling inarticulacy contribute to the sense of eternal human values—courage, fairness, resignation, pride—which war cannot extinguish.

It is perhaps to be expected that Hardy, with his profound and tragic response to death, should show some of his most successful fusions of ballad mode and modern sensibility in those narratives which rely on a sense of the supernatural. Narratives which are not otherwise remarkable suddenly spring to life for a moment when the supernatural touches human life with a mysterious finger. The poetic conception contained in stanza VI of 'The Bird-catcher's Boy'—a poem constantly threatened by inept diction and sentimentality—

> Through the long passage, where
> Hang the caged choirs:
> Harp-like his fingers there
> Sweep on the wires

—lifts the poem momentarily onto another plane when its repetition-with-a-difference coincides with the boy's death at sea. The child's supernatural knowledge that 'My false father/Has murdered my true' turns the strangely-worded melodrama of 'The Flirt's Tragedy' into opera for a moment, and the archetypal demon lover of 'Burning the Holly' adds a shiver to a tale of seduction. The Unquiet Grave theme, when the dead begin to speak, lurks behind several poems—'Her Immortality', 'The Harvest Supper', "Ah, are you Digging on my Grave?", and 'The Dead and the Living One', for example. But Hardy appeals to his own century in the tension that exists between the familiar framework and the subject of the dead person's reproaches to the living. When primitive familiarity with the Otherworld has given way to belief in everlasting death,

> 'Oh who sits weeping on my grave
> And will not let me sleep?'

is replaced by the ghosts pleading, not for repose, but remembrance:

> 'A Shade but in its mindful ones
> Has immortality.'

Hardy told William Archer that he would give ten years of his life to see an authenticated ghost. His failure to do so is reflected in the insubstantiality of his revenants. Though Hardy's peasants show as little surprise as their primitive forebears at encountering a ghost, his revenants do not normally bring all the attributes of the physical corpse from the grave as ballad ghosts do. "My old love rises from the worms" in 'The Harvest Supper' has some echo of the realistic physical details of grave-life found in 'The Unquiet Grave', 'The Wife of Usher's Well', and 'Sweet William's Ghost': the tardy lover of 'The Second Night' does not recognize that the girls he meets is a ghost, though a sense of strangeness inheres in her mysterious relationship to the 'mad star' that 'crossed the sky to the sea':

> The sparks of the star in her pupils gleamed,
> She was vague as a vapour now . . .

But these are exceptions to Hardy's general rule. His revenants are more often incorporeal, dreams, or hallucinations. The 'Cruel Mother' of folk tradition does not recognize the 'twa pretty babes playing at the ba'' as ghosts of her murdered children: the girl who procures an abortion in Hardy's 'Reluctant Confession' sees 'in hell-dark dreams' . . . 'a newborn child in the clothes I set to make'. Guilt takes a subjective form in 'A Sound in the Night', 'The Catching Ballet of the Wedding Clothes', and 'The Sacrilege'. Modern dream psychology backs up the folk-motif of a physical feature inherited not from the natural parents but from a projection of desire, which Hardy used both in 'San Sebastian' and the short story 'An Imaginative Woman', and Ibsen in 'The Lady from the Sea'. The supernatural manifestations are left unexplained, but the state of mind of the narrators places them as hallucinations correlative to guilt or suspicion, as in 'At Shag's Heath' and 'A Tramp-woman's Tragedy'. The motifs are traditional; the temper which ascribes them to natural rather than supernatural causes is modern.

The neutral or plural narrator is another favourite Hardeian device for disclaiming responsibility for the truth of a ghost story. The Mellstock quire, and personages from it, take responsibility for 'The Paphian Ball' and 'The Choirmaster's Burial', distanced from the reader by time and memory:

> Such the tenor man told
> When he had grown old.

In 'The Lost Pyx', 'some say the spot is banned', but 'the ancient Vale-folk tell' a different story. Hardy does not vouch for either.

But though the manifestation of ghosts may be insubstantial and doubtful, their environment is not. Hardy's strong sense of the physical and local life of Wessex gives validity to expressions of the metaphysical. The 'viewless quire' of Mellstock follows a well-trodden path,

> Dogged by the living; till it reached
> The bottom of Church Lane.

The traditional storm of romantic balladry sweeps over Wessex landmarks in 'The Lost Pyx', and the miracle of the found Pyx is vividly incarnated in the local nature of its animal guardians,

> Of Blackmore's hairy throng,
> Whereof were oxen, sheep, and does,
> And hares from the brakes among . . .

God's heavy humour and the Last Judgment vision of the dead sitting upright in their coffins in 'Channel Firing' are earthed by the particular detail:

> The mouse let fall the altar-crumb,
> The worms drew back into the mounds.

The melodrama and bathos that threatens the ghostly apparition of Monmouth in 'At Shag's Heath' is boldly turned aside by the sudden descent to a homely dialect word:

> "I love you still, would kiss you now,
> But blood would stain your nighty-rail!"

The memories of the 'local hearts and heads' who speak from the grave in 'Friends Beyond' are intimate and local. Mutability and the values of a particular Wessex community speak through William Dewey's old bass viol, Farmer Ledlow's favourite heifer, and the concern implied by farmer, squire, squire's lady, and peasants for the proper upkeep of land and property. The supernatural event, fused with the sharply accurate local detail, expresses that sense of local continuity and community in which narrative and dramatic art have their roots.

The supernatural mode of balladry, when it controls the telling of the tale as tautly as it does in 'The Dead and the Living One', catches perfectly the essence of the human life, pausing beside a grave, trapped in a network of ironic convergences that impinge on it from the Overworld and the Underworld:

> The dead woman lay in her first night's grave,
> And twilight fell from the clouds' concave,
> And those she had asked to forgive forgave.

The cosmic irony that mocks the living woman's gratitude for her rival's death in the form of 'a martial phantom of gory dye' which provides the surprise twist in the Unquiet Grave theme, weights the supernatural ballad mode with the emotion of nineteen disillusive centuries. The result of the fusion is an intense impersonality that could only be achieved through a deep personal response to the human predicament.

> There was a cry by the white-flowered mound,
> There was a laugh from underground,
> There was a deeper gloom around.

The cry is the cry of all humanity caught in the situations of violence (the poem was written in 1915) that have inspired narrative and dramatic art from *The Iliad* to *The Royal Hunt of the Sun*. The laugh is with the dead, for the ironies that attend the passions of the living cannot touch them. The gloom that is deeper than the cloud's concave expresses the compassion of the poet who sees in the drama of events the enduring values and sorrows of Everyman, working out his destiny in the shadow of the darkness which forms the backdrop to authentic balladry ancient and modern.

Poetry and Narrative: Minor Fiction

It is commonly accepted that Hardy wrote a number of great novels and some others with flashes of greatness. The number placed in each category varies with the reader. However, *Far from the Madding Crowd, The Return of the Native, The Mayor of Casterbridge, The Woodlanders, Tess of the d'Urbervilles*, and *Jude the Obscure* are frequently assessed as pillars of his achievement, with *Under the Greenwood Tree* and *The Trumpet Major* as notable minor supports. It is not easy to define precisely what is missing from the rest of his fiction. However, one may usefully adapt T. S. Eliot's distinction between poetic and prose drama to suggest that the lacking quality is a consistent poetic 'underpattern' which produces 'a kind of doubleness in the action, as if it took place on two planes at once.'

The poetic impulse is never absent from Hardy's fiction. But in the minor works it appears in isolated flashes and pulls against the narrative and dramatic impulses instead of creating a fruitful tension with them 'to intensify the expression of things . . . so that the heart and inner meaning is made vividly visible' (*Life*). The great novels are memorable not only for plot but for the poetic-dramatic scenes that carry the inner meaning of the plot. In *The Return of the Native*, the gambling scene by glow-worm light on Egdon Heath, besides being crucial to plot development, is also a unit in the organic conflict of light and darkness, chance and control.

Reading one of the successful novels inspires poetic emotion. It has become a cliché of criticism to say that Hardy's novels are 'poetic'. The word needs closer definition to establish the factors which give Hardy's novels this quality, and to distinguish the poetry of a Hardy novel from the poetry of *Wuthering Heights* or *The Waves*. As David Cecil points out in *Hardy the Novelist*, 'the English literary genius is, most characteristically, a poetic genius', which shows itself in other forms besides poetry. Cecil has made a study of the poetic aspects of Hardy's imagination. He defines the poetic imagination as 'of a type that more often chooses verse as its mode of expression'. Hardy was inspired by those aspects of experience which required the emotional and imaginative intensity of lyric, ballad and poetic drama. His vision of life was not primarily of man's relation to man, but of man's relation to the forces of ultimate reality. His characters live most fully not in the social encounters of Jane Austen's Bath or George Eliot's Middlemarch, but in the great emotional crises that express their heroic resistance to fate, the conflict of reason and instinct, or their harmonies and disharmonies with the natural world.

Hardy's revelations of meaning through surface action are made through the weapons of a poet. It has often been noticed how close to balladry is Hardy's vision of basic passions and strong highlights. Donald Davidson ('The Traditional Basis of Hardy's Fiction', *Southern Review*, 1940) measures his success in terms of his debt to balladry and folklore; his failures are 'attempts to be a fully modern and literary novelist'. This view does not account for the power of Hardy's most 'modern' novel, *Jude the Obscure*, where the ballad echoes are fainter than the modern climate of opinion. But in general it is true to say that plot, situation, character and setting of the major fiction have a unity of tone that owes much to ballad ancestry, while the better moments of the minor fiction elicit an emotional response that has been conditioned by folklore archetypes: the demonic element in Miss Aldclyffe, Aeneas Manston, and William Dare; the sinister prophetic dream of Cytherea Graye and Ethelberta's Kafkaesque view of Neigh's estate; the tower that reaches from the world of nature to the stellar universe; the Cliff without a Name that faces Knight with his littleness; and the series of ironic conjunctions and parallel motifs in *A Pair of Blue Eyes*, for example, that call up the incremental repetition of ballad stanzas.

Fundamental ballad types abound: patient Griseldas of both sexes, inconstant lovers, often with a streak of the supernatural demon lover; the dashing soldier and the sailor returned from the sea to claim his kin; forlorn milkmaids; girls driven by a wild impulse to reject the true and love the false; lords and ladies of high degree; and the lowly man who, like Gabriel Oak, rises by hard work and, like Henchard, falls again. The furmity hag, the mysterious reddleman who emanates from the heath, old John South, whose life is linked to a tree—these are folklore symbols of a reality beyond man. Perhaps Little Father Time owes as much to them as to Ibsen's anti-naturalistic dramatic symbols, which are equally rooted in folklore. The plots are as tightly-knit, in the major fiction, as 'Edward' or 'Chevy Chase', They develop, stanza-like, through encounters with human and fatal forces. Event dominates motive. Situations and characters balanced usually for tragic resolution, repeat the staple material of balladry. The triangle of man or woman poised between constant and inconstant lover is a frequent motif, varied as in *Far from the Madding Crowd* by another lover from the dramatis personae of balladry, the rich squire, or linked, as in *The Mayor of Casterbridge*, with another theme, of rise and fall.

The situations that produce tragedy are ballad situations: family tensions, the clash of irreconcilable passions, the inconvenient return and the long-kept secret, social barriers, unpredictable accidents. The dramatic highlights objectify the clash of fatal forces which dominate the ballad world. Eustacia's romantic meeting in boy's disguise with Clym, Mrs Yeobright's death by snakebite on the indifferent heath, the simultaneous drowning of two fleeing lovers in stormy darkness to weird incantations over a wax image, the fight between Henchard and Farfrae in the loft, the macabre scene by Fanny's coffin, Grace Melbury's capture in a mantrap, like Mollie Vaughan in the ballad of that name, the wife-sale that begins *The Mayor of Casterbridge*, the sleep-walking and final scenes of *Tess*—these and countless other episodes carry the resonances of myth and folklore. Ritual, omens, the workings of chance and coincidence which replace ballad expressions of supernatural agency, the grotesque distortions of reality which objectify the workings of the cosmic will; the moral comment which acts like ballad tags; the irony revealed by stylized pattern; the choral interludes, the importance of physical things, and the involvement of human action with the natural world, place Hardy's major fiction securely in the ballad world made inherently poetic by its stark delineation of man's tragic predicament.

However, the fact remains that Hardy's novels are novels and his ballads ballads. 'The Revisitation' and 'A Sunday Morning Tragedy' are genuine ballad poetry, stripped to the essence of character, situation, and scene. In Hardy's novels, ballad techniques and overtones combine with a full-length picture of human lives in developing relationships to men, environment, and fate to present a vision that speaks to the complex modern spirit. In this combination, Hardy resembles Emily Brontë. Both need the distorted reality of the sensational ballad incident—heroic, romantic, wild, irregular, grotesque, mysterious, sublime—pitched in a high emotional key, to point through superficial naturalism to the deeper reality of their vision. Both need more space than a ballad can give to show the effect of time and to accumulate the mass of observed fact, rooted in common experience, that suspends disbelief in their unprosaic metaphors of reality. That Hardy's canvas is fuller than Emily Brontë's is due to the difference in their vision. Because Emily Brontë's vision of the ultimate resolution of elemental disharmonies is mystical, she can keep closer to the balladist's familiarity with the supernatural. In Darwin's scientific universe, Hardy had to deny himself the aid of the supernatural in persuading his readers to accept strange events. Hence the meticulous evocation of Wessex in all its aspects, for which *Wuthering Heights* offers no comparison.

Nature, the visible world as pointer to the invisible, has long been a poetic symbol to English lyric writers. We know Hardy's Wessex in all its moods and seasons, in the intimate detail of heath, pasture, arable, woodland, and water; its vegetable, animal and human outgrowths; its occupations; and its past of earthworks, barrows, extinct species, flints, and geological strata—its record of the eternal processes of time. As Cecil points out, Hardy's vision of nature combines breadth and intimacy. The ever-widening perspective from the familiar natural detail of grass-bent or heath-bell to the unfamiliar stellar reaches makes of the local scene a poet's metaphor of the unknowable, without departing from the objective fact.

It is appropriate to Hardy's post-Darwinian vision that nature dominates the scene, as in *Wuthering Heights* it does not, though the changing face of the Yorkshire moor, like Hardy's Wessex, reflects the conflict of elemental forces which move the passions of men. Often a Hardy novel begins with a powerful evocation of the natural scene before a tiny human being appears to give it meaning. Emily Brontë's Yorkshire moor appears piecemeal throughout the novel, as actual scene and as psychic image. Lockwood, after the strange events at Wuthering Heights that blur the limits of normal human experience, sees 'dark night coming down prematurely, and sky and hills mingled in one bitter whirl of wind and suffocating snow.' In Chapter XI of *Far from the Madding Crowd*, the sheer physical weight of Hardy's description of the snowy scene makes Fanny Robin an image of human unimportance to the cosmos. The evocation includes not only the present objective scene, but also the subjective mood called up by the rhythmic melancholy associations of past seasonal changes:

'the retreat of the snakes, the transformation of the ferns, the filling of the pools, a rising of fogs, the embrowning by frost, the collapse of the fungi, and an obliteration by snow.'

Exact physical details are massed and placed in relation to time and space to conjure up the mood of Fanny's isolation. We are given both the fact, and its significance to the imagination. It is a poet's way of working, familiar to readers of Hardy's verse. And always in his vision, the metaphysical perspective never loses sight of the physical fact in which it is rooted. The apocalyptic birds which universalize Tess's situation in a chaotic universe are also starving creatures who watch the girls disturbing the earth for signs of food. The rabbit in the trap whose long and useless sufferings adumbrate Jude's own becomes a correlative for the human condition through the grim physical sound of the trap dragged about in its writhings.

Any meaning in Hardy's vision must rise from his truth to the physical world. But its beauty and terror blend with the romantic poet's subjective presentation of nature as a symbol of the inner life, transforming and transformed by the angle of vision. Clym's despair at obstructive cross-purposes both rises from and is embodied by the uncompromising flatness of Egdon heath. Boldwood's unbalanced state of mind is not analysed in terms of complexes and obsessions, but sensuously felt in his view of the brittle frozen grass and birds' footprints, and the unnatural reversed light of the snow.

This is the poet's way. As Cecil points out, Hardy's greatest poetic asset is the power to make us see—and, coming not very far behind, to make us hear and feel the different qualities of sound and texture in the physical world. To cut out the appeal to the senses in Hardy's novels would rob the libretto of the music that makes it meaningful. His stories are a series of scenes, not photographic, but lyric, dramatic, sometimes distorted in Kafkaesque fashion to show the deeper reality underlying the scenic. The unstable effect of firelight, picking out 'shadowy eye-sockets, deep as those of a death's head', stresses the burden of mortality carried by the dancers round the bonfire in *The Return of the Native*. Words, gestures, movement, setting, are lit up with the tragic sense— which is the poet's sense—of the pain and glory of life.

However, Hardy is not blind to that other kind of poetry that lies in the trivial round, as his poems show. Truth to fact saves his presentation of the countryman's working relationship to nature— another poetic device as old as Virgil—from being sentimental. Marty is blue with cold as she plants pines, and Tess finds reed-drawing and threshing a severe trial of strength. The rustic chorus has a realistic share of untrustworthy members; but their collective function is poetic through their concern with daily bread and the rituals that mark human and natural seasons. Commonplace life is heightened by their eternal actions and their ruminating Wessex speech, with its delight in word-play that suddenly charges the basic rhythms of living with a new perspective. There is a Shakespearian poetry of incongruity in their juxtaposition of comic and tragic—their discussion on folklore remedies for snake-bite while Mrs Yeobright lies dying; their 'tendency to talk on principles which is characteristic of the barley-corn' in the *Buck's Head* while Fanny's coffin with its explosive secret lies outside.

Hardy's poetic power lies in the detail of style that expresses subject. The evocative word, phrase, or figure of speech; the emotive verb that gives anthropomorphic force to nature; the comparisons from nature and art which illuminate both terms of the comparison; the grotesque or unusual angle or light that exposes a fundamental relationship to reality; the hint of myth below the surface—'He looked and smelt like Autumn's very brother'; the simple statement that holds the weight of *lacrimae rerum* or the ecstasy of love—'Winterborne was gone, and the copses seemed to show the want of him', 'There was hardly a touch of earth in her love for Clare'; the rhythms of speech and narrative cadence which precisely express the emotion or movement of a scene: all these weapons amalgamate the disparate experiences of life into a new whole compounded of complexity and simplicity.

The poetic detail is rarely superfluous. In Chapter xxii of *Far from the Madding Crowd*, the sharply realized shape and colour of the 'fern-sprouts like bishops' croziers' and the 'odd cuckoo-pint,— like an apoplectic saint in a niche of malachite' equate the forces of nature with the deity in the preceding sentence, 'God was palpably present in the country, and the devil had gone with the world to town,' and prepare for the natural conception of religion in the long description of the Shearing Barn, where 'the defence and salvation of the body by daily bread is still a study, a religion, and a desire'. In *Tess*, where contrast between reality and image is central, frequent references to religious works of art underline the theme. The returned Angel as 'Crivelli's dead *Christus*', the two girls in the swede field as 'some early Italian conception of the two Marys', Angel and 'Liza-Lu as Giotto's 'Two Apostles' at Tess's death, are sharply described, universalized, and contrasted in their living reality by the fixed images of art. The prospect of Wintoncester as 'an isometric drawing', to which Lionel Johnson objected because the architectural term spoilt the emotional tone of Tess's death, can also be justified by the theme. Stonehenge carried the crisis of emotion: the architect's abstract of the city distances the emotion to stress the inhuman blueprint of reality to which Tess is sacrificed.

Such attention to detail as part of the total conception looks forward to Virginia Woolf's poetic organization of the novel. However, one must distinguish the poetic method of Virginia Woolf or James Joyce from the poetic method of Hardy or Emily Brontë. In the modern writers, associative structure of themes largely replaces the narrative of a succession of events in time as the pattern of meaning. Hardy and Emily Brontë include the narrative line as part of a contrapuntal symphony of images and scenes that have the power of images. Cecil points out that 'Hardy's strain of poetry shows itself not just in atmosphere but in the actual turn of the action, not in the scenery but in the play'. The narrative provides action in time. The poetic underpattern, with its accumulation of echoes, parallels, and contrasts, shows the significance of that action.

The result of lack of space to develop the delicate counterpoint between narrative and poetic impulses can be seen in many of Hardy's tales.

'They give us, in varying forms and manners, his characteristic vision of life; what we miss in them is the subtle declaration of what that vision profoundly *means* to his inmost emotion.'

(Lascelles Abercrombie: *Thomas Hardy*)

Many tales suffer from an overbalance of one or the other. Sometimes it is an excess of poetic feeling. 'A Tryst at an Ancient Earthwork' builds up a powerful mood picture of Maiden Castle that recalls Egdon heath in *The Return of the Native*. But its 'obtrusive personality' overpowers the slight incident of the scholar's discovery, and probable theft, of a Roman statuette. On the other hand, the slow-paced evocation of night, storm and pastoral setting that begins 'The Three Strangers' contributes to its meaning. The ironic but unlikely conjunction of life and death embodied in the meeting of hangman and intended victim gains imaginative belief from the echoes of Christian ritual—the shepherd's cottage at the cross-roads, the christening, the three strangers, the three knocks, the victim's drink at the door, the ritual withdrawal in a 'remote circle' from the *cinder*-gray stranger, 'whom some of them seemed to take for the Prince of Darkness himself'—blended with the sharp details of the pastoral world that is at once part of the myth and a guarantee of authenticity in the world of sense experience; 'the tails of little birds trying to roost on some scraggy thorn were blown inside-out like umbrellas', and the earthy Wessex humour of the guests. The swift telling of the tale, with its skilful use of primary narrative effects of suspense, surprise, expectation, ritual repetition, false inference, and true conclusion, all converging on a single dramatic crisis, makes a satisfactory poetic image of life such as one finds in poems of situation like 'Life and Death at Sunrise', 'At the Railway Station, Upway', and the title poems of *Satires of Circumstance*.

The most obvious lack of balance comes in those tales where plot dominates. The power of events and the effects of time are among Hardy's major themes. An extended form, almost a skeleton novel, is used to develop the consequences of missed chances, possibilities of rechoice, the righting or consolidation of old wrongs, the maturing of ambition, revenge, compassion, or indifference, and the quirks of fate that complete a design in an unexpected manner. But the sensational happenings and coincidences that embody Hardy's sense of the cosmic Absurd become less credible in a crowded synopsis unprepared for by poetic atmosphere. The sudden deaths of Mrs Downes and Mrs Barnet, Helena Hall, Selina's Dragoon lover, Baptista's newly-wed husband, the village youth who married the Marchioness of Stonehenge, and the Duchess of Hamptonshire, are little more than improbable plot devices to set in motion the endeavour 'to rectify early deviations of the heart by harking back to the old point'.

Hardy's art is descriptive, not impressionistic in the Chekhov or Hemingway tradition. But when he gives credence to the irrational events from the shadow side which disrupt normal living, by a blend of strong shaping action, overtones of folklore, descriptive evocation of the world of sense, and a pervading poetic symbol, the tales have a consistent poetic force which carries their meaning beyond the limited human action. The blasting but involuntary jealousy of Rhoda Brook (the rejected Bonnie Annie figure of 'The Withered Arm') based on a distorted image of her supplanter, and objectified in the nightmare incubus and her beautiful rival's growing deformity, is surrounded by the rhythms of a simple agricultural community, where belief in sympathetic magic is not abnormal. Sleepy Stickleford, the Great Exhibition, and the sights and sounds of Farmer Tucker's dairy accompany the strange manifestations of the death-yearning for the absolute state which assail the robust Margery Tucker of 'The Romantic Adventures of a Milkmaid' as well as the sensitive Car'line Aspent in 'The Fiddler of the Reels', in the traditional form of a demon lover. Mop Ollamoor's irresistible 'chromatic subtleties', which force Car'line, Hardy's Fair Janet, to dance a sexual dance against her will, his sudden appearances and disappearances, and mirror reflection, are demonic properties. Baron von Xanten, first revealed significantly contemplating suicide in a wooden structure which shelters its occupant from the seasonal weathers of an imperfect world, who shows Margery all the kingdoms of the world, is a more complex demonic symbol than the fiddler. His efforts to return Margery to her normal sphere, with truelove Jim's help, give him the ambivalence of a modern shadow symbol like Michael Tippett's King Fisher; the provocative force which initiates a needed transformation process. Margery's translation from milkmaid to fairy princess fit to go to a ball is accomplished by evocative description that keeps us in the natural world among the birds and hares of Chillington wood, while at the same time suggesting archetypal symbols of translation to a dangerously abnormal sphere of inflated possession. Margery's imprisonment in her airy creation inside the tree where she had found it—'huge, hollow, distorted, and headless, with a rift in its side' until the Baron 'tore away pieces of the wooden shell which enshrouded Margery and all her loveliness', sounds the note of birth into death that is repeated in her inverted vision of the ballroom 'floored with black ice; the figures of the dancers appearing upon it upside down'.

The central symbol in 'Barbara of the House of Grebe', the statue of Edmund Willowes, evoking echoes of Pygmalion and Beauty and the Beast, controls a network of images taken from art and the theatre. This image cluster defines, against various 'masks' of appearance, the heroic worth of Edmund's character ('beauty . . . was the least of his recommendations') and Barbara's maladjustment to the changing reality of the world of time that would ultimately have turned her handsome husband into the 'thing of the charnel-house' hidden by the face mask. The burning of the theatre, from which Edmund emerges physically disfigured but morally a hero, offers Barbara a chance to destroy *her* world of masquerade. Her failure to do so leads to her puppet submission to the diabolic stage-management of Uplandtowers, whose resolve to win her at all costs started the story with a hint of the Immanent Will controlling his actions. The stage-shrine which he sets up in her bedroom, with 'a wax-candle burning on each side of it to throw the [statue's] cropped and distorted features into relief', faces her with a foreshortened image of reality which is really appearance. The end of the tale, telling of Barbara's strange revenge in depriving Uplandtowers of a male image of the only kind of nobility he believes in, and the final discovery of the broken statue, which was considered to be either 'a mutilated Roman satyr; or, if not, an allegorical figure of Death', gains resonance from the powerful poetic underpattern of fixed image and fluid reality that controls its metaphysic.

The inner meaning of 'On the Western Circuit' is pointed immediately by the powerful image of the 'pleasure-machine' which is going to whirl Charles Raye, Anna and her mistress into a merry-go-round of cross-purposes and passions as arbitrary as the decision of the 'inexorable stoker, grimly lurking behind the glittering rococo-work' (brother to the engineer in *Tess*) that 'this set of riders had had their pennyworth'.

'A smoky glare, of the complexion of brass-filings, ascended from the fiery tongues of innumerable naphtha lamps affixed to booths, stalls, and other temporary erections which crowded the spacious market-square. In front of this irradiation scores of human figures, more or less in profile, were darting athwart and across, up, down, and around, like gnats against a sunset.'

The details of light, shape, and texture point to the infernal (i.e. meaningless) nature of the mechanical process, and the diminution of human importance, counterpointing Anna's illusion of being a fixed point in an 'undulating, dazzling, lurid universe' moving and 'countermoving in the revolving mirrors.'

There are poetic elements, of course, even in the less successful tales, which stand out in the memory. The active power of what is absent is conveyed through symbols—Joseph Halcomb's walking stick flowering in the sedge after his drowning, the re-donned wedding dress and mummied cake of 'Enter a Dragoon', the photograph of the poet Ella had never seen, immortalized, like the Stranger in Ibsen's *Lady from the Sea*, in the eyes of the baby son whose birth fulfilled her death-wish. The power of actions which do not remain passive in the past, but start up to drive the process to its appointed end, is embodied in people and things: the gown intended for Sally Hall's wedding but worn by her lover's old flame Helena, so that 'he seemed to feel that fate had impishly changed his *vis-à-vis* in the lover's jig he was about to foot'; the long-lost Bellston's clothes, delivered to his wife on the eve of her marriage to her old lover, which stops the marriage even when Bellston has been found dead; the corpse of Baptista's first husband lying in the next room on her honeymoon with her second; the sea-sickness that reveals the relationship of Millborne and his daughter by investing their features with 'the spectral presence of entombed and forgotten ancestors'; the snobbish son of 'The Son's Veto' set against the 'green bastions of cabbages' journeying to Covent Garden, which remind his uprooted mother of the lost securities of her country home. Ghosts do not appear in Hardy's fiction, but the power of a past image assumes control of the action. 'The insistent shadow of that unconscious one', the dead hero Maumbry, prevents his widow's second marriage. Mrs Petrick's fantasy about her son's noble birth influences his real father's treatment of the boy; and Milly's refusal to relinquish the role of widow with child foisted on to her to save the reputation of the Marchioness of Stonehenge contributes to the noble lady's death.

Most of the tales recall balladry. Some, such as 'The Lady Penelope' and 'What the Shepherd Saw', would have gained intensity and credibility in the stripped ballad form suggested by their stanzaic shape and incremental repetition. The theme of missed and second chances is emphasized by the ballad device of repetition, and resolved tragically or ironically, in 'The Son's Veto', 'For Conscience' Sake', 'Fellow-Townsmen', 'Interlopers at the Knap', 'The Marchioness of Stonehenge', 'The Duchess of Hamptonshire', 'The Lady Icenway', 'The Waiting Supper', 'Alicia's Diary', and 'Enter a Dragoon'. The balladist's irony blends with the modern poet's sense of the ambiguity of things to question the rightness of certain choices: Millborne's belated impulse to marry the lady he wronged twenty years ago; the rising solicitor's marriage to the 'unlettered peasant' who was to bear his child; the curate's refusal to elope with the Duchess of Hampton-shire, whom he later unwittingly buried at sea; Alicia's unselfish encouragement of her lover's marriage to her sister; the conversion of the dashing Sergeant Maumbry to a dull parson; Barnet's decision to save, and the brothers Halcombe's decision not to save, the life of their obstructive relation; and the ballad ethic of *crime passionel* which kills innocent people in 'What the Shepherd Saw' and 'Master John Horseleigh, Knight'. But there is also the poet's feeling for simple human values and loyalties, and humour, and the ability to snatch limited victories from boredom and despair, in the lively smuggling story 'The Distracted Preacher'; in Baptista Trewthen's growing love for her four dull stepdaughters; the happiness of Betty Countess of Wessex with the husband, 'old enough to be compassionate', who had passed the challenge—of kissing her with the smallpox—failed by her lover; and the deter-mination of Sally Hall to retain her unmarried independence.

The problem of striking the right balance between poetry and narrative makes the tales unequal in quality. However, there are two collections, *A Group of Noble Dames* and *A Few Crusted Characters*, in which the total effect is greater than the sum of its parts. Hardy has borrowed the method of Chaucer's *Canterbury Tales* to create a group mood. It is compounded of the social occasion, the inter-linked stories of local hearts and heads, the spirit of place, and the characteristics of the orally-descended tale which is Hardy's medium rather than the written short story—its personal flourishes and digressions, changes of pace and rhythm, and consciousness of a shared tradition between narrator and audience. The occasion of *A Group of Noble Dames* is a weather-bound meeting of the Wessex Field and Antiquarian Club. The Museum fossils, and the tales told by the members, of women (naturally, in a male gathering) whose sexual desires, image of the impersonal cosmic will, cannot be bounded by facile formulae or paper pedigrees, measure with compassionate irony the blindness of these comfortable types who 'still praise the Lord with one voice for His best of all possible worlds.' The return of a native by carrier's van provides the occasion of *A Few Crusted Characters*. The reminiscences of his fellow-passengers about the village characters he knew in his youth—humorous sketches, anecdotal, fabliau-like, ballad-like tales with folklore never very far behind and fundamental human values stressed with warmth and sanity, rich in Wessex idiom and

148

rhythm—build up a mood of nostalgia for the vigorous life that has passed, which finds its climax in the traveller's realization that the roots he was searching for are in the churchyard.

The unresolved tension between poetic and narrative impulses robs the minor novels, except in flashes, of universal meaning. *Two on a Tower* and *The Well-Beloved*, as Cecil points out, lean towards the poetic impulse. After the first thrill in *Two on a Tower* at the central contrast between the inhuman stellar universe and human passions, which informs the lyrics 'In Vision I Roamed' and 'At a Lunar Eclipse', the uninhabited sky proves to be an unresponsive partner in the conflict between man and the nature of things. In *The Return of the Native* or *The Woodlanders*, the conflict grows from the nature of Egdon or the Hintocks. The poor man and the lady theme, and the unlikely intrigue-plot that fills up the rest of the novel with a caricatured bishop, a brother who is invariably where he is least wanted, and a shoal of coincidences and chances missed by a minute, could have developed without the stars.

The beginning promises well, with the sunlit tower, isolated like the two chief characters, rising unimpeded into the sky from a sunless, sobbing forest rooted in palaeolithic dead men and rocking 'in seconds, like inverted pendulums', to evoke the deeper reality of absolute aspiration rooted in human pain, darkness, and time. The romantic tragi-comedy of Swithin's descent from his 'primitive Eden of unconsciousness' on the tower to the lower world of passions, Viviette's mature control over natural instincts to release her young lover, and their defeat by time, has some relevance to the scene. The Wessex chorus has a fine comic choir practice, but is forgotten for long periods. Swithin's sudden appearance in Sir Blount's clothes foreshortens in an anti-realistic image the legal resurrection of the husband and Swithin's usurpation of his place. But these scattered poetic evocations do not coalesce into an underpattern of meaning that pervades the whole novel, though the tower as an imaginative symbol acts as focus to concentrate the plot and draw all the characters into its magnetic field, and gives ballast to the mind adrift on change.

In *The Well-Beloved*, the poetry of place proves too rocky to carry the fantasy of the sculptor's pursuit of his ideal love through three generations of one family. The theme of the immortal face in perishable flesh has been treated adequately in Hardy's poetry; notably 'Heredity' and 'The Pedigree'. The contrast between fixed image and living individuality found lyrical expression in several poems, and a fable to incarnate it in fiction in 'Barbara of the House of Grebe' and *Tess*. The powerful evocation in time and space of 'the peninsula carved by Time out of a single stone'; of unity made out of diversity, as in Deadman's Bay, 'a presence—an imaginary shape or essence from the human multitude lying below', demands the strength of Tess's personality and tragedy to oppose it. The scene is stronger than the repetitive, conventional narrative and the characters. A prophetic example of the film 'fade-in' which dissolves the human faces at a fashionable dinner into the rocky features of the Isle is symbolic of Hardy's failure, apart from Pierston's realistic choice of the aging Marcia, to bring the narrative into unity with the overpowering factual poetry of the scene.

A Pair of Blue Eyes is, as Coventry Patmore told Hardy, 'not a conception for prose', but he succeeds intermittently in uniting poetic and narrative strains to suggest underlying causes. Its lyrical Cornish setting, romantic heroine, anti-realistic symbols and stylized form (an overplus of ironic coincidences, sensational and macabre episodes, repeated situations with cast changes, and characters whose force depends on situation rather than depth of personality) ask for ballad treatment. Mrs Jethway's unmotivated appearances would be less improbable in ballad form; in prose, she is a less credible symbol of the fatal past than the furmity hag of *The Mayor of Casterbridge*, whose appearance in a court of law sometime was quite probable. The effort to fill out a poetic conception of young love with event leads to disunited impulses in the narrative itself. The tone varies from romantic comedy and social comedy to tragi-comedy, melodrama and ironic tragedy. The comic parson and Stephen's robust Wessex parents hardly seem to inhabit the world of the last scenes and the Cliff without a Name, which as a presence of cosmic indifference is worthy to stand beside Egdon Heath. However, juxtaposition of comic and tragic can sometimes have a complex poetic effect that recalls Shakespeare or Ibsen. Hardy scratches the surface of a tragedy to find a comedy in Knight's rescue from the cliff by Elfride's underwear, the Hamlet-like gravediggers and Knight's pompous lecture on mortality in the vault while Elfride and Stephen suffer agonies of emotion, the absurd self-esteem of the two lovers quarrelling over their precedence in the dead Elfride's affections, and Knight's catechism of Elfride on Jethway's tomb:

' "Did you say you were sitting on that tomb?" he asked moodily.
"Yes; and it was true."
"Then how, in the name of Heaven, can a man sit upon his own tomb?"
"That was another man. Forgive me, Harry, won't you?"
"What, a lover in the tomb and a lover on it?" '

The Cornish scene is not linked to Elfride's character as it is to Emma's in *Poems of 1912–13*, where it gives universal dimension to the personal tragedy. However, the scene does yield elements of a poetic underpattern in one prominent image: the recurring skeletons, real and metaphorical, which warn of the dangers of indecision. The leaf-skeletons in the pool where Elfride, like its primitive insect life, lets chance choose her course, are recalled in the 'dancing leaf-shadows', awakened gnats and earthworms, and 'the horizontal bars of woodwork, which crossed their forms like the ribs of a skeleton' when Stephen sees Elfride with Knight in the summer-house; in the Luxellian vault and Jethway's tomb; in the final irony when Elfride's two lovers unknowingly travel on the same train as her coffin to ask her hand; and, most impressively of all, in the anatomical structure of the Cliff without a Name and the fossil trilobite which shows Knight, hanging over the cliff, not only their common insignificance to space and time, but also the difference that can be made to their fate by human intelligence and forethought and, on this occasion, Elfride's unaccustomed decision and resourcefulness. Dr C. J. P. Beatty, in his London Ph.D. thesis *The Part played by Architecture in the Life and Works of Thomas Hardy*, points out that the evocation of chaos circumscribed by shape in Hardy's description of cliff and sea adumbrates the theme of man's efforts at construction; and the problem of reconciling nature's fixed forms with individual ephemera is mirrored in the rigid Knight's relationship to the mercurial Elfride. But these traces of poetic pattern demonstrate the lack of a shaping action or characters of tragic stature, which in *Tess of the d'Urbervilles* turns the intolerance of Angel and the suffering of Tess into great tragic myth.

In *The Hand of Ethelberta*, where the impulses to poetry, romance, comedy of manners, farce, and social satire cannot reconcile their differences, the narrative of Ethelberta's manoeuvres to climb into high society cannot compete with Hardy's powerful poetic evocation of the corruption at its heart which her conscious aim will not admit. On Neigh's estate, on the site 'where, by every law of manorial topography, the mansion would be situate', Ethelberta sees

'numerous horses in the last stage of decrepitude, the animals being such mere skeletons that at first Ethelberta hardly recognized them to be horses at all; they seemed rather to be specimens of some attenuated heraldic animal, scarcely thick enough through the body to throw a shadow . . .'

The cumbrous formality of the language describing her walk down the drive, the heraldic associations of the de-natured and two-dimensional creatures, flesh and blood reduced by Neigh's ambition to an ironic travesty of pedigree, the 'chronological sequel' of rotting horseflesh hung on trees which have been lopped to a distorted parody of life for the purpose, mock Ethelberta's expectations with the life-denying qualities of the upper classes. The context of the lopped trees makes the emotional tone very different from that created in the Talbothays idyll (*Tess*, xxvii):

'At the door the wood-hooped pails, sodden and bleached by infinite scrubbings, hung like hats on a stand upon the forked and peeled limb of an oak fixed there for that purpose; all of them ready and dry for the evening milking.'

As a warning of evil from what Jung and Eliot would recognize as Ethelberta's 'Guardians', this expressionistic scene indicates a three-dimensional humanity in her and sets overtones vibrating which disrupt the unemotional comedy of situation in which she moves.

A Laodicean and *Desperate Remedies* suffer in different ways from too much plot. The scenes that begin *A Laodicean*—Somerset copying transitional architecture against a sunset that irradiates ephemeral insects, Paula's rejection of total immersion, and the conjunction of ancient castle with modern telegraph—introduce the poetic contrast of new and old. But the limited interest of Paula's Laodicean tactics is padded out with inorganic incidents. Somerset's fall down the turret staircase, unlike Knight's down the Cliff without a Name, leads nowhere in plot or poetic vision. The sudden return of Uncle Abner, and his equally unexpected revolutionary past, revealed by Dare in a melodramatic scene where they face each other across the vestry table with revolvers and mutual blackmail, are motivated only by the need to provide opposition to

Somerset's romance. There are poetic symptoms, however, of another story under the one Hardy actually wrote, which lights up at rare moments the daemonic energies that disturb the surface of modern life. The 'appearance, as from the tomb, of this wintry man' (Abner) is marked by his connection with non-human elements: his face has been 'the plaything of strange fires or pestilences'. De Stancy's Protean gift of assuming the features of his ancestral portraits aligns him with the impersonal past. Both have a negative quality that links them to the grotesque figure from which the book derives most of its energy, though the link remains seminal. The demonic Dare is not an impossible figure: Rimbaud could provide a contemporary parallel. He is, however, closer to folklore and the nihilistic medievalism of Thomas Mann's devil in *Dr Faustus*. His presentation as 'a being of no age, no nationality and no behaviour' . . . 'a complete negative'; a photographer who distorts Paula's romantic image of her lover; a student and taker of chances; a diabolic showman of the human absurdity that allows him to manipulate people and events (a view that modifies Cecil's objection to 'a romance . . . inspired by the sight of physical jerks in pink flannel'); makes him a symbol of impersonal destructive cosmic chaos, which is turned aside by the human determination of Paula in the last scenes and the unselfishness of Charlotte.

Desperate Remedies, unlike *A Laodicean*, does not flag in the telling. Its complicated plot would provide material for several different novels—a romantic comedy, a detective novel, a sensation novel, an expressionistic novel, a Wessex pastoral, a psychological study of a frustrated woman, even, as D. H. Lawrence observed, a morality play. These different impulses do not, as in the major novels, blend into a unity of poetic effect. But they show flashes of poetic energy which brand this first novel with Hardy's mark. The most impressive character, Miss Aldclyffe, lives through suggestive details that present her as a tragic, tormented figure motivated by daemonic sources that contradict her will and the virago-type of Mrs Henry Wood which she outwardly resembles. The relationship between her and Manston reaches beyond the mother-and-son actuality through the elemental imagery that surrounds them both. Cytherea's first sight of Miss Aldclyffe, in a crimson room lit by a late sun, of a woman 'like a tall black figure standing in the midst of fire', is duplicated in her first encounter with Manston, an unnaturally tall silhouette against a gathering thunderstorm, who proves to have the devil's power of staring open-eyed at lightning and, like the demonic Fiddler of the Reels, of sexually fascinating an impressionable girl by his music. The death-wish implicit in contact with daemonic sources is suggested by the recurring sound of the waterfall that accompanies the death of Miss Aldclyffe's father, Cytherea's meeting with Manston, and the typically Hardeian conjunction of watchers depending on the chain that starts with Manston burying his wife's corpse; and in Cytherea's masochistic nightmare on her wedding eve, expressive of guilt in the conflict between instinct and reason, that she was being whipped by a masked Manston 'with dry bones suspended on strings, which rattled at every blow like those of a malefactor on a gibbet'. Nature is used variously, but always poetically; as objective fact, to mirror and affect human emotions, to measure human conduct and reflect the cosmos. The happy and ephemeral creatures in the rain-butt inspire Manston to follow nature; the slow, minutely described fire of couch-grass, which grew out of hand only because of human casualness, shows the consequences of doing so. The 'sensuous natures of the vegetable world' encourage Manston's animal passions; the 'helpless flatness of the landscape' takes away Cytherea's impulse to resist. The sinister mandrakes and weeds flourish in a garden where there is no Gardener. The tragic elements of the underpattern pull against the comic trend of the sensation novel whose tidy development implies the cosmic order missing from Hardy's universe.

The Trumpet Major and *Under the Greenwood Tree* are the best of the minor novels because their poetic elements are not inconsistent with the other impulses. Both narrative and poetry are at ease in the rustic community Hardy knew well. His lesser novels suffer from his unease with 'high life', and lack of a rustic chorus, or at best one which appears infrequently. These two novels miss the Hardeian tragic intensity, but give more scope to the rich humour of caricature, character, situation and Wessex idiom which contribute to a poetic meditation on the importance of the small eternal things of life that go on in time of the breaking of nations and ancient traditions. The vacillations of Anne Garland and Fancy Day, the domestic comedy and country humour, are none the worse for an honourable descent from balladry and folklore, the traditional guardians of basic values. The grotesque scenes and sensational events of the major novels would destroy the quiet unity of tone that encloses one novel with the cycle of the seasons and the other with the coming and going of the dragoons. The coincidences, such as John's recognition of Matilda and Maybold's meeting with Dick just after he has written to accept a living in Yorkshire for himself and Dick's fiancée, do not strain credulity.

In *The Trumpet Major* the war itself is kept in the background. The foreground is occupied by the physical and emotional realities of daily life which oppose their values to its impersonal power. Food and drink and gay gatherings are lovingly detailed. The mill becomes a poetic symbol of the eternal struggle for daily bread that touches everyone: Mrs Garland does not mind the noise or the flour on her furniture, 'being as it was, not nasty dirt, but the blessed staff of life'. The 'genial and historical value' of its human associations is inferred by the description of the spring-cleaning process which removes 'the tawny smudges of bygone shoulders in the passage' and other visible marks and ancient smells of long human occupation (one can compare the description of Geoffrey Day's cottage, in which every object has a human association or interest); and the paving stones worn by the ebb and flow of feet since Tudor times.

Descriptive detail accumulates to a total vision that reaches beyond the logical meaning of the words, and beyond the close-up of ordinary life in a particular period. The processes of nature frame wars and human passions. The sun rises, as usual, on the unusual scene of the King's review, giving the resplendent trumpet major a lilac shadow (the colour of death) and the transitory significance of 'a very god of war'. Hardy reminds us that the connection of the characters with nature is deeper than their involvement in war. Anne, whose vacillations are an outgrowth of impersonal cosmic movement, inspires natural imagery: her yellow boots 'looked like a pair of yellow-hammers flitting under her dress'. The miller's weather-vane, metamorphosed from soldier to sailor, and the intensely poetic conception of the Aeolian harp, whose 'strange mixed music of water, wind, and strings' is an objective correlative of Anne's emotional relationship to John, become symbolic of human emotion played on by irrational elemental forces which bring love to the less worthy and death to the better man.

The total effect of the novel depends on the mood of muted elegy that has been built up through details of ordinary living, with all their emotional association, and an interplay between recollection and the present moment that recalls the structure of many poems. At moments when the viewpoint moves back to reveal the action, the war itself, and the future death of the actors in battles that are now the facts of history, as episodes in a long perspective of time, it reveals that the objective play is controlled by the subjective mood and personal voice of the poet; which selects 'through the mists of the seventy or eighty years that intervene between then and now' the details that conjure up the spirit and colour of the time. The candles, brilliant uniforms, and heads outlined against a dark background of his evocation are a recurring image which returns and is distanced, in the final paragraph, to hold in solution noble but transient human qualities and the long but meaningless stretch of time that dims the light and silences the assertive trumpet in the darkness.

All the elements of *Under the Greenwood Tree* evoke a poetic mood compounded of nostalgia for old rural ways and hope for the resilience of life in the new order. Fancy Day, educated above her station, is the structural pivot, both in her vacillation between the rustic virtues of Dick Dewy and the refinements of the innovating parson, and in her ability to play the organ which displaces the Mellstock quire. The scenes that show the rustics in communal action, working, feasting, dancing, celebrating the seasons of the natural and Christian calendar, measuring all the small repetitive events that give their lives significance in the rich Wessex speech and gesture that shows respect for self and others, build up a solid image of the sustaining ritual of a community that gives the dispersal of an obscure band of musicians more than local significance. The quiet pathos of their appearance in church on the day of Fancy's installation, scattered among the congregation, 'awkward, out of place, abashed, and inconvenienced by their hands', points to the loss of communal involvement in religion that deepens in the later novels to a tragic alienation from the stabilities of religious and natural harmony.

But the sustaining power of ritual close to nature has not yet left Mellstock. The ritual processions, feasts and dances which frame the story between Christmas and Fancy's summer wedding realize the controlling image of permanence in transience. Out of the dark wood whose individual voices evoke a whole range of emotions, Dick and the quire evolve, first of all as merely another quality of sound, and then as two-dimensional black profiles against the sky, 'which suggested some processional design on Greek or Etruscan pottery'. It recurs in Grandfather William's 'Titanic shadow at least thirty feet in length', which stretches to infinity as the natural world knows it, 'his head finally terminating upon the trunk of a grand old oak-tree': and in the ancient greenwood tree outside Keeper Day's cottage, that for generations has nurtured the great continuous movement of mating, birth, and supersession.

Nature pervades the novel to contribute, in Hardy's distinctive manner, to a poetic underpattern of resonances. The overflow of human emotions into external phenomena gives the story deeper significance. Stable tree trunks 'writhed like miserable men' in the rain to mirror the feelings of Dick and Fancy at her father's opposition, and the compelling power of the witch's 'charm' that removes it. The fertile promise of their wedding day is mirrored in the noisy activity of birds and bees and the fullness of blossom. There are times, too, when man's juxtaposition with nature defines cosmic absurdity and disharmony. The honey-taking, with its unimpassioned working rhythm, shows up the absurd rivalry of Dick and Shiner to fetch hartshorn for Fancy's sting. The desolate stillness that marks Dick's unsuccessful attempt to ask Geoffrey Day for Fancy's hand is intensified and disturbed by

'some small bird that was being killed by an owl in the adjoining wood, whose cry passed into the silence without mingling with it.'

But this note is rare in the poetic texture of this early novel that celebrates the continuance of life through all its changes.

The poetic strain in Hardy is too complex to yield to labels. What is clear is that the novelist could not exist without the poet. It is the poet's eye for the ultimates of the human situation, for the metaphysic in the physical fact, for the truth in distortion, and for the underpattern of symphonic connections running parallel with surface cause and effect, which gives Hardy's major novels their tragic greatness.

Far from the Madding Crowd:
A Pastoral Novel

Far from the Madding Crowd is the first of Hardy's novels to rise to tragic stature through interplay between surface narrative and poetic underpattern. The calm of *Under the Greenwood Tree* and *The Trumpet Major* is scarcely rippled by Fancy's deviation from Dick, Mr Maybold's rejection, Anne's vacillation, rumours of invasion, or John Loveday's muted death far away in time and space on the battlefields of Spain. But Troy's sexual charm, Bathsheba's caprice, and Boldwood's madness—the fatal consequence of both—provide not only incidents in the plot but also intimations of an archetypal pattern of behaviour tragically asserting itself against conscious human purpose.

The means by which Hardy probes under the surface of events are poetic. The plot itself, a dramatic metaphor that touches the mystery of things with its scenes of heightened passion, lyrical feeling and celebration of seasonal rites that link man to nature, reveals the stylized shape and basic characteristics of balladry.

'There are the neat, rounded, and intertwining groups of events, the simple and decisive balancing of characters . . . There is the narrative method whereby encounter (whether of person with person, or person with Fate) is the life of the tale.'

(Douglas Brown: *Thomas Hardy*)

Fanny Robin is the betrayed maiden, Oak the faithful lover tested by his lady, Troy the inconstant soldier whose conquest by 'winning tongue' is ironically foretold in the ballad of Allan Water that Bathsheba sings at the shearing supper. Qualities of character are taken for granted. Much is revealed through dialogue, tone, movement and gesture. The shepherd's rise from rags to riches to marry his lady of high degree, and Boldwood's crime of passion and swift self-punishment are in true ballad tradition. The story has the simplicity of a ballad plot that pushes the characters into tragic relationships which converge on a climax of love, passion and death.

The action in the eleven serial instalments (Chapters I–V, VI–VIII, IX–XIV, XV–XIX, XX–XXIV, XXV–XXIX, XXX–XXXIII, XXXIV–XXXVIII, XXXIX–XLII, XLIII–XLVII, XLVIII–LVII) advances the story by definite stages like the stanzas of a ballad. Each section strongly concludes a certain stage in the fortunes of the characters and hints at future developments which may change the emotional current. In the first instalment, for example, Gabriel's rejection by Bathsheba and loss of his sheep require a response in the following instalment. The central part (Chapters XXV–XXIX) destroys Boldwood's rising hopes when Bathsheba capitulates to Troy, and ends with Gabriel's attempt to warn her against him. The penultimate instalment prepares for Troy's return, and the last chapters move swiftly to the final tragic consequence of Troy's infidelity to Fanny and Bathsheba's infatuation.

The poetic qualities of the novel could not be felt without the clearly-defined plot. It provides the melody to Hardy's poetic counterpoint in the texture, and focuses on the central chapters— Bathsheba's fatal attraction to Troy—to suggest that poetic 'doubleness in the action' which

'should remove the surface of things, expose the underneath, or the inside, of the natural surface appearance. It may allow the characters to behave inconsistently, but only with respect to a deeper consistency. It may use any device to show their real feelings and volitions, instead of just what, in actual life, they would normally profess or be conscious of; it must reveal, underneath the vacillating or infirm character, the indomitable unconscious will; and underneath the resolute purpose of the planning animal, the victim of circumstance and the doomed or sanctified being.'

(T. S. Eliot: Introduction to S. L. Bethell, *Shakespeare and the Popular Dramatic Tradition*)

The 'deeper consistency' of a poetic reading troubles readers who are looking for the novel Hardy did not write. Its most obvious manifestation, perhaps, is in the Hardeian stress on chance and coincidence. A naturalistic appraisal of the novel might consider Gabriel Oak exceptionally unlucky to lose his sheep before they were insured, and exceptionally lucky to get a lift to Weatherbury in Bathsheba's waggon, to be at hand when fire breaks out on her farm, and to be recalled so soon after his dismissal to cure blasted sheep. It is unfortunate that Boldwood is the one man who would take a valentine seriously, or that Troy should invade Weatherbury twice as 'the impersonator of Heaven's persistent irony towards him'. The *deus ex machina* which rescues Troy from drowning or the favourable conjunction of events that enables him to snatch Penny-ways' note from Bathsheba's hand may come too pat on their cue. The mockery of the weather and the gurgoyle, the fog coinciding with the journey of the most fearful of the rustics, Bathsheba's decision to be guided by the position of the tossed Bible instead of her reason, Fanny's mistake in the church: the workings of chance and coincidence add up rapidly to a poetic vision of the 'silent workings of an invisible hand', irrational and unknowable, directing the buried life away from merely human purposes to fulfil the 'indomitable unconscious will'. For all its wealth of agricultural detail, *Far from the Madding Crowd* is a non-naturalistic novel that exposes the underneath of surface appearance.

A poetic talent is at home in stylization. Though specific chapters do not tally with the rigidity of an architectural blueprint, there is a careful placing of parallel scenes in a before-and-after relationship to the central chapters that invites the comparisons and contrasts of a poetic reading. They show how the central action of human choice releases a fatal force which reverses the current of all fortunes except Gabriel Oak's. Gabriel proposes twice, and Boldwood three times. Boldwood's rise in Bathsheba's favour from his first proposal (rejected) to his second (half accepted) is offset on the other side of the central episode by his second rejection, so much more terrible in Chapter xxxi because it is accompanied by a loss of control that hints at a tragic outcome to his obsession. There is a shearing feast and a wedding feast, linked thematically by Troy's harvest/wedding revel that profanes both. Time and chance jeer twice at Troy, through their grotesque embodiment in clockwork and stone in All Saints and Weatherbury Churches. The second occasion, when Fanny is past his help, points up with tragic irony his failure to persist after the first mockery. Troy takes two locks of hair, and abandons both women: Bathsheba's discovery of the colour of Fanny's hair precipitates her own crisis. The effect of Bathsheba's valentine—serious but not yet tragic—on Boldwood's temperament is set off by his intensified agony in Chapter xxxvii. On both occasions Oak meets his solitary figure at daybreak. In the later meeting, Boldwood's incoherent grief and evidence of diminished responsbility recall the earlier Boldwood, who felt 'twinges of shame and regret at having so far exposed his mood by those fevered questions to a stranger', and had discussed Fanny's elopement with intelligent responsibility. The complete isolation of Fanny Robin in an indifferent landscape, helped only by a dog, in Chapter XL comments on Chapters VII and XI, when her lonely figure at least had Oak's practical sympathy and the uncertain support of Troy's promise. The comfortable Wessex ritual of drinking in Warren's Malthouse (VIII) has its less pleasant counterpart in the Buck's Head, where Gabriel Oak, who had been received as 'one of us' in the earlier ritual, takes charge of the muddle caused by Joseph Poorgrass's multiplying eye. At Warren's, news was heard of Fanny's disappearance: the delay at the Buck's Head is the cause of her dramatic reappearance to direct events from her coffin, and the disappearance of Troy, which in its turn forges another link in the tragic chain of cause and effect when *he* reappears. At the farthest points of radiation from the centre, the novel begins and ends with the fortunes of Gabriel Oak who, as his name suggests, watches and endures throughout.

There is hardly a scene, a character, or an image which has not its reflections on either side of the central crisis. It is characteristic of Hardy that their poetic force is carried by the relationship of characters to their environment. Nature dominates an agricultural community: 'Weatherbury' is well named. The adjustment or maladjustment of the characters to its seasonal rituals and emergencies—that is, to the reality of life—controls the deeper meaning of the story.

Hardy knows Nature too well to limit its presentation to the pathetic fallacy. There are scenes where Nature seems to be in sympathy with the human actors. Incidents in the story of human love run a diurnal and seasonal course. Oak is rejected in January, the intense passion of Bathsheba and Troy reaches its peak in high summer, Fanny dies at the onset of winter, Troy at Christmas, and hope begins to revive for Bathsheba and Oak in the new year. Dawn initiates action, reveals, and challenges: Bathsheba's spirit is revealed to Oak in her early morning ride in Chapter III, Oak discovers the loss of his flock in V, the effect of the valentine on Boldwood in XIV, and in Chapter XXXVIII the depth of the farmer's unbalance in neglecting his farm. In Chapter IX Boldwood pays his first visit to Bathsheba, and in XLIV and XL the dawn reveals Bathsheba's and Fanny's plight and their efforts to control it. Evenings often darken in storm and passion (XXXI, XXXIV, XXXVI, LXIV). When the distracted Bathsheba faces the stormy sunset after Boldwood's passionate reproaches in Chapter XXXI, 'the unresting world wheeled her round to a contrasting prospect eastward, in the shape of indecisive and palpitating stars'. But the subjective view of nature is corrected by the objective. As Boldwood walks across the meadow after he has received the valentine, 'the ground was melodious with ripples, and the sky with larks', but nature ruins his crops and Troy's romantic repentance, snows on an unprotected Fanny, and kills Gabriel's sheep.

Subjective and objective are fused when Nature becomes a correlative for those impulses which, because of their complexity or the character's failure in 'mapping out my mind upon my tongue', or ignorance of true motives, or Victorian taboos, cannot be expressed directly. The pool which 'glittered like a dead man's eye' is a vivid expression of Oak's unspoken impulse to suicide after the accident to his flock. The morning breeze which blew, 'shaking and elongating the reflection of the [skeleton] moon without breaking it' as he rejects the impulse conveys a basic concept of his resilient character.

Gabriel Oak's vital relationship to the natural world provides a touchstone by which the other characters are measured, a central leitmotif that links scenes, incidents and characters symphonically, and a powerful example of the poetic force of Hardy's Wessex. While Hardy takes some licence with his environment—the gurgoyles on Weatherbury (Puddletown) Church, for example, have probably been imported from the church of Sydling St Nicholas, and 'the heroine's fine old Jacobean house [Waterston Manor] would be found in the story to have taken a witch's ride of a mile or more from its actual position'—it has the physical solidity of actual place. In Chapter II Norcombe Hill, 'not far from lonely Toller-Down', is given an identity that distinguishes it from any other hill by its minutely detailed features. The 'desolating wind' which creates different sound responses from the differing textures of wood, leaves, grasses, and hedgerows; the decaying plantation of beeches, 'whose upper verge formed a line over the crest, fringing its arched curve against the sky, like a mane', bring Norcombe Hill sharply to the senses in its varying shapes, textures, and qualities of sound, as one of the ultimates of the human situation, an active agent of fate with a will and effective power of its own.

As in the poetry, Hardy's truth to physical detail adds a metaphysical dimension: Norcombe Hill is also 'a mysterious sheet of fathomless shade'. The poet's power of leaping from the known to the unknown resides first of all in the evocative exactness of his vocabulary. The 'sound' words, 'smote', 'floundered', 'grumbling', 'gushed', 'weakened moan', 'simmered', 'boiled', 'rattled', 'rubbing', 'raking', 'brushing', evoke familiar human emotions and moods in tension with the non-human processes of time, wind and weather bending every digit to their unalterable course. Sound combines with sense, stress, sentence and paragraph structure, rhythm and control of tempo to make 'the roll of the world eastward . . . almost a palpable movement' to the reader. Short objective statements of time and place give way in the second paragraph to a Latinate weight of rhythm and vocabulary appropriate to Hardy's definition of Norcombe Hill as 'a shape approaching the indestructible as nearly as any to be found on earth,' and to the more personal rhythms and subjective evocations of the two paragraphs following. The cosmic pulse established rhythmically in the first two paragraphs sweeps with cumulative force through complex sentences and balanced clauses which place speech stress on the 'sound' qualities of Norcombe Hill, until the carefully built-up mood dies away, after the last sound climax of 'hurrying gust', on the soft consonants and open vowels of 'plunged into the south, to be heard no more'. The change of rhythm and tempo is typical of the whole novel. Sentences, paragraphs and chapters are juxtaposed as artistically as the fast and slow movements of a symphony.

Many of the poems can parallel in miniature the swing back from the heightened sense of awe at the sweep of mysterious natural forces to the sharp objective detail that anchors Hardy's Nature to the physical world. The adjectives which define the colour of the stars above Norcombe Hill—'a steely glitter', 'a fiery red'—stress with their non-human extremes 'the complete abstraction from all its compass of the sights and sounds of man'. Norcombe Hill, despite the emotional music of its wind cadences and poetry of motion, is a place without consciousness, and therefore without significance to Hardy except as reflected sensation 'derived from a tiny human frame'. The unordered motions of nature are suddenly jolted into perspective by the crowning climax of Farmer Oak's flute, whose notes 'had a clearness which was to be found nowhere in the wind, and a sequence which was to be found nowhere in nature'.

The focus now moves to Gabriel Oak. It is perhaps not accidental that Hardy's extended character studies of Oak, Boldwood, Troy and Bathsheba in Chapters I, XVIII, XXV and XXIX are juxtaposed with episodes in which their relationship to nature defines and judges their attitude to physical reality. Oak is linked vitally to the natural world in the novel's first sentence: his smile wrinkles his face 'like the rays in a rudimentary sketch of the rising sun'. His practical dress, unromantic capacity to wear well, the unassuming movements that suggest his conviction that 'he had no great claim on the world's room', and his special 'static' power, give him a likeness in certain respects to the indestructible 'featureless convexity' of Norcombe Hill going on its 'stately progress through the stars.' He appreciates the sky as 'a useful instrument' more reliable than his man-made timepiece, and as 'a work of art superlatively beautiful'. But his human capacity to make order, morality and beauty in the spinning universe isolates the movement of his life, in spite of its adjustment to seasonal rhythms, from the throb of the impersonal pulse with which it is counterpointed. Norcombe Hill now appears transformed by Oak's human purpose. The 'wild slope' is dotted with protective hurdles and the lambing hut, whose practical contents challenge the unordered natural furnishings of the hillside.

The introduction of Gabriel Oak on Norcombe Hill shows that his relationship to nature is one of open-eyed reality. After the lapses of attention that cost him his consciousness in an unventilated hut and his precious flock, he never relaxes his watch against nature's indifference. He knows how far he can utilize its resources to control the chaos of a spinning universe. The poetic texture throughout the novel shows Oak true to his role of creating order out of chaos. Hardy's description of the fire in Chapter VI and the storm in Chapters XXXVI and XXXVII stress the 'remarkable confusion of purpose' that invades both men and macrocosm. The men's 'shadows danced merrily up and down, timed by the jigging of the flames, and not at all by their owners' movements': flames of all shapes, sizes and noises consume the rick haphazardly in all directions. The factual details modulate into a poetic truth, linked to the grotesque mechanism of the All Saints jackaclock and the Weatherbury gurgoyle,

'Individual straws in the foreground were consumed in a creeping movement of ruddy heat, as if they were knots of red worms, and above shone imaginary fiery faces, tongues hanging from lips, glaring eyes, and other impish forms, from which at intervals sparks flew in clusters like birds from a nest . . .'

to reveal the world of strange chaotic forces to which Gabriel must oppose his intelligence and moral order. Characteristically, there is a swing back to the physical reality of the fire through the 'nest' simile that carries the mind back to the straw rick. In the storm Gabriel opposes an infuriated universe, strengthened by Troy's irresponsibility, with his experienced reading of the weather-lore of lower creatures, his improvised lightning conductor, endurance and devotion. The details of animal behaviour, transformation of landscape by light and shade, and *unfulfilled* warnings of the 'dance of death', throw into sharp relief the triumph of human contrivance against time and chance, and when Bathsheba joins him, the harmonious bond of mutual responsibility to life that is more enduring than the sexual attraction between Bathsheba and Troy. The lightning which brings them close to death reveals blinding truths in vivid image about their relationship to reality: Bathsheba's figure, running to join the solitary Oak; her confession of irrational impulse to marry Troy, which accords with the wild confusion of the storm raging about them; and an enlarged shadow-image of 'two human shapes, black as jet', that compels comparison with the mangled shadows of Troy and Bathsheba in the fir plantation (xxiv) as archetypes of her relationship to the two men.

Bathsheba's entry into the story implies the dominance of impulse over reason and intelligence which allows nature to assert its power. Her showy red jacket, a dissonant note in the 'featureless convexity' where survival depends on adjustment to the unexciting daily round, links her on the poetic level with the alien red coat Troy, who wins her by the dazzle of passion, and the tragic one-sidedness of Boldwood, which leads to bloodshed. (In Chapter L the colour leitmotif and her raised position in the tent, 'enthroned alone in this place of honour, against a scarlet background', suggests how far her infatuation for Troy has isolated her from her natural background.) Her irrational impulse to admire her image on Norcombe Hill is a visual metaphor of the blindness to reality which links the three in a tragic trio. All three mistake a projection of their own desires for love, and are too sensitive to the mockery of men and nature. Oak's sensible clothes and purposeful movements throw into relief Bathsheba's longing to escape the demands of life. She would like to be a bride at a wedding, 'if I could be one without having a husband'. 'That's a terrible wooden story' says Oak.

Hardy's moral judgement of Bathsheba is made in the chapter that follows her capitulation to Troy in the hollow in the ferns. Chapter xxviii, when examined with xliv, suggests by poetic means the nature of her blindness, and her recovery from it, in terms that would hardly have been acceptable to the Victorian reader in straight statement. To readers of the surface story, and to Bathsheba herself, she was captured by a soldier's 'winning tongue'. But the poetic texture makes it clear that she was won as a woman by the phallic sword. The sword exercise is a correlative in action of the appeal of danger, death, and the dominant male.

Hardy's setting is essential to the meaning of both chapters. The film of *Far from the Madding Crowd* (1968) set the scene in grim, angular Maiden Castle. But Hardy's sensuous description of the lush ferns, 'their soft, feathery arms caressing her up to her shoulders', the thick, flossy, yielding carpet of moss and grass, make clear Bathsheba's inarticulate sexual desires. We are prepared for her to make a response to Troy that is emotional, not rational, by the shape of the pit, 'shallow enough to allow the sunshine to reach their heads'. The shadow in which their bodies stand looks back to the intimate sexual darkness of the fir plantation in which she becomes so dramatically 'entangled' with Troy. His sudden appearance in the hollow is like the suddenness of the 'fairy transformation' revealed by Bathsheba's dark lantern, and as diabolically 'magic' as his mastery of the sword and scarlet garb. The transformation is into something below the human level. If one views the sword exercise as a dazzling courtship ritual, Bathsheba's rejection of the less glamorous Oak and Boldwood becomes clear.

The complexity of the attraction is evoked by the swift action and evocative power of the words. An accumulation of active verbs and words of rapid hissing movement build up a powerful impression of Troy's slipperiness and Bathsheba's fascinated response to the fatal attraction of the sword. Troy's role as bringer of death is defined at the end of the chapter in an image that brings back, with a difference, Gabriel's rejection of suicide:

'He was altogether too much for her, and Bathsheba seemed as one who, facing a reviving wind, finds it blow so strongly that it stops the breath.'

Bathsheba submits: Gabriel resists, and the reviving breeze distorts the moon's reflection without breaking it.

Reminders of the earlier scene in Chapter XLIV stress the difference. The scene of Troy's mating display is now a refuge from him. The summer 'ferns with their feathery arms' are now 'yellowing' in the winter: the 'blades' of 'a peculiar species of flag' which 'glistened in the emerging sun, like scythes' recall Troy's explanation of his cuts in terms of sowing and harvesting. Bathsheba's advice to Liddy—really to herself—'Stand your ground, and be cut to pieces' recalls her danger, and the courage she has transferred from that romantic situation to the present hard reality. The fungi, 'marked with great splotches, red as arterial blood', remind of Troy's appearance on the natural scene as 'a dim spot of artificial red' and his role as bringer of death. Even the language in Chapter XXVIII, full of hissing and explosive consonants, has changed to an evocation in sound and sense of oozing and rotting. The difference lies in Bathsheba's new assessment of reality after Fanny's revelation. Her eyes are now open to the presence of evil. The beautiful flossy carpet has hidden a malignant swamp.

But she does not allow the evil to distort her vision. It is from here, her Slough of Despond, that the dawn reveals to her the rebirth of natural life, the comforting ritual of the daily round—the schoolboy learning his collect—in contrast to the dazzling mating ritual which had 'well-nigh shut out earth and heaven', and her own choice to endure, which aligns her with Gabriel Oak. Her poetic link to her surroundings shows the distorted perception of her youth giving way to the clear sight of maturity. The reflected image of her solitary self at the beginning of the novel, which blinded her to the consequences of toying with the affections of the reserved farmer who did not bow down to her image, is replaced at the end by a contrasting picture of Bathseba in harmony with man and nature. Her wedding to Oak is marked by practical plainness; clogs, cloak and umbrella acknowledging the weather and the Weatherbury band acknowledging renewed harmony with rustic tradition. The whole novel, with its picture of Bathsheba presiding over the minutely described affairs of household and farm, is a great evocation of that 'mass of hard prosaic reality' which she accepts as the basis of marriage in marrying Oak, after the failure of high romance.

Troy's relationship to his environment is marked from beginning to end by distortion. He makes his entry in Chapter XI as a voice 'so much a part of the building, that one would have said the wall was holding a conversation with the snow.' The implied inflexibility marks his attitude at All Saints, where he 'stood still with the abnormal rigidity of the old pillars around.'

The stone rigidity of what should be humanly flexible is balanced in Chapter xlvi by the grotesque Walpurgis-night writhing of flowers which should be rooted in Fanny's grave. The resulting chaos enacts visibly the 'element of absurdity' in his belated repentance. His acceptance of chaos as his element is pointed by his response to the mockery of the gurgoyle, and Bathsheba's contrasting attempt to restore order in the churchyard, though it means acknowledgment of her own unimportance: 'she wiped the mud spots from the tomb as if she rather liked its words than otherwise, and went home again.' Troy, unlike Bathsheba, never realizes that independence involves responsibility and order.

The laughter of an absurd universe which constantly opposes Troy's self-importance is realized in a cluster of images that defines his attitude to reality. It is heard first in Chapter xi, 'hardly distinguishable from the tiny whirlpools outside', and realized finally in the grotesque gurgoyle that creates another whirlpool on Fanny's grave. The chuckling of the two 'bowed and toothless old almsmen' in All Saints modulates into the cosmic mockery of the gurgoyle, whose 'lower row of teeth was quite washed away'. Time itself is distorted: visibly, in the grotesque shapes of the clockwork mannikin and gurgoyle which embody time's revenge on Troy's illusion that past errors can be retrieved, and warn him, in vain, not to let time and chance direct his actions; and aurally, in the very movement of the prose. The coarse directness of 'The gurgoyle spat' develops into a rhythmic spate, and in Chapter xi Troy's suspense, and the reader's, is sustained by recounting in detail the mechanism of the striking of the hours, halves, and quarters in language that is heavy with consonants and monosyllables.

Troy's first encounter with Bathsheba is seen as a grotesque distortion of surface reality. One has only to compare Chapter xxiv with the first meeting of Dorothea and Casaubon in George Eliot's *Middlemarch* to notice how Hardy has changed the appearance of the world of common experience to bring out the deeper reality, the 'real feelings and volitions' of Bathsheba's relation to Troy. Dorothea meets her future husband at dinner with her uncle. Her false estimate of Casaubon arises out of trivial table talk about home and political economy. Her practical sister's comment on his looks and lack of social graces fixes him in George Eliot's world of prosaic reality and measures the extent of Dorothea's illusion. Bathsheba's walk round the farm begins in the familiar world of cows that can be identified in the darkness by mundane sounds, friendly contact, visual memory of features, and individual names. The fir plantation through which she then passes, a 'vast, low, naturally formed hall' with a 'plumy ceiling' and yielding carpet of 'dead spikelets and mildewed cones' takes her gradually on a Jungian night journey from the familiar world of everyday experience to a grotesque, irrational, Kafkaesque expression of subconscious motives and warnings. Her first encounter with Troy is of touch. Its violence, which 'nearly threw Bathsheba off her balance', is sexual. The phallic spur caught in the soft tissues of her dress (which, as Hardy has remarked earlier, is part of a woman's personality) define Bathsheba's attraction to Troy as a wish for domination by the virile male 'cockbird' rather than its rationalization as 'It was a fatal omission of Boldwood's that he had never once told her she was beautiful.' The dialogue which rises out of the darkness expresses the primal recognition of sex between Man and Woman.

> ' "We have got hitched together somehow, I think."
> "Yes."
> "Are you a woman?"
> "Yes."
> "A lady, I should have said."
> "It doesn't matter."
> "I am a man." '

Finally, the flamboyant scarlet figure revealed by the lantern, which 'had upon her the effect of a fairy transformation', joins with the dazzled Bathsheba in a Gothic dance of shadows that warns of the suffering in store if they persist in a relationship that breeds distorted vision. The lantern

> 'radiated upwards into their faces, and sent over half the plantation gigantic shadows of both man and woman, each dusky shape becoming distorted and mangled upon the tree-trunks till it wasted to nothing.'

Hardy constantly draws attention to Troy's military dress as a visible symbol of his relationship to nature. In its realistic aspect of army uniform, it opposes the rootlessness of the soldier to a way of life rooted in seasonal ritual. The red coat, alien to the landscape with which Oak's working clothes harmonize, carries traditional charges of danger, death, pride, and passion. It also carries diabolic overtones. Troy has touches of the resistless demon lover, the devil's sudden appearances and disguises (soldier, civilian, haymaker, Dick Turpin), the devil's luck and the devil's trickery in his cruel teasing of Boldwood in Chapter xxxiv. The grotesque pictorial composition that meets Oak's gaze in the barn, focused on the Mephistophelian figure of Troy,

'. . . the wretched persons of all the work-folk, the hair of their heads at such low levels being suggestive of mops and brooms. In the midst of these shone red and distinct the figure of Sergeant Troy, leaning back in a chair . . .'

suggests the devil's power to distort human dignity. It is a striking contrast to the previous picture of genuine though precarious harmony at the Shearing feast, where Bathsheba and Boldwood at the peak of their relationship are framed by the window, with Oak accompanying them, outside, on his flute. The soldier is death to the farm. The 'Soldier's Joy' with which he profanes the harvest home, enforcing it with threats of dismissal, violates traditional customs and responsibilities and the spontaneity of rustic music, seen in its true function both at the shearing feast and Bathsheba's wedding to Oak. His sword as an instrument of deception and destruction carries an implied contrast with Gabriel's lance—borrowed, significantly, from Boldwood—which heals the stricken sheep and saves the economy of the farm. It places him as a human agent of cosmic dissonance. The 'deathy' cuts of the sword exercise are recalled in Chapter xxxvii by the 'dance of death' of an infuriated universe, described in terms of mailed armies and military manoeuvres. The distortion he has created by his drunken revel has entered the cosmos. 'The night had a haggard look, like a sick thing.'

Boldwood's tragic distortion of reality compels comparison with Troy's. He too enters the story as a voice, but a voice sharply distinguished from the outside world, not reproaching Fanny, but asking kindly for news of her. His first appearance at the Corn Exchange picks out his Roman features and erect carriage as components of his pre-eminent trait, dignity. He is a more worthy man than Troy, yet his kind of inflexibility leads to a self-absorbed concern with his own image that links him to the playboy. His mirror reflection in Chapter xiv (compare Bathsheba's colourful image) is 'wan in expression, and insubstantial in form'. Together with his various settings, it defines his defective vision of physical reality as an inversion of life. As the valentine rests on 'a time-piece, surmounted by a spread eagle'—suggestive not only of Roman dignity but also of 'the symmetry of his existence' which he felt 'to be slowly getting distorted in the direction of an ideal passion', the reflected moonlight

'had that reversed direction which snow gives, coming upward and lighting up his ceiling in an unnatural way, casting shadows in strange places, and putting lights where shadows had used to be'.

His vision is blocked prophetically by a correlative of blind and death-marked passion. 'The large red seal became as a blot of blood on the retina of his eye.' It fixes the natural features of the snowy landscape in a frozen 'glaze'. 'Withered grass-bents, encased in icicles, bristled through the smooth wan coverlet in the twisted and curved shapes of old Venetian glass'. The brittle rigidity of old Venetian glass, not of stone pillars, suggests the fragility of Boldwood's mental balance. But a brilliant modulation of the unnatural 'rayless' sun (which recalls by contrast Gabriel's smiling face) 'like a red and flameless fire shining over a white hearthstone', introduces the reality against which Boldwood's inversion is measured. 'On the ridge, up against the blazing sky, a figure . . . like the black snuff in the midst of a candle-flame', the eternal shepherd Gabriel Oak, creates order as the snuff vitalizes and controls the candle-flame, and directs the chapter to the life-giving warmth of 'the scarlet and orange glow' inside Warren's.

Boldwood's interest—good for the serial—as a man on the dangerous edge of things is heightened emotionally by Hardy's presentation of his solitary figure against dawns and sunsets of unpredictable weather. As chaos is Troy's element, extremity is Boldwood's. Chapter XVIII, which shows him in his element, suggests the nature of the subconscious disturbance that is to overthrow his fine 'balance of enormous antagonistic forces.' His round of the stables recalls Bathsheba's round of the cowsheds before her ill-fated liaison. But thoroughbred horses are more delicately balanced than cows: their contented munching is varied by 'the restless and shadowy figure of a colt' who mirrors 'the celibate' restlessly pacing 'his almonry and cloister'. The religious image, the traditional association of horses with the extremes of sexual and imaginative power, the poles of stillness and restlessness that constitute the atmosphere, define Boldwood's tragic flaw as similar to

Angel Clare's—a devotion to the absolute ideal at the expense of suppression of the flesh. His wild happiness at the prospect of 'six years of intangible ethereal courtship' and the psychotic clothes fetishism are correlative to his desire to worship Bathsheba's image in place of the flesh and blood woman.

Outside his cloister, in the social or natural world, he is ill at ease. When all nature is bursting with new life, 'Boldwood went *meditating* down the slopes with his eyes on his boots, which the yellow pollen from the buttercups had bronzed in artistic gradations.' (My italics.) Scenes of social ineptness stress his unfitness for the world of human concerns. He is forced to ask whether Bathsheba is considered handsome, and whether any late tie-knot is in fashion. Even Troy in Chapter XXXIV shows up his scheme to bargain with human counters.

' "Bad as I am, I am not such a villain as to make the marriage or misery of any woman a matter of huckster and sale . . . You say you love Bathsheba; yet on the merest apparent evidence you instantly believe in her dishonour. A fig for such love!" '

His self-consuming passion abstracts dignity from the man and responsibility from the farmer. The tragic picture in XXXVIII of the solitary self-alienated man in the rain that has ruined his crops through his neglect of husbandry, is an effective comment on Boldwood's unbalanced view of reality.

Fanny Robin's relationship to nature is marked by assimilation. Always alone, usually anonymous—she is described as 'a form', 'the shape', 'the blurred spot', 'a mere shade upon the earth', 'the woman', 'the wayfarer', 'the pedestrian', 'a shapeless heap', 'the panting heap of clothes'—slight and colourless against a colourless indifferent expanse of earth, she inherits the common burden of journeying, death, dissolution into the elements, and transformation. She melts into the shade of a tree and evolves out of the snowy landscape as imperceptibly as a snowflake. Chapter XI consists largely of mood-painting details that build up to a general poetic impression of the basic human predicament. The natural transformations that mark the changes of the seasons, ending inevitably in 'an obliteration by snow', the null snow-covered moor—'its irregularities were forms without features; suggestive of anything, proclaiming nothing'; the flatness of the river, the vertical mass of wall that is part of Troy's unresponsiveness; the muffled bell, the darkness and drabness, make up an oppressive image of the negation of human significance by the density of physical matter, against which Fanny's weak aim at her lover's window is inadequate.

Yet Chapter XL defines the anonymous woman as a significant human being by virtue of her ability to make use of nature. The only action of the chapter is that a dying pregnant woman covers two miles of highway to the workhouse. But interest is sustained by constant tension between the 'blind obtuseness of inanimate things' and the Oak-like ingenuity of the girl to direct nature. The crust of cloud shuts out 'every speck of heaven': no superhuman help will guide her to the earthly 'haven of rest' marked by the Casterbridge aurora. Contrasts between light and darkness, silence and sound—the attenuated clock striking one, the dull boom of the morning wind over the flats, the funereal note of the fox's bark, her own voice encouraging herself and the dog—stress her isolation in a non-human world. Her actions are described in short direct statements from the outside, with Brechtian alienation. As she selects sticks for crutches, she begins to control her environment by 'feeling with her hands.' The phrase links her to Gabriel Oak, who worked entirely by feeling with his hands, an image of human ignorance and intelligence, in the darkness of the storm, to repair another consequence of Troy's carelessness. The link with Oak, Hardy's measure of man's adjustment to nature, implies criticism of Fanny's earlier compliance. Her heroic efforts to save herself and her baby—too late—suggest that arriving at the right church should not have been beyond her capacity.

When her physical aids fail, Fanny demonstrates the power of mind over matter. When 'the faculty of contrivance was worn out', help appears from nature. Hardy's dog, as might be expected, is a real dog, 'as homeless as she', and frantic with distress when Fanny falters. His fate at the end of the chapter comments on man's inhumanity and ignorance of the potentialities of lower nature directed by human intelligence. But Hardy's double vision endows a suffering fellow-creature with mythical overtones. Like Fanny, he is anonymous, 'being thus assignable to no breed'. He is 'a portion of shade' which detaches itself from 'the stripe of shadow' on the bridge. 'Night, in its sad, solemn, and benevolent aspect, apart from its stealthy and cruel side, was personified in this form.' Jungians would recognize him as a projection of the subconscious reserves of power that rise from stress and despair to order a transformation of personality. The dog in Egyptian mythology is the divine helper and sacred animal of death. This mysterious helper from the lower world leads Fanny towards the death that transforms her scarcely perceptible life into an instrument of dramatic power.

Fanny's 'resurrection' as a power from the grave is stressed ritually by the association of her death with flowers. They are the sign of Troy's repentance, and Bathsheba's atonement to the dead girl in Chapter XLII: and Bathsheba gives orders, reminiscent of Ophelia's death, that the new spring waggon, washed very clean, which carries her body should be covered in hardy flowers and various evergreens. The result of Fanny's power is to make the other characters realize their unimportance in the cosmic scheme. Her first victim is Joseph Poorgrass. His 'pale companion' joins with the monotonous enveloping fog—a typically Fanny Robin scene—to rob him of his sense of identity. Its restoration at the Buck's Head leads to the discovery that inspires Bathsheba's wild, egoistic bid for Troy's attention by the open coffin, Troy's departure and return, and Boldwood's final act of madness.

Fanny Robin and Oak, while involved with the fortunes of the tragic trio of unadjusted lovers, are also part of that aspect of Wessex evoked by Hardy's chorus of rustics. Fanny belongs to their class, and when she moves out of it to follow Troy and initiate the tragedy Hardy stresses her isolation by juxtaposing Chapters VII, XI, XVI, XL–XLII with scenes that portray the communal life of rural Wessex. Gabriel Oak, on the other hand, is to be found taking an active part in these choric scenes of rural gossip, work, play, and ritual. He is accepted as an equal and part of the traditional scene because the old maltster, symbol of natural continuance with 'his frosty white hair and beard overgrowing his gnarled figure like the grey moss and lichen upon a leafless appletree', 'knowed yer grandfather for years and years!' and the features of the local landscape which are a shared heritage. He shares with them the sheep-washing, shearing and other seasonal rituals that control the rhythms and crises of the story, and as 'a clever man in talents' takes charge of their confused fire-fighting and the muddle caused by Joseph's multiplying eye.

The functions of Hardy's rustic chorus have often been appreciated, and its loss felt in *Tess of the d'Urbervilles* and *Jude the Obscure* as a loss of humour and balance. It has a poetic function. The lyrical and meditative poetry of the countryman's close involvement with nature and the basic realities presents the ultimates of immutability in the human situation, to set off the passionate search for personal stability through love that moves the more sensitive characters to strange and momentous actions. The rustics are a natural outgrowth of the 'functional continuity' of the medieval shearing barn, for both 'embodied practices which had suffered no mutilation at the hands of time'—the long perspective of birth, marriage, death, ritual, superstition, and custom that make up the Wessex past, so changeless that the rooting of an apple-tree and the pulling down of a wooden cider-house are taken as evidence of 'stirring times'. Occasionally they commit or fail to commit an action that changes the tenor of the story. Joseph's weakness at the Buck's Head and Liddy's encouragement of Bathsheba's whim to send the valentine are trivial actions that enliven the monotonous daily round but have tragic consequences. (Liddy, as Bathsheba's confidante, has a multiple function. Her shallowness and dependence on Bathsheba's favour make her an unsafe guide for superior minds to follow, as in the valentine episode. Her attempts to keep on the right side of her mistress while passing the judgement of common humanity on her behaviour, as in Chapter xxx; her symbolic negotiation of the swamp in ignorance of its existence in Chapter xliv, and her parody of her mistress' airs in Chapters x, make her an effective foil to Bathsheba's wise and foolish actions.)

Hardy has no illusions that his rustics live in a golden age. Their confusion does nothing to fight fire or storm, and wastes precious minutes while the sheep are in the clover and Troy is on his way to Boldwood's party. But their chief function is not to act, but to be. Their conversation, full of a pithy humour and proverbial wisdom that is Shakespearean as well as Hardeian, builds up a poetic texture of simple eternal values to live by that make limited opportunities endurable. It ranges widely through birth and death, love and marriage, the strange behaviour of their superiors and Providence, religion of church and chapel and the more pagan religion evinced by a wealth of superstition and ritual, the wonders of the city of Bath transformed by their miraculous expectations, to the local hero-myths—Joseph's encounter with the owl, Pa'son Thirdly's charity, Farmer Everdene's ruse to keep himself faithful—which build up a sense of man's significance. Their kindly if sometimes exaggerated appreciation of rustic talent—Gabriel's learning and performance on the flute, Joseph's efforts at ballad-singing, even Pennyways' unwonted honesty at the shearing supper—shows a respect for the 'otherness' of people which Troy and Boldwood never learn. Their insistence on marks of individuality—(which Hardy presents, as he presents the jackaclock and gurgoyle, with a relish for the strange manifestation) the maltster's age, Joseph's shyness, Jacob's milestone-like tooth, Henery Fray's eccentric spelling and intimations of wasted genius—are the marks of self-sufficiency which constitute their defiance of darkness; a self-sufficiency which the modern habit of taking too much thought has undermined.

The story of *Far from the Madding Crowd* plots the tragic cross-purposes of five people fighting for happiness through love. The poetic aspects of the underpattern 'intensify the expression of things . . . so that the heart and inner meaning is made vividly visible'. The vivid visibility of what the action *means* is achieved through the organization of the novel like a poem through interconnecting ideas, images, and phrases; through the vitality of figure, metaphor, and simile taken from nature and art; through intensely dramatic and sometimes grotesque scenes charged with inherent emotion and the mystery of subconscious impulses leaping theatrically to the surface, set against a running river of quiet lyric meditation on old ways and changeless things; through moments of spiritual revelation rising out of sense experience of the physical world. It is backed up aurally by personal rhythms of speech and gesture (worth noting are Boldwood's gradual disintegration from the solemnity of his first proposal to his disjointed outpourings and feverish search for reassurance in the later part of the novel; and Bathsheba's varying speech patterns in her talk to Liddy and the rustics, her skittish play with Oak changing to mature respect, and the verbal love-fencing with Troy that ends in confused submission) counterpointing the larger rhythms of seasonal ebb and flow punctuated by crises of human emotion that temporarily impose a different rhythm, as in Chapters XI and XXXIV. Hardy's stern moral comment on the failure of all but Oak to control reality underlines the insignificance of their struggles to an indifferent universe. But the poetic relation to environment of these ephemeral creatures living and suffering in a remote part of Wessex lifts their story onto the cosmic plane of archetypal conflict of great ultimates—chaos and order, adjustment and non-adjustment, suffering and peace, tragedy and comedy, good and evil, and life and death.

The Return of the Native:
A Novel of Environment

The Return of the Native strikes a harsher note than *Far from the Madding Crowd*. Egdon Heath, the resistant matter of the cosmos on which the action takes place, bears, shapes, nourishes, and kills conscious organisms possessed of its striving will without its unconsciousness of suffering. The six main characters take their key from Egdon. They all feel its pull through some affinity of temperament. Clym, Mrs Yeobright and Diggory Venn share its look of isolation; Thomasin, Clym and Venn its endurance; Eustacia and Wildeve, though they hate it, share its primal vitality and indifference to others. The rustics, too, take a more subdued tone from the heath. The accent of their talk falls on time passing, change and decay. Their environment is one in which change and chance, death and darkness, prevail, and 'the overpowering of the fervid by the inanimate' is a recognized conclusion to human effort.

It is fashionable in this denigrating age to decry Hardy's description of the heath in Chapter 1 as pretentious. An earlier critic was nearer the mark in likening it to the entry of the Gods in Wagner. Large orchestras are not out of place in making the power of cosmic forces felt on the pulse. Egdon is presented as a visual correlative of space and time and the modern view of life 'as a thing to be put up with'. It is characteristic of Hardy's poetic style to begin with the specific—'A Saturday afternoon in November'—and widen the local view gradually to a philosophic vision of cosmic processes which the heath has power to affect:

'The face of the heath by its mere complexion added half an hour to evening; it could in like manner retard the dawn, sadden noon, anticipate the frowning of storms scarcely generated, and intensify the opacity of a moonless midnight to a cause of shaking and dread.'

The description of the heath in terms of a face, 'a face on which time makes but little impression', which will later be recalled by the face (Clym's) on which time has recorded disillusive experience, introduces the theme of shape that opposes the chaos of Egdon's primal matter. But in this first chapter the details emphasize storm and darkness. Jungians will recognize in Hardy's hint of the tragic climax the subconscious hinterland of elemental myth that presents man's painful predicament in relation to a demonic landscape of barren earth, isolating wind, stormy water, and creative/destructive fire.

'The storm was its lover, and the wind its friend. Then it became the home of strange phantoms; and it was found to be the hitherto unrecognized original of those wild regions of obscurity which are vaguely felt to be compassing us about in midnight dreams of flight and disaster, and are never thought of after the dream till revived by scenes like this.'

Its 'Titanic form' widens the perspective still further to invest the heath with heroic echoes of classical myth; particularly the Prometheus myth of rebellion against darkness. There is a swing back again, characteristic of Hardy's poetic method, from these long philosophical perspectives to 'intelligible facts regarding landscape', its emotional and practical connection with man and his efforts to civilize it. The evocation ends with another swing from localized human vision to a vista of geological aeons. The Latinate dignity of the language, the balanced pauses, the unhurried rhythm, the slow build-up of paragraph structure, enact a persistent hammering at intractable physical substance which is part of the character and theme of Egdon.

'The great inviolate place had an ancient permanence which the sea cannot claim. Who can say of a particular sea that it is old? Distilled by the sun, kneaded by the moon, it is renewed in a year, in a day, or in an hour. The sea changed, the fields changed, the rivers, the villages, and the people changed, yet Egdon remained. Those surfaces were neither so steep as to be destructible by weather, nor so flat as to be the victims of floods and deposits. With the exception of an aged highway, and a still more aged barrow . . . themselves almost crystallized to natural products by long continuance—even the trifling irregularities were not caused by pickaxe, plough, or spade, but remained as the very fingertouches of the last geological change.'

The Return of the Native is concerned with the Promethean struggle of conscious life against the unconscious 'rayless' universe from which it sprang. The poetic-dramatic structure of the first chapters initiates the underlying metaphor of the novel, the ancient conflict of light and darkness. The white man-made road that crosses the brown heath, the red glow of bonfires, the 'blood-coloured' figure of Diggory Venn, challenge the dark drabness of the earth.

'To light a fire is the instinctive and resistant act of man when, at the winter ingress, the curfew is sounded throughout Nature. It indicates a spontaneous, Promethean rebelliousness against the fiat that this re-current season shall bring foul times, cold darkness, misery and death. Black chaos comes, and the fettered gods of the earth say, Let there be light.'

The almost supernatural figure of Diggory Venn modulates be-tween the heath and the human beings whose desire for joy and purpose troubles the scene. He is dyed into an identification of the heath and its products. Yet his conspicuous fiery colour suggests a character that will master reality through involvement with it.

Chapter II begins with one of Hardy's familiar images of the human condition, the meeting of two lonely figures on a deserted road. One wonders about the meaning of the two walking figures and the woman concealed in the van. The chapter ends with an-other anonymous figure rising from the central point of Rain-barrow as the apex of plain, hill, and tumulus. Between the two scenes of human interest stands the modulating chord of the heath. Hardy is careful to plant his descriptions of scene where they will direct emotion. The reader's eye is forced to follow the reddle-man's musing survey upwards from the 'speck on the road' that defines the vanishing Captain to the protruberance of the barrow and the ambiguous potential of the crowning figure to make or mar human significance.

The shifting perspective, that enlarges and diminishes the human figure ('a spike from a helmet', 'the only obvious justi-fication of [the hills'] outline', 'it descended . . . with the glide of a water-drop down a bud'), and transforms the barrow itself from 'a wart on an Atlantean brow' to 'the pole and axis of this heathery world', leaves in suspension the comparative significance of scene and human actors. The figure of unknown potential has been associated with the Celts who built the barrow as a bulwark of order against chaos; but what it marks is a place of death. It gives a perfect aesthetic finish to the mass; yet the Greek ideal of perfect beauty has been defined in Chapter I as an anachronism. As it disappears, the surprise of the movement where all seemed fixity stresses the function of human consciousness on the natural scene. It can change and be changed.

Change is the keynote of the distanced 'sky-backed pantomime of silhouettes' which replaces the composition of barrow and lonely figure. In Chapter III the focus shifts from the permanent mass of the heath, with solitary wanderers crawling like ants over its surface and the still figure on its central point, to a firelit impression of movement and evanescence.

'All was unstable; quivering as leaves, evanescent as lightning. Shadowy eye-sockets, deep as those of a death's head, suddenly turned into pits of lustre: a lantern-jaw was cavernous, then it was shining; wrinkles were emphasized to ravines, or obliterated entirely by a changed ray.'

Stillness gives way to motion; the solitary figure reaching for the sky to several 'burdened figures' bowed down under the furze they carry, playing out the next stage of human development. The pyramid-shaped bonfire they build to top the barrow enacts a wordless ritual of human function to shape and control. The heath, detached from them by the radiant circle of light they have created, becomes the 'vast abyss' of Milton's, Dante's and Homer's hell. By implication, the distorted human features evoke tormented souls acting out a timeless doom.

Hardy modulates from ritual to the human plane by bringing the fragmented Grandfer Cantle gradually forward from the composition to speak and act as a mortal limited by time and the need for warmth and self-assertion. The elemental ritual of light and darkness recedes as the kindly rustic voices gather strength. But it remains in the imagination to colour the talk of local human concerns with its larger rhythms. The conflict of wills that emerges from the gossip about Mrs Yeobright forbidding the banns, Tamsin's rash choice of Wildeve, Wildeve's character and attainments, the criticism of Eustacia's non-communal bonfire, the anticipation of Clym's Promethean role—'What a dog he used to be for bonfires!'—the nostalgia for youth and quiet acceptance of death as part of the seasonal cycle: all are marked with the preceding evocation of the limitations of the earth and the desire to transcend them; the fire of life and passion and the distortion of reality it brings with its comfort; the double vision of man's speck-like insignificance on the face of the heath and the poetic light that gives his ephemeral features the eternal grandeur of ravines and caverns.

The human drama evolves, as it were, from the scene and its implications. The character of Egdon encourages resistance and determines the kind of action that can take place within its bounds. Isolation fosters Eustacia's attraction to Clym and to a man of inferior calibre, the misunderstanding between Clym and his mother, the misapprehension about Mrs Yeobright's guineas. The openness of the country enables bonfire signals to be seen for miles; and kills Mrs Yeobright after her exhausting walk from one isolated cottage to another. Much of the action consists of solitary journeys across the heath to keep up communications or assignations, to spy out the land, or pursue erring mortals who have lost their way literally and figuratively on the dark criss-crossing paths that become symbolic of their antagonistic purposes. The presence of the vast passionless heath puts the human movements into perspective as the scurrying of ephemeral ants.

The plot resembles *Far from the Madding Crowd* in the tragic chain of love relationships and the situation of Wildeve, the gay man vacillating between the innocent girl he is engaged to and the woman of greater passion and complexity. The pattern is again complicated by an idealist with an obsession, though Clym Yeobright's ambition, unlike Boldwood's, is unconnected with the irrational force of sexual love. Mrs Yeobright adds another colour to the figure in the carpet in the conflict between generations and their ideals of progress. As usual, the poetic stylization contributes to meaning. Douglas Brown (op. cit.) notes that

'the very grouping of the protagonists tells much. On one far side is Thomasin ("All similes concerning her began and ended with birds") and on the other, Wildeve, the ineffectual engineer, invading the country to become a publican. Clym (the native home from exile) and Eustacia (seeking exile, and confusing that with home) stand between them. At the centre, between Clym and Eustacia, Mrs Yeobright is subtly placed, a countrywoman upholding urban attitudes whose true nature and effect she cannot perceive.'

R. W. Stallman, in his ingenious article 'Hardy's Hour-Glass Novel' (*Sewanee Review*, LV, 1947) sees in the novel a chain of seven 'hour-glass' plots, in which Fate keeps turning the hour-glass over to reverse events, situations, and partners.

The tragic action was designed originally to lead to the double death in the weir, involving the earlier tragedy of Mrs. Yeobright's death. The original five-part structure, the strict regard for unities of place, time (the year and a day of folklore quest) and action, may recall Shakespearean and Classical drama. The two signal fires are the novel's poles of time and action, and Rainbarrow its axis in space. But such stylization is part of Hardy's normal poetic technique. The five parts clearly graph the stages in the inter-related love affairs, and the disillusionment which reality brings to Eustacia's romantic dreams of happiness and Clym's dreams of finding a purpose.

Book First introduces the three women whose relationship to the two men is to promote a tragic antagonism of ideals. The wedding complications of Tamsin and Wildeve introduce the blind obstruc-tiveness of things (the marriage licence, and the subconscious reluctance of Wildeve that allowed the mistake to happen; Mrs Yeobright's 'Such things don't happen for nothing' anticipates the psychology of Freudian error), and the countermoves of human intelligence (Mrs Yeobright's unscrupulous use of Venn as a rival lover to bring Wildeve to heel, and Venn's active determination to look after Tamsin's interests). Book Second, 'The Arrival', re-solves the marriage complications and changes the emotional cur-rent by the return of Clym Yeobright. Interest is sustained by the potential of conflict and attraction between a man who has re-jected the worldly vanity of Paris and a woman for whom he repre-sents an avenue of escape to its delights. Book Third, 'The Fasci-nation', charts the blind sexual attraction between Clym and Eustacia, each a distorted projection of fulfilment to the other, and the serious division it causes between Clym and his mother. Mrs Yeobright's attempt to heal the breach by her gift of money to Tamsin and Clym sows the seeds of the catastrophe by a combina-tion of carelessness (she entrusts the money to the weak-witted Christian Cantle), blind chance (Wildeve wins the guineas from Cantle), and ignorance (Venn does not know that half the money he wins back from Wildeve was destined for Clym).

Book Fourth, 'The Closed Door', shows more than one door closing on human possibilities. Clym's blindness limits his ambi-tions to knowledge of a few square feet of furze. Simultaneously it dashes Eustacia's hopes of escaping Egdon through Clym, and sends her back to Wildeve. Wildeve's presence in the cottage with Eustacia when Mrs Yeobright calls keeps the door closed against her, and Clym's heavy sleep is another closed door. Hope of reconciliation is closed for ever by Mrs Yeobright's lonely death on the heath. But Johnny Nunsuch's dramatic restatement of Mrs Yeobright's words, 'she said I was to say that I had seed her, and she was a broken-hearted woman and cast off by her son' opens the door to Clym's painful discovery in Book Fifth of the circumstances of her death and Eustacia's part in it. 'The Discovery' charts the steps Clym takes to find out the truth, and the Oedipus-like irony that each step he takes drives him deeper into a hell of remorse, self-knowledge, and division from the other woman he loves. The final step drives Eustacia from his anger to seek escape through Wildeve, and to a despairing death with him in storm and darkness.

Hardy gave way to editorial necessity and common probability to add Book Sixth, which presents 'the inevitable movement onward' that restores order after tragic catastrophe. Tamsin and Diggory Venn find happiness in marriage, and Clym partial fulfilment as an itinerant preacher, to the accompaniment of the rituals of May Day and the waxing of a feather bed for the married pair, which involve them all in the seasonal rite of fertility and regeneration.

One can point to the usual incidents in the working out of plot which compel comparisons vital to structure. The different purposes, selfish and altruistic, which motivate the characters to seek conflicting manifestations of fulfilment; which animate the various figures who crown Rainbarrow, and inspire the lonely journeys taken across the heath, are worth close study. The different attitudes to Egdon and its limitations and traditions are embodied, as Dr Beatty has shown, in Hardy's descriptions of Mistover Knap and Blooms-End. Captain Vye's house at Mistover Knap has 'the appearance of a fortification'. Blooms-End is separated from the heath only by a row of white palings and a little garden (which orders nature by control, not defence). The traditional mummers find a warm welcome at Blooms-End, the family home of the Yeobrights; while 'for mummers and mumming Eustacia had the greatest contempt'. At Blooms-End, the loft over the fuel-house 'was lighted by a semicircular hole, through which the pigeons crept to their lodgings in the same high quarters of the premises', and the sun irradiated Tamsin as she selected apples from their natural packing of fern, with 'pigeons . . . flying about her head with the greatest unconcern'. At the fuel-house of Mistover Knap, the outsider Eustacia looks in from the darkness at the mummers' rehearsal to relieve her boredom, through 'a small rough hole in the mud wall, originally made for pigeons', but now disused, and the building is lit from the inside.

What the contrasts reveal is that all the stylizations draw their meaning from the underpattern of conflicting light and dark. This central opposition moves the conflict between Clym and Eustacia, to which all the other characters stand in dramatic relationship. Their association with the elemental forces in conflict is defined by the fire and light images which identify them with the Promethean myth, and the images of darkness and death that endow Eustacia additionally with some of the attributes of Persephone Queen of the Shades.

The different manifestations of light and fire which define the characters also define their responses to the leitmotif question 'What is doing well?' Wildeve has the 'curse of inflammability'; Eustacia is a smouldering subterranean fire reaching by blind instinct for the sun; they snatch at the heat of momentary passion in a rebellion that speaks to the twentieth-century rebellion against the permanence of things. Clym's way of opposing the gods of darkness is to bring light rather than fire to mankind. (The name 'Yeobright' is significant in both its parts.) Tamsin is marked by the image of benevolent sunshine. Mrs Yeobright, who has ignored the primitive power of the cosmos in her 'civilized' desires for Clym's advancement, meets death by fire in a parched waste land with a poisonous serpent and a sun that foreshadows the hostile antagonist of Camus' *The Outsider*. Diggory Venn is permeated with the colour of fire, and shares the craft and symbolic ambiguity of the early fire-god Loki. Fire as an answer to darkness can be creative or destructive; an instrument of mastery or chaos. The scenes that carry the underpattern show the characters acting out their ritual roles as bringers of light or darkness to the pattern of human fate.

Clym Yeobright plays the double role of Promethean hero and ironic parody of primitive heroic attitudes. There is no doubt about his altruistic Promethean aspirations. 'The deity that lies ignominiously chained within an ephemeral human carcase shone out of him like a ray'. His absence has taught him that Egdon realities are realities the world over. Yet the context in which we first see Clym at close quarters (Book Second, vi) qualifies our approval of his aim to teach the Egdon eremites 'how to breast the misery they are born to'. At the Blooms-End Christmas party the snug picture framed by the settle does not show much evidence of misery.

'At the other side of the chimney stood the settle, which is the necessary supplement to a fire so open that nothing less than a strong breeze will carry up the smoke. It is, to the hearths of old-fashioned cavernous fireplaces, what the east belt of trees is to the exposed country estate, or the north wall to the garden. Outside the settle candles gutter, locks of hair wave, young women shiver, and old men sneeze. Inside is Paradise. Not a symptom of a draught disturbs the air; the sitters' backs are as warm as their faces, and songs and old tales are drawn from the occupants by the comfortable heat, like fruit from melon-plants in a frame.'

Hardy's selection of concrete detail to build up poetic mood and sequence takes us from the physical effects of the coldness outside to the simple statement that sums up human yearning for fulfilment, 'Inside was Paradise'. The simile of melon-plants in a frame clinches the natural sequence of comfort and growth that order this earthly Paradise—which Clym would jump in his ascetic plans for higher development.

'To argue upon the possibility of culture before luxury to the bucolic world may be to argue truly, but it is an attempt to disturb a sequence to which humanity has been long accustomed.'

Outside the ordered frame of unreflective comfort are Clym, who has passed beyond it, and Eustacia, who has not yet reached it. The conjunction of traditional scene of conviviality, blind animal will to enjoy that has motivated Eustacia's presence, and Clym's 'typical countenance of the future' marked by consciousness of man's tragic predicament in an uncaring universe, questions whether modern perceptiveness may be an unmixed blessing to men untouched by the disillusive centuries and adapted to the world they live in.

Clym's troubles spring from his failure to respect the laws of physical reality. His blindness is both a natural consequence of ignoring physical strain on his eyes, a simplification of the modern complexity of life which denies him 'any more perfect insight into the conditions of existence', and a complex poetic symbol of the figurative blindness displayed by this representative of 'modern perceptiveness' who 'loved his kind', to the needs of the individuals closest to him, and to the nature of his illusions. He is blind to the reality which is in the heath, himself, his mother, Eustacia, and the 'Egdon eremites' he had come to teach how to bear it. He meets its obstructiveness in the common resistance to the kind of progress that jumps the stage of social advance, in the irrational demands of sexual love, in the reality of Eustacia's primitive nature that runs counter to his projected image of her (a fault that makes him brother to Angel Clare and Knight). His sense of affinity with the dead and virgin moonscape (Book Third, iv), and the appearance of the 'cloaked figure' of Eustacia, who is repeatedly associated with night, death, and the moon, at the base of Rainbarrow simultaneously with the eclipse ('for the remote celestial phenomenon had been pressed into sublunary service as a lover's signal') are correlative to his destructive and self-destructive attachment to Absolute Reality.

The failure of Clym's Promethean aim leads one to consider his role as an ironic reversal of the traditional hero-myth. R. Carpenter, in *Thomas Hardy*, sees the heroic archetype in Clym's quest for meaning. His originality is recognized at an early age, he serves his apprenticeship in a foreign land guarding treasure, and becomes possessed of deeper knowledge which he wishes to pass on to his people. His temporary withdrawal from the world suggests the initiation of a sun-god-hero into a religious cult. He returns to his birthplace, a dark and fallen world (Tartarus, the prison of the exiled Titans) but is not really recognized. He is diverted from his quest by a dark and beautiful enchantress against the wishes of his goddess mother, undergoes a period of spiritual trial and is symbolically blinded, like Oedipus and Milton's Samson, so that he may achieve true insight. The counterpointing strain of the hero who triumphs over obstacles to shape destiny, questions the validity, to the modern mind aware of 'the obstructive coil of things', of simple heroic resistance. To Louis Crompton ('The Sunburnt God: Ritual and Tragic Myth in *The Return of the Native*', *Boston University Studies in English*, iv, 1960) Clym is a compound of the free hero of romance, the hero of classical tragedy, subject to fate and moral judgement, whose *hubris* leads to his downfall, and the diminished hero of modern realism, subject to biological and economic laws which limit human responsibility. But the wry comment on ancient heroic standards should not hide the genuine heroism achieved by a man who must painfully scale down his notions of progress to the limitations that condition the slow rate of evolutionary change. ('This was not the repose of actual stagnation, but the apparent repose of incredible slowness.')

The new concept of heroic action redefines Clym's quest as the quest of fallen man to re-establish harmony with nature. Clym takes his first steps towards Paradise regained when he accepts his primitive roots, puts on his old brown clothes, and becomes of no more account than a parasitic insect fretting the surface of the heath. Knowledge is redefined, in a poetic passage that emphasizes each unit of the physical scene with a major stress and pause, as 'having no knowledge of anything in the world but fern, furze, heath, lichens, and moss'. His movements over the heath, feeling, sensing through the dark, bring an intense regenerative contact with the physical world that is a source of strength in misery, even though conscious man can never achieve complete harmony. Hardy's description of Clym working among the small heath creatures, with its details of colour and movement, its varying rhythms of natural activity, its acceptance of the sun's meaning as simple warmth and beauty for the earth's creatures, its delight in vitality, and its superbly simple climax, celebrates like his poetry an enlargement of the horizon within those limited areas where man can still find certainty.

'His daily life was of a curious microscopic sort, his whole world being limited to a circuit of a few feet from his person. His familiars were creeping and winged things, and they seemed to enrol him in their band. Bees hummed around his ears with an intimate air, and tugged at the heath and furze-flowers at his side in such numbers as to weigh them down to the sod. The strange amber-coloured butterflies which Egdon produced, and which were never seen elsewhere, quivered in the breath of his lips, alighted upon his bowed back, and sported with the glittering point of his hook as he flourished it up and down. Tribes of emerald-green grasshoppers leaped over his feet, falling awkwardly on their backs, heads, or hips, like unskilful acrobats, as chance might rule; or engaged themselves in noisy flirtations under the fern-fronds with silent ones of homely hue. Huge flies, ignorant of larders and wire-netting, and quite in a savage state, buzzed about him without knowing that he was a man. In and out of the fern-dells snakes glided in their most brilliant blue and yellow guise, it being the season immediately following the shedding of their old skins, when their colours are brightest. Litters of young rabbits came out from their forms to sun themselves upon hillocks, the hot beams blazing through the delicate tissue of each thin-fleshed ear, and firing it to a blood-red transparency in which the veins could be seen. None of them feared him.'

Clym has recently been demoted from protagonist, and Eustacia promoted, on the grounds that she has the heroic force which he lacks. But it is surely intentional that a character possessing the animal vitality of a more primitive era should make a greater sensuous impact than the new heroic type, 'slighted and enduring', distinguished by contemplative rather than active heroism. The two characters are perfectly balanced in their vital opposition to carry the meaning of the story.

Eustacia's delineation as 'Queen of Night' indicates her function as a reverse parallel to Clym. Her first and last appearance is on the barrow, house of the dead. She shares, while she suffers from, the heath's darkness, 'Tartarean dignity', indifference, and slumbrous vitality. But her relation to Clym is not a simple opposition of darkness to light. It is also the antagonism of illumination at different stages of development.

The first sentence of Chapter VII, Book First, where she is defined as Queen of Night, stresses the two qualities that associate her on one side with the heath and on the other with the Promethean Clym. 'Eustacia Vye was the raw material of a divinity.' Her animal nature, unreflecting and unpurposive ('she would let events fall out as they might sooner than wrestle to direct them') partakes of the blind chaos of the heath's raw material, which has not yet reached Promethean forethought. The many Classical and Romantic metaphors and the 'geometric precision' of her perfect beauty define Eustacia as an anachronistic reincarnation of the Hellenic age whose 'old-fashioned revelling in the general situation' is being replaced by the record of disillusive time (destroyer of beauty) that scars the other faces, of Clym and the heath. But the subterranean fire of divinity is there, chained to an ideal of fulfilment antagonistic to Clym's and out of tune with the haggard times.

Her poetic context in VI defines the sun she seeks for her soul. The cumulative evocation of the wind over the heath, that begins in distinguishing the special notes of the 'infinitesimal vegetable causes' which harmonize to produce 'the linguistic peculiarity of the heath', and rises to a philosophical contemplation of Infinity as it is made sensuously manifest in the sound of the combined multitudes of mummied heath-bells scoured by the wind, is a rich image that evokes simultaneously the timelessness of nonhuman time that diminishes human importance, against which Eustacia rebels, and the absolute loneliness that is the price of her god-like rejection of human compromise. Her challenge to the forces that render beauty ephemeral is 'a blaze of love, and extinction, . . . better than a lantern glimmer . . . which should last long years', and a too thorough identification, suggested by hour-glass and telescope, with the metaphysic of transience.

Eustacia's will to enjoy in the present moment is the universal thrust of life to grow out of the primal stage of blind, self-absorbed groping towards the sun to a state of being where light, form and meaning are imposed on matter. But she is false to her humanity by acquiescing in the lower state, as Clym is false to his by wanting to jump the intermediate stage of evolution to reach the higher. Consequently her environment controls her as it controls the ear of corn in the ground. The two movements down from and up beyond the human norm meet in a god-like desire for absolute reality, which Hardy's poetic transformations of light into darkness define as a form of the death-wish.

Eustacia's dream (Book Second, III) is the first of a series of related ritual enactments of her subconscious drive to self-destruction. A comparison with her mumming adventure (Book Second, V, VI), the Egdon gipsying (Book Fourth, III) and her death (Book Fifth, VII–IX) reveals the fantastic action of the dream ironically transformed and realized in a complex love/death sequence. The shining knight with whom she dances and plunges into the water is transformed from her Paradisal Clym to the commonplace Wildeve. The visor that hides his face turns into the mummers' ribbons that hide hers, as their true natures are concealed by their projected roles. The ecstatic dance becomes a Dionysiac revel that replaces a 'sense of social order' with the self-destructive sexual impulse. The expected consummation under the pool is revealed first as her ritual death at the hands of the Christian Knight in the mummers' play, and finally as the real embrace of death with Wildeve in the weir, for which her ideal knight is partly responsible. The woman who feels she is in Paradise becomes the woman who is excluded, with Clym, from the earthly Paradise inside the settle. The brilliant rainbow light modulates to the moonlight of the mumming and the gipsying, the familiar illusory moonlight existence of Eustacia's imagination, which stresses the fantastic, trance-like ritual aspect of movement and mask-like features. It resolves finally into the hellish red glow from Susan Nunsuch's cottage that reveals the 'splendid woman' who arraigns the Prince of the World as a mere waxen image of pride and vanity, and reconciles Eustacia's death by water to the death by fire consuming her in effigy. The heath that is only dimly felt in the dream looms larger and blacker in the following scenes to block her desire for absolute heroic existence. The shining knight who falls into fragments as the dreamer's translation of 'the cracking . . . of the window-shutter downstairs, which the maid-servant was opening to let in the day', foreshadows the disintegration of her ideal world in face of the obstructive reality of Clym's nature and the world's daylight triviality. Her death sets her in her only 'artistically happy background', where her conflicting drives to darkness and sunlight are reconciled. 'Pallor did not include all the quality of her complexion, which seemed more than whiteness; it was almost light.'

Clym and Eustacia each have a partial truth that bears on the question of how to live. Mrs Yeobright provides another. Her conception of doing well is coloured by Egdon, which she neither loves nor hates, but tries to ignore in her desire to civilize the wilderness. She is one of T. S. Eliot's women of Canterbury, fearful of the 'disturbance of the quiet seasons' and human order from the ultimate powers of the cosmos which Clym and Eustacia know as light and heat and darkness.

Mrs Yeobright is related poetically to the heath and to the elemental struggle of light and darkness by Hardy's visual presentation. When she steps forward into the light of the bonfire in Book First, III, 'her face, encompassed by the blackness of the receding heath, showed whitely, and without half-lights, like a cameo.' The profile etched distinctly on a dark ground, repeated in our first sight of Clym's face (Book Second, VI) and Eustacia's (Book First, VI) suggests inflexible resistance to cosmic darkness.

Her journey across the heath to her death builds up a complex poetic image of her confrontation by the ultimate reality of the cosmos which civilization does not cope with. Its absurdity and hostility to human purpose are demonstrated in the action of the closed door. Poetically, they are embodied in the merciless sun and the parched obstructive earth she has to cross; major symbols of the elemental conflict between Clym and Eustacia which destroys her in its working out. Every image, every word, is selected for sound and sense to evoke a harsh waste land on fire with the blazing sun that 'had branded the whole heath with his mark': the scorched and flagging plants, the air 'like that of a kiln', the 'incineration' of the quartz sand, the 'metallic mirrors' of smooth-fleshed leaves, the moan of lightning-blasted trees. Echoes of Lear and his Fool on the stormy heath in Johnny Nunsuch's innocent questions and statements of fact and Mrs Yeobright's answers charged with experience of human misery, heighten the poetic emotion. But it is controlled by the changing perspective that measures Mrs Yeobright's human effort objectively against the lowly species of the heath 'busy in all the fulness of life' and indifferent to her prostration.

'Independent worlds of ephemerons were passing their time in mad carousal, some in the air, some on the hot ground and vegetation, some in the tepid and stringy water of a nearly dried pool. All the shallower ponds had decreased to a vaporous mud amid which the maggoty shapes of innumerable obscure creatures could be indistinctly seen, heaving and wallowing with enjoyment.'

Human isolation from primal harmony is complete. The 'vaporous mud' and 'maggoty shapes . . . heaving and wallowing' evoke a preconscious world in which human emotion and purpose are anachronisms. If these lowly creatures recall Eustacia's preconscious will to enjoy, the gleaming wet heron who flies towards the sun recalls the unworldly aspirations of Clym, equally antagonistic to Mrs Yeobright's desire for civilization. The ants who share with her the shepherd's-thyme where she lies dying, 'where they toiled a never-ending and heavy-laden throng' in a miniature city street, define the futile bustle of her 'doing well' in face of the sun, which 'stood directly in her face, like some merciless incendiary, brand in hand, waiting to consume her.'

Wildeve's relationship to Egdon and the Promethean light that rebels against it denotes a man who is not great enough to become a force of nature instead of a helpless instrument. Even his vices are petty; his little meannesses about Tamsin's allowance, his trumpery schemes of revenge. Our first sight of him through the window of the Quiet Woman is not of a sharp profile, but an indeterminate 'vast shadow, in which could be dimly traced portions of a masculine contour'. His tendency 'to care for the remote, to dislike the near' recalls Eustacia's and Clym's dissatisfaction with human limitations. But Wildeve cannot initiate rebellion. He can only respond to Eustacia's fire, and be consumed in her flame, like the moth-signal he releases to her.

Tamsin Yeobright and Diggory Venn are grouped together to reflect the passive and active principle of acquiescence in the human condition that is Egdon. Tamsin, the gentle point of rest between the major antagonists, has no awkward ideas about doing well to thrust her out of her environment. Doing simply means marrying for Tamsin, and her firmness on this point helps to retrieve the error of the unfulfilled wedding that begins the novel. The sun-lighted ritual of braiding her hair on the wedding day stresses her adherence to the traditional ordering of birth, marriage, children, and death—one of the few ambitions that tally with the Egdon rate of progress. The images of light and music which introduce her (Book First, IV) imply a relationship to the earth that has not yet become discordant. Benevolent sunshine is her natural form of light, but even on the night of storm and chaos which is a perfect complement to the chaos within Eustacia, Tamsin's sense of proportion and lack of that pride which demands a personal antagonist preserves her from harm.

'To her there were not, as to Eustacia, demons in the air, and malice in every bush and bough. The drops which lashed her face were not scorpions, but prosy rain; Egdon in the mass was no monster whatever, but impersonal open ground. Her fears of the place were rational, her dislikes of its worst moods reasonable.'

Diggory Venn, acquiescing in human limitations while working at the same time, like Oak, with the grain of his environment, has a link with darkness and fire that is ambiguous. When action depends on intimate knowledge of the heath—when he uses the camouflage of turves to eavesdrop on the plans of Eustacia and Wildeve, or when his familiarity with Shadwater Weir enables him to devise a plan of rescue—his triumph is due to the light of human intelligence controlling events. But his sudden appearances and disappearances, his colour, his devil's luck in gambling, his tricksy pranks with their unpredictable outcome, invest him with the poetry of a supernatural folkore character; not so much a 'Mephistophilian visitant' of the Christian era as a primitive fire daemon capable of good or evil. John Hagan points out ('A Note on the Significance of Diggory Venn', *Nineteenth Century Fiction*, XVI, 1961–2) that his well-intentioned interventions solve immediate problems, but initiate unwittingly the long-range tragedy of cosmic cross-purposes: Eustacia's decision to abandon Wildeve for Clym, and the events connected with the closed door.

Hardy's extended description of the reddleman stresses the ambiguity in his character which mirrors the ambiguity of the cosmos. The domestic picture (Book First, VIII) of a peaceful red man smoking a red pipe and darning a red stocking, kindly binding Johnny's wounds with a red bandage, gives way in IX to an evocation of his shadow side. His link with the heath is stressed in the 'blood-coloured figure' which is, like Egdon in storm, 'a sublimation of all the horrid dreams' of the human race. 'Blood-coloured', an alteration from the simple 'red' of the manuscript, takes up the theme of guilt suggested in 'the mark of Cain' simile which defines the effects of reddle, and amplified in the evocation of the reddleman as an isolated 'Ishmaelitish' character (the same adjective describes both the heath and the reddleman) who had taken to the trade as a lifelong penance for criminal deeds. The imaginative details of a legendary inheritance of guilt superimposed on the good and well-balanced human character of Diggory Venn suggest, paradoxically, a harmony with what Egdon means through acceptance of isolation and the guilt inherent in existence. After Clym's agonized self-reproach at Eustacia's death, it is Venn who puts it into perspective.

' "But you can't charge yourself with crimes in that way," said Venn. "You may as well say that the parents be the cause of a murder by the child, for without the parents the child would never have been begot." '

The heightened poetic tone of Chapter VIII, Book Third, where Venn wins back the Yeobright guineas, defines his ambiguous relation to light and darkness in a brilliant sensuous correlative. The overpowering darkness of the heath at night is fitfully broken by various forms of light which illuminate the flat stone, reminiscent of the flatness of the heath, and human participation in a game of chance, which becomes an image of the human predicament. It is natural that Venn's familiarity with the heath should give him an advantage over the excitable Wildeve, who is disturbed by the humbler heath-dwellers. Wildeve's confused actions and Venn's calmness, chance and direction, range themselves with the antagonisms of darkness and light that motivate the novel. The visual presentation of Venn as a 'red automaton' raises him to the plane of a supernatural agent of fate. But his human lack of knowledge that half the guineas were destined for Clym qualifies his control of the situation.

The ritual patterns in the scene intensify its effect as a glimpse of destiny working itself out on another plane. In the heightened poetic tension, Venn's ballad-like incantation of the incremental phrases of Wildeve's gambling stories as the money coils in in reverse direction; the night moths which circle the lantern twice; the heath-croppers who encircle the gamblers twice, 'their heads being all towards the players, at whom they gazed intently'; the thirteen glow-worms placed in a circle round the dice, take on the aspect of mechanical functions of fate controlled by the 'red automaton'. The moths attracted to the light and the death's-head moth which extinguishes the lantern to the accompaniment of 'a mournful whining from the herons which were nesting lower down the vale', foreshadow in symbol and detail the deaths of Wildeve and Mrs Yeobright.

The transformation of a folklore character into a mundane dairy farmer with a bank balance in Book Sixth worries some critics. While Hardy's note to Chapter III indicates that his 'austere artistic code' did not originally plan such a transformation, Venn's change tallies with the laws that condition Egdon's rate of progress. The cycle of aeons as well as the cycle of seasons directs his evolution from a 'nearly perished link between obsolete forms of life and those which generally prevail'. It is part of the movement of the novel from primitive darkness to conscious understanding appropriate to the modern era.

The poetic development of the novel is completed by a return to the visual image of 'a motionless figure standing on the top of the tumulus, just as Eustacia had stood on that lonely summit some two years and a half before'. But the transformation of Eustacia into Clym has replaced the dark winter night with summer afternoon, isolation with relationship to man and the lower species, and the self-absorbed unconscious drives of nature with hope of redemption through man's consciousness of the roots from which he sprang. Clym's suffering has taught him that love of place or woman is not enough without understanding, and that in order to move forward on Egdon one must move back.

To know Egdon is to know the great forces that move the world. It is not isolated from the rest of space, and time. Vapours from other continents arrive upon the wind, and rare migrants as well as native species watch the alien movements of man in a setting that 'seemed to belong to the ancient carboniferous period'. Egdon contains all the elements of the world before the Fall, including a secluded Paradise and a serpent. All its Promethean characters are seeking a place where they will feel at home after the development of isolating consciousness. Their survival depends on their reassessment of the place where they are. Hardy's sensuous evocation of the heath and its effect on human fate makes its physical presence impossible to ignore. At moments of crisis its 'oppressive horizontality' gives Clym, and others, 'a sense of bare equality with, and no superiority to, a single living thing under the sun'. There is no special place in nature for man. But from the heath's dark negation springs that affirmation of its raw vitality and that yearning for the light which combine to enable conscious man, as part of the general Will, to

> Bend a digit the poise of forces,
> And a fair desire fulfil.
>   ('He Wonders about Himself')

The Mayor of Casterbridge:
A Novel of Character and Environment

The Mayor of Casterbridge, like *The Return of the Native*, is primarily a novel of environment in relation to character. But instead of the almost changeless face of Egdon heath, with its few scattered inhabitants, the factor that controls the action is the evolving social organism of Casterbridge the county town. The novel reflects the changes that were taking place in Casterbridge, and beyond, in the nineteenth century: the increasing mastery over environment, the advance of mechanization, the development of new business methods to keep pace, the importance of education for a rapidly changing world, the breaking down of social barriers, the spread of co-operative and humanitarian principles. The concept of a static world in which changes are only superficial was being replaced by the evolutionary concept of change as ultimate reality.

The plot, with its epic hero representing a whole culture and way of life, the characters, situations, and rhythms of narrative movement, are subtly balanced in relation to the Casterbridgean environment of space, time, and society, to form a poetic correlative of the inevitable on-going of the world. The two chief characters, Michael Henchard and Donald Farfrae, are engaged in a commercial struggle that brings in the new order to supersede the old.

'The break between Henchard and Farfrae is not so much between personalities as between methods, the capacities of different generations to meet changing needs. For Henchard's muscle, Farfrae substitutes brain, for energy system, for antiquated drudgery the efficiency of the machine. Thus Henchard's downfall is more than personal; like the downfall of the archetypal tragic hero it signifies the passing of an era, of ways which have outlived their purpose. By the end of the novel Henchard is one with the patriarchal shepherd who appears briefly in the market place to survey an alien world that has no use for him.'

(D. A. Dike: 'A Modern Oedipus: *The Mayor of Casterbridge*'
Essays in Criticism II, 1952)

The movement of the plot, divided clearly into a prologue and six acts, or the stanzaic steps of a ballad, is one of reversal that recalls Greek tragedy. It climbs upward through intensifying conflict and complication to a peak point—Henchard's bankruptcy, and the hag's disclosure—from which he falls and Farfrae rises. The movement is repeated, fugue-like, a little later in the fall of Lucetta and the rise of Elizabeth-Jane. The Prologue tells, in the simple rhythms of fable, of Henchard's sale of wife and daughter, the act to which all subsequent action looks back. The rest of the story plots his double pursuit of the affection he has sold to his ambition, and of the self-destruction he unconsciously invites to punish the guilt of self-assertion against the limitations of the human condition.

The twenty-year gap between prologue and the drama proper stresses the link between crime and punishment. The first act shows his wilful violation of human relationship apparently bearing fruit. He is rich, successful, and the Mayor of Casterbridge. But the seeds of his destruction are already there; in the corruption of bread, for which his ignorance is responsible (which, as a spoiling of nature, recalls the furmity hag's corruption of wholesome furmity and its consequences); in the return of Susan and her daughter, hand in hand—a detail that compels comparison with the isolation of Henchard from his wife at the beginning of the story—and in his appointment of the astute Farfrae as his manager. But the re-marriage of Susan and Henchard brings the act to a close on a note of apparent retrieval of past error.

The second act robs Henchard of affection—friend and manager Farfrae, wife, and child. Farfrae is lost to him through the possibilities of division that are present, together with the possibilities of creative partnership, in the new ideas of the man 'frae far'. Susan is lost through death, and Elizabeth-Jane through his disregard of Susan's instructions not to open, until the girl's wedding day, the letter which discloses that she is Newson's daughter. The irony of reversal operates again when Elizabeth-Jane's removal to the house of Lucetta, the lady whom Henchard 'ought' to marry for conventional reasons, and Henchard's withdrawal of his objection to Farfrae's courtship of Elizabeth-Jane, results in Farfrae's attraction to Lucetta.

The third act graphs the competition in business and love between Henchard and Farfrae, and Henchard's failure in the ambition which he substituted for affection. In the conflict between old and progressive ideas, in the foresight and judgement needed to safeguard Casterbridge crops and Casterbridge entertainment from uncertain weather, Farfrae gains ground and Henchard's wrong-headed impulsiveness leads to bankruptcy. His social status receives 'a startling fillip downwards' by the furmity hag's disclosure in court of his sale of Susan, which robs him of the moral right to lead the flourishing town. Reversal of roles with his rival is complete when Farfrae buys his house and business, employs him as work-man, marries the woman he was going to marry and eventually Henchard's stepdaughter, and becomes Mayor of Casterbridge.

Act four charts the degradation and increasing isolation of the former Mayor. The close of his period of teetotalism marks viola-tions of human dignity that recall the beginning of the novel; the anathema on Farfrae, the fight in the loft, the self-humiliation at the Royal visit. Twenty-four hours sees violent reversals. The pomp of the Royal visit is parodied by the grotesque skimmity in the evening; Lucetta is dead in the dawn after her triumph; Hen-chard's murderous attack on Farfrae in the morning is balanced by his desperate attempt to warn Farfrae of Lucetta's illness in the evening. Finally, his new hope of affection from Elizabeth-Jane is qualified by the return of Newson, who brings with him, like Far-frae in act two, possibilities for good or ill, and is sent away with a lie.

The fifth stage is a period of regeneration for Henchard; of renewed contact with love through Elizabeth-Jane, and with the natural world untouched by big business through his little seed-shop. He schools himself to accept Elizabeth-Jane's growing love for Farfrae, but the uneasy interval comes to an end with Newson's second return and Henchard's departure from Casterbridge, out-wardly the hay-trusser who had entered it twenty years ago. The final act brings him to full stature as the tragic, isolated, self-alienated scapegoat, whose impulse to self-destruction sends him to die like an animal on the heath after Elizabeth-Jane's rebuff and his refusal 'to endeavour strenuously to hold his own in her love'.

Hardy's poetic readings of life, the stylized ironies of reversal and substitution, are evident in a mere recital of the events. Hardy was conscious of the packed incidents.

'It was a story which Hardy fancied he had damaged more recklessly as an artistic whole, in the interest of the newspaper in which it appeared serially, than perhaps any other of his novels, his aiming to get an incident into almost every week's part causing him in his own judgment to add events to the narrative somewhat too freely . . . though it must be said in favour of the plot, as he admitted later, that it was quite coherent and organic, in spite of its complication.'

(Life)

The incidents that affect Henchard's life are like violent hammer blows set in motion by his first violent act. A chain of eventful arrivals which substitutes something else for the thing desired—Farfrae's friendship for wife and child, Susan and Elizabeth-Jane for Farfrae, Lucetta for the daughter lost in Elizabeth-Jane, and Farfrae for Henchard in Lucetta's affections—leads the mind back inevitably to the first link in the chain, the substitution of ambition for love. The crises are brought about by revelation of hidden acts: the sale of wife and child, Henchard's association with Lucetta, the secret of Elizabeth-Jane's birth. Accidents and coincidences add their effect to acts of human wilfulness. Some can hardly be called accidents; Henchard's impulse to self-punishment places him in the way of bad luck. Nothing else can account for his entrusting Lucetta's letters to his enemy Jopp, or his rashness in acting on the long-range forecast of the weather-prophet without waiting for the oracle's full development. The return of Susan, Newson, Lucetta, and the furmity hag (who appears in court on the one day when Henchard is sitting as substitute magistrate): the appearance of Farfrae at the very moment when Henchard needs his knowledge to get out of a difficulty; the bad weather that intensifies his failure by the failure of others involved in his speculations—stress the long arm of coincidence. But not all the coincidences are disastrous—Henchard's sight of his substitute self, the effigy, in the water saves him from suicide—and the poetic mood created by the stylized plot makes them credible as correlatives of the past and its claim to atonement.

The plot owes some of its emotional force to the feeling that it is archetypal. The myth of human responsibility and rebellion against the human condition is deep-seated. Henchard is overtly or implicitly compared with Achilles, Ajax, Oedipus, Orestes pursued by the Furies, Cain, Saul, Samson working in the mill of the Philistines after his fall, Job, Coriolanus, King Lear, and Faust. Farfrae can be regarded as the Creon to his Oedipus and David to his Saul; Elizabeth-Jane as the Cordelia to his Lear. The Abel to his Cain, and Fool to his Lear, is provided by Abel Whittle, who represents, at Henchard's first clash of principle with Farfrae (xv) and at Henchard's death, the brotherhood which the self-alienated man had rejected and finally embraced. His self-alienation and impulse to self-destruction recall more modern heroes: Emily Brontë's Heathcliff, Melville's Captain Ahab, Conrad's Lord Jim and Razumov, the ambiguous heroes of Gide and Dostoievsky, Camus' Meursault. Older than any literary manifestation is the seasonal rite of the corn-king supplanted, after ritual combat and supernatural agency (furmity hag and weather-prophet) by his adopted 'son' in his role as virile leader of an agricultural community. The ancient myth of the scapegoat-king meets the modern saga of the nineteenth-century self-made man deposed by the new order of big business, in a penetrating study of the alienation from self and natural harmony that follows the guilt of wilfully imposing conscious desires on the human condition.

The alienation suffered by Henchard and his feminine counterpart, Lucetta (who suffers in a pathetic, not tragic, capacity) is expressed through scenes that function as dramatic metaphor. The scenes of civic ritual point to the gulf between appearance and reality that is a vital theme of the story. The bow window that separates the banqueters at the King's Arms from the 'plainer fellows [that] bain't invited' also puts a stage-frame round the feast. The disharmony within, the distorted shapes of the diners, the straight-backed figure in the Mayoral chair, distance the scene to a mock representation of Mayoral responsibility. Elizabeth-Jane's relationship to the public image—'the natural elation she felt at discovering herself akin to a coach'—is later balanced by the bankrupt Henchard's sight, through the same window, of the reality of the love he has missed in Elizabeth-Jane. It is the public image which Henchard wishes to preserve. When he is superseded in his civic role, he crumbles to the nothingness implied by his will.

The high drama of the police court faces his public image with the reality of the past action his appearance has denied. The furmity hag is part of his past, and so part of the self he cannot escape. The power of that other self is one of the notes that creates the rich resonance of Chapter XLI, where Henchard gazes at his effigy-self in Ten Hatches Weir. The savage ritual of the skimmity which placed effigies of himself and Lucetta in positions of inverted honour, recalls the past of that other self and points to his future fate as scapegoat outcast for the sins of existence. Yet at this juncture the sense of a magical substitution saves the life of the man who cannot escape from himself. The phenomenon has a natural cause, yet the theatrical, hallucinatory effect of the scene becomes symbolic of a Dostoievskian ultimate reality of the divided self.

The skimmity ride is a caricature of the Royal visit, whose pomp has already been parodied within itself by the drunken Henchard, drawing down on his grotesque image of Mayoralty the degradation imposed by the real Mayor Farfrae. The maid's description of the effigies' dress—an effective adaptation of the Greek messenger technique—dramatically diminishes the civic importance of Henchard and Lucetta to a puppet show of hollow pomp and poses covering an inharmonious past.

> ' "The man has got on a blue coat and kerseymere leggings; he has black whiskers, and a reddish face. 'Tis a stuffed figure, with a falseface. . . . Her neck is uncovered, and her hair in bands, and her back-comb in place; she's got on a puce silk, and white stockings, and coloured shoes." '

The market place, where many of the important scenes of the novel are enacted, takes on the character of a commercial stage. 'The *carrefour* was like the regulation Open Place in spectacular dramas, where the incidents that occur always happen to bear on the lives of the adjoining residents.' There, men assume the roles and 'market-faces' required by buying and selling. Seen from Lucetta's window, they take on distortions ('men of extensive stomachs, sloping like mountain sides; men whose heads in walking swayed as the trees in November gales') that compel comparison with the dehumanizations of the banqueters: gigantic inflations caused by the ready money they represent to Casterbridge, which misshapes reality. Lucetta, who believes that she can remain in the wings as a mere spectator ('I look as at a picture merely') is forced onto the stage because her house is part of the *carrefour*. High Place Hall has a market face of Palladian reasonableness, counterpointed by the distorted mask, recalling the grotesque theatrical masks that hang over the proscenium arch, that marks a past of intrigue and violence. It is significant that Henchard chooses this entrance to make his renewed contact with Lucetta.

The commercial stage, viewed through Lucetta's window, defines her relationship with Farfrae. Their common sympathy for the predicament of the old shepherd and the courting couple, whose relationship is threatened by the commercial standards of the hiring fair, and its resolution by Farfrae's compassion, draw hem together. The old shepherd remains in the memory as a poetic symbol of the human cost of the new market techniques introduced in the next scene. Lucetta is linked to the seed-drill by the assumption of a role that foreshadows, through the leitmotif of colour, both her triumph and tragedy. Her decision to be 'the cherry-coloured person at all hazards' links her to the red machine, to the future of Farfrae and the commercial values of Casterbridge, and to the 'puce silk' of her effigy that comments on the hollowness of her role. The artificial brightness of her appearance is suddenly placed by the reality of the sun, which is in harmonious relationship with the drill.

'The sun fell so flat on the houses and pavement opposite Lucetta's residence that they poured their brightness into her rooms. Suddenly, after a rumbling of wheels, there were added to this steady light a fantastic series of circling irradiations upon the ceiling, and the companions turned to the window. Immediately opposite a vehicle of strange description had come to a standstill, as if it had been placed there for exhibition.'

The metaphor of the stage, in fact, is one which pervades the novel. The action grows out of dramatic conflict, and life is seen as a vast arena where the battle for survival takes place. The Ring has always been an arena for violent and tragic spectacle. Its ghosts and skeletons are a memorial to the military power of the Romans. Reverberations of gladiatorial combat, the law of force, add pathos to Henchard's furtive meetings there with Susan and Lucetta. As Henchard leaves Casterbridge, the metaphor sums up his experience. 'He had no wish to make an arena a second time of a world that had become a mere painted scene to him.' It recalls, with compassionate irony, Elizabeth-Jane's hopeful entry into Casterbridge, which was to her a romantic sunset backdrop of 'towers, gables, chimneys, and casements'—romantic, but not insubstantial—and the earlier sunset backdrop that defines Henchard's act of human violation as part of a great cosmic drama.

'The sun had recently set, and the west heaven was hung with rosy cloud, which seemed permanent, yet slowly changed. To watch it was like looking at some grand feat of stagery from a darkened auditorium. In presence of this scene after the other there was a natural instinct to abjure man as the blot on an otherwise kindly universe; till it was remembered that all terrestrial conditions were intermittent, and that mankind might some night be innocently sleeping when these quiet objects were raging loud.'

The prologue concentrates into a dramatic scene, which has the starkness of a ballad, the themes that operate in the wider world of Casterbridge to drive Michael Henchard to destruction. He enters the novel anonymously, as the 'skilled countryman' defined by his clothes, his tools, and 'measured, springless walk'. The atmosphere of 'stale familiarity' that surrounds him and Susan identifies him with the universal drabness of the human condition, embodied in the long dusty road,

'neither straight nor crooked, neither level nor hilly, bordered by hedges, trees, and other vegetation, which had entered the blackened-green stage of colour that the doomed leaves pass through on their way to dingy, and yellow, and red.'

The 'noises off' of Weydon Fair counterpoint the drabness with the search for gaiety that is another familiar Hardy image. Henchard's sale of his wife, to the background noises of 'the sale by auction of a few inferior animals, that could not otherwise be disposed of', in a blaze of narrative intensity, challenges human limitation with a self-assertive act that violates the deepest human, natural and moral instincts.

The swallow, seeking escape from the mercenary perversion of nature inside the tent, provides a moment of equilibrium, always present in Hardy's work, when human choice could give fate a different turn; and looks forward to the caged goldfinch of XLV, which symbolizes the consequences of the act that made Henchard unfree. But Henchard assumes his role and his destiny. The result is to turn a stage play into reality, with 'the demand and response of real cash' which is to become a symbol of power in Casterbridge.

'The sight of real money in full amount, in answer to a challenge for the same till then deemed slightly hypothetical, had a great effect upon the spectators. Their eyes became riveted upon the faces of the chief actors, and then upon the notes as they lay, weighted by the shillings, on the table.'

The meaning of the scene—Henchard's obsessive desire to sacrifice human relationships to the power of money—is pointed by the similarity of Susan's warning, 'If you touch that money, I and this girl go with the man. Mind, it is a joke no longer', to Farfrae's, when he clashes with Henchard over respect for Abel Whittle.

> ' "I say this joke has been carried far enough."
> "And I say it hasn't! Get up in the waggon, Whittle."
> "Not if I am manager," said Farfrae. "He either goes home, or I march out of this yard for good." '

The prologue ends with a return of leitmotifs. The morning after, the drabness of the cosmos is accentuated by the buzzing fly and the barking dog; Henchard's isolation by routine family matters proceeding at all levels: 'He went on in silent thought, unheeding the yellowhammers which flitted about the hedges with straws in their bills'. But the movement from lurid candlelight through darkness to the newly risen sun, from the temporary man-made structure of the tent and its man-made commercial atmosphere to the fresh September morning on the uplands 'dotted with barrows, and trenched with the remains of prehistoric forts', to the church where Michael Henchard is defined for the first time by name and the conscious purpose of his oath, stresses the rhythm of defeat and regeneration, degradation and redefinition, that marks the life of Michael Henchard in Casterbridge. The whole movement, with its foreshadowing in stark dramatic terms of the delicate balance between human dignity and vaulting ambition, its market ethics, and its denial of nature and responsibilities formed in the past, ends with a widening out from the claustrophobic tent to the social world where the balance will be worked out.

> 'Next day he started, journeying south-westward, and did not pause, except for nights' lodgings, till he reached the town of Casterbridge, in a far distant part of Wessex.'

The solidity of Hardy's evocation of Casterbridge, both concrete and poetic, vouches for its effect on the characters. The plane of myth and fable in the prologue modulates to the plane of physical reality as Elizabeth-Jane moves from the fairy-tale transformation of Henchard to the local voices and local issues of bad bread which prove the fairy-tale Mayor vulnerable. But continuity with the prologue is there, in the evocation of Casterbridge as a town in vital contact with the forces which Henchard's act had denied or embraced—nature, the past, and the values of the market.

The environment that changes lives is itself in a continuous process of change, without which there is no progress. The passing of time finds its correlative in the clocks, chimes, and curfews; the seasonal character of the shop-window display; references to Casterbridge features no longer in existence. And while Casterbridge is growing in stature by virtue of its size and favourable position, the three visits to Weydon stress that 'pulling down is more the nater of Weydon', where 'the new periodical great markets of neighbouring towns were beginning to interfere seriously with the trade carried on here for centuries.' These cyclic rhythms of rise and fall, seen and heard through the observant senses of Elizabeth-Jane as she approaches the town, prepare us for their re-enactment in the career of the man they are seeking. The squareness she notes in Casterbridge is repeated in the descriptions of the Mayor, its representative citizen; its conservative distrust, 'huddled all together', in his inflexible attitude to new inventions.

The approach of the two women, downhill towards the town, is sensuously realized in a description that moves from the architect's plan ('to birds of the more soaring kind') to an elevation drawn in increasing detail as its features are encountered by 'the level eye of humanity'. Yet it is not a blueprint. The details are selected to form an impressionist picture of an interlocking 'mosaic-work of subdued reds, browns, greys, and crystals' in vital pattern-relation to the 'rectangular frame of deep green' and the 'miles of rotund down and concave field' that held the individual pieces in shape. The architect's eye and the poet's selective detail provide a comment on the relationship of Casterbridge individuals to their surroundings. The weather- and time-nibbled church, the individual voices of curfew and clocks, add the dimension of time to Hardy's evocation of Casterbridge in space. The cumulative poetic effect is to make the entry of the two unassuming women into the boxed-in 'snugness and comfort' of the town through the dark avenue of trees, an image of the tragic solitary human condition. Then, the individual sounds modulate into the communal brass band, and the still-life picture begins to move with the rhythms of vigorous natural life.

The physical position of Casterbridge, 'a place deposited in the block upon a corn-field', without transitional mixture of town and down, is essential to its growth as a living organism. It retains a vital link with nature, which Henchard corrupts and Farfrae respects, in his treatment of the corrupted grain, his purchase of the seed-drill that takes the chance out of sowing, his creative use of the tree-lined walk for his entertainment, and his respect for human dignity.

'Casterbridge was the complement of the rural life around; not its urban opposite. Bees and butterflies in the cornfields at the top of the town, who desired to get to the meads at the bottom, took no circuitous course, but flew straight down High Street without any apparent consciousness that they were traversing strange latitudes. And in autumn airy spheres of thistledown floated into the same street, lodged upon the shop fronts, blew into drains; and innumerable tawny and yellow leaves skimmed along the pavement, and stole through people's doorways into their passages with a hesitating scratch on the floor, like the skirts of timid visitors.'

The poet's sensitive ear for sound quality—'circuitous', 'innumerable', 'skimmed', 'stole', 'a hesitating scratch', soft feminine consonants and singing vowel progressions, realizes the insidious creep of nature into the lives of Casterbridge citizens. The simile that ends the paragraph prepares for the timid visitors who are about to remind Henchard of his offence against natural law.

Dr Beatty (op. cit.) has made a fruitful comparison of Hardy's Casterbridge with Dickens' Coketown (*Hard Times*, 1, Chapter x), which is what Casterbridge was not—one of the 'many manufacturing towns which are as foreign bodies set down, like boulders on a plain, in a green world with which they have nothing in common.'

'In the hardest working part of Coketown, in the innermost fortifications of that ugly citadel, where Nature was as strongly bricked out as killing airs and gases were bricked in, at the heart of the labyrinth of narrow courts upon courts, and close streets upon streets, which had come into existence piecemeal, every piece in a violent hurry for some one man's purpose, and the whole an unnatural family, shouldering, and trampling, and pressing one another to death; in the last close nook of this great exhausted receiver, where the chimneys, for want of air to make a draught, were built in an immense variety of stunted and crooked shapes, as though every house put out a sign of the kind of people who might be expected to be born in it; among the multitude of Coketown, generically called "the hands"—a race who would have found more favour with some people, if Providence had seen fit to make them only hands, or, like the lower creatures of the seashore, only hands and stomachs—lived a certain Stephen Blackpool, forty years of age.'

Nature is bricked out: consequently Coketown reflects denial of life in its piecemeal shapelessness, deformity, and embrace of death.

The individuals and buildings of Casterbridge 'which spoke so cheerfully of individual unrestraint as to boundaries' reflect the penetrating forces of life and growth (which can, however, be destructively distorted by the power of money). Casterbridge is not an 'exhausted receiver', but 'the pole, focus, or nerve-knot of the surrounding country life'. Coketown depends on utilitarian 'hands' minus the creative brain to direct them. The 'unnatural family' of Coketown, put there for the sole purpose of making money, compels contrast with the interrelationship of all the Casterbridge people, from the Mayor to the labourers, with the staff of life that grows in the surrounding cornfields.

Differences of style in Dickens and Hardy stress the difference between the two towns. The complex sentence that takes up most of the page mirrors the piecemeal labyrinthine construction of Coketown. The subject, closing the sentence, suggests the neglect of the human being who should provide meaning to the heaped-up phrases. The picture of Casterbridge in Chapter xiv as 'the complement of the rural life around; not its urban opposite', is built up by an accumulation of complementary details—farmer's boy/town clerk, judge/sheep-stealer, barns/main thoroughfare.

'Here lived burgesses who daily walked the fallow; shepherds in an intra-mural squeeze. A street of farmers' homesteads—a street ruled by a mayor and corporation, yet echoing with the thump of the flail, the flutter of the winnowing-fan, and the purr of the milk into the pails—a street which had nothing urban in it whatever . . .'

The synthesis of incongruities, the rhythmic cadences, and the onomatapoeic diction of the final sentence, evoke the sensuous vitality of Casterbridge as only a poet can.

The reality of the evocation gives authenticity to the mythical aspects of the story. The diminished perspective, through Elizabeth-Jane's eyes, of Farfrae and Henchard 'ascending to the upper end of the long street till they were small as two grains of corn' is an image natural to the evocation of man linked with nature, but it remains in the memory to qualify, a moment later, the correlative of Henchard's importance, the five loaded waggons of hay marked with his name. The shifting perspective of the link established here returns as leitmotif in xxvii, to invest the collision of Henchard's loaded waggon and Farfrae's with the mythic significance of ritual combat between corn-king and successor.

The link with nature in Casterbridge is often integrated with evidence of past layers of Casterbridge life. The wall of Henchard's house 'was studded with rusty nails speaking of generations of fruit-trees that had been trained there', and the open doors of the houses passed by Elizabeth-Jane reveal a floral blaze 'backed by crusted grey stone-work remaining from a yet remoter Casterbridge than the venerable one visible in the street'.

The 'past-marked prospect' of Casterbridge, dotted with tumuli, earth-forts, Roman remains, and evidence of violent blood sports and man's continuing inhumanity to man, is a physical reminder of the barbarity of a ruthless competitive battle for survival, still present (as in Mixen Lane) under the civilized front. Henchard is placed in a setting that speaks of the primitive past (II, XI, XXXV, etc.), which both diminishes and enhances his ephemeral dignity, whenever he tries to disown his own past. Significantly, it is from the massive prehistoric fort of Mai-Dun that he sees the past he tried to deny catching up on the present, in the figure of Newson striding relentlessly along 'the original track laid out by the legions of the Empire', to claim his daughter.

Casterbridge as a market town has symbolic value. The market, as D. A. Dike points out, organizes the values and desires of the citizens. The perennial problem of a market town is to preserve respect for the individuality of human beings who are cogs in a machine for making money. Henchard and Lucetta, who buy and sell human relationships, fail to keep the balance. Lucetta's offer of money to pay Henchard's debts on the day she had broken faith with him to marry his rival; Henchard's gift to her sent 'as plaster to the wound'; the annuity he settles on Elizabeth-Jane to rid himself of her presence when the discovery of her parentage makes her worthless stock in his eyes; his gift of five guineas to buy Susan back again; his free entertainment; his reaction to Farfrae's disinterested help, 'What shall I pay you for this knowledge?'; his insult to the self-respect of Jopp and Whittle when business cannot wait for their tardy arrival; all are repetitions of the original violation of love by measuring it in the commercial terms of the market place. Farfrae, on the other hand, manages to keep the delicate balance between humanity and business. It is in the market place, appropriately, that he shows respect for the family unit of the old shepherd as well as for the revolutionary seed-drill. Abel Whittle, another man who has cause to thank Farfrae's respect for human dignity, sums up the meaning of the change from Henchard's ownership of the corn business to Farfrae's.

' "Yaas, Miss Henchet,' he said, 'Mr. Farfrae have bought the concern and all of we work-folk with it; and 'tis better for us than 'twas—though I shouldn't say that to you as a daughter-law. We work harder, but we bain't made afeard now. It was fear made my few poor hairs so thin! No busting out, no slamming of doors, no meddling with yer eternal soul and all that; and though 'tis a shilling a week less I'm the richer man; for what's all the world if yer mind is always in a larry, Miss Henchet?" '

Casterbridge is a more complex Egdon heath, in that it represents the given conditions of life which the characters variously adjust to or defy. Their responses to the values of nature, the past, and the market control the curves of their lives. Henchard's career, after the bid for freedom that enslaves his life and liberates his awareness, is a hard-won progress through rejection of market ethics to integration with the past and the family he had cast off, and finally to the realization that he can love what is beyond market price and not his own, in Elizabeth-Jane.

The primitive past and primitive nature operate in Michael Henchard's instinctive impulses, usually disastrous in a modern civilization that must progress morally. The elemental and animal imagery that defines him ('moving like a great tree in a wind', 'leonine', 'tigerish', 'a bull breaking fence'); his energy and inarticulacy, his retrogression to brutal loneliness after his defiance of the moral order; his recourse to rivalry for love, territory, and possessions; his admiration for ruthless business methods in and out of the market; the touchstone of brute strength in all things which makes him despise Farfrae's slight physique while admiring his brains, and give himself a handicap before he fights Farfrae in the loft—are all traits that link Henchard to the pre-human world. The instructions he leaves for his burial are appropriate for an animal—one whose conscious self-assertion against nothingness has failed. When, stripped of everything that built up his public image as man and Mayor, he accepts the nothingness under the robes of office; a nothingness that is physically present in the mud hovel where he dies, scarcely distinguishable from the ancient natural world of Egdon Heath, and advances to the unselfish love which alone can make him significant, Henchard has risen, paradoxically, from the status of a magnificent animal to the nobility of man.

In Casterbridge Farfrae is faced with the same chances and conditions of success or failure. But his character and the needs of the time are on his side. In a social organism where further progress depends as much on co-operation as competition, Farfrae is the man whose chariot they will follow to the Capitol. No-one could be less of a gloomy being who had quitted the ways of vulgar men. While Henchard believes that superiority can only be maintained by standing aloof, Farfrae can be found dancing reels at his co-operative entertainment and singing songs at the Three Mariners, where, we remember, Henchard violated the social ritual of music by forcing the choir to sing an anathema on his rival. He has no past to hide, and no market face required by a role that is different from his reality. He provides the education, method, intelligence, foresight, drive, judgment, sympathy and respect for others, and swift adaptation to conditions of environment, which is lacking in Henchard's 'introspective inflexibility.' The reign of chance and rule of thumb comes to an end under Farfrae's leadership. The new seed drill is symbolic of man's increasing mastery of his environment: 'Each grain will go straight to its intended place, and nowhere else whatever!' His ability to live with honour and dignity within human limitations balances the other great value of Henchard's defiance.

The relation of Henchard's other rival, Newson, to the market ethics of the place where he is an alien passing through (as his name suggests) is double-edged. He holds the rights of property, by which Henchard has lived, and which deal the last blow to his hopes of Elizabeth-Jane. His unpossessiveness is an effective foil to Henchard's possessiveness, yet it is a bitter irony that soon after the wedding he leaves his daughter. Henchard is not capable of the abnegation of identity by which Newson drops out of Susan's life, until the terrible negation of his Will. Yet Newson's too facile acceptance of another man's wife and contribution to the skimmity suggest that the character he negates is not deep. However, he is more socially acceptable to Casterbridge than the deeper-souled Henchard, because he never attempts to disguise his real character, slight as it is. Hence his closeness to the ballad stereotype of the genial, open-handed sailor is a merit rather than a defect in characterization.

Newson shares with Susan Henchard, that other lightly-sketched but convincing ghost from the past, a fidelity to the basic human loyalties expressed for her by the simple moral code of the unlettered peasant. It is founded on acceptance of cosmic injustices and the cyclic movement of lives and seasons. Market ethics is something Susan suffers from, as a woman dependent on a man, but does not subscribe to in her individual values. Her momentary flash of independence at Weydon Fair has the fatalistic assumption of property rights behind it—

' "Will anybody buy her?" said the man.
' "I wish somebody would," said she firmly. "Her present owner is not at all to her liking!" '

—but her feeling for the continuity of past with present (it is fitting that she should be buried in the old Roman burial ground) and present with future, in her desire for a wider horizon for her daughter, liberates her from Lucetta's need to snatch feverishly at evanescent present pleasures.

Lucetta and Elizabeth-Jane compel comparison in their response to Casterbridge. The values of the market impel Lucetta's emotions and actions.

' "I was so desperate—so afraid of being forced to anything else—so afraid of revelations that would quench his love for me, that I resolved to do it off-hand, come what might, and purchase a week of happiness at any cost!" '

The commercial terms in which her confession of marriage to Farfrae is worded, her assessment and use of her ephemeral beauty as an asset of marketable worth, her treatment of Elizabeth-Jane as a counter in her pursuit of a man, now as bait for Henchard, now as 'a watch-dog to keep her father off' when 'a new man she liked better' appears, her concern for external appearance, suggest how thoroughly Lucetta has embraced market ethics. She has tried to repudiate her past in the change of environment from Jersey to Casterbridge, and the change of name from Le Sueur to Templeman 'as a means of escape from mine, and its wrongs.' She has also rejected the role she could have taken in Casterbridge. Ostensibly she is the stranger, like Farfrae, who brings new ideas into the town. Her furniture, contrasting with Henchard's old-fashioned, pretentious Spanish mahogany, is fifty years ahead of the Casterbridge times. Her ability to distinguish between true culture and false in Elizabeth-Jane, as Henchard cannot (' "What, not necessary to write ladies'-hand?" cried the joyous Elizabeth') provides an ironic comment on the gulf she makes in her own life between appearance and reality, past and present. What might have been remains in the mind as the external image she has built up crumbles under the skimmity ride's rude revelation of what lies underneath. It kills her, but keeps Henchard alive, because his will to defy circumstances makes him more than the puppet of his role.

It is fitting that Hardy draws Lucetta from the outside, while Elizabeth-Jane's thoughts and feelings guide the reader's emotions. She is trustworthy and balanced, because she does not admit any gulf between appearance and reality, past and present, nature and civilization. Consequently the values of the market cannot touch her. She can see nothing wrong in waiting on at the Three Mariners to pay her board, speaking dialect, or picking up coals for the servant—all 'social catastrophes' to Henchard. She refuses to be treated as a chattel either by Henchard or Lucetta. The confusions that surround her name do not affect the intrinsic worth of her character, which Henchard comes to value. The social forms of a simple moral code are not artificial conventions to which she pays only lip-service, but expressive of her deepest convictions. However, there is a final appeal from them to the basic instinctive loyalties she inherits from her parents. It is the same woman who shares the adversity of the man she believes to be her father, and who would 'root out his image as that of an arch-deceiver' to return to a still deeper loyalty of the past, even though by current social standards recognition of Newson's paternity makes her illegitimate. The mood built up by Hardy's picture of Casterbridge in its natural setting, in Chapter XIV, leads to the poetic suggestion of her affinity with that world, when the wheat-husks on her clothes make the instinctive contact with Farfrae that her mother had desired. Her vision of the past as continuous with the present is reflected in her 'study of Latin, incited by the Roman characteristics of the town she lived in', in contrast to Lucetta's irreverent attitude. Though she balances the enterprise of Farfrae by keeping 'in the rear of opportunity', her desire for knowledge, to make the furnishings of her mind match the furnishings of her beauty, faces her towards a future of complex change—the future of Tess and Jude—where the simple unquestioning values of the older generation will prove inadequate to human experience.

The meaning of those values, expressed through characters and action, is assessed by the Casterbridge people, who both suffer from change and have the elective power to bring it about. The Hardeian chorus is divided into one main and two subsidiary groups, whose social and moral status is marked by their inns. At the top and bottom of the social scale, the King's Arms and Peter's Finger groups are both deceived by appearances. The King's Arms, where Henchard is seen in his success, tests his worth by his actions. But the story reveals that the truth about the curse sung on Farfrae, the hag's disclosure, and Henchard's failure to preserve correspondence between bulk and sample, is more complex than their simple definitions of hatred, immorality, and dishonesty.

If the vision of the King's Arms is distorted by wealth and the power of the civic image, the grotesque effigy of vice created by Mixen Lane is just as far from the truth. Mixen Lane is a negative place, doomed to extinction. The negative way of life is threatened by the vitality of Henchard's bid to achieve meaning. (One can compare the situation in John Whiting's play, *The Devils*.) Reality for them is measured by the failings, not the virtues, of the more vital characters. Hardy's presentation of Mixen Lane makes it less of a place than a human problem correlative to the unlocalized guilt of godless man. Physical description is limited, but a selection of details—the white aprons covering vice, the swivelling eye at a man's footfall, the concealed plank that significantly connects the cancerous tissue with the body of Casterbridge, the dampness, the ruined Priory, the patched structure of Jopp's cottage that conceals the broken lives within, and the symbols of crime—gaol, hangman's cottage, gallows—poetically evoke the misery and guilt that operate, in Henchard and Lucetta, to provide the 'missing feature' needed to complete the design of the gallows—'the corpse of a man' (xix). Their sense of guilt accepts the judgment of Mixen Lane too seriously. One must wait for Jude Fawley to find a man capable of bearing personal and inherited guilt alone.

The 'philosophic party' of rustics who frequent the friendly, unpretentious Three Mariners provide the most realistic judgement on Casterbridge affairs. Their concern with the essentials of labouring and victualling, bringing up their children, and burying their dead leaves them little time to be influenced by appearances. The two-dimensional inn sign of traditional worthies symbolizes the values of their traditional community. There are no barriers at the Three Mariners. Even the horses stabled at the back mingle with the guests coming and going, and the inn has given hospitality to the Mayor and to members of the Peter's Finger group. The ale lives up to its promise, and no one sings out of tune until Henchard chooses the Three Mariners to break his vow and their traditional Sunday custom. Though they do not put too fine a point on honour ('why *should* death rob life of fourpence? I say there was no treason in it') they take a kindly interest in the careers of Farfrae and Elizabeth-Jane, and their judgement of Elizabeth-Jane (xxxvii and xliii) severs her intrinsic worth from accidents of family connection and environment. Their response to Farfrae's mixture of commonsense and idealism (which does not preclude criticism of his musical sentiment, 'What did ye come away from yer own country for, young maister, if ye be so wownded about it?') places the promise of the new age firmly in the commonalty of the Three Mariners.

Yet it is through the workfolk of Casterbridge that Hardy sounds the deep elegiac note for the passing of the old order, in the deaths of Susan and Michael Henchard. Direct death-bed scenes do not attract Hardy, for the meaning of a life that defies death is to be found in its effect on the survivors. The biblical and Shakespearean cadences of Mrs Cuxsom's elegy on Susan join with homely Wessex idiom, and the refusal to be overawed by sentiment in contemplation of Coney's theft of the penny weights, to celebrate her patience and endurance, her closeness to the facts of the earth, and the necessity for preserving human dignity in death, 'that 'a minded every little thing that wanted tending.'

The sublime tragic simplicity of Whittle's elegy on Henchard, with its physical details of his last hours offset by the bond of compassionate love (' "What, Whittle," he said, "And can ye really be such a poor fond fool as to care for such a wretch as I!" ') which has become Henchard's ultimate value, defines the meaning of his life with a fierce affirmation of love and pain that makes the negations of his Will positive. The Biblical rhythms of deep emotion in the elegiac Wessex voice are the pervading rhythms of Hardy's poetic images of the human condition; of a lonely heroic man, outside the traditional rituals that celebrate the human dignity which his Will refuses, creating his own moral order and meaning.

'Then Henchard shaved for the first time during many days, and put on clean linen, and combed his hair; and was as a man resuscitated thenceforward.'

(xli)

' ". . . God is my witness that no man ever loved another as I did thee at one time. . . . And now—though I came here to kill 'ee, I cannot hurt thee!" '

(xxxviii)

214

'   "If I had only got her with me—if I only had!" he said. "Hard work would be nothing to me then! But that was not to be. I—Cain—go alone as I deserve—an outcast and a vagabond. But my punishment is *not* greater than I can bear!"

He sternly subdued his anguish, shouldered his basket, and went on.'

(XLIII)

Henchard's tragic plight is threefold: cosmic (representative of man's predicament in an uncaring universe), social (showing the plight of a rural community when old methods are swept away by new) and personal. But it is intense poetic response to the personal tragedy that makes *The Mayor of Casterbridge* cosmic tragedy that will stand comparison with the Greeks and Shakespeare.

X

The Woodlanders:
A Novel of Assimilation

'On taking up *The Woodlanders* and reading it after many years I think I like it, *as a story*, the best of all. Perhaps that is owing to the locality and scenery of the action, a part I am very fond of.'

(*Life*)

Hardy's explanation of his preference for *The Woodlanders* '*as a story*' by 'the locality and scenery' implies a close organic connection between plot and the poetry of place. The story hinges on Melbury's struggles to lift his daughter above the levelling processes of life. The larger rhythms of woodland and orchard counterpoint the assertion of his will with intimations of 'how the whitey-brown creeps out of the earth over us' to assimilate the personal movement of human life to the impersonal drive of nature. The tension between the two movements, expressed with a poet's sensitivity to language and rhythm, generates an emotion of lyrical force. It could not, however, have been expressed in a lyric. The insidious creep of time towards absorption into the earth demands the extended action of a novel.

The plot is a metaphor of the Unfulfilled Intention that pervades the natural world with manifestations of frustrated desire. Social status, a weapon of sexual selection in the human species, is integral to the tragedy. The emotional relationship which combines a group in chain formation where each character loves the one who is a step higher in social grade, leads to frustration for everyone. The permutations of the group are changed, as Hardy so often changes them, by intervention from another environment; the aristocrats Fitzpiers and Felice Charmond, who disturb the simple workable moralities of the woodlanders, rooted in nature and tried by tradition, with their urban values and complex psychology. 'In the simple life he [Melbury] had led it had scarcely occurred to him that after marriage a man might be faithless.' Melbury's misplaced trust in civil law, foreign to the unwritten 'household laws' that kept Hintock stability, gives a blow to Winterborne's revived hopes which weakens him and leads, with other apparently trivial causes, to the most tragic unfulfilment of all—his death and assimilation into the woods.

In no other novel perhaps, does the natural environment permeate human life so thoroughly. Egdon Heath dominates by its physical mass: the atmosphere of the Hintocks, composed of myriads of frail individual lives of many species struggling for survival, creeps into the very bones and minds of the woodlanders. Egdon concentrates: the woodland disperses the characters in a confusion of purposes that recalls Shakespeare's dark wood near Athens, and Matthew Arnold's darkling plain. Its character-limitations, scene, climate, crafts, traditions, and folklore deter, mine the kind of action that takes place there.

'It was one of those sequestered spots outside the gates of the world where may usually be found more meditation than action, and more listlessness than meditation; where reasoning proceeds on narrow premisses, and results in inferences wildly imaginative; yet where, from time to time, dramas of a grandeur and unity truly Sophoclean are enacted in the real, by virtue of the concentrated passions and closely-knit interdependence of the lives therein.'

The woodlanders are involved closely in the battle of natural selection that links all species in a mystery of suffering. Trees, woodland creatures and human beings alike sound the dominant note of pain at the disharmony of natural things interrelated in 'one great network or tissue which quivers in every part when one point is shaken, like a spider's web if touched' (*Life*); a disharmony made poignant so often by the human character given through imagery to vegetation:

'They went noiselessly over mats of starry moss, rustled through interspersed tracts of leaves, skirted trunks with spreading roots whose mossed rinds made them like hands wearing green gloves; elbowed old elms and ashes with great forks, in which stood pools of water that overflowed on rainy days, and ran down their stems in green cascades. On older trees still than these huge lobes of fungi grew like lungs. Here, as everywhere, the Unfulfilled Intention, which makes life what it is, was as obvious as it could be among the depraved crowds of a city slum. The leaf was deformed, the curve was crippled, the taper was interrupted; the lichen ate the vigour of the stalk, and the ivy slowly strangled to death the promising sapling.'

Trees rub each other into wounds; dripping hedges ruin garden plots; Giles sets traps to catch the rabbits who eat his winter-greens; the cramps of Melbury's old age are the long credits of time and nature, 'the net product of the divers sprains and over-exertions that had been required of him in handling trees and timber when a young man': the creeping damps and heavy rains kill Giles when he is too weak to fence them off. The sombre isola-tion of the woodland drives the two aliens, Fitzpiers and Felice Charmond, to seek interest and human assertion in each other. The enclosed situation of Hintock House, built 'when shelter from the boisterous was all that men thought of in choosing a dwelling place, the insidious being beneath their notice', is 'a stimulus to vegetation' and 'prejudicial to humanity'.

The action takes colour from the meditative spirit of the Hin-tocks and the insidious nature of evolutionary change. There are some traces of the more sensational Hardy: in Fitzpiers' bloody head at Mrs Charmond's window, in the stereotyped picture of the *femme fatale* which Mrs Charmond presents to Fitzpiers' eyes, and in the passionate lover from South Carolina whose sole function is to shoot Mrs Charmond. But they do not destroy the unity of tone imposed by the woodland context. Fitzpiers' bloody head is expressionistic of the pain and guilt of an affair which the appari-tion prevents from being broken off. It is not necessary for Mrs Charmond to be more than another subjective reflection of 'joy accompanied by an idea' which promises Fitzpiers escape from the levelling influence of the Hintocks. The lover from South Caro-lina, in his one physical appearance, can be defended as part of the symbolic context. His incongruous appearance in evening dress at the ancient Midsummer rites, his theatrical aspect, his definition as 'Satan pursuing us with his hour-glass', his rout of girls and animals which drives both Grace and Suke Damson into Fitzpiers' arms, mark him as an expressionistic dramatic symbol of modern values and the irrational power of time and circumstance imping-ing grotesquely on the woodland world; not inappropriate to an evening that begins in divination and ends in the ritual of nature's larger purposes (Fitzpiers' sexual pursuit of a village girl in the moonlit hayfield). But in general, the plot is developed less through sensational coincidences and catastrophic events than through an accumulation of small acts and isolated purposes rubbing each other into wounds through the close interdepen-dence of Hintock lives. Grace's early arrival at Sherton, and Melbury's at Winterborne's party, cutting across his unhurried country rhythm; the slug well-boiled in its natural home which somehow came upon Grace's plate; Mrs Charmond's decision to go abroad without Grace, which Melbury erroneously attributed to the ill-fated party held just before; the coincidence of Grace's flight with Winterborne's illness and the Autumn rains, and of Fitzpiers' accident with Mrs Charmond's determination to fly from him—these seemingly trivial concurrences are signs of cosmic cross-purposes as surely as the struggling species in the woodland scene. Marty's letter, 'the tiny instrument of a cause deep in nature', produces a mixed bag of delayed consequences that she could scarcely have wished, since they included two violent deaths as well as the desired object of returning Fitzpiers to his wife. The battle for right of way in a narrow lane between Mrs Charmond's carriage and Winterborne's loaded timber waggon, resulting in her refusal to disturb 'the natural course of things' by renewing the lease of his house, dooms her affair with Fitzpiers as well as Winterborne's romance with Grace, and undermines his health by the loss of his shelter. The houses themselves, doomed to be absorbed into an estate Mrs Charmond did not want, hung on a group of lives, at last attenuated to 'the one fragile life—that had been used as a measuring-tape of time by law'. And old South's life, the measuring-tape of time, depended on the life of a tree.

The poetic underpattern of *The Woodlanders* is appropriately a close network of interrelated images which make it the despair and delight of the critic. Every scene and every character triggers off a wealth of thematic reflection and cross-reflection that develop under the human action the stylized ritual of nature's larger purposes working themselves out through character and event. Sometimes Hardy's voice makes comparison explicit. When Grace tends the dying Winterborne, Hardy reminds us of Mrs Charmond's care of the wounded Fitzpiers: 'Outwardly like as it had been, it was yet infinite in spiritual difference; though a woman's devotion had been common to both.' Sometimes a simple juxta-position points forward to an implied contrast. 'The lights in the village went out, house after house, till there only remained two in the darkness.' One comes from the house of 'the young medical gentleman in league with the devil', the other lights Marty South in league with nature at her woodland work. The force of the juxtaposition comes home a few pages later. The rapidly changing colour of Fitzpiers' light does not augur well for the adjustment to

Marty's woodland world of a doctor reputed to be in league with the powers of chaos.

'Almost every diurnal and nocturnal effect in that woodland place had hitherto been the direct result of the regular terrestrial roll which produced the season's changes; but here was something dissociated from these normal sequences, and foreign to local knowledge.'

The literal situation may imply a comparison that is metaphorical. Mrs Charmond lost in the woods is matched by Melbury, out of his depth in the laws and deceptions of a complex civilization. Different actors placed in the same situation comment on both actors and situation. The party given by Giles, where the Melburys are ill at ease, adds resonance to and gains from the supper given by Mrs Melbury where Fitzpiers is the outsider. Hardy is adept at setting up tensions between different social classes and different levels of sensitivity by the small thing that jars—oil on the chair, a slug in the wintergreens, Creedle's rough and ready method of serving, the desire of the woodland community to welcome Fitzpiers as one of themselves when he wants to preserve his identity by keeping aloof.

As an artist, Hardy knew the value of a 'frame' which concentrates attention on a pictorial or dramatic composition, and points to vital comparisons by altering a few details when the image recurs. We get our first view of Marty South through the window of her cottage, in a shaft of light, hard at work. The scene, to Barber Percomb,

'composed itself into an impression-picture of extremest type, wherein the girl's hair alone, as the focus of observation, was depicted with intensity and distinctness, while her face, shoulders, hands, and figure in general were a blurred mass of unimportant detail lost in haze and obscurity'.

Marty's hair, thus picked out as the central feature in a framed composition, links the scene to two more portraits framed by the window. In the second, Grace sees her writing what proves to be the fatal letter to Fitzpiers about Mrs Charmond's borrowed attraction. In the third, Fitzpiers, returning repentant to the Hintocks after the death of Mrs Charmond, sees Marty, hard at work again, polishing the dead Winterborne's tools. 'His glance fell upon the girl's rare-coloured hair, which had grown again.' His reference to the cause of his regeneration, and his help in buying Winterborne's cider-making equipment so that Marty can continue his seasonal work, stresses the cumulative force of Marty's hair as a fertility talisman. Its 'rape' in the first chapters (likened to the rape of Sif's hair in Norse fertility myth by Loki, the capricious and deceiving god who bears some resemblance to Mrs Charmond) has been retrieved, at the cost of suffering and death, by the continuance of natural growth.

Grace's meetings with Fitzpiers, contrasted with her fruitful association with Giles, are framed and reflected in images whose details invest her choice between two men and two worlds with the significance of a choice between the forces of life and death, appearance and reality. Her first sight of Fitzpiers, asleep, inspires a simile of death—'a recumbent figure within some canopied mural tomb of the fifteenth century'—which looks forward to the sparse ruins of the Oakbury Fitzpiers property, melancholy evidence of the near-extinction of the doctor's ancient family. (The man of modern scientific notions springing out of primitive medievalism is an interesting forerunner of Thomas Mann's definition of the daemonic death wish, combining progression and regression, in *Dr Faustus*.) Their significant experience of each other at this meeting is of reflections in the mirror. It is a warning from the subconscious powers of the dangers of Fitzpiers' platonic idealism—'Nature has at last recovered her lost union with the Idea!'—and wish-projection of 'joy accompanied by an idea which we project against any suitable object in the line of our vision', which Giles bluntly defines as 'what we call being in love down in these parts, whether or no.' Grace's mysterious compulsion by the reflected image, which differs from the reality in having its eyes open, recalls 'The Fiddler of the Reels' and folklore of demonic possession through the reflected image. Her hurried exit and return to the house so that Fitzpiers sees her coming instead of going, out of the natural order of things; the imagery taken from theatrical speech and gesture, the overtones of deception to come, add to the dream-like quality of the scene, and invest it with the importance of a compressed subconscious drama of the action that depends on Grace's choice. The scene ends with a reminder of Fitzpiers' association with death and dissection, in the view of John South's brain reflected under a microscope. It throws the mind back to the true woodlander's living link with trees, and the very different first meeting of Grace and Giles under the apple tree,

221

indubitably real and muddy but symbolic of future bloom and growth.

Fitzpiers' reflected world of reality recurs in action and scene, contrasted with the physical world as it is, in Chapter XIX. He surveys the woodland scene, and makes his approach to Grace on the strength of his impression, from the sentimental viewpoint of an observer, reading his book inside the shelter while the physical process of bark-ripping, its sights, sounds, smells, textures, surrounds him with the reality at the heart of the sylvan scene. The reality includes 'great undertakings on the part of vegetable nature' which he is too indolent to copy, ancient timber stories and traditions which his lack of association with place and people present and past cannot make meaningful, and the economic facts of woodland life which are inextricably involved with the display of Marty's superior skill. Her position 'encaged amid the mass of twigs and buds like a great bird' in branches which had 'caught the earlier rays of the sun and moon while the lower part of the forest was still in darkness' may tinge her with the light of a tree-spirit but the poetic fact depends on the economic fact. ''Tis only that they've less patience with the twigs, because their time is worth more than mine.' As Grace and her father leave the magic firelit circle which has shaped a new stage in the relationship of Grace and Fitzpiers, and they spare a thought for the distanced Giles contemplating his apple bloom while their carriage wheels crush the minute forms of life underneath, the feeling built up by the interplay of narrative, scene, and memory of that first meeting with Fitzpiers charges their departure with the force of a rejection of Winterborne's world of life and growth and reality.

Hardy's dramatic and pictorial composition of scenes where human relationships are interwoven with the seasonal movements of woodland work, from planting to felling, gives the poetic under-pattern the resonance of myth where human beings ritually act out their archetypal roles. The shrouding and felling of the tree to which John South's life is mysteriously linked is one of the inter-related generative images of the poetic network which sharply focuses the theme of man's connection with the natural world. It involves all the main characters, to whose fortunes the tree, a kind of Hintock Yggdrasil, is central, in a compressed symbolic drama, but never loses sight of the modern facts that carry the ancient ritual. While South's belief in his link with the tree reflects the sympathetic magic that expressed primitive man's sense of kinship with nature, there is a rational explanation of his 'terrifying illusion' in the action of the wind. The disaster that overtakes him and his kin when the tree is felled, attested by primitive belief in the tree-soul, has its modern cause in the lifehold conditions attached to South's cottages. Much of the scene's evocative power lies in the poetic interplay between mystery and fact, rational and irrational, different expressions of the same thing—a close natural interdependence that can only be broken at great risk.

It is broken, symbolically by Mrs Charmond, to whom the tree belongs and the cottages revert at South's death, and actually by Fitzpiers, whose rational remedy does not allow for the strength of old forest faiths (reinforced by Grammar Oliver's reversion to type). These two aliens drive a destructive wedge between the kinship loyalties, sacred to the woodland code, that arose out of the mutual interdependence imaged in the world of nature. Giles Winterborne, forced to operate on the tree by Fitzpiers' orders, seals the loss of his houses and his own death as well as South's. His ascent up the tree, 'cutting away his perches as he went', gathers layer upon layer of meaning. It dramatizes the destructive power of modern thought and codes, which cut away the stability of man's roots in nature and the past. As he works higher up the tree in darkness and mist which is likened to Niflheim, the Norse region of cold and death, 'cutting himself off more and more from all intercourse with the sublunary world', the distancing becomes more than physical. Grace's snub moves him fatally out of the everyday world of human concerns. 'He could only just be discerned as a dark grey spot on the light grey zenith', as the sound of boughs falling and the stroke of his billhook, and, when he descends, by a shiver and sigh from the tree that expresses his emotion. His identification with tree and sky, his distance from the human world on the ground, the loneliness and shade of the woodland reflected in his position and gesture, invest him with the impersonal role of wood-god climbing towards the otherworld doomed to death and absorption into his non-human environment. The ritual aspect comes out in his contact with Grace, which places her share of responsibility for destroying the fruitful connection between man and nature. He calls her twice; twice she passes by. On the third passing, she calls twice to him. His decision to move higher up after her snub, which pushes him out of his merely human into his archetypal role, may also carry an implied criticism of his acquiescence in his fate.

'Had Giles, instead of remaining still, immediately come down from the tree to her . . . the probabilities are that something might have been done . . .'

The episode gains retrospective ritual force from later episodes, which gather richness from it in turn. Giles Winterborne's call to Grace from the heights of South's tree—'Thinking that she might not see him, he cried, "Miss Melbury, here I am" '—presents Grace with a vital appeal to recognize his, and her, identity with the natural world. The cost of her failure to do so recalls this scene when she sits luxuriously in the 'Earl of Wessex', the poor little rich girl of folklore, figuring as a fine lady on the balcony above, separated from Giles cider-making in the yard by the window, the height, and the nature of the choice she made under South's tree. The appeal is ritually reversed. Twice she calls down to him to recognize her superiority to the workaday world. He recognizes her finally by a stern rebuke for her choice of separation, which has contributed to his misery. And Winterborne's last illness gains accumulated resonance from these two scenes by the repetition of his separation from Grace, though both are now at ground level, by a window. Through the window of his hut she gives him his meals, calls but fails to make him hear, and knows him only through a handclasp in the darkness. His isolation from human contact and her separation from the organic world are complete.

The deeper meaning that accumulates into myth and the factual, sensuous descriptions of Giles at his seasonal work are inseparable. Grace's desire to escape from the levelling processes of the Hintocks embodies the modern alienation from physical conditions, including the march of time, that is treated more fully in *Tess* and *Jude*. Her meetings with Giles, actively engaged in his seasonal work, at points of crisis and conflict between her two worlds, surround her with the mud, the whitey-brown, the natural transformations which are inescapable. Winterborne's control of the physical world through working with its produce imposes a pattern of meaning on the physical chaos that is sombre but satisfying. It is the pattern of fertility ritual, which involves Grace, like all the heroes and heroines of the major novels, in a process of regeneration through contact with her roots in the earth, and deepens the social theme with anthropological significance.

The pervading sight and smell of apples, which characterizes the

Hintocks to Barber Percomb in the first chapter, becomes a recurring metaphor for the regenerative process. Winterborne's first meeting with Grace, fresh from her expensive education, 'looking glorified and refined to much above her former level', occurs under the boughs of the specimen apple tree he is trying to sell in Sherton market place.

'Winterborne, being fixed to the spot by his apple-tree, could not advance to meet her: he held out his spare hand with his hat in it, and with some embarrassment beheld her coming on tip-toe through the mud to the middle of the square where he stood.'

The distance between their worlds is already implied by the mud, the embarrassed gestures, the identification of Winterborne with his tree, 'being fixed to the spot' by it like a local tree-god; and re-iterated later by Grace's inability to distinguish between bitter-sweets and John-apples. The pictorial composition of the cider-making at the 'Earl of Wessex' recalls her earlier reluctance in the same town to cross the mud to more abundant life. 'She had felt superior to him then, and she felt superior to him now.' The named varieties of apples quivering in the hopper, the rich colours, the stress on verbs of energetic action, the poet's sensitivity to rhythm and diction, bring the physical process to our senses, and recall the vitality of a link with nature that Grace has rejected. But the ritual movements, and the appearance of Giles, coated with apple-rind and pips like a primitive fruit-god, bring to the surface an intuitive response to her need. When Fitzpiers defines himself as a different species to the workers in the yard, Grace replies, 'And from me, too, then. For my blood is no better than theirs.'

Grace's recognition of identity prepares for the regenerative process that starts with her third meeting with Giles in his ritual aspect, in the rich Autumn landscape that places him as 'Autumn's very brother', as she returns from watching Fitzpiers ride away to his new love on the gentle horse that was Winterborne's gift to Grace. Every detail of colour, movement, gesture, and speech in the chapter contributes to a pattern of association that opposes the vitality of a controlled relationship with nature's fertility to its abuse in Fitzpiers' infatuation. The scene begins with a memory of Chapter xix, that links the spring promise of that scene to its Autumn fulfilment in human and natural life. Fitzpiers, looking towards Mrs Charmond's residence, leans over the gate on High

Stoy Hill where in the earlier scene, fresh from a romantic encounter with Fitzpiers, Melbury and Grace had noticed the rejected Giles contemplating his apple blossom. The recapitulation
points the ironical difference from the original: the emotional dis-
turbances experienced between the two scenes have changed the
underlying harmonies to re-direct the story. A transitional minor
harmony has been supplied by the memory that High Stoy Hill
was also the spot from which Melbury pointed out the decayed
Fitzpiers property, now significantly used by a local farmer for his
young stock. The rustic opinion that Darling has been 'hag-rid'
after her long journey to Middleton Abbey points to the irrational 'black magic' character of Fitzpiers' infatuation, later
opposed by the 'white magic' of the horse's natural instinct (embodying Winterborne's natural wisdom) which brought her unconscious rider safely home—a scene that has some of the resonance of the sleepwalking episode in *Tess*. Her pale colour, which
defines her rider clearly against the background—'the sky behind
him being deep violet she could still see white Darling in relief
upon it'—looks back to Winterborne's identification with the grey
sky surrounding South's tree, and forward to his blending with the
Autumn landscape.

As Fitzpiers moves away from her, Grace accepts the evil that is
part of nature's carefully detailed natural bounty. 'In all this
proud show some kernels were unsound as her own situation.' It is
the turning point of her recovery. Fitzpiers' movement *away* from
her is answered ritually by Giles and Creedle 'moving up the
valley towards her', defined as god-like symbols of fertility and
regeneration by the reflected sunlight on their tools and the sensuous perceptions.

'He looked and smelt like Autumn's very brother, his face being sunburnt to wheat-colour, his eyes blue as corn-flowers, his sleeves and
leggings dyed with fruit-stains, his hands clammy with the sweet juice
of apples, his hat sprinkled with pips, and everywhere about him that
atmosphere of cider which at its first return each season has such an
indescribable fascination for those who have been born and bred among
the orchards. Her heart rose from its late sadness like a released bough;
her senses revelled in the sudden lapse back to Nature unadorned.'

The dance-like figure which replaces the destructive Fitzpiers with
the regenerative Giles who 'had arisen out of the earth ready to her
hand'; the vital sensuousness of his description in terms of autumn's

colour, texture, smell, produce, and process; the rhythm, that rises to little climaxes of stress on nature's seasonal products, and leads to a relaxation in sound and sense, 'Her heart rose from its late sadness like a released bough', vividly embody Grace's return to a living relationship with nature through love for a human being. Their shared experience of the sunset, a correlative of 'her abandonment to the seductive hour' and the natural passion ritually expressed in Giles' caress of the flower at her breast, compels comparison with the sunset that defines Fitzpiers' caprice when he refuses the Budmouth practice to stay near Mrs Charmond. 'His motive was fantastic, glowing, shapeless as the fiery scenery about the western sky.' The passion of Giles and Grace has its surrogate climax in complete identification with the 'bottomless medium of soft green fire', but it is anything but shapeless. Its development is controlled by the creative art of nature.

'They passed so far round the hill that the whole west sky was revealed. Between the broken clouds they could see far into the recesses of heaven . . . the eye journeying on under a species of golden arcades, and past fiery obstructions, fancied cairns, logan-stones, stalactites and stalagmite of topaz. Deeper than this their gaze passed thin flakes of incandescence, till it plunged into a bottomless medium of soft green fire.'

The regenerative power of Giles acting out his deeper purposes sustains Grace while she waits for news of a divorce. His ritual death completes for her the meaning of his role as Autumn's brother. 'Autumn, this year, was coming in with rains', which kill as well as fertilize. The vital colour of the earlier Autumn figure is recalled by the absence of colour in the dark wood and the destructive violence of the storm that is 'only an invisible colourless thing'. The living sunlight that defined the scene is shut out by lush foliage. The darkness and images of death remind us that much of Autumn's colour and fertility is provided by decaying vegetation. Hardy gets every ounce of emotive value out of the traditional elegiac associations of rain, darkness, and decay, which invest the objective world of the woodland with Grace's state of mind and the reader's expectation of tragedy.

'The plantations were always weird at this hour of eve—more spectral far than in the leafless season, when there were fewer masses and more minute lineality. The smooth surfaces of glossy plants came out like weak, lidless eyes: there were strange faces and figures from expiring lights that had somehow wandered into the canopied obscurity; while now and then low peeps of the sky between the trunks were like sheeted shapes, and on the tips of boughs sat faint cloven tongues.'

The absence of definition by colour and 'lineality' robs the human being, isolated in a wood full of decaying vegetable presences, of personal identity. Grace 'seemed almost to be apart from herself—a vacuous duplicate only. The recent self of physical animation and clear intentions was not there.' Giles' gentle slide towards death mirrors the absorption of all human, animal and vegetable purposes into the whitey-brown of the earth, that is the obverse side of Autumn fertility. The man who was 'fixed to the spot' by his apple-tree, house and local ties is gradually pushed out of the social structure of the Hintocks till he is revealed as essentially continuous with nature. After the loss of his houses he 'retired into the background of human life and action thereabout' to become a wanderer, like Tess and Jude. From a shadow of his former self he dissolves into the wood by imperceptible degrees. As Grace's isolation from him increases—the isolation of the conscious human being in a non-human universe—she and the reader are overwhelmed by woodland sights, sounds, and textures. 'The stopping of the clock for want of winding' places her in a world of non-human time. The eft that rustles out to bask in the last sun-rays, the lower species investigating Winterborne's hut with a view to winter quarters, the thrush who steals his untouched food; the evocation in sound and sense of decaying vegetation whose individual struggles for fulfilment are backed by evidence of past defeats by time, 'Dead boughs were scattered about like ichthyosauri in a museum', and linked inextricably to human life and death in the image of 'rotting stumps of those of the group that had been vanquished long ago, rising from their mossy setting like black teeth from green gums'; all add up to an overpowering sense of transience and trespass. As Giles moves down the evolutionary scale, distinguished at first by a cough that sounds like a squirrel or a bird, then as a 'voice . . . floating upon the weather as though a part of it', and finally indistinguishable, as 'an endless monologue, like that we sometimes hear from inanimate nature in deep secret places where water flows, or where ivy leaves flap against stones', the meaning of identity with the natural world, so often sounded as his keynote, comes home with tragic force to the modern reader,

developed beyond the primitive, hardly conscious needs answered once by fertility ritual.

The three elegies that mark Winterborne's death bring together the natural, social and cosmic themes which make his life and death an inevitable poetic outgrowth of the woodland evocation that began the novel. The first is the lament of nature (recalling the lament for Baldur the Beautiful) for the loss of his controlling power.

'The whole wood seemed to be a house of death, pervaded by loss to its uttermost length and breadth. Winterborne was gone, and the copses seemed to show the want of him; those young trees, so many of which he had planted, and of which he had spoken so truly when he said that he should fall before they fell, were at that very moment sending out their roots in the direction that he had given them with his subtle hand.'

The simplicity, the poetic precision that infuses the fact with deep elegiac emotion, is achieved through the run of the sentences—the first cut off abruptly with short vowels and hard consonants; the second, after a check at 'want of him', gathering strength as it expresses the continuity of life in which Winterborne was involved, with stress falling on the words that develop the regenerative process from death to new growth. It casts the mind back to Giles in the fullness of his life planting firs with Marty, and harmonizes the two deep notes sounded then that immortalize his quality both as a natural genius (in both senses of the word) and as a man; his 'marvellous power of making things grow', and Marty's perception of universal *lacrimae rerum* in the sighing of the young pines. It stresses the regenerative power of his life and death, which functions even as he lies dying while Grace runs for help: 'The spirit of Winterborne seemed to keep her company and banish all sense of darkness', the same rain that killed him lighting the path with phosphorescent gleams; and looks forward to the muted regeneration of Grace and a more considerate Fitzpiers, whose gift to Marty of Giles' cider-making equipment ensures the continuation of his memory, genius and work. It sounds again the dominant keynote of the novel, sounded at the beginning, where the descriptive details (the trees which make the 'wayside hedges ragged by their drip and shade', the leaves which *bury* the track, the *tomb-like stillness*, the melancholy associations called up by emotion and scene of past charioteers now *perished*, the 'blistered soles that have trodden [the highway] and the tears that have wetted it') introduce the novel with overtones of pain and death, loss, transience, vanished generations in the agelessness of natural process, assimilation to the earth, human isolation, and the insignificance to the larger movements of nature of the human figure who stands on the deserted road uncertain of his way: overtones which are now fulfilled.

The elegy of Robert Creedle mourns the loss of Winterborne to a community. Spoken in the simple, rhythmic idiom of Wessex workfolk whose contact with concrete things and the earth evokes the loss of a physical human presence, it laments the practical agricultural worker, the end of a local family, and the goodness that makes Giles a mainstay of Hintock tradition.

> ' "Forgive me, but I can't rule my mourning nohow as a man should, Mr Melbury," he said. "I ha'nt seen him since Thursday se'night, and have wondered for days and days where he's been keeping. There was I expecting him to come and tell me to wash out the cider-barrels against the making, and here was he . . . Well, I've knowed him from table-high; I knowed his father—used to bide about upon two sticks in the sun afore he died!—and now I've seen the end of the family, which we can ill afford to lose, wi' such a scanty lot of good folk in Hintock as we've got. And now Robert Creedle will be nailed up in parish boards 'a b'lieve; and nobody will glutch down a sigh for he!" '

Creedle speaks for the rustic chorus (less comic, less prominent and more integrated into tone and movement than in the previous major novels) whose communal memory holds the codes and traditions of the locality. They measure character and action by their adjustment to the Hintock world. Mrs Charmond is 'the wrong sort of woman for Hintock, hardly knowing a beech from a woak'. Fitzpiers is censured for his roving eye, and Grace for making workfolk traipse seven miles needlessly in search of her at the end of the novel. Melbury deplores Grace's equivocal status, neither married nor single, because it 'will always be remembered against us in Hintock'. Though Hintock law cannot provide the last word on modern problems of a complex civilization, the rustics dramatize the ability to make limited opportunities endurable through fixed responses hallowed by local tradition; lack of ambition; a way of life that remains close to nature while improving on its morality by control, mutual loyalties, respect for others and the sacredness of life; respect for truth; and a long memory that enshrines the transient life in the hero-myths of Hintock. It is the

Hintock memory that inspires Winterborne's sacrifice for Grace's reputation, which some modern critics find absurd or proof of impotence—a view not shared by Hardy. Creedle's elegy ensures a place for Giles as a local hero.

The last elegiac voice in the novel is Marty South's, sounding the simultaneous chords of love, pain, life and death that combine in the elegies to Emma Hardy. It combines personal sorrow with remembrance of the immortal good in Winterborne's way of life as a woodland worker and human being. While intensifying the elegiac tone of the opening chapters to shape the novel to a harmonious close, Marty's elegy stresses the loss of moral fineness in the human consciousness that makes the fall of a man so much more tragic than the fall of a leaf. 'You was a good man, and did good things.' It is appropriate that Marty—Winterborne's counterpart as the spirit of the woods in its purity, versed like him in the language of the woods and now his living heir—should begin and end the novel by pointing the difference between the purposes of man and the purposes of nature. In the first chapters she evolves out of the poetic evocation of natural selection and assimilation as an image of human involvement in the process. Her hair, symbol of the vitality of life close to nature, is destined to follow the downward trend of assimilation into an impersonal movement, evidenced by the coffin stool in her cottage, Mr Melbury's house, Winterborne's cottages, the vanished charioteers, and the fallen leaves. Her final elegy is enriched by her consciousness of the cost of involvement to human sensitivity in pain and unfulfilment. Pain is the dominant emotion of the novel. Marty, more sensitive even than Giles to the pain of all living things, brings it poetically to the reader's senses. Her sense of unfulfilment when she overhears Mr Melbury's plans for Giles to marry Grace enters the cosmos in a physical metaphor charged with emotional force: 'The bleared white visage of a sunless winter day emerged like a dead-born child.' It is Marty who hears the pines sigh, envies the pheasants whose lack of human consciousness gives them nothing more than the weather to think of, and comments on the symbolism of the two quarrelling pigeons who fall into the ashes of the fire by which Fitzpiers declared his feelings: 'That's the end of what is called love.' It is Marty who comes to share with Grace the pain of Giles' death, with a dignity and truth that compels comparison with the tragi-comedy of Grace's treatment of Fitzpiers' two other 'wives' when they come for news of his accident.

' "He belongs to neither of us now, and your beauty is no more powerful with him than my plainness. I have come to help you, ma'am. He never cared for me, and he cared much for you; but he cares for us both alike now." '

Quietly she accepts the truth of pain as part of the great impersonal movement of nature without accepting the morality of nature uncontrolled by man. Her elegy restores the poetic keynote after the deliberately commonplace slackening of tension which marks Grace's reunion with Fitzpiers, and which, far from being a fault, enacts the gradual reassertion of life, including Grace's response to Fitzpiers' sexuality, after the numbness caused by Winterborne's death. It stresses Marty's function as Giles Winterborne's heir in a scene where woodland and orchard speak of nature unrestrained and nature held in check—to keep the tools that control and direct in good order. It distances Winterborne's death by opening up a long perspective of man's fruitful and continuing contact with the perpetual renewal of the earth. Her lonely figure, sexless, colourless, hardly distinguishable from the misty landscape, speaks the sublime simple words that affirm both the good of the individual human life rooted in but not controlled by nature (as South was controlled by his tree) and the pain that defines its value. It is a lament for all human beings who deserve the name, and for a simple way of life whose passing creates the complex problems of *Tess of the d'Urbervilles* and *Jude the Obscure*.

' "Now, my own, own love,' she whispered, 'you are mine, and only mine; for she has forgot 'ee at last, although for her you died! But I—whenever I get up I'll think of 'ee, and whenever I lie down I'll think of 'ee again. Whenever I plant the young larches I'll think that none can plant as you planted; and whenever I split a gad, and whenever I turn the cider wring, I'll say none could do it like you. If ever I forget your name let me forget home and heaven! . . . But no, no, my love, I never can forget 'ee; for you was a good man, and did good things!" '

XI

Tess of the d'Urbervilles:
A Novel of Assertion

' ". . . what's the use of learning that I am one of a long row only—
finding out that there is set down in some old book somebody just like
me, and to know that I shall only act her part; making me sad, that's
all. The best is not to remember that your nature and your past doings
have been just like thousands' and thousands', and that your coming
life and doings 'll be like thousands' and thousands'." '

(Tess of the d'Urbervilles)

Tess of the d'Urbervilles is not about a pure woman betrayed by
man, morality, and the President of the Immortals; her fight for
re-acceptance and happiness; 'the incessant penalty paid by the
innocent for the guilty' (*Academy* review) or the decay of the
peasantry. All these aspects are there, but all are contributory to
the major conflict suggested by the two parts of the title. ' "Call
me Tess," she would say askance' when Angel Clare 'called her
Artemis, Demeter, and other fanciful names half teasingly', and it
is as the dairymaid Tess, an individual human being, that she 'had
set herself to stand or fall by her qualities'. But she is also Tess 'of
the d'Urbervilles', and the novel is shaped by the tension between
the personal and impersonal parts of her being. The right to be
human is not easy to assert against the laws of nature, heredity,
society and economy which abstract from people 'the differences
which distinguished them as individuals'.

The surface story of Tess narrates the events that defeat her
struggle for personal happiness. But the poetic underpattern
reveals 'underneath the resolute purpose of the planning animal,
the victim of circumstance and the doomed or sanctified being'
—a more archetypal direction to her life, hostile to personal
claims.

The plot is simple and unoriginal. Its familiarity springs from
two sources. The eternal triangle, the wronged woman who cannot
escape her past, 'the woman pays', the double standard of morality

for men and women, were themes known to Victorian literature. Balladry can produce Patient Griselda, the highborn lady in disguise, the seduced milkmaid, the murder of a betrayer, and retribution on the gallows. Hardy's poetic power lies first of all in crossing and challenging the Victorian moral tale with the ethic of folk tradition. The Victorian assumption that the fallen woman did not rise again is questioned by the timeless values of the ballad world, closer to natural law.

> 'Though a knave hath by me leyne,
> Yet am I noder dede nor slowe;
> I trust to recouer my harte agayne,
> And Crystes curse goo wyth yow!'
> ('Crow and Pie')

The ballad mode, non-naturalistic and poetic, also lends belief to those unlikely incidents which disturb a naturalistic view of the novel but fall into place as manifestations of 'the indomitable unconscious will' that directs the underpattern. Angel's sleepwalking, Alec's conversion and his blood soaking through the ceiling, the gift of an empty mansion in the New Forest; the impish operations of time, chance, coincidence and cross-purpose, mock the resolute purpose of the planning animal with intimations of her archetypal destiny. Such are the collision of the mailcart with the Durbeyfield waggon, the coincidence of Chaseborough Fair with the market, the drunken revel and Tess's fatigue; the mistiming that dooms Tess 'to be seen and coveted that day by the wrong man', and Angel to dance with the wrong girl and return from Brazil too late; the events which frustrate her attempts to confess and seek aid from Angel's parents; the tenant-farmer of the 'starve-acre' farm turning out to be the Trantridge man who owed her a grudge; Angel's chance glimpse of the d'Urberville portraits as he hesitates outside Tess's bedroom; the build-up of her family's misfortunes just after she has refused Alec's help; and the omens—all add up to an impressive vision of the workings of a Fate familiar to folklore, irrational and unknowable, ordering the affairs of men to a non-human rhythm.

The plot is organized round the seven 'phases' of Tess's personal story to give pointers to the direction in which her impersonal life is moving. Her first phase as 'The Maiden' ends when Alec seduces her.

'An immeasurable social chasm was to divide our heroine's personality thereafter from that previous self of hers who stepped from her mother's door to try her fortune at Trantridge poultry farm.'

The second phase follows Tess's return home with the consciousness of original sin on her—'she looked upon herself as a figure of Guilt intruding into the haunts of Innocence'—to the birth and death of her baby, and her reintegration into country ritual. 'The past was past; whatever it had been was no more at hand.'

'On one point she was resolved: there should be no more d'Urberville air-castles in the dreams and deeds of her new life. She would be the dairymaid Tess, and nothing more.'

In Phase the Third, 'The Rally', the experience and personality of the dairymaid Tess are enlarged at Talbothays by Angel Clare. The unpremeditated kiss that ends this phase means that 'something had occurred which changed the pivot of the universe for their two natures'. That 'something', in the next phase, is that Tess hands over part of her self to the impersonal force of love. This phase follows the maturing natural relationship of two lovers 'converging, under an irresistible law, as surely as two streams in one vale,' until Tess's fatal confession on her wedding night. In Phase the Fifth, 'The Woman Pays', the personal Tess is gradually depersonalized, first of all by the abstract ideal of purity which Angel prefers to her real human self, and secondly, when he has abandoned her, by the increasingly automatic mode of her life.

'There was something of the habitude of the wild animal in the unreflecting instinct with which she rambled on—disconnecting herself by littles from her eventful past at every step, obliterating her identity.'

Now seeking not happiness, but mere survival, she has a second recovery through endurance of winter weather and rough work at Flintcombe Ash. This time it is halted on her return from Emminster, when a meeting with Alec gives her 'an almost physical sense of an implacable past which still engirdled her'.

The closing in of her implacable past to submerge her personal identity occupies the sixth phase. She makes her last helpless gesture as an independent woman in the d'Urberville vaults, where her homeless family have camped for the night. 'Why am I on the wrong side of this door!' In the last phase, the 'coarse pattern' that had been traced 'upon this beautiful feminine tissue, sensitive as gossamer', is fulfilled at Stonehenge, a place of religious sacrifice, and Wintoncester, ancient social capital of Wessex. Alec's murder and Tess's execution identify the personal Tess with the d'Urberville family type, the scapegoat victim of fertility rites, and those innate and external pressures which level down the human being into something less than human—'her breathing now was quick and small, like that of a lesser creature than a woman.'

The pivotal points in Tess's fight to be herself show fundamental parallels that compel comparisons and contrasts. These draw the lines of the 'coarse pattern' for us. Tess has three 'deaths' and three rebirths: the first at Talbothays into the fullness of human and natural existence; the second at Flintcombe Ash into a lower plane of animal survival; the third in a metaphysical sense, when she hands over the meaning of her life to 'Liza-Lu and Angel standing, significantly, in the position of Giotto's 'Two Apostles'. Her two violations, physical and spiritual, invite comparison as well as contrast between Alec d'Urberville and Angel Clare. Both deny Tess the right to be human, Alec in obedience to the sub-human impulse of sex, Angel to the superhuman power of the image that substitutes essence for existence. Both are incompletely characterized when compared with the rounded humanness of Tess, but this is surely stratagem rather than error. Alec's resemblance to the Victorian stage villain and the morality Vice, and Angel's to one of his own unreal (angelic) conceptions of human nature, indicate their role as complementary agents of dehumanization. Both betray Tess in a world of paradisal lushness, though the resemblance should not blind one to the essential differences between Trantridge and Talbothays. Both feed her with fruit (v, xxx). Both are associated in action and commentary with fire; Alec in its red, murky aspect and Angel with its radiance—the fire of hell and heaven.

There are other parallels stressed by radiation outwards from the central crisis of Tess's confession. The fertility of her experience at Talbothays in Phase the Third, rising to its climax of hope in her engagement to Clare, is balanced in Phase Five by the sterility at Flintcombe Ash, which touches the bottom of despair at Alec's return. Her reintegration into natural rhythms in Phase Two is offset by her increasing subjection to mechanical rhythms in Phase Six, and pointed up by the repetition of the word 'past' at the end of each phase. The final swallowing up of the particular aim in the general doom in Phase the Seventh is an ironical development of

John Durbeyfield's claim to definition by family in Phase the First.

Such parallels suggest a rich layer of archetypal myth directing the course of Tess's life. Hardy's rich poetic and narrative resources combine to bring out the deeper meaning of the novel by imaginative description of the way characters move and speak and relate to their environment. The central events are described in Darwinian terms of struggle and adaptation, extinction and renewal of the species. But the discovery of Tess's ancestry initiates all the myths about the meaning of being human; myths that are explored in the rest of the novel through an intricate network of poetic cross-references. It may be dismissed as top dressing, but a responsiveness to poetic overtones in the first chapters reveals why Hardy placed the d'Urberville theme in a key position.

'Sir John d'Urberville—that's who I am,' declares shiftless peasant Jack Durbeyfield. His prostrate position 'upon the bank among the daisies' suggests the effigies in the d'Urberville vault. The attempt of insecure man, no longer able to give himself meaning by reference to a creator with a holy plan, to define himself through the name and fame of his human pedigree, becomes an ironical definition through death. 'I've—got—a—gr't—family—vault—at—Kingsbere—and—knighted-forefathers-in-lead-coffins-there!' Ancestry becomes a metaphor for all the impersonal forces which swallow up individual effort and lethargy alike in the final and inclusive impersonality of death.

Hardy's poetic and dramatic presentation of the various layers of Tess's past prepares us to view her in the double aspect indicated by the title. The lyrical meditation that begins Chapter II, on the 'fertile and sheltered tract of country' where Tess was born gives way to a shot, nearer in space and time but still distanced, of the transformed fertility rite that connected primitive man to the cycle of nature. Jack Durbeyfield's mock-heroic progress, with its absurd hero chanting his meaningless identification with things that are dead, provides an ironical backdrop to this 'local Cerealia'—an inheritance older than the d'Urbervilles that once gave religious and social definition, if a violent one, to man in the mass—and draws attention to Tess taking part. The colour combination which picks her out—'She wore a red ribbon in her hair, and was the only one of the white company who could boast of such a pronounced adornment'—persistently links her with a complex of passion, guilt, sacrifice, and purity. Here it associates her with the noble white hart killed violently in the forest, the first of the hunting images that run through the book as types of Tess's fate. As we move to close-up in the present moment, Tess comes before us not only as herself, but also as a product of the same nonhuman forces that produced landscape, ritual and heredity. On the outskirts of the scene stands Angel Clare, urban invader of the unconscious harmony with his disease of modern thought and 'creeds which futilely attempt to check what wisdom would be content to regulate', watching a primitive try at regulation. The dramatic composition is masterly.

The need for wisdom to regulate is made clear in Chapter III, where the picture of Tess's inheritance is completed. Joan Durbeyfield, fixed forever at the cradle and the washtub, opposes 'the muck and muddle of rearing children' to the memory Tess brings with her of an ordered ritual that once gave religious significance to fertility. Tess, as a budding woman, is cast for the role of childbearer too. But the dramatic juxtaposition questions the value of the primitive, unaware fertility of shiftless Marlott for modern conditions of self-conscious responsibility.

The dramatic and poetic vision that links Tess to her inheritance as animal, woman, and human being has already suggested the three fundamental and interconnecting myths that she will be lived by. They are the fertility scapegoat, Paradise Lost, and that twentieth century response to the 'ache of modernism', the exile. Marlott and Trantridge, sheltered and languorous, smaller in scale than the Valley of the Great Dairies where Tess reaches maturity, present the first of these, the world of fertility myth, or primal harmony before the birth of consciousness. (Richard Beckman, in 'A Character Typology for Hardy's Novels', *English Literary History*, xxx, 1963, suggests that the pattern of moods built up in the novels parallels the pattern of evolution in 'Before Life and After'——Nescience—Consciousness—Nescience.)

'They followed the road with a sensation that they were soaring along in a supporting medium, possessed of original and profound thoughts, themselves and surrounding nature forming an organism of which all the parts harmoniously and joyously interpenetrated each other. They were as sublime as the moon and stars above them, and the moon and stars were as ardent as they.'

The figures in this world take on the Dionysian attributes of vegetation gods:

238

'Of the rushing couples there could barely be discerned more than the high lights—the indistinctness shaping them to satyrs clasping nymphs—a multiplicity of Pans whirling a multiplicity of Syrinxes; Lotis attempting to elude Priapus, and always failing . . .'

and it is on this night of traditional licence that Tess is seduced. But Hardy's poetic presentation casts doubt on the meaning of fertility myth for modern man. The elements of the 'supporting medium' which contribute to the harmony of all the parts—moonlight, candlelight, pollen dust (the first of the many pollen images that link Tess with fertility throughout the book), fog, and 'the spirit of wine' lend it a nightmare quality, and distance it as an illusion of the irresponsible. Tess becomes aware of the need for a more advanced harmony, which will not affront the dignity of a self-conscious human being by ignoring the dissonance of personal pain, when the inharmonious accident to Prince proves the universe's 'serene dissociation from these two wisps of human life'. The birds, who 'shook themselves in the hedges, arose, and twittered' as usual, and the incongruous beauty of spilt blood in the sunrise suggest a duplicity in the cosmos too complex for communal fertility ritual to cope with.

Nevertheless, the sexual guilt of causing life subconsciously demands a scapegoat whose purity will carry off the sins of the world. Tess's role as victim is stressed in those scenes where the symbolic overtones of red and white set up rich dissonances of pain and purity, guilt and innocence, life and death, the paradox of living. The red is often the red of real blood. Prince's blood glares against the paleness of dawn, the lane, and Tess's white features as [Correct] she tries to stop the hole with her hand. The violent colour contrast, the crimson stain Tess receives as the result of her effort, the suggestion of sexual guilt in the blood ('Princely' but worn-out like the d'Urbervilles) that pours from a hole pierced by the phallic spike on a dark night, foreshadow her seduction and doom of murder and sacrifice. Such foreshortenings of reality, as Morrell points out in *Thomas Hardy: The Will and the Way*, are not necessarily images of what *must* happen, but of what *may* happen if steps are not taken to avert disaster. Tess's association with blood is often neutral, or at least ambivalent. Another dawn scene, when she humanely kills the bleeding pheasants, reveals to her not only her own predicament in the cosmos as a creature 'brought into being by artificial means' in order to be killed, but also her superior freedom as a human being not to hurry to her destiny. The nest she had made for herself under the boughs recalls the nest of leaves Alec made for her in The Chase but the plight of the pheasants restores her to human nature from the animal nature Alec's act implied: 'I be not mangled, and I be not bleeding, and I have two hands to feed and clothe me.' As she stands hesitant at the door of Emminster Vicarage,

'a piece of bloodstained paper, caught up from some meat-buyer's dust-heap, beat up and down the road without the gate; too flimsy to rest, too heavy to fly away; and a few straws kept it company.'

The blood-stained paper and straw, here literally a floating omen, is transmuted by her crucial loss of courage at Emminster into a fixed image of the fate she has helped to release. When she strikes Alec on the rick with a gauntlet, 'the blood began dropping from his mouth upon the straw', and Tess, 'with the hopeless defiance of the sparrow's gaze before its captor twists its neck', accepts the domination of her impersonal role. 'Once victim, always victim—that's the law!'

Even Hardy's figurative description of Alec, when Tess first meets him, as 'one who stood fair to be the blood-red ray in the spectrum of her young life' modulates before long through the forced strawberries and early roses he has given her to another blood omen in the thorn that pricks her chin. The suspicion that he has been decking a sacrificial victim, in this region 'wherein Druidical mistletoe was still found on aged oaks' (a phrase recalled when Tess confesses to an impulse of suicide under Angel's ironical gift of mistletoe over the wedding bed) is strengthened when Joan washes her daughter's hair (a fertility symbol) for the second visit to Trantridge, and

'put upon her the white frock that Tess had worn at the club-walking, the airy fulness of which, supplementing her enlarged *coiffure*, imparted to her developing figure an amplitude which belied her age, and might cause her to be estimated as a woman when she was not much more than a child.'

She is wearing the same white dress when she is seduced.

Descriptions of natural phenomena, used so variously in Hardy's work, combine with colour symbolism to define Tess's role as ritual victim. The sun-god, who demanded blood to perpetuate his life-giving powers, is much in evidence. Hardy's accuracy in conveying the effect of sunlight at different times of the day and year make these effects a poetic correlative to Tess's acceptance of her role. At Wellbridge Manor, just before she confesses, the low afternoon winter sunlight 'stretched across to her skirt, where it made a spot like a paint-mark set upon her'. The stain sets up reverberations not only of Prince's blood, which splashed her 'from face to skirt', but also of the text-painter who embodied her conventional sense of guilt in red letters, 'THY, DAMNATION, SLUMBERETH, NOT'. At Flintcombe Ash, where the red threshing machine drives Tess with the impersonality of immutable law, 'a wrathful shine' from the March sunset dyes the tired faces of the enslaved threshers with 'a coppery light', giving to the human features the look of ritual masks that marked the men who surrounded Tess on the Stone of Sacrifice at sunrise, 'their faces and hands as if they were silvered, the remainder of their figures dark'. Even the benevolent morning sun of the Marlott harvest, 'a golden-haired, beaming, mild-eyed, God-like creature', throws 'stripes like red-hot pokers' on cottage furniture and intensifies the ruddy hue of the 'revolving Maltese cross' on the reaping machine, reminding us that sun worship had its sacrificial aspect. At all times Tess is linked intimately to the natural world from which her consciousness isolates her. Hardy's double vision presents her both as an extension of nature moved by forces beyond her control—most obviously in the Talbothays idyll, where her sexuality blossoms with the maturing season—and as a subjective being whose moral awareness pushes her beyond the world of fertility myth to the world of knowledge gained and Paradise lost.

One world can be seen modulating into the other in Chapter xiv. The Marlott harvest shows the highest achievement possible to a way of life still closely linked to fertility ritual. It is a good life. All the details contribute to a picture of natural harmony: the youthful sun-god, taking a personal interest in the ritual, the reaping machine which starts with a non-mechanical ticking 'like the love-making of the grasshopper', and the horses who pull it, made as much a part of the sun-directed pattern by their glistening brasses as the men by their twinkling trouser buttons. The women too are 'part and parcel of outdoor nature', timing their dance-like movements to the unhurried pace of machine and horses. Once again, as in Chapter ii, Tess is seen first as an integral part of landscape and ritual; as one of the field-women, who has 'somehow lost her own margin, imbibed the essence of her surrounding, and assimilated herself with it'. As Hardy describes the 'clock-like monotony' of Tess's work in great detail, the tense changes to the eternal present (a common feature of Hardy's style when describing the unchanging rhythms of country labour) and the rhythm of binding controls the rise and fall of the sentences. The quiet rhythms, soft consonants and subtle vowel progressions are halted abruptly by the hardness of the last word as Hardy draws attention to the girl's bare arm: '. . . and as the day wears on its feminine smoothness becomes scarified by the stubble, and bleeds.' The abrupt halt serves to remind us of Tess's connection, by now well-established through colour imagery, with the motif of sacrifice. The undertones are strengthened by the red 'Maltese cross' to which Hardy draws attention and the ritual encirclement of small animals, which tallies closely with Frazer's description in *The Golden Bough* of the killing of the corn spirit/vegetation god/scapegoat at harvest. But even this does not destroy the harmony. It is distanced by time, '. . . the doom that awaited them later in the day', and by the ritual pattern of their death, that abstracts individuality from participants in the dance. The choreography is continued by the children carrying the baby, who 'rose above the stubbly convexity of the hill' to repeat the earlier movement pattern of the reaper and horses. Feeding the baby adds another feminine rhythm to the eternal ritual. The baby, the friendliness of the rustics, the unhurried rhythm of work and repose where nature, animal, man and machine work together in unforced harmony, build up a vision of a world where primal rightness has not yet taken the tinct of wrong.

The good life, doing what it must, with no hope, no despair, no human awareness or choice of action, has its own dignity. But certain elements in the scene—the moonlight progress, the sense of oneness with nature—throw the mind back to the drunken revel at Chaseborough, and the two scenes held in balance with Hardy's comment on Tess's subjective sensations demonstrate the falseness of a philosophy of harmony for the modern thinking and feeling human being, who has emerged from innocence to awareness of alienation. 'The familiar surroundings had not darkened because of her grief, nor sickened because of her pain.'

There is something in Tess at war with nature which she needs the qualities denoted by Angel's name to bring out. Communal fertility ritual cannot cope with a personal 'misery which transcended that of the child's simple loss'. Her concern for the baby's individual soul belongs to the kind of Christianity practised, if not preached, by Angel's parents. Her passage thus from 'simple girl to complex woman' is embodied in a striking visual image in the second half of the chapter, the baptism of her baby, which carries overtones still sounding from the harvest ritual. The modulation begins in the paragraph that joins the two parts. The picture of Tess taking part in the traditional ride home on the harvest wagon, at one with her ballad-singing companions and the rhythms of life and death denoted by harvest and balladry, is lit by

'a broad tarnished moon that had risen from the ground to the east-wards, its face resembling the outworn gold-leaf halo of some worm-eaten Tuscan saint.'

The worm-eaten saint superimposed on the symbol of fertility/ purity prepares both for Tess's growth towards a more advanced kind of religion and for the deadness of its outer forms. The eye moves from the moonlit and sunlit communal ritual to the solitary candlelit figure of Tess performing a sacred rite of the Christian church. 'The ecstasy of faith almost apotheosized her.' The priest-like white nightgown, the basin and jug and other properties of this 'act of approximation' are made divine and meaningful not by any virtue in the rite of baptism itself, but by the value of the individual human being that stands at the centre of Christ's religion.

'The children gazed up at her with more and more reverence, and no longer had a will for questioning. She did not look like Sissy to them now, but as a being large, towering, and awful—a divine personage with whom they had nothing in common.'

The sign of the cross that marks the baby baptizes Tess as a suffering human being. Conception in sorrow, toil for daily bread, frailty, freedom of will and awareness of human alienation are to define the new-created woman in place of nobility human and divine and innocence lost. Her 'desires are limited to man and his humble yet formidable love' (*The Plague*)—the basic human rights to live, love, work and be happy. She also takes with her to Tal-bothays an inheritance of vital animal instincts with which human values must come to terms. These are constantly present in Hardy's minutely detailed evocations of the maturing summer in the fertile Valley of the Great Dairies, where growth is felt as an active sexual force that affects vegetation, animals, maids and men alike. The details that denote the observant naturalist are selected by the poet to evoke simultaneously the mystery of the 'great passionate pulse of existence' that orders the movement of the natural world, and a solid sense of everyday reality.

'Rays from the sunrise drew forth the buds and stretched them into long stalks, lifted up sap in noiseless streams, opened petals, and sucked out scents in invisible jets and breathings.'

'During the day the animals obsequiously followed the shadow of the smallest tree as it moved round the stem with the diurnal roll; and when the milkers came they could hardly stand still for the flies.'

'On the gray moisture of the grass were marks where the cows had lain through the night—dark-green islands of dry herbage the size of their carcases, in the general sea of dew. From each island proceeded a serpentine trail, by which the cow had rambled away to feed after getting up, at the end of which trail they found her; the snoring puff from her nostrils, when she recognized them, making an intenser little fog of her own amid the prevailing one.'

The sense of reality is vital to the novel. It is the reality of the physical world in which a human being without God finds meaning and definition. Tess's response to it takes the obvious form of response through a lover. Angel and Tess are constantly seen as an image of the highest fulfilment in the human pair not divorced from the natural setting that is their present meaning and past history.

'The sun was so near the ground, and the sward so flat, that the shadows of Clare and Tess would stretch a quarter of a mile ahead of them, like two long fingers pointing afar to where the green alluvial reaches abutted against the sloping sides of the vale.'

Talbothays stands fair to become Paradise regained. It is a fully human paradise, that does not exclude moral awareness and unmerited personal suffering. It provides constant reminders of the doom of death and the shortness of life: butterflies trapped in the milkmaids' gauze skirts, 'another year's instalment of flowers, leaves, nightingales, thrushes, finches, and such ephemeral creatures',

'wooden posts rubbed to a glossy smoothness by the flanks of infinite cows and calves of bygone years, now passed to an oblivion almost inconceivable in its profundity.'

Work is transformed from God's curse to a harmony with country rhythms and one of the factors in the growth of love, for every emotional crisis happens during the course of the dairy chores. The three milkmaids, suffering as individuals from a gratuitous passion which reduces each to 'portion of one organism called sex' accept their pain with dignity and generosity. Sex itself is not evil at Talbothays: only thinking makes it so. Tess's spiritual quality of purity is rooted in her vital sexual nature. Talbothays gives hope of reconciliation between the natural harmony of a pre-conscious state and a respect for the conscious human self.

Angel Clare is seen as the 'god-like' Adam to Tess's Eve. With his modern consciousness, advanced views and vaunted respect for the variegated Hodge, he has qualities of spiritual delicacy that could benefit an untutored Paradise. But the poetic undercurrents flowing through his encounters with Tess suggest that his angelic qualities have some kinship with the snake that deceived her in the earlier unconscious Eden. The snake is still there, in the form of her sex. 'She was yawning, and he saw the red interior of her mouth as if it had been a snake's.' It was a moment 'when the most spiritual beauty bespeaks itself flesh'. The unweeded garden where Tess 'undulated upon the thin notes of the second-hand harp' looks back to the sinister lushness of Marlott. Her inability to leave the spot, 'like a fascinated bird' looks forward to her bird-like submission to her sexual master Alec on the rick. The distortion of reality produced by Angel's music on her subjective consciousness—

'The floating pollen seemed to be his notes made visible, and the dampness of the garden the weeping of the garden's sensibility. Though near nightfall, the rank-smelling weed-flowers glowed as if they would not close for intentness, and the waves of colour mixed with the waves of sound . . .'

—the confusion of senses and distances, the pollen, the sense of exaltation—'Tess was conscious of neither time nor space'—even the rhythm of the sentences, echo the self-deception of the Trantridge revellers. Yearning for absolute harmony is the other side of the coin of sexual attraction.

Hardy's double stress on the objective reality of the garden, full of attractive but foul-smelling weeds and sticky blights that stain Tess as she is drawn towards the angelic music (played, as Hardy is careful to point out, on a *second-hand* harp and with poor execution) and its subjective beauty when filtered through Tess's unweeded emotions, point the dangers as well as the advantages of the angelic power to transform the physical world into the spiritual. Tess's comment, after confessing her fears of life, 'But *you*, sir, can raise up dreams with your music, and drive all such horrid fancies away!' marks the kind of deceiver Angel will be in this new conscious garden of Eden. The sham d'Urberville raised hopes of definition by human pedigree; the sham angel appeals to the human yearning for the absolute, which leads likewise to death. But ideal dreams persist. Angel is introduced into the story by a typically idealistic remark on William Dewey's deception of the bull with the Nativity hymn, which caricatures Angel's attempts to impose his superhuman vision on the living physical world. In a godless world human beings depend on each other for definition. But Angel betrays the humanness of Tess by his distorted perception. To him she 'was no longer the milkmaid, but a visionary essence of woman'—Artemis, Demeter, Eve, a goddess. His preference of essence to existence adds a modern Existentialist slant to Hardy's version of the Paradise myth.

Angel's replacement of the living Tess by a lifeless image is realized in a closely-woven poetic texture. It links together the various manifestations of automatic impulsion which drive Tess to her death when she leaves Talbothays. This can be seen clearly in Chapter xx, where the identification with Adam and Eve is explicit. The chapter is built on tension between physical reality and distorted perception of it which is central to the novel.

'Whilst all the landscape was in neutral shade his companion's face, which was the focus of his eyes, rising above the mist stratum, seemed to have a sort of phosphorescence upon it. She looked ghostly, as if she were merely a soul at large. In reality her face, without appearing to do so, had caught the cold gleam of day from the north-east; his own face, though he did not think of it, wore the same aspect to her.'

The strange poetic effects of light and mist are just as natural, and just as neutral, as the physical solidity of the cows. It is the self-deceiving mind of Angel that takes appearance for reality. Hardy stresses the 'preternatural' 'non-human' quality of those early morning hours, yet 'it was then . . . that [Tess] impressed him most deeply', not as a human being who craved warmth but as 'a visionary essence of woman'. The 'dignified largeness both of disposition and physique' which 'Tess seemed to Clare to exhibit' compels comparison not only with the physical 'luxuriance of

246

aspect' that rivets Alec's eyes, but also with the baptism of the baby, where the divinity of this being, 'large, towering, and awful' is created by what Angel forgets—the imperfect human being at the centre of the ritual. The 'minute diamonds of moisture' that temporarily give Tess a 'strange and ethereal beauty' look back to 'the miniature candle-flame inverted in her eye-pupils', in the baptism scene, which 'shone like a diamond', and forward to the brilliants which help Angel to create another Tess. The unreal essence of fine lady he has created, dramatically embodied in the debased d'Urberville portraits 'builded into the wall' like his fixed definition of purity, moves him to turn from the living woman.

'Sinister design lurked in the woman's features, a concentrated purpose of revenge on the other sex—so it seemed to him then. The Caroline bodice of the portrait was low—precisely as Tess's had been when he tucked it in to show the necklace; and again he experienced the distressing sensation of a resemblance between them.'

The fog in Chapter xx, and the remoteness imposed on human figures by effects of light and distorted subjective perception, carry echoes of the confused, unreflective life of Marlott and Trantridge, which add overtones of the subhuman to this scene of superhuman harmony with nature.

'At these non-human hours they could get quite close to the water-fowl. Herons came, with a great bold noise as of opening doors and shutters, out of the boughs of a plantation which they frequented at the side of the mead; or, if already on the spot, hardily maintained their standing in the water as the pair walked by, watching them by moving their heads round in a slow, horizontal, passionless wheel, like the turn of puppets by clockwork.'

Like the heron that Mrs Yeobright watches as she lies near death on Egdon Heath, these herons, with their 'noise as of opening doors and shutters', suggest the freedom of the absolute. The mechanical similes that describe their movements fuse the unreflecting animal life with that other mode of automatic impulsion, machinery, to imply the mechanical nature of the universe that crushes the vital qualities of Tess's nature after Angel's rejection of her personal self for a 'passionless' 'non-human' image of purity.

Careful attention to the details of such scenes where Angel is a chief actor reveals his archetypal role as human agent of the impersonal powers which, once released, will destroy Tess's life. In Chapter xx the poetic force comes from the accumulation of lyrical details: in the sleepwalking scene, from dramatic details which form a poetic image. This scene, like the Stonehenge episode, has been criticized for its theatricality. But they are theatrical for a purpose. The staginess reinforces Hardy's Aeschylean image of Tess as 'sport' for the President of the Immortals. Tess at Stonehenge and Angel in the sleepwalking episode are playing roles assigned to them by their buried selves. Psychology bears witness to the theatrical nature of the subconscious. Movement, gesture, speech, positioning, and props of the scene grow rings of evocation. The rigid stone coffin of an abbot in which Tess's living body is placed suggests the logical end of absolute aspirations, and the destructive force of the ascetic image which will hound Tess to the Stone of Sacrifice. To Angel, the human Tess is 'Dead! Dead! Dead!' and his unconscious actions are eloquent of the repressed sexual guilt and fear of the powers of life that demand a sacrifice to purity. The precariousness of their position on the plank, Tess's trust and impassivity, and her failure to follow up her chance to take control, are all dramatic correlatives of the poetic under-pattern which drives Tess from Paradise a second time.

Tess's expulsion from the human Paradise thrusts her into the modern myth of the lonely, rootless exile from meaning. Talbothays has given her human awareness, meaning through love, and roots in the natural rhythms of life and work in a simple traditional community. Hardy's poetic treatment of Tess's new relationship to her surroundings after Angel's betrayal—the betrayal of god-in-man—shows what Camus calls 'this divorce between man and his life, the actor and his setting' which constitutes the feeling of absurdity. The divorce begins immediately after Tess's confession. 'All material objects around announced their irresponsibility with terrible iteration.' Angel's absolute mode of perceiving is revealed as inadequate. The physical world that took its meaning from human emotion now exists only as a lumpish, alien factor in the elemental struggle to survive and endure.

Flintcombe Ash brings sharply to the senses the bleak sterility of life without illusions, without love, without God, without a future goal or anything that gives a reason for living to the human being, irrelevant and abandoned on the surface of the earth in a wintry death-marked universe that does not add up. A patient accumulation of the manifestations of rain, wind and snow and their physical effects on Tess and Marian builds up a feeling of the obliteration of human identity by the 'achromatic chaos of things'. Tess's mutilation of her distinctive beauty is reflected in the huge, high swede field, over which the two girls crawl like flies: 'it was a complexion without features, as if a face, from chin to brow, should be only an expanse of skin.' Once again she is part of the landscape. But the arrival of apocalyptic Northern birds, 'gaunt spectral creatures with tragical eyes' but no memory of the cataclysmic horrors they had witnessed, gives the lie to the impression that she is 'a thing scarcely percipient, almost inorganic'. The human consciousness that has brought Tess pain and exile has also brought her knowledge and memories of the Talbothays paradise which define her as a human being against the levelling flintiness of trivial existence.

Flintcombe Ash also provides the modern false gods which step into the void created by lack of roots in heaven and earth. The threshing should be compared in every detail with the Marlott reaping as processes that are respectively meaningless and meaningful. The dawn of the cold March morning is 'inexpressive' in contrast to the August sunrise which gave definition to men, horses and furnishings. The personal sun-god has been replaced by the impersonal 'engine which was to act as the *primum mobile* of this little world': the horses and local driver who understood every stage of the reaping ritual, by an itinerant Northern engineer, described less as a person than as a mechanical function, who 'had nothing to do with preparatory labour' and remained isolated from the agricultural scene. His engagement on another farm the following day forces the breakneck pace of the work; a sad reminder of the unhurried rhythm of the Marlott harvest. The friendly rick which gave Tess shelter as she ate her lunch and fed her baby in harmonious companionship has been transformed into a threatening abstract 'trapezoidal' shape which exposes her to Alec's attentions. The thresher is a soulless 'red tyrant' that gears all the workers to its insatiable demands and drives Tess by its incessant throbbing to a state of puppet-like action independent of will. The dominance of the mechanical image over the vital qualities of life suggests that the patterned ritual dance which gave harmonious meaning to life and death has been replaced by the order of immutable law which, like the engineer, does not require process to have purpose.

'His fire was waiting incandescent, his steam was at high pressure, in a few seconds he could make the long strap move at an invisible velocity.

Beyond its extent the environment might be corn, straw, or chaos; it was all the same to him.'

The details that evoke a mechanistic universe include all the impersonal forces that abstract meaning from a human being unprotected by providential design, ritual pattern, or love. One of them is time. The accelerated motion of the machine that dominates Tess, reinforced by Alec's renewed attentions, warns that time will not stand still. Nothing but her submission to conventional judgements stands in the way of another visit to Emminster; yet still Tess fails to stamp a meaningful pattern on the flow of time by decisive action. The pathos of Tess practising Angel's favourite ballads against his return should not hide Hardy's comment: 'Tess was so wrapt up in this *fanciful dream* [my italics] that she seemed not to know how the season was advancing.' Time in the shape of heredity controls her actions in the prophetic blow she deals to Alec with a gauntlet. Time combines with another false god of the void, economic interest, to rob the human being of significance. Hardy's metaphysical meaning, as usual, comes out of a physical situation. The dominance of machinery in late nineteenth-century Wessex was one of the factors which exiled man from work rooted in nature, and defined him by the profit motive and the production schedule. The homelessness of Tess's family ties the metaphysical sense of exile from meaning to concrete economic pressures which drive man unresting over the earth with no place to go.

The logical end of all depersonalizing forces is the d'Urberville vaults where Tess, in terms of the hunt metaphor, is run to earth. The reproachful gleam of the unloaded furniture, and the spoliation of the d'Urberville tombs, build up a powerful picture of a world dead to human values. It is completed when the sham d'Urberville rises from the 'mere stone reproduction' on the oldest altar tomb, to challenge the 'hollow echo from below' with the false values that too often define the modern exile in a universe shaped by death—money and sex uncontrolled by meaningful ritual. The scene looks back to the stone coffin in which Angel places a Tess who is dead to him in her human aspect, and forward to the Stone of Sacrifice.

Alec's role as devil of negation in an absurd universe (his loud clothes, diabolical disguises, and sudden manifestations call to mind the negating devils of Dostoievsky and Thomas Mann) is defined by his poetic connection with the threshing. He turns up at the rat-hunt which is done not by harvesters engaged in the ritual dance of life and death as at Marlott, but by 'men unconnected with the threshing' as a casual sport, 'amid the barking of dogs, masculine shouts, feminine screams, oaths, stampings, and confusion as of Pandemonium'. The Plutonic engineer foreshadows Alec's satanic association with fire and smoke on the Marlott allotment, where they isolate him in a *pas de deux* with Tess. The 'red tyrant' recalls the colour through which he is linked to Tess's fate: his red house, just as alien to the landscape, 'built for enjoyment pure and simple', where strawberries, roses, fowls and Tess are forced out of the order of nature for pleasure. His element is chaos. Tess kills him, and takes responsibility (like Camus' Meuersault), to assert human purpose against the temptations of purposeless process. The murder, while it aligns Tess with inherited automatic tendencies which direct the cosmic process towards death (a *Daily Chronicle* review of Galton's *Hereditary Genius* in 1892 called heredity 'the scientific equation of the theological dogma of original sin'), paradoxically restores to her life an order she has chosen; to live and love with an intensity sharpened by knowledge of the imminent death sentence she had pronounced on herself.

After Alec's murder, Tess and Angel re-live with the poetic intensity of a drowning man a telescoped and accelerated version of Tess's life, which points her archetypal role by blending motifs from all three myths. Tess's lonely journeys over the surface of Wessex have defined her archetypal exile from harmony. Since leaving Talbothays all her journeying, with the significant exception of the abortive trip to Emminster, has pointed in the direction of Stonehenge. In a universe shaped by death, it is the only journey to end in fulfilment. The realization that 'to stay, or make a move—it came to much the same' (Camus: *The Outsider*) when all effort ends in death adds a dissonant undermelody to the paradisal interlude in the New Forest with an Angel fallen to human virtues—'Tenderness was absolutely dominant in Clare at last.' The lush woodland which recalls the richness of Talbothays and the barren Salisbury plain which recalls the Flintcombe Ash period flank the belated fulfilment of the wedding night in a mansion whose furnishings recall Wellbridge Manor. The fulfilment is as childlike, as 'temporary and unforefending' as their plans of escape. Ironical echoes of the earlier innocence at Marlott —seclusion, the dream-like atmosphere, the sense of suspended time—hint at the impossibility of Paradise for two responsible living human beings. 'Within was affection, union, error forgiven: outside was the inexorable.' Tess and Angel can only achieve absolute harmony by 'ignoring that there was a corpse'.

Tess's fate acknowledges the power of death, which allows no-one to remain unsoiled.

'. . . we can't stir a finger in this world without the risk of bringing death to somebody . . . each of us has the plague within him; no one, no one on earth, is free from it . . . What's natural is the microbe. All the rest—health, integrity, purity (if you like)—is a product of the human will, of a vigilance that must never falter.'

(Camus: The Plague)

Tess, in spite of her vigilance, collaborates at times with the power of death—with her desire for oblivion, her submission to impersonal forces and concepts through her love for Angel, her relapses to waiting on Providence when her responsible consciousness tells her that there is no Providence to wait on. Stonehenge and Winton-cester, with their symbols of an order based on death defined blackly against the empty sky, provide a fitting end to this modern myth about the maintenance of human identity against the void. Hardy gives full weight to the impersonal agents of that order. Yet while his cosmos robs the human individual of meaning, his poetry puts it back again.

The poetic vision gives supreme importance to Tess's inner, unique experience of the world through her sensations and emotions; unusually detailed for Hardy. She is also defined by the poetry of her work. Even the harsh work at Flintcombe Ash borrows poetic beauty from the transformations of frost and snow and the tragic evocations of the Northern birds who share and universalize Tess's will to live. The differing kinds of work take their special rhythm from the rhythms of her life, sensitively realized in narrative and speech structure. The rhythms of Talbothays, slow and contemplative or simple and passionate, reflecting her sweep to maturity with its hesitations, crises, reprieves and rallies, build up a very different emotional response from the monotonous, consonantal rhythm of mechanical work at Flintcombe Ash, or the deadness of shocked existence, detail after dragging detail in flat bald sentences, at Wellbridge Manor. Hardy's dialogue is not always inspired: perhaps even Angel would hardly have met the greatest crisis of his life with 'My God—how can forgiveness meet such a grotesque—prestidigitation as that!'—

but Tess's stupefied simplicity in the quarrel, her bare statements of truth—'It is in your own mind what you are angry at, Angel; it is not in me'—catch the intimate cadences of a noble and passionate woman. Her qualities even infect the rougher speech of her companions. Izz Huett's 'She would have laid down her life for 'ee. I could do no more', and 'Her mind can no more be heaved from that one place where it do bide than a stooded wagon from the hole he's in' have the noble ballad simplicity of Tess's personal rhythms. This personal rhythm is set frequently against the dance-like rhythm of scenes where human beings become part of an automatic process—the harvest, the garlic picking, the threshing. Yet the personal rhythm prevails in an overwhelming sense of Tess's beauty of character.

Tess dies, but the meaning of her life, and of the whole book, lies in her vibrant humanity, her woman's power of suffering, renewal, and compassion, which has restored Angel to his rightful nature as Man, conscious of guilt and imperfection. One could not wish to be angel or animal while Tess exists in her human love, passion, beauty, trust, forgiveness, pity, sensitivity, responsibility, endurance, dignity, integrity, and spiritual light. To accept her mortality and the terrible beauty of the earth, to discover the absurdity of immutable law that makes of her fineness a death-trap, and yet to oppose her will against the universe as she found it and make moral choice that it is better to do this than that, is to answer the question of 'The Blinded Bird', 'Who is divine?'

XII
Jude the Obscure:
A Novel of Affirmation

Jude the Obscure begins with a farewell. Phillotson's farewell to Marygreen as he sets off for Christminster starts a novel that was Hardy's farewell to novel-writing, to his lyrical evocation of nature, to the comic relief of the Wessex chorus (even in so subdued a form as Dairyman Crick's stories in *Tess*), to the traditional beliefs and securities of unreflective rural life, and to the nineteenth century. *Jude* initiates the modern novel with its ambitious working-class hero and its neurotic heroine; city life in the back streets; the problems of adaptation to a rapidly changing world; of commercial and material values; of sexual and social maladjustment of the 'abnormal' variation from the species. It foreshadows the modern themes of failure, frustration, and futility, disharmony, isolation, rootlessness, and absurdity as inescapable conditions of life. It charts rebellion against orthodox labels which inhibit spontaneity and personal growth. It probes the existentialist's terrible freedom and the burden of unlocalized guilt; the search for self-definition, self-knowledge, self-sufficiency, and purpose without significance, gods, homeland, religious myths, or absolute values. It stresses the importance and self-destructive exclusiveness of personal relationships; the value of doubt and fluidity; the intellectual over-development that endangers the primary appetites for life; the ascendancy of the death-wish; the absurd and tragic predicament of human beings developed to a high degree of sensitivity in an insentient universe bearing all things away; the primacy of suffering. Jude Fawley differs from most anti-heroes, to his credit, in knowing what he wants to escape from and where he wants to go to, in holding fast to his ideal Christminster, and in refusing to demean his integrity in order to survive, Lucky Jim fashion, in the real defective world. But the line of descent is there.

Hardy's style and structure, too, have moved nearer to the modern psychological novel, without losing his traditional characteristics. His penetration into unconscious motives enabled him to embody the impulse to self-destruction, long before Freud, as self-punishment for the guilt of aspiring personal being. It can be seen at work in Jude's compulsion to degrade himself by drink, and in Sue's reversals of feeling, unnecessary housework (vi–ix), and sudden explosions of suppressed feminine desires. The psychology of evasion finds expression in Jude's half-acknowledged self-deceptions. When attracted by Arabella, 'he kept his impassioned doings a secret almost from himself'. His articulated desire to find in Sue 'a companion in Anglican worship, a tender friend', soon betrays its sexual origin; and the false logic which convinces him that he should meet Arabella instead of studying the Greek Testament is betrayed by Hardy's comment that 'foreseeing such an event he had already arrayed himself in his best clothes'. Occasionally Hardy makes use of the limited viewpoint to throw another light on a relationship that is too close to be balanced: Sue and Jude at the Great Wessex Show are seen through Arabella's vulgar but shrewd gaze. But the modern psychological subtlety contributes to the old Hardeian pattern of basic archetypes playing out a ritual of human destiny. The contrasts of style and structure reflect the discordances of modern life moving between a dead world and a world waiting to be born. The range moves from the realism of Jude's sexual relations to Sue and Arabella, and the pig-killing, to the grotesque symbolism of Little Father Time's triple murder. Epic grandeur and ironic low comedy combine in the familiar arraignment of the fundamental injustice of conscious being.

Nevertheless, *Jude* differs from the earlier novels in that its deeper reality lies less in the action than in the flow of perceptions, feelings and thoughts which make up an Ibsenite discussion drama of the inner life. The mental process by which Jude arrives at the decision to meet Arabella is a case in point. Dialogue, in a novel that embodies so much of the advanced argument of the day, takes on symbolic and cumulative importance. Hardy's touch is not always certain when he presents the play of intellectual minds, and Sue's criticism that Jude is 'too sermony' could be applied to much of the speech. But his touch is sure when human passion informs diction and rhythm, as in the last meeting of Sue and Jude, and in speeches (really monologues, true to the novel's theme of isolation) whose differing contexts dramatize the stages of Jude's career.

The revealing action, gesture, and symbol still have their place.

But a novel which rejects the old concepts of rational order and stable character looks forward in some respects to the more fluid conception which admits a sequence of external events in time to be meaningless and the human psyche to be a battleground of baffling contradictory impulses. The significance of the plot relies less on a chain of related actions than on a series of situations, created from inner tensions, which lead to 'moments of vision'—the poetic technique of later writers such as Virginia Woolf and James Joyce.

In spite of its bleakness, sexual frankness, social concern, and prosaic realism, *Jude the Obscure* is as poetic a novel as its predecessors. Its kind of poetry looks back to the epic, defiant poetry of the Book of Job and forward to the grey modern note of expected pain. The poetic strain blends several elements. Though Hardy's characteristic poetry of nature and man rooted in nature's seasonal rhythms cannot play a large part in an epic of rootlessness, the poetry of buildings and ancient cities stresses the essential themes of change and loneliness. The novel's serious concern with the ultimates of man's fate—loneliness, loss, frustration, failure, death—makes its subject as inherently poetic as the Bible or Greek tragedy. Basic myths are felt moving behind this modern pilgrim's progress to define the archetypal psychic impulsions that link Jude to earlier epics of man's relation to destiny. The seeker for knowledge to expand the limited human horizon recalls Faust. His relationship to Sue takes him into the region of legend dominated by La Belle Dame sans Merci, the enchanted maiden immured between heaven and earth (Sue's inaccessibility is stressed by the windows which separate her from Jude), and the fatal mermaid sexually attractive but impossible to mate, correlative to the fear of life that yearns for absolute existence. The most prominent mythic echoes come from the Bible and Greek literature. Jude's consistent heroic prototypes are the defiant, suffering Job, Tantalus and Sisyphus—the hero who provided Camus with an image for modern man's doom of futile effort. Jude's fate is likened to the curse on the houses of Atreus and Jeroboam. These resonances from two great shaping cultures help to define the Hebraic and Hellenic attitudes, self-denial and self-assertion, to the modern predicament.

Jude's name and appearance (curly black beard and hair) help to identify him with Jewish hero-myth as well as with St Jude, patron saint of craftsmen and impossible things. The references to

Samson and Delilah in portrait (i–vii) and metaphor (vi–vii) are an obvious comment on Jude's relationship with Arabella and his fight against the Philistines. Norman Holland, Jr., in an article ' "Jude the Obscure": Hardy's Symbolic Indictment of Christianity' (*Nineteenth Century Fiction*, ix, 1954), finds a denial of the relevance of Christianity in the reverberations of Jewish and pagan myth. The Jewish image pattern identifies Jude with the Judaic character, combining sensuality with aspiration, Sue with the Virgin mother as well as pagan deities, Arabella the pig-breeder's daughter with the unclean animal of the Jews (and Phillotson, by implication), and Little Father Time with Christ. Mr Holland's interpretation sees Jude as the potentially Christian Jew of the Old Testament and Sue as the potentially Christian pagan; and Little Father Time's function to enact a substitute Crucifixion for the 'poor Christ' Jude has become, to point the futility of atonement in a spiritual waste land. But it seems to be less of a substitution than a parody. Father Time is introduced as 'an enslaved and dwarfed Divinity', recalling E. M. Forster's conception of absolute infinity as something mean and small. If he is another Christ, he is, like Camus' Meuersault, 'the only Christ we deserve'; a grotesque anti-Saviour, created to mock the absurdity of the cosmic process.

The personal movement of Jude's life, the modern Everyman caught in the violent contrasts of his own being and the changing world, gains poetic depth from its power to represent the larger mythical, historical and evolutionary rhythms of the cosmos. He is Everyman as Tess is Everywoman. Elfride defines to Smith the essential difference (blurred by Sue Bridehead, the modern intellectual woman) between masculine and feminine assertion of being: 'I am content to build happiness on any accidental basis that may lie near at hand; you are for making a world to suit your happiness' (*A Pair of Blue Eyes*). Jude's personal search for knowledge (a magic formula that would invest life with meaning) and a place in life takes its rise in the post-Darwinian climate of insecurity and doubt. The end of his search is a bitter contrast to the beginning. Orthodox images of scholarship and religion crumble before the true religious scholar, whose first duty as a thinker, according to Hardy's admired thinker John Stuart Mill, was 'to follow his intellect to whatever conclusions it may lead'. The Biblical and Classical counterpoint to Jude's life raises the question of the place of intellect in any Holy Plan. 'Thou shalt not' of Old Testament letter is too negative and too external a creed to control those who live by their intellects and those strong inner impulses of love recognized by the spirit of the New Testament. The conflict is imaged in the two parts of *Christ/minster*.

The search for meaning in knowledge leads to knowledge of futility. 'The yearning of his heart to find something to anchor on, to cling to' leads to experience of the void. Jude's arhythmic wanderings and sexual relationships trace his progress towards self-definition. His quest is the basic myth of twentieth-century man; of Gide's Oedipus and Sartre's Orestes, isolated from conventional securities and comforting myths of a Holy Plan, free, without hope, to create ethics without dogma and the terms of his own being:

'I had gushed up from the unknown; no longer any past, no longer any father's example, nothing to lean on any more; everything to be built up anew—country, forefathers—all to be invented, all to be discovered.'

(André Gide, *Oedipus*, tr. John Russell)

His progress from a desire to find fulfilment in College and Church to the simple need to live as a human being involves an examination of the earlier myths that man has lived by, in the scientific spirit advocated by contemporary advanced thinkers. The result denies their relevance to the modern predicament. The spirit that characterized pagan and Christian civilizations—'that zest for existence' and 'the view of life as a thing to be put up with', the clarity of 'Classic' and the spontaneity of 'Gothic'—is embodied in the story and character of Jude and Sue. Their failure to find a compromise between the best of Hebraism and the best of Hellenism contributes to their personal tragedy. Their inability to stand alone as human beings without myth, most strongly marked in Sue, leads only to a reversal of their pagan and Christian standpoints. The values and defects of both have been so thoroughly measured against human needs that Sue's return to religious orthodoxy and Jude's Saturnalian re-marriage to the 'substantial female animal' are felt as defilements of their humanity.

That Hardy does not for the most part rely on the highly-charged poetic imagery of the epic genre to develop this modern epic, but on bare narration and dialogue, acceptable to the prosaic modern spirit, is a measure of his achievement. The typical tension in Hardy's verse between jerky personal rhythm and rigid form is repeated in the structure of the novel. Jude's arhythmic wanderings (Marygreen—Christminster—Melchester—Shaston—Aldbrickham and elsewhere—Christminster) are counterpointed and held together with hoops of steel by the poetic stylization of the plot. Hardy stresses that the plot is 'almost geometrically constructed—I ought not to say *constructed*, for, beyond a certain point, the characters necessitated it, and I simply let it come'.

'The "grimy" features of the story go to show the contrast between the ideal life a man wished to lead, and the squalid real life he was fated to lead. The throwing of the pizzle, at the supreme moment of his young dream, is to sharply initiate this contrast . . . It is, in fact, to be discovered in *everybody's* life . . .'

'Of course the book is all contrasts—or was meant to be in its original conception . . . e.g. Sue and her heathen gods set against Jude's reading the Greek Testament; Christminster academical, Christminster in the slums; Jude the saint, Jude the sinner; Sue the Pagan, Sue the saint; marriage, no marriage; &c., &c.'

(*Life*)

The structure of Jude's quest for meaning is marked by contrasting 'epiphanies' that define his progress from medieval to modern man. At Marygreen the pig's pizzle cutting across his abstract reflections makes him aware of his double nature. His brief marriage with Arabella brings into question the logic of social and natural law which show indifference to his finer aspirations. But the milestone to Christminster still carries his vision. At Christminster he encounters Sue Bridehead and the obstructive physical reality of his vision. His past relationship with Arabella and his growing love for Sue affect his studies and reflect the complexities of his nature. Arabella frustrates his nobler aspirations, Sue his sexual desires, and Christminster, attuned to a celibate ideal of scholarship, his complete fulfilment as a human being. Sue is closely linked with Christminster and its atmosphere of light. Her intellect promises Jude the freedom which the real Christminster denies him. But she is as ethereal as his vision of the city; emancipated, as he is not, from sexual appetites. His ideal intellectual city and his ideal intellectual woman frustrate his human impulses equally. The Christminster episode balances the vision of Part I—the ideal life frustrated by the physical—with his recognition of the incompleteness of the ideal alone. On the day he awakens from his dream, his vision embraces the reality of

259

Christminster from the heights and the depths. The unattainable Pisgah-panorama from Wren's theatre and the tavern where he drinks steadily and recites the creed in Latin to an uncomprehending rabble express his complex nature in a juxtaposition of the ideal and its negation (a structural concept basic to Hardy's poetry).

At ecclesiastical Melchester Jude's desire 'to do some good thing' as a humble man of God is disturbed by his developing passion for Sue and the influence of her free-ranging intellect on his beliefs. The epiphany that grows out of Part III is an awareness that 'the human was more powerful in him than the Divine'. Correlative to this recognition, the abstract ordinances of the Church on intimate relationships, when measured by the practical needs of the human being, are found wanting. Its concepts are based either on the subhuman or the superhuman: regarding sex as sin, yet recognizing animal desire as the sole grounds for marriage or divorce. It is typical of the modern novel that the moment of vision comes in an episode that seems extraneous to the main development of the novel, yet it grows out of dominant mood and theme: Jude's impulsive visit to the composer who, he discovers, is prostituting his talent to the mean bread-and-cheese question.

Shaston, that other 'city of a dream' where Sue lives in sexless marriage with Phillotson, the temporary quarters of eccentric itinerants, is the place where Jude sets up his standard as no more than a human individual. The unpremeditated kiss between him and Sue, each married to someone else, is the signal for Jude to burn his religious books so that 'in his passion for Sue he could now stand as an ordinary sinner, and not as a whited sepulchre'. It is also the signal for Sue to realize her false position as Phillotson's 'wife', and Phillotson, whose name suggests his Philistine role ('I hate such eccentricities, Sue. There's no order or regularity in your sentiments') to retreat from his legal rights into spontaneous human charity. ('I am not going to be a philosopher any longer! I only see what's under my eyes.') The vision gained at Shaston widens into universal significance through not being confined to Jude. The respect of both Jude and Phillotson (an older, more conventional reflection of Jude in the story) for Sue's sexual fastidiousness, for the special being of Sue Bridehead instead of for an abstraction 'the average woman', is a triumph for human individuality. It is inevitably qualified by a negation. The reverse side of individuality is anarchy. Part IV ends with the ironic low comedy of Phillotson's public defence of his charity, wrecked by his drop-out supporters. The major ironic contrast of the absurdity that vulgarly intrudes on the noblest human instincts marks the moments of vision at every stage of Jude's progress.

The title of Part v, 'At Aldbrickham and elsewhere', indicates the increasing rootlessness and isolation which follow on Jude's and Sue's attempt to live according to their own standards of truth. Social ostracism and their own sensitiveness to difference from the mass force them into an increasingly nomadic life. Fighting to keep their standards of spontaneity in a vacuum reduces both to a basic level of human existence. Jude's aspirations shrink to baking the staff of life. Sue submits to Jude's sexual desires to keep him from his lawful wife. Only the animal and unaspiring survive in an unimaginative world. The ideal vision appears only in flashes at temporary halting-places: the sense of bodiless oneness in the 'enchanted palace' of flowers at the Great Wessex show, and the Christminster cakes which embody Jude's ruling passion at Kennetbridge fair (significantly qualified by Little Father Time's sense that the roses are doomed to wither, and Arabella 'unceremoniously munching one of the cakes' which are made to be eaten.) Part v brings into prominence the forces that will crush individuality: Arabella (sex), Phillotson (convention) and Jude's son Little Father Time, whose name suggests the impersonal abstraction which assimilates human endeavour to general non-existence.

It is inevitable that Jude's progress to knowledge of self and the world he lives in should end at Christminster. His early vision is all that is left to him. Now not deceived by the reality, he sets against the hollow pomp, pride, and cruelty of Remembrance Day the justification for an obscure man's life. His great speech to the crowd compels comparison with his rehearsal of the creed, in a language not his own, of beliefs that did not square with his human experience. This spontaneous performance, the result of deep thought and painful living, is his climactic moment of triumph and vision. His physical stance, child on his arm, and the pregnant Sue at his side, stresses a vision of the dignity of a human being stripped to nothingness.

' "I am in a chaos of principles—groping in the dark—acting by instinct and not after example. Eight or nine years ago when I came here first, I had a neat stock of fixed opinions, but they dropped away one by one; and the further I get the less sure I am. I doubt if I have anything more for my present rule of life than following inclinations which do me and nobody else any harm, and actually give pleasure to those I love best. There, gentlemen, since you wanted to know how I was getting on, I have told you." '

The justification is followed by the climactic negation. Little Father Time's triple murder is the logical outcome of the absurdity at the heart of the cosmos that Jude's career has revealed. Jude's despairing remarriage to Arabella, gin-drunk, and Sue's prostitution, creed-drunk, to the religious and social orthodoxy which she thinks can take from her the responsibility of guilt for creating life doomed to death, are recognitions of absurdity. Jude's lonely death, murmuring Job's bitter indictment of life to the uncomprehending cheers of the Festival crowd outside, completes the sum of his knowledge. It is not an answer but a question. *'Wherefore is light given to him that is in misery, and life unto the bitter in soul?'*

Jude's inner development, geared as it is to the ferment of nineteenth-century advanced thought, runs the risk of being more of a tract than a novel. Its basic structure of contrasts could have turned it into a lifeless mechanical blueprint. But Hardy's poetic power of visualization clothes the abstract skeleton in a series of dramatic and interlocking scenes of sensuous human response to life that are not easily forgotten. The structural contrasts grow naturally from the details that evoke life in its variety as it falls in a sequence of related impressions on the mind of a sensitive child. Jude is Hardy's only detailed portrait of a child. The difference between *Jude the Obscure* and a manifesto on the marriage question can be gauged by examining the resonances of a scene, based on a personal childhood experience, which has reached us in three different forms; the poem 'Childhood among the Ferns', an early experience recorded in the *Life*, (pp. 15–16) and an incident in the novel.

> I sat one sprinkling day upon the lea,
> Where tall-stemmed ferns spread out luxuriantly,
> And nothing but those tall ferns sheltered me.
>
> The rain gained strength, and damped each lopping frond,
> Ran down their stalks beside me and beyond,
> And shaped slow-creeping rivulets as I conned,

With pride, my spray-roofed house. And though anon
Some drops pierced its green rafters, I sat on,
Making pretence I was not rained upon.

The sun then burst, and brought forth a sweet breath
From the limp ferns as they dried underneath:
I said: "I could live on here thus till death";

And queried in the green rays as I sate:
"Why should I have to grow to man's estate,
And this afar-noised World perambulate?"

'He was lying on his back in the sun, thinking how useless he was, and covered his face with his straw hat. The sun's rays streamed through the interstices of the straw, the lining having disappeared. Reflecting on his experiences of the world so far as he had got, he came to the conclusion that he did not wish to grow up . . . Yet this early evidence of that lack of social ambition which followed him through life was shown when he was in perfect health and happy circumstances.'

'Jude went out, and, feeling more than ever his existence to be an undemanded one, he lay down upon his back on a heap of litter near the pig-sty. The fog had by this time become more translucent, and the position of the sun could be seen through it. He pulled his straw hat over his face, and peered through the interstices of the plaiting at the white brightness, vaguely reflecting. Growing up brought responsibilities, he found. Events did not rhyme quite as he had thought. Nature's logic was too horrid for him to care for. That mercy towards one set of creatures was cruelty towards another sickened his sense of harmony. As you got older, and felt yourself to be at the centre of your time, and not at a point in its circumference, as you had felt when you were little, you were seized with a sort of shuddering, he perceived. All around you there seemed to be something glaring, garish, rattling, and the noises and glares hit upon the little cell called your life, and shook it, and warped it.
'If he could only prevent himself growing up! He did not want to be a man.'

The fear of adult responsibilities is common to all three. But the details vary to evoke different emotions. In poem and statement the response is nostalgic, but not potentially tragic. 'His experiences of the world' in the statement are not specified. 'Happy circumstances' and 'lack of social ambition' do not invest the incident with the significance of a protest against the conditions of being. The poem replaces the straw hat with a natural shelter of fern, a more adequate protection for the child who wants to regress, and dyes the sunlight to the fern's green shade. The fear of life, of which the poem is a correlative, is muted. The child has nothing worse to face than the discomforts of rain.

The incident as it is transmuted in the novel retains more features of the original. The less protective straw hat and Jude's prostrate position stress the defencelessness and defeat that have just been painfully brought home in Farmer Troutham's chastisement of the boy for his kindness to the birds. His wish to avoid responsibility grows out of the facts of his experience of the tragic dissonance that will destroy his life. The 'something glaring, garish, rattling', enacted in the prose that comes to a painful halt at every revolution of the child's thoughts, is an obvious correlative of his punishment with the rattle, and a prophecy of the vulgar sexual impulses that will cut across his finer aspirations. The pigsty, not present in poem or statement, defines the vulgarity more closely. It is the place to which he returns when defeated by lumpish physical conditions—the sheer plod of Classical grammar, the passion for Sue that makes him burn his religious books. It introduces the persistent pig imagery that is part of Jude's complex destiny as an animal being. Pigs are prominently featured in his courtship of Arabella, and it is the killing of a pig that hastens their parting and contributes to Jude's nurture by the insight it gives into their two opposed attitudes to nature's logic—the attitudes of adaptation and protest.

The details are not all of negative potentiality. Jude's affirming vision of Christminster exists in embryo in the 'white brightness' of the sun that reaches him through the translucent fog. It grows out of his moments of despair as a 'city of light', a 'heavenly Jerusalem' of all that is absolute and meaningful in a dissonant world. Its light is associated with various shades of fog and darkness that shift their meaning to define Jude's progress in disillusion. His early views of the distant city, an impressionistic mirage filtered through morning mist, an evening 'halo or glow-fog' of lamps and the romantic mists of his yearning mind, make the city seem deceptively near and the physical foreground chimaerically unreal and funereally dark. Night hides the unwelcoming countenances of the colleges when he gets there, and fog hangs over the city in the days of his final despair, chaos of principles, and bitter realization of the muddle that should have been a clear intellectual centre of light.

Unlike the statement and the poem, the incident in the novel cannot stand alone. It is part of a complex of interrelated affirmations and negations that define Jude as sufferer from the inharmonious 'ache of modernism' from beginning to end. His nature and destiny as Jude the obscure and superfluous are suggested from the start. He has no roots in family or village. His conflicting drives are obscure to his consciousness. He is caught up and lost in the atmosphere of change that prophetically begins the novel.

The inhabitants of Marygreen, particularly Aunt Drusilla and Widow Edlin, are relics of the old stable rural culture, free from 'the chronic melancholy which is taking hold of the civilized races with the decline of belief in a beneficent power'. But Aunt Drusilla tells tales of matrimonial misery, the old church is put to debased uses, and the old well into which Jude stares 'was probably the only relic of the local history that remained absolutely unchanged'. The well is a stable point to which Jude returns at moments of crisis and defeat in his changeful history. Its 'long circular perspective ending in a shining disk of quivering water', its natural encrustations, suggest the infinity he yearns for, and the mystery and continuity of life; a paradox which he is to seek in sexual experience. Phillotson, the schoolmaster who has inspired Jude with scholastic ambition, is now joining the movement of change, to seek a degree in Christminster.

The incident that draws attention to Jude—his offer of Aunt Drusilla's fuel-house to store Phillotson's piano—subtly defines the difference between master and pupil in terms of a spiritual force (music) that resounds thematically through the novel. Phillotson, who 'had never acquired any skill in playing', fails later to touch emotional chords in Sue which Jude reaches at this very piano (IV–i). It is a piquant irony that they are so moved by the emotional hymn whose composer had deserted music for the wine trade. The irony grows in power as Jude's inharmonious 'failures' —his passion for Sue, emancipation from Christian belief, the death of the children, and his own obscure death—are counterpointed by incongruous musical harmonies—psalm, hymn, waltz—entering his isolated consciousness from the communal life of Christminster and Melchester. Sue's feeling, after the death of their children,

'that the world resembled a stanza or melody composed in a dream; it was wonderfully excellent to the half-aroused intelligence, but hopelessly absurd at the full waking . . .'

is not intrusive philosophical comment, but an integral (though partial) summing up in a novel where music is a recurrent image of the harmony absent from the cosmos.

The scene that sickened his sense of harmony in Farmer Troutham's field is emotionally connected to Jude's feeling of disorientation after his teacher's departure. Like Flintcomb Ash, the field presents the earth as a lumpish, 'meanly utilitarian' antagonist to be reckoned with in desires that flout the morality of Nature. Yet Hardy never sees the opposition as simple. The comment of the young idealist out of love with life as it is—'How ugly it is here!'—leads to an evocation of the field in positive terms that Jude has missed, of its human associations with the eternal pursuits of men and women. It is here that Jude's first moment of vision, his 'perception of the flaw in the terrestrial scheme, by which what was good for God's birds was bad for God's gardener', is brought violently to our senses by Hardy's dramatic and poetic power.

'Troutham had seized his left hand with his own left, and swinging his slim frame round him at arm's-length, again struck Jude on the hind parts with the flat side of Jude's own rattle, till the field echoed with the blows, which were delivered once or twice at each revolution.

' "Don't 'ee, sir—please don't 'ee!" cried the whirling child, as helpless under the centrifugal tendency of his person as a hooked fish swinging to land, and beholding the hill, the rick, the plantation, the path, and the rooks going round and round him in an amazing circular race.'

Jude suffers a symbolic foreshortening of his fate, placed with no secure foothold in an alien mechanical world that whirls him round on its own inscrutable punishing purposes; his pain misinterpreted by man and ignored by God (the blows 'echoing from the brand-new church tower just behind the mist'). The effect is sharpened by the poet's concern with both the objective appearance of physical things and their subjective distortion through the eyes of the 'whirling child'; and with the selective language, which ranges from the simple vitality of the 'hooked fish swinging to land' to the abstract ponderousness of 'centrifugal tendency'—both appropriate to a dramatic image that evokes the helpless individual's painful dependence on impersonal forces.

But it is characteristic of Hardy that he does not leave the scene without resisting its negation with Jude's human tenderness. He swings from the long perspective of the child as a whirling atom at the mercy of mechanical law to a close-up of him picking his way on tiptoe among 'scores of coupled earthworms lying half their length on the surface of the damp ground' (perhaps another oblique forecast of the sexual and compassionate impulses that are going to keep him in rotatory submission to the earth)' without killing a single one'.

The whole novel is shaped by meaningful contrasts and repetitions growing organically from the physical life of the poetically-conceived scenes. The most obvious symbolic contrast of ideal and real, letter and spirit, intention and result, lies in the structural relationship of the characters. Arabella and Sue as Caliban and Ariel to Jude's Everyman can be seen on one level as a projection of conflicting inner forces. Arabella's role as agent of the assimilating earth is clear. The ethereal and aptly-named Sue Bridehead, who shares with Catherine Earnshaw a death-wish longing to get back to the life of her infancy and freedom, seems to evoke the paradisal innocence Jude has lost (a concept familiar to readers of twentieth-century French writers, who often, like Hardy, present the longing for the paradisal ideal in terms of strong family affinity). The picture Sue presents dressed in Jude's best clothes after her escape from the Training College, 'a slim and fragile being masquerading as himself on a Sunday', strikingly foreshadows Conrad's study of projection in 'The Secret Sharer'. Phillotson can be seen as projecting the alternative career of a more conventional Jude.

Yet the characters live first and foremost as vitally rounded people who suffer as human beings from the conflicting forces at work in themselves and the cosmos. Their inner contradictions are presented in sensuous terms, in scenes whose elements link across the novel to light character and theme from several angles. The psychological complexities of Sue, for example, swinging between 'pagan' and 'saint', love and fear of life, are evoked in scenes that are linked by religious 'props'. Jude's first romantic glimpses of her in a photograph—a prophetically insubstantial image—'in a broad hat with radiating folds under the brim like the rays of a halo', between two brass candlesticks on his aunt's mantelpiece, and at her 'sweet, saintly, Christian business' among the religious bric-à-brac of the Christminster shop, provides an ironic underharmony to the shrine-image of the large white naked statues of Venus and Apollo, set between two candles on her chest of drawers,

'in odd contrast to their environment of text and martyr, and the Gothic-framed Crucifix-picture that was only discernible now as a Latin cross, the figure thereon being obscured by the shades.'

The complexity of Sue's response to her pagan gods invests every action, to contribute to the poetic mood surrounding her: her rebellious impulse to buy them, the white pipeclay that comes off on her gloves (evoking the incompleteness of her paganism), her nervous reaction to their nakedness, which leads her to wrap them in vegetation of sexual potency, her heretical reading of Gibbon and Swinburne as she sits in front of their home-made shrine. The Calvary print that is almost obscured, except for the Latin cross, by the pagan statues and darkness gains retrospective meaning from the huge solidly constructed Latin cross, brightly jewelled, that dominates the church of St Silas where Jude discovers a distraught Sue (vi–iii) who has sacrificed her free human individuality (reduced to 'a heap of black clothes') to take on the role of the martyred 'figure . . . obscured by the shades'. The changed perspective of the religious accessories in these two scenes tells us, as surely as Jamesian psychological nuances, of the reversals taking place in Sue's highly-strung mind.

The return to certain places connected with significant action is a well-tried narrative technique, which Hardy does not disdain to use in his most modern novel to mark the ironies in human progress. The white milestone to Christminster, the brown ploughed field of his punishment which Jude has to cross to reach the high vantage point of the Brown House, the Brown House itself, the ancient white Ridgeway and high road to Alfredston which intersect there, the neighbouring cottage where Jude and Arabella spend their short married life, form a cluster of associations that embody Jude's moments of intense affirmative vision and the moments of agony that are likewise permanent. Part of the poetic force is carried by Hardy's colour symbolism. The brown of the earth and the white light of absolute reality are repeated throughout the book, notably in the brown-fleshed Arabella and the pale, scintillating brightness of Sue, who is associated with the 'city of light' Jude first seeks from the top of the Brown House. The lofty ridge which gives him his first glimpse of subjective meaning stresses the related and essential loneliness of the human being, even as he lies there with Arabella, in 'the most apparent of all solitudes, that of empty surrounding space.' It is here that Jude kneels, like Tess, to adore the pagan gods of life in the ecstasy of the 'Carmen Saeculare', and here that he falls victim to Arabella's earthy wiles. The central scenes of their courtship and marriage are played out in the locality. The Brown House barn was 'the point at which he had planned to turn back' to his studies after walking out with Arabella. The consequences of his failure to do so bring the earlier scenes to mind when he repasses the scene with Sue, married to Phillotson. It is here that Arabella, also moved by a vision of the past, flings her religious tracts in the hedge when she determines to win Jude back from Sue. It is here that the hereditary doom of the Fawley family was enacted, where Jude's unhappily married parents parted and an ancestor was hanged after a marital tragedy that contained the elements of Jude's final tragedy—a dead child, a parting, madness. It is here that Jude elects to fulfil the doom of his house by committing virtual suicide after his last journey in the rain, ill and exhausted, to see Sue.

'He was by this time at the corner of the green, from which the path ran across the fields in which he had scared rooks as a boy. He turned and looked back, once, at the building which still contained Sue; and then went on, knowing that his eyes would light on that scene no more.

'There are cold spots up and down Wessex in autumn and winter weather; but the coldest of all when a north or east wind is blowing is the crest of the down by the Brown House, where the road to Alfredston crosses the old Ridgeway. Here the first winter sleets and snows fall and lie, and here the spring frost lingers last unthawed. Here in the teeth of the north-east wind and rain Jude now pursued his way, wet through, the necessary slowness of his walk from lack of his former strength being insufficient to maintain his heat. He came to the milestone, and, raining as it was, spread his blanket and lay down there to rest. Before moving on he went and felt at the back of the stone for his own carving. It was still there; but nearly obliterated by moss. He passed the spot where the gibbet of his ancestor and Sue's had stood, and descended the hill.'

The symphonic reiteration of familiar landmarks of his ecstasy and agony, the strong, rhythmic simplicity of diction and sentence structure, the evocation of a past beyond his own, the gesture of feeling the milestone for the marks of his identity and youthful hope, 'nearly obliterated by moss', even as he lies prostrate from the physical weight of the world, as he had done many years before, charges the connection of man and scene with a tragic emotion only the greatest of epic writers can command.

Christminster, of course, is the most pervasive double-edged metaphor of Jude's complexity. His architectural evocation of the city, as Dr C. J. P. Beatty has ably demonstrated in his London Ph.D. thesis, *The Part played by Architecture in the Life and Works of*

Thomas Hardy, has caught its many aspects as ideal and physical obstructiveness. Jude's 'heavenly Jerusalem' is dissected in Parts II and VI into all the earthly reality that defeats the vision: slum lodgings, seedy taverns, and above all the insuperable barrier of cold stone college walls that he can live at the back of and restore (as the religious medievalism that founded Christminster cannot be restored to direct complex modern life) but never enter as a scholar. His experience of Christminster swings between the impressionistic subjective—the romantic moonlight dream that enrols him among the saints and visionaries of the past, and conjures up the city from the architectural details revealed by the flash of a lamp and the feel of moulding under his fingers—and the daylight reality.

'What at night had been perfect and ideal was by day the more or less defective real. Cruelties, insults, had, he perceived, been inflicted on the aged erections. The condition of several moved him as he would have been moved by maimed sentient beings. They were wounded, broken, sloughing off their outer shape in the deadly struggle against years, weather, and man.'

The double face of the colleges, inhumanly obstructive and humanly suffering, links them to Jude himself. 'There in the old walls were the broken lines of the original idea; jagged curves, disdain of precision, irregularity, disarray': an architectural commentary on the broken design of his life, shattered by the inharmonious physical processes that corrupted the crumbling walls, and the power of the mean bread-and-cheese question that elbowed the poor scholar off the pavement.

It is significant in a novel that celebrates respect for individuality that the 'original idea' is conjured up, not by the total vision of a college or colleges, but by details, and that most of these details are Gothic. Hardy has declared his allegiance to Gothic principles of spontaneity in art and life. It was not until *The Magic Mountain* and *Dr Faustus* that another great artist, Thomas Mann, studied in depth the self-destructive aspect of the Gothic ideal which Hardy saw existing in tension with its vitality.

The only Classical building to have importance in the fable is Wren's circular theatre. It is from this structure that Jude awakens to a balanced sense of his limitations in his panoramic view of the promised land, and admits defeat of spontaneity in a speech that is a triumph of spontaneity. It is here that another child's vision—

Little Father Time's—comments ironically on his father's. His view of the colleges as 'gaols' and the procession of the Doctors in their 'blood-red' robes as the Judgement Day, soon to be tragically realized in his bloody judgement on superfluous life enacted on this tragic Remembrance Day which honours the dignity of man, is a correlative of man's tragic futility that has become more familiar through the 'prison' images of Kafka, Camus, and Bernard Malamud.

One could go on listing other scenes which dramatize the contrasts of the novel. Jude's moonlight dream of Christminster, interrupted by the 'real and local voice' of a policeman and the fact 'that he seemed to be catching a cold', is recalled to disturb the emotional current of his repassing the spot with Arabella in Part VI, seriously ill, defeated by Sue's orthodoxy, and too disillusioned to take exception to her judgement of his delirious rambling: 'Phantoms! There's neither living nor dead hereabouts except a damn policeman!' Jude's imaginary procession of welcoming worthies is set against the real procession and their ignorance of the obscure scholar in their midst. Meetings and partings comment ironically on each other. Jude's first encounters with Arabella and Sue forecast their meaning to his life. Sue's sensitivity about their place of meeting, her freedom from flirtatious scheming, her unpredictable mystery, are set against Arabella's lack of these qualities as she courts Jude over the pig's pizzle hanging from the bridge. The meeting near the Martyr's Cross is balanced by the parting by the children's graves, which leads Sue to a living martyrdom and Jude to his death. Phillotson's meetings and partings with Sue reflect on Jude's. His human motives for letting Sue go are more admirable, and more Jude-like, than his conventional motives for taking her back. The Aldbrickham pub where Jude takes Sue to begin their life together and where she refuses to 'live with' him in the usual sense, is shadowed by the temporary physical union he had there with Arabella, which strikes him as the worse offence.

The marriage/no-marriage theme is richly varied in a series of scenes that set the spirit against the letter: the two legal marriages and divorces set against the unlicensed marriage of the spirit; the wedding rehearsal that Sue forces on Jude which comments piquantly, together with the weddings (or sacrifices) they observe, on the ceremony they never have and the affinity they have; the concepts of honour, upheld by the officiating clergymen, which push Jude and Sue into a grotesque parody of honour and marriage;

the unhappy alliances of their family that ghost their own. The theme has vivid concrete portrayal in the repeated attempts to cast away flesh or spirit in obedience to orthodox conceptions—Jude burning his books, Sue burning her 'adulterous' nightgown to Widow Edlin's expostulation, 'Upon my life I don't call that religion!'—honestly placed in their futility by Arabella pitching her tracts into the hedge. 'I've tried that sort o' physic and have failed wi' it. I must be as I was born!'

The theme of separation is embodied in dramatic visual terms throughout the book: Arabella parading her dishevelled state in front of the cottage after her quarrel with Jude; the separate rooms that Jude and Sue occupy; Sue caressing Jude through a window or by letter, where the barrier of distance enables her to find release in tenderness from her fear of physical life; Jude dramatically marking Sue's decision to return to Phillotson: 'He went to the bed, removed one of the pair of pillows thereon, and flung it to the floor.'

Hardy's mixture of poetic styles conveys the basic contrasts and nightmare conjunctions of prosaic physical reality and the grotesque abstract Absurdity that disrupts it. Ibsen and Strindberg, Absurd Theatre, and the novels of Sartre, Camus, and Iris Murdoch, to name no more, have familiarized us with a mixture of planes of reality essential to a vision of absurdity. Hardy's symbolic presentation of Little Father Time is such a vision, not a mistake in a novel of social realism. The paradox of absurdity comes home with full force embodied in a child, when one remembers Jude's youthful hopes. Hardy places him firmly in the objective world (compare the poem 'Midnight on the Great Western') of train, passengers, ticket, and lamplight, until his lack of response to the playing kitten modulates to another more remote key. The solemn rhythms of the prose, the abstract Latinate sonority the language takes on ('He was Age masquerading as Juvenility' . . .) the child's movement ('a steady mechanical creep which had in it an impersonal quality—the movement of the wave, or of the breeze, or of the cloud') and unnerving incuriosity about details of the landscape, invest him as an expressionistic agent of the automatic cosmic process which abstracts significance from individual things.

'To him the houses, the willows, the obscure fields beyond, were apparently regarded not as brick residences, pollards, meadows; but as human dwellings in the abstract, vegetation, and the wide dark world.'

His meaningless and monstrous act, told with the swift movement of an absurd 'happening', is a poetic foreshortening of the reality that comes to all, though hidden by human hope, purpose, and reproduction. It is the logical end of modern perceptiveness and the disillusive centuries which, aware of the futile repetition of life without redemption, has turned the death-wish into a modern social problem.

Yet Little Father Time's negation does not constitute the total effect of this great and terrible vision of the human condition. Time and the suffering it brings is the modern affirmation of spiritual maturity. The naked pain felt in *Jude the Obscure* intensely affirms the value of life's potentialities. How great is the affirmation of love in the agonized gesture with which Sue denies Jude's last appeal for a new beginning:

'As he passed the end of the church she heard his coughs mingling with the rain on the windows, and in a last instinct of human affection, even now unsubdued by her fetters, she sprang up as if to go and succour him. But she knelt down again, and stopped her ears with her hands till all possible sound of him had passed away.'

Their suffering affirms the life that will evolve beyond their own. In i–ii, the manuscript defines Jude as 'the *coming* sort of man who was born to ache a good deal before the fall of the curtain upon his unnecessary life should signify that all was well with him again.' (My italics.) The tragedy of the children's death brings Jude and Sue to a recognition of their role as pioneers of a new, more sensitive stage of development. It was left to G. B. Shaw, at the end of *Back to Methuselah*, to envisage the final stage of creative evolution to which they are moving.

'After passing a million goals they press on to the goal of redemption from the flesh, to the vortex freed from matter, to the whirlpool in pure intelligence that, when the world began, was a whirlpool in pure force.'

The shape of things to come can be seen side by side with the conditions that resist a new awakening. Individuals are not universally unkind. Sue Bridehead is the most imaginatively realized type of the future. Her suffering springs from the contradictions of character that are inevitable because, as a pioneer variation from the parent species, her evolution is necessarily incomplete. The obsessive self-created ritual pattern of attracting a man, living with him in selfish sexless intimacy, rejecting him, feeling guilt, and submitting herself to punishment out of all proportion to the crime betrays her allegiance to original sin. Her vitality is ambiguous. Destructive and self-destroying without roots in sexual or social conformity, it is yet productive of Jude's maturity and self-control. In a world where Sue's sexlessness has offended more than Tess's sexuality, social conceptions that have become shop-soiled through insistence on the physical aspect—'marriage', 'to live with', 'sin', 'adultery'—become revitalized by Sue.

Hardy is not uncritical of Jude's and Sue's attempts to find self-fulfilment. Jude makes the usual mistakes in defining it. Hardy, as always, draws attention to those neutral moments when an exercise of human will could have turned things in another direction. Jude saw Arabella's meaning 'with his intellectual eye, just for a short fleeting while'. Brains, too, are natural. Jude and Sue abuse theirs by living too exclusively in a 'dreamy paradise', when, for example, marriage or removal would have dealt with the taunts of Little Father Time's schoolmates. Jude had the sense of responsibility and sexual control that could have risen above non-resistance to a law of nature. The boy's *Done because we are too menny* has point in a world where there is an overpopulation problem. The tragedy is to some extent avoidable.

Some critics have questioned whether a novel whose heroine is suffering from a special maladjustment can be defined as tragedy, which requires some responsible re-ordering of moral chaos. Both Sue and Jude begin in the belief, like traditional tragic heroes, that they can mould circumstances. Both have tragic recognitions of their failure in standards of sincerity, responsibility, and respect for individual being which they themselves have set up. Even after the horror, Jude has profited sufficiently by his suffering to see hope of a new start free of everything except fidelity to human needs and values. 'Is there anything better on earth than that we should love one another?' But Sue's inability to bear human burdens alone, which betrays her humanity and Jude's needs, is the real tragedy.

Tragedy in *Jude the Obscure* is the natural condition. One can only attain a modern harmony by trying to understand it. What remains to affirm the life and endeavour of Jude and Sue is a memory of their love, ennobled by its comparative freedom from physical grossness; their courageous assertion of Hellenic joy and meaning and human dignity against the abstractions of society and the looming dark of death; their compassion for all living creatures bound to them in a common mystery of suffering. In the event, it is Jude's qualities that affirm this epic of modern existentialist man. His astonishing resilience and adaptation to ever-narrowing limitations, without being reconciled to the present stage of evolution; his emotional impulses of affection and tenderness; his sensitivity, his ideal of Christminster's meaning which outlasts his disillusion with the place; his unflinching self-examination and devotion to sincerity, make him worthy to stand for man, 'neither commonplace, unmeaning, nor tame . . . but slighted and enduring', in an age of futility, darkness, and scepticism.

XIII
The Dynasts:
An Epic-Drama of Evolution

The Dynasts promotes a sharp divergence of opinion between Hardy's older and newer critics.

> 'Sensitive poet-critics like Lascelles Abercrombie and Edmund Blunden have declared *The Dynasts* a masterpiece, yet at the present moment the work seems to have few enthusiastic critics and, I would surmise, not many more readers.
>
> (Irving Howe: *Thomas Hardy*)

Its size, resistance to classification, narrative/poetic/dramatic form, strange diction, long stretches of the blankest blank verse, Overworld choruses, account of 'human action in spite of human knowledge' (Hardy's psychology of the Unconscious), bleak philosophy of the Immanent Will, and vision of futile battle upon battle, are disconcerting if one looks for the quickfire dramatic conflicts, passionate human relationships, and nature poetry of the poems and novels. But if one differs from Howe's opinion that 'we are today not much concerned with questions of ultimate causation', Hardy's original treatment of those questions has turned 'the real, if only temporary, thought of the age' into a projection of the eternal quest for meaning that has as much validity as *The Iliad* or *War and Peace*. The difficulties of the conglomerate form become powerful aids to 'the modern expression of a modern outlook' (Preface) if *The Dynasts* is read with the kind of dramatic imagination that one would apply, not to Shakespearean or Ibsenite drama, or to a film script, but to the form of mixed media that embodies Brecht's epic drama.

It is futile to speculate whether Hardy would have limited *The Dynasts* to mental performance only (two stage productions of selected scenes were given later) if the modern film and lighting techniques which he so obviously anticipates had been available to him. Brecht had both means and vision to translate into terms of actual theatre the radical conceptions of total drama common to them both. Though Hardy had less faith than Brecht in the human control of fate, the futility of mass self-slaughter was clear to both. The heroism that war inspires can be found in both *Mother Courage* and *The Dynasts*, but the narrative comment that distances the illustrative drama strongly questions the waste of heroism.

Hardy's rejection as anachronistic of 'the importation of Divine personages from any antique Mythology as ready-made sources or channels of Causation' (Preface) forced a radical change of form which, while it looks back to models like Shelley's *Prometheus Unbound* and Goethe's *Faust*, and ironically to the *Persae* and *Oresteia* of Aeschylus, who employs human conflict to postulate cosmic order and justice, looks forward to Brecht's special definition of 'Epic' theatre.

'While the theatre of illusion is trying to re-create a spurious present, by pretending that the events of the play are actually taking place at the time of each performance, the 'epic' theatre is strictly *historical*; it constantly reminds the audience that it is merely getting a *report* of past events.'

(Martin Esslin: *Brecht: A Choice of Evils*)

The tension and unity of *The Dynasts* comes from the ironic incongruities of historical drama and Overworld report; of ancient epic and modern epic-drama. And the effects of form are poetic. A work that sensuously embodies such a central mystery as the Will could hardly be anything but a poem, of Hardy's inclusive ilk. The three Parts are framed and qualified by the unchanged, emaciated figure of a humanized Europe at beginning and end, and the visual metaphor of 'Life's impulsion by Incognizance' which is realized six times in the drama when the Pities ask for reasons for the futile suffering. The historical drama illustrates the poetic metaphor in action, and the epic comment frames the drama as a cosmic show.

Sound dramatic principles unite the three parts of the display. Part First begins with the apex of Napoleon's usurping career, his coronation at Milan, and ends with expectation delicately balanced between the disaster at Austerlitz and victory at Trafalgar, whose true measure is known only to the Overworld—'*Utter defeat, ay, France's naval death*' (vi, vii). The result of France's naval death is seen in Part Second. It draws together the diverse material of the Spanish, Prussian, and Austrian campaigns through Napoleon's dynastic plans. The birth of his son to Maria Louisa of Austria, whose marriage to Napoleon proved to be the knot which began severance from Russia, and the dearly-bought British victory at Albuera, raise dramatic expectation at the end of Part Second with the conflicting threads of birth and death, alliance and enmity, woven by the Will-web, to be unravelled in Part Third. The final Part brings into prominence the Russian thread that is to weave Napoleon's military and dynastic defeat. French defeats balance the previous French victories. French refugees from Vitoria (3, II, iii) balance Sir John Moore's retreating army (2, III, i). The drowning of French by Russians at the Bridge of the Beresina (3, I, x) revenges the massacre of Russians by French on the Satschan Lake (1, VI, iv). Napoleon's desertion of 'these stricken shades in a limbo of gloom' (3, I, xi) on the retreat from Moscow parallels the cosmic desertion of the forgotten army at Walcheren (2, IV, viii). Wellington's rise to prominence and control balances Napoleon's in Part Second; his grasp of reality and contingencies gains ground as Napoleon loses his sense of reality in a wild dream of reconquering Europe with 'seven hundred sabres'. Nevertheless, the final battle of Waterloo is presented as a clash of well-matched opposites. Hardy's first stage direction (VII) points the coincidence that both commanders were forty-six, and both mounted on chargers who are named in true epic tradition. In the battle itself, the helplessness of both is stressed by parallel appeals for reinforcements which neither can send. Hardy's eye for symmetry plays no small part in giving design to an epic of purposelessness.

As surprise can play little part in the structure of a narrative already known, the scenes are selected and juxtaposed to afford comment on the workings of the Immanent Will. Artistic form occasionally takes precedence over strict chronology. Villeneuve's suicide is antedated, as Hardy's note tells us (1, v, vi), 'to include it in the Act to which it essentially belongs'. This act is analysed by W. R. Rutland (*Thomas Hardy*) to show Hardy's imaginative use of history. But well-constructed as it is, Act v only shows to advantage when embedded in the whole panorama of rhythmic flux and reflux, tension and relaxation.

The scenes that make up Act I of the first Part present the wide-flung interrelationships that tie together the folk of Wessex, their Parliamentary leaders, and the people of France, in the web of the Will that is weaving a convulsion of nations. The central visual image (iv) of

'countless companies of soldiery, engaged in a drill-practice of embarking and disembarking, and of hoisting horses into the vessels and land-
ing them again'

crystallizes the futility of rumour, debate, plan, and action, implies the theatrical nature of the preceding scenes of busy purpose,
and dissolves that purpose into meaningless fragmentation, when
'the Show presently dims and becomes broken, till only its flashes
and gleams are visible'. The whole tenor of the Act has prepared
us to see Napoleon's assumption of the crown in Milan Cathedral
as a climactic piece of role-playing staged by the Will, and the
drama as a conflict between man's stage-management and the
Will's.

Act II introduces the counter-check. ' "*Where, where is Nelson?*"
questions every tongue'. The humane principles and sense of reality
that motivate both Nelson and his worthy opponent, Villeneuve,
in this Act, counterpoint the stagery which has so far surrounded
the absent or distanced figure of Napoleon, and introduce into this
dramatic conflict of Free-will and Necessity the possibility that
human and humane choice can swerve the course of the Will.
Napoleon's presentation in (iii) as little more than a planning
brain, 'in trim for each alternative', is offset by the following
scenes which present in human roundness the men and decisions
that will annul his stage directions, and by the two Wessex scenes
following, which place human figureheads and designs and wars
in the perspective of eternal human values.

'Lard, Lard, if 'a [George III] were nabbed, it wouldn't make a deal
of difference! We should have nobody to zing to, and play single-stick
to, and grin at through horse-collars, that's true. And nobody to sign
our few documents. But we should rub along some way, goodnow.'

The leitmotif tension of human design and human blindness to
cosmic design, which welds together the scenes of Acts III and IV
and culminates in Nelson's reputation, 'He's staunch. He's watching, or I am much deceived', prepares for Trafalgar as the climactic emotional correlative. Napoleon's designs for the conquest
of Europe are counterpointed by the blindness of George III to
Pitt's need for a Coalition, that prolongs the war and shortens
Pitt's life (IV, i). The reputations of Villeneuve (III, i) and Mack
(IV, vi) for far-sightedness are seen from another angle (IV, iii) as
ignorance and confusion, stressed by the 'murk of evening' that

'obscures the prospect' of military preparations before Ulm. At Trafalgar, the confusion of smoke, noise, blood, life, and death, brought vividly to all the senses by Hardy's stage directions, is set against the purposeless ballet of attack and defence, while the view-point alternates between the 'Victory' and the 'Bucentaure', where the two most sensitive heroes of the drama, driven to compass each other's death by events they did not cause, are shown at the height of their concern for human flesh. Unlike the constantly diminished Napoleon, both Nelson and Villeneuve are allowed to meet a death consonant with heroic dignity, each exercising the limited choice accorded to him by the Will. The epic roll-call of ships captured and men dead or wounded, a device by which Homer gave individual dignity to his combatants, counterpoints the realistic portrayal of pain and meaningless fragmentation of men and things in war:

> arms, legs, trunks, heads,
> Bobbing with tons of timber on the waves,
> And splinters looped with entrails of the crew.

Yet the same incident, the explosion in the French ship 'Achille', provides one of Hardy's eternal touchstones; the grotesque humour of the captain's woman, 'desperate for life' swimming naked:

> Our men in charge,
> Seeing her great breasts bulging on the brine,
> Sang out, 'A mermaid 'tis, by God!'—then rowed
> And hauled her in.

The interrelated complex of death and glory, peace and war, finds its still point when, with Nelson dying, Captain Hardy's mind swings back to his native Wessex, and the local but eternal values for which men have always fought. The Guildhall scene which follows, placing the fame of Trafalgar and of Pitt's 'last large words' as accidents of time and place, Villeneuve's suicide, muted complementary to Nelson's death in action; the Wessex gossip of the thirsty sailors who 'broached the Adm'l'; and the ballad of Trafalgar which ends Act v, wind down the tension of the battle by crystallizing particular event into universal myth.

Act vi, after an act which stresses human action and values, returns to the theme of 'stark sightlessness' and futility at Auster-litz, Napoleon's countercheck to Trafalgar. The Russian conjectures (ii) introduce us to another kind of Hardeian hero, very different from the romantic, vigilant Nelson. The wisdom of the significantly one-eyed, sleeping Kutúzof, the only wisdom that could sustain the different nature of Napoleon's future campaigns, lies in accepting human ignorance.

> Such plans are—paper! Only tomorrow's light
> Reveals the true manoeuvre to my sight!

Part First ends with the death of a dispirited Pitt, realizing so soon after his acclamation as saviour in v that 'I am as though I had never been!' But as one wave falls, another prepares to rear. The brief mention of Wellesley's visit to Pitt introduces the man who is to redress the balance of Austerlitz at Waterloo.

To detail the structure Act by Act and scene by scene would take too long. The same care is shown throughout to select and juxtapose incidents which illustrate the ironies inherent in the conflict of human and unconscious design. Part Second ends, for example, with a cluster of scenes (VI, iii–vii) which question Napoleon's assertion of identity through his son (iii). Bloody Alburera melts down human order and definition (iv):

> 'The lines of the Buffs, the Sixty-sixth, and those of the Forty-eighth
> . . . in a chaos of smoke, steel, sweat, curses, and blood, are beheld
> melting down like wax from an erect position to confused heaps. Their
> forms lie rigid, or twitch and turn, as they are trampled over by the
> hoofs of the enemy's horse. . . .'

and turns men into grotesque faceless black-masked puppets (Hardy understood the massed anonymity of modern warfare), 'their mouths blackened by cartridge-biting', 'discharging musketry in each other's faces when so close that their complexions may be recognized'. The evocation of a cosmic masquerade is strengthened by the *'regal puppet-shows'* (v–vii). The mad King George III,

> *Mocked with the forms and feints of royalty*
> *While scarified by briery Circumstance*

poignantly evaluates human responsibility for the 'victory' of Albuera:

> He says I have won a battle? But I thought
> I was a poor afflicted captive here,

and the Prince Regent plays out the sub-comedy of his 'wives' at the Carlton House celebration, where he sits 'like a lay figure' in royal state, in the incongruous dress of a Field Marshal, at a table whose romanticized centrepiece recalls the now battle-scarred landscape of Albuera. But the last hope of the Pities—that the Will may wake and *'with knowledge use a painless hand'* stresses the increasing importance in Parts Second and Third of limited human choice and partial control of the Will.

This theme imposes unity and pattern on the flux and reflux of the Prussian and Spanish campaigns of Part Second—the mid-way neutral ground of the drama on which human action may stamp a design. Napoleon's one unselfish choice, to save the mother and not his child (2, vi, iii) and its happy outcome inspires the comment (qualified though it is by its source) from the Ironic Spirits, *'The Will Itself is slave to him.'* Between the dilemma of Fox, which appropriately opens Part Second, when he is faced with Napoleon's would-be assassin, and the last Chorus of the Pities in Part Third with its hope of human consciousness infiltrating the Will of which it forms part, lies a tissue of opportunities missed or taken, juxtaposed with the consequences of choice.

'If only' weaves through the texture of history. If only Villeneuve had been as conscienceless as his master; if only Pitt had been allowed to form a coalition; if only Fox had accepted the assassin's offer; if only Queen Louisa had married the Prince of Wales, or had met Napoleon before dynastic ambition had driven out susceptibility to women; if only Maria Louisa had been persuaded to join Napoleon after his escape from Elba; if only Grouchy's reinforcements had arrived in time—the list is endless—history might have taken a different turn. The defeat of Coruña follows a second chance to kill Napoleon (iii, ii) missed because the deserter had thrown away his firelock. Expediency, not morality, may control the Will that *'neither good nor evil knows'*. Constant readiness to adapt to the workings of chance and time has a cumulative effect on the course of the war. Chance location *'evolved the fleet of the Englishry'*, but Nelson's vigilance and Wellington's modern methods of warfare kept England safe. The scenes of the Prussian defeat (2, i, iii–viii) imply criticism of Prussia's unadaptive sluggishness which, lost in romantic devotion to the warrior queen who embodied the myth of their military past,

> *takes no count of the new trends of time,*
> *Trusting ebbed glory in a present need.*

'The slow clocks of Muscovy', on the other hand, are instrumental in Napoleon's defeat because they are backed by the chance factor of the Russian winter and Napoleon's sense of his own dignity, though after Russia's belated answer to his marriage proposals Champagny points his freedom to choose: 'You might, of course, sire, give th'Archduchess up.'

Vigilant control is man's only defence against the unknown concomitants that affect the course of destiny. In two juxtaposed scenes (2, ii, ii, iii) Hardy shows that the Prince of Wales' dalliance with the ladies in an insular and phlegmatic country misses the disastrous consequences of Godoy's affair with the Spanish queen. But the Bourbon throne might have been saved by the self-control that is so conspicuously lacking when the queen visits her lover on the night his palace is wrecked by the mob. 'I could not help it—nay, I *would* not help!'

Part Third brings into prominence the man and the qualities which defeated Napoleon. The 'prim ponderosities' of Wellington's defence works outside Torrès Védras (2, vi, ii) introduce a concrete correlative of the endurance that was needed to survive the third phase of the war—

> They are Lord Wellington's select device
> And, like him, heavy, slow, laborious, sure

—fought over ground that manifests the basic hostilities facing man's endeavour; space, time, the elements, and insignificance. The square blocks of men who withstand the French charges at Waterloo 'like little red-brick castles' are a physical image of the control needed to do nothing but endure. 'They writhe to charge— or anything but stand!' Wellington's grasp of reality, and intelligent use of the limited foresight granted to men after a full look at the worst, comes into the ascendant as Napoleon retreats into paranoid fantasy and deception of his men, that finds its climax and hubris at Waterloo.

Through the third Part of *The Dynasts*, Napoleon's stage management is constantly juxtaposed with the reality that refuses to be directed. The silence that greets his entry into Moscow (i, viii) is an unnerving anti-climax to his posturing plans for the city's surrender (vii). The Act (v) that begins with Napoleon's rally— his escape from Elba—ends with the burning of his effigy at Durnover Green. The man who made Europe dance to his tune is seen as a puppet, devoid of significance:

'. . . only a mommet they've made of him, that's got neither chine nor chitlings. His innerds be only a lock of straw from Bridle's barton.'

From Hardy's dramatic shaping of the historical narrative he drew a poetic underpattern compounded of a complex of assent and dissent to traditional epic, which creates for him a modern myth. The historical drama provides much epic material for that 'Iliad of Europe' with Napoleon as 'a sort of Achilles' that was Hardy's earliest conception of *The Dynasts* (1875 to 1881). The problem of writing an epic, embodying a philosophical statement and the values of contemporary culture in an age when the writer 'can neither assume a core of beliefs common to himself and his audience nor adopt the long forms which artists have traditionally used for such statements' (Hynes: *The Pattern of Hardy's Poetry*) was solved by Hardy's ironic vision and the epic/dramatic/poetic form to which it gave birth.

The epic can show two broad and often interrelated genres: the epic of war (*The Iliad*) and the search for identity (*The Odyssey*). War is a measure of man's relationship to the controlling forces of the universe, his god-like potentialities for destruction and self-creation in the face of ever-present death. It raises urgently the metaphysical questions of the value of life, the basis of individual identity, and how far war is an inevitable part of human character and destiny. These questions arise both in Primary epic, which is defined by C. S. Lewis (*Preface to Paradise Lost*) as the *Iliad* type, where personal tragedy is set against the meaningless flux of history and no achievement is permanent; and in Secondary epic, where some event—the founding of Rome, the Fall of Man—invests history with pattern and suffering with meaning. The epic hero dramatizes the potentialities of his culture to deal with these questions.

The first conception of Napoleon as 'a sort of Achilles' compels comparison with the traditional epic hero. Achilles had a special relationship to the Absolute, having enough god-like force to challenge things as they are. Though nothing can happen beyond fate, his heroic energy reshapes the will of the gods to some extent, and wins him the right to self-determination within the pattern of fate. Napoleon, conscious of his role as Man of Destiny and '*unwavering, keen, and irresistible/As is the lightning prong*' (1, I, ii), is associated with the fire that was for Achilles the symbol of his part in the nature of godhead—complex of wrath, war, divinity, and death; irreconcilable and self-destructive to mortals.

> Great men are meteors that consume themselves
> To light the earth. This is my burnt-out hour.
>
> (3, VII, ix).

Napoleon's aspirations to godhead, 'to shoulder Christ from out the topmost niche/In human fame' are measured and found wanting to the needs of a godless age by the compassion of the Christian ideal he rejects, evoked in the incongruity of his definition (by the Spirit Ironic) as 'the Christ of War'. It is significant that the one act of Napoleon's which seems to reshape the Will is not of heroic self-assertion but of compassion for the mother of his child. 'Every generous, selfless action in the drama expresses resistance to the selfish, egocentric impulse of the Immanent Will' (J. O. Bailey, *Thomas Hardy and the Cosmic Mind*), and adumbrates the ultimate effect of the human mind upon the cosmic. Napoleon is the man of heroic force and '*suasive pull of personality*' who refuses the challenge to become this new kind of hero, falling back instead on an outmoded epic pattern. (There is some analogy with the Eustacia/Clym opposition.) This erstwhile champion of Liberty (1, I, vi) becomes a mechanism of the Will, and declares it responsible for his self-assertive drive to power (3, I, i) though the Spirit of the Pities challenges his determinist view: (3, I, v)

> *So he fulfils the inhuman antickings*
> *He thinks imposed upon him. . . .*

The Will, symbol of *primitive* energy, impels him into immediate channels and immediate successes. Where endurance and the later acquisition of foresight is needed, his law of the jungle does not always prevail. As he struggles towards his own conception of destiny, he becomes more and more aware that his Absolute aspirations are limited by mortal conditions—lack of heirs, his increasing fatness and drowsiness, the physical expanse of Russia to be crossed by exhausted men. The Overworld perspective evaluates this Man of Destiny as no more than an unheroic puppet of the Will, '*the brazen rod that stirs the fire/Because it must.*' Hardy's presentation of Napoleon selects those aspects which diminish his traditional courage and human feeling. He comes over as little more than a mechanism, a constantly planning will, weaving '*eternal artistries in Circumstance*'; a modern Sisyphus, whose whole being has been exerted to accomplishing nothing. But Hardy, as always, leaves open the question whether the compassionate choices he did not make in 'moments of equilibrium' would have altered his fate.

Like Homer, Hardy illuminates his conception of heroic character by comparing his Achilles with other leaders. In addition, the echoes of Homeric counterparts question the values of traditional epic. The English leaders, military and Parliamentary, contrast favourably in concern for their people with Napoleon's egotistical genius. Napoleon's Hector may be found in Nelson, the thoroughly human hero, who asserts himself bravely to defend the domestic values he cherishes from the war he abhors. His death ironically achieves the god-like status of death/glory which Napoleon desired. The Overworld debate that rises from his protracted suffering questions the ideals of heroism which bring needless pain to creatures so sensitively developed. But Hector did not carry the burden of modern self-alienated man, 'who is with himself dissatisfied' (1, II, i), which operates as a death-wish in Nelson: that was the doubtful privilege of Achilles alone. It enables Nelson to determine his mode of life and death within the narrow freedom allowed by the Will. Minor heroes bear the same modern burden; Picton, 'riding very conspicuously', and Brunswick, whose 'solemn and appalling guise' embodying his devotion to death attracted the bullet. They might have saved their lives if they had heeded warnings from the Overworld.

Sir John Moore presents another kind of modern hero. His painful death in defeat, his concern for the battle and those in it, his attachment to his sword (the traditional epic object that acquires symbolic honour and a life of its own)—'I wish it to go off the field with me'—mark him as the youthful romantic hero of the epic of chivalry. But he owes his immortality to the modern evaluation of failure as the human condition. (2, III, v)

> His was a spirit baffled but not quelled,
> And in his death there shone a stoicism
> That lent retreat the rays of victory.

The French can show their heroes of chivalry too, in Villeneuve and Ney. The nearest Homeric equivalent to Ney is the rash, romantic, constantly charging Diomedes, for whom heroic action is uncomplex—and immature. The danger of Ney's romantic appeal is embodied by the colourful trappings of his cavalry, *that would persuade us war has beauty in it*. (3, VII, iv). But whereas

Siborne (Hardy's historical source here) admires 'the gorgeous, yet harmonious, colouring of this military spectacle', Hardy's Spirit of the Pities points to the un-epic disharmony of the tragic feeling of the modern soldiers who constitute the spectacle. The Overworld evaluates it ('the barbaric trick') and, with regret, Ney's gallantry, as outmoded and misguided.

> *Simple and single-souled lieutenant he . . . .*
> *Why should men's many-valued motions take*
> *So barbarous a groove?*

While the awareness to suffering of Nelson and Moore, caught in the trap of an ancient mechanism for which they are too highly evolved, implies a cautious hope that awareness will one day break into the Will, the hero who is best adjusted to the present is the man, not over-sensitive, who challenges things as they are by adjusting intelligently to the environment he finds himself in. The old Russian commander Kutúzov, 'bravely serving though slowly dying', embodies the qualities which defeated Napoleon on Russian soil—inaction, silence, endurance, and realization of man's ignorance and mortality. Wellington, like Ajax, gives the impression of being rooted to the earth; stubborn, blunt, not over-imaginative, impatient of irregularities, squarely enduring and defensive. His sober look at the worst and ballad-like expectation of human endurance in face of it—

> to hold out unto the last,
> As long as one man stands on one lame leg
> With one ball in his pouch!—

contrasts with Napoleon's betrayal of his troops into false optimism. His grasp of reality and intelligent deductions from fact accord with the Spirit of the Years' refusal to live beyond factual knowledge (3, vi, viii):

> The noonday sun, striking so strongly there,
> Makes mirrors of their arms. That they advance
> Their growing radiance shows. Those gleams by Marbais
> Suggest fixed bayonets.

Hardy's women are no exception to the tradition that epic women are depicted as victims of the death and division that war brings into their domestic lives. Josephine's distressful position, womanly charm, and lifelong devotion to Napoleon and even to his son make her a more attractive heroine than Maria Louisa. But Hardy's myth-making faculty presents them both as victims of the human condition rather than the opportunistic schemings of an Empire-builder. Napoleon's demand that Josephine should act in the formalities of divorce 'as if you shaped them of your own free will' is an image of the human action of the whole drama. Maria Louisa's cry of pain in childbirth, 'Why should I be tortured even if I am but a means to an end!' universalizes her situation to stand for all women travailing ceaselessly for a mysterious and seemingly futile end. Other women too take on mythopoeic dimension. Queen Louisa's dramatically silent image passes across the stage as the militant warrior-queen expected by a Prussia which has failed to keep up with the times, at odds with the feminine nature displayed in her dialogue with Napoleon. Colonel Dalbiac's Wessex wife, who rode to the charge at Salamanca behind her husband, and Mrs Prescott, who found hers 'lying dead and bloody there', take on mythical stature as the eternal price of a war that forces them out of their normal creative functions.

The likeness to Homeric heroic character stresses the differences that make *The Dynasts* a modern epic. Hardy does not celebrate the noble relationship of arms and the man. The temper of *The Dynasts*, nevertheless, is not anti-epic or anti-heroic. What it celebrates is a kind of heroism acceptable to the self-conscious modern world.

Epic action in *The Dynasts* is ineffective sound and fury. Though the battle-joy is felt by some of Hardy's heroes as by Homer's and Tolstoy's, '*driven to demonry/By the Immanent Unrecking*' (3, VII, viii), the needlessness of war as a testing ground of man's quality is strongly presented. Hardy's war is bestial and dehumanizing; the generous Homeric impulse is rare. Wellington, though moved to admiration by Ney's action, will not move to save him from ignominious death (3, VII, iv). All Hardy's resources are directed to a vision of war as futile and insignificant. No other epic of war can have so much of the major action relegated to comment. Wagram (2, IV, iii), Coruna (2, III, iii–iv) and much of Trafalgar and Waterloo are presented as running commentary, with all the misunderstandings, inaccuracies, and differences of opinion that attend a partial view. Napoleon exists, for much of the drama, as a voice heard through walls, in dictation, or in proclamations to his officers. Nothing could convey more dramatically the limits of human awareness and action. Napoleon realizes his inability to direct events at Waterloo. 'Life's curse begins, I see,/With helplessness. The reportage of epic action places man's function as observer and commentator on events he can neither control nor understand.

Another form of comment is the Dumb Show, which becomes a poetic and dramatic metaphor for the human condition of uncomprehended activity. The ceremony of Alexander's alliance with Napoleon on the river Niemen (2, I, vii) is qualified by the silence, the dwarfing perspective, the simultaneous balletic movements of the two barges, and the effect (like Cocteau's raised platform in *The Infernal Machine*) of the action in the 'gorgeous pavilion of draped woodwork' isolated in a void of water that imparts to the man-made stage 'a rhythmical movement, as if it were breathing'. The spectacle of man trying futilely to stage his own show while being moved by a more powerful current is broken by the Overworld's reminder of *'the prelude to this smooth scene'* in the lyric that begins

Snows incarnadined were thine, O Eylau, field of the wide white spaces.

The poetic incongruities contained in 'snows incarnadined', 'frozen limbs', 'blood iced hard', echoed in the musical dissonances of open vowels, sliding vowel progressions, and hard consonants, places the staginess of the Dumb Show inside the reality of suffering. The combination of Dumb Show and lyric comment expresses better than the Homeric dignity of ceremonial dialogue the futility of the alliance.

Hardy's aerial view from the Overworld, often glazed by mists and water, 'provides both an expansive perspective of vast "epic" actions, and an ironically contracting philosophical perspective of what those actions mean' (Hynes, op. cit.). It diminishes epic ritual to model theatre. After the coronation in Milan Cathedral, 'the point of view recedes, the whole fabric smalling into distance and becoming like a rare, delicately carved alabaster ornament' (a comment too on the relativity of *'the creed that these rich rites disclose'*). Napoleon himself is 'diminished to the aspect of a doll' after his declaration of war on Russia. The relegation of the endless processions to stage direction—coronation and wedding ceremonies, triumphal progresses and submissions, military retreats and advances, disorganized flights of refugees—diminishes human effort to find meaning in ritual to a confusion of human and cosmic cross-purposes. The modern film device suggested in Maria Louisa's ceremonial progress to meet her future husband (2, v, v)—

'The puny concatenation of specks being exclusively watched, the surface of the earth seems to move along in an opposite direction, and in infinite variety of hill, dale, woodland, and champaign'

—like the revolving stage under Mother Courage's wagon, proves the illusion of forward movement. The foreshortened view of messengers shuttling across the Channel (2, I, ii) exposes the ritual (stressed as ritual by the Rumours 'chanting in antiphons') of diplomatic negotiation as a ruthless game of skill in which *'lives are ninepins to these bowling hands'*. The simultaneous proclamations of war made by Napoleon and the Russians (3, I, i), each blaming the other and pretending to read enemy motives, are placed by a stage direction whose dramatic grouping anticipates Beckett's experiments in language and Schoenberg's in serial sound to project a closed circle of mechanical, meaningless echoes:

'When the reconnoitrers again come back to the foreground of the scene the huge array of columns is standing quite still, in circles of companies, the captain of each in the middle with a paper in his hand. He reads from it a proclamation. They quiver emotionally, like leaves stirred by a wind. NAPOLÉON and his staff reascend the hillock, and his own words as repeated to the ranks reach his ears, while he himself delivers the same address to those about him.'

Human communication merges into the meaningless sounds of nature. The sounds of celebration and agony are the same. Speech and hand-clapping become the babbling of waves. The groans of the soldiers drowning under fire in the Satschan Lake 'reach the ears of the watchers like ironical huzzas' (1, VI, iv).

All manifestations of the life process appear as equally significant or insignificant. Great armies are reduced to crawling caterpillars or cheesemites, Maria Louisa's wedding procession to 'a file of ants crawling along a strip of garden-matting', Napoleon himself to a puppet twitched by the Immanent Will and his victims to animalcula gyrating from his impetus. Naval convoys 'float on before the wind almost imperceptibly, like preened duck-feathers across a pond' (2, II, v). Soldiers 'wheel into their fighting-places . . . their arms glittering like a display of cutlery at a hill-side fair' (3, VII, i).

Much of the perspective is expressed in stage directions. The sensuous impact, diction, rhythm, and emotional force of Hardy's stage directions make them a potent poetic instrument in the creation of a modern myth. As the historical action moves from futile battle to futile battle, the mythopoeic underpattern moves in counterpoint from illusion of the human condition as purposeful action (Part First) through the flux and reflux of futility (Part Second) to acceptance of the reality of insignificant man in relationship with indifferent earth (Part Third). Jena, Trafalgar, and Austerlitz are questioned as victories for man's purpose and action by the flux and reflux of the Peninsular campaigns. The deserters in the cellar near Astorga (2, III, i) can still find meaning in the basic necessities of wine, women, and song. But their human reality and stability are threatened by the ultimate expressionistic nightmare reality of 'a straggling flock of military objects' retreating in ceaseless silent logicless flux.

'The Retreat continues. More of ROMANA's Spanish limp along in disorder; then enters a miscellaneous group of English cavalry soldiers, some on foot, some mounted, the rearmost of the latter bestriding a shoeless foundered creature whose neck is vertebrae and mane only. While passing it falls from exhaustion; the trooper extricates himself and pistols the animal through the head. He and the rest pass on.'

The coughing sergeant who drills his crippled invalids into the role of a pursuing platoon; the dehumanized, unemotional executions of the horse and the prisoner chosen by lot, cause no disturbance in the current.

The Absurd juxtapositions of human order and cosmic disorder prepare for a response to Sir John Moore's funeral (2, III, iv) which is very different from the response accorded to Wolfe's poem. The gravediggers 'hastily digging a grave there with extemporised tools', the punctuating shots, the voice of the Chaplain intoning the Burial service that stresses the shortness of time, the ritual that expresses human attempt at ordering death, make an effect through the simultaneity of drama that resembles the rich counterpoint between modern futility and eternal order which Benjamin Britten catches in his *War Requiem* through juxtaposing Owen's war poetry with the Mass.

Trial in battle by fire and water of mortal men not equipped with Achilles' god-like force to overcome the elements, leads to a sojourn in Limbo. Walcheren (2, IV, viii) requires the 'dingy doom'

291

of assimilation to the earth. It is the place where illusions of definition and meaning die; the home of the deceiving Jack-lantern and the illusory beauty of 'brass-hued and opalescent bubbles, compounded of many gases', and undefinable 'strange fishy smells, now warm, now cold'. The lament of its 'skeletoned men' forgotten and imprisoned to await futile, purposeless death in an island that is primitive earth, Homeric Underworld, and the modern Limbo of despair, is for meaningful action. All is diminished. The *'ancient Delta'* is an *'ignoble sediment of loftier lands'*. The doom of dissolution is enacted lyrically, in the sound of language and choice of words. The physical power of earth's insignificance to cover man's striving invests phrasing and rhythm:

> *The ever wan morass, the dune, the blear*
> *Sandweed, and tepid pool, and putrid smell,*
> *Emaciate purpose to a fractious fear,*
> *Beckon the body to its last low cell—*
> *A chink no chart will tell.*

The Russian campaign, accumulating resonance from the myth, finds the only meaning of life in life itself. Overworld perspective and stage direction present it as an epic struggle for bare survival in the primal indifference of nature. The point of observation, 'high amongst the clouds' (3, 1, ix) reveals the earth 'as a confused expanse merely'. The Pities' question *'Where are we? And why are we where we are?'* reverberates beyond the geographical confines of Russia. Gradually, the scene unfolds the fragmentary *'skinny growths'* that mean *'sustenance elsewhere yclept starvation'*. The archaic *'yclept'* and

> *the rolling brume*
> *That parts, and joins, and parts again below us*
> *In ragged restlessness*

roll back the years of racial memory so that the primitive *'object like a dun-piled caterpillar'* shuffling painfully along is no surprise. The Recording Angel's definition ('in minor plain-song') of the Grand Army in terms of the myth of God's chosen but exiled people strengthens by irony this modern myth of man's abandonment and insignificance, lost in a snowy silent monochrome, broken only by 'the incessant flogging of the wind-broken and lacerated horses'—the sounds of man's inhumanity to his fellow-sufferers that makes human life an inharmonious blot on the primitive landscape, and death a restoration of harmony as parts of the caterpillar shape drop off, 'are speedily flaked over, and remain as white pimples by the wayside'.

Groups break off to enact the ritual of primitive survival, which blends with the modern existentialist myth of men deserted by leader, God, and meaning. Only the poetically incongruous simile, 'icicles dangling from their hair that clink like glass-lustres as they walk' (xi) as they search for firewood, reminds us of the civilized existence that is men's right. The final stage direction points to the logical end of the myth, in language that stresses the sharp hostility of the environment: 'the stars come out in unusual brilliancy, Sirius and those in Orion flashing like stilettos; and the frost stiffens' as the exhausted soldiers, crouched round the fire unconscious of differences of rank, stiffen into an eternal sculpture of human suffering dehumanized by their trials of fire and ice, their dissonances harmonized in death.

> They all sit
> As they were living still, but stiff as horns;
> And even the colour has not left their cheeks,
> Whereon the tears remain in strings of ice.—
> It was a marvel they were not consumed:
> Their clothes are cindered by the fire in front,
> While at their back the frost has caked them hard.

The Dante-esque echoes define their experience as an experience of Hell.

Epic has always explored man's relationship to the natural world. The old anthropomorphic relationship gives poignant resonance to Hardy's myth of the earth, the most powerful physical fact of man's life, indifferent to his aims and sufferings, transforming his orderly patterns into preconscious human shapes which comment on the nature of warfare and prophesy his ultimate doom of reversion to unconsciousness (3, IV, i):

'All these dark and grey columns, converging westward by sure degrees, advance without opposition. They glide on as if by gravitation, in fluid figures, dictated by the conformation of the country, like water from a burst reservoir; mostly snake-shaped, but occasionally with batrachian and saurian outlines. In spite of the immensity of this human mechanism on its surface, the winter landscape wears an impassive look, as if nothing were happening.'

Natural descriptions in the context of *The Dynasts* are made grotesquely expressionistic of the deeper reality, woven by the tranced Will, underlying the scenic. The Overworld framework makes man's relation to his environment the objective correlative for a dream relationship, as Emma Clifford suggests ('The Impressionistic View of History in *The Dynasts*', *Modern Language Quarterly*, XXII, 1961). Together, the two dimensions of the historical drama and the Will which dreams it project Ultimate Reality where men and nature meet in a moment of vision that records a truth of suffering.

Yet the double function of earth as womb and tomb provides some effective poetic Hardeian tensions. The very similes which diminish naval or military manoeuvres to duck feathers or cutlery expand the importance of these homely appurtenances of peace. At the height of the carnage there are interludes which evoke, through the rhythms of war, the rhythms of peace and man's creative partnership with the earth which makes the fall of cities a catastrophe that is not final. As Nelson dies in unjustified pain, Captain Hardy remembers 'the red apples on my father's trees,/Just now full ripe'. It is a device Thomas Hardy could have learnt from Homer. On the eve of Waterloo (3, VI, viii)

> *Cavalry in the cornfields mire-bestrowed,*
> *With frothy horses floundering to their knees*

(Hardy is particularly sensitive to the bewildered agony of horses used in war) evoke the pastoral relationship of horses and corn to show the present conjunction as unnatural. The domestic words such as 'hamlet-roofs', 'chambers', 'household', referring to the small nesting creatures of Waterloo field to whom the mechanized butchery looms in magnified destructiveness, bring a sense of ultimate stability into the terror. Hardy's glimpses of women too, at their ordinary tasks, at fashionable balls, bearing children, comforting lovers, tending the wounded, balance the destruction with creation, like Homer's domestic similes. The incongruity of image and context is a powerful epic comment. Perhaps Hardy's most poetically incongruous and original adaptation of the Homeric domestic simile is his conception of the Immanent Will, unconsciously weaving a fabric of war and suffering *'like a knitter drowsed,/Whose fingers play in skilled unmindfulness'* (Forescene). The domestic image diminishes the First Cause to something terrible in its smallness.

The modern myth is completed and defined by the poetic power of Hardy's home-made theology. It could not end with a vision of insignificance. Though Hardy's regard for truth gave the vision full weight, the eternal questioning of events in space and time counterpoints it with a positive poetic emotion that implies the significance of human consciousness in the further evolution of the myth. The question, whether existence has meaning, is the total subject of the Dynasts, and *'the lobule of a Brain/Evolving always that it wots not of'* is its metaphor. The Overworld performs a vital dramatic function by keeping the Will present to the imagination when it is not embodied on the stage. They discuss its attributes, and though they are themselves swayed by Necessity, they dramatize transmission of impulses from the Unconscious by psychic phenomena, intuitions, and subconscious voices (1, v, vi; 2, v, viii, 2, vi, vii; 3, i, i, 3, vi, ii, 3, vi, iii, 3, vii, vi, 3, vii, ix) as 'Channels of Causation'. Though they share the super-knowledge of Homer's gods, they define their difference from the traditional 'celestial machinery' which takes a lively part in human affairs: *'Our scope is but to register and watch'* (Forescene).

However, Hardy makes good dramatic use of spectators with superior consciousness. They justify through the simultaneity that is possible to drama his choice of a semi-dramatic form.

> *We'll close up Time, as a bird its van,*
> *We'll traverse Space, as spirits can,*
> *Link pulses severed by leagues and years,*
> *Bring cradles into touch with biers;*
> *So that the far-off Consequence appears*
> *Prompt at the heel of foregone Cause.—*

Telescoped space and time bring into significant juxtaposition the battles of Salamanca in Spain and Borodino in Russia (3, 1, iv). Telescoped time shows the futility of military plans when the result of a battle is foreseen before it begins (2, vi, iv) as *'red smears upon the sickly dawn'*. Premonitions of death bring foreknowledge of Quatre-Bras and Waterloo into the desperate gaiety of the ball at Brussels. The falling of Marie Antoinette's portrait forecasts division in the unnatural marriage between France and Austria. The Spirit Ironic breaks into Archduke Ferdinand's fears of capture by an upstart adventurer to note the future shape of things (1, iv, iii):

> *Note that. Five years, and legal brethren they—*
> *This feudal treasure and the upstart man!*

The rounded perspective stresses the opposition between the partial vision of men and the almost total consciousness of the Spirits.

The Overworld debates from its superior knowledge the inner meaning of the action, explains motives, interprets, narrates, summarizes, and makes transitions between scenes. The multiple function of the Spirits makes them important, not as gods, but as the latent divinity in human life that may supersede Necessity through a process of evolution. They represent different human responses, indicated by their names, to human suffering, if human beings were completely aware of their place in the cosmos. They are certainly the most 'realistic' individuals in the drama. Men are distanced and blurred into the workings of the Will.

The basic dramatic experience of conflict could be negated by the spectacle of conflict without meaning. But Hardy's meaning is the whole work. The war—a perfect correlative of futility—is placed in dramatic tension with the Overworld debate, which has its own inner drama. The Ancient Spirit of the Years, Showman and spokesman of the Will, represents things unemotionally as they are. Feelings and judgements which are pointless to his factual statement of existence, and which evolved with human consciousness, oppose him in the Spirit Ironic and the Spirit of the Pities. As part of the Will, feelings are as valid as facts. The Spirits of Irony and Pity challenge the determinism of the action with the possibility of limited free choice between impulses from the Unconscious and conscious sources of action—reason, intelligence, the consciousness of absurdity, unselfishness, compassion. The Pities independently disobeys the Will to suggest compassion to Napoleon (1, I, vi) and suicide to Villeneuve. At the Talavera brook (2, IV, v) *'the spectacle of Its instruments, set to riddle one another through, and then to drink together in peace and concord'*, pointed out in their different fashions by both Spirits, provokes the Spirit Sinister (evil for its own sake) into a fear that awareness of such piteous ironies *'may wake up the Unconscious Itself, and tempt It to let all the gory clock-work of the show, run down to spite me!'*

The poetic development of the debate lies in the push of the Will, dramatized by its pioneers the Overworld in their capacity as *'the flower of Man's Intelligence'*, to become conscious. It is carried by the poetic peaks, in the Fore Scene and After Scene, at the end of each Part, and at major crises of suffering—Trafalgar, Austerlitz, Talavera, Walcheren, Albuera, Waterloo—which bring the question of purpose under urgent review. The intense poetic emotion is generated by arrangement of language and rhythm which takes us beyond the usual bounds of space and time. But the obsolete, coined, abstract, philosophical words which embody the strange dimension of the Overworld are usually in fruitful tension with some homely vivid word of emotional charge that relates the Overworld to our human experience.

The poetry of the Overworld can be justified dramatically. It speaks of ultimate concepts, but constantly translates the abstract mystery of the Will into immediate sensuous terms through imagery and precision in expressing emotion. The language of each Spirit is appropriate to his function. This includes the vulgar, Gilbertian, music-hall or doggerel terms and jaunty rhythms which have pained critics. When the Overworld expresses itself in such terms, it is to diminish the epic grandeur of Napoleon's coronation, the armistice between France and Austria (1, VI, v), the British battalions under sail for Spain (2, II, v), the meeting of Napoleon and Maria Louisa (2, v, vi) and Napoleon's escape from Elba (3, v, i). Another idiosyncratic dissonance between form and subject is felt in their expression of the chaos, horror, futility, and obscenity of modern warfare in forms borrowed from Campbell, Southey, Byron, Scott, Browning, Swinburne, Tennyson, Barnes, ballad, hymn, and psalm, which had mellifluously, jubilantly, or jauntily sung of its glory or the peacefulness of peace.

The lyrics of the Overworld have been admired enough to be included in selections of Hardy's poetry. But they owe their power in *The Dynasts* to the context of many kinds of poetry and prose which express a world of multiple reality. The Overworld has almost a monopoly of lyrical poetry affirming individual feeling and personality. Their language is rich in metaphor which establishes relationship between points of experience, because their perspective is total and not fragmentary. The blank verse of the dynasts is flat and factual. Men have the experience but not the meaning. Nevertheless their verse is a dramatic instrument. It enacts the plodding obstructiveness of the human condition that defeats Napoleon, and creates the illusion of the characters acting out a cosmic play. The humble ranks speak in the humorous half-poetic prose of the novels. The stage directions, like the novels and poems, relate realistic and poetic, abstract and concrete, in powerful images that hold in tension the irreconcilables of the Will.

'So massive is the contest that we soon fail to individualize the combatants as beings, and can only observe them as amorphous drifts, clouds, and waves of conscious atoms, surging and rolling together; can only particularize them by race, tribe, and language. Nationalities from the uttermost parts of Asia here meet those from the Atlantic edge of Europe for the first and last time. By noon the sound becomes a loud droning, uninterrupted and breve-like, as from the pedal of an organ kept continuously down.'

(3, iii, ii).

It is characteristic of Hardy's ironic double vision that the non-human 'atoms' are qualified by 'conscious', and the individual 'race, tribe, and language' levelled down in a musical image that incongruously evokes from the dissonance of the conflict the harmony that *should* reign at a meeting of nations.

The Fore Scene sets in motion the dramatic clash of style and idea that develops the opposition of conscious and unconscious will. The first and basic question, '*What of the Immanent Will and Its designs?*' develops the ambiguity of 'designs' into the dissonances of '*Eternal artistries//in Circumstance*', '*patterns, wrought//by rapt aesthetic rote*', '*listless//aim*'. The agitated speech rhythms that characterize the Pities, '*Still thus? Still thus?/Ever unconscious?*' oppose their warm impulsive human melody to the measured onomatapoeic tick of the Years' exposition of being.

> *You cannot swerve the pulsion of the Byss,*
> *Which thinking on, yet weighing not Its thought,*
> *Unchecks Its clock-like laws.*

The Years' language is full of imagery from the automatic motion of mechanical, biological, and astronomical law, miraculously defining the abstract Undefinable by negatives. It is reiterated and redefined in response to the unanswerable 'Why?' at scenes of suffering.

The leitmotif of the harmony that should reign instead of the dissonance that is, which threads the whole debate, is introduced by the Pities in the musical, dignified diction of basic truths. They would establish the rule of

> *Those, too, who love the true, the excellent,*
> *And make their daily moves a melody.*

The creative evolution theme that backs up their irrational hope is hinted in the Years' answer to the Earth's revolt against the futile interchange of Dynasts, '*when all such tedious conjuring could be shunned/By uncreation*':

> *Nay, something hidden urged*
> *The giving matter motion; and these coils*
> *Are, maybe, good as any.*

The dissonance of issues and styles, abstraction and concrete, returns at scenes of suffering, where human flesh is torn by an abstract force. The language dramatizes '*The intolerable antilogy/Of making figments feel*'. But at Trafalgar and Austerlitz the debate takes place in a context of evolutionary lyric that counterpoints the despair with a larger hope of eventual fulfilment to emerge from the 'sublime fermenting-vat'. '*O pause, till all things all their days fulfil!*' The Pities' Prayer to the 'Great Necessitator' to dull the suffering at Austerlitz leads by poetic logic to the quiet close of Part First where the Years seems to respond to the Pities to '*show ruth/At man's fag end, when his destruction's sure*' at Pitt's peaceful death. He has already shown pity for Villeneuve's suffering, and anger at the cynicism of the Spirit Sinister (1, I, vi).

Throughout Part Second, the defiance of the Pities to the Years' iteration of determinism grows stronger. They take on the lament of mortal futility at Walcheren, and after Alburera and the madness of George III they defy the Ironic Spirits' vision of empty stellar spaces, hammered home by the one rhyme, with their irrational determination to pray

> *To some Great Heart, who haply may*
> *Charm mortal miseries away.*

And at the end of Part Second, the evolving compassion which has developed from question to prayer which almost conjures a god from the emptiness, defies the Years' picture of the whole world obeying the Will, to assert faith in Its waking to consciousness.

In Part Third, the Pities batter the emotions to wake the Will. The confusion of battle and horror of pain, brought vividly to the senses, become more evident in their reporting. At Borodino they oppose the Years' vision of 'mechanized enchantment' with their report that the '*ugly horror*' has woken even Napoleon '*to all its vain uncouthness*'. The Choruses, which heighten the lyric mood of the Spirit's comments, sing not of the movements of battle but of exhausted and dying men. At Waterloo they transform the Years' Borodino vision of a '*web of rage/That permeates as one stuff the weltering whole*' to a web of suffering that includes all creatures in its fabric, in a lyric that is significantly shared by the Chorus of the Years. Waterloo, a victory for English virtues in the world of men, in the larger world of human potentialities is a victory for compassion at the sufferings involved, and a possible indication that to feel such suffering and act on the feelings is the purpose of man's existence as pioneer of the Will in universal pity. Regret—always a positive emotion for Hardy—informs the Pities' report of Waterloo; for the unfulfilment of promise in crops and youths impartially crushed, and in men of fine calibre like Ney. The response of the Pities so far dominates Part Third that the Spirit of the Years picks out for observation examples of vindictiveness in men deserted by '*all wide sight and self-command*' which the Pities would foster. Earlier, the protest of the Pities at the intolerable antilogy of making figments feel (1, IV, v) has ranged the Spirit of the Ironies on his side because '*Logic's in that.*' Irony and Pity are two sides of the same coin, both trying to find human response in the Will. At Waterloo, the Ironic Spirits comment in a question and answer lyric that is emotionally inspired by the Pities' irrational faith.

> *Of Its doings if It knew,*
> *What It does It would not do!*

And it is the Spirit Ironic who asks Napoleon, '*Has all this been worthwhile?*'

The After Scene is a coda that brings back the themes of the conflict. But the conflict is musically resolved in one of Hardy's modern chords of dissonance. The Years reiterates the ceaseless urging of the Will-web weaving unconsciously in the stellar void

> *Where hideous presences churn through the dark—*
> *Monsters of magnitude without a shape,*
> *Hanging amid deep wells of nothingness*

and diminishes the horrifying abstract sublimity of the infinite with the ambiguity of '*this vast and singular confection*', defined as '*inutile all—so far as reasonings tell*'. But his saving clause indicates that the Pities have not agonized in vain. Their response picks up the dignified Latinate roll of the Years' style, but the inexorable law it illustrates is the law of evolution.

> *Thou arguest still the Inadvertent Mind.—*
> *But, even so, shall blankness be for aye?*
> *Men gained cognition with the flux of time,*
> *And wherefore not the Force informing them,*
> *When far-ranged aions past all fathoming*
> *Shall have swung by, and stand as backward years?*

From this point the Spirit of the Pities directs the course, emotion, and language of the debate as he would direct evolution. In the Pities' hymn to the Will of their dream the abstraction so long defined by the terrifying neuter 'It' and many resounding names of abstract and negative quality, is humanized as 'Thee' and the merciful and controlling God of Christian tradition evoked as an alternative possibility. But this God is not yet in being, except as an ideal in the compassionate faith of his pioneers. The Years admits to sympathy for their conception.

> *You almost charm my long philosophy*
> *Out of my strong-built thought, and bear me back*
> *To when I thanksgave thus . . .*

The vision of cosmic harmony aroused by the Pities' hymn brings back the musical imagery. The Years is moved to complete the hymn, in terms that blend the responses of Years and Pities, by assuming the role of questioner from which the Pities' maturity developed. '*To what tune danceth this Immense?*' The Pities complete the epic-drama with a prophecy of '*Consciousness the Will informing, till It fashion all things fair!*' But the concluding chord is that of the seventh. Hardy's power of poetry and vision makes *The Dynasts* a vast musical composition awaiting fulfilment of the final harmonizing chord.

XIV

Afterwards

Thomas Hardy, born in the nineteenth century and dying in the twentieth, bridges the two worlds. His Janus face may account for his appeal to young readers and writers today. The integrity of his personal search for meaning and self-supporting attitudes in an absurd world, his refusal to be comforted by ready-made formulae, myths and illusions, or to take refuge in cynicism, the unpretentious rough-hewn voice talking quietly of intense suffering and joy, speak to their own condition, while the backbone of certainties about fundamental human values which he inherited from his own century offsets the modern permissive confusion.

Though Hardy has been defined at various periods as an 'unfashionable' author, and the poetry largely neglected in favour of the novels in his unfashionable phases, it is in the field of modern verse that his influence can be detected most distinctly. Kenneth Marsden, in *The Poems of Thomas Hardy*, has listed some of the twentieth-century expectations which contributed to the neglect of his poetry by the common reader and critic. They include hostility to 'ideas' in poetry; dislike of Hardy's world-view, limited themes, and poetic persona, which had to contend with Eliot's influential theory of impersonality in poetry; the doctrine of expressive form and *vers libre* which drew attention away from the different kind of freedom expressed in Hardy's counterpoint of natural speech stress and traditional formalism; the modern impatience of anything less than a very high standard of competence throughout the whole body of a poet's works; and lastly, Hardy's reputation as an innovator, which disappointed preconceptions of a sensational revolution and bold avant-garde experiment. But whatever the prevailing critical opinion, practising poets have never ceased to pay tribute to his art and influence. They include Ezra Pound, Siegfried Sassoon, Edmund Blunden, Edward Thomas, Robert Graves, C. H. Sorley, Andrew Young, C. Day Lewis, James Reeves, W. H. Auden, Dylan Thomas, Philip Larkin, Philip Oakes, and Roger Frith.

However, it is not the kind of influence that is easy to pinpoint. One can usually pick out a disciple of Eliot or Hopkins through echoes of style, tone or theme. But even about those poets who have admitted Hardy's influence, 'no-one . . . seems willing to give details or even ask some obvious questions' (Marsden). Marsden quotes instances of imitation, pastiche and parody of Hardy's themes and style from C. H. Sorley, John Crowe Ransom, de la Mare, C. Day Lewis, William Plomer, John Betjeman and Philip Larkin. Larkin, a thoroughgoing admirer, who has confessed that

'one reader at least would not wish Hardy's *Collected Poems* a single page shorter, and regards it as many times over the best body of poetic work this century so far has to show . . .'

helps to define the nature of Hardy's influence on modern poets. His work shows Hardeian preoccupations, set down in the common language of common man, with the relationships of death, life, and love, with time and memory, with moments missed and moments of vision lighting the flat stretches of boredom and daily triviality, with the multiple interpretation of experience, with the assertion of human identity against cyclic flux, with the conflict of image and reality, with the sad agnosticism of honest disbelief, with the failure of things to bear out their promise.

> The glare of that much-mentioned brilliance, love,
>   Broke out, to show
> Its bright incipience sailing above,
> Still promising to solve, and satisfy,
> And set unchangeably in order. So
>   To pile them back, to cry,
> Was hard, without lamely admitting how
> It had not done so then, and could not now.
>   ('Love Songs in Age')

But the language and poetic persona are his own, while the themes are not peculiar to Hardy and Larkin; they have become part of common twentieth-century experience. Hardy has played a vital though unobtrusive role in educating us to an awareness of the common human predicament.

The difference between Hardy and his admirers constitutes, paradoxically, his major influence.

'It should be fairly obvious . . . that for another poet to be *seriously* influenced by Hardy is rather unlikely, because as the real Hardy, the one who is worth being influenced by, started from subject, the poet being influenced would do the same. He might well take over, or rather perceive anew, Hardy's subject matter, but since he would be attempting to render *his* perception it is not likely that he would employ Hardy's peculiarities of vocabulary.'

(Marsden: op. cit.)

His importance to modern poets and novelists was not as a maker of new traditions like Eliot, Hopkins and Joyce, but as a writer who battered the older forms into speaking with the idiosyncratic voice of his own persona, which invested traditional forms with a new originality. W. H. Auden, who claimed Hardy as his poetic father, recognised that he owed his independence to the older poet —the best tribute a son can pay to his father:

'Such unusual verse forms help the imitator to find out what he has to say: . . . in addition [he] taught me much about direct colloquial diction, all the more because his directness was in phrasing and syntax, not in imagery.'

('A Literary Transference', *Southern Review*, vi, 1940)

Hardy's integrity in saying what he had to say in his own way, against opposition and expectation, encouraged younger poets to achieve a self-supporting persona in the absence of 'the habits of the community formulated, corrected, and elevated by the continuous thought and direction of the Church' (T. S. Eliot, *After Strange Gods*).

Hardy's rejection of inherited dogmas led to a sifting and modification of inherited poetic methods which showed the way for modern poets to emancipation from the rich sensuous music of Victorian verse. Tennyson's doubts and Swinburne's attacks on the 'supreme evil, God' had not been reflected, as Hardy's reluctant agnosticism was, in a fundamental dissonance of form which recalls modern music. His original treatment of traditional forms makes them reflect the poignant tensions of modern verse. The hymn tune behind 'The Impercipient' and the *In Memoriam* stanza behind 'A Sign-Seeker' carry their own irony. Marsden has pointed out that Hardy's 'obsession with time and his wish to arrest the flux'—a modern trait—'could have encouraged a desire for strict and perhaps complicated forms', as in 'Looking Across'.

'The substance of the poem is the undeviating, inevitable, progression to Death, those close to him being taken one by one . . . The structure, however, seems to have been designed, consciously or not, to allow very little movement. The twenty-five lines contain only two rhymes! which run through and link every stanza; in addition one of the b rhymes of each stanza, the last line, is identical (the last line is, in fact, a modified refrain). No less than ten lines begin with 'and' which—so to speak—adds, without chronological progression; this is quite apart from the effect of the mere repetition of the word itself. Furthermore, of the remaining fifteen lines, four begin with the same word 'that'. Individually these points may be trivial; collectively I think that they are significant. The consciousness of Time and Death produces, in the last stanza, apparent acquiescence; the structure of the poem tells a different, contradictory story.'

The allusions to European culture which Eliot and Pound integrated into their poetry to counteract the break-up of a European tradition is anticipated, in a modest way, by Hardy's synthesis of language drawn from many levels of a native culture. The reflection of a world increasingly scientific, the determination that poetry should not be restricted to a special range of language or subject, the determination not to avoid triviality and ugliness (without, in Hardy's case, going to the opposite extreme by avoiding nobility and beauty) can all be found in Hardy's poetry. The failure of logic to explain an absurd godless world is enacted in the juxtaposition, without synthesis, of multiple and contradictory facets of experience—not a far cry from the fragmentation of 'The Waste Land', though Hardy never abandons strict form for free verse or the conscious level of statement in favour of the subconscious logic of association. ('I am very anxious not to be obscure' he explained to V. H. Collins: *Talks with Thomas Hardy at Max Gate 1920–1922.*)

Even where there has been no conscious imitation or confession of influence, Hardy's poetic response to the changing world opened the way to sincerity of response and boldness of experiment in the generations following. Even Eliot, for all his religious antipathy to Hardy's ability to live without God, touches the older poet's tragic vision in 'Dry Salvages'; and the futility, boredom, and unsensational recording of facts in Eliot's earlier poetry—'The Journey of the Magi', for example—can be paralleled in much of Hardy's poetry.

> A tedious time
> I found it, of routine, amid a folk
> Restless, contentless, and irascible.—
> ('Panthera')

Eliot's 'patient etherised upon a table' is simply a more violently realized image of Hardy's persistent poetic persona; of modern man as the bewildered helpless observer, born out of his time and place, powerless to alter the tragic predicament which he endures in alienated awareness.

While Hardy's own poems were still coming out, younger poets were experimenting in several different directions. Their aims were diverse, but had to some extent been anticipated in Hardy's varied output. Some of the Imagist tenets—'Everything can go, but this stark, bare, rocky directness of statement, this alone makes poetry today' (D. H. Lawrence): Ezra Pound's conviction that poetry should be 'austere, direct, free from emotional slither', . . . 'as much like granite as it can be, its force will lie in its truth'—and their concern for centrality of subject allied to craftsmanship, had been carried into practice since the beginning of Hardy's poetic career. A more surrealistic direction was pointed by some of the experiments in *Wheels*, a collection of poetry which appeared annually from 1916 to 1921. The poets represented expressed a general disgust with life and its mechanical motiveless malignity. Their response, though very different from Hardy's tragic affirmative joy in man and nature, took forms which *The Dynasts* and the five volumes of poetry so far published had introduced. The First Cause, minimized in the *Dynasts* by the domestic imagery of weaving and knitting, fares no better in *Wheels*, where elemental forces are described in terms of man-made products, as in Edith Sitwell's 'smooth black lacquer sea'. The soulless mechanical process that drives the action in Hardy's universe is recalled by the younger poets' geometric and mechanical metaphors, substituted (as they were not in Hardy) for metaphors from the world of nature. Though Hardy was not tempted to the extremes of expression reached by these two schools, the climate of opinion created by his anticipation of their themes and techniques encouraged interest in their experiments.

As a countryman, Hardy's greatest gift to a century which produced many Georgian 'nature' poets was to invest man's experience of his natural environment with cosmic implications. The best of his followers in this respect—D. H. Lawrence, Andrew Young, Robert Frost, Walter de la Mare, James Reeves—have been faithful to Hardy's detailed affirmative recording of the sensuous world, the sense of human solitude and alienation from the natural harmony which nevertheless commands his obedience, the acceptance of cosmic indifference, the inextricable weaving of life and death in the natural cycle, the preservation of local feeling and local word as symbols of identity against the encroachments of standardization.

Hardy's novels, no less than his poems, put into circulation themes and techniques which have become the commonplaces of twentieth-century thought. The poetic response to life which marks his prose as well as his poetry has nurtured a consciousness of the multiple and ambiguous faces of experience, the inextricable beauty and terror, which finds expression across the span of eighty years in similar terms.

'The huge pool of blood in front of her was already assuming the iridescence of coagulation; and when the sun rose a hundred prismatic hues were reflected from it.'

(*Tess of the d'Urbervilles*, 1891)

'On the fourth day the rats began to come out and die in batches . . . In the mornings the bodies were found lining the gutters, each with a gout of blood, like a red flower, on its tapering muzzle.'

(Camus, *The Plague*, 1947)

Even the sun-clouds this morning cannot manage such skirts.
Nor the woman in the ambulance
Whose red heart blooms through her coat so astoundingly—

(Sylvia Plath, 'Poppies in October',
Ariel, 1965)

I know the colour rose, and it is lovely,
but not when it ripens in a tumour;
and healing greens, leaves and grass, so springlike
in limbs that fester are not springlike.

(Dannie Abse, 'Pathology of
Colours', *A Small Desperation*, 1968)

The modern novel and drama have moved nearer to poetry in their Hardeian awareness of discordant and various experience which cannot be explained by any system. The relativity of truth and the unchronological pattern created by 'moments of vision' help to determine theme and shape of experimental novels written by the generation following Hardy; James Joyce, Virginia Woolf, E. M. Forster. Events and characterization are provisional, taking their significance from other events and characters in a web of leitmotif. All action is equally significant in the void of the Marabar caves or the perspective of *The Dynasts* which reduces marching armies and snowflakes to the same dead level. Though literature since the Second World War has made a partial return to straightforward narrative and plot, which mirrors the shift in interest away from post-Freudian free association in the subjective stream of consciousness to a web of continually changing exterior relationships through which man defines his identity, it owes its distinctive form to depiction of the incongruous worlds in which existentialist man has to create himself and his purposes. The incursion of irrational forces into the systems of order man tries to impose on the chaotic universe, one of Hardy's major themes, forms a vital source of tension in many modern novels. The rational society created in Angus Wilson's modern parable of what Hardy called 'human action in spite of human knowledge', *The Old Men at the Zoo*, is upset by animal violence. The Christian structures built up by Graham Greene's characters and the boys in William Golding's *Lord of the Flies* are knocked down by irrational and incomprehensible evil in human nature. The rationally planned ways of life in Iris Murdoch's novels, of which her titles are an image (*Under the Net, The Bell, The Sandcastle, A Severed Head*), are shown to be illusions when disrupted by the human passions of the planners and the inexplicable casual event. One need not look far in Hardy's work to find symbols of incomprehensible cosmic irrationality like the gipsy who shadows the disruptive love affair in *The Sandcastle*, or Felicity's unsuccessful attempt (in Dorset) to impose her will on the cosmos with an aid of a burning image of her enemy. Lucky Jim's luck is just as irrational as the bad luck of Hardy's characters, and rather less credible. The psychological evasions practised by modern fictional characters to hide their irrational behaviour is prefigured, as Morrell points out, in Hardy's stories. The self-deception of Kingsley Amis's Bowen (*I Like it Here*) who 'by an internal holding of telescope to blind eye, . . . had been keeping off what he had been up to', is no different in kind from Bathsheba's evasion of her true purpose in following Troy to Bath.

The 'doubleness in the action' which is the mark of poetic writing, and which has moulded the shape of so much modern fiction, was anticipated by Hardy in his use of symbolic leitmotifs to create a pattern of subconscious action that strains against the narrative level of conscious action. Bathsheba's sexual perception of the hollow in the ferns where she meets Troy defines the sword exercise as a desired seduction. In L. P. Hartley's *The Go-Between*, the adolescent boy's discovery of the belladonna just after meeting his friend's beautiful sister defines his subconscious perception of the ambiguous creative/destructive nature of sex, which consciously he cannot articulate. The older novelist does not depend, as Hartley does, on nothing but associative juxtaposition to make his point. Unlike the sword exercise, which marks a crisis in the relations of Troy and Bathsheba, Hartley's belladonna serves no narrative function in the plot. But a similar consciousness of multiple layers of personality begets similar methods of expression.

The sub-structure of symbolic leitmotif which reveals actions and desires obeying a different morality from conscious action has become a commonplace of modern novels. D. H. Lawrence, whose long essay on Hardy proves subjectively how much he owes to the older man, put into circulation a concept of personality and action whose springs were in the non-personal sexual force that moves Hardy's wilful characters to burst into being in defiance of conventional surface morality. The response of the two girls to the fox and the young man who kills it in Lawrence's short story *The Fox* realigns their personal relationships according to the non-personal sexual rhythms hidden underneath their conscious desires and moral values. Lawrence is Hardy's only true English successor in his feeling for the rhythms of eternity that bind the natural world to the ragged inconsequential lives of human beings; in his fear of mechanization and respect for individuality; in his power to depict the subconscious sexual tensions that motivate close relationships. Even in so autobiographical a novel as *Sons and Lovers*, the mother/son relationship recalls that of Clym and Mrs Yeobright, and Miriam tampering sensuously with the flowers as a substitute for the sexual experience she fears is sister to Sue Bridehead burying her face in the blooms at the Great Wessex Show. But though Hardy recognized the subconscious basis of much action and the consequent need for compassionate judgement of frailties, he saw no salvation in surrender to the dark gods. Though in the interests of realistic fiction he deplored the Victorian edict that 'the crash of broken commandments shall not be heard' ('Candour in English Fiction', *New Review*, January 1890) he was firm about the moral duty of authors.

'The higher passions must ever rank above the inferior—intellectual tendencies above animal, and moral above intellectual—whatever the treatment, realistic or ideal. Any system of inversion which should attach more importance to the delineation of man's appetites than to the delineation of his aspirations, affections, or humors, would condemn the old masters of imaginative creation from Aeschylus to Shakespeare.'

('The Profitable Reading of Fiction', *New York Forum*, March 1888)

The essential difference of outlook that marks Hardy off from modern authors with whom he shares so many preoccupations, explains why his *forte* is tragedy while the typical form of the modern novel is tragi-comedy. Hardy's heroes and heroines find moral assertion of the best values humanity has known, still possible in a chaos of indifference without fixed standards of value. Tess and Alec still represent the two choices open to modern man:

' "Why, you can have the religion of loving-kindness and purity at least, if you can't have—what do you call it—dogma."

' "O no! I'm a different sort of fellow from that! If there's nobody to say, 'Do this, and it will be a good thing for you after you are dead; do that, and it will be a bad thing for you,' I can't warm up. Hang it, I am not going to feel responsible for my deeds and passions if there's nobody to be responsible to; and if I were you, my dear, I wouldn't either!" '

(Chapter XLVII)

Alec's *credo* leads logically to the hedonistic standards of Alan Sillitoe's characters, or the opportunistic hero of Kingsley Amis, John Wain and John Braine whose aim is simply adjustment to the society in which he lives.

'. . . the sane man does not allow any of his roles to become abstract manifestations of general truth or guides to conduct. Existence is the only necessary condition, and the opportunistic hero plays any role he can in any world he can (the fantastic, the limited, or the deceitful) in order to get what he simply happens to want.'

(James Gindin, *Postwar British Fiction*)

Modern *homo fictus* is often a Lucky Jim who keeps a battery of faces to meet the various contingencies of his multiple and incongruous environment. Lacking a consistent essence against which to define himself, he continuously creates his life, values and purpose, and is cast by others, in a series of roles. Avoiding commitment to a role renders him powerless against circumstances (the tendency of Tess and Eustacia to let things drift has the same result). Lucky Jim's bad luck ceases when, in his new role of masterful man, he seizes every opportunity, at the expense of others, to act out the role.

'More than ever he felt secure: here he was, quite able to fulfil his role, and, as with other roles, the longer you played it the better chance you had of playing it again. Doing what you wanted to do was the only training, and the only preliminary, needed for doing more of what you wanted to do.'

(Kingsley Amis: Lucky Jim)

The clash of roles causes tragedy in Hardy (though there is a touch of comic absurdity about Knight's and Angel's casting of Elfride and Tess as 'the pure woman') because the roles his characters assume *are* consistent 'guides to conduct'. *Tess* and *Jude* plead passionately against the inflexibility of 'abstract manifestations of general truth', but Tess and Jude nevertheless do not betray their steady ideals by assuming the faces required to adapt to society. The multiplicity of roles and values in the modern novel, the existentialist vision of man, responsible to no god, doomed to freedom of choice and commitment in an indifferent and Janus-faced world where the action by which he must define himself has no ultimate significance, invites the comic as well as the tragic perspective. Hardy comes nearest to the modern comic perspective in his less successful novels, where emotional identification with character is less intense. The comic perspective intrudes on serious or romantic matter to convey the bizarre duplicity of things and the lack of cosmic order. Even Graham Greene's Catholic universe cannot escape the absurd vision. Wilson's declaration of love to Scobie's wife, who does not return it, is made ludicrous by a nosebleed, the motherly concern of both Scobie and his wife, and the undignified prostrate position he is obliged to adopt.

'Louise struck at his cheek and missing got his nose, which began to bleed copiously. She said, "That's for calling him Ticki. Nobody's going to do that except me. You know he hates it. Here, take my handkerchief if you haven't got one of your own."
'Wilson said, "I bleed awfully easily. Do you mind if I lie on my back?" He stretched himself on the floor between the table and the meat safe, among the ants.'

(The Heart of the Matter)

In *The Sandcastle*, the stereotype of a passionate quarrel between husband and wife about Bill's affair with the young artist is punctured by Nan's hiccups and her undignified entry through the window when she cannot find her key. Sex, so tragically disruptive in Hardy, but even in *Jude the Obscure* tinged with the Absurd perspective when the pig's pizzle rudely dislocates Jude's sublime dream of Christminster, is the greatest incongruity of all. The attempted suicide of the would-be postulant Catherine in *The Bell* is made bizarre by Dora's ham-fisted rescue operations, the more resourceful life-saving of the 'aquatic nun' in her underclothes, and Catherine's public expression of love to the horror-stricken and homosexual Michael. The comic and multiple perspective questions the ultimate importance both of the sexual crisis and the ideals it disrupts.

The multiple perspective and singular form of *The Dynasts* anticipates much modern experimental drama. An epic action framed by various forms of narrative comment and other alienation techniques was placed firmly on the modern stage by Bertolt Brecht, author of that other great outcry against the futility of war, *Mother Courage*. Both dramatists see destiny as alterable by the action of men, so there are moments of choice for the protagonists when an alternative action is glimpsed; but both Napoleon and Mother Courage choose war. Brechtian spirits of Pity and Irony (Grusha and Azdak, and the two faces of the Good Woman) inspire the fundamental structure of *The Caucasian Chalk Circle* and *The Good Woman of Setzuan*. Brecht's use of mixed media can be paralleled in Hardy's varied presentation of his drama through realistic and non-realistic action and characters, dialogue, dumb show, changing perspectives, spectacle, poetry, prose, song. Only the quirk of Time prevented the use of film projection as the most appropriate medium for Hardy's stage directions and battle scenes. Brecht's instructions to his actors that the role should be demonstrated rather than acted, in the interests of alienation, recalls Hardy's suggestion of anti-naturalistic speech and gesture:

'In respect of such plays of poesy and dream a practicable compromise may conceivably result, taking the shape of a monotonie delivery of speeches, with dreamy conventional gestures, something in the manner traditionally maintained by the old Christmas mummers . . .'

(Preface, *The Dynasts*)

The 'automatic style—that of persons who spoke by no will of their own' of this mode of delivery has an unexpected descendant in

T. S. Eliot's use of the tranced chorus of aunts and uncles in *The Family Reunion.*

The repetitive futility of human action demonstrated in the modern anti-drama owns *Waiting for Godot* as parent and *The Dynasts* as prime fugleman of the line. The multiple representation of both showman and show, abstract reality and image, actor and role, which forms an essential part of the technique of Cocteau, Anouilh, Pirandello, and many playwrights of the Absurd Theatre, is anticipated in the structure of *The Dynasts* and the novels. The abstract reality of the Immanent Will concretely represented by the heaving brain-tissue has many descendants in symbolic stage props: Pinter's dumb waiter in the play of that name, which suggests cosmic cross-purposes as vividly as the jackaclock and gurgoyle in *Far from the Madding Crowd*; the platonic castle-model-cum-altar of the huge mysterious castle in which Albée's *Tiny Alice* is set; the gallows with corpse that opens *The Devils* with the question asked throughout the play:

> MANNOURY: What's left, man? After that.
> ADAM: Ah, you've something in your head.
> MANNOURY: Has he? That's the point.

The seeker for good brave causes (Jimmy Porter, *Look Back in Anger*), for self-definition and evolution away from simple peasant standards which yet provide a stability and lovingkindness lost to the seeker (Beatie Bryant, *Roots*), for shelter against the terror of insecurity (Pinter's Rose, Davies, Stan); the inadequate failures who cast themselves and others in satisfying roles (*The Caretaker, The Brithday Party, The Cocktail Party, A Sleep of Prisoners, Hadrian VII*), and reject the love they need because it does not come in the romantic form they desire; all these modern archetypes are represented in Hardy's work. The problems of evil, death, and the death of God, of the mechanization of personality in a mechanical universe, inform his books as they inform every serious drama today. The unacknowledged death-wish, so dramatically expressed in the figure of Little Father Time and the trend of the later novels, drives man to assume the role of sacrificial victim or executioner (*The Devils, Saint's Day, Tiny Alice*). More rarely in an anti-heroic age suspicious of ideals and professions of faith, the dignified resistance of a human being (Sir Thomas More in *A Man for All Seasons*, Proctor in *The Crucible*, Grandier in *The Devils*) against assimilation into Absurdity and lack of meaning, recalls the integrity of Hardy's heroic characters faced with the temptation to nihilism. The realization of suffering as an essential element in the higher development of consciousness, and the meaning discovered in personal relationships which, in Peter Shaffer's plays *The Royal Hunt of the Sun* and *The Battle of Shrivings*, creates the only god there is, were also Hardy's positives against the darkness.

To find the purest inheritors of Hardy's cosmos, however, one must cross the Channel. His inscription (dated October 1904) in Jerome Kern's copy of *Jude the Obscure* pays tribute to European recognition: 'It was left to the French & Germans to discover the author's meaning, through the medium of indifferent translations.' Thomas Mann, backed by his German inheritance of logic and philosophy, metaphysics and music, found a powerful two-fold symbol in *Dr Faustus* for the evil that gave birth to two world wars, in Leverkuhn's twelve-tone method of composition and a hallucinatory devil, equated in their appeal to rational nihilism and regressive primitivism. They recall not only similar manifestations of Absurd evil in Kafka and Gide, but Hardy's Mephistophelian visitants—William Dare and Fitzpiers, both rationalist dilettantes, and Mop Ollamoor, whose 'chromatic subtleties' distort the diatonic harmonies of sleepy Stickleford, and who had nothing but 'devil's tunes in his repertory'.

In France, the nostalgia for an impossible purity, and the Existentialist vision developed since the two world wars, have produced a kind of novel and drama anticipated in Hardy's themes. Proust indicates a familiarity with Hardy's novels in Volume 10 ('The Captive', Part Two) of *Remembrance of Things Past*. The whole novel develops familiar Hardeian themes: the subjectivity of love, the impossibility of union with the reality of one's desire, life as a series of substitutions, the tendency to swing between memory and desire and desire and boredom, the incessant process of time and change, the past as both a positive and negative influence. Proust's subjective technique of presenting emotions and mental states indirectly through what a character notices was anticipated in, for example, Boldwood's distorted view of the snowy landscape and the summer glow of Talbothays that reflected Tess's love for Angel. R. Giannoni, in an article on 'Alain-Fournier et Thomas Hardy' (*Revue de Littérature Comparée*, XLII, 1968) discovers a link between the French author's reading of *Tess* in 1906 and his treatment of the theme of nostalgia for a lost homeland of paradisal purity, a theme which has occupied French writers at least since *Madame Bovary*.

'C'est en lisant *Tess*, par exemple, que Fournier commença à méditer sur le thème de la pureté perdue qui allait être au centre de ses preoccupations morales.'

Giannoni is careful to point out, however, that the nature of Fournier's debt to Hardy was independent. 'Alain-Fournier, lecteur enthousiaste de Thomas Hardy, ne fut ni un imitateur ni un disciple' but 'en la personne de Hardy, il trouva un guide précieux qui l'aida à voir clair en lui-même.'

The search for reunion with the pure part of one's being in Proust, Gide, Anouilh, Cocteau, often takes the form of an abnormal relationship, which includes the death wish. The closeness of Orpheus and Eurydice, the incestuous bond explicit in Gide's *Oedipus* and Cocteau's *The Infernal Machine* and implicit in the children of *Les Enfants Terribles*; the homosexual relationships of Gide's characters and his Narcissus' compulsion towards his mirror image, recall the special relationship between the cousins Jude and Sue. The purity of Hardy's characters is stained by the impurity of the cosmos of which they are part. Anouilh's pure lovers, like Hardy's Tess and Elfride, have unparadisal parents. His pure Thérèse (*La Sauvage*) succumbs finally, like Tess, to the compulsion of inherited impurity and the memory of past degradation. The contrast between sordid reality and the ideal dream, as clearly defined in *Antigone* or *La Sauvage* as in *Jude* and *Tess*, leaves only the choice of death or the deliberate assumption of a compromised role and acceptance of suffering in a fallen world.

All the characters in Romain Gary's *The Roots of Heaven* (1956), driven by the need for purity that involves a search for the source of man's sense of alienation from his roots, have an obsessive relationship with the wild elephants who become 'the very image of an immense liberty', of non-utilitarian natural splendour and individual dignity, almost extinct in a mechanistic and mechanized world. The desire of Camus' Tarrou for an impossible purity, the possibility of being a saint without God, is carried on with the recognition that all living creatures are tainted with the plague (the will to cause and suffer death in a universe whose only end and purpose is death). His refusal to collaborate willingly, his desire to maintain instead a constant vigilance against infection, is typical of the integrity of Hardy's tragic heroes and heroines. 'There are pestilences and there are victims, and it's up to us, so far as possible, not to join forces with the pestilences' (*The Plague*).

The refusal to be overawed by death into accepting the abstraction of significance from individuals placed many French writers, as Hardy had been placed, in opposition to social conventions. Gide's fight for the rights of the abnormal member of society, after recognition of his own homosexuality, continued Hardy's plea for greater tolerance. *Jude the Obscure* and *Tess of the d'Urbervilles*, as much as *The Immoralist* and *The Counterfeiters* and *Oedipus*, contain a rejection of authoritarian systems in favour of a personal morality which binds as much as it liberates, the courageous acceptance of one's desires, the difficulties of living with the new-found freedom of the godless and fatherless alien, the struggle not to slip back into a morality not one's own, the evolutionary and existentialist power of 'disponibilité'—the power of remaining unsatisfied and undefined, capable of change and growth. It is this power which Sue betrays by choosing to imprison herself in a rigid religious convention.

The integrity of the Hardeian response to an absurd universe is nowhere more apparent than in the work of Sartre and Camus, who brought the concepts of Absurdity and Existentialism into common consciousness on both sides of the Channel. All three writers are concerned with the practical problem of how to live in chaos. Caligula's collaboration with Absurdity, consequent on his discovery that 'men die; and they are not happy' (Camus, *Caligula*) like the collaboration of Alec, Troy, Eustacia, Fitzpiers, and Little Father Time, is rejected by his creator. Freedom for Sartre's Orestes, Camus' Clamance, Hardy's Tess, Jude, and Sue—the limited freedom of the prisoner condemned to death, and until then answerable to no authority but his own—brings a heavy burden of unatonable guilt and responsbility for all that lives and suffers.

The full look at the worst which these three authors steadily sustained brings recognition—the true tragic recognition—of both acceptance and revolt as man's destiny.

' ". . . since the order of the world is shaped by death, mightn't it be better for God if we refuse to believe in Him, and struggle with all our might against death, without raising our eyes towards the heaven where He sits in silence?" '

asks the doctor in *The Plague*. 'Fighting against creation as he found it' is the privilege and penalty of being human. Anguish and exile from paradisal harmony—'that sensation of a void within which never left us, that irrational longing to hark back to the past', realized in Hardy's concrete portrayal of a vanishing Wessex, are the marks of modern self-consciousness. Resistance involves an ordering of one's life. Existentialist man, unable to be defined by 'essences' or stereotypes of human nature (and how often the stereotyped conception causes tragedy in Hardy!) creates himself by commitment to purpose and action. His life is therefore a series of choices. A rash choice, such as Henchard's decision to make an early marriage, forges fetters that close round his fate. On the other hand, Hardy's pattern of reprieves, rallies, and re-choices shows the characters engaging in the constant process of re-defining and re-interpreting the past, and in some cases gaining partial control over the future, in a new context which proves how the first choice has changed the chooser. Morrell points out that the list of those who make, unmake, and then remake their original choice includes Fitzpiers, Grace, Angel, Eustacia, Wildeve, Pierston, Marcia, Sue, Jude, Farfrae, and Bob Loveday. Hardy's most typical tragic hero or heroine is one who fails to stand firmly by the chosen commitment. Henchard allows misunderstanding to develop at Elizabeth-Jane's wedding; Tess drifts into her mother's outmoded morality of waiting on Providence. Nevertheless Tess's constant ideal of purity makes her more than the existentialist sum of her acts.

The meaning of an author's work lives after him. Hardy has created, not a host of imitators and disciples, but an individual awareness of and thoughtful response to the human predicament that defines his spiritual successors. One cannot say with certainty whether Camus, that most upright and compassionate champion of human individuality against the abstractions of Absurdity, was influenced by reading Hardy. But he was born conscious of Hardy's universe. The values of physical life, love, friendship, emotion, happiness, goodness, clear-sightedness, daily work, heroism, personal integrity, and the love of life that is found on the other side of despair, which Camus opposes in *The Plague* to the 'nights and days filled always, everywhere, with the eternal cry of human pain'; the value of pain itself to develop sympathy with a common suffering, maintain their power across half a century of permissiveness, cynicism, and the savagery of two world wars because Hardy taught us to recognize them as the eternal truths to live by. The end of *The Plague*, reaffirming that trust in men slighted and enduring but nobler than the unconscious cosmos which crushes them, might stand as a tribute from the younger writer to his spiritual father; one of those who, 'while unable to be saints but refusing to bow down to pestilences, strive their utmost to be healers'; whose works, like his own, bore witness

'in favour of those plague-stricken people; so that some memorial of the injustice and outrage done them might endure; [and stated] quite simply what we learn in a time of pestilence: that there are more things to admire in men than to despise.'

Bibliography

I. THOMAS HARDY

References are taken from the definitive Wessex edition of Hardy's works published by Macmillan in 24 vols between 1912 and 1931. First publication dates in magazine and book form are also given. Further bibliographical information may be found in R. L. Purdy's invaluable *Thomas Hardy, A Bibliographical Study* (Oxford), 1954.

1. NOVELS

The Poor Man and the Lady. Written 1868; unpublished.

Desperate Remedies. London 1871. Wessex edn. London 1912.

Under the Greenwood Tree, or the Mellstock Quire. London 1872. Wessex edn. London 1912.

A Pair of Blue Eyes, serialized *Tinsley's Magazine,* Sept. 1872–July 1873. London 1873. Wessex edn. London 1912.

Far from the Madding Crowd, serialized *Cornhill Magazine,* Jan–Dec. 1874. London 1874. Wessex edn. London 1912.

The Hand of Ethelberta, A Comedy in Chapters, serialized *Cornhill Magazine,* July 1875–May 1876. London 1876. Wessex edn. London 1912.

The Return of the Native, serialized *Belgravia,* Jan–Dec. 1878. London 1878. Wessex edn. London 1912.

The Trumpet-Major, serialized *Good Words,* Jan–Dec. 1880. London 1880. Wessex edn. London 1912.

A Laodicean, A Story of Today, serialized *Harper's New Monthly Magazine* (European edn.), Dec. 1880–Dec. 1881. New York and London, 1881. Wessex edn. London 1912.

Two on a Tower, serialized *Atlantic Monthly* (Boston), May–Dec. 1882, simultaneously in London. London 1882. Wessex edn. London 1912.

The Mayor of Casterbridge, The Life and Death of a Man of Character, serialized *Graphic,* Jan–May 1886. London 1886. Wessex end. London 1912.

The Woodlanders, serialized *Macmillan's Magazine,* May 1886–Apr. 1887. London and New York 1887. Wessex edn. London 1912.

Tess of the d'Urbervilles, A Pure Woman Faithfully Presented, serialized *Graphic,* July–Dec. 1891. London 1891. Wessex edn. London 1912.

Jude the Obscure, serialized *Harper's New Monthly Magazine* Dec. 1894–Nov. 1895, simultaneously in New York and London. London 1896. Wessex edn. London 1912.

The Well-Beloved, A Sketch of a Temperament, serialized as *The Pursuit of the*

Well-Beloved in *The Illustrated London News*, Oct.–Dec. 1892. London 1897.
Wessex edn. London 1912.

2. SHORT STORIES

'An Indiscretion in the life of an Heiress', *New Quarterly Magazine*, July 1878, simultaneously *Harper's Weekly*. London (privately printed) 1934. *Wessex Tales*, London and New York, 1888. Wessex edn. London 1912. Contents in 1888: 'The Three Strangers' (*Longman's Magazine*, March 1883); 'The Withered Arm', (*Blackwood's Edinburgh Magazine*, Jan. 1888); 'Fellow-Townsmen' (*New Quarterly Magazine*, Apr. 1880): 'Interlopers at the Knap', (*The English Illustrated Magazine*, May 1884); 'The Distracted Preacher' (as 'The Distracted Young Preacher', *New Quarterly Magazine*, April 1879). 'An Imaginative Woman' (*Pall Mall Magazine*, April 1894) added to the Osgood, McIlvaine edn. of *Wessex Tales* 1896. In Wessex edn. 1912, 'An Imaginative Woman' was removed to *Life's Little Ironies*, and 'A Tradition of Eighteen Hundred and Four' and 'The Melancholy Hussar' transferred from *Life's Little Ironies* to *Wessex Tales*.

A Group of Noble Dames, London 1891. Wessex edn. London 1912. Contents: 'The First Countess of Wessex' (*Harper's New Monthly Magazine*, Dec. 1889); 'Barbara of the House of Grebe', 'The Marchioness of Stonehenge', 'Lady Mottisfont', 'The Lady Icenway', 'Squire Petrick's Lady', 'Anna Lady Baxby' (*Graphic*, Christmas Number, 1890); 'The Lady Penelope' (*Longman's Magazine*, Jan. 1890); 'The Duchess of Hamptonshire' (as 'The Impulsive Lady of Croome Castle', *Light*, Apr. 1878); 'The Honourable Laura' (as 'Benighted Travellers', *Bolton Weekly Journal*, Dec. 1881).

Life's Little Ironies, London 1894. Wessex edn. London 1912. Contents in 1894: 'The Son's Veto' (*The Illustrated London News*, Christmas Number 1891); 'For Conscience' Sake' (as 'For Conscience Sake', *Fortnightly Review*, March 1891); 'A Tragedy of Two Ambitions', (*The Universal Review*, Dec. 1888); 'On the Western Circuit' (*The English Illustrated Magazine*, Dec. 1891); 'To Please His Wife' (*Black and White*, June 1891); 'The Melancholy Hussar of the German Legion' (as 'The Melancholy Hussar' in the *Bristol Times and Mirror*, Jan. 1890); 'The Fiddler of the Reels' (*Scribner's Magazine*, New York, May 1893); 'A Tradition of Eighteen Hundred and Four' (as 'A Legend of the Year Eighteen Hundred and Four', *Harper's Christmas*, Dec. 1882); 'A Few Crusted Characters' (as 'Wessex Folk', *Harper's New Monthly Magazine*, American and European editions, March–June 1891. In Wessex edn. 1912, 'An Imaginative Woman' was transferred from *Wessex Tales*, and 'A Tradition of Eighteen Hundred and Four' and 'The Melancholy Hussar of the German Legion' removed to *Wessex Tales*.

A Changed Man and Other Tales. London 1913. Wessex edn. London 1914. Contents: 'A Changed Man' (The Sphere, Apr. 1900); 'The Waiting Supper' (Murray's Magazine, Jan-Feb. 1888, and Harper's Weekly (America) Dec.-Jan. 1887–8); 'Alicia's Diary' (*The Manchester Weekly Times*, Oct. 1887): 'The Grave by the Handpost' (*St. James's Budget*, Christmas Number 1897); 'Enter a Dragoon' (*Harper's Monthly Magazine*, New York, Dec. 1900); 'A Tryst at an

Ancient Earthwork' (as 'Ancient Earthworks and What Two Enthusiastic Scientists Found Therein', *Detroit Post*, March 1885; and as 'Ancient Earthworks at Casterbridge', *English Illustrated Magazine*, Dec. 1893); 'What the Shepherd Saw' (*The Illustrated London News*, Christmas Number 1881); 'A Committee Man of "The Terror"' (*The Illustrated London News*, Christmas Number 1896); 'Master John Horseleigh, Knight' (*The Illustrated London News*, Summer Number 1893); 'The Duke's Reappearance' (*The Saturday Review*, Christmas Supplement, 1896); 'A Mere Interlude', *The Bolton Weekly Journal*, Oct. 1885); 'The Romantic Adventures of a Milkmaid' (*Graphic*, Summer Number 1883).

3. POETRY

Wessex Poems and Other Verses. London 1898. Wessex edn., *Wessex Poems, Poems of the Past and the Present*, London 1912.
Poems of the Past and the Present. London 1902 [1901] Wessex edn., *Wessex Poems, Poems of the Past and the Present*, London 1912.
Time's Laughingstocks and Other Verses. London 1909. Wessex edn., *The Dynasts*, Part Third, *Time's Laughingstocks*, London 1913.
Satires of Circumstance, Lyrics and Reveries, London 1914. Wessex edn., *Satires of Circumstance, Moments of Vision*, London 1919.
Moments of Vision and Miscellaneous Verses. London 1917.
Late Lyrics and Earlier with Many Other Verses. London 1922. Wessex edn., *Late Lyrics and Earlier, The Famous Tragedy of the Queen of Cornwall*, London 1926.
Human Shows, Far Phantasies, Songs, and Trifles, London 1925. Wessex edn., *Human Shows, Winter Words*, London 1931.
Winter Words, in Various Moods and Metres. London 1928. Wessex edn., *Human Shows, Winter Words*, London 1931.

My references have been taken from *Collected Poems*, London 1930.

4. DRAMA

The Dynasts, A Drama of the Napoleonic Wars, in Three Parts, Nineteen Acts, and One Hundred and Thirty Scenes. Part First, London 1903 [1904]. Part Second, London 1905 [1906]; Part Third, London 1908. Wessex edn., *The Dynasts*, Parts First and Second, London 1913; Part Third, & *Time's Laughingstocks*, London 1913. *The Famous Tragedy of the Queen of Cornwall at Tintagel in Lyonnesse*, London, 1923; Wessex edn., *Late Lyrics and Earlier, The Famous Tragedy of the Queen of Cornwall*, London 1926.

5. ARTICLES, ETC.

'How I built myself a House' (Chambers's Journal, Mar. 1885).
'The Dorsetshire Labourer' (Longman's Magazine, July 1883).
The Dorset Farm Labourer, Past and Present. Dorchester 1884.
'The Rev. William Barnes, B.D.' (*The Athenaeum*, Oct 1886)
'The Profitable Reading of Fiction' (*The Forum*, New York, Mar. 1888).
'Candour in English Fiction' (*New Review*, Vol. ii, No. 8, 1890).
'Why I Don't Write Plays' (*The Pall Mall Gazette*, Aug. 1892).
Selected Poems of William Barnes, ed. with Preface and gloss, London 1908.
Further information may be found in Purdy, *op. cit.*, and Harold Orel (ed.) *Thomas Hardy's Personal Writings*, London & Melbourne, 1967.

II. REFERENCE AND CRITICISM

1. BIBLIOGRAPHY

R. L. Purdy, *Thomas Hardy, A Bibliographical Study*, Oxford 1954.

C. J. Weber, *The First Hundred Years of Thomas Hardy: a Centenary Bibliography of Hardiana*, New York 1965.

2. BIOGRAPHY AND CRITICAL BIOGRAPHY

F. E. Hardy, *The Life of Thomas Hardy, 1840–1928* (the official biography), London 1962.

William Archer, *Real Conversations*, London 1904.

C. J. P. Beatty (ed.), *The Architectural Notebook of Thomas Hardy* (in facsimile), Dorchester 1966.

C. J. P. Beatty, *The Part Played by Architecture in the Life and Work of Thomas Hardy, with particular reference to the novels* (unpublished Ph.D. Thesis, University of London 1963).

Edmund Blunden, *Thomas Hardy*, London 1941.

V. H. Collins, *Talks with Thomas Hardy at Max Gate, 1920–1922*, London 1928.

Evelyn Hardy, *Thomas Hardy: A Critical Biography*, London 1954.

Evelyn Hardy, & R. Gittings, *Some Recollections by Emma Hardy together with Some Relevant Poems by Thomas Hardy*, London 1961.

C. J. Weber (ed.), *The Letters of Thomas Hardy*, Waterville, Maine 1954.

C. J. Weber, *Hardy of Wessex: his Life and Literary Career* (Revised edn.), New York and London 1965.

3. CRITICISM

1. GENERAL

The following list is limited to books and articles which find reflection in the present work. Many other works were consulted *en route* which may have been unconsciously absorbed without acknowledgement. Some may have missed acknowledgement in the text through the author's concern for uninterrupted flow and brevity. Gaps are inevitable unless the length of the Bibliography is going to challenge the length of the book.

L. Abercrombie, *Thomas Hardy: a Critical Study*, London 1919.

Douglas Brown, *Thomas Hardy* (2nd edn.), London 1961.

R. C. Carpenter, *Thomas Hardy*, New York 1964.

David Cecil, *Hardy the Novelist*, London 1943.

M. E. Chase, *Thomas Hardy from Serial to Novel*, Minneapolis 1927.

Samuel C. Chew, *Thomas Hardy, Poet and Novelist*, Bryn Mawr and New York 1921.

H. H. Child, *Thomas Hardy*, London 1916.

H. C. Duffin, *Thomas Hardy: a study of the Wessex Novels, the Poems, and The Dynasts* (3rd edn. revised), Manchester 1937.

P. d'Exideuil (tr. F. W. Crosse), *The Human Pair in the Work of Thomas Hardy*, London 1930.

Ruth A. Firor, *Folkways in Thomas Hardy*, Philadelphia 1931.

H. B. Grimsditch, *Character and Environment in the Novels of Thomas Hardy*, New York 1962.

ed. A. J. Guerard, *Hardy: a Collection of Critical Essays by various authors*, Englewood Cliffs, N.J. 1963.

A. J. Guerard, *Thomas Hardy: the Novels and Stories*, Cambridge, Mass. 1949.

A. D. Hawkins, *Thomas Hardy*, London 1950.

Irving Howe, *Thomas Hardy*, London 1968.

H. A. T. Johnson, *Thomas Hardy*, London 1968.

L. D. Johnson, *The Art of Thomas Hardy* (revised), London 1968.

ed. Laurence Lerner and John Holmstrom, *Thomas Hardy and his readers: a selection of contemporary reviews*, London 1968.

R. C. R. Morrell, *Thomas Hardy: the Will and the Way*, Kuala Lumpur 1965.

Arthur McDowall, *Thomas Hardy: a Critical Study*, London 1931.

A. E. Newton, *Thomas Hardy, Novelist or Poet?* Philadelphia, privately printed, 1929.

F. B. Pinion, *A Hardy Companion: a guide to the Works of Thomas Hardy and their Background*, London 1968.

W. R. Rutland, *Thomas Hardy: a study of his Writings and their Background*, Oxford 1938.

Hildegard Schill, *The Criticism of Thomas Hardy's Novels in England from 1871–1958* (unpublished Ph.D. thesis, University of London, 1963).

H. C. Webster, *On a Darkling Plain; the Art and Thought of Thomas Hardy*, Chicago and Cambridge, 1947.

George Wing, *Hardy*, Edinburgh and London, 1963.

SHORT STUDIES, ARTICLES, PAMPHLETS, ETC.

Carol Reed Anderson, 'Time, Space, and Perspective in Thomas Hardy': *Nineteenth Century Fiction*, IX, 1954–5.

J. O. Bailey, 'Hardy's "Mephistophelian Visitants"': P.M.L.A., LXI, 1946.

J. O. Bailey, 'Hardy's Visions of the Self': *Studies in Philology*, LVI, 1959.

Jacques Barzun, 'Truth and Poetry in Thomas Hardy': *Southern Review* (Hardy Centennial Issue), VI, 1940.

Richard Beckman, 'A Character Typology for Hardy's Novels': *E.L.H.* (Journal of English Literary History), XXX, 1963.

R. C. Carpenter, 'Hardy's "Gurgoyles"': *Modern Fiction Studies* (Hardy Special Number), VI, 1960.

F. Chapman, 'Revaluations (IV): Hardy the Novelist': *Scrutiny*, III, 1934.

Donald Davidson, 'The Traditional Basis of Thomas Hardy's Fiction': *Southern Review* (Hardy Centennial Issue), VI, 1940.

Bonamy Dobree, in *The Lamp and the Lute* (2nd edn.), London 1964.

T. S. Eliot, in *After Strange Gods*, London 1934.

Havelock Ellis, 'Thomas Hardy's Novels': *Westminster Review*, n.s., LXIII, 1883.

Eugene Goodheart, 'Thomas Hardy and the Lyrical Novel': *Nineteenth Century Fiction*, XII, 1957–8.

Ian Gregor, 'What Kind of Fiction did Hardy Write?': *Essays in Criticism*, XVI, 1966.

Barbara Hardy, in *The Appropriate Form*, London 1964.

L. J. Henkin, in *Darwinism in the English Novel 1860–1910*: N.Y. 1963.

Philip Larkin, 'Wanted: Good Hardy Critic': *Critical Quarterly*, VIII, 1966.

D. J. de Laura, '"The Ache of Modernism" in Hardy's Later Novels': *ELH*, XXXIV, 1967.

D. H. Lawrence, ed. E. D. McDonald, 'Study of Thomas Hardy', in *Phoenix; the Posthumous Papers of D. H. Lawrence*, New York 1950.

Gilbert Neiman, 'Thomas Hardy, Existentialist': *Twentieth Century Literature*, I, 1956.

Katharine Anne Porter, 'Notes on a Criticism of Thomas Hardy': *Southern Review* (Hardy Centennial Issue), VI, 1940.

Mary C. Richards, 'Thomas Hardy's Ironic Vision': *Nineteenth Century Fiction*, III, 1948–59, and IV, 1949–50.

James F. Scott, 'Thomas Hardy's Use of the Gothic: An Examination of Five Representative Works'; *Nineteenth Century Fiction*, XVII, 1962–3.

Alastair Smart, 'Pictorial Imagery in the Novels of Thomas Hardy': *Review of English Studies*, XII, n.s. 1961.

T. R. Spivey, 'Thomas Hardy's Tragic Hero': *Nineteenth Century Fiction*, IX, 1954.

J. I. M. Stewart, 'The Integrity of Hardy': *English Studies*, I, 1948.

Virginia Woolf, 'The Novels of Thomas Hardy', in *The Common Reader* (Second Series), London 1935.

Morton Dauwen Zabel, 'Hardy in Defense of his Art: The Aesthetic of Incongruity': *Southern Review* (Hardy Centennial Issue), VI, 1940.

Maurice Beebe, Bonnie Culotta, and Erin Marcus, 'Criticism of Thomas Hardy: A Selected Checklist': *Modern Fiction Studies* (Hardy Special Number), VI, 1960.

2. POETRY

E. C. Hickson, *The Versification of Thomas Hardy*, Philadelphia 1931.

Samuel L. Hynes, *The Pattern of Hardy's Poetry*, Chapel Hill and London 1961.

Kenneth Marsden, *The Poems of Thomas Hardy: a Critical Introduction*, London 1969.

J. G. Southworth, *The Poetry of Thomas Hardy* (2nd edn.), New York 1966.

SHORT STUDIES, ARTICLES, PAMPHLETS, ETC.

W. H. Auden, 'A Literary Transference': *Southern Review* (Hardy Centennial Issue), VI, 1940.

Howard Baker, 'Hardy's Poetic Certitude': *Southern Review* (Hardy Centennial Issue), VI, 1940.

J. E. Barton, *The Poetry of Thomas Hardy*, Guernsey 1969.

R. P. Blackmur, 'The Shorter Poems of Thomas Hardy': *Southern Review* (Hardy Centennial Issue), VI, 1940.

C. M. Bowra, *The Lyrical Poetry of Thomas Hardy* (Byron Foundation Lecture), Nottingham 1946.

G. Bullough, in *The Trend of Modern Poetry* (2nd edn.), Edinburgh and London 1941.

G. R. Elliott, 'Spectral Etching in the Poetry of Thomas Hardy': *P.M.L.A.*, XLIII, 1928.

ed. P. N. Furbank, in Introduction, *Selected Poems of Thomas Hardy* (Macmillan's English Classics), London and New York 1967.

A. J. Guerard, 'The Illusion of Simplicity: The Shorter Poems of Thomas Hardy': *Sewanee Review*, LXXII, 1964.

F. R. Leavis, 'Hardy the Poet': *Southern Review* (Hardy Centennial Issue), VI, 1940.

F. R. Leavis, in *New Bearings in English Poetry*, London 1950.

F. R. Leavis, 'Reality and Sincerity: Notes in the Analysis of Poetry': *Scrutiny*, XIX, 1952.

C. Day Lewis, 'The Lyrical Poetry of Thomas Hardy': *Proceedings of the British Academy*, XXXVII, 1951.

David Perkins, 'Hardy and the Poetry of Isolation': *ELH*, XXVII, 1959.

John Crowe Ransom, 'Honey and Gall': *Southern Review* (Hardy Centennial Issue), VI, 1940.

Delmore Schwartz, 'Poetry and Belief in Thomas Hardy': *Southern Review* (Hardy Centennial Issue) VI, 1940.

Lionel Stevenson, in *Darwin among the Poets*, New York 1963.

Allen Tate, 'Hardy's Philosophic Metaphors': *Southern Review* (Hardy Centennial Issue), VI, 1940.

John Wain, 'The Poetry of Thomas Hardy': *Critical Quarterly*, VIII, 1966.

G. M. Young, in Introduction, *Selected Poems of Thomas Hardy*, London 1940.

3. SPECIFIC WORKS

THE DYNASTS

J. O. Bailey, *Thomas Hardy and the Cosmic Mind*: a *New Reading of the Dynasts*, Chapel Hill, N. Carolina 1956.

Ernest Brennecke, *Thomas Hardy's Universe: A Study of a Poet's Mind*, London 1924.

A. Chakravarty, *The Dynasts and the Post-War Age in Poetry*, Oxford 1938.

Harold Orel, *Thomas Hardy's Epic-Drama: A Study of 'The Dynasts'* (2nd printing), Kansas 1963.

W. F. Wright, *The Shaping of 'The Dynasts': a Study in Thomas Hardy*, Lincoln-Nebraska 1967.

SHORT STUDIES, ARTICLES, PAMPHLETS, ETC.

Richard Church, 'Thomas Hardy as revealed in *The Dynasts*': *Etudes Anglaises*, VII, 1954.

Emma Clifford, 'The Impressionistic View of History in *The Dynasts*': *Modern Language Quarterly*, XXII, 1961.

Emma Clifford, 'Thomas Hardy and the Historians': *Studies in Philology*, LVI, 1959.

Bonamy Dobrée, 'The Dynasts': *Southern Review* (Hardy Centennial Issue), VI, 1940.

Barker Fairley, 'Notes on the Form of *The Dynasts*': *P.M.L.A.*, XXXIV, 1919.

NOVELS: SHORT STUDIES, ARTICLES, PAMPHLETS, ETC.

DESPERATE REMEDIES

Laurence O. Jones, '*Desperate Remedies* and the Victorian Sensation Novel': *Nineteenth Century Fiction*, XX 1965–6.

UNDER THE GREENWOOD TREE

N. T. Carrington, *Notes on Under the Greenwood Tree* ('Brodies' Notes on Chosen English Texts), Bath, undated.

Harold E. Toliver, 'The Dance under the Greenwood Tree. Hardy's Bucolics': *Nineteenth Century Fiction*, XVII, 1962–3.

FAR FROM THE MADDING CROWD

Howard Babb, 'Setting and Theme in *Far from the Madding Crowd*': *E.L.H.*, xxx, 1963.

I. L. Baker, *Notes on Far from the Madding Crowd* (Brodie's Notes on Chosen English Texts): Bath, undated.

R. C. Carpenter, 'The Mirror and the Sword: Imagery in *Far from the Madding Crowd*': *Nineteenth Century Fiction*, xviii, 1963–4.

Ralph Elliot, Hardy: *Far from the Madding Crowd* (Macmillan Critical Commentaries), London 1966.

THE RETURN OF THE NATIVE

M. L. Anderson, 'Hardy's Debt to Webster in *The Return of the Native*': *Modern Language Notes*, liv, 1939.

Louis Crompton, 'The Sunburnt God: Ritual and Tragic Myth in *The Return of the Native*': *Boston University Studies in English*, iv, 1960.

Leonard W. Deen, 'Heroism and Pathos in Hardy's *Return of the Native*', *Nineteenth Century Fiction*, xv, 1960–1.

John Hagan, 'A Note on the Significance of Diggory Venn': *Nineteenth Century Fiction*, xvi, 1961–2.

M. A. Goldberg, 'Hardy's Double-Visioned Universe': *Essays in Criticism*, vii, 1957.

John Paterson, *The Making of The Return of the Native*, Berkeley and Los Angeles, 1960.

John Paterson 'The "Poetics" of "The Return of the Native"': *Modern Fiction Studies* (Hardy Special Number), vi, 1960.

John Paterson, '*The Return of the Native* as Anti-Christian Document': *Nineteenth Century Fiction*, xiv, 1959–60.

Morse Peckham, 'Darwinism and Darwinisticism': *Victorian Studies*, iii, 1959.

R. W. Stallman, 'Hardy's Hour-Glass Novel': *Sewanee Review*, lv, 1947.

THE MAYOR OF CASTERBRIDGE

James R. Baker, 'Thematic Ambiguity in *The Mayor of Casterbridge*': *Twentieth Century Literature*, i, 1955.

Howard O. Brogan, '"Visible Essences" in *The Mayor of Casterbridge*': *E.L.H.*, xvii, 1950.

Douglas Brown, *Thomas Hardy: The Mayor of Casterbridge* (Studies in English Literature), London 1964.

N. T. Carrington, *Notes on The Mayor of Casterbridge* (Brodie's Notes on Chosen English Texts), Bath, undated.

D. A. Dike, 'A Modern Oedipus: *The Mayor of Casterbridge*': *Essays in Criticism*, ii, 1952.

Robert. B. Heilman, 'Hardy's *Mayor*: Notes on Style': *Nineteenth Century Fiction*, xviii, 1963–4.

F. R. Karl, '"The Mayor of Casterbridge": A New Fiction Defined': *Modern Fiction Studies* (Hardy Special Number), vi, 1960.

Robert Kiely, 'Vision and Viewpoint in *The Mayor of Casterbridge*': *Nineteenth Century Fiction*, xxiii, 1968–9.

John Paterson, '*The Mayor of Casterbridge* as Tragedy': *Victorian Studies*, iii, 1959.

F. B. Pinion, *Hardy: The Mayor of Casterbridge* (Macmillan Critical Commentaries), London, 1966.

Robert C. Schweik, 'Character and Fate in Hardy's *Mayor of Casterbridge*': Nineteenth Century Fiction, xxi, 1866–7.

G. G. Urwin, *The Mayor of Casterbridge* (Notes on English Literature), Oxford 1964.

THE WOODLANDERS

Robert Y. Drake Jr. '"The Woodlanders" as Traditional Pastoral': *Modern Fiction Studies* (Hardy Special Number), vi, 1960.

William J. Matchett, '*The Woodlanders*, or Realism in Sheep's Clothing': *Nineteenth Century Fiction*, ix, 1954–5.

TESS OF THE D'URBERVILLES

Allan Brick, 'Paradise and Consciousness in Hardy's *Tess*': *Nineteenth Century Fiction*, xviii, 1962–3.

N. T. Carrington, *Notes on Tess of the D'Urbervilles* (Brodie's Notes on Chosen English Texts), Bath, undated.

Langdon Elsbree, '*Tess* and the Local Cerealia': *Philological Quarterly*, xl, 1961.

Elliot B. Gose, Jr., 'Psychic Evolution: Darwinism and Initiation in *Tess of the d'Urbervilles*': *Nineteenth Century Fiction*, xviii, 1963–4.

Arnold Kettle, in *An Introduction to the English Novel*, Vol. ii, London, 1953.

JUDE THE OBSCURE

Havelock Ellis, 'Concerning *Jude the Obscure*': *Savoy*, iii, 1896.

Robert B. Heilman, 'Hardy's Sue Bridehead': *Nineteenth Century Fiction*, xx, 1966.

Norman Holland, Jr., '*Jude the Obscure*: Hardy's Symbolic Indictment of Christianity': *Nineteenth Century Fiction*, ix, 1954–5.

William J. Hyde, 'Theoretic and Practical Unconventionality in *Jude the Obscure*': *Nineteenth Century Fiction*, xx, 1965–6.

F. P. W. McDowell, 'Hardy's "Seeming or Personal Impressions": the Symbolical Use of Image and Contrast in "Jude the Obscure"': *Modern Fiction Studies* (Hardy Special Number), vi, 1960.

Arthur Mizener, '*Jude the Obscure* as a Tragedy': *Southern Review* (Hardy Centennial Issue), vi, 1940.

SHORT STORIES

James. L. Roberts, 'Legend and Symbol in Hardy's "The Three Strangers"': *Nineteenth Century Fiction*, xvii, 1962–3.

Index

'Dead and the Living One, The', 133, 135
'Dead "Wessex" the Dog to the House-
hold', 79
Death of Tragedy, The (Steiner), 16, 103
Desperate Remedies, 13, 23, 138, 152, 153–4
Devils, The (Whiting), 213, 313
Dewy, Dick (*Under the Greenwood Tree*),
155, 156–7, 158
Dickens, Charles, 206–7
Dike, D. A., 196, 208
'Distracted Preacher, The', 148
Dobrée, Bonamy, 14, 15, 16
Dr Faustus (Mann), 153, 221, 270, 314
Donne, John, 96
'Doom and She', 26, 28
Dostoievsky, Fyodor, 200, 201, 250
'Dream Question, A', 25, 26, 27
'Drinking Song', 43, 44
'Drizzling Easter Morning A', 41
'Drummer Hodge,' 76
'Duchess of Hamptonshire, The', 147
'Duel, The', 130
d'Urberville, Alec (*Tess of the d'Urber-
villes*), 234, 235, 236, 240, 245, 247, 249,
250, 251, 310, 316; compared with
Angel, 236
Durbeyfield, Joan (*Tess of the d'Urbervilles*),
238, 240
Durbeyfield, John (*Tess of the d'Urber-
villes*), 237, 246
'During Wind and Rain', 58, 71–2
Dynasts, The, 8, 9, 14, 16, 23, 35, 113, 114,
115, 130, 276–301, 306, 312, 313

Edlin, Widow (*Jude the Obscure*), 265, 272
'Edward', 117, 122, 123, 139
Egdon Heath (*The Return of the Native*),
description of, 177–80,
Elfride (*A Pair of Blue Eyes*), 13, 150, 151,
257, 311, 315
Eliot, George, 168–9
Eliot, T. S., 20, 47–8, 52, 69, 137, 152,
159, 190, 302, 304, 305, 306, 312–13
Elizabeth-Jane (*The Mayor of Caster-
bridge*), 18, 22, 197–214, 317
'Elopement, The', 130
'Enter a Dragoon', 147
Esslin, Martin, 277
Ethelberta (*The Hand of Ethelberta*), 13,
138, 151–2
Eustacia (*The Return of the Native*), *see*
Vye, Eustacia

'Face at the Casement, The', 108
'Fallow Deer at the Lonely House, The', 59

Fanny (*Far From the Madding Crowd*), *see*
Robin, Fanny
Far From the Madding Crowd, 8, 13, 18, 19–
20, 21, 22, 120, 137, 138, 139, 140–1,
142, 158–76, 177, 308, 309, 313, 314,
316; action linked to seasons, 161; film
of, 166
Farfrae, Donald (*The Mayor of Caster-
bridge*), 8, 19, 22, 139, 196–214, 317
Faust (Goethe), 49, 277
Fawley, Jude (*Jude the Obscure*), 12, 13, 14,
15, 19, 22, 141, 254–75, 311, 312, 315,
316, 317
'Fellow-Townsmen', 147
Few Crusted Characters, A, 148
'Fiddler of the Reels, The', 145, 154, 221
'Figure in the Scene, The', 71
Fitzpiers (*The Woodlanders*), 12, 216–32,
314, 316, 317; relationship with Grace,
23, 221–2, 226
'Five Students, The', 71–2
'Flirt's Tragedy, The', 130, 133
Folklore, Hardy's debt to, 138–9, 144,
148, 153, 154, 217
'For Conscience' Sake', 147
'For Life I had never Cared Greatly', 60
Forster, E. M., 90, 91, 257, 307
Fournier, Alain-, 314–15
Fray, Henery (*Far From the Madding
Crowd*), 18, 176
Frazer, Sir James, G., 242
'Friends Beyond', 135
Frith, Roger, 302
Frost, Robert, 306

Galton, Sir Francis, 251
Garland, Anne (*The Trumpet Major*), 154,
155, 158
Gary, Romain, 315
George III (*The Dynasts*), 279, 281, 299
Giannoni, R., 314–15
Gide, André, 200, 258, 314, 315, 316
Giles (*The Woodlanders*), *see* Winterborne,
Giles
Gindin, James, 310
'God-Forgotten', 25, 26, 39–40
'God's Education', 38
'God's Funeral', 41, 43
Goethe, Johann Wolfgang von, 49, 277
'Going, The', 96, 97–8, 106
Golden Bough, The (Frazer), 242
Golding, William, 308
Grace (*The Woodlanders*), *see* Melbury,
Grace
Granite and Rainbow (Woolf), 11–12

330